TAKING SIDES

Clashing Views in

Anthropology

FIFTH EDITION

TAKING SIDES

Clashing Views in

Anthropology

FIFTH EDITION

Selected, Edited, and with Introductions by

Robert L. Welsch
Franklin Pierce University

and

Kirk M. Endicott
Dartmouth College

Mc
Graw
Hill

Connect
Learn
Succeed™

The McGraw·Hill Companies

Mc Graw Hill

Connect
Learn
Succeed™

TAKING SIDES: CLASHING VIEWS IN ANTHROPOLOGY, FIFTH EDITION

Published by McGraw-Hill, a business unit of The McGraw-Hill Companies, Inc., 1221 Avenue of the Americas, New York, NY 10020. Copyright © 2013 by The McGraw-Hill Companies, Inc. All rights reserved. Printed in the United States of America. Previous edition(s) © 2009, 2005, and 2004. No part of this publication may be reproduced or distributed in any form or by any means, or stored in a database or retrieval system, without the prior written consent of The McGraw-Hill Companies, Inc., including, but not limited to, in any network or other electronic storage or transmission, or broadcast for distance learning.

Some ancillaries, including electronic and print components, may not be available to customers outside the United States.

This book is printed on acid-free paper.

Taking Sides® is a registered trademark of the McGraw-Hill Companies, Inc.
Taking Sides is published by the **Contemporary Learning Series** group within the McGraw-Hill Higher Education division.

1 2 3 4 5 6 7 8 9 0 DOC/DOC 1 0 9 8 7 6 5 4 3 2

MHID: 0-07-805034-0
ISBN: 978-0-07-805034-3
ISSN: 1530-0757

Managing Editor: *Larry Loeppke*
Developmental Editor II: *Debra A. Henricks*
Senior Permissions Coordinator: *Shirley Lanners*
Marketing Specialist: *Alice Link*
Lead Project Manager: *Jane Mohr*
Design Coordinator: *Brenda A. Rolwes*
Cover Graphics: *Rick D. Noel*
Buyer: *Nicole Baumgartner*
Media Project Manager: *Sridevi Palani*

Compositor: MPS Limited
Cover Image: © Getty Images RF

www.mhhe.com

Editors/Academic Advisory Board

Members of the Academic Advisory Board are instrumental in the final selection of articles for each edition of TAKING SIDES. Their review of articles for content, level, and appropriateness provides critical direction to the editors and staff. We think that you will find their careful consideration well reflected in this volume.

TAKING SIDES: Clashing Views in Anthropology
Fifth Edition

EDITORS

Robert L. Welsch
Franklin Pierce University

and

Kirk M. Endicott
Dartmouth College

ACADEMIC ADVISORY BOARD MEMBERS

Preface

Many courses and textbooks present anthropology as a discipline that largely consists of well-established facts. In *Taking Sides: Clashing Views in Anthropology,* we present the discipline in quite a different light. Here we focus on active controversies that remain unresolved. These issues represent the kinds of arguments and debates that have characterized anthropology for more than a century. They show the varied ways that anthropologists approach the subject of their research and the kinds of anthropological evidence needed to bolster an academic argument.

Generally, we have chosen selections that express strongly worded positions on two sides of an issue. For most issues, several other reasonable positions are also possible, and we have suggested some of these in our introductions and especially following the readings in the *Critical Thinking and Reflection* questions and the section called *Is There Common Ground?*

Taking Sides: Clashing Views in Anthropology is a tool to encourage and develop critical thinking about anthropological research questions, methods, and evidence. Both students and professors should note that we consider it vital for anthropology students to understand the questions that anthropologists raise in their research. Only by understanding anthropological questions can you understand anthropology. We have selected a range of readings and issues to illustrate the kinds of topics that anthropologists study. Another goal of this volume is to provide opportunities for students to explore how anthropologists frame and defend their interpretations of anthropological evidence. We have also chosen issues that raise questions about research methods, testable hypotheses, and the quality or reliability of different kinds of data. All of these complex matters go into shaping the positions that anthropologists debate and defend in their writings. We hope that in discussing these issues students will find opportunities to explore how anthropologists think about the pressing theoretical issues of the day.

Plan of the Book

This book is made up of 18 issues that deal with topics that have provoked starkly different positions by different anthropologists. We have divided the volume into five units reflecting the discipline's four main subfields (Biological Anthropology, Archaeology, Linguistic Anthropology, and Cultural Anthropology) as well as Ethics in Anthropology. Each issue begins with an issue question, *Learning Outcomes,* a summary of the two positions, and an *introduction,* which set the stage for the debate as argued in the YES and NO selections. Following these two selections is *Exploring the Issue,* which consists of a series of *Critical Thinking and Reflection* questions and *Is There Common Ground?,* a section that makes some final observations and considers other less extreme positions. Finally, to conclude each issue is a selection of *Additional Resources* identifying further readings, videos, and Web pages.

In reading an issue and forming your own opinions, you should remember that there are often alternative perspectives that are not represented in either the YES or NO selections. Many anthropologists might even support a less extreme position over either the YES or NO positions. Many issues may have reasonable positions that might appear to be intermediate between the two more extreme viewpoints represented here in the selections. There are often quite reasonable positions that lie totally outside the scope of the debate as presented in these readings, and even different framing of the question. The notes in the *Additional Resources* section will help you find further resources to continue your study of any topic. Students researching any of these issues or related ones for a research paper will find these a useful place to begin a more intensive analysis.

At the end of the book, we have also included a list of all the *contributors to this volume*, which will give you some relevant information on the anthropologists and other commentators whose views are debated here. An *Internet References* page accompanies each unit opener. This page gives some Internet Web addresses (URLs) that are relevant to the issues discussed in that part of the book. Many of these sites contain links to related sites and bibliographies for further study.

Changes to This Edition

In this edition, we have expanded the introductions for every issue in this volume to give a much broader and more comprehensive background to each issue. In most cases, the introduction is three times as long as in previous editions, which should help students understand how these issues have emerged in the discipline. We have also replaced the *postscript* found in previous editions with a series of questions for *Critical Thinking and Reflection* and a new section called *Is There Common Ground?* In previous editions, we included references to other sources and resources in the postscript, but these appear here with annotations in the *Additional Resources*.

This edition has also been updated to reflect several current and ongoing controversies that can help undergraduates understand the breadth and range of anthropological research within the four fields of the discipline. Five issues are new to this edition and we have tried to make several other issue questions clearer for students. The new issues are "Are Female Primates Selected to Be Monogamous?" (Issue 3), "Can Archaeologists Determine the Cultural Background of the Earliest Americans from the Ancient Skeleton Known as Kennewick Man?" (Issue 6), "Was There a Goddess Cult in Prehistoric Europe?" (Issue 7), "Does Language Shape How We Think?" (Issue 9), "Is Black American English a Separate Language from Standard American English, with Its Own Distinctive Grammar and Vocabulary?" (Issue 10).

An *Instructor's Resource Guide with Test Questions* is available through the publisher for the instructor using *Taking Sides* in the classroom. Also available is a general guidebook called *Using Taking Sides in the Classroom,* which discusses methods and techniques for integrating the pro–con approach into any classroom setting. An online version of *Using Taking Sides in the Classroom* and a correspondence service for *Taking Sides* adopters can be found at www .mhhe.com/cls.

Taking Sides: Clashing Views in Anthropology is only one of many titles in the *Taking Sides* series. If you are interested in seeing the table of contents for any of the other titles, please visit the Taking Sides Web site www.mhhe .com/cls.

Acknowledgments

We are thankful for the many helpful comments we received from many friends and colleagues, including Hoyt Alverson, Colin Calloway, Elizabeth Carpenter, Brian Didier, Dale Eickelman, Rachel Flemming, Laura Garzon, Rosemary Gianno, Paul Goldstein, Albert Gomes, Robert Goodby, Robert Gordon, Lauren Gulbas, Nathan Hedges, Allen Hockley, Peter Jenks, Sergei Kan, Steve Kangas, Katherine Keith, Kenneth Korey, Christine Kray, Laura Litton, Deborah Martin, Deborah Nichols, Ventura Perez, Debra Picchi, Lynn Rainville, Kevin Reinhart, John Edward Terrell, Robert Tonkinson, John Watanabe, Lindsay Whaley, and Luis Vivanco. We also want to thank Becca Cahill and Jill Wixom, librarians at Frank S. DiPietro Library at Franklin Pierce University and also John Cocklin, Lucinda Hall, Francis X. Oscadal, Cindy Shirkey, Reinhart Sonnenberg, and Amy Witzel in the Baker-Berry Library Reference Department at Dartmouth College, all of whom helped track down many of the sources and background readings we have used in setting up these issues. We also want to thank our student research assistants at Franklin Pierce University, Shannon Perry, Scott Spolidoro, and Michael Surrett, who helped with this new edition, and our student research assistants at Dartmouth College, all of whom assisted with issues that appeared in earlier editions of this book: Todd Rabkin Golden, Joseph Hanlon, Russell Herman, Tate LeFevre, Adam Levine, Adam Slutsky, Lauren Weldon, Whitney Wilking, and Rachel Yemeni. We also want to thank Debra Henricks of McGraw-Hill in Dubuque, Iowa, for her help in making this latest edition a reality. Finally, we want to thank our wives, Sarah L. Welsch and Karen L. Endicott, for their support and encouragement during the preparation of this volume.

Robert L. Welsch
Franklin Pierce University

Kirk M. Endicott
Dartmouth College

Contents in Brief

Contents

UNIT 1   BIOLOGICAL ANTHROPOLOGY   1

Biological and forensic anthropologist George Gill argues that the concept of race is useful because races—conceived of populations originating in particular regions—can be distinguished by combinations of external and skeletal features. The concept of race is especially useful for the forensic task of identifying human skeletons. The notion of race also provides a vocabulary for discussing human biological variation and racism that can be understood by students. Biological anthropologist C. Loring Brace argues that distinct races cannot be defined because human physical features vary gradually (in clines) and independently from region to region, without sharp discontinuities between physical types. He says races exists in people's perceptions but not in biological reality. In his view the peculiar historical pattern in which Native Americans, Africans brought to the United States as slaves, and European immigrants largely from northern Europe artificially makes it seem that these three groups form distinct races.

Biological anthropologist Richard Wrangham and science writer Dale Peterson maintain that male humans and chimpanzees, our closest nonhuman relatives, have an innate tendency to be aggressive and to defend their territory by violence. They state that sexual selection, a type of natural selection, has fostered an instinct for male aggression because males who are good fighters mate more frequently and sire more offspring than weaker and less aggressive ones. Biological anthropologist Robert W. Sussman rejects the theory that human aggression is an inherited propensity, arguing instead that violence is a product of culture and upbringing. He also rejects the contention that male chimpanzees routinely commit violent acts against other male chimps. Sussman regards the notion that human males are inherently violent as a Western cultural tradition, not a scientifically demonstrated fact.

Issue 3. Are Female Primates Selected to Be Monogamous? 40

Evolutionary psychologist David M. Buss draws on evolutionary theory to argue that humans like other primates have been shaped by evolution. For him, one key aspect of our evolutionary past is that male and female humans have evolved to have different evolutionary desires. Men desire multiple sexual partners, whereas females seek protection, security, and proven fertility in their mates. In this view, females favor monogamy and a stable relationship with the father of their children because such stability increases the likelihood of male investment in their children. Social psychologist Carol Tavris challenges the claims of sociobiologists and evolutionary psychologists that evolution has programmed women to seek monogamy. Suggesting that primate females have been selected for promiscuity, she argues that having multiple partners provides benefits for human females just as it might for males. The best evolutionary strategy for females is to get pregnant as quickly as possible, and having multiple partners is the quickest way to achieve this goal.

UNIT 2 ARCHAEOLOGY 67

Issue 4. Did Humans Migrate to the New World from Europe in Early Prehistoric Times? 68

Archaeologists Bruce Bradley and Dennis Stanford maintain that there is no evidence that the ancestors of the Clovis big-game hunting people of North America originated in Siberia and migrated down an ice-free corridor from Alaska. They argue that Clovis stone tool technology probably developed among the Solutreans of Europe, and that these Solutrean hunters traveled across the North Atlantic ice sheet to North America, where they became the ancestors of the Clovis people. Archaeologist Lawrence Guy Straus counters that the Solutrean culture of Europe ended at least 5000 years before the Clovis culture appeared in the New World. He contends that the North Atlantic Ocean would have been an insurmountable barrier to human travel during the last glacial maximum. He argues that the similarities between the Clovis and Solutrean tool technologies are limited and coincidental.

Archaeologists Donald Grayson and David Meltzer argue that the evidence for human predation as the cause of the Pleistocene megafauna's extinction is circumstantial. They contend that this explanation is based on four premises that find little archaeological evidence to support them. Since there is limited evidence to support the overkill hypothesis, they suggest that climate change is a more likely explanation for these extinctions in North America as they seem to have been in Europe. Archaeologists Stuart Fiedel and Gary Haynes are strong supporters of the overkill hypothesis that argues that humans overhunted large mammals to extinction in North America. They contend that Grayson and Meltzer have misinterpreted older archaeological evidence and largely ignore more recent data. They maintain that there is little evidence for climate change as the cause of the extinctions, which happened within a relatively short period of about 400 years. They feel the empirical evidence supports the "overkill hypothesis."

In 1997, biological anthropologist and archaeologist James Chatters set off a firestorm when he described one of the earliest skeletons found in North America as "Caucasoid-like," based on a very preliminary analysis of what has come to be known as Kennewick Man. Here, he provides a more thorough analysis and a much more cautious analysis of this same skeleton, finding that these remains are not similar to any modern Native American skeletons. He concludes that the 8000+ year old Kennewick skeleton, together with several other early skeletons, indicates that settlement of North America was not by a single Asian population, but a much more complex pattern of in-migration from multiple populations than most archaeologists and biological anthropologists have assumed. Forensic anthropologist Michelle Hamilton challenges Chatters's original description of the Kennewick skull as "Caucasoid." She argues that Chatters and others have subsequently backed away from this description in favor of a new model they have called the "Paleoamerican Paradigm." She contends that this new paradigm implies that the ancestors of modern Native Americans are not the first human settlers on the continent, much as in Chatters's original assessment. After considering the analysis of the Kennewick skull and Native American reactions to the entire controversy, she concludes that the strident approach by Chatters and his colleagues has increased tensions between archaeologists and Indians like no other event in the past 20 years.

Archaeologist Marija Gimbutas argues that the civilization of pre-Bronze Age "Old Europe" was matriarchal—ruled by women—and that the religion centered on the worship of a single great Goddess. Furthermore, this civilization was destroyed by patriarchal Kurgan pastoralists (the Indo-Europeans), who migrated into southeastern Europe from the Eurasian steppes in the fifth to third millennia B.C. Archaeologist Lynn Meskell considers the belief in a supreme Goddess and a matriarchal society in prehistoric Europe to be an unwarranted projection of some women's utopian longings onto the past. She regards Gimbutas's interpretation of the archaeological evidence as biased and speculative.

UNIT 3   LINGUISTIC ANTHROPOLOGY   169

Psychologist and primate specialist E. S. Savage-Rumbaugh argues that, since the 1960s, there have been attempts to teach chimpanzees and other apes symbol systems similar to human language. These studies have shown that although apes are not capable of learning human language, they demonstrate a genuine ability to create new symbolic patterns that are similar to very rudimentary symbolic activity. Linguist Joel Wallman counters that attempts to teach chimps and other apes sign language or other symbolic systems have demonstrated that apes are very intelligent animals. But up to now these attempts have not shown that apes have any innate capacity for language.

Sociolinguists John Gumperz and Stephen C. Levinson contend that recent studies of language and culture suggest that language structures human thought in a variety of ways that most linguists and anthropologists had not believed possible. They argue that culture through language affects the ways that we think and the ways that we experience the world. Cognitive neuropsychologist Steven Pinker draws on recent studies in cognitive science and neuropsychology to suggest that Edward Sapir and Benjamin Whorf were wrong when they suggested that the structure of any particular language had any effect on the ways human beings thought about the world in which they lived. He argues that previous studies have examined language but have said little, if anything, about thought.

Linguist Ernie Smith argues that the speech of many African Americans is a separate language from English because its grammar is derived from the Niger-Congo languages of Africa. Although most of the vocabulary is borrowed from English, the pronunciations and sentence structures are changed to conform to Niger-Congo forms. Therefore, he says, schools should treat Ebonics-speaking students like other non–English-speaking minority students. Linguist John McWhorter counters that Black English is just one of many English dialects spoken in America that are mutually intelligible. He argues that the peculiar features of Black English are derived from the dialects of early settlers from Britain, not from African language. Because African American children are already familiar with standard English, he concludes, they do not need special language training.

Cultural anthropologist Clifford Geertz views anthropology as a science of interpretation, and he argues that anthropology should never model itself on the natural sciences. He believes that anthropology's goal should be to generate deeper interpretations of cultural phenomena, using what he calls "thick description," rather than attempting to prove or disprove scientific laws. Cultural anthropologist Robert Carneiro argues that anthropology has always been and should continue to be a science that attempts to explain sociocultural phenomena in terms of causes and effects rather than merely interpret them. He criticizes Geertz's cultural interpretations as arbitrary and immune to disconfirmation.

Issue 12. Was Margaret Mead's Fieldwork on Samoan Adolescents Fundamentally Flawed? 264

YES: **Derek Freeman**, from *Margaret Mead and Samoa: The Making and Unmaking of an Anthropological Myth* (Harvard University Press, 1983) *268*

NO: **Lowell D. Holmes and Ellen Rhoads Holmes**, from "Samoan Character and the Academic World," in *Samoan Village: Then and Now,* 2nd ed. (Harcourt Brace Jovanovich College Publishers, 1992) *278*

Social anthropologist Derek Freeman argues that Margaret Mead was wrong when she stated that Samoan adolescents had sexual freedom. He contends that Mead went to Samoa to prove anthropologist Franz Boas's cultural determinist agenda and states that Mead was so eager to believe in Samoan sexual freedom that she was consistently the victim of a hoax perpetrated by Samoan girls and young women who enjoyed tricking her. He contends that nearly all of her conclusions are spurious because of biases she brought with her and should be abandoned. Cultural anthropologists Lowell Holmes and Ellen Holmes contend that Margaret Mead had a very solid understanding of Samoan culture in general. During a restudy of Mead's research, they came to many of the same conclusions that Mead had reached about Samoan sexuality and adolescent experiences. They accept that Mead's description of Samoan culture exaggerates the amount of sexual freedom and the degree to which adolescence in Samoa is carefree but these differences, they argue, can be explained in terms of changes in Samoan culture since 1925 and in terms of Mead's relatively unsophisticated research methods compared with field methods used today.

Issue 13. Do Men Dominate Women in All Societies? 290

YES: **Steven Goldberg**, from "Is Patriarchy Inevitable?" *National Review* (November 11, 1996) *294*

NO: **Kirk M. Endicott and Karen L. Endicott**, from "Understanding Batek Egalitarianism," in *The Headman Was a Woman: The Gender Egalitarian Batek of Malaysia* (Waveland Press, 2008) *299*

Sociologist Steven Goldberg contends that in all societies men occupy most high positions in hierarchical organizations and most high-status roles, and they also tend to dominate women in interpersonal relations. He states that this is because men's hormones cause them to compete more strongly than women for status and dominance. Cultural anthropologists Kirk and Karen Endicott argue that the Batek people of Peninsular Malaysia form a gender egalitarian society in the sense that neither men nor women as groups control the other sex, and neither sex is accorded greater value by society as a whole. Both men and women are free to participate in any activities, and both have equal rights in the family and camp group.

Cultural anthropologist Roger Ivar Lohmann argues that a supernaturalistic worldview or cosmology is at the heart of virtually all religions. For him, the supernatural is a concept that exists everywhere, although it is expressed differently in each society. For him, supernaturalism attributes volition to things that do not have it. He argues that the supernatural is also a part of Western people's daily experience in much the same way that it is the experience of the Papua New Guineas with whom he worked. Lutheran pastor and anthropological researcher Frederick (Fritz) P. Lampe argues that "supernatural" is a problematic and inappropriate term like the term "primitive." If we accept the term "supernatural," it is all too easy to become ethnocentric and assume that anything supernatural is unreal and therefore false. He considers a case at the University of Technology in Papua New Guinea to show how use of the term "supernatural" allows us to miss out on how Papua New Guineans actually understand the world in logical, rational, and naturalistic terms that Westerners would generally see as illogical, irrational, and supernaturalistic.

Indian social researcher Sudhir Kakar analyzes the origins of ethnic conflict from a psychological perspective to argue that ethnic differences are deeply held distinctions that from time to time will inevitably erupt as ethnic conflicts. Ethnic anxiety arises from preconscious fears about cultural differences. In his view, no amount of education or politically correct behavior will eradicate these fears and anxieties about people of differing ethnic backgrounds. American sociologist Anthony Oberschall considers the ethnic conflicts that have recently emerged in Bosnia to conclude that primordial ethnic attachments are insufficient to explain the sudden emergence of violence among Bosnian ethnic groups. He adopts a complex explanation for this violence, identifying circumstances in which fears and anxieties were manipulated by politicians for self-serving ends. It was only in the context of these manipulations that ethnic violence could have erupted.

Cultural anthropologist Roger M. Keesing argues that what native peoples in the Pacific now accept as "traditional culture" is largely an invented and idealized vision of their past. He contends that such fictional images emerge because native peoples are largely unfamiliar with what life was really like in pre-Western times and because such imagery distinguishes native communities from dominant Western culture. Hawaiian activist and scholar Haunani-Kay Trask asserts that Keesing's critique is fundamentally flawed because he only uses Western documents. She contends that native peoples have oral traditions, genealogies, and other historical sources that are not reflected in Western historical documents. Anthropologists like Keesing, she maintains, are trying to hold onto their privileged position as experts in the face of growing numbers of educated native scholars.

UNIT 5   ETHICS IN ANTHROPOLOGY   375

Assistant professor of justice studies and member of the Pawnee tribe James Riding In argues that holding Native American skeletons in museums and other repositories represents a sacrilege against Native American dead. Non-Native Americans would not allow their cemeteries to be dug up and their ancestors bones to be housed in museums. Thus, all Indian remains should be reburied. Professor of anthropology and archaeologist Clement W. Meighan believes that archaeologists have a moral and professional obligation to the archaeological data with which they work. Such field data are not just about Native Americans and their history but about the heritage of all humans. He concludes that such data are held in the public good and must be protected from destruction.

Anthropologist Terence Turner contends that journalist Patrick Tierney's book *Darkness in El Dorado* accurately depicts how anthropologist Napoleon Chagnon's research among the Yanomami Indians caused conflict between groups and how Chagnon's portrayal of the Yanomami as extremely violent aided gold miners trying to take over Yanomami land.

Anthropologists Edward Hagen, Michael Price, and John Tooby counter that Tierney systematically distorts Chagnon's views on Yanomami violence and exaggerates the amount of disruption caused by Chagnon's activities compared to those of such others as missionaries and gold miners.

Correlation Guide

The *Taking Sides* series presents current issues in a debate-style format designed to stimulate student interest and develop critical thinking skills. Each issue is thoughtfully framed with an issue summary, an issue introduction, and key end-of-issue instructional and discussion tools. The pro and con essays—selected for their liveliness and substance—represent the arguments of leading scholars and commentators in their fields.

Taking Sides: Clashing Views in Anthropology, 5/e is an easy-to-use reader that presents issues on important topics such as *culture, language, and fieldwork*. For more information on *Taking Sides* and other *McGraw-Hill Contemporary Learning Series* titles, visit www.mhhe.com/cls.

This convenient guide matches the issues in **Taking Sides: Anthropology** with the corresponding chapters in two of our best-selling McGraw-Hill Anthropology textbooks by Kottak.

Taking Sides: Clashing Views in Anthropology, 5/e	Window on Humanity: A Concise Introduction to Anthropology, 5/e by Kottak	Anthropology: Appreciating Human Diversity, 14/e by Kottak
Issue 1: Is Race a Useful Concept for Anthropologists?	**Chapter 4:** Evolution, Genetics, and Human Variation **Chapter 17:** Ethnicity and Race	**Chapter 5:** Evolution and Genetics **Chapter 6:** Human Variation and Adaptation **Chapter 15:** Ethnicity and Race
Issue 2: Are Humans Inherently Violent?	**Chapter 2:** Culture **Chapter 4:** Evolution, Genetics, and Human Variation	**Chapter 2:** Culture **Chapter 5:** Evolution and Genetics **Chapter 6:** Human Variation and Adaptation
Issue 3: Are Female Primates Selected to Be Monogamous?	**Chapter 5:** The Primates	**Chapter 7:** The Primates
Issue 4: Did Humans Migrate to the New World from Europe in Early Prehistoric Times?		**Chapter 10:** The Origin and Spread of Modern Humans
Issue 5: Did Climate Change Rather Than Overhunting Cause the Extinction of Mammoths and Other Megafauna in North America?		
Issue 6: Can Archaeologists Determine the Cultural Background of the Earliest Americans from the Ancient Skeleton Known as Kennewick Man?	**Chapter 6:** Early Hominins	**Chapter 8:** Early Hominins **Chapter 10:** The Origin and Spread of Modern Humans

(Continued)

Taking Sides: Clashing Views in Anthropology, 5/e	Window on Humanity: A Concise Introduction to Anthropology, 5/e by Kottak	Anthropology: Appreciating Human Diversity, 14/e by Kottak
Issue 7: Was There a Goddess Cult in Prehistoric Europe?	**Chapter 2:** Culture **Chapter 14:** Gender	**Chapter 2:** Culture **Chapter 18:** Gender
Issue 8: Can Apes Learn Language?	**Chapter 5:** The Primates **Chapter 10:** Language and Communication	**Chapter 7:** The Primates **Chapter 14:** Language and Communication
Issue 9: Does Language Shape How We Think?	**Chapter 10:** Language and Communication	**Chapter 14:** Language and Communication
Issue 10: Is Black American English a Separate Language from Standard American English, with Its Own Distinctive Grammar and Vocabulary?	**Chapter 10:** Language and Communication	**Chapter 14:** Language and Communication
Issue 11: Should Cultural Anthropology Stop Trying to Model Itself as a Science?	**Chapter 1:** What is Anthropology? **Chapter 3:** Doing Anthropology **Chapter 18:** Applying Anthropology	**Chapter 1:** What is Anthropology? **Chapter 3:** Applying Anthropology **Chapter 13:** Theory and Methods in Cultural Anthropology
Issue 12: Was Margaret Mead's Fieldwork on Samoan Adolescents Fundamentally Flawed?	**Chapter 1:** What is Anthropology? **Chapter 3:** Doing Anthropology **Chapter 18:** Applying Anthropology	**Chapter 1:** What is Anthropology? **Chapter 3:** Applying Anthropology **Chapter 13:** Theory and Methods in Cultural Anthropology
Issue 13: Do Men Dominate Women in All Societies?	**Chapter 14:** Gender	**Chapter 18:** Gender
Issue 14: Does the Distinction Between the Natural and the Supernatural Exist in All Cultures?	**Chapter 1:** Culture **Chapter 15:** Religion	**Chapter 2:** Culture **Chapter 21:** Religion
Issue 15: Is Conflict Between Different Ethnic Groups Inevitable?	**Chapter 2:** Culture **Chapter 17:** Ethnicity and Race	**Chapter 2:** Culture **Chapter 15:** Ethnicity and Race
Issue 16: Do Native Peoples Today Invent Their Traditions?	**Chapter 2:** Culture **Chapter 17:** Ethnicity and Race	**Chapter 2:** Culture **Chapter 15:** Ethnicity and Race
Issue 17: Should the Remains of Prehistoric Native Americans Be Reburied Rather Than Studied?	**Chapter 1:** What is Anthropology? **Chapter 3:** Doing Anthropology **Chapter 15:** Religion **Chapter 18:** Applying Anthropology	**Chapter 1:** What is Anthropology? **Chapter 3:** Applying Anthropology **Chapter 13:** Theory and Methods in Cultural Anthropology **Chapter 21:** Religion
Issue 18: Did Napoleon Chagnon's Research Methods Harm the Yanomami Indians of Venezuela?	**Chapter 1:** What is Anthropology? **Chapter 3:** Doing Anthropology **Chapter 18:** Applying Anthropology	**Chapter 1:** What is Anthropology? **Chapter 3:** Applying Anthropology **Chapter 13:** Theory and Methods in Cultural Anthropology

Topic Guide

T his topic guide suggests how the selections in this book relate to the subjects covered in your course. You may want to use the topics listed on these pages to search the Web more easily. On the following pages, a number of Web sites have been gathered specifically for this book. They are arranged to reflect the units of this *Taking Sides* reader. You can link to these sites by going to www.mhhe.com/cls.

All issues, and their articles that relate to each topic are listed below the bold-faced term.

African Americans

1. Is Race a Useful Concept for Anthropologists?
9. Does Language Shape How We Think?

Asian Societies

10. Is Black American English a Separate Language from Standard American English, with Its Own Distinctive Grammar and Vocabulary?
12. Was Margaret Mead's Fieldwork on Samoan Adolescents Fundamentally Flawed?

Biological Determinism

2. Are Humans Inherently Violent?
3. Are Female Primates Selected to Be Monogamous?
8. Can Apes Learn Language?
11. Should Cultural Anthropology Stop Trying to Model Itself as a Science?
12. Was Margaret Mead's Fieldwork on Samoan Adolescents Fundamentally Flawed?
13. Do Men Dominate Women in All Societies?
15. Is Conflict Between Different Ethnic Groups Inevitable?
16. Do Native Peoples Today Invent Their Traditions?

Conflict and Violence

2. Are Humans Inherently Violent?
17. Should the Remains of Prehistoric Native Americans Be Reburied Rather Than Studied?

Cultural Determinism

2. Are Humans Inherently Violent?
3. Are Female Primates Selected to Be Monogamous?

8. Can Apes Learn Language?
11. Should Cultural Anthropology Stop Trying to Model Itself as a Science?
12. Was Margaret Mead's Fieldwork on Samoan Adolescents Fundamentally Flawed?
13. Do Men Dominate Women in All Societies?
15. Is Conflict Between Different Ethnic Groups Inevitable?
16. Do Native Peoples Today Invent Their Traditions?

Cultural Construction Models

8. Can Apes Learn Language?
9. Does Language Shape How We Think?
13. Do Men Dominate Women in All Societies?
14. Does the Distinction Between the Natural and the Supernatural Exist in All Cultures?
15. Is Conflict Between Different Ethnic Groups Inevitable?
16. Do Native Peoples Today Invent Their Traditions?
17. Should the Remains of Prehistoric Native Americans Be Reburied Rather Than Studied?

Essentialist Models

8. Can Apes Learn Language?
9. Does Language Shape How We Think?
13. Do Men Dominate Women in All Societies?
14. Does the Distinction Between the Natural and the Supernatural Exist in All Cultures?
15. Is Conflict Between Different Ethnic Groups Inevitable?
16. Do Native Peoples Today Invent Their Traditions?
17. Should the Remains of Prehistoric Native Americans Be Reburied Rather Than Studied?

(Continued)

European Societies

14. Does the Distinction Between the Natural and the Supernatural Exist in All Cultures?
17. Should the Remains of Prehistoric Native Americans Be Reburied Rather Than Studied?

Feminist Approaches

11. Should Cultural Anthropology Stop Trying to Model Itself as a Science?
12. Was Margaret Mead's Fieldwork on Samoan Adolescents Fundamentally Flawed?
13. Do Men Dominate Women in All Societies?

Fieldwork

11. Should Cultural Anthropology Stop Trying to Model Itself as a Science?
18. Did Napoleon Chagnon's Research Methods Harm the Yanomami Indians of Venezuela?

Gender and Sexuality

11. Should Cultural Anthropology Stop Trying to Model Itself as a Science?
12. Was Margaret Mead's Fieldwork on Samoan Adolescents Fundamentally Flawed?
13. Do Men Dominate Women in All Societies?
14. Does the Distinction Between the Natural and the Supernatural Exist in All Cultures?

Human Skeletal Remains

6. Can Archaeologists Determine the Cultural Background of the Earliest Americans from the Ancient Skeleton Known as Kennewick Man?
18. Did Napoleon Chagnon's Research Methods Harm the Yanomami Indians of Venezuela?

Interpretative Approaches

10. Is Black American English a Separate Language from Standard American English, with Its Own Distinctive Grammar and Vocabulary?

Language

7. Was There a Goddess Cult in Prehistoric Europe?
8. Can Apes Learn Language?
9. Does Language Shape How We Think?

Migration

4. Did Humans Migrate to the New World from Europe in Early Prehistoric Times?
6. Can Archaeologists Determine the Cultural Background of the Earliest Americans from the Ancient Skeleton Known as Kennewick Man?

North American Societies

1. Is Race a Useful Concept for Anthropologists?
4. Did Humans Migrate to the New World from Europe in Early Prehistoric Times?
5. Did Climate Change Rather Than Overhunting Cause the Extinction of Mammoths and Other Megafauna in North America?
6. Can Archaeologists Determine the Cultural Background of the Earliest Americans from the Ancient Skeleton Known as Kennewick Man?
9. Does Language Shape How We Think?
14. Does the Distinction Between the Natural and the Supernatural Exist in All Cultures?
15. Is Conflict Between Different Ethnic Groups Inevitable?
18. Did Napoleon Chagnon's Research Methods Harm the Yanomami Indians of Venezuela?

Oceanic Societies

11. Should Cultural Anthropology Stop Trying to Model Itself as a Science?
13. Do Men Dominate Women in All Societies?
15. Is Conflict Between Different Ethnic Groups Inevitable?
16. Do Native Peoples Today Invent Their Traditions?

Primates

3. Are Female Primates Selected to Be Monogamous?
7. Was There a Goddess Cult in Prehistoric Europe?

Race and Ethnicity

1. Is Race a Useful Concept for Anthropologists?
6. Can Archaeologists Determine the Cultural Background of the Earliest Americans from the Ancient Skeleton Known as Kennewick Man?
9. Does Language Shape How We Think?
17. Should the Remains of Prehistoric Native Americans Be Reburied Rather Than Studied?

Reification and Cultural Labeling

1. Is Race a Useful Concept for Anthropologists?
6. Can Archaeologists Determine the Cultural Background of the Earliest Americans from the Ancient Skeleton Known as Kennewick Man?
8. Can Apes Learn Language?
9. Does Language Shape How We Think?
17. Should the Remains of Prehistoric Native Americans Be Reburied Rather Than Studied?

Religion and Worldviews

16. Do Native Peoples Today Invent Their Traditions?
17. Should the Remains of Prehistoric Native Americans Be Reburied Rather Than Studied?

Research Methods

6. Can Archaeologists Determine the Cultural Background of the Earliest Americans from the Ancient Skeleton Known as Kennewick Man?
7. Was There a Goddess Cult in Prehistoric Europe?
10. Is Black American English a Separate Language from Standard American English, with Its Own Distinctive Grammar and Vocabulary?

11. Should Cultural Anthropology Stop Trying to Model Itself as a Science?
18. Did Napoleon Chagnon's Research Methods Harm the Yanomami Indians of Venezuela?

Social Organization

12. Was Margaret Mead's Fieldwork on Samoan Adolescents Fundamentally Flawed?
14. Does the Distinction Between the Natural and the Supernatural Exist in All Cultures?
15. Is Conflict Between Different Ethnic Groups Inevitable?

Sociobiology and Environmental Psychology

2. Are Humans Inherently Violent?
3. Are Female Primates Selected to Be Monogamous?
11. Should Cultural Anthropology Stop Trying to Model Itself as a Science?

South American Societies

18. Did Napoleon Chagnon's Research Methods Harm the Yanomami Indians of Venezuela?

Introduction

Robert L. Welsch
Kirk M. Endicott

Anthropology is the study of humanity in all its biological, social, cultural, and linguistic diversity. Some of the founders of American anthropology, such as Franz Boas, made important contributions to the understanding of human biology, culture, and language. During their field research projects, some of his students like A. B. Lewis, who spent four years surveying the cultures of New Guinea and the Melanesian islands, talked with villagers and made notes about his conversations, took photographs of their daily tasks, collected contemporary objects they used including some half-finished to show how they were made, collected word lists and names for objects in dozens of languages, measured skulls that government officers had seized from headhunting groups, and excavated a small part of a midden containing dozens of broken pots called potsherds. For these early anthropologists, all these different kinds of data were anthropological data. Few such renaissance men and women can found today, because to master the concepts, methods, and literature involved in studying the different aspects of human variation, anthropologists need to specialize on a narrow aspect of the discipline. Boas and his students could read the entire anthropological literature on African society or California Indian in less than a month; today it might take a lifetime. As a result of specialization at times it seems that no two anthropologists actually study the same things, yet they are all wording toward a great understanding of the commonalities and differences that define the human species. But as several issues in this volume suggest, several broad, general questions link studies across the discipline.

Today anthropology encompasses four major subdisciplines—biological anthropology, prehistoric archaeology, linguistic anthropology, and cultural anthropology, as well as many smaller subdisciplines of each. Controversial issues in each of these subfields are included in the first four units of this volume. The fifth unit considers the ethics of anthropology.

Biological anthropology, also called physical anthropology, concerns the anatomy, physiology, mental capabilities, and genetics of humans and our nearest relatives, the primates. Traditionally, biological anthropologists, like other biologists, have understood human variation in evolutionary terms. Increasingly, as geneticists have introduced new ways of analyzing genetic data encoded in our DNA, some biological anthropologists have described and explained human biological variation at the molecular level.

Fundamental questions for biological anthropologist include: How did our species evolve from early nonhuman primates? How similar are human and nonhuman primates anatomically and in terms of their capabilities? When did our species take on attributes that are associated with anatomically modern humans? Where did our species arise? What were the evolutionary forces that contributed to our anatomical and behavioral evolution? How much has human behavior been shaped by evolution? How and why did the hominins—the ancestors of humans—develop the capacity for culture—socially learned and transmitted patterns of behavior, thought, and feeling? Does our human biology program us to behave in certain ways?

Paleoanthropologists (those anthropologists who study humankind's ancient ancestors) search for and excavate fossil bone fragments of long-dead primates, reconstruct their skeletons, and make inferences about their behavior patterns from bones, teeth, and other clues. They also use sophisticated dating techniques, computer models, and studies of living primates, both in the laboratory and in their natural environments, to create plausible models of human evolution and the relationships among different branches of the primate order.

Archaeology, which is sometimes referred to as *prehistory,* involves documenting, understanding, and explaining the history of human communities and civilizations that existed before written records. Like other historians, these anthropologists seek evidence about how people lived, what they subsisted on, and the kinds of social institutions they established. But unlike most historians who can turn to documents and papers to detail the life and times of their subjects, archaeologists must usually find evidence for their reconstructions of the past through excavations of sites where people formerly lived or worked at some particular task. Over the past century, archaeologists have developed specialized methods for excavating and analyzing artifacts, stone tools, animal bone, shell, pollen, and carbon from old fires to determine a great deal about ancient environments, people's subsistence patterns and living arrangements, and when sites were occupied.

One issue at the heart of most archaeological controversies is how we can or should interpret these varied kinds of data to reconstruct the ways of life of earlier times. Recurrent questions include: What is the use and meaning of an artifact? To what extent can we use current lifeways of tribal or foraging groups as analogies for how prehistoric communities lived? Like detective work, archaeology involves constructing plausible scenarios from scanty clues, then testing these scenarios against existing archaeological data or with newly excavated data. As we will see, different scholars do not always draw the same conclusions for a given set of data.

A set of questions that archeologists continue to ask is when, why, and how people first settled in different parts of the world, such as the Americas or the Pacific Islands. They also ask why innovations like agriculture developed at particular times and places. Why did some societies develop into complex civilizations, while others remained village-based societies, free of centralized political authority? Why did some complex civilizations break down, leaving tribal or village-based societies and enormous ruins that recall the complex political organizations of the past?

A frequent point of debate among archaeologists is the dates of archaeological deposits. Accurate dating, even if only relative to other artifacts in a site, is clearly essential for accurate interpretations, although dating alone does not reveal the processes that led to particular changes in the archaeological record. Stratification—the principle that the lower layers of a deposit are older than the upper layers—is still the most reliable basis for relative dating within a site. Now archaeologists also draw on a wide battery of high-tech absolute dating methods—including Carbon-14 dating, Potassium-Argon dating, and thermoluminescence dating—which have varying degrees of accuracy for different time spans of the past. Archaeologists (and paleoanthropologists) use as many different methods of dating a site as they can, but sometimes the results do not fully coincide. Dating always requires interpretation because, for example, carbon samples may be contaminated by more recent organic material like tree roots, and scholars do not always agree on the correct interpretation.

Linguistic anthropology includes the study of language and languages, especially non-Western and unwritten languages, and the study of the relationship between language and other aspects of culture. Language provides the categories within which much of culture is expressed. Some anthropologists regard linguistic anthropology as a subdivision of cultural anthropology because language is so much a part of culture and is the medium by which much of culture is transmitted from one generation to the next.

A classic question for linguistic anthropologists has been: Do the categories of a language shape how human beings perceive and understand the world? For example, if a language has terms for certain categories, do these categories encourage speakers to assume the reality of these categories. This question was first developed by Edward Sapir early in the twentieth century and expanded on by Benjamin Whorf in the 1950s and has become known as the Sapir–Whorf Hypothesis. Other enduring linguistic controversies concern whether there are universal grammatical categories and whether some linguistic categories are determined by human biology, such as basic color terminologies. Another question that linguistic anthropologists have debated for several decades concerns whether chimpanzees and other apes have the innate ability to use symbols in ways that resemble human language. This question is important because if apes are capable of complex symbolic activity, then language and culture are probably not the exclusive capabilities of humans but have their origins in our primate past.

Cultural anthropology, which is also called *social anthropology* in Great Britain or sometimes *sociocultural anthropology* in the United States, is concerned with the cultures and societies of living communities. Cultural anthropologists have proposed many different definitions of "culture." Most emphasize that cultural behavior, thought, and feelings are socially created and learned, rather than generated by biologically transmitted instincts (innate behavioral tendencies). Anthropologists differ considerably among themselves on the relative weight they assign to culture and instincts in explaining human behavior, as some of the issues in this volume show. Because cultures are human creations, they differ from one society to another, often in quite significant ways.

Data for most cultural anthropologists come from observations, informal conversations, and interviews made while living within a study community. The hallmark of cultural anthropology is "fieldwork," in which the anthropologist lives with another cultural group and learns their language, their customs, and their patterns of interaction. Anthropological fieldwork involves *participant observation*—observing while participating in the life of the community. Nearly all cultural anthropologists use participant observation to some extent, and methodologically it is what distinguishes most anthropological research from that of sociologists, psychologists, human geographers, and economists.

As in the other subfields of anthropology, cultural data must be interpreted. Interpretation begins with the creation of the research questions themselves. The research questions reflect what investigators consider important to find out and direct their observations and interviews in the field. At each step of data collection and analysis, the investigators' theories and interests shape their understandings of other cultures.

Much explanation in cultural anthropology is based on comparison of cultural features in different societies. Some anthropologists explicitly make cross-cultural comparisons, using statistics to measure the significance of apparent correlations between such things as childrearing practices and adult personalities. Even anthropologists who concentrate on explaining or interpreting features of particular cultures use their knowledge of similar or different features in other societies as a basis for insights.

Like other anthropologists, cultural anthropologists look for uniformities in human behavior as well as variations. Understanding what patterns of human behavior are possible has been at the center of many controversies in cultural anthropology. Questions touched on in this book include: Is gender equality possible? Is violence inevitable? Do ethnic differences lead to conflict? Does the amount of sexual freedom offered to adolescents make a difference in their transition to adulthood?

Recently, cultural anthropologists have begun asking questions about anthropologists and the culture of anthropology, specifically about possible biases in the ways we depict and represent other cultures through our writing, films, and other media. This movement has been called "post-modern anthropology" or "critical anthropology." Post-modernists ask, among other things: Do our theories and methods of representation inadvertently portray the people we study as exotic "Others," in exaggerated contrast with Western peoples? Are our fieldwork methods biasing the data we collect?

Ethics in anthropology. Concerns about the ethics of research have become increasingly important in contemporary anthropology. The American Anthropological Association has developed the Code of Ethics covering both research and teaching (see the AAA Web site at www.aaanet.org). It recognizes that researchers sometimes have conflicting obligations to the people and animals studied, host countries, the profession, and the public. One basic principle is that researchers should do nothing that could harm or distress the people or animals they study. Cultural anthropologists must obviously be aware of the possibility of harming the living people with whom they work. But similar considerations also affect archaeologists and biological anthropologists because the artifacts of past communities often represent the ancestors of living communities. Skeletons preserved and ready for study are also the remains of someone's dead ancestors. Here the interests of anthropologists and native peoples may diverge. For example, in Issue 18 we ask: "Should the Remains of Prehistoric Native Americans be Reburied Rather Than Studied?" Similarly, we may ask what the ethical responsibilities of Western anthropologists should be when they find certain cultural practices of other peoples abhorrent or unjust. Should anthropologists work to change these practices? Just what are our responsibilities to native communities? For example, Issue 18 asks: "Did Napoleon Chagnon's Research Methods Harm the Yanomami Indians of Venezuela?" All of these issues raise questions about how involved anthropologists should become with the peoples with whom they work. Should anthropologists take a passive, objective, and even scientific position, treating people as objects of study, or should they use what they know to support or change these native communities?

Some Basic Questions

On the surface, the issues presented in this book are very diverse. Anthropologists from different subfields tend to focus on their own specialized problems and to work with different kinds of evidence. Most of the controversial issues we have chosen for this volume can be read as very narrow focused debates within a subfield. But many of the issues that confront anthropologists in one subfield arise in other subfields as well. What has attracted us to the issues presented here is that each issue raises much broader questions that affect the entire discipline. In this section, we briefly describe some of the basic questions lying behind specific issues.

Is Anthropology a Science or a Humanity?

Science is a set of ideas and methods intended to describe and explain phenomena in a naturalistic way, seeing individual things and events as the outcome of discoverable causes and as conforming to general laws or emerging according to general principles. Anthropologists taking a scientific approach are concerned with developing broad theories about the processes that lead to observed patterns of variation in human biology, language, and culture. The humanities, on the other hand, are concerned with understanding people's cultural creations in terms of their meanings to their creators and the motivations behind their creation.

Biological anthropology seeks the reasons for human evolution and biological diversity largely in the processes of the natural world, and it uses the methods of the physical sciences for investigating those phenomena. Archaeology too uses natural science concepts and methods of investigation, but it also draws on understandings of human behavior that take account of culturally influenced motivations, values, and meanings. Cultural anthropologists are divided over whether cultural anthropology should model itself on the natural sciences or on the humanities. Some cultural anthropologists try to discover the causes of particular cultural forms occurring at specific places and times, while others try to interpret the meanings (to the people themselves) of cultural forms in other societies in ways that are intelligible to Western readers. Many of those who try to interpret cultural behavior in other communities see their role at translating the cultural meanings of activities in one society to people in American or European societies. Issue 11, "Should Cultural Anthropology Stop Trying to Model Itself as a Science?", directly addresses the question of whether anthropology is science or humanities.

Is Biology or Culture More Important in Shaping Human Behavior?

Most anthropologists accept that both genetically transmitted behavioral tendencies (instincts) and cultural ideas and norms influence human behavior, thought, and emotion. However, anthropologists diverge widely over the amount of weight they assign to these two influences. *Biological determinists* believe that all human behavior is ultimately determined by the genes, and culture merely lends distinctive coloration to our genetically driven behaviors. At the other extreme, *cultural determinists* believe that any instincts humans may have are so weak and malleable that cultural learning easily overcomes them. The conflict between supporters of the two extreme views, called the *nature-nurture debate*, has been going on for many years and shows no sign of being resolved soon.

Issue 12, "Was Margaret Mead's Fieldwork on Samoan Adolescents Fundamentally Flawed?", considers the Margaret Mead–Derrick Freeman controversy, which has its roots in the question of whether biology or culture is most important in shaping human behavior. From her research in Samos, Mead claimed that nurture was not important, while some decades later Freeman concluded from his research in Samoa precisely the opposite. Other issues in this volume also deal directly with the nature-nurture question, particularly Issue 2, "Are Humans Inherently Violent?", Issue 3, "Are Female Primates Selected to Be Monogamous?", Issue 8, "Can Apes Learn Language?", Issue 9, "Does Language Shape How We Think?", Issue 13, "Do Men Dominate Women in All Societies?", and Issue 14, "Does the Distinction Between the Natural and the Supernatural Exist in All Cultures?"

To What Extent Do Cultural Patterns Develop Locally or Do They Diffuse from Other Societies?

Although this kind of question used to be of great concern to cultural anthropologists like Franz Boas and his students, it has become much more important for archaeologists in recent decades. At its heart is whether societies develop in situ or locally, or whether their cultural patterns are borrowed from other societies. Issue 4, "Did Humans Migrate to the New World from Europe in Early Prehistoric Times?", and Issue 6, "Can Archaeologists Determine the Cultural

Background of the Earliest Americans from the Ancient Skeleton Known as Kennewick Man?", are both of this character since they are about the cultural origins of the earliest inhabitants of North America.

Issue 5, "Did Climate Change Rather Than Overhunting Cause the Extinction of Mammoths and Other Megafauna in North America?", is a variant on this general kind of question, asking whether human cultural activity or environmental change brought the end of the wooly mammoths and mastodons in North America.

To What Extent Are Certain Cultural Patterns Essential Traits or Are They Culturally Constructed?

In recent years, cultural anthropologists have tended to see cultural patterns, and especially the meanings associated with them, as constructed from the society's social patterns and humans' tendency to treat whatever patterns are familiar as normal or natural, and to consider whatever new patterns they encounter as fundamentally wrong. Anthropologists, of course, are used to encountering any number of unexpected social patterns during field research. Most anthropologists examine these forms in terms of the other cultural features and social patterns in the community under study. Our rejection of ethnocentrism encourages anthropologists to reject our initial aversion to many social practices in favor of understanding why these practices occur.

Some practices may exist in a few societies but are not typical of humans generally. For example, homosexual acts are well known to have occurred frequently among upper class men in ancient Greece and Rome, but such pairings were never given the same legal status as marriage. Moreover, anthropologists have recorded diverse forms of marriage, including plural marriage for both men and women. But until the past decade or so, nowhere have societies accepted same-sexed pairings as marriage. Does this distribution of varied marriage patterns suggest that marriage between people of opposite genders is more natural than gay marriage? Just how constructed are the social patterns we identify as marriage around the world?

A number of other issues we raise in this volume are also about just how humanly constructed are the social forms observed in different societies around the world. For example, Issue 9, "Does Language Shape How We Think?", asks whether language constructs the world we perceive by conditioning us to think in certain ways rather than others? Similarly, Issue 10, "Is Black American English a Separate Language from Standard American English, with Its Own Distinctive Grammar and Vocabulary?", asks about whether the differences between languages and between dialects of the same language are innate or constructed. In this case, the answer has implications according to state law in California and other places to provide different kinds of instruction in the classroom. Issue 1, "Is Race a Useful Concept for Anthropologists?", Issue 14, "Does the Distinction Between the Natural and the Supernatural Exist in All Cultures?", and Issue 15, "Is Conflict Between Different Ethnic Groups Inevitable?", ask whether the very basic ideas of race, the supernatural, and ethnicity are culturally constructed or inherent in the facts or even biology of human life.

Is a Feminist Perspective Needed in Anthropology?

Although female anthropologists—like Margaret Mead and Ruth Benedict—have been very influential in the development of anthropology, there was a bias in early anthropological studies emphasizing the social and political lives of men. Over the past 40 years, feminist anthropologists have argued that these male-biased accounts have overlooked much of what goes on in traditional societies because male anthropologists have been preoccupied with men's activities and points of view, ignoring the lives, activities, and worldviews of women. Feminist anthropologists want ethnographers and theorists to give full weight to the activities and perspectives of women and to recognize that gender identities and values pervade all cultures.

Issue 2, "Are Humans Inherently Violent?", and Issue 3, "Are Female Primates Selected to Be Monogamous?", ask whether there are fundamental biological differences between males and females. While on the one hand, these are questions about whether violence and monogamy are driven by nature or nurture, they are also questions about whether anthropologists have accepted American cultural biases and a more sophisticated analysis would incorporate feminist views.

Other issues, such as Issue 12, "Was Margaret Mead's Fieldwork on Samoan Adolescents Fundamentally Flawed?", can be viewed as a challenge by a male anthropologist to an early feminist interpretation of Samoan cultural patterns. Issue 13, "Do Men Dominate Women in All Societies?", considers among other things whether a feminist perspective is needed to recognize sexual equality. Feminist anthropologists have also claimed that male bias affects anthropological methodology as well.

Does Reification Pose a Problem for Anthropological Interpretation of Data?

Anthropologists and other social scientists use the term *reification* to refer to the fact that when people have names for things, the very fact that we use these names in conversation makes them seem real and authentic. An early example of reification occurred in the middle ages when scholars discussed with great vigor the pressing theological question of the day, "How many angels could dance on the head of a pin?" Having a name for some sort of being we call an "angel" implies that there are such beings, even if we cannot see them. But if we accept the existence of angels, we can logically ask about their mass and materiality and whether more than one could perch on a pin's tiny head. Few students actually debate such issues today because the existence of angels is no longer considered a scientific question. But this old example of a trivial question illustrates how making a "thing" out of a phenomenon by giving a name to it—the process of reification—shapes the conversation and discourse about many topics. In its broadest sense, reification is about labels and whether the labels anthropologists give to phenomena help our interpretations and analysis or whether they stand in the way of good interpretations and our understanding of phenomena.

Several issues in this volume involve reification and labeling. Issue 1, "Is Race a Useful Concept for Anthropologists?", for example, is as much about the label "race," which means so much to Americans as an explanation for why people look different from one another, as it is about human biological variation. Issue 6, "Can Archaeologists Determine the Cultural Background of the Earliest Americans from the Ancient Skeleton Known as Kennewick Man?", concerns what we call the Kennewick Man. Is he "Caucasoid-like" or a "Paleoindian" or a "Paleoamerican"? Each label reifies the complex history of early settlement in North America. And Issue 9, "Does Language Shape How We Think?", is about whether the categories our language provides for us shapes or reifies our interpretations of the world around us.

In similar ways, Issue 10, "Is Black American English a Separate Language from Standard American English, with Its Own Distinctive Grammar and Vocabulary?", is about what we call Black English; is it a separate language or merely a different dialect? Issue 14, "Does the Distinction Between the Natural and the Supernatural Exist in All Cultures?", is about whether all societies have a category of the supernatural, which like the dancing angels of the middle ages are at best an unproven and unobserved phenomenon. And Issue 15, "Is Conflict Between Different Ethnic Groups Inevitable?", is also about how we label ethnic differences. As all of these issues suggest, reification is considered a problem for interpretation by many anthropologists.

How Much Do Our Preconceptions Affect Our Interpretations of Anthropologists?

Like the question of reification, our preconceptions also affect how we interpret anthropological data. Preconceptions are assumptions that may or may not fit with the facts. The challenge for anthropologists is distinguishing good preconceptions from less viable ones. Most of the issues in this volume involve this kind of problem at one level or another.

Some Methodological Concerns

Research Methods in Anthropology

Many of the issues in this volume address one or more of the basic questions outlined above. But some of these issues also point out fundamental differences in the methods different anthropologists use to answer research questions. For example, Issue 1, "Is Race a Useful Concept for Anthropologists?", deals with important biological facts that have driven anthropological studies for more than a century. But one position uses the methodology of comparing biological variables in communities across the globe, while the other focuses exclusively on variations in the American population. In Issue 4, "Did Humans Migrate to the New World from Europe in Early Prehistoric Times?", and Issue 6, "Can Archaeologists Determine the Cultural Background of the Earliest Americans from the Ancient Skeleton Known as Kennewick Man?", the authors use slightly different methods largely because they choose to consider slightly different data sets or give more significance to some evidence over others.

Issue 11, "Should Cultural Anthropology Stop Trying to Model Itself as a Science?", most directly addresses this concern because it highlights the major rift in anthropology today. Some anthropologists, particularly biological anthropologists, archaeologists, and some cultural anthropologists, see anthropology as a science, whereas others reject this notion arguing that anthropology is one of the humanities. Clearly, these two positions invoke different methods for their research.

Some issues, such as Issue 12, "Was Margaret Mead's Fieldwork on Samoan Adolescents Fundamentally Flawed?", are fundamentally about the quality of Margaret Mead's fieldwork. While Derek Freeman argues that Mead's fieldwork was flawed, it is not clear that Freeman's data collection was any better. But this issue centerpieces the question of good ethnographic field research.

Testable Hypotheses

If one accepts that anthropology is a science, one should expect that researchers will put forward hypotheses that can be tested by further research. One of the problems encountered in some of the issues is that one position or the other does not really propose well designed hypotheses. Issue 12, "Was Margaret Mead's Fieldwork on Samoan Adolescents Fundamentally Flawed?", hinges on the hypothesis that Mead felt she was testing, namely culture shapes the anxiety around sexuality experienced during adolescence. Freeman accepts this hypothesis, but finds no evidence to uphold it. In this case, anthropologist Martin Orans has argued that neither Mead nor Freeman has used a hypothesis that is testable. Their hypothesis sounds like it is a hypothesis, but it offers no clear way to confirm or invalidate the hypothesis. This same problem is at the heart of several of the debates in biological anthropology and archaeology, and even among some of the linguistic anthropology issues.

Some Theoretical Approaches

Anthropologists draw on many theories of widely varying scope and type. We present below brief summaries of a number of theoretical approaches used by authors in this book so that you will recognize and understand them when you see them. We have arranged these theories in a rough continuum from most scientific in approach to most humanistic.

Biological evolution. Biological anthropology is based predominantly on the modern theory of biological evolution. This builds upon the ideas of Charles Darwin in the mid-nineteenth century. Darwin combined the idea of evolution—the development of species by means of incremental changes in previous species—with the concept of natural selection. Natural selection means that in a variable population the individuals that best adapted to the environment are most likely to survive and reproduce, thus passing on their favorable characteristics (called *survival of the fittest*). The modern theory of biological evolution adds an understanding of genetics, including the concepts of *genetic drift* (random variation in gene frequencies), *gene flow* (transmission of genes between populations), and random *mutation*. Most biological anthropologists today also subscribe to the notion of *punctuated equilibrium*, which says that evolutionary change takes place in fits and starts, rather than at an even pace.

Virtually all biological anthropologists use the modern theory of evolution, so their disagreements arise not over which theory to use, but over interpretation of evidence and questions of how the theory applies to specific cases.

Sociobiology. Sociobiology is a theory that attempts to use evolutionary principles to explain all behavior of animals, including humans. The best-known practitioner is biologist E.O. Wilson, whose book *Sociobiology: The New Synthesis* (Harvard University Press, 1975) sets out the basic concepts. Sociobiologists believe that human behavior is determined by inherited behavioral tendencies. The genes promoting behaviors that lead to survival and successful reproduction are favored by natural selection and thus tend to become more common in a population over several generations. For sociobiologists such behaviors as selfishness, altruism to close kin, violence, and certain patterns of marriage are evolutionarily and biologically determined. They see individual and cultural explanations of these behaviors as mere rationalizations of innate patterns of behavior. In their view, no culture will persist that goes against the "wisdom of the genes."

Cultural evolution. Drawing on an analogy with biological evolution, nineteenth-century cultural anthropologists developed the idea that complex societies evolve out of simpler ones. The unilineal schemes of such cultural evolutionists as Lewis Henry Morgan, E.B. Tylor, and James G. Fraser postulated that all societies pass through a fixed series of stages, from savagery to civilization. They regarded contemporary simple societies, like the tribal peoples of the Amazon, as "survivals" from earlier stages of cultural evolution.

Unilineal schemes of cultural evolution have now been discredited because they were speculative, ignored differences in patterns of culture change in different places, and were blatantly ethnocentric, regarding all non-Western cultures as inferior to those of Europe. But some archaeologists and cultural anthropologists still espouse more sophisticated versions of cultural evolution regarding at least some aspects of culture change. An example is the widely used scheme of political evolution in which band societies are seen as developing into tribes and tribes into states.

Cultural ecology. The theory of cultural ecology was developed by cultural anthropologist Julian Steward in the 1930s as a corrective to the overly simple schemes of cultural evolution. Emphasizing the process of adaptation to the physical environment, he postulated that societies in different environments would develop different practices, although the general trend was toward higher levels of complexity, a process he called *multilinear evolution*. (See his book *Theory of Culture Change* [University of Illinois Press, 1955].) His idea of adaptation, like natural selection, explained why some societies and practices succeeded and were perpetuated, while other less well-adapted ones died out.

Many archaeologists and cultural anthropologists use versions of cultural ecology to explain why certain cultural practices exist in certain environments. Marvin Harris's widely used theory of *cultural materialism* is a further development of cultural ecology. The basic idea behind all versions of cultural ecology is that societies must fulfill their material needs if they are to survive. Therefore, the institutions involved with making a living must be well adapted to the environment, while others, like religions, are less constrained by the environment.

Culture history. One of the founders of American cultural anthropology, Franz Boas, rejected the cultural evolution schemes of the nineteenth century, with their fixed stages of cultural development. He pointed out that all societies had unique histories, depending on local innovations and diffusion of ideas from neighboring societies. Also, change is not always toward greater complexity; civilizations crumble as well as rise. Boas advocated recording the particular events and influences that contributed to the makeup of each culture.

World system theory. Some of the earlier theories in anthropology, like cultural ecology, treated societies as though they were isolated from outside influences. The world system theory, which has gained great prominence in the social sciences in recent years, claims, on the contrary, that all societies large and small are—and long have been—integrated in a single worldwide political-economic system. This theory was popularized in anthropology by Eric Wolf in his book *Europe and the People Without History* (University of California Press, 1982). This approach emphasizes the connections among societies, especially the influence of politically powerful societies over weak ones, as in colonialism, rather than local development of culture.

Cultural interpretation. Humanist anthropologists emphasize their role as interpreters, not explainers, of culture. They focus on the task of describing other cultures in ways that are intelligible to Western readers, making sense of customs that at first glance seem incomprehensible. The most prominent practitioner of cultural interpretation is Clifford Geertz, who coined the term "thick description" for this process. (See, for example, his book *The Interpretation of Cultures* [Basic Books, 1973].)

Feminist anthropology. Feminist anthropology began in the 1970s as the anthropology of women, an approach meant to correct the lack of coverage of women and women's views in earlier anthropology. It has now developed into a thoroughgoing alternative approach to the study of culture and society. Its basic idea is that gender is a cultural construction affecting the roles and meanings of the sexes in particular societies. The aim of feminist anthropology is both to explain the position of women and to convey the meanings surrounding gender. Feminist anthropologists emphasize that all social relations have a gender dimension.

How Anthropologists Reach Conclusions

None of the issues considered in this volume has been resolved, and several are still the subject of heated and at times acrimonious debate. The most heated controversies typically arise from the most extreme points of view. When reading these selections, students should bear in mind that only two positions are presented here formally, although in the introductions and follow-up questions and the section called "Is There Common Ground?", we raise questions that should guide you to consider other positions as well. The perspectives of the authors represented here are often diametrically opposed, and many anthropologists would see at least one selection in each issue as an extreme or radical position, while other anthropologists might find other selections overly simplistic, unsupported, or naive. We encourage you to question all of the positions offered before coming to any conclusions of your own. Remember, for more than a century anthropology has prided itself on revealing how our own views of the world are culturally biased. Try to be aware of how your own background, upbringing, ethnicity, religion, likes, and dislikes affect your assessments of the arguments presented here. Many anthropological perspectives that emerge from unexamined assumptions are not necessarily the best answers to important issues.

In our own teaching, we have often used controversial issues as a way to help students understand how anthropologists think about research questions. We have found that six questions often help students focus on the most important points in these selections:

1. Who is the author? (Here we especially mean the author's disciplinary or subdisciplinary background, since the names of these authors may not be familiar to you.)
2. What question is the author trying to answer?
3. What are the author's assumptions?
4. What methods and data does an author use?

5. What are the author's conclusions?
6. How does the author reach his or her conclusions from the data?

For each issue we suggest that you consider what school of thought, what sort of training, and what sort of research experience each author has. We often find it useful to ask why this particular author finds the topic worth writing about. Does one or the other author seem to have any sort of bias? What assumptions does each author hold? Do both authors hold the same assumptions?

For any anthropological debate, we also find it useful to ask what methods or analytical strategies each author has used to reach the conclusions he or she presents. For some of the issues presented in this book, authors share many of the same assumptions and are generally working with the same evidence, but disagree as to how this evidence should be analyzed. Some authors disagree most profoundly on what kinds of data are most suitable for answering a particular research question. Some even disagree about what kinds of questions anthropologists should be asking.

Finally, we suggest that you consider how the author has come to his or her conclusions from the available data. Would different data make any difference? Would a different kind of evidence be more appropriate? Would different data likely lead to different conclusions? Would different ways of analyzing the data suggest other conclusions?

If you can answer most of these questions about any pair of selections, you will be thinking about these problems anthropologically and will understand how anthropologists approach controversial research questions. After weighing the various possible positions on an issue, you will be able to form sound opinions of your own.

Internet References . . .

American Anthropological Association's Statement on "Race"

In 1998 the executive board of the American Anthropological Association issued a Statement on "Race." This statement was compiled by anthropologists from many different research backgrounds and aimed to be general and broad. It does not, however, reflect the consensus of all members of the association.

www.aaanet.org/stmts/racepp.htm

Nova: Does Race Exist?

This Web page explores the issues pro and con on the reality of race.

www.pbs.org/wgbh/nova/evolution/does-race-exist.html

Power of an Illusion: Notes for a Three-Part Film on Race Distributed by California Newsreel That Critiques the Concept of Race

http://newsreel.org/guides/race/pressreleasecredit.htm

Psychology Today

This online source explores the MOA gene ("warrior gene"). It is said that a person with this gene is more aggressive, even though there may be cultural influences that trigger the aggressiveness of this gene.

www.psychologytoday.com/blog/psychology-writers/201104/ triggering-the-warrior-gene-in-villain-or-hero

This link argues that chimpanzees (the closest ancestor to humans) are no more violent than any other primate; therefore humans have not genetically inherited violence. This study states that chimpanzee behavior is peaceful, but if their culture is manipulated they act out in a more violent manner.

www.psychologytoday.com/blog/moral-landscapes/201103/male-chimps- and-humans-are-genetically-violent-not

Some Forensic Anthropology Web Sites

www.nd.edu/~stephens/Forensics.pdf

http://web.utk.edu/~fac/facilities.html

Biological Anthropology

*B*iological anthropologists, also called physical anthropologists, study the bodies, bones, and genetics of humans and of our nearest relatives, the other primates. Their basic goals are to understand human evolution scientifically and to explain contemporary human diversity. Fundamental questions include: How did our species evolve from early nonhuman primates? When did our species take on attributes that are associated with anatomically modern humans? Where did our species develop as a species, and what were the evolutionary forces that contributed to our anatomical evolution? These questions have traditionally required detailed comparisons of bones from living species and fossilized bones from extinct species. However, increasingly anthropologists asking these kinds of questions are developing new models about evolution from observing and studying living primates either in the laboratory or in their natural environment.

- Is Race a Useful Concept for Anthropologists?
- Are Humans Inherently Violent?
- Are Female Primates Selected to Be Monogamous?

ISSUE 1

Is Race a Useful Concept for Anthropologists?

YES: **George W. Gill**, from "Does Race Exist? A Proponent's Perspective," *NOVA Online* (October 12, 2000)

NO: **C. Loring Brace**, from "Does Race Exist? An Antagonist's Perspective," *NOVA Online* (October 12, 2000)

Learning Outcomes

After reading this issue, you should be able to:

- Understand why forensic anthropologists may find race a useful concept for identifying skeletal material.
- Discuss the difference between the biological concept of race and the social aspects of race provided by our society.
- Explain some of the problems with the common sense view of race in America.
- Discuss the disconnect between why average Americans perceive races while biological anthropologists argue that biologically speaking there are no identifiable races.
- Understand why forensic analysis might be able to use the race concept even though when looked at over the entire globe there are no distinct races.

ISSUE SUMMARY

YES: Biological and forensic anthropologist George Gill argues that the concept of race is useful because races—conceived of populations originating in particular regions—can be distinguished by combinations of external and skeletal features. The concept of race is especially useful for the forensic task of identifying human skeletons. The notion of race also provides a vocabulary for discussing human biological variation and racism that can be understood by students.

NO: Biological anthropologist C. Loring Brace argues that distinct races cannot be defined because human physical features vary gradually (in clines) and independently from region to region, without

2

sharp discontinuities between physical types. He says races exists in people's perceptions but not in biological reality. In his view the peculiar historical pattern in which Native Americans, Africans brought to the United States as slaves, and European immigrants largely from northern Europe artificially makes it seem that these three groups form distinct races.

The European idea of humanity being divided into physically distinct types—races—developed after the Age of Exploration in the fifteenth and sixteenth centuries. Before the era of rapid transportation and mass population movements, most people were born, lived, and died without seeing anyone who looked appreciably different from themselves. But when European explorers reached Africa, East Asia, and the Americas, they were confronted with people who were very different from them in appearance and in their ways of life. Europeans tried to understand this unforeseen human diversity in terms of the religious worldview of the time. High Councils of the Church debated whether particular peoples in the New World, for example, had souls that missionaries could save. Not only was their physical appearance different from Europeans, but their ways of life often seemed primitive or repugnant—although it must be said that in the Americas, East Asia, and Africa most peoples found Europeans' appearance and practices extremely unappealing as well. Enslaving or killing colonized peoples seemed justified by the view that these peoples were inherently inferior beings that were not fully human.

By the nineteenth century, the idea that populations looked and acted differently because of their different hereditary endowments was widely believed. Scholars assumed that the European way of living with its advanced technology and complex social hierarchy was the highest stage that humankind had yet reached. They viewed different groups around the world as being at different stages of progress on the march to becoming a European-style civilization, and they considered those that lagged behind technologically to have been held back by their inferior physical, mental, and moral endowments.

One aspect of these early views of the varied endowments of people from different cultural backgrounds is that Europeans in the eighteenth and nineteenth centuries relied on the clothing of their countrymen as a marker of someone's place in society, social worth, intellectual ability, and, of course, wealth and social refinement. The poor in England, France, or Spain wore ragged clothes, while upper class people competed to wear more expensive and trendy outfits. Explorers were nearly always over dressed for the climate when they visited the New World, Africa, or the Far East. Since people in the warm tropical countries typically wore little clothing and had very simple technologies, it was often assumed that their darker skin tone was a sign of intellectual limitations and an inability to master the technologies and social refinements of European society. These were racist views about the characteristics of peoples around the world. The development of cultural evolutionary schemes in the second half of the century, inspired in part by Darwin's theory of the evolution of species, seemed to give a scientific basis for this view of other people's inferiority. In short, racism and the idea of race developed together.

During the twentieth century, anthropology in America developed somewhat differently. One of the founding figures in American anthropology, Franz Boas, challenged the relationship between biological traits and cultural traits. He fought a life-long battle against racism, hoping to counter the idea that cultural and psychological characteristics could be explained in terms of inherited biology. He recognized that there were broad differences among Africans, Europeans, Native Americans, and East Asians, but he rejected the idea that these differences were the basis of several stages of intellectual evolution. His most important study on this topic used physical measurements of Eastern European and Mediterranean immigrants who were arriving in New York and other large cities in large numbers. Because they often had few possessions, little education, and spoke no English, immigration officers assumed these immigrants were mentally deficient. From a study of 18,000 immigrants, Boas showed that the physical characteristics of European immigrants and their descendants were changing once they reached the United States, showing that physical type was not nearly as fixed as previous scholars had assumed.

Toward the middle of the twentieth century, biological anthropologists tried to refine the concept of race by separating biological differences from cultural ones. They also began to focus on populations, rather than individuals, and genetic variations, rather than superficial physical differences like head shape. One seemingly intractable problem emerged in the resulting analyses. Different set of races appeared depending on the number and nature of the specific physical features considered. No matter how many races were distinguished, there were always some groups of individuals that did not fit in.

The two selections presented here were produced for *NOVA Online*, specifically to explore how modern scholars understood the biological notion of race. All anthropological researchers are aware of the racial stereotypes that have been the basis of racial prejudice and racial inequality in the United States. The question they are debating here is whether the biological (as opposed to the sociological) notion of race is useful.

Here, George W. Gill argues that races should be understood as populations derived from particular geographical regions. Such races can be distinguished not only through their external characteristics, such as skin color, but also by skeletal features. By using a combination of distinctive osteological characteristics, which are found in varying proportions in different geographical races, forensic anthropologists can make highly accurate guesses about the ancestry of persons whose bones they examine. Gill also notes the danger of removing the topic of race from public discourse.

On the other side of the debate, C. Loring Brace contends that race is a meaningless biological concept. He argues that there are no clear-cut boundaries between geographical "races" because human physical features vary gradually and independently from region to region. Brace does not, however, deny that race is a social reality. He recognizes that Americans tend to view physical variations in terms of a concept of race, but he contends that discrete and clear races cannot be scientifically defined and distinguished, no matter what traits one considers.

This issue touches on a number of thorny questions for anthropologists, some scientific and some ethical. What sorts of concepts are needed for discussing and analyzing human hereditary differences? Can geographical races be defined in terms of varying proportions of characteristics that together form a distinctive profile? What is the relationship between individuals and racial categories? Does the very idea of classifying humans into clear-cut categories inherently misrepresent the gradual nature of genetic variation and change? Is the term *race* so loaded with racist connotations that it must be replaced by a more neutral term before dispassionate discussion of human hereditary variation can proceed?

YES ↵

Does Race Exist?
A Proponent's Perspective

Slightly over half of all biological/physical anthropologists today believe in the traditional view that human races are biologically valid and real. Furthermore, they tend to see nothing wrong in defining and naming the different populations of *Homo sapiens*. The other half of the biological anthropology community believes either that the traditional racial categories for humankind are arbitrary and meaningless, or that at a minimum there are better ways to look at human variation than through the "racial lens."

Are there differences in the research concentrations of these two groups of experts? Yes, most decidedly there are. As pointed out in a recent 2000 edition of a popular physical anthropology textbook, forensic anthropologists (those who do skeletal identification for law-enforcement agencies) are overwhelmingly in support of the idea of the basic biological reality of human races, and yet those who work with blood-group data, for instance, tend to reject the biological reality of racial categories.

I happen to be one of those very few forensic physical anthropologists who actually does research on the particular traits used today in forensic racial identification (i.e., "assessing ancestry," as it is generally termed today). Partly this is because for more than a decade now U.S. national and regional forensic anthropology organizations have deemed it necessary to quantitatively test both traditional and new methods for accuracy in legal cases. I volunteered for this task of testing methods and developing new methods in the late 1980s. What have I found? Where do I now stand in the "great race debate?" Can I see truth on one side or the other—or on both sides—in this argument?

Findings

First, I have found that forensic anthropologists attain a high degree of accuracy in determining geographic racial affinities (white, black, American Indian, etc.) by utilizing both new and traditional methods of bone analysis. Many well-conducted studies were reported in the late 1980s and 1990s that test methods objectively for percentage of correct placement. Numerous individual methods involving midfacial measurements, femur traits, and so on are

From *NOVA Online*, October 12, 2000. Copyright © 2000 by George W. Gill. Reprinted by permission of the author.

over 80 percent accurate alone, and in combination produce very high levels of accuracy. No forensic anthropologist would make a racial assessment based upon just *one* of these methods, but in combination they can make very reliable assessments, just as in determining sex or age. In other words, multiple criteria are the key to success in all of these determinations.

I have a respected colleague, the skeletal biologist C. Loring Brace, who is as skilled as any of the leading forensic anthropologists at assessing ancestry from bones, yet he does not subscribe to the concept of race. Neither does Norman Sauer, a board-certified forensic anthropologist. My students ask, "How can this be? They can identify skeletons as to racial origins but do not believe in race!" My answer is that we can often *function* within systems that we do not believe in.

As a middle-aged male, for example, I am not so sure that I believe any longer in the chronological "age" categories that many of my colleagues in skeletal biology use. Certainly parts of the skeletons of some 45-year-old people look older than corresponding portions of the skeletons of some 55-year-olds. If, however, law enforcement calls upon me to provide "age" on a skeleton, I can provide an answer that will be proven sufficiently accurate should the decedent eventually be identified. I may not believe in society's "age" categories, but I can be very effective at "aging" skeletons. The next question, of course, is how "real" is age biologically? My answer is that if one can use biological criteria to assess age with reasonable accuracy, then age has some basis in biological reality even if the particular "social construct" that defines its limits might be imperfect. I find this true not only for age and stature estimations but for sex and race identification.

The "reality of race" therefore depends more on the definition of reality than on the definition of race. If we choose to accept the system of racial taxonomy that physical anthropologists have traditionally established—major races: black, white, etc.—then one can classify human skeletons within it just as well as one can living humans. The bony traits of the nose, mouth, femur, and cranium are just as revealing to a good osteologist as skin color, hair form, nose form, and lips to the perceptive observer of living humanity. I have been able to prove to myself over the years, in actual legal cases, that I am *more* accurate at assessing race from skeletal remains than from looking at living people standing before me. So those of us in forensic anthropology know that the skeleton reflects race, whether "real" or not, just as well if not better than superficial soft tissue does. The idea that race is "only skin deep" is simply not true, as any experienced forensic anthropologist will affirm.

Position on Race

Where I stand today in the "great race debate" after a decade and a half of pertinent skeletal research is clearly more on the side of the reality of race than on the "race denial" side. Yet I do see why many other physical anthropologists are able to ignore or deny the race concept. Blood-factor analysis, for instance, shows many traits that cut across racial boundaries in a purely *clinal* fashion with very few if any "breaks" along racial boundaries. (A cline is a gradient of change, such as from people with a high frequency of blue eyes, as in Scandinavia, to people with a high frequency of brown eyes, as in Africa.)

Morphological characteristics, however, like skin color, hair form, bone traits, eyes, and lips tend to follow geographic boundaries coinciding often with climatic zones. This is not surprising since the selective forces of climate are probably the primary forces of nature that have shaped human races with regard not only to skin color and hair form but also the underlying bony structures of the nose, cheekbones, etc. (For example, more prominent noses humidify air better.) As far as we know, blood-factor frequencies are *not* shaped by these same climatic factors.

So, serologists who work largely with blood factors will tend to see human variation as clinal and races as not a valid construct, while skeletal biologists, particularly forensic anthropologists, will see races as biologically real. The common person on the street who sees only a person's skin color, hair form, and face shape will also tend to see races as biologically real. They are not incorrect. Their perspective is just different from that of the serologist.

So, yes, I see truth on both sides of the race argument.

Those who believe that the concept of race is valid do not discredit the notion of clines, however. Yet those with the clinal perspective who believe that races are not real do try to discredit the evidence of skeletal biology. Why this bias from the "race denial" faction? This bias seems to stem largely from socio-political motivation and not science at all. For the time being at least, the people in "race denial" are in "reality denial" as well. Their motivation (a positive one) is that they have come to believe that the race concept is socially dangerous. In other words, they have convinced themselves that race promotes racism. Therefore, they have pushed the politically correct agenda that human races are not biologically real, no matter what the evidence.

Consequently, at the beginning of the 21st century, even as a majority of biological anthropologists favor the reality of the race perspective, not one introductory textbook of physical anthropology even presents that perspective as a possibility. In a case as flagrant as this, we are not dealing with science but rather with blatant, politically motivated censorship. But, you may ask, are the politically correct actually correct? Is there a relationship between thinking about race and racism?

Race and Racism

Does discussing human variation in a framework of racial biology promote or reduce racism? This is an important question, but one that does not have a simple answer. Most social scientists over the past decade have convinced themselves that it runs the risk of promoting racism in certain quarters. Anthropologists of the 1950s, 1960s, and early 1970s, on the other hand, believed that they were combating racism by openly discussing race and by teaching courses on human races and racism. Which approach has worked best? What do the intellectuals among racial minorities believe? How do students react and respond?

Three years ago, I served on a NOVA-sponsored panel in New York, in which panelists debated the topic "Is There Such a Thing as Race?" Six of us sat on the panel, three proponents of the race concept and three antagonists. All had authored books or papers on race. Loring Brace and I were the two anthropologists "facing off" in the debate. The ethnic composition of the panel was three white and three black scholars. As our conversations developed, I was struck by how similar many of my concerns regarding racism were to those of my two black teammates. Although recognizing that embracing the race concept can have risks attached, we were (and are) more fearful of the form of racism likely to emerge if race is denied and dialogue about it lessened. We fear that the social taboo about the subject of race has served to suppress open discussion about a very important subject in need of dispassionate debate. One of my teammates, an affirmative-action lawyer, is afraid that a denial that races exist also serves to encourage a denial that racism exists. He asks, "How can we combat racism if no one is willing to talk about race?"

Who Will Benefit?

In my experience, minority students almost invariably have been the strongest supporters of a "racial perspective" on human variation in the classroom. The first-ever black student in my human variation class several years ago came to me at the end of the course and said, "Dr. Gill, I really want to thank you for changing my life with this course." He went on to explain that, "My whole life I have wondered about why I am black, and if that is good or bad. Now I know the reasons why I am the way I am and that these traits are useful and good."

A human-variation course with another perspective would probably have accomplished the same for this student if he had ever noticed it. The truth is, innocuous contemporary human-variation classes with their politically correct titles and course descriptions do not attract the attention of minorities or those other students who could most benefit. Furthermore, the politically correct "race denial" perspective in society as a whole suppresses dialogue, allowing ignorance to replace knowledge and suspicion to replace familiarity. This encourages ethnocentrism and racism more than it discourages it.

Does Race Exist? An Antagonist's Perspective

I am going to start this essay with what may seem to many as an outrageous assertion: There is no such thing as a biological entity that warrants the term "race."

The immediate reaction of most literate people is that this is obviously nonsense. The physician will retort, "What do you mean 'there is no such thing as race'? I see it in my practice everyday!" Jane Doe and John Roe will be equally incredulous. Note carefully, however, that my opening declaration did not claim that "there is no such thing as race." What I said is that there is no "biological entity that warrants the term 'race'." "You're splitting hairs," the reader may retort. "Stop playing verbal games and tell us what you really mean!"

And so I shall, but there is another charge that has been thrown my way, which I need to dispel before explaining the basis for my statement. Given the tenor of our times at the dawn of the new millennium, some have suggested that my position is based mainly on the perception of the social inequities that have accompanied the classification of people into "races." My stance, then, has been interpreted as a manifestation of what is being called "political correctness." My answer is that it is really the defenders of the concept of "race" who are unwittingly shaped by the political reality of American history. . . .

But all of this needs explaining. First, it is perfectly true that the long-term residents of the various parts of the world have patterns of features that we can easily identify as characteristic of the areas from which they come. It should be added that they have to have resided in those places for a couple of hundred thousand years before their regional patterns became established. Well, you may ask, why can't we call those regional patterns "races"? In fact, we can and do, but it does not make them coherent biological entities. "Races" defined in such a way are products of our perceptions. "Seeing is believing" will be the retort, and, after all, aren't we seeing reality in those regional differences?

I should point out that this is the same argument that was made against Copernicus and Galileo almost half a millennium ago. To this day, few have actually made the observations and done the calculations that led those Renaissance scholars to challenge the universal perception that the sun sets in the evening to rise again at the dawn. It was just a matter of common sense to believe that the sun revolves around the Earth, just as it was common sense to "know" that the Earth was flat. Our beliefs concerning "race" are based on the same sort of common sense, and they are just as basically wrong.

The Nature of Human Variation

I would suggest that there are very few who, of their own experience, have actually perceived at first hand the nature of human variation. What we know of the characteristics of the various regions of the world we have largely gained vicariously and in misleadingly spotty fashion. Pictures and the television camera tell us that the people of Oslo in Norway, Cairo in Egypt, and Nairobi in Kenya look very different. And when we actually meet natives of those separate places, which can indeed happen, we can see representations of those differences at first hand. But if one were to walk up beside the Nile from Cairo, across the Tropic of Cancer to Khartoum in the Sudan and on to Nairobi, there would be no visible boundary between one people and another. The same thing would be true if one were to walk north from Cairo, through the Caucasus, and on up into Russia, eventually swinging west across the northern end of the Baltic Sea to Scandinavia. The people at any adjacent stops along the way look like one another more than they look like anyone else since, after all, they are related to one another. As a rule, the boy marries the girl next door throughout the whole world, but next door goes on without stop from one region to another.

We realize that in the extremes of our transit—Moscow to Nairobi, perhaps—there is a major but gradual change in skin color from what we euphemistically call white to black, and that this is related to the latitudinal difference in the intensity of the ultraviolet component of sunlight. What we do not see, however, is the myriad other traits that are distributed in a fashion quite unrelated to the intensity of ultraviolet radiation. Where skin color is concerned, all the northern populations of the Old World are lighter than the long-term inhabitants near the equator. Although Europeans and Chinese are obviously different, in skin color they are closer to each other than either is to equatorial Africans. But if we test the distribution of the widely known ABO blood-group system, then Europeans and Africans are closer to each other than either is to Chinese.

Then if we take that scourge sickle-cell anemia, so often thought of as an African disease, we discover that, while it does reach high frequencies in some parts of sub-Saharan Africa, it did not originate there. Its distribution includes southern Italy, the eastern Mediterranean, parts of the Middle East, and over into India. In fact, it represents a kind of adaptation that aids survival in the face of a particular kind of malaria, and wherever that malaria is a prominent threat, sickle-cell anemia tends to occur in higher frequencies. It would appear that the gene that controls that trait was introduced to sub-Saharan Africa by traders from those parts of the Middle East where it had arisen in conjunction with the conditions created by the early development of agriculture.

Every time we plot the distribution of a trait possessing a survival value that is greater under some circumstances than under others, it will have a different pattern of geographical variation, and no two such patterns will coincide. Nose form, tooth size, relative arm and leg length, and a whole series of other traits are distributed each in accordance with its particular controlling selective force. The gradient of the distribution of each is called a "cline" and those clines are completely independent of one another. This is what lies behind the aphorism, "There are no races, there are only clines." Yes, we can recognize people from a given area. What we are seeing, however, is a pattern of features derived from common ancestry in the area in question, and these are largely without different survival value. To the extent that the people in a given region look more like one another than they look like people from other regions, this can be regarded as "family resemblance writ large." And as we have seen, each region grades without break into the one next door.

There is nothing wrong with using geographic labels to designate people. Major continental terms are just fine, and sub-regional refinements such as Western European, Eastern African, Southeast Asian, and so forth carry no unintentional baggage. In contrast, terms such as "Negroid," "Caucasoid," and "Mongoloid" create more problems than they solve. Those very terms reflect a mix of narrow regional, specific ethnic, and descriptive physical components with an assumption that such separate dimensions have some kind of common tie. Biologically, such terms are worse than useless. Their continued use, then, is in social situations where people think they have some meaning.

America and the Race Concept

The role played by America is particularly important in generating and perpetuating the concept of "race." The human inhabitants of the Western Hemisphere largely derive from three very separate regions of the world—Northeast Asia, Northwest Europe, and Western Africa—and none of them has been in the New World long enough to have been shaped by their experiences in the manner of those long-term residents in the various separate regions of the Old World.

It was the American experience of those three separate population components facing one another on a daily basis under conditions of manifest and enforced inequality that created the concept in the first place and endowed it with the assumption that those perceived "races" had very different sets of capabilities. Those thoughts are very influential and have become enshrined in laws and regulations. This is why I can conclude that, while the word "race" has no coherent biological meaning, its continued grip on the public mind is in fact a manifestation of the power of the historical continuity of the American social structure, which is assumed by all to be essentially "correct."

Finally, because of America's enormous influence on the international scene, ideas generated by the idiosyncrasies of American history have gained currency in ways that transcend American intent or control. One of those ideas is the concept of "race," which we have exported to the rest of the world without any realization that this is what we were doing. The adoption of the biologically indefensible American concept of "race" by an admiring world has to be the ultimate manifestation of political correctness.

EXPLORING THE ISSUE

Is Race a Useful Concept for Anthropologists?

Critical Thinking and Reflection

1. What are the origins of the concept of race as most Americans understand it?
2. To what extent is the social problem of racial inequality dependent upon the biological reality of race as a scientific concept? Does the fact that scientists have talked about race for more than a century encourage racial discrimination?
3. Should people concerned with social justice be concerned about whether there are biologically defined races or not? What if biological anthropologists stopped using the term race altogether?
4. How does the fact that the American population includes people selectively brought to the New World from only a few world regions lead most Americans to see them as belonging to a series of discontinuous races? Could this fact account for Gill's ability to identify the "race" of his forensic cases?
5. Is it possible for Gill to be correct that in forensic analysis he can use racial groupings, yet Brace is also correct when he argues that there really are no discrete races when worldwide populations are considered?

Is There Common Ground?

No one denies that variations in hereditary features between individuals and populations exist. The disagreement between these two biological anthropologists is over whether the concept of race, understood as "subspecies" of human beings, accurately expresses these variations. Gill argues that combinations of superficial and skeletal characteristics cluster together, making it possible to distinguish geographical populations as separate races. He sees the race concept as particularly useful for forensic anthropologists trying to determine the identity of dead people from their bones alone. Brace counters that distinct races cannot be defined objectively on the basis of biological variations because physical characteristics are not discrete, meaning that there are no clear breaks in physical type between nearby geographical populations. Instead groups of people vary gradually as one goes from region to region. In addition, he adds that characteristics vary independently of each other, rather than in clusters.

Most scholars—including Gill and Brace—agree, however, that the idea and perception of race is deeply embedded in American culture. The view that races do not exist seems nonsensical to the average American, who has grown up steeped in the idea that humanity is made up of different races. Racial categories are so ingrained in our vocabulary and thought that we identify people by race as readily as by sex or age. We are asked our race on official census forms, and many government policies, such as affirmative action, depend on the reality of race. What is needed, Brace would say, is recognition that this notion of race is a cultural—not biological—construction. On this point, few biological anthropologists would disagree with the view that the cultural view of race is a cultural construct and not the same construct that people in Brazil or the Congo, or India have.

Additional Resources

The literature on race, including the concept of race, is enormous. For further reading on the concept of race a good place to start is the American Anthropological Association's "Statement on 'Race,'" which can be found on the AAA Web site at: www.aaanet.org/stmts/racepp.htm

Informative overviews of the concept of race in anthropology include the following:

Banton, Michael. 1998. *Racial Theories*. Second Edition. Cambridge: Cambridge University Press.

Shanklin, Eugenia. 1994. *Anthropology and Race*. New York: Wadsworth Publishing Company.

Two landmark books in the development of anthropological views of race are:

Boas, Franz. 1940. *Race, Language, and Culture*. New York: Macmillan.

Montagu, Ashley. 1945. *Man's Most Dangerous Myth: The Fallacy of Race*. New York: Columbia University Press.

For further discussion of race as a cultural construct:

Marks, Jonathan. 1994. "Black, White, Other." *Natural History* (December 1994).

For an accessible source on forensic anthropology that includes a discussion on identifying race:

Rhine, Stanley. 1998. *Bone Voyage: A Journey in Forensic Anthropology*. Albuquerque: University of New Mexico Press.

ISSUE 2

Are Humans Inherently Violent?

YES: Richard Wrangham and Dale Peterson, from *Demonic Males: Apes and the Origins of Human Violence* (Houghton Mifflin Harcourt Publishing Company, 1996)

NO: Robert W. Sussman, from "Exploring Our Basic Human Nature: Are Humans Inherently Violent?" *Anthro Notes* (Fall 1997)

Learning Outcomes

After reading this issue, you should be able to:

- Understand the debate between those biological anthropologists who believe that violence is an inherent human trait and those who feel we are not biologically hardwired to be aggressive.
- Discuss the evidence that researchers use when offering arguments either in favor of or against the argument that humans are inherently violent.
- Explain the goals of studies of behavioral evolution, often called sociobiology.
- Understand the limitations of evolutionary arguments when we cannot observe evidence of actual behavior.
- Evaluate the strengths and weaknesses of the argument that humans are evolutionarily adapted to violence.

ISSUE SUMMARY

YES: Biological anthropologist Richard Wrangham and science writer Dale Peterson maintain that male humans and chimpanzees, our closest nonhuman relatives, have an innate tendency to be aggressive and to defend their territory by violence. They state that sexual selection, a type of natural selection, has fostered an instinct for male aggression because males who are good fighters mate more frequently and sire more offspring than weaker and less aggressive ones.

NO: Biological anthropologist Robert W. Sussman rejects the theory that human aggression is an inherited propensity, arguing instead that violence is a product of culture and upbringing. He also rejects the contention that male chimpanzees routinely commit violent acts against other male chimps. Sussman regards the notion that human males are inherently violent as a Western cultural tradition, not a scientifically demonstrated fact.

Human history is rife with wars between groups of all types, from clans to nation-states, and interpersonal violence is common enough that all societies attempt to control it. But is violence a part of human nature, or is violence merely one of many human capabilities that may be either encouraged or discouraged by culture?

The question of whether humans have an instinct for aggression has been around since the formative years of anthropology, and it is still being debated today. Some nineteenth century scholars interpreted Darwin's concepts of "natural selection" and "survival of the fittest" to mean that the strong would kill off the weak. The strongest and most aggressive individuals, therefore, would have the most offspring, and their strength and instinct for aggression would gradually come to predominate in the population.

The idea of an instinct for aggression sprang up again in the 1960s. The South African anthropologist Raymond Dart, who discovered the first Australopithecines—very early African bipedal hominins—hypothesized that they evolved from earlier primates when they became carnivorous and developed bone tools to kill their prey (Raymond A. Dart with Dennis Crag, *Adventures with the Missing Link*, Harper and Row, 1959). The notion that hominins were born in violence and that we still carry the genes predisposing us to mayhem was expanded and popularized by Robert Ardrey in his books *African Genesis* (Atheneum, 1961), *The Territorial Imperative* (Atheneum, 1966), and *The Social Contract* (Atheneum, 1970). Drawing on the behavior of certain birds and fish, he expanded Dart's concept to include instincts for aggressive defense of territories, thus making the concept of private property a part of human nature as well. These and similar works, such as Desmond Morris's book *The Naked Ape* (McGraw-Hill, 1967) and *The Human Zoo* (McGraw-Hill, 1969), gained a wide and approving audience. The argument that humans, especially males, were innately aggressive and territorial because of natural selection not only explained human violence, but to some also excused it.

Most cultural anthropologists from the 1950s onward rejected the explanation of human aggression in terms of instincts, emphasizing instead the social and cultural causes of violence. They pointed out that the amount of aggression tolerated varies widely from one society to another and that individuals can become aggressive or peaceful depending on how they are raised. They held up such groups as the Semai of Malaysia (Robert K. Dentan, *The Semai: A Nonviolent People of Malaya*, Holt, Rinehart, and Winston, 1968) as proof that culture could create a people who abhorred all forms of aggression and coercion. Whatever instinct for aggression humans might have, they argued, must be very weak indeed.

The question behind this issue concerns human nature. Have we a set of innate behavioral predispositions when, when set off by certain stimuli, are very likely to be expressed? Or are any such predispositions at best weak tendencies that can be shaped or even negated by cultural conditioning? Many apparently innate behaviors in humans turn out to be highly variable in their strength and form. Although the suckling instinct of babies operates predictably in all newborns, a hypothesized "mothering instinct" seems quite diverse in expression and variable in strength from one woman to another. The question then is whether the hypothesized aggression instinct is a powerful drive, which all human males must express in one way or another, or a weak and pliable tendency, which some males may never act upon.

At its core, this issue is one of several examples of the nature-nurture debates that anthropologists and other researchers have been debating for the past century. Is the tendency for male violence that we can observe in many contemporary human societies the result of some basic instinct or basic human nature or is it the result of nurture and how our particular human cultures shape our behavioral patterns?

In the first selection, biological anthropologist Richard Wrangham and science writer Dale Peterson argue that human wars and interpersonal violence are driven by inherited behavioral tendencies that have evolved under the pressures of sexual selection—the natural selection of traits that enhance the reproductive success on one sex. Among both humans and chimpanzees, for example, males who are aggressive use their fighting ability to dominate other males and prevent them from mating with the available females. Therefore, they argue, the genes causing aggression are passed on to succeeding generations in greater numbers than the genes causing nonaggressive behavior. Wrangham and Peterson have not identified any particular genes as "aggressive genes" but hypothesize that there must be some to account for the patterns of aggressive behavior found among the world's diverse peoples. Wrangham and Peterson's argument is a classic argument in sociobiology, the branch of biological anthropology that seeks biological explanations for modern human behavior by drawing on arguments about natural selection. Sociobiological explanations consist of two basic claims: (1) that all human behavior is ultimately driven by instincts and (2) that those instincts result from natural selection favoring the behaviors they cause.

In his rejoinder, biological anthropologist Robert Sussman rejects Wrangham and Peterson's claim that natural selection favors aggressive human males and that aggressiveness is an inherited trait or tendency. He sees aggressiveness as a result of environment and upbringing, in other words, as culturally shaped traits rather than biological ones. He contends that human hunter-gatherers and most apes are remarkably nonaggressive, as were our earliest human ancestors, the Australopithecines. On this point, he also rejects Raymond Dart's entire model about what drove human evolution from the Australopithecines to modern humans. Sussman sees the evidence that chimpanzee males routinely attack other males as weak. He also questions the relevance of chimpanzee behavior for understanding human behavior.

These articles raise a number of questions regarding the nature and causes of human aggression. How can we determine whether a person's aggressive act is due to instinct, upbringing, or both? If male aggression in humans is based on instinct, how can scholars explain variations in the amount and type of aggression found in different individuals and cultures? If male aggression is not based on instinct, why is violence between men so widespread? What role would women have had in the evolution of an instinct for male violence? To what extent can studies of animal behavior be applied to humans?

YES

**Richard Wrangham
and Dale Peterson**

Demonic Males: Apes and the Origins of Human Violence

Paradise Lost

The killer ape has long been part of our popular culture: Tarzan had to escape from the bad apes, and King Kong was a murderous gorilla-like monster. But before the Kahama observations [in which males of one chimpanzee group killed the males of a neighboring group], few biologists took the idea seriously. The reason was simple. There was so little evidence of animals killing members of their own species that biologists used to think animals killed each other only when something went wrong—an accident, perhaps, or unnatural crowding in zoos. The idea fit with the theories of animal behavior then preeminent, theories that saw animal behavior as designed by evolution for mutual good. Darwinian natural selection was a filter supposed to eliminate murderous violence. Killer apes, like killers in any animal species, were merely a novelist's fantasy to most scientists before the 1970s.

And so the behavior of people seemed very, very different from that of other animals. Killing, of course, is a typical result of human war, so one had to presume that humans somehow broke the rules of nature. Still, war must have come from somewhere. It could have come, for example, from the evolution of brains that happened to be smart enough to think of using tools as weapons, as Konrad Lorenz argued in his famous book, *On Aggression,* published in 1963.

However it may have originated, more generally war was seen as one of the defining marks of humanity: To fight wars meant to be human and apart from nature. This larger presumption was true even of nonscientific theories, such as the biblical concept of an original sin taking humans out of Eden, or the notion that warfare was an idea implanted by aliens, as Arthur C. Clarke imagined in *2001: A Space Odyssey.* In science, in religion, in fiction, violence and humanity were twinned.

The Kahama killings were therefore both a shock and a stimulus to thought. They undermined the explanations for extreme violence in terms of uniquely human attributes, such as culture, brainpower, or the punishment of an angry god. They made credible the idea that our warring tendencies go back into our prehuman past. They made us a little less special.

And yet science has still not grappled closely with the ultimate questions raised by the Kahama killings: Where does human violence come from, and why? Of course, there have been great advances in the way we think about these things. Most importantly, in the 1970s, the same decade as the Kahama killings, a new evolutionary theory emerged, the selfish-gene theory of natural selection, variously called inclusive fitness theory, sociobiology, or more broadly, behavioral ecology. Sweeping through the halls of academe, it revolutionized Darwinian thinking by its insistence that the ultimate explanation of any individual's behavior considers only how the behavior tends to maximize genetic success: to pass that individual's genes into subsequent generations. The new theory, elegantly popularized in Richard Dawkins's *The Selfish Gene,* is now the conventional wisdom in biological science because it explains animal behavior so well. It accounts easily for selfishness, even killing. And it has come to be applied with increasing confidence to human behavior, though the debate is still hot and unsettled. In any case, the general principle that behavior evolves to serve selfish ends has been widely accepted, and the idea that humans might have been favored by natural selection to hate and to kill their enemies has become entirely, if tragically, reasonable.

Those are the general principles, and yet the specifics are lacking. Most animals are nowhere near as violent as humans, so why did such intensely violent behavior evolve particularly in the human line? Why kill the enemy, rather than simply drive him away? Why rape? Why torture and mutilate? Why do we see these patterns both in ourselves and chimpanzees? Those sorts of questions have barely been asked, much less addressed.

Because chimpanzees and humans are each other's closest relatives, such questions carry extraordinary implications, the more so because the study of early human ancestry, unfolding in a fervor as we approach the century's end, is bringing chimpanzees and humans even closer than we ever imagined. Three dramatic recent discoveries speak to the relationship between chimpanzees and humans, and all three point in the same direction: to a past, around 5 million years ago, when chimpanzee ancestors and human ancestors were indistinguishable.

First, fossils recently dug up in Ethiopia indicate that over 4.5 million years ago there walked across African lands a bipedal ancestor of humans with a head strikingly like a chimpanzee's.

Second, laboratories around the world have over the last decade demonstrated chimpanzees to be genetically closer to us than they are even to gorillas, despite the close physical resemblance between chimpanzees and gorillas.

And third, both in the field and in the laboratory, studies of chimpanzee behavior are producing numerous, increasingly clear parallels with human behavior. It's not just that these apes pat each other on the hand to show affection, or kiss each other, or embrace. Not just that they have menopause, develop lifelong friendships, and grieve for their dead babies by carrying them for days or weeks. Nor is it their ability to do sums like 5 plus 4, or to communicate with hand signs. Nor their tool use, or collaboration, or bartering for sexual favors. Nor even that they hold long-term grudges, deliberately hide their feelings, or bring rivals together to force them to make peace.

No, for us the single most gripping set of facts about chimpanzee behavior is what we have already touched on: the nature of their society. The social world of chimpanzees is a set of individuals who share a communal range; males live forever in the groups where they are born, while females move to neighboring groups at adolescence; and the range is defended, and sometimes extended with aggressive and potentially lethal violence, by groups of males related in a genetically patrilineal kin group.

What makes this social world so extraordinary is comparison. Very few animals live in patrilineal, male-bonded communities wherein females routinely reduce the risks of inbreeding by moving to neighboring groups to mate. And only two animal species are known to do so with a system of intense, male-initiated territorial aggression, including lethal raiding into neighboring communities in search of vulnerable enemies to attack and kill. Out of four thousand mammals and ten million or more other animal species, this suite of behaviors is known only among chimpanzees and humans.

Humans with male-bonded, patrilineal kin groups? Absolutely. *Male bonded* refers to males forming aggressive coalitions with each other in mutual support against others—Hatfields versus McCoys, Montagues versus Capulets, Palestinians versus Israelis, Americans versus Vietcong, Tutsis versus Hutus. Around the world, from the Balkans to the Yanomamö of Venezuela, from Pygmies of Central Africa to the T'ang Dynasty of China, from Australian aborigines to Hawaiian kingdoms, related men routinely fight in defense of their group. This is true even of the villages labeled by anthropologists as "matrilineal" and "matrilocal," where inheritance (from male to male) is figured out according to the mother's line, and where women stay in their natal villages to have children—such villages operate socially as subunits of a larger patrilineal whole. In short, the system of communities defended by related men is a human universal that crosses space and time, so established a pattern that even writers of science fiction rarely think to challenge it.

When it comes to social relationships involving females, chimpanzees and humans are very different. That's unsurprising. Discoveries in animal behavior since the 1960s strongly suggest that animal societies are adapted to their environments in exquisitely detailed ways, and obviously the environments of chimpanzees and humans are a study in contrast. But this just emphasizes our puzzle. Why should male chimpanzees and humans show such similar patterns?

Is it chance? Maybe our human ancestors lived in societies utterly unlike those of chimpanzees. Peaceful matriarchies, for example, somewhat like some of our distant monkey relatives. And then, by a remarkable quirk of evolutionary coincidence, at some time in prehistory human and chimpanzee social behaviors converged on their similar systems for different, unrelated reasons.

Or do they both depend on some other characteristic, like intelligence? Once brains reach a certain level of sophistication, is there some mysterious logic pushing a species toward male coalitionary violence? Perhaps, for instance, only chimpanzees and humans have enough brainpower to realize the advantages of removing the opposition.

Or is there a long-term evolutionary inertia? Perhaps humans have retained an old chimpanzee pattern which, though it was once adaptive, has now acquired a stability and life of its own, resistant even to new environments where other forms of society would be better.

Or are the similarities there, as we believe, because in spite of first appearances, similar evolutionary forces continue to be at work in chimpanzee and human lineages, maintaining and refining a system of intergroup hostility and personal violence that has existed since even before the ancestors of chimpanzees and humans mated for the last time in a drying forest of eastern Africa around 5 million years ago? If so, one must ask, what forces are they? What bred male bonding and lethal raiding in our forebears and keeps it now in chimpanzees and humans? What marks have those ancient evolutionary forces forged onto our twentieth-century psyches? And what do they say about our hopes and fears for the future? . . .

Sexual selection, the evolutionary process that produces sex differences, has a lot to answer for. Without it, males wouldn't possess dangerous bodily weapons and a mindset that sanctions violence. But males who are better fighters can stop other males from mating, and they mate more successfully themselves. Better fighters tend to have more babies. That's the simple, stupid, selfish logic of sexual selection. So, what about us? Is sexual selection ultimately the reason why men brawl in barrooms, form urban gangs, plot guerrilla attacks, and go to war? Has it indeed designed men to be especially aggressive?

Until we have carefully examined the evidence, our answer should be: not necessarily. Because the social, environmental, genetic, and historical circumstances for any single species are so extremely complex, we can't assume a priori that sexual selection has acted in any particular way for any single species. Among the 10 million or more animal species on earth, you can find interesting exceptions to almost every rule. On the one hand, you can find species like spotted hyenas, where such extraordinary ferocity has evolved among females that it outshines even the stark sexual aggression shown by males. And on the other, you will discover the pacifists. . . .

So there is no particular reason to think that human aggression is all cultural, or that our ancestors were as pacific as muriquis [nonaggressive monkeys of South America]. The only way to find out whether sexual selection has shaped human males for aggression is to leave the theory and go back to the evidence. There are two places to look for an answer. We can look at our bodies, and we can think about our minds. The easier part is our bodies.

❧◈❧

A biologist from Mars looking at a preserved human male laid out on a slab might find it hard to imagine our species as dangerous. Lined up next to male specimens from the other apes, or from virtually any other mammal species, human males don't look as if they are designed to fight at all. They are rather slender, their bones are light, and they appear to have no bodily weapons. People don't think of humans in the same way that they think of dangerous animals.

That first impression is misleading, however. Humans are indeed designed to fight, although in a different way from most of the other primates.

Here's one clue. Men are a little larger and more heavily muscled than women. For other primate species, larger male size links strongly to male aggression. But with humans, that apparent evidence seems to conflict with the absence of fighting canine teeth. Could it be that humans break the general rule linking larger males to an evolved design for aggression?

Consider our teeth. The upper canines of most primates are longer and sharper than any other tooth. These long teeth are obvious weapons, bright daggers ground to a razor-sharp edge against a special honing surface on a premolar tooth in the lower jaw. Baboons, for example, have canines five to six centimeters long. Male baboons trying to impress each other grind their canines noisily, occasionally showing off their teeth in huge, gaping yawns. When male baboons make those display yawns, they are acting like cowboys twirling their revolvers.

By comparison, human canines seem tiny. They barely extend beyond the other teeth, and in males they are no longer than in females. Those canines may help us bite an apple, we love to imagine them elongated for the Halloween scare, and we unconsciously display them when we sneer, but our canines virtually never help us fight. In fact, the fossil record indicates that ever since the transition from rainforest ape to woodland ape, our ancestors' canines have been markedly smaller than they are in chimpanzees. In the woodlands, those teeth quickly became muriqui-like in appearance—one reason why some people wonder if woodland apes were as pacific as modern muriquis are.

But we should not allow ourselves to become misled by the evidence of canine teeth. The importance of a species' canines depends entirely on how it fights. . . .

Apes can fight with their fists because they have adapted to hanging from their arms, which means that their arms can swing all around their shoulders, the shoulder joint being a flexible multidirectional joint. So chimpanzees and gorillas often hit with their fists when they fight, and they can keep most canine-flashing opponents at bay because their arms are long. If chimpanzees and gorillas find punching effective, then surely the woodland apes, who were standing up high on hind legs, would have fought even better with their arms.

Fists can also grasp invented weapons. Chimpanzees today are close to using hand-held weapons. Throughout the continent, wild chimpanzees will tear off and throw great branches when they are angry or threatened, or they will pick up and throw rocks. Humphrey, when he was the alpha male at Gombe, almost killed me once by sending a melon-size rock whistling less than half a meter from my head. They also hit with big sticks. A celebrated film taken in Guinea shows wild chimpanzees pounding meter-long clubs down on the back of a leopard. (Scientists were able to get that film because the leopard was a stuffed one, placed there by a curious researcher. The chimpanzees were lucky to find a leopard so slow to fight back.) Chimpanzees in West Africa already have a primitive stone tool technology, and there could well be a community of chimpanzees today, waiting to be discovered, who are already using heavy sticks as clubs against each other. Certainly we can reasonably imagine that the woodland apes did some of these things.

. . . The shoulders of boys and girls are equally broad until adolescence; but at puberty, shoulder cartilage cells respond to testosterone, the male sex hormone newly produced by the testes, by growing. (In an equivalent way, pubertal girls get wider hips when their hip cartilage cells respond to estrogen, the female sex hormone.) The result is a sudden acceleration of shoulder width for boys around the age of fourteen, associated with relative enlargement of the upper arm muscles. In other words, the shoulders and arms of male humans—like the neck muscles of a red deer, the clasping hands of a xenopus frog, or the canine teeth of many other primates—look like the result of sexual selection for fighting. All these examples of male weaponry respond to testosterone by growing. They are specialized features that enlarge for the specific purpose of promoting fighting ability in competition against other males. Small wonder, then, that men show off to each other before fights by hunching their shoulders, expanding their muscles, and otherwise displaying their upper-body strength. . . .

If the bipedal woodland apes fought with fists and sometimes with weapons, those species should have had especially broad shoulders and wellmuscled arms, like modern men. We haven't enough fossils yet to know if that's true. Indeed, it is not yet absolutely certain that male woodland apes were larger than females, though most of the current fossil evidence suggests so. If they were, we can confidently imagine that the males were designed for aggression. Perhaps the early development of club-style weapons might also explain why the skulls of our ancestors became strikingly thicker, particularly with *Homo erectus* at 1.6 to 1.8 million years ago. That's a guess, but it's clear in any case that our present bodies carry the same legacy of sexual selection as other mammals whose males fight with their upper bodies. The broad shoulders and powerful, arching torso we so admire in Michelangelo's *David* are the human equivalent of antlers. The mark of Cain appears in our shoulders and arms, not in our teeth.

⁂

What about our minds? Has sexual selection shaped our psyches also, in order to make us better fighters? Can sexual selection explain why men are so quick to bristle at insults, and, under the right circumstances, will readily kill? Can our evolutionary past account for modern war?

Inquiry about mental processes is difficult enough when we deal just with humans. Comparison with other species is harder still. The supposed problem is that animals fight with their hearts, so people say, whereas humans fight with their minds. Animal aggression is supposed to happen by instinct, or by emotion, and without reason. Wave a red rag in a bull's face and the bull charges thoughtlessly—that's the model. Human wars, on the other hand, seem to emerge, so Karl von Clausewitz declared, as "the continuation of policy with the admixture of other means." According to historian Michael Howard, human wars "begin with conscious and reasoned decisions based on the calculation, made by both parties, that they can achieve more by going to war than by remaining at peace." The principle seems as true for the measured deliberations on the top floor of the Pentagon as for the whispered councils among the Yanomamö, and it suggests a wholly different set of psychological processes from the supposedly rigid, instinctual, emotional drives of animals. The fact that we possess consciousness and reasoning ability, this theory says, takes us across a chasm into a new world, where the old instincts are no longer important. If there is no connection between these two systems, the rules for each cannot be the same. In other words, aggression based on "conscious and reasoned decisions" can no longer be explained in terms of such evolutionary forces as sexual selection.

The argument sounds fair enough, but it depends on oversimplified thinking, a false distinction between animals acting by emotion (or instinct) and humans acting by reason. Animal behavior is not purely emotional. Nor is human decision-making purely rational. In both cases, the event is a mixture. And new evidence suggests that even though we humans reason much more (analyze past and present context, consider a potential future, and so on) than nonhuman animals, our essential process for making a decision still relies on emotion. . . .

People have always accepted that animals act from emotions; humans . . . can never act without them. Suddenly the apparent chasm between the mental processes of chimpanzees and our species is reduced to a comprehensible difference. Humans can reason better, but reason and emotion are linked in parallel ways for both chimpanzees and humans. For both species, emotion sits in the driver's seat, and reason (or calculation) paves the road.

We are now ready to ask what causes aggression. If emotion is the ultimate arbiter of action for both species, then what kinds of emotions underlie violence for both? Clearly there are many. But one stands out. From the raids of chimpanzees at Gombe to wars among human nations, the same emotion looks extraordinarily important, one that we take for granted and describe most simply but that nonetheless takes us deeply back to our animal origins: pride.

Male chimpanzees compete much more aggressively for dominance than females do. If a lower-ranking male refuses to acknowledge his superior with one of the appropriate conventions, such as a soft grunt, the superior will become predictably angry. But females can let such insults pass. Females are certainly capable of being aggressive to each other, and they can be as politically adept as males in using coalitions to achieve a goal. But female chimpanzees act as if they just don't care about their status as much as males do.

By contrast, we exaggerate only barely in saying that a male chimpanzee in his prime organizes his whole life around issues of rank. His attempts to achieve and then maintain alpha status are cunning, persistent, energetic, and time-consuming. They affect whom he travels with, whom he grooms, where he glances, how often he scratches, where he goes, and what time he gets up in the morning. . . .

Eighteenth-century Englishmen used less dramatic tactics than wild chimpanzees, but that acute observer Samuel Johnson thought rank concerns were as pervasive: "No two people can be half an hour together, but one shall acquire an evident superiority over the other." Pride obviously serves as a stimulus for much interpersonal aggression in humans, and we can hypothesize confidently that this emotion evolved during countless generations in which males who achieved high status were able to turn their social success into extra reproduction. Male pride, the source of many a conflict, is reasonably seen as a mental equivalent of broad shoulders. Pride is another legacy of sexual selection. . . .

Our ape ancestors have passed to us a legacy, defined by the power of natural selection and written in the molecular chemistry of DNA. For the most part it is a wonderful inheritance, but one small edge contains destructive elements; and now that we have the weapons of mass destruction, that edge promotes the potential of our own demise. People have long known such things intuitively and so have built civilizations with laws and justice, diplomacy and mediation, ideally keeping always a step ahead of the old demonic principles. And we might hope that men will eventually realize that violence doesn't pay.

The problem is that males are demonic at unconscious and irrational levels. The motivation of a male chimpanzee who challenges another's rank is not that he foresees more matings or better food or a longer life. Those rewards explain why sexual selection has favored the desire for power, but the immediate reason he vies for status is simpler, deeper, and less subject to the vagaries of context. It is simply to dominate his peers. Unconscious of the evolutionary rationale that placed this prideful goal in his temperament, he devises strategies to achieve it that can be complex, original, and maybe conscious. In the same way, the motivation of male chimpanzees on a border patrol is not to gain land or win females. The temperamental goal is to intimidate the opposition, to beat them to a pulp, to erode their ability to challenge. Winning has become an end in itself.

It looks the same with men.

Robert W. Sussman

→ **NO**

Exploring Our Basic Human Nature: Are Humans Inherently Violent?

Are human beings forever doomed to be violent? Is aggression fixed within our genetic code, an inborn action pattern that threatens to destroy us? Or, as asked by Richard Wrangham and Dale Peterson in their recent book, *Demonic Males: Apes and the Origins of Human Violence,* can we get beyond our genes, beyond our essential "human nature"?

Wrangham and Peterson's belief in the importance of violence in the evolution and nature of humans is based on new primate research that they assert demonstrates the continuity of aggression from our great ape ancestors. The authors argue that 20–25 years ago most scholars believed human aggression was unique. Research at that time had shown great apes to be basically nonaggressive gentle creatures. Furthermore, the separation of humans from our ape ancestors was thought to have occurred 15–20 million years ago (Mya). Although Raymond Dart, Sherwood Washburn, Robert Ardrey, E.O. Wilson and others had argued through much of the 20th century that hunting, killing, and extreme aggressive behaviors were biological traits inherited from our earliest hominid hunting ancestors, many anthropologists still believed that patterns of aggression were environmentally determined and culturally learned behaviors, not inherited characteristics.

Demonic Males discusses new evidence that killer instincts are not unique to humans, but rather shared with our nearest relative, the common chimpanzee. The authors argue that it is this inherited propensity for killing that allows hominids and chimps to be such good hunters.

According to Wrangham and Peterson, the split between humans and the common chimpanzee was only 6–8 Mya. Furthermore, humans may have split from the chimpanzee-bonobo line after gorillas, with bonobos *(pygmy chimps)* separating from chimps only 2.5 Mya. Because chimpanzees may be the modern ancestor of all these forms, and because the earliest australopithecines were quite chimpanzee-like, Wrangham speculates (in a separate article) that "chimpanzees are a conservative species and an amazingly good model for the ancestor of hominids" (1995, reprinted in Sussman 1997:106). If modern chimpanzees and modern humans share certain behavioral traits, these traits have "long evolutionary roots" and are likely to be fixed, biologically inherited parts of our basic human nature and not culturally determined.

From *Anthro Notes,* Fall 1997, pp. 1–6, 17–19. Copyright © 1997 by Anthro Notes, National Museum of Natural History Bulletin for Teachers. Reprinted by permission

Wrangham argues that chimpanzees are almost on the brink of humanness:

> Nut-smashing, root-eating, savannah-using chimpanzees, resembling our ancestors, and capable by the way of extensive bipedalism. Using ant-wands, and sandals, and bowls, meat-sharing, hunting cooperatively. Strange paradox . . . a species trembling on the verge of hominization, but so conservative that it has stayed on that edge. . . . (1997:107).

Wrangham and Peterson (1996:24) claim that only two animal species, chimpanzees and humans, live in patrilineal, male-bonded communities "with intense, male initiated territorial aggression, including lethal raiding into neighboring communities in search of vulnerable enemies to attack and kill." Wrangham asks:

> Does this mean chimpanzees are naturally violent? Ten years ago it wasn't clear. . . . In this cultural species, it may turn out that one of the least variable of all chimpanzee behaviors is the intense competition between males, the violent aggression they use against strangers, and their willingness to maim and kill those that frustrate their goals. . . . As the picture of chimpanzee society settles into focus, it now includes infanticide, rape and regular battering of females by males (1997:108).

Since humans and chimpanzees share these violent urges, the implication is that human violence has long evolutionary roots. "We are apes of nature, cursed over six million years or more with a rare inheritance, a Dostoyevskyan demon . . . The coincidence of demonic aggression in ourselves and our closest kin bespeaks its antiquity" (1997:108–109).

Intellectual Antecedents

From the beginning of Western thought, the theme of human depravity runs deep, related to the idea of humankind's fall from grace and the emergence of original sin. This view continues to pervade modern "scientific" interpretations of the evolution of human behavior. Recognition of the close evolutionary relationship between humans and apes, from the time of Darwin's *Descent of Man* (1874) on, has encouraged theories that look to modern apes for evidence of parallel behaviors reflecting this relationship.

By the early 1950s, large numbers of australopithecine fossils and the discovery that the large-brained "fossil" ancestor from Piltdown, in England, was a fraud, led to the realization that our earliest ancestors were more like apes than like modern humans. Accordingly, our earliest ancestors must have behaved much like other non-human primates. This, in turn, led to a great interest in using primate behavior to understand human evolution and the evolutionary basis of human nature. The subdiscipline of primatology was born.

Raymond Dart, discoverer of the first australopithecine fossil some thirty years earlier, was also developing a different view of our earliest ancestors.

At first Dart believed that australopithecines were scavengers barely eking out an existence in the harsh savanna environment. But from the fragmented and damaged bones found with the australopithecines, together with dents and holes in these early hominid skulls, Dart eventually concluded that this species had used bone, tooth and antler tools to kill, butcher and eat their prey, as well as to kill one another. This hunting hypothesis (Cartmill 1997:511) "was linked from the beginning with a bleak, pessimistic view of human beings and their ancestors as instinctively bloodthirsty and savage." To Dart, the australopithecines were:

> confirmed killers: carnivorous creatures that seized living quarries by violence, battered them to death, tore apart their broken bodies, dismembered them limb from limb, slaking their ravenous thirst with the hot blood of victims and greedily devouring livid writhing flesh (1953:209).

Cartmill, in a recent book (1993), shows that this interpretation of early human morality is reminiscent of earlier Greek and Christian views. Dart's (1953) own treatise begins with a 17th century quote from the Calvinist R. Baxter: "of all the beasts, the man-beast is the worst/ to others and himself the cruellest foe."

Between 1961–1976, Dart's view was picked up and extensively popularized by the playwright Robert Ardrey (*The Territorial Imperative, African Genesis*). Ardrey believed it was the human competitive and killer instinct, acted out in warfare, that made humans what they are today. "It is war and the instinct for territory that has led to the great accomplishments of Western Man. Dreams may have inspired our love of freedom, but only war and weapons have made it ours" (1961:324).

Man the Hunter

In the 1968 volume *Man the Hunter,* Sherwood Washburn and Chet Lancaster presented a theory of "The evolution of hunting," emphasizing that it is this behavior that shaped human nature and separated early humans from their primate relatives.

> To assert the biological unity of mankind is to affirm the importance of the hunting way of life. . . . However much conditions and customs may have varied locally, the main selection pressures that forged the species were the same. The biology, psychology and customs that separate us from the apes . . . we owe to the hunters of time past . . . for those who would understand the origins and nature of human behavior there is no choice but to try to understand "Man the Hunter" (1968:303).

Rather than amassing evidence from modern hunters and gatherers to prove their theory, Washburn and Lancaster (1968:299) use the 19th-century concept of cultural "survivals": behaviors that persist as evidence of an earlier time but are no longer useful in society.

Men enjoy hunting and killing, and these activities are continued in sports even when they are no longer economically necessary. If a behavior is important to the survival of a species . . . then it must be both easily learned and pleasurable (Washburn & Lancaster, p. 299).

Man the Dancer

Using a similar logic for the survival of ancient "learned and pleasurable" behaviors, perhaps it could easily have been our propensity for dancing rather than our desire to hunt that can explain much of human behavior. After all, men and women love to dance; it is a behavior found in all cultures but has even less obvious function today than hunting. Our love of movement and dance might explain, for example, our propensity for face-to-face sex, and even the evolution of bipedalism and the movement of humans out of trees and onto the ground.

Could the first tool have been a stick to beat a dance drum, and the ancient Laetoli footprints evidence of two individuals going out to dance the "Afarensis shuffle"? Although it takes only two to tango, a variety of social interactions and systems might have been encouraged by the complex social dances known in human societies around the globe.

Sociobiology and E.O. Wilson

In the mid-1970s, E.O. Wilson and others described a number of traits as genetically based and therefore human universals, including territoriality, male–female bonds, male dominance over females, and extended maternal care leading to matrilineality. Wilson argued that the genetic basis of these traits was indicated by their relative constancy among our primate relatives and by their persistence throughout human evolution and in human societies. Elsewhere, I have shown that these characteristics are neither general primate traits nor human universals (Sussman 1995). Wilson, however, argued that these were a product of our evolutionary hunting past.

For at least a million years—probably more—Man engaged in a hunting way of life, giving up the practice a mere 10,000 years ago. . . . Our innate social responses have been fashioned through this life style. With caution, we can compare the most widespread hunter-gatherer qualities with similar behavior displayed by some of the non-human primates that are closely related to Man. Where the same pattern of traits occurs in . . . most or all of those primates—we can conclude that it has been subject to little evolution. (Wilson 1976, in Sussman 1997:65–66).

Wilson's theory of sociobiology, the evolution of social behavior, argued that:

1. the goal of living organisms is to pass on one's genes at the expense of all others;
2. an organism should only cooperate with others if:

   (a) they carry some of his/her own genes (kin selection) or
   (b) if at some later date the others might aid you (reciprocal altruism).

To sociobiologists, evolutionary morality is based on an unconscious need to multiply our own genes, to build group cohesion in order to win wars. We should not look down on our warlike, cruel nature but rather understand its success when coupled with "making nice" with *some* other individuals or groups. The genetically driven "making nice" is the basis of human ethics and morality.

> Throughout recorded history the conduct of war has been common . . . some of the noblest traits of mankind, including team play, altruism, patriotism, bravery . . . and so forth are the genetic product of warfare (Wilson 1975:572–3).

The evidence for any of these universals or for the tenets of sociobiology is as weak as was the evidence for Dart's, Ardrey's and Washburn and Lancaster's theories of innate aggression. Not only are modern gatherer-hunters and most apes remarkably non-aggressive, but in the 1970s and 1980s studies of fossil bones and artifacts have shown that early humans were not hunters, and that weapons were a later addition to the human repertoire. In fact, C.K. Brain (1981) showed that the holes and dents in Dart's australopithecine skulls matched perfectly with fangs of leopards or with impressions of rocks pressing against the buried fossils. Australopithecines apparently were the hunted, not the hunters (Cartmill, 1993, 1997).

Beyond Our Genes

Wrangham and Peterson's book goes beyond the assertion of human inborn aggression and propensity towards violence. The authors ask the critical question: Are we doomed to be violent forever because this pattern is fixed within our genetic code or can we go beyond our past?—get out of our genes, so to speak.

The authors believe that we can look to the bonobo or pygmy chimpanzee as one potential savior, metaphorically speaking.

Bonobos, although even more closely related to the common chimpanzee than humans, have become a peace-loving, love-making alternative to chimpanzee-human violence. How did this happen? In chimpanzees and humans, females of the species select partners that are violent . . . "while men have evolved to be demonic males, it seems likely that women have evolved to prefer demonic males . . . as long as demonic males are the most successful reproducers, any female who mates with them is provided with sons who themselves will likely be good reproducers" (Wrangham and Peterson 1996:239). However, among pygmy chimpanzees females form alliances and have chosen to mate with less aggressive males. So, after all, it is not violent males that have caused humans and chimpanzees to be their inborn, immoral, dehumanized selves, it is rather, poor choices by human and chimpanzee females.

Like Dart, Washburn, and Wilson before them, Wrangham and Peterson believe that killing and violence is inherited from our ancient relatives of the past. However, unlike these earlier theorists, Wrangham and Peterson argue this is not a trait unique to hominids, nor is it a by-product of hunting. In fact, it is just this violent nature and a natural "blood lust" that makes both humans and chimpanzees such good hunters. It is the bonobos that help the authors come to this conclusion. Because bonobos have lost the desire to kill, they also have lost the desire to hunt.

> . . . do bonobos tell us that the suppression of personal violence carried with it the suppression of predatory aggression? The strongest hypothesis at the moment is that bonobos came from a chimpanzee-like ancestor that hunted monkeys and hunted one another. As they evolved into bonobos, males lost their demonism, becoming less aggressive to each other. In so doing they lost their lust for hunting monkeys, too . . . Murder and hunting may be more closely tied together than we are used to thinking (Wrangham and Peterson 1996:219).

The Selfish Gene Theory

Like Ardrey, Wrangham and Peterson believe that blood lust ties killing and hunting tightly together but it is the killing that drives hunting in the latter's argument. This lust to kill is based upon the sociobiological tenet of the selfish gene. "The general principle that behavior evolves to serve selfish ends has been widely accepted; and the idea that humans might have been favored by natural selection to hate and to kill their enemies has become entirely, if tragically, reasonable" (Wrangham and Peterson 1996:23).

As with many of the new sociobiological or evolutionary anthropology theories, I find problems with both the theory itself and with the evidence used to support it. Two arguments that humans and chimpanzees share biologically fixed behaviors are: (1) they are more closely related to each other than chimpanzees are to gorillas; (2) chimpanzees are a good model for our earliest ancestor and retain conservative traits that should be shared by both.

The first of these statements is still hotly debated and, using various genetic evidence, the chimp-gorilla-human triage is so close that it is difficult to tell exact divergence time or pattern among the three. The second statement is just not true. Chimpanzees have been evolving for as long as humans and gorillas, and there is no reason to believe ancestral chimps were similar to present-day chimps. The fossil evidence for the last 5–8 million years is extremely sparse, and it is likely that many forms of apes have become extinct just as have many hominids.

Furthermore, even if the chimpanzee were a good model for the ancestral hominid, and was a conservative representative of this phylogenetic group, this would not mean that humans would necessarily share specific behavioral traits. As even Wrangham and Peterson emphasize, chimps, gorillas, and bonobos all behave very differently from one another in their social behavior and in their willingness to kill conspecifics.

Evidence Against "Demonic Males"

The proof of the "Demonic Male" theory does not rest on any theoretical grounds but must rest solely on the evidence that violence and killing in chimpanzees and in humans are behaviors that are similar in pattern; have ancient, shared evolutionary roots; and are inherited. Besides killing of con-specifics, Wrangham "includes infanticide, rape, and regular battering of females by males" as a part of this inherited legacy of violent behaviors shared by humans and chimpanzees (1997:108).

Wrangham and Peterson state: "That chimpanzees and humans kill members of neighboring groups of their own species is . . . a startling excep-tion to the normal rule for animals" (1996:63). "Fighting adults of almost all species normally stop at winning: They don't go on to kill" (1996:155). How-ever, as Wrangham points out there are exceptions, such as lions, wolves, spot-ted hyenas, and I would add a number of other predators. In fact, most species do not have the weapons to kill one another as adults.

Just how common is conspecific killing in chimpanzees? This is where the real controversy may lie. Jane Goodall described the chimpanzee as a peaceful, non-aggressive species during the first 24 years of study at Gombe (1950–1974). During one year of concentrated study, Goodall observed 284 agonistic encounters: of these 66% were due to competition for introduced bananas, and only 34% "could be regarded as attacks occurring in 'normal' aggressive contexts" (1968:278). Only 10 percent of the 284 attacks were clas-sified as 'violent', and "even attacks that appeared punishing to me often resulted in no discernable injury. . . . Other attacks consisted merely of brief pounding, hitting or rolling of the individual, after which the aggressor often touched or embraced the other immediately (1968:277).

Chimpanzee aggression before 1974 was considered no different from pat-terns of aggression seen in many other primate species. In fact, Goodall explains in her 1986 monograph, *The Chimpanzees of Gombe,* that she uses data mainly from after 1975 because the earlier years present a "very different picture of the Gombe chimpanzees" as being "far more peaceable than humans" (1986:3). Other early naturalists' descriptions of chimpanzee behavior were consistent with those of Goodall and confirmed her observations. Even different com-munities were observed to come together with peaceful, ritualized displays of greeting (Reynolds and Reynolds 1965; Suguyama 1972; Goodall 1968).

Then, between 1974 and 1977, five adult males from one subgroup were attacked and disappeared from the area, presumably dead. Why after 24 years did the patterns of aggression change? Was it because the stronger group saw the weakness of the other and decided to improve their genetic fitness? But surely there were stronger and weaker animals and subgroups before this time. Perhaps we can look to Goodall's own perturbations for an answer. In 1965, Goodall began to provide "restrictive human-controlled feeding." A few years later she realized that

> the constant feeding was having a marked effect on the behavior of the chimps. They were beginning to move about in large groups more often than they had ever done in the old days. Worst of all, the adult males were becoming increasingly aggressive. When we first offered the chimps bananas the males seldom fought over their food;. . . . now . . . there was a great deal more fighting than ever before. . . . (Goodall 1971:143).

The possibility that human interference was a main cause of the unusual behavior of the Gombe chimps was the subject of an excellent, but generally ignored book by Margaret Power (1991). Wrangham and Peterson (1996:19) footnote this book, but as with many other controversies, they essentially ignore its findings, stating that yes, chimpanzee violence might have been unnatural behavior if it weren't for the evidence of similar behavior occurring since 1977 and "elsewhere in Africa" (1996:19).

Further Evidence

What is this evidence from elsewhere in Africa? Wrangham and Peterson provide only four brief examples, none of which is very convincing:

(1) Between 1979–1982, the Gombe group extended its range to the south and conflict with a southern group, Kalande, was suspected. In 1982, a "raiding" party of males reached Goodall's camp. The authors state: "Some of these raids may have been lethal" (1996:19). However, Goodall describes this "raid" as follows: One female "was chased by a Kalande male and mildly attacked. . . . Her four-year-old son . . . encountered a second male—but was only sniffed" (1986:516). Although Wrangham and Peterson imply that these encounters were similar to those between 1974–77, no violence was actually witnessed. The authors also refer to the discovery of the dead body of Humphrey; what they do not mention is Humphrey's age of 35 and that wild chimps rarely live past 33 years!

(2) From 1970 to 1982, six adult males from one community in the Japanese study site of Mahale disappeared, one by one over this 12 year period. None of the animals were observed being attacked or killed, and one was sighted later roaming as a solitary male (Nishida et al., 1985:287–289).

(3) In another site in West Africa, Wrangham and Peterson report that Boesch and Boesch believe "that violent aggression among the chimpanzees is as important as it is in Gombe" (1986:20). However, in the paper referred to, the Boesches simply state that encounters by neighboring chimpanzee communities are more common in their site than in Gombe (one per month vs. 1 every 4 months). There is no mention of violence during these encounters.

(4) At a site that Wrangham began studying in 1984, an adult male was found dead in 1991. Wrangham states: "In the second week of August, Ruizoni was killed. No human saw the big fight" (Wrangham & Peterson 1996:20). Wrangham gives us no indication of what has occurred at this site over the last 6 years.

In fact, this is the total amount of evidence of warfare and male-male killing among chimpanzees after 37 years of research!! The data for infanticide and rape among chimpanzees is even less impressive. In fact, data are so sparse for these behaviors among chimps that Wrangham and Peterson are forced to use examples from the other great apes, gorillas and orangutans. However, just as for killing among chimpanzees, both the evidence and the interpretations are suspect and controversial.

Can We Escape Our Genes?

What if Wrangham and Peterson are correct and we and our chimp cousins are inherently sinners? Are we doomed to be violent forever because this pattern is fixed within our genetic code?

After 5 million years of human evolution and 120,000 or so years of *Homo sapiens* existence, is there a way to rid ourselves of our inborn evils?

> What does it do for us, then, to know the behavior of our closest relatives? Chimpanzees and bonobos are an extraordinary pair. One, I suggest shows us some of the worst aspects of our past and our present; the other shows an escape from it. . . . Denial of our demons won't make them go away. But even if we're driven to accepting the evidence of a grisly past, we're not forced into thinking it condemns us to an unchanged future (Wrangham 1997:110).

In other words, we can learn how to behave by watching bonobos. But, if we can change our inherited behavior so simply, why haven't we been able to do this before *Demonic Males* enlightened us? Surely, there are variations in the amounts of violence in different human cultures and individuals. If we have the capacity and plasticity to change by learning from example, then our behavior is determined by socialization practices and by our cultural histories and not by our nature! This is true whether the examples come from benevolent bonobos or conscientious objectors.

Conclusion

The theory presented by Wrangham and Peterson, although it also includes chimpanzees as our murdering cousins, is very similar to "man the hunter" theories proposed in the past. It also does not differ greatly from early European and Christian beliefs about human ethics and morality. We are forced to ask:

Are these theories generated by good scientific fact, or are they just "good to think" because they reflect, reinforce, and reiterate our traditional cultural beliefs, our morality and our ethics? Is the theory generated by the data, or are the data manipulated to fit preconceived notions of human morality and ethics?

Since the data in support of these theories have been weak, and yet the stories created have been extremely similar, I am forced to believe that "Man the Hunter" is a myth, that humans are not necessarily prone to violence and aggression, but that this belief will continue to reappear in future writings on human nature. Meanwhile, primatologists must continue their field research, marshaling the actual evidence needed to answer many of the questions raised in Wrangham and Peterson's volume.

References

Ardrey, Robert. 1961. *African Genesis: A Personal Investigation into Animal Origins and Nature of Man.* Atheneum.

——. *The Territorial Imperative*. Atheneum, 1966.

Brain, C.K. 1981. *The Hunted or the Hunter? An Introduction to African Cave Taphonomy*. Univ. of Chicago.

Dart, Raymond. 1953. "The Predatory Transition from Ape to Man." *International Anthropological and Linguistic Review* 1:201–217.

Darwin, Charles. 1874. *The Descent of Man and Selection in Relation to Sex*. 2nd ed. The Henneberry Co.

Cartmill, Matt 1997. "Hunting Hypothesis of Human Origins." In *History of Physical Anthropology: An Encyclopedia*, ed. F. Spencer, pp. 508–512. Garland.

——. 1993. *A View to a Death in the Morning: Hunting and Nature Through History*. Harvard Univ.

Goodall, Jane. 1986. *The Chimpanzees of Gombe: Patterns of Behavior*. Belknap.

——. 1971. *In the Shadow of Man*. Houghton Mifflin.

Goodall, Jane. 1968. "The Behavior of Free-Living Chimpanzees in the Gombe Stream Reserve." *Animal Behavior Monographs* 1:165–311.

Nishida, T., Hiraiwa-Hasegawa, M., and Takahtat, Y. "Group Extinction and Female Transfer in Wild Chimpanzees in the Mahali Nation Park, Tanzania." *Zeitschrift für Tierpsychologie* 67:281–301.

Power, Margaret. 1991. *The Egalitarian Human and Chimpanzee: An Anthropological View of Social Organization*. Cambridge University.

Reynolds, V. and Reynolds, F. 1965. "Chimpanzees of Budongo Forest." In *Primate Behavior: Field Studies of Monkeys and Apes*, ed. I. DeVore, pp. 368–424. Holt, Rinehart, and Winston.

Suguyama, Y. 1972. "Social Characteristics and Socialization of Wild Chimpanzees." In *Primate Socialization*, ed. F.E. Poirier, pp. 145–163. Random House.

Sussman, R.W., ed. 1997. *The Biological Basis of Human Behavior*. Simon and Schuster.

Sussman, R.W. 1995. "The Nature of Human Universals." *Reviews in Anthropology* 24:1–11.

Washburn, S.L. and Lancaster, C. K. 1968. "The Evolution of Hunting." In *Man the Hunter*, eds. R. B. Lee and I. DeVore, pp. 293–303. Aldine.

Wilson, E. O. 1997. "Sociobiology: A New Approach to Understanding the Basis of Human Nature." *New Scientist* 70(1976):342–345. (Reprinted in R.W. Sussman, 1997.)

——. 1975. Sociobiology: *The New Synthesis*. Cambridge: Harvard University.

Wrangham, R.W. 1995. "Ape, Culture, and Missing Links." *Symbols* (Spring):2–9, 20. (Reprinted in R. W. Sussman, 1997.)

Wrangham, Richard and Peterson, Dale. 1996. *Demonic Males: Apes and the Origins of Human Violence*. Houghton Mifflin.

EXPLORING THE ISSUE

Are Humans Inherently Violent?

Critical Thinking and Reflection

1. What evidence are Wrangham and Peterson using to support their position on violence and aggression as inherent human traits? Are they using experimental data?
2. What kinds of evidence does Sussman use to dismiss Wrangham and Peterson's claims? To what extent are these claims based on thought experiments and to what extent observed animal behavior?
3. To what extent are arguments in favor of human aggression as an inherited trait parallel to mainstream American views about "human nature" and male aggression? Can these American cultural views be disentangled from the evidence?
4. Since chimpanzees and bonobos have rather different patterns of mating and aggression, why would we expect chimpanzee behavior to be more useful in understanding human behavior than the rather nonviolent bonobos?
5. If the human lineage separated from that of the other apes about 8 million years ago, why would we use chimpanzee data to help us resolve this question?

Is There Common Ground?

There really is very little common ground between the two positions represented in these selections. One position hopes to explain behavior as a consequence of natural selection, whereas the other position looks to cultural conditioning that comes from living in a particular society.

In recent years, sociobiological explanations have become very popular. They began in biology and ethology (the study of animal behavior) and spread to the social sciences, including psychology, where it is now called "evolutionary psychology." The goal of these studies is to explain many confusing variations in behavior by a few simple, scientific principles. Any human social behavior—from selfishness to altruism—can be explained by sociobiology. It's all in the genes. If we ask why human males are often aggressive, the answer is because natural selection favored our more aggressive ancestors, allowing them to have more children than our less aggressive ancestors. Thus, selection allowed these aggressive individuals that have more children than nonaggressive ones, ensuring that the tendency for male aggression increased in our species.

Although many biological anthropologists accept the behavioral patterns like the observed aggressive behavior of many males, they argue that human violence is basically a product of social and cultural conditions. This argument comes from the tradition of cultural anthropology in the United States. Sussman challenges Wrangham and Peterson's assumptions that human behaviors are driven by instincts. He argues that behaviors, like violence, territoriality, and male dominance over females, are not in fact universal among humans and lower primates. He also questions whether an instinct must exist if a particular behavior is universal among humans, is easy to learn, and is pleasurable to perform. By these criteria, Sussman says, dancing must also be caused by an instinct to dance. Presumably a long list of similar activities, such as playing games and telling jokes, must also have their governing instincts. The cultural conditioning argument also challenges, if natural selection was selecting for aggressiveness since the Australopithecines, aren't all males equally aggressive? It is hard to see why female chimps (or humans) would actively select males that were very aggressive to be fathers to their children. The mechanisms that Wrangham and Peterson point to could, in Sussman's view, actually be cultural patterning rather than selection of particular genes.

Between these two positions, anthropologists continue to study how universal and how patterned various behaviors are. Both sides have tended to use reductionist arguments, also Sussman—as a biological anthropologist—seems more willing to appreciate the power of natural selection than most cultural anthropologists. There are also a number of sociobiologists who accept a more complex role for culture in addition to biological factors.

Additional Resources

To learn more about sociobiology in general, the best starting point is probably E. O. Wilson's seminal work:

Wilson, E. O. 1975. *Sociobiology: The New Synthesis.* Cambridge, MA: Harvard University Press.

Several books explaining the human propensity for violence in terms of instincts include:

Daly, Martin and Wilson, Margo. 1988. *Homicide.* New York: A de Gruyter.

Ghiglieri, Michael. 1999. *The Dark Side of Man: Tracing the Origins of Male Violence.* Reading, MA: Perseus Books.

Lorenz, Konrad. 1967. *On Aggression.* New York: Harcourt, Brace, and World.

Wrangham, Richard and Peterson, Dale. 1996. *Demonic Males: Apes and the Origins of Human Violence.* Boston: Houghton Mifflin Company.

This study expands on sociobiological explanations of violence to argue that human males have an instinct for rape because in the evolution of hominins rape was an effective way for males to pass on their genes:

Thornhill, Randy and Palmer, Craig T. 2000. *A Natural History of Rape: Biological Bases of Sexual Coercion.* MIT Press.

Important works challenging the sociobiological explanation of human violence include:

Bock, Kenneth. 1980. *Human Nature and History: A Response to Sociobiology.* New York: Columbia University Press.

Cartmill, Matt. 1993. *A View to a Death in the Morning: Hunting and Nature through History.* Cambridge, MA: Harvard University Press.

Lewontin, Richard, Kamin, Leon, and Rose, Stephen. 1984. *Not in Our Genes: Biology, Ideology, and Human Nature.* New York: Pantheon Books.

Montague, Ashley. 1976. *The Nature of Human Aggression.* New York: Oxford University Press.

For descriptions and analyses of societies in which aggression is minimized, see:
Howell, Signe and Willis, Roy. eds. 1989. *Societies at Peace: Anthropological Perspectives.* London: Routledge.

Sponsel, Leslie E. and Gregor, Thomas A. eds. 1994. *The Anthropology of Peace and Nonviolence.* Boulder: L. Rienner.

ISSUE 3

Are Female Primates Selected to Be Monogamous?

YES: David M. Buss, from *The Evolution of Desire: Strategies of Human Mating* (Basic Books, 1994)

NO: Carol Tavris, from *The Mismeasure of Women* (Simon and Schuster, 1992)

Learning Outcomes

After reading this issue, you should be able to:

- Discuss sociobiological arguments that primate males and females have evolved with different behavioral preferences.
- Understand why Darwin and many sociobiologists today accept the view that women have been adapted to be monogamous, whereas men have been adapted not to be.
- Explain why many primatologists and anthropologists challenge sociobiological arguments about the evolution of monogamy among primates.
- Discuss the problem of relying on untested stereotypes about our own society to explain the evolution of human and primate behavior.
- Understand how important data from empirical observation is for testing many of these evolutionary arguments.

ISSUE SUMMARY

YES: Evolutionary psychologist David M. Buss draws on evolutionary theory to argue that humans like other primates have been shaped by evolution. For him, one key aspect of our evolutionary past is that male and female humans have evolved to have different evolutionary desires. Men desire multiple sexual partners, whereas females seek protection, security, and proven fertility in their mates. In this view, females favor monogamy and a stable relationship with the father of their children because such stability increases the likelihood of male investment in their children.

NO: Social psychologist Carol Tavris challenges the claims of sociobiologists and evolutionary psychologists that evolution has programmed women to seek monogamy. Suggesting that primate females have been selected for promiscuity, she argues that having multiple partners provides benefits for human females just as it might for males. The best evolutionary strategy for females is to get pregnant as quickly as possible, and having multiple partners is the quickest way to achieve this goal.

In 1975, biologist E.O. Wilson published his seminal statement on *sociobiology* (Harvard University Press), which attempted to bring about a new synthesis that used the evolutionary principles first identified by Charles Darwin and the studies of animal behavior that he and other biologists had conducted over the previous decades. It was the first systematic attempt to show the relationship between evolution and social behavior. When Darwin proposed his model of evolution, he suggested that nature—through the natural forces of the physical environment—could give advantages to individuals with certain useful traits in a particular population because they would be more successful in reproducing. More specifically, these individuals with the favorable traits would have more offspring that would survive to adulthood and would themselves have more offspring than individuals with less favorable traits. He likened the process of natural selection to what a pigeon breeder like Darwin himself did when he chose individual pigeons with a particularly interesting pattern of plumage over plainer individuals. In each breeding generation, he selected the individuals with the most exciting plumage for breeding and within a few generations the preferred plumage pattern became more dominant in numbers among his pigeons. Nature and the environment might work more slowly than pigeon breeders in selecting particular forms, but select it did.

Darwin also noticed among birds in natural settings that females frequently had drab or even dull patterns of plumage. Males on the other hand often had the most remarkable arrays of feathers, colorful and eye-catching both to human observers and to females. He also observed that the same eye-catching and colorful sprays of plumage also attracted the attention of predators who liked to eat birds. He hypothesized that the colorful plumage attracted the attention of possible mates and predators alike. The most successful individuals in the flock would be those who could attract the attention of females as possible mates while avoiding the eyes of deadly predators, at least until they had mated with enough females to pass on their traits to the next generation.

Darwin hypothesized that certain species of birds—an example would be the many species of birds of paradise found on the island of New Guinea—whose male plumage was highly sought after for their hats by European and American women for most of the nineteenth century. Female birds of paradise have remarkably drab and plain appearance, whereas males have huge sprays of delicate plumes, iridescent patches, bouncing quills, and the like, all of which they use during mating dances hoping to attract the attention of possible mates. We now know that most species have some sort of courting or mating behaviors during which unattached males and females go through distinctive behaviors apparently aimed at choosing mates. These sorts of behaviors involved with the mating performances seem to be behaviors that evolutionary processes have selected for over many hundreds or thousands of generations. Linking these social or behavioral aspects of animal life with evolutionary forces of selection is what sociobiology and its related field evolutionary psychology is all about.

This issue concerns primate behavior associated with the social behavior after mating has occurred and asks whether female primates are being selected to be monogamous. If monogamy for primates is being selected, then we would expect that having a single mate for an extended period of time should favor the survival of her offspring. If not, we would expect to find that females who were monogamous and those who had mated with numerous males would have equal success in producing healthy, fertile adult offspring. Unlike the birds considered above, primate infants take an extended period of time to mature, often more than a year, and for a part of that period the offspring are quite defenseless and unable to care for themselves. So evolutionary psychologists and sociobiologists have looked at survival rates among these offspring to determine which individuals would pass on their genes in the largest numbers to the next generations.

Here evolutionary psychologist David M. Buss draws on evolutionary theory to argue that humans like other primates have been shaped by evolution. He suggests that one key aspect of our evolutionary past is that among humans, males and females have evolved to have different desires about their relationships with individuals of the other sex. Much like the birds of paradise, males have adapted to have colorful plumage and a wide repertoire of performance skills, while their female mates are drab and less animated in their behavior. Although Buss's argument is framed as one about primates, his primary focus concerns humans. He argues that men desire multiple sexual partners, whereas females seek protection, security, and proven fertility in their mates. In his view, females favor monogamy and a stable relationship with the father of their children because such stability increases the likelihood of male investment in their children. Males, on the other hand, want to play the field and would prefer not to settle down. Reproductive success for males may involve passing their genes onto offspring from many different females, whereas for females it may involve protecting their offspring to maturity, an issue that Buss sees as less compelling for males.

Social psychologist Carol Tavris challenges the claims of sociobiologists and evolutionary psychologists that evolution has programmed women to seek monogamy over promiscuity. Suggesting that primate females have been selected for promiscuity, she argues that having multiple partners provides benefits for human females just as it might for males. She argues that the best evolutionary strategy for females is to get pregnant as quickly as possible, and having multiple partners is the quickest way to achieve this goal. Once she has children, it may be a useful strategy to have a stable male partner who can protect her children, but how she got pregnant in the first place may not require monogamy at all, and in fact monogamy might get in the way of getting pregnant.

For Tavris, the evolutionary biology and sociobiology arguments are attempts to find an evolutionary basis or justification for American stereotypes about men's and women's behavior. The public discourse about men and women in America often surrounds several inaccurate stereotypes that she refers to as myths. For her, the arguments of sociobiologists and evolutionary psychologists are designed to fit the popular culture images of women and men, rather than designed to observe what men and women actually do and then determine whether these observed patterns actually lead to reproductive success. Then drawing upon a variety of species as examples, she suggests that there is a wide variety of patterns that animals have chosen that do not fit patterns like that suggested by Buss.

As you read these selections, consider what kinds of empirical data the two authors have chosen for their analysis. Are they observing mating behavior from natural settings or are they using deductive reasoning alone to test their hypotheses? Are these selections about all primates or about just one species of primate—our own? Can either of these arguments be falsified with new data collected from actual observations of human or primate behavior? Would a careful analysis of more observational data about behavior support or refute these arguments?

YES ↵

David M. Buss

The Evolution of Desire: Strategies of Human Mating

What Women Want

We are walking archives of ancestral wisdom.

—Helena Cronin, *The Ant and the Peacock*

What women actually want in a mate has puzzled male scientists and other men for centuries, for good reason. It is not androcentric to propose that women's preferences in a partner are more complex and enigmatic than the mate preferences of either sex of any other species. Discovering the evolutionary roots of women's desires requires going far back in time, before humans evolved as a species, before primates emerged from their mammalian ancestors, back to the origins of sexual reproduction itself.

One reason women exert choice about mates stems from the most basic fact of reproductive biology—the definition of sex. It is a remarkable circumstance that what defines biological sex is simply the size of the sex cells. Males are defined as the ones with the small sex cells, females as the ones with the large sex cells. The large female gametes remain reasonably stationary and come loaded with nutrients. The small male gametes are endowed with mobility and swimming speed. Along with differences in the size and mobility of sex cells comes a difference between the sexes in quantity. Men, for example, produce millions of sperm, which are replenished at a rate of roughly twelve million per hour, while women produce a fixed and unreplenishable lifetime supply of approximately four hundred ova.

Women's greater initial investment does not end with the egg. Fertilization and gestation, key components of human parental investment, occur internally within women. One act of sexual intercourse, which requires minimal male investment, can produce an obligatory and energy-consuming nine-month investment by the woman that forecloses other mating opportunities. Women then bear the exclusive burden of lactation, an investment that may last as long as three or four years.

No biological law of the animal world dictates that women invest more than men. Indeed, among some species, such as the Mormon cricket, pipefish seahorse, and Panamanian poison arrow frog, males invest more. The male Mormon cricket produces through great effort a large spermatophore that is loaded with nutrients. Females compete with each other for access to the males that hold the largest spermatophores. Among these so-called sex-role reversed species, it is the males who are more discriminating about mating. Among all four thousand species of mammals, including the more than two hundred species of primates, however, females bear the burden of internal fertilization, gestation, and lactation.

The great initial parental investment of women makes them a valuable, but limited, resource. Gestating, bearing, nursing, nurturing, and protecting a child are exceptional reproductive resources that cannot be allocated indiscriminately. Nor can one woman dispense them to many men.

Those who hold valuable resources do not give them away cheaply or unselectively. Because women in our evolutionary past risked enormous investment as a consequence of having sex, evolution favored women who were highly selective about their mates. Ancestral women suffered severe costs if they were indiscriminate—they experienced lower reproductive success, and fewer of their children survived to reproductive age. A man in human evolutionary history could walk away from a casual coupling having lost only a few hours of time. His reproductive success was not seriously compromised. A woman in evolutionary history could also walk away from a casual encounter, but if she got pregnant as a result, she bore the costs of that decision for months, years, and even decades afterward.

Modern birth control technology has altered these costs. In today's industrial nations, women can have short-term dalliances with less fear of pregnancy. But human sexual psychology evolved over millions of years to cope with ancestral adaptive problems. We still possess this underlying sexual psychology, even though our environment has changed.

Components of Desire

Consider the case of an ancestral woman who is trying to decide between two men, one of whom shows great generosity with his resources to her and one of whom is stingy. Other things being equal, the generous man is more valuable to her than the stingy man. The generous man may share his meat from the hunt, aiding her survival. He may sacrifice his time, energy, and resources for the benefit of the children, furthering the woman's reproductive success. In these respects, the generous man has higher value as a mate than the stingy man. If, over evolutionary time, generosity in men provided these benefits repeatedly and the cues to a man's generosity were observable and reliable, then selection would favor the evolution of a preference for generosity in a mate.

Now consider a more complicated and realistic case in which men vary not just in their generosity but also in a bewildering variety of ways that are significant to the choice of a mate. Men vary in their physical prowess, athletic skill, ambition, industriousness, kindness, empathy, emotional stability, intelligence, social skills, sense of humor, kin network, and position in the status hierarchy. Men also differ in the costs they impose on a mating relationship: some come with children, bad debts, a quick temper, a selfish disposition, and a tendency to be promiscuous. In addition, men differ in hundreds of ways that may be irrelevant to women. Some men have navels turned in, others have navels turned out. A strong preference for a particular navel shape would be unlikely to evolve unless male navel differences were somehow adaptively relevant to ancestral women. From among the thousands of ways in which men differ, selection over hundreds of thousands of years focused women's preferences laser-like on the most adaptively valuable characteristics.

The qualities people prefer, however, are not static characteristics, Because characteristics change, mate seekers must gauge the future potential of a prospective partner. A young medical student who lacks resources now might have excellent future promise. Or a man might be very ambitious but have already reached his peak. Another man might have children from a previous marriage, but because they are about to leave the nest, they will not drain his resources. Gauging a man's mating value requires looking beyond his current position and evaluating his potential.

Evolution has favored women who prefer men who possess attributes that confer benefits and who dislike men who possess attributes that impose costs. Each separate attribute constitutes one component of a man's value to a woman as a mate. Each of her preferences tracks one component.

Preferences that favor particular components, however, do not completely solve the problem of choosing a mate. Women face further adaptive hurdles. First, a woman must evaluate her unique circumstances and personal needs. The same man might differ in value for different women. A man's willingness to do a lot of direct child care, for example, might be more valuable to a woman who does not have kin around to help her than to a woman whose mother, sisters, aunts, and uncles eagerly participate. The dangers of choosing a man with a volatile temper may be greater for a woman who is an only child than for a woman with four strapping brothers around to protect her. The value of potential males, in short, depends on the individualized, personalized, and contextualized perspective of the person doing the choosing.

In selecting a mate, women must identify and correctly evaluate the cues that signal whether a man indeed possesses a particular resource. The assessment problem becomes especially acute in areas where men are apt to deceive women, such as pretending to have higher status than they do or feigning greater commitment than they are willing to give.

Finally, women face the problem of integrating their knowledge about a prospective mate. Suppose that one man is generous but emotionally unstable. Another man is emotionally stable but stingy. Which man should a woman choose? Choosing a mate calls upon psychological mechanisms that make it possible to evaluate the relevant attributes and give each its appropriate weight in the whole. Some attributes are granted more weight than others in the final decision about whether to choose or reject a particular man. One of these heavily weighted components is the man's resources.

Economic Capacity

The evolution of the female preference for males who offer resources may be the most ancient and pervasive basis for female choice in the animal kingdom. Consider the gray shrike, a bird that lives in the Negev Desert of Israel. Just before the start of the breeding season, male shrikes begin amassing caches of edible prey, such as snails, and other useful objects, such as feathers and pieces of cloth, in numbers ranging from 90 to 120. They impale these items on thorns and other pointed projections within their territory. Females look over the available males and prefer to mate with those having the largest caches. When the biologist Reuven Yosef arbitrarily removed portions of some males' caches and added edible objects to others, females shifted to the males with the larger bounties. Females avoided entirely males without resources, consigning them to bachelorhood. Wherever females show a mating preference, the male's resources are often the key criterion.

Among humans, the evolution of women's preference for a permanent mate with resources would have required three preconditions. First, resources would have had to be accruable, defensible, and controllable by men during human evolutionary history. Second, men would have had to differ from each other in their holdings and their willingness to invest those holdings in a woman and her children—if all men possessed the same resources and showed an equal willingness to commit them, there would be no need for women to develop the preference for them. Constants do not count in mating decisions. And third, the advantages of being with one man would have to outweigh the advantages of being with several men.

Among humans, these conditions are easily met. Territory and tools, to name just two resources, are acquired, defended, monopolized, and controlled by men worldwide. Men vary tremendously in the quantity of resources they command—from the poverty of the street bum to the riches of Trumps and Rockefellers. Men also differ widely in how willing they are to invest their time and resources in long-term mateships. Some men are cads, preferring to mate with many women while investing little in each. Other men are dads, channeling all of their resources to one woman and her children.

Women over human evolutionary history could often garner far more resources for their children through a single spouse than through several temporary sex partners. Men provide their wives and children with resources to an extent that is unprecedented among primates. Among most other primate species, for example, females must rely solely on their own efforts to acquire food, because males usually do not share food with their mates. Men, in contrast, provide food, find shelter, and defend territory. Men protect children. They tutor them in the art of hunting, the craft of war, the strategies of social influence. They transfer status, aiding offspring in forming reciprocal alliances later in life. Such benefits are unlikely to be secured by a woman from a temporary sex partner. Not all potential husbands can confer all of these benefits, but over thousands of generations, when some men were able to provide some of these benefits, women gained a powerful advantage by preferring them as mates.

So the stage was set for women to evolve a preference for men with resources. But women needed cues to signal a man's possession of those resources. These cues might be indirect, such as personality characteristics that signaled a man's upward mobility. They might be physical, such as a man's athletic ability or health. They might include reputational information, such as the esteem in which a man was held by his peers. Economic resources, however, provide the most direct cue. . . .

Social Status

Traditional hunter-gatherer societies, which are our closest guide to what ancestral conditions were probably like, suggest that ancestral men had clearly defined status hierarchies, with resources flowing freely to those at the top and trickling slowly to those at the bottom. Traditional tribes today, such as the Tiwi, an aboriginal group residing on two small islands off the coast of Northern Australia; the Yanomamo of Venezuela; the Ache of Paraguay; and the !Kung tribe of Botswana, are replete with people described as "head men" and "big men" who wield great power and enjoy the resource privileges of prestige. Therefore, an ancestral man's social status would provide a powerful cue to his possession of resources.

Henry Kissinger once remarked that power is the most potent aphrodisiac. Women desire men who command a high position in society because social status is a universal cue to the control of resources. Along with status come better food, more abundant territory, and superior health care. Greater social status bestows on children social opportunities missed by the children of lower-ranked males. For male children worldwide, access to more mates and better quality mates typically accompanies families of higher social status. In one study of 186 societies ranging from the Mbuti Pygmies of Africa to the Aleut Eskimos, high-status men invariably had greater wealth, better nourishment for children, and more wives. . . .

Age

The age of a man also provides an important cue to his access to resources. Just as young male baboons must mature before they can enter the upper ranks in the baboon social hierarchy, human adolescents and young men rarely command the respect, status, or position of more mature older men. This tendency reaches an extreme among the Tiwi tribe, a gerontocracy in which the very old men wield most of the power and prestige and control the mating system through complex networks of alliances. Even in American culture, status and wealth tend to accumulate with increasing age. . . .

In traditional societies, part of this linkage may be related to physical strength and hunting prowess. Physical strength increases in men as they get older, peaking in their late twenties and early thirties. Although there have been no systematic studies of the relationship between age and hunting ability, anthropologists believe that ability may peak when a man is in his thirties, at which point his slight decline in physical prowess is more than compensated

for by his increased knowledge, patience, skill, and wisdom. So women's preference for older men may stem from our hunter-gatherer ancestors, for whom the
resources derived from hunting were critical to survival. . . .

In cultures where people marry young, often the economic capacity of a
man cannot be evaluated directly but must be deduced indirectly. Indeed, in
hunter-gatherer groups that lack a cash economy, the target of selection cannot be financial resources per se. Among the Tiwi tribe, for example, young
men are scrutinized carefully by both women and older men to evaluate which
ones are "comers," destined to acquire status and resources, and which are
likely to remain in the slow lane, based in part on their personality. The young
men are evaluated for their promise, the key signs being good hunting skills,
good fighting skills, and especially a strong proclivity to ascend the hierarchy
of tribal power and influence. Women in all cultures, past and present, can
select men for their apparent ability to accrue future resources, based on certain personality characteristics. And women who value the personality characteristics likely to lead to status and sustained resource acquisition are far better
off than women who ignore these vital characterological cues. . . .

Size and Strength

When the great basketball player Magic Johnson revealed that he had slept
with thousands of women, he inadvertently revealed women's preference for
mates who display physical and athletic prowess. The numbers may be shocking, but the preference is not. Physical characteristics, such as athleticism, size,
and strength, convey important information that women use in making a
mating decision.

The importance of physical characteristics in the female choice of a mate
is prevalent throughout the animal world. In the species called the gladiator
frog, males are responsible for creating nests and defending the eggs. In the
majority of courtships, a stationary male is deliberately bumped by a female
who is considering him. She strikes him with great force, sometimes enough
to rock him back or even scare him away. If the male moves too much or bolts
from the nest, the female hastily leaves to examine alternative mates. Most
females mate with males who do not move or who move minimally when
bumped. Only rarely does a female reject a male who remains firmly planted
after being bumped. Bumping helps a female frog to decide how successful the
male will be at defending her clutch. The bump test reveals the male's physical
ability to perform the function of protection.

Women sometimes face physical domination by larger, stronger men,
which can lead to injury and sexual domination by preventing them from
exercising choice. Such domination undoubtedly occurred regularly during
ancestral times. Indeed, studies of many nonhuman primate groups reveal
that male physical and sexual domination of females has been a recurrent
part of our primate heritage. The primatologist Barbara Smuts lived among
baboons in the savanna plains of Africa while studying their mating patterns.
She found that females frequently form enduring "special friendships" with
males who offer physical protection to themselves and their infants. In return,

these females grant their "friends" preferential sexual access during times of estrus. In essence, female baboons exchange sex for protection.

Analogously, one benefit to women of permanent mating is the physical protection a man can offer. A man's size, strength, and physical prowess are cues to solutions to the problem of protection. The evidence shows that women's preferences in a mate embody these cues. In the study of temporary and permanent mating. American women rated the desirability or undesirability of a series of physical traits. Women judge short men to be undesirable as a permanent mate. In contrast, they find it very desirable for a potential permanent mate to be tall, physically strong, and athletic. Another group of American women consistently indicates a preference for men of average or greater than average height, roughly five feet and eleven inches, as their ideal marriage partner. Tall men are consistently seen as more desirable dates and mates than men who are short or of average height. Furthermore, the two studies of personal ads described earlier revealed that, among women who mention height, 80 percent want a man who is six feet or taller. Perhaps even more telling is the finding that ads placed by taller men receive more responses from women than those placed by shorter men. Tall men date more often than short men and have a larger pool of potential mates. Women solve the problem of protection from aggressive men at least in part by preferring a mate who has the size, strength, and physical prowess to protect them.

Tall men tend to have a higher status in nearly all cultures. "Big men" in hunter-gatherer societies—men high in status—are literally big men physically. In Western cultures, tall men make more money, advance in their professions more rapidly, and receive more and earlier promotions. Few American presidents have been less than six feet tall. Politicians are keenly aware of voters' preference. Following the televised presidential debate in 1988, George Bush made a point of standing very close to his shorter competitor, Michael Dukakis, in a strategy of highlighting their disparity in size. As the evolutionary psychologist Bruce Ellis notes:

> Height constitutes a reliable cue to dominance in social interactions . . . shorter policemen are likely to be assaulted more than taller policemen . . . suggesting that the latter command more fear and respect from adversaries . . . taller men are more sought after in women's personal advertisements, receive more responses to their own personal advertisements, and tend to have prettier girlfriends than do shorter men.

This preference for taller men is not limited to Western cultures. Among the Mehinaku tribe of the Brazilian Amazon, the anthropologist Thomas Gregor notes the importance of men's wrestling skills as an arena where size differences become acute:

> A heavily muscled, imposingly built man is likely to accumulate many girlfriends, while a small man, deprecatingly referred to as a *perissi*, fares badly. The mere fact of height creates a measurable advantage. . . . A powerful wrestler, say the villagers, is frightening . . . he commands fear and respect. To the women, he is "beautiful" (awitsiri), in demand as a

paramour and husband. Triumphant in politics as well as in love, the champion wrestler embodies the highest qualities of manliness. Not so fortunate the vanquished! A chronic loser, no matter what his virtues, is regarded as a fool. As he wrestles, the men shout mock advice. . . . The women are less audible as they watch the matches from their doorways, but they too have their sarcastic jokes. None of them is proud of having a loser as a husband or lover.

Barbara Smuts believes that during human evolutionary history physical protection was one of the most important things a man could offer a woman. The presence of aggressive men who tried to dominate women physically and to circumvent their sexual choices may have been an important influence on women's mate selection in ancestral times. Given the alarming incidence of sexual coercion and rape in many cultures, a mate's protection value may well remain relevant to mate selection in modern environments. Many women simply do not feel safe on the streets, and a strong, tall, athletic mate acts as a deterrent for sexually aggressive men.

Attributes such as size, strength, and athletic prowess are not the only physical attributes that signal high mating value. Another physical quality critical for survival is good health.

Good Health

Women worldwide prefer mates who are healthy. In all thirty-seven cultures included in the international study on choosing a mate, women judge good health to be anywhere from important to indispensable in a marriage partner. In another study on American women, poor physical conditions, ranging from bad grooming habits to a venereal disease, are regarded as extremely undesirable characteristics in a mate. The biologists Clelland Ford and Frank Beach found that signs of ill health, such as open sores, lesions, and unusual pallor, are universally regarded as unattractive.

In humans, good health may be signaled by behavior as well as by physical appearance. A lively mood, high energy level, and sprightly gait, for example, may be attractive precisely because they are calorically costly and can be displayed only by people brimming with good health.

The tremendous importance we place on good health is not unique to our species. Some animals display large, loud, and gaudy traits that are costly and yet signal great health and vitality. Consider the bright, flamboyant, ostentatious plumage of the peacock. It is as if the peacock is saying: "Look at me; I'm so fit that I can carry these large, cumbersome feathers, and yet still I'm thriving." The mystery of the peacock's tail, which seems so contrary to utilitarian survival, is finally on the verge of being solved. The biologists William D. Hamilton and Marlena Zuk propose that the brilliant plumage serves as a signal that the peacock carries a light load of parasites, since peacocks who carry more than the average number of parasites have duller plumage. The burdensome plumage provides a cue to health and robustness. Peahens prefer the brilliant plumage because it provides clues to the male's health.

In ancestral times, four bad consequences were likely to follow if a woman selected a mate who was unhealthy or disease-prone. First, she put herself and her family at risk of being contaminated by the disease. Second, her mate was less able to perform essential functions and provide crucial benefits to her and her children, such as food, protection, health care, and child rearing. Third, her mate was at increased risk of dying, prematurely cutting off the flow of resources and forcing her to incur the costs of searching for a new mate and courting all over again. And fourth, if health is partly heritable, she would risk passing on genes for poor health to her children. A preference for healthy mates solves the problem of mate survival and ensures that resources are likely to be delivered over the long run.

Love and Commitment

A man's possession of such assets as health, status, and resources, however, still does not guarantee his willingness to commit them to a particular woman and her children. Indeed, some men show a tremendous reluctance to marry, preferring to play the field and to seek a series of temporary sex partners. Women deride men for this hesitancy, calling them "commitment dodgers," "commitment phobics," "paranoid about commitment," and "fearful of the M word." And women's anger is reasonable. Given the tremendous costs women incur because of sex, pregnancy, and childbirth, it is reasonable for them to require commitment from a man in return.

The weight women attach to commitment is revealed in the following true story (the names are changed). Mark and Susan had been going out with each other for two years and had been living together for six months. He was a well-off forty-two-year-old professional, she a medical student of twenty-eight. Susan pressed for a decision about marriage—they were in love, and she wanted to have children within a few years. But Mark balked. He had been married before; if he ever married again, he wanted to be absolutely sure it would be for good. As Susan continued to press for a decision, Mark raised the possibility of a prenuptial agreement. She resisted, feeling that this violated the spirit of marriage. Finally they agreed that by a date four months in the future he would have decided one way or another. The date came and went, and still Mark could not make a decision. Susan told him that she was leaving him, moved out, and started dating another man. Mark panicked. He called her up and begged her to come back, saying that he had changed his mind and would marry her. He promised a new car. He promised that there would be no prenuptial agreement. But it was too late. Mark's failure to commit was too strong a negative signal to Susan. It dealt the final blow to their relationship. She was gone forever.

Women past and present face the adaptive problem of choosing men who not only have the necessary resources but also show a willingness to commit those resources to them and their children. This problem may be more difficult than it seems at first. Although resources can often be directly observed, commitment cannot be. Instead, gauging commitment requires looking for cues that signal the likelihood of fidelity in the channeling of resources. Love is one of the most important cues to commitment. . . .

Kindness is an enduring personality characteristic that has many components, but at the core of all of them is the commitment of resources. The trait signals an empathy toward children, a willingness to put a mate's needs before one's own, and a willingness to channel energy and effort toward a mate's goals rather than exclusively and selfishly to one's own goals. Kindness, in other words, signals the ability and willingness of a potential mate to commit energy and resources selflessly to a partner.

The lack of kindness signals selfishness, an inability or unwillingness to commit, and a high likelihood that costs will be inflicted on a spouse. The study of newlyweds, for example, identified unkind men on the basis of their self-assessment, their wives' assessment, and the judgment of male and female interviewers, and then examined the wives' complaints about these husbands. Women married to unkind men complain that their spouses abuse them both verbally and physically by hitting, slapping, or spitting at them. Unkind men tend to be condescending, putting down their wife's opinions as stupid or inferior. They are selfish, monopolizing shared resources. They are inconsiderate, failing to do any housework. They are neglectful, failing to show up as promised. Finally, they have more extramarital affairs, suggesting that these men are unable or unwilling to commit to a monogamous relationship. Unkind men look out for themselves, and have trouble committing to anything much beyond that.

Because sex is one of the most valuable reproductive resources women can offer, they have evolved psychological mechanisms that cause them to resist giving it away indiscriminately. Requiring love, sincerity, and kindness is a way of securing a commitment of resources commensurate with the value of the resource that women give to men. Requiring love and kindness helps women to solve the critical adaptive mating problem of securing the commitment of resources from a man that can aid in the survival and reproduction of her offspring. . . .

Women's Many Preferences

We now have the outlines of an answer to the enigma of what women want. Women are judicious, prudent, and discerning about the men they consent to mate with because they have so many valuable reproductive resources to offer. Those with valuable resources rarely give them away indiscriminately. The costs in reproductive currency of failing to exercise choice were too great for ancestral women, who would have risked beatings, food deprivation, disease, abuse of children, and abandonment. The benefits of choice in nourishment, protection, and paternal investment for children were abundant.

Permanent mates may bring with them a treasure trove of resources. Selecting a long-term mate who has the relevant resources is clearly an extraordinarily complex endeavor. It involves at least a dozen distinctive preferences, each corresponding to a resource that helps women to solve critical adaptive problems.

That women seek resources in a permanent mate may be obvious. But because resources cannot always be directly discerned, women's mating preferences are keyed to other qualities that signal the likely possession, or future acquisition, of resources. Indeed, women may be less influenced by money per se than by qualities that lead to resources, such as ambition, status, intelligence, and age. Women scrutinize these personal qualities carefully because they reveal a man's potential.

Potential, however, is not enough. Because many men with a high resource potential are themselves discriminating and are at times content with casual sex, women are faced with the problem of commitment. Seeking love and sincerity are two solutions to the commitment problem. Sincerity signals that the man is capable of commitment. Acts of love signal that he has in fact committed to a particular woman.

To have the love and commitment of a man who could be easily downed by other men in the physical arena, however, would have been a problematic asset for ancestral women. Women mated to small, weak men lacking in physical prowess would have risked damage from other men and loss of the couple's joint resources. Tall, strong, athletic men offered ancestral women protection. In this way, their resources and commitment could be secured against incursion. Women who selected men in part for their strength and prowess were more likely to be successful at surviving and reproducing.

Resources, commitment, and protection do a woman little good if her husband becomes diseased or dies or if the couple is so mismatched that they fail to function as an effective team. The premium that women place on a man's health ensures that husbands will be capable of providing these benefits over the long haul. And the premium that women place on similarity of interests and traits with their mate helps to ensure the convergence of mutually pursued goals. These multiple facets of current women's mating preferences thus correspond perfectly with the multiple facets of adaptive problems that were faced by our women ancestors thousands of years ago. . . .

Carol Tavris   ➡ **NO**

The Mismeasure of Woman

The Myth of the Coy Female

> [Thus] we arrived at the important conclusion that polygamy is the natural order among human beings, just as it is in most species of the animal kingdom. . . . monogamy is responsible for the high incidence of divorce and female grievances in modern society, as well as the genetic deevolution and behavioral degeneration of civilization as a whole. . . . Culture is to blame, and fortunately *culture can be changed*. Mating is the key. [Emphasis in original.]

> —Sam Kash Kachigan, *The Sexual Matrix*

Sam Kash Kachigan is not a social scientist; he's just a regular fellow who thinks that the theories of sociobiology offer the best hope of improving relations between women and men. "Mating is the key," he argues. The mating he has in mind, it turns out, would (if we were truly to follow our evolutionary heritage) occur between rich old men and beautiful young girls. Among the annoying contemporary practices that Kachigan laments is the habit of beautiful young girls marrying boys their own age. To Kachigan, in any truly civilized society— that is, one in which our practices fit our sociobiological natures—girls would marry men who were old enough to demonstrate their "true potential":

> In every respect, then, it makes much more sense for young women to mate with *older* men, who will have *proven* their genetic endowment as well as their financial and emotional capacity for raising children. [Emphasis in original.]

Why do I suspect that Kachigan is such a man?

The basic ideas behind sociobiology date back to Charles Darwin, who in 1871 described what he considered to be a basic dichotomy in the sexual natures of males and females of all species. Males actively pursue females; they are promiscuous; and those who are strongest, most fit in evolutionary terms, succeed in their sexual conquest. Females, said Darwin, are "comparatively passive"; they may choose their preferred suitor, but then remain monogamous and faithful. That this dichotomy conveniently fit Victorian dating and mating patterns was, naturally, pure coincidence.

For a century after Darwin, research on sexual selection and sexual behavior was based on the belief that males are passionate and undiscriminating (any female in a storm will do), whereas females are restrained, cautious, and highly discriminating in their choice of partner (only a male who meets her shopping list of qualifications will do). According to primatologist Sarah Blaffer Hrdy, this stereotype of "the coy female" has persisted in the public mind—and she adds a phrase that by now should be familiar to us—"*despite the accumulation of abundant openly available evidence contradicting it*" [my emphasis].

The stereotype of the coy female got a major boost in an important paper published in 1948 by Angus John Bateman. Bateman was a distinguished plant geneticist who did dozens of experiments with Drosophila, the tiny fruit fly that many people remember from science experiments in junior high school. Bateman found that successful male fruit flies could, with multiple matings, produce nearly three times as many offspring as the most reproductively successful female. As Hrdy explains, "whereas a male could always gain by mating just one more time, and hence benefit from a nature that made him undiscriminatingly eager to mate, a female, already breeding near capacity after just one copulation, could gain little from multiple mating and should be quite uninterested in mating more than once or twice."

What, you may ask, does a human man have in common with a fruit fly? When it comes to sexual strategies, said Bateman, the answer is everything. Generalizing from his sixty-four experiments with Drosophila to all species, Bateman concluded that there is a universally lopsided division in the sexual natures of all creatures, apart from "a few very primitive organisms." Quite simply, males profit, evolutionarily speaking, from frequent mating, and females do not. This is why, said Bateman, "there is nearly always a combination of an undiscriminating eagerness in the males and a discriminating passivity in the females."

The modern field of sociobiology took this idea still further, attempting to account for complex human social arrangements and customs—warfare and corporate raiding, feeding infants and giving children karate lessons—in terms of the individual's basic need to reproduce his or her genes. Women and men, sociobiologists believe, adopt highly different strategies in order to do this. Males compete with other males for access to desirable females, and their goal is to inseminate as many females as possible. Females, in contrast, are motivated to attach themselves to genetically "superior" males because of the female's greater "investment" in terms of time and energy in her offspring; this, according to sociobiologists, is why females are more faithful and nurturant than males. As biologist Ruth Hubbard observes, "Thus, from the seemingly innocent asymmetries between eggs and sperm [say the sociobiologists] flow such major social consequences as female fidelity, male promiscuity, women's disproportional contribution to the care of children, and the unequal distribution of labor by sex."

Sociobiological explanations of competitive, promiscuous men and choosy, inhibited but flirtatious women fit right in with many elements within the popular culture. "And so it was," Hrdy says, "that 'coyness' came to be the single most commonly mentioned attribute of females in the literature on sociobiology."

It all seems a cruel joke of nature. Certainly many people are convinced, as the King of Siam sings in *The King and I*, that the male is like the honeybee, flitting from flower to flower, "gathering all he can," whereas the female has "honey for just one man." But notice that it is the King who sings that song; until relatively recently, no one was asking Queens for their view of things. Nor were male observers asking why, if human females were so naturally chaste, coy, and monogamous, social taboos from ostracism to death had to be placed on females who indulged in forbidden sexual relationships. For that matter, why did nonmarital affairs need to be forbidden anyway, if females have "honey for just one man"?

Sociobiologists attempt to explain human social customs by drawing on research on nonhuman animals, from the fields of primatology, evolutionary biology, anthropology, and related disciplines. In the last two decades, however, there has been an explosion of new research that casts doubt on many sociobiological assumptions, a change that is largely a result of the growing numbers of women who have entered these fields. Most of the women saw animal behavior in a different light from most of the male observers who had preceded them. Male primatologists, for example, had tended to observe and emphasize male-male competition and the number of times the male animals "got lucky"; the female animals, to the human men observing them, seemed mysterious and unpredictable. This is not unlike the ways in which human females have seemed mysterious and unpredictable to the human males who have observed *them*.

At first, women who went into these research fields saw the world as they had been taught to see it, through the academic perspective of their mentors. But after a while, they began to ask different questions and to bring different expectations to their observations. Hrdy recalls her own first glimpse of a female langur

> . . . moving away from her natal group to approach and solicit males in an all-male band. At the time, I had no context for interpreting behavior that merely seemed strange and incomprehensible to my Harvard-trained eyes. Only in time, did I come to realize that such wandering and such seemingly "wanton" behavior were recurring events in the lives of langurs.

Eventually, Hrdy learned that female langurs often leave their troops to join up with bands of males; and she also found that often a female, for reasons unknown, "simply takes a shine to the resident male of a neighboring troop." In fact, female langurs (and many other primate species) are able to shift from being in heat once a month to being continuously receptive for weeks at a time, a state not unlike the first phase of (human) love. In many primates, female receptivity is often *situation specific*, rather than being dependent exclusively on cyclical periods of being in heat.

As a result of the efforts of many pioneers like Hrdy, we now know that the females of many animal species do not behave like the patient, coy fruit fly. On the contrary, the females are sexually ardent and can even be called polyandrous (having many male partners). Further, their sexual behavior does not depend simply on the goal of being fertilized by the male, because in many cases females actively solicit males when they are not ovulating, and even when they are already pregnant. Here are a few illustrations from hundreds of research studies:

- Many species of female birds are promiscuous. In one study, researchers vasectomized the "master" of a blackbird harem . . . but the females nevertheless conceived.
- Many species of female fish are promiscuous. A female shiner perch who is not ovulating will nevertheless mate with many males, collecting sperm and storing them internally until she is ready to ovulate.
- Many species of female cats, notably leopards, lions, and pumas, are promiscuous. A lioness may mate dozens of times with many different partners during the week she is in estrus.
- Many species of female primates are promiscuous. Among savanna baboons and Barbary macaques, females initiate many different brief sexual encounters. Among chimpanzees, Hrdy reports, some females form partnerships with one male, but others engage in communal mating with all males in the vicinity. And among wild tamarin monkeys, a species long thought to be monogamous (at least in captivity), supposedly faithful females will mate with several males. So do female Hanuman langurs, blue monkeys, and redtail monkeys, all primates that were formerly believed to be one-man women. The old notion that primate females typically form "one-male breeding units," as primatologists would say, is now seriously called into question.

In spite of rapidly accumulating evidence that females of many different and varied species do mate "promiscuously" (a word that itself has evaluative overtones), it was not until 1980 or so that researchers realized that this fact threw, well, a monkey wrench into traditional evolutionary theories. Why would females have more copulations than are necessary for conception? Why would they go off with some guy from a neighboring town, whom none of their friends approves of? Why risk losing the genetic father's support by joining the baboon equivalent of Hell's Angels? And the brooding question over all of them, why did female primates develop continuous sexual receptivity?

These questions stimulated a flurry of new theories to explain why female philandering would make as much survival sense as its male counterpart. Most of these new explanations directly resulted from considering the world from the female's point of view. Traditional theories of sexual selection, after all, were based exclusively on the perspective of the male: Males compete for *access* to the female, who apparently is just hanging around waiting to go out and party with the winner. And it's only from a male point of view that multiple female matings can be considered "excessive," or that female sexual interest is even described as her time of "receptivity." Is she passively "receptive" to the active intentions of the male? The word implies that she's just putting up with his annoying lustfulness yet again.

New hypotheses argue that there are genetic benefits for the offspring of sexually adventurous mothers. According to Hrdy's review of these explanations, the "fertility backup" hypothesis assumes that females need sperm from a number of males in order to assure conception by the healthiest sperm. The "inferior cuckold" hypothesis suggests that a female who has a genetically inferior mate will sneak off with a genetically superior male when she is likely to conceive. (I suppose she knows this by the size of his income.) And the "diverse paternity" hypothesis argues that when the environment is unpredictable, females diversify. Over a reproductive lifetime, females who have numerous partners, and thus different fathers for their offspring, improve their offspring's chances for survival.

Other theories look for the social and environmental benefits of female promiscuity to the mother and her infants. The "therapeutic hypothesis" suggests that having lots of partners and multiple orgasms (in some species) makes intercourse and conception more pleasurable, and therefore more likely to occur. The "keep 'em around" hypothesis maintains that females actively solicit lower-status males (with the tacit approval of dominant males), a behavior that prevents weaker males from leaving the group. Hrdy's own favored theory is what she calls the "manipulation hypothesis," the idea that females mate with numerous males precisely because paternity becomes uncertain. The result is that male partners will be more invested in, and tolerant of, the female's infants. This idea, Hrdy explains,

> grew out of a dawning awareness that, first of all, individual females could do a great deal that would affect the survival of their offspring, and second, that males, far from mere dispensers of sperm, were critical features on the landscape where infants died or survived. That is, females were more political, males more nurturing (or at least not neutral), than some earlier versions of sexual selection theory would lead us to suppose.

Both of these points are essential: Not only are females more than passive receptacles of sperm, but also males are more than "mere dispensers of sperm." They don't just mate and run. They have a key role in determining whether infants survive or die. Among primates, there is enormous variation in the extent to which males nurture and protect offspring:

- Among the ruffed lemur, the male tends the nest while the female forages for food.
- Among New World monkeys, males directly care for offspring in half of all species; often, the male is the primary caretaker, carrying the infant on his back, sharing food with it.
- In a rare study of a monogamous species of night monkey, an observer found that during one infant's first week of life, the mother carried it 33 percent of the time, the father 51 percent of the time, and a juvenile member of the troop the remaining time.
- Among baboons, males do not have much direct contact with infants, but they hover nearby protectively and offer what Hrdy calls "quality" time in a very real sense: They increase the infant's chances of survival. They discourage attacks on the infant from males who are unknown, in both the literal and the Biblical sense, to the mother.

Hrdy's "manipulation hypothesis" assumes that primate males respond more benevolently to the offspring of females with whom they have mated, so the females derive obvious benefits from mating with more than one male. In numerous primate species, the mother's multiple sexual partners act like godfathers to the infant, as primatologist Jeanne Altmann calls them. Each of these males will help care for the female's offspring. Baboon males, many of whom could have served as the model for *Three Men and a Baby*, develop special relationships with the infant, carrying it on their backs in times of danger and protecting it from strangers and hazards. These affectionate bonds are possible because of the mother's closeness to the males, says Hrdy, and because the infant comes to trust these males and seek them out.

The manipulation hypothesis may or may not hold up with further research, as Hrdy acknowledges. It certainly does not apply to most human societies, where husbands do not look too kindly on their wives' "special relationships" with other men, let alone their previous lovers, husbands, and wooers. Hrdy's work, nonetheless, shows that theories depend, first and foremost, on what an observer *observes,* and then on how those observations can be blurred by unconscious expectations. Hrdy initially regarded those "wanton" female langurs as aberrations because their behavior did not fit the established theory. Not until researchers began to speculate on the potential benefits of female promiscuity did they come up with different questions and answers about female sexual behavior than had sociobiologists.

In evolutionary biology, if not in the popular press, the myth of the coy female (and, for that matter, the myth of the absent father) is dead. Hrdy is encouraged by the speed with which primatologists, once aware of the male bias that permeated their discipline, have produced "a small stampede by members of both sexes to study female reproductive strategies." This she takes to be a healthy sign, as do I. But Hrdy cautions against "substituting a new set of biases for the old ones":

> That is, among feminist scholars it is now permissible to say that males and females are different, provided one also stipulates that females are more cooperative, more nurturing, more supportive—not to mention equipped with unique moral sensibilities. . . .

Perhaps it is impossible, as biologist Donna Haraway suggests, for any of us to observe the behavior of other species, let alone our own, in a way that does not mirror the assumptions of our own way of life. It is disconcerting, says Hrdy wryly, that primatologists were finding "politically motivated females and nurturing males at roughly the same time that a woman runs for vice president of the United States and [Garry] Trudeau starts to poke fun at 'caring males' in his cartoons." Informally, scientists admit that their prejudices—such as the tendency to identify with the same sex of the species they are studying—affect their research. One woman primatologist told Hrdy, "I sometimes identify with female baboons more than I do with males of my own species."

The recognition of a male-centered bias in primatology and biology proved to be an enormous step forward, allowing scientists of both sexes to revise their theories of animal behavior. Sociobiologists (and their fans like Sam Kash Kachigan) can no longer justify traditional sex roles, particularly male dominance and female nurturance and chastity, by appealing to the universality of such behavior in other species. Other species aren't cooperating.

But that is not the only moral of the Parable of the Primates. The female perspective is invaluable, but, as Hrdy warns, a female-centered bias will provide its own set of distortions. Cultural feminists who look to evolutionary biology to explain women's allegedly sweeter, more cooperative ways are on as shaky ground as the antifeminists they would replace.

If the sociobiological heroine is the coy female who is so different from males, the heroine of modern sexology is the lusty female who is just like them. I like her better, but I'm afraid that she, too, is (as a student of mine once inadvertently said) a fig leaf of the imagination. . . .

EXPLORING THE ISSUE

Are Female Primates Selected to Be Monogamous?

Critical Thinking and Reflection

1. To what extent does Buss rely on Darwin's original formulation of natural selection to explain different patterns of behavior among men and women?
2. Has Buss relied on observational data to form his hypothesis? How does he test this hypothesis?
3. Tavris outlines several attacks against arguments like those suggested by Buss. Outline these different lines of attack.
4. Why should researchers be careful in accepting their own cultural stereotypes as facts? What can we do to avoid this pitfall in our analysis?
5. Do either of these selections support their position on the monogamy question with systematic empirical evidence? What should they do to get more and better empirical evidence?

Is There Common Ground?

As early as 1871, Darwin had argued that males were selected to be promiscuous because an increased number of partners meant more chances that his traits would be passed on to the next generation. He also believed that females had more success if they were coy and selective in choosing their mates, all of which were ways that Victorian England used to describe their stereotypes of behavior in English society. But Darwin's assumptions about male and female behavior in his own society seemed so compelling that they were never seriously questioned until the 1960s. One can hypothesize that the so-called "sexual revolution" that was sweeping through England and America, itself, was what was driving researchers to look more closely at Darwin's assumptions. But these new assumptions were not at all the same as observational behavior, but built from new stereotypes that were arising as society was changing.

Darwin knew nothing about genetics, but thought only about "traits." Because of advances in biology, genetics, and DNA, we now know that Darwin's traits are generally encoded in genetic material and passed from one generation to the next through successful mating. Recent advances in genetics and DNA research suggest that many traits we assumed a generation ago to be coded in particular genes may actually be encoded in several parts of the DNA sequence, often in several genes rather than a single one. Thus, even if our behavior was being selected for by a combination of the natural and social environment, it is unlikely to be so simply coded as a single gene for monogamy, criminal behavior, sexual orientation, or any of the myriad behaviors that social researchers since E.O. Wilson have tried to associate with genetic patterning and natural selection.

A systematic analysis of whether human females—unlike males—have been selected for monogamy requires more observational evidence that some of the deductive experiments have been preferred by some sociobiologists. Most researchers are willing to use deductive logic for establishing a hypothesis, but there is no substitute for empirical data when it comes to supporting or disconfirming a hypothesis. Of course, systematic field observations are time-consuming, expensive, and difficult under the best conditions.

Both of these selections should lead us to be wary of imposing our own cultural stereotypes as a substitute for observed behavior. Our own stereotypes feel inherently "right" and "correct" to us, but they are often inaccurate as a description of empirical reality, both in Darwin's time and in our own.

Additional Resources

For more on the reproductive strategies of female primates, see the following. These are probably the most compelling and comprehensive analyses of the evolution of behavior relevant to the question of monogamy to date:

Fuentes, Agustin. 1998. "Reevaluating Primate Monogamy." *American Anthropologist* 100(4):890–907.

Fuentes, Agustin. 2009. *Evolution of Human Behavior*. New York: Oxford University Press.

For other, somewhat earlier, perspectives see:

Small, Meredith. 1993. *Female Choices: Sexual Behavior of Female Primates*. Ithaca: Cornell University Press.

Small, Meredith. 1995. *What's Love Got to Do With It?: The Evolution of Human Mating*. New York: Anchor Books.

For studies of primate behavior, a number of classic studies are useful:

Goodall, Jane. 1986. *The Chimpanzees of Gombe: Patterns of Behavior*. Cambridge, MA: Harvard University Press.

Haraway, Donna. 1989. *Primate Visions: Gender, Race and Nature in Modern Science*. New York: Routledge.

Smut, Barbara. 1999. *Sex and Friendship in Baboons*. Cambridge, MA: Harvard University Press.

Strum, Shirley. 1987. *Almost Human: A Journey into the World of Baboons*. New York: Random House.

To learn more about sociobiology in general, the best starting point is probably E.O. Wilson's seminal work:

Wilson, E.O. 1975. *Sociobiology: The New Synthesis*. Cambridge, MA: Harvard University Press.

A sociobiological analysis that relies heavily on systematic observational data would include:

Borgerhoff Mulder, Monique. 2009. "Serial Monogamy as Polygyny or Polyandry: Marriage in the Tanzanian Pimbwe." *Human Nature* 20:130–150.

Much of the research in primate behavioral evolution in recent years has focused on cognition, asking, how do primates think? While we remain far from understanding primate cognition, students may find the following useful:

Cheney, Dorothy R. and Robert M. Seyfarth. 2007. *Baboon Metaphysics: The Evolution of a Social Mind.* Chicago: University of Chicago Press.

Dobson, Seth D. 2012. "Coevolution of Facial Expression and Social Tolerance in Macaques." *American Journal of Primatology* 147–149.

Internet References . . .

A Useful Web Site on the Early Settlement Debate

http://cogweb.ucla.edu/Chumash/EntryDate.html

American Museum of Natural History on the Overkill Hypothesis

www.amnh.org/science/biodiversity/extinction/Day1/overkill/Bit1.html

Archaeology Magazine

This is the Web site of *Archaeology* magazine. This site has a searchable database with links to various articles about recent issues in archaeology, including a number of articles on the goddess cult in Europe.

www.archaeology.org

Center for the Study of the First Americans

The Center for the Study of the First Americans works to promote interdisciplinary scholarly dialogue and to stimulate public interest concerning the colonization of the Americas. This Web site provides articles that describe several theories on how the Americas were first colonized.

www.centerfirstamericans.com/cat.html?c=4

Earliest Americans Theme Study

This Web site by the National Park Service covers a wide range of issues involving early Paleoindian inhabitants of the United States. It addresses a variety of issues and topics that students may find useful for further research and offers citations of other articles and sources. The focus is on the Southeastern United States.

www.nps.gov/history/seac/outline/02-paleoindian/se_paleo/01-intro.htm

www.nps.gov/history/seac/outline/

Kennewick Man Documents

The most recent set of documents about Kennewick Man can be found on the National Park Service Web site. This collection of official reports is the most comprehensive available.

www.nps.gov/archeology/kennewick/Index.htm

Nova

This site presents a fairly balanced view of the Overkill Hypothesis debate.

www.pbs.org/wgbh/nova/evolution/end-big-beasts.html

Archaeology

*A*rchaeologists *are prehistorians concerned with questions about the unrecorded history of human communities and civilizations. Like other historians, archaeologists seek evidence about how people lived, what they subsisted on, and the kinds of social institutions they established. But, unlike most historians who can turn to documents and papers to detail the lives and times of their subjects, archaeologists must find evidence in excavations. Over the past century, archaeologists have developed specialized methods for excavating and analyzing artifacts, stone tools, animal bones, shells, pollen, and carbon from old fires to determine a great deal about the environment, vegetation, subsistence patterns, living arrangements, and also when sites were occupied. At issue is how these varied kinds of data from ancient sources can be interpreted to reconstruct the lifeways of earlier times. A traditional set of questions that archaeologists ask is when, why, and how did people first settle different parts of the world, such as the Americas. They also ask questions about the meaning and significance of certain kinds of artifacts, such as the goddess figures of ancient Europe and the Middle East. Archaeologists also ask questions about why complex civilizations rose and fell.*

- Did Humans Migrate to the New World from Europe in Early Prehistoric Times?

- Did Climate Change Rather Than Overhunting Cause the Extinction of Mammoths and Other Megafauna in North America?

- Can Archaeologists Determine the Cultural Background of the Earliest Americans from the Ancient Skeleton Known as Kennewick Man?

- Was There a Goddess Cult in Prehistoric Europe?

ISSUE 4

Did Humans Migrate to the New World from Europe in Early Prehistoric Times?

YES: Bruce Bradley and Dennis Stanford, from "The North Atlantic Ice-Edge Corridor: A Possible Palaeolithic Route to the New World," *World Archaeology* (December 2004)

NO: Lawrence Guy Straus, from "Solutrean Settlement of North America? A Review of Reality," *American Antiquity* (April 2000)

Learning Outcomes

After reading this issue, you should be able to:

- Understand the possible problems with the so-called Solutrean migration hypothesis and the kinds of evidence that might be used to support this hypothesis.
- Discuss what kinds of evidence archaeologists have made available for determining where the first human immigrants to the New World actually were.
- Explain the problems with the evidence for settlement of the New World from both Asia and Europe.
- Discuss the problem with stylistic similarities between the Solutrean tool kit and the Clovis tool kit.
- Evaluate some of the strengths and limitations of the evidence for the Solutrean hypothesis and the "out of Asia" hypothesis.

ISSUE SUMMARY

YES: Archaeologists Bruce Bradley and Dennis Stanford maintain that there is no evidence that the ancestors of the Clovis big-game hunting people of North America originated in Siberia and migrated down an ice-free corridor from Alaska. They argue that Clovis stone tool technology probably developed among the Solutreans of Europe, and that these Solutrean hunters traveled across the North Atlantic ice sheet to North America, where they became the ancestors of the Clovis people.

NO: Archaeologist Lawrence Guy Straus counters that the Solutrean culture of Europe ended at least 5000 years before the Clovis culture appeared in the New World. He contends that the North Atlantic Ocean would have been an insurmountable barrier to human travel during the last glacial maximum. He argues that the similarities between the Clovis and Solutrean tool technologies are limited and coincidental.

Archaeologists have long wondered when and how human beings first arrived in the Americas. The conventional view has been that the first humans arrived from Asia over a land bridge across the Bering Strait that connected Siberia and Alaska during the last Ice Age, when the sea level was lower due to a vast amount of water being trapped in glacial ice. The ice sheet covering northern North America would have presented an impenetrable barrier to human passage until the end of the Ice Age, when a narrow ice-free corridor opened up along the eastern flank of the Rocky Mountains about 14,500 years ago. The theory was that big game hunters then advanced southward, following mammoths and other megafauna into the Great Plains. From there they spread rapidly throughout North and South America.

In the early 1930s, archaeologists discovered a site near Clovis, New Mexico, that contained large stone points with a distinctive thinning at the base (called "fluting") where they would have been attached to wooden shafts. Similar points were later found at other sites throughout what is now the United States as well as Canada and Central America, some of them in conjunction with bones of now extinct animals. Archaeologists called the complex of tools the "Clovis culture." Carbon-14 dating suggests that it first appeared about 11,500 years ago. Until the 1980s, the orthodox view in American archaeology was that the Clovis people were the immediate descendants of the first immigrants into the Americas and the ancestors of the native peoples of North and South America. For many decades, archaeologists assumed that Clovis people were the earliest humans in North America and that they (or their immediate ancestors) were the ancestors of all people in South America before the arrival of Spanish and Portuguese colonizers in the fifteenth and sixteenth centuries.

In recent decades, archaeologists have found and excavated a small number of North and South American sites that may predate the Clovis culture. The best-known such site is Monte Verde in south-central Chile. The Monte Verde people apparently lived in a long communal tent and had a complex hunting and gathering economy that exploited numerous species of plants and animals, including large extinct species such as mastodons. Significantly, their stone tools bore no resemblance to Clovis tools. The main occupation layer at Monte Verde has been carbon-14 dated at about 12,500 years ago, 1000 years earlier than the earliest Clovis sites!

A further challenge to the theory that the Clovis people were the first immigrants to the Americas and the sole ancestors of the native peoples of the Americas comes from the recent discovery of ancient human remains that do not resemble contemporary Native Americans. The best-known example, Kennewick Man, died near the Columbia River in eastern Washington about 9400 years ago. Some experts say his skull resembles those of the Ainu people of northern Japan more than modern Native Americans. Other ancient skeletal remains have been compared with Australian Aborigines, Africans, South Asians, Polynesians, and Europeans. The implication is that there may have been a number of migrations into the Americas from different points of origin.

The discovery of apparently pre-Clovis cultures in the Americas has once again thrown open the questions of who were the first immigrants to the Americas, where did they come from, and how did they get here. If they came before the ice-free corridor opened up, they must somehow have circumvented the vast ice sheet that covered northern North America. One possibility is that immigrants from Asia came down the west coast of Alaska and British Columbia in boats, stopping at ice-free islands and beaches and living mostly off the resources of the sea. Some early sites on islands off the coast of Alaska and California seem to support this scenario.

Another possibility, represented by Bradley and Stanford's article, is that early Europeans made their way across the North Atlantic in small boats, living off fish and sea mammals and camping on the edge of the ice sheet, much like the Central Inuit of Canada in historical times. Bradley and Stanford argue that these migrants brought the Solutrean stone tool tradition with them from Europe. They argue that this stone tool tradition developed into the Clovis culture in North America.

Straus takes issue with this claim, pointing out that there is a gap of about 5000 years between the last Solutrean toolmakers in Europe and the first Clovis toolmakers in America. In his view, the pre-Clovis tools that have so far been found in North America bear little resemblance to Solutrean tools found in Europe. He also questions whether people could have crossed the stormy and ice-clogged Atlantic Ocean in primitive boats, arguing that the ice sheet would have been too dangerous and small water craft would have been even more dangerous.

In their article, Bradley and Stanford maintain that the Clovis stone tool tradition of North America was derived from the Solutrean tool tradition of southern Europe. They hypothesize that some Solutrean people who had adapted to hunting and fishing on the edge of the ice sheet crossed the Atlantic in boats, and their descendants developed the Clovis culture in North America. Straus, however, regards it as unlikely that Solutreans could have crossed the Atlantic in boats during the last glacial maximum, and he considers the similarities between the Solutrean and Clovis tool traditions to be superficial and coincidental.

Archaeologists are continuing to pursue the answers to the questions of when the first humans reached the Americas, where they came from, and how they got here. They are concentrating their attention on the presumed pre-Clovis sites—such as Monte Verde in Chile, Meadowcroft Rockshelter in Pennsylvania, the Topper site in South Carolina, and Cactus Hill in Virginia. They focus especially on issues of dating and the question of how the artifacts in those sites relate to those of the later Clovis culture. Proponents of the theory that the first immigrants came down the west coast of North America in boats are looking for evidence of early human presence on islands and coastal areas.

A major problem is that most of the places where such people would have camped or settled are now as much as 50 or 100 feet under water, because as the glaciers melted, sea level rose to its current level. In addition, these simple hunters did not make much of an impact on the land whenever the first humans arrived. Nevertheless, promising sites include On Your Knees Cave on an island off the Alaska coast, Daisy Cave on an island off the California coast, and Cedros Island off the coast of Baja California. Recently, a team of geoarchaeologists from Liverpool John Moores University in Britain caused a controversy when they claimed that apparently human footprints preserved in volcanic ash in Puebla, Mexico, were 40,000 years old (see Robert Adler, "The First Americans," *NewScientist,* April 2006).

As you read these selections, ask yourself what kinds of evidence would be needed to resolve this question. At the heart of this issue is the scanty evidence for either of these two hypotheses. What do the authors agree on and where do they disagree about evidence? Are they using the same kinds of rationales for evaluating the evidence? Do the authors agree on the processes by which stone tool traditions arise and evolve? How many and what kinds of similarities must exist between two tool traditions to show that they are historically connected rather than independently invented?

YES ↵

Bruce Bradley and
Dennis Stanford

The North Atlantic Ice-Edge Corridor: A Possible Palaeolithic Route to the New World

Introduction

Because of the fully modern anatomical features of Native Americans, early twentieth-century anthropologists staunchly denied the possibility that humans were present in the Americas before about 4000 B.C. By contrast, a dedicated group of amateur archaeologists, erroneously believing that simple crude stone tools were comparable in age to the early Palaeolithic tools of Europe, advocated a more ancient occupation. The resolution of these debates came in 1926 with the documentation of a direct association between projectile points and extinct Pleistocene bison at a site near Folsom, New Mexico. A few years later, another distinctive type of fluted spear point was found in direct association with mammoth bones near Clovis, New Mexico. Although these early discoveries were not directly dated, the associations with extinct animals confirmed that the North American continent was populated by the end of the Pleistocene. Since their initial discovery, fluted Clovis-like points have been found from the Atlantic to the Pacific coast and from southern Canada to Central America.

After the late Pleistocene human presence in North America was established, archaeologists sought to explain the origin of the unique Clovis technology. It was thought that the ancestors of Clovis people must have come from Asia by crossing a land bridge, known as Beringia, that connected Siberia and Alaska. This land bridge formed when Ice Age sea levels dropped during the build up of the continental glaciers. The hypothesis continued that, after early populations arrived in Alaska, the glaciers began to melt, creating an 'ice-free corridor' between the Arctic and the rest of the Americas. Using the corridor as a migration route, Clovis people spread southward.

This theory seems eminently logical as Siberia is only a short distance from Alaska, and North American Indians share many physical traits with north-eastern Asians. Thus, practically all scholars accept the proposition that the bearers of Clovis culture must have come from north-eastern Asia and were the ancestors of modern Native Americans. Alternative routes were

From *World Archaeology*, vol. 36, no. 4, December 2004. Copyright © 2004 by Taylor & Francis Group. Reprinted by permission via Rightslink.

not considered since they would have required the use of watercraft, and it is inconceivable that Palaeolithic people had either the technical skills or the material culture to have crossed an Ice Age sea.

We must remember that these ideas on New World origins are based on informed speculation and are not supported by archaeological evidence. Through time and repetition, and in the absence of any clear alternatives, the theory has become dogma, and ultimately ideology, appearing in all text-book and popular publications. Over the past fifty years, archaeologists have expended a great deal of effort and resources trying to find evidence of Clovis ancestors in Alaska and north-eastern Siberia. In addition, anybody who suggested that there might be an alternative theory relative to either place or time of origin has been immediately discounted. The profession has come full circle, with the time of origin simply moved from 4000 years ago to the end of the Pleistocene, and the only acceptable place of origin being north-east Asia. However, there is a lack of data supporting an Asian connection and the origin of Clovis culture and technology still remains a mystery.

The Clovis Baseline

Although it is well established that Clovis people were in North America by 11,500 14 C BP [carbon: 14 years before present] years ago, there is very little evidence regarding early colonization. New dating techniques have placed many sites in a chronological context, but most Clovis sites are surface manifestations and cannot be directly dated. This is especially true in eastern North America where preservation of organic remains is poor. Nevertheless, it has been possible to document a basic assemblage of stone tool types and technologies that are readily identifiable as Clovis or at least related to Clovis.

Although there is some variability in tools and technologies, especially in relation to site function, the basic Clovis tool-kit is surprisingly consistent across diverse environments, ranging from the sub-tropics to the sub-arctic. This broad geographic distribution suggests that the tool-kit was designed for effective exploitation of almost any environment. As more sites are found our understanding of this early culture grows, and scholars are recognizing its complexity. Nevertheless, regardless of either time or space, Clovis artefacts retain an amazing technological consistency.

Clovis flint knappers used two basic flaked-stone technologies: bifacial thinning and large blade production. Both of these technologies are characterized by complex reduction strategies and specific sequences of flake and blade removal. Although space does not permit detailed description of these highly sophisticated technologies, we can summarize their salient characteristics.

Biface thinning was accomplished by highly organized reduction sequences and the application of a very difficult technique known as overshot flaking. When using this method flakes are struck that cross the entire width of the biface, many times removing a small portion of the edge opposite the striking platform. . . .

Along with controlled percussion thinning, most Clovis bifaces are basally thinned, with distinctive, well-controlled flakes called flutes. It is fluting that caught the attention of archaeologists because of its rarity in biface industries around the world. Flutes are negative flake scars desired as an end product on the finished artefacts. Inordinate attention has been placed on this interesting technological innovation, to the near exclusion of other traits. But is fluting really so special? In terms of Clovis biface technology, it is evident that fluting was done throughout the flaking sequence and is not technically different from other thinning flake removals; it just originates from the base of the preform rather than the side. Its distinctiveness comes from the intentional retention of the flake scar on finished pieces. . . .

Large blade production is typical of Clovis assemblages, and is especially common at habitation sites located on abundant sources of good flaking stone in south-eastern North America. Interestingly, blades and blade tools are much less common in the kill/processing sites that dominate the Rocky Mountain and Plains records. As with the bifaces, it is the details of blade production that are of special interest. The most frequent blade production technology resulted in large wedge-shaped cores. These cores have a single acute-angle platform, a single blade production face and a flat back (either cortical or prepared). The reduction sequence of this technology has yet to be completely reconstructed.

Retouched Clovis tools were made both from blades and from large biface thinning flakes. The former are most common at the large settlements, such as Gault in Texas and the latter at most large game kill/processing sites. Formal retouched tool types are limited in number, with side and end scrapers, biface knives, small gravers and weapon points being most prevalent. The number of formal tool forms increases with the size of assemblages and especially at habitation sites, where end scrapers, borers, adzes and backed pieces occur. Conspicuously lacking or rare are burins.

Among specific Clovis behaviours relative to lithic artefacts were caching large bifaces and a preference for exotic raw materials tools. Although they rarely resorted to heat-treating intractable tool-stone, Clovis flint knappers would occasionally heat raw material to improve its flaking quality. Recently recognized additions to Clovis lithic assemblage are small limestone slabs and pebbles. They mainly exhibit geometric designs, but at least two may have animal depictions. . . .

Although rare and poorly represented, bone and ivory artefacts, including sagaie (single bevelled points), bi-bevelled rods, awls, a shaft straightener, two barbed harpoons, a billet, an eyed needle and several dart throwing board hooks, have been found in Clovis assemblages. Most of these items have been recovered from sites with exceptional preservation and their rarity results from preservation problems rather than their uniqueness in Clovis assemblages.

So what are the implications for seeking a Clovis progenitor? It is our opinion that the well-developed Clovis bone and lithic technologies did not spring up overnight and there should be archaeological evidence of a transitional technology. Thus, we believe that a developmental Clovis assemblage should minimally include a formal tool assemblage with biface thinning, large blades, large bifaces, thin bifacial projectile points, end and side scrapers and a range of bone and ivory tools, including simple sagaies, awls and needles. In addition, we expect to see detailed similarities in specific manufacturing techniques, including overshot flaking, basal thinning of projectile points and pressure flaking.

What Evidence of Asian Origins?

The Ushki site on the Kamchatka Peninsula, was once thought to have been occupied over 14,000 years ago and was considered by many to be the origin point for the first Americans. Unfortunately, a recent re-evaluation of the site has demonstrated that its earliest occupation occurred only 10,700 years ago, much too late to figure in a first Americans scenario. As a result, one has to look over a thousand kilometres west of the Bering Strait to find technologies older than Clovis or to even find artefacts that are remotely similar. The bottom line is that there are no pre-12,000-year-old sites in Beringia that contain a lithic technology that remotely resembles anything we would be expecting as a precursor to Clovis. . . .

With the conviction that Clovis culture originated in north-eastern Asia, American archaeologists have focused their attention on Alaska. However, after over seventy years of research, there is no evidence of an early lithic technology related to Clovis in Alaska, in spite of concerted efforts to find it. So far, the oldest Alaskan lithic assemblages contain Asian microblades and wedge-shaped microblade cores. These eastern Beringian industries used inset technologies that have little in common with Clovis technology; moreover, they are contemporary with Clovis and persist into later Holocene times. . . .

As in Alaska, years of concentrated research in the ice-free corridor of Canada have failed to find unequivocal archaeological evidence of the passage of either Clovis or any other people through the corridor in the late Pleistocene. The few fluted projectile points found in the area appear to be related to weapon tips found in Alaska, and the few radiocarbon assays indicate a post-Clovis age. . . .

Thus, it is clear to us that there is no archaeological evidence that Clovis ancestors came out of Siberia by crossing the land bridge or that they passed down an ice-free corridor linking north-east Asia to America. When the ice-free corridor finally became habitable, it appears that the first people to move through it came from the south rather than the north. This should not be surprising because the gateway became biologically viable much sooner in the south than the north and we now know there was a resident Clovis-related population poised to move northward. Although there is no doubt that later people of Asian ancestry did indeed populate the territory of the former ice-free corridor, we reject the standard New World origins hypothesis.

Asian Alternatives?

Given the relative unlikelihood of a pre-Clovis terrestrial trek down the ice-free corridor, early immigrants must have used alternative routes to the New World. Fladmark and Dixon have proposed that people using watercraft established a foothold in the Americas while exploiting the coastal environments of the Pacific Rim and continental shelf, which were ice-free by 13,000 years ago.

This proposal is supported by recent reconstructions of former environments and ecosystems verifying that Pleistocene animals flourished along the Ice Age coastline. In addition, artefacts have been found in off-shore island sites, and drowned terrestrial and intertidal deposits. To date, these discoveries are too young to be ancestral Clovis, nor are the artefacts technologically related. Nevertheless, these discoveries indicate that early inhabitants had maritime capabilities and were utilizing the now-inundated continental shelf. . . .

Unfortunately, direct archaeological evidence of ancient watercraft is problematic at best. Materials used in early boat construction were perishable and would not readily survive in most environments. In addition, such craft are usually stored near water and would have suffered degradation through erosion by the tides of rapidly rising sea levels associated with deglaciation. This situation applies to many coastal habitation sites as well. . . .

Regardless of how issues of the antiquity and use of watercraft are resolved, and even though it is clear that Asian cultures contemporary with Clovis moved into the Americas, technological evidence for a pre-Clovis Asian ancestor is still totally absent. . . .

A European Alternative?

Over the years, scholars have observed significant similarities between Clovis and the older Upper Palaeolithic Solutrean technologies of south-western Europe. Jelinek identified the Solutrean culture in the Vasco-Cantabrian region of northern Spain as having the most striking resemblance to Clovis tools and technology. He noted a great many correspondences, including bifacially flaked lanceolate projectile points with concave bases and basal/edge grinding, a blade industry, small end scrapers with graver tips, large side scrapers made on flakes, cylindrical bevel-based bone points (sagaie) and a relative scarcity of burins. Yet he concluded that a direct historical relationship between Clovis and Solutrean was unlikely because Solutrean is more than 6,000 years older than Clovis, and the crossing of the glacial Atlantic Ocean would have been a major obstacle. More recently, Straus reaffirmed these concerns and attributed the similarities to independent invention. Although these observations are valid and must be resolved, neither author supported his opinions with archaeological or theoretical data demonstrating why this extraordinary convergence occurred. We suggest that the lack of evidence from Siberia and a new appreciation of the antiquity of watercraft warrant re-evaluation of the Solutrean hypothesis.

A Solutrean Solution?

Solutrean is the only Old World archaeological culture that meets our criteria for an ancestral Clovis candidate. It is older than Clovis, its technology is amazingly similar to Clovis down to minute details of typology and manufacture technology, and the two cultures share many unique behaviours. Indeed, the degree of similarity is astounding.

Solutrean sites are primarily found in south-western France, especially in the Aquitaine, and in Cantabria and Asturias in northern Spain. A variant also occurs in Portugal and on the Mediterranean coast. Solutrean sites date between 22,000 and 16,500 BP, the period of the Last Glacial Maximum (LGM) when continental glaciers covered much of Europe. . . .

The most impressive similarity is the basically identical manufacturing technology of thin bifaces using an overshot flaking method. Although we have studied many biface-thinning technologies, the only deliberate and systematic use of this technique occurs in Solutrean and Clovis. The complexity and difficulty of this technique and its rarity argue against it being independently developed. In addition, Solutrean is credited with introducing pressure flaking, intentional pre-treatment of stone by controlled heating to improve flaking quality, basal thinning and intentional margin grinding, possibly to dull edges for hafting. Individually these techniques may have been developed in different places and times, but a duplication of the complete comprehensive technological system seems unlikely to have occurred without a historical connection.

Large Solutrean bifaces, called laurel leafs, are bipointed, thin (width to thickness ratio greater than 5 to 1), have their widest dimension approximately ⅓ of the distance from the base to the tip, and exhibit heavy lower lateral margin grinding. This also describes Clovis points except they usually have indented bases with distinctive flutes. Some Solutrean projectile points, mainly in northern Spain, are shaped like Clovis weapon tips. The main difference is that just under half of the Solutrean indented base points are primarily unifacially flaked.

At least one method of producing large blades is shared by Solutrean and Clovis flint knappers. This includes specific pre-core shaping, the way the core face is set up, and blade detachment techniques. This Solutrean blade technology is more like Clovis than it is like any other European blade core technology used either before or after Solutrean.

Many other Solutrean chipped-stone tool types resemble Clovis tools made on blades and over-shot flakes, among them distinctive end scrapers, retouched biface flakes, strangulated blades, borers and multiple gravers. Burins are rare in both Solutrean and Clovis assemblages, but occasionally appear. Backed blade tools are also rare in Clovis, but as more campsites are excavated they are becoming more common, although some Solutrean tools, such as the distinctive shouldered points and 'willow leaves,' are not present in Clovis. However, all Clovis tool types including fluted bifaces occur in Solutrean assemblages. By contrast, only a few ubiquitous flaked tool types are shared between Clovis and any Siberian technology. . . .

The similarity between Solutrean and Clovis is also evident in the bone, antler and ivory tools, especially projectile points (sagaie). Bone shaft wrenches occur in both assemblages, and an eyed ivory needle has been found in Florida. Stones engraved with geometric and zoomorphic designs have been found in both cultures.

How much similarity is necessary before an interpretation of convergence gives way to an historical relationship? When a single artefact similar to Clovis

Figure 1

Clovis and Solutrean tools. a–k: Clovis; l–v: Solutrean; a, m–n: end
scrapers on blades; b, o: borers; c: retouched bladelet; d: retouched
blade; p: shouldered point; e, f, r: notches; g, s: burins; h–j, t–v: gravers.
(a: Gault Site; b, c, j: Bostrum site; d, e: Simon Cache; f, g, i: Murray
Springs; h: Blackwater Draw Locality 1; k: Fenn Cache; l: Solutré; m, q:
Fourneau-du-Diable; n, r, s, t, u: Laugerie-Haute Ouest; o: Oulen;
p: La Placard; v: La Riera.)

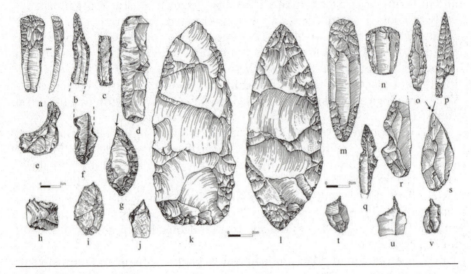

discovered in Siberia, no matter how remote in time and space or even if out of
context and misidentified, rates publication in *Science,* we believe that scholars
should seriously consider the ramifications of the overwhelming number of
unique technological and cultural similarities shared between Solutrean and
Clovis. If a Solutrean assemblage were found in Siberia, everyone would consider the question of Clovis origins resolved.

Crossing the Water

During the LGM, the Polar Front was pushed to latitudes as far south as Portugal,
turning the Iberian peninsula into a steppe-tundra environment with lowered
temperatures, shortening growing seasons and reducing the extent and quality of natural grasslands. Game animals may have abandoned or become rare
in the interior regions of Western Europe, forcing both animal and human
populations into more favourable areas along the rivers and the coastlines of
south-western Europe. In northern Spain, the Solutrean population lived in a
narrow strip of coastal plain and foothills wedged between mountains with
glaciers and heavy snow pack and an ice-covered ocean for much of the year.
Although hunting was probably seasonally effective in the nearby mountains,

Figure 2

Early indented base projectile points. a: unifacial Clovis point, Delmarva Peninsula, Maryland; b: Page-Ladson point, Page-Ladson site, Florida; c: Page-Ladson point, Delmarva Peninsula, Maryland; d, e: Cactus Hill points, Cactus Hill, Virginia; f, g, h: Solutrean points, Las Caldas, Spain.

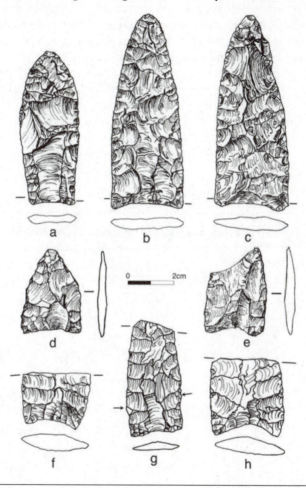

people augmented their food supply by turning to alternative food resources, including hunting and fishing along the river estuaries and beaches.

The perennial Arctic ice formed much further south during the LGM, covering major portions of the North Atlantic and connecting Europe and North America with an ice bridge. This pushed the active young ice-edge margin and the animals adapted to sub-Arctic waters southward. The ice margin is a region with intense biological productivity, providing a major food source for much of the marine food chain. . . .

These conditions resulted in a major annual influx of migratory sea mammals, birds and fishes into the Bay of Biscay from early fall through spring.

By comparison, over 4 million harp seals were counted in the western rookery during the most recent census, an amazing figure considering the reduced productivity of food along the Canadian coast and the impact of major long-term hunting fishing pressures. A Solutrean hunter must have been awe-struck when he watched for the first time a pristine seal colony stretching for as far as he could see, basking on an ice floe as it drifted towards the shore. . . .

Solutrean artists left evidence in their rock art depicting sea mammals, deep-water fish and great auks that they were giving these resources serious thought. With their talent for innovation and several thousand years to observe the environment, Solutreans would have learned to target these resources.

Faunal collections from Solutrean sites in northern Spain contain abundant evidence that people were utilizing coastal and estuarian resources, and there was an increasing dependence on marine resources through time. Even though the sea coast was farther away than today, people were transporting substantial quantities of limpets up to 10km from the shore

Figure 3

The North Atlantic region at the Last Glacial Maximum.

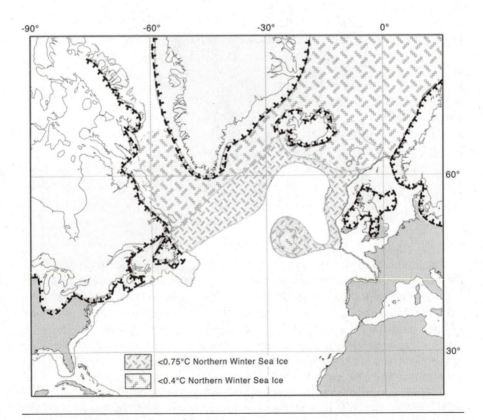

to La Reira Cave. Based on this evidence, Straus suggested that, since many pleniglacial coastal sites are under the sea, marine resources may have been even more significant as dietary supplements than the present evidence would indicate. . . .

Although upland hunting sites were periodically used to stage ibex and red deer hunts, the marine resources would have been available year round. Sea mammal hunting on winter sea ice, hunting leads and ice edge in the late spring and summer would have provided food and fuel throughout the year. Sea birds such as the great auk and fish were seasonally abundant and would have augmented the Solutrean larder.

In the process of adapting to a coastal marine economy, tool-kits would have been elaborated to exploit the sea more efficiently; waterproof clothing, nets, harpoon gear and watercraft were necessary to exploit the marine resources and would have been useful on inland rivers during the LGM. It would not have taken long for the people to recognize the signs of impending storms and changing weather conditions. Nor would it have taken long to understand various sea-ice types, dangers and advantages. Hunters would learn that ice leads are not only excellent hunting locations, but provide havens during storms as the surrounding ice greatly reduces wave formation. Large ice floes are also good hunting locations and provide pullout 'islands' for camping or temporarily sitting out a storm in an overturned, well-secured skin boat.

Survival along the ice edge is possible with only a few skills and a little knowledge, particularly when following the harp and grey seal migrations. These seals feed along the northward receding ice edge during the summer, and move south in the fall as the winter ice begins to form. Successful hunting of these animals alone would provide all the resources necessary to sustain human life. Beyond a food source, seals provide oil for heating and cooking, and there is melting ice for fresh water, all of which can be accomplished with a single flame burning in a basin chipped into the ice. Seal body parts contribute soft tissue and bone for the manufacture of tools, waterproof garments, ropes and lashing, and covers and repair patches for tents and boats. There are many documented tales of groups of hunters set adrift on ice islands surviving for months, and being swept across the sea when the floe was trapped in an oceanic gyre. . . .

Solutrean hunters probably developed their techniques for exploiting the marine environment during a colder climatic period when the annual ice regularly formed in the Bay of Biscay. Once this tradition was established, there would have been increasing reliance on the use of ice-edge resources. Inevitably, this cool climate phase began to collapse, with slow warming and the distance between land's end and the ice-edge habitat continually increasing: good for seals, bad for seal hunters, especially if they did not have boats. Thus, in order to maintain the ice-edge economy, the hunters had to travel further and further out to sea to find the seals. These hunts likely became major extended treks with entire kin groups participating in the events. Inevitably, a group following the European seals on their northward migration would have ended up at the western end of the gyre, not knowing until too late that they were hunting Canadian seals heading southward to rookeries along the Atlantic coast of North America. Once they understood the seal migration patterns, the hunters could work the pattern back and forth. The entire distance along the ice bridge would have been around 2500km, shorter than the Thule Inuit migrations from Alaska to Greenland. Some families eventually established camps along the Western Atlantic seaboard and did not return to Europe.

The Missing Links

In recent years, three sites in eastern North America—Meadowcroft rock shelter in Pennsylvania, Cactus Hill in Virginia and Page-Ladson in Florida—have yielded stratified deposits with pre-Clovis radiocarbon dates associated with undeniable artefacts. Although the number of artefacts from these sites is small, most of the technological characteristics we propose for the developmental Clovis technology are present. These include thinned bifaces, indented base projectile points (that are pressure thinned, without true flutes), blades and bladelettes, backed blades and overshot flaking.

The early dates from Meadowcroft have been vociferously challenged, but microstratigraphic research has concluded that there are no geochemical reasons to reject the dates. Likewise, the radiocarbon dates from pre-Clovis features at Cactus Hill suggesting occupations between 15,000 and 18,000 14 C BP have come under scrutiny, but Wagner and McAvoy have adequately resolved these issues. At the Page-Ladson site, two points of a Suwannee variety, now redefined as Page-Ladson, were recovered from a displaced context, but are probably associated with artefacts and mastodon remains dated to nearly 14,345 C BP.

The oldest radiocarbon dates for a Clovis site are from the south east, whereas the youngest dates are from the west. There is a clear overlapping of declining radiocarbon ages from Solutrean, Cactus Hill, Meadowcroft, Page-Ladson and the earliest Clovis in the East and western Clovis. We therefore suggest that the pre-Clovis technologies are transitional between Solutrean and Clovis as, not only do they fill the time gap, they are also conveniently located near the Atlantic Coasts of Europe and North America.

Conclusion

Although there have been numerous efforts to find the origin of Clovis culture in Alaska and north-eastern Siberia, little new evidence has been encountered during the past seven decades. In fact, the more remains we find, the less they look like Clovis. The better our dating has become, the younger the sites turn out to be. It now seems that the materials most closely resembling Paleoindian in the north probably originated from groups travelling up through the opening ice-free corridor, rather than the other way around.

We contend that the overwhelming and diverse number of similarities between Solutrean and Pre-Clovis/Clovis mediate against the simple explanation of convergence. The location, dating and technology represented by the

Cactus Hill, Meadowcroft and Page-Ladson sites provide the 'missing' chronological and technological links between Solutrean and Clovis. The hypothesis that a Solutrean Palaeolithic maritime tradition ultimately gave rise to Clovis technology is supported by abundant archaeological evidence that would be considered conclusive were it not for the intervening ocean. None of the competing hypotheses for Clovis origins are supported by archaeological data. Therefore, we argue that the hypothesis that a Solutrean Palaeolithic maritime tradition gave rise to pre-Clovis and Clovis technologies should be elevated from moribund speculation to a highly viable research goal.

Lawrence Guy Straus   ➡ **NO**

Solutrean Settlement of North America? A Review of Reality

Recent popular—albeit influential—writings on the peopling of the New World in the wake of Kennewick Man, cite some prominent Paleoindian authorities (notably Dennis Stanford and Bruce Bradley) as suggesting a European origin for at least one episode of settlement of North America during the late Upper Pleistocene. . . .

Although I have tried to set the factual record straight, my attempts to publish letters to the editors of *The New Yorker* and *Newsweek* have been rebuffed. As an Old World prehistorian who lives and teaches in the United States, I feel an obligation to clarify the factual archeological record, especially since the issue has been overtly linked to the supposed "caucasoid" appearance of certain Paleoindian skeletal remains, with all the implications that would carry for public policy and the practice of both biological anthropology and archaeology in the United States (and presumably Canada). I am concerned that scientific debate must not be conducted *primarily* in the news media, where standards of argument and proof are very different than in academic discourse, but where the ramifications may be most serious, given mass dissemination and easy misunderstanding.

According to the Stanford-Bradley hypothesis as interpreted by reporters, a European peopling of America would supposedly have taken place by crossing the ice-laden northernmost Atlantic on foot or by boat. Specifically, similarities are claimed between certain lithic and osseous artifacts of the Solutrean "culture" of southern France and Iberia and some items typical of the Clovis "tradition" in the eastern three-quarters of the United States. These putative resemblances are then translated into an hypothesis of migration, "explaining" Clovis with reference to the Solutrean. This is in fact an old theory, having been proposed by Emerson Greenman in 1960. Seductive though such hyper-migrationist ideas apparently still seem to be in the archaeology of 2000, they are no more based in reality than they were 40 years ago. As a specialist in the Upper Paleolithic of western Europe in general and in the Solutrean in particular, I propose to set the record straight on the Solutrean and to show that the appearance of bifacial foliate "points" and bone "rods" in Clovis is merely one more instance of widespread technological convergence or parallelism in prehistory. Rather than requiring the presence of "sophisticated" paleo-European immigrants to develop the Clovis technology, it was the work of Native Americans, undoubtedly of trans-Beringian Asian origin.

Chronology

Stanford, in his Web page, states that the Solutrean is "not that much older" than Clovis. However, even the oldest bifacial foliate point (unfluted and straight-based) from the supposed "pre-Clovis" context in Meadowcroft Rockshelter is bracketed by radiocarbon dates of 11,300 and 18,800 B.P.[1]—and that is taking these controversial dates at face value. The Clovis techno-complex has now been carefully dated between 11,200–10,900 B.P.

The Solutrean of France, Spain, and Portugal is now dated by over 80 credible radiocarbon dates (both conventional and AMS). In France, the distinctive Solutrean lithic technology (i.e., bifacial and unifacial leaf-shaped, shouldered and stemmed points made on flakes and blades) lasted a short time, from about 20,500 B.P. to about 18,500 B.P., when it was replaced by the flake-based Badegoulian (aka Magdalenian 0+1) technology in the southwest and by the derivative Salpêtrian industry in the southeast. In Cantabrian (Atlantic) Spain, the dates for the Solutrean range from about 20,500 to 17,000 B.P., after which it was gradually replaced by backed bladelet-rich assemblages labeled "early Magdalenian." In Mediterranean Spain (Catalonia, Levante and Andalusia), the Solutrean dates between about 21,000 and 16,500 B.P. and is followed by an early Magdalenian or "Badegoulian". In Portugal, recent research, principally by J. Zilhao, shows that Solutrean technology developed as early as 21,000 B.P. and was replaced at some time between 17,000–16,500 B.P. by a bladelet-rich "early Magdalenian." In short, the *latest* Solutrean stone points are more than *5,000 radibcarbon years older* than the oldest Clovis points.

Geographic Distribution

The Solutrean techno-complex coincided with (and clearly represented a behavioral adaptation to) the Last Glacial Maximum, centered on 18,000 B.P. Prior to ca. 25,000–22,000 B.P., northwestern Europe (i.e., northern France, southern England and Wales, Belgium and Germany) was occupied by humans making backed and/or tanged lithic projectile points associated with the Gravettian technological tradition. With the onset of the extreme cold and, especially, the aridity of the Last Glacial Maximum (LGM), the human geographic range gradually contracted, resulting in the total (or near-total) abandonment of these previously occupied regions. They were not to be reoccupied until the Late Glacial. Specifically, although there *may* have been some ephemeral "visits" to or "explorations" of northern France, Belgium and southern Germany by around 16,000 B.P. or slightly earlier, actual resettlement of the Paris Basin, the Belgian Meuse Basin, southern England, and Germany only occurred between 13,000–12,500 B.P. This recolonization came during the distinct warming trend that was well underway by ca. 13,000 B.P. Culturally, this period corresponds to the late Magdalenian, materially defined by the frequent presence of antler harpoons, whereas the earlier Late Glacial corresponds to the "early Magdalenian," often rich in antler spear points and backed bladelets, but with no foliate or tanged lithic projectiles.

But during the LGM (i.e., during the Solutrean), the human occupation in western Europe was restricted to several refugia in southwest and southeast France and (mainly) to the lowland peripheries of the Iberian Peninsula (Vasco-Cantabrian, eastern and southern Mediterranean Spain, and Portugal). The very northernmost Solutrean site, Saint-Sulpice-de-Favières, is south of Paris at ca. 48°30′ N. Although this site is undated, the absence of shouldered points and the presence of many large bifacial laurel leaf points and blanks at this specialized lithic quarry-workshop camp might suggest repeated brief visits at a relatively early Solutrean date, before the height of the LGM. Otherwise, the northern frontier of Solutrean settlement seems to have corresponded to the Loire River valley, at ca. 47°30′ N, where there is a cluster of sites, notably Fritsch, Fressignes, and Tannerie, with radiocarbon dates between 19,000–18,000 B.P. In sum, there were simply *no people* living in (or even visiting with any degree of frequency) the regions north of Paris during the period from about 22,000–16,000 B.P., which is when the peopling of the New World now seems to have occurred. And there were certainly no people even in the southern part of England until ca. 12,500 B.P., so humans could not have crossed on pack ice between the British Isles and the Maritime Provinces. On the other hand, the distance from Portugal to Virginia is *5,000 km* straight across the open mid-North Atlantic Ocean.

Technology

Despite a few superficial similarities—which can easily be attributed to independent invention—there are vast differences between the Solutrean and Clovis technologies.

The technological traditions of the Franco-Iberian Solutrean were firmly rooted in those of the Gravettian (middle Upper Paleolithic) of western Europe. Depending on the local availability and quality of lithic raw materials, as well as on site function, blanks used for making stone implements were flakes, blades, and bladelets ("micro-blades" in American terminology), although the Solutrean leaf, shouldered, and stemmed points were usually made on blades often produced from diverse specific forms of prismatic cores. The hallmark of Solutrean lithic technology is indeed its projectile component, consisting of both a variety of single-element tips (of widely varying sizes and weights, including many "laurel leaves" that may actually have been used as knives) *and* (especially in later Solutrean contexts) backed bladelets that were used multiply as barbs and/or tips of projectiles, whose other elements were basally beveled antler points. Modern-quality Solutrean excavations (using fine-screening techniques) are yielding backed bladelets in quantities up to 40 percent of the total retouched tool fraction, although 5–20 percent is a more common range of proportions.

The classic Solutrean stone points include unifacial and bifacial pieces, often worked by invasive percussion (and sometimes pressure) flaking, with occasional evidence of heat treatment. The finest pieces are finished with ribbon removals that sometimes overshoot the opposite edge. But most pieces are far less sophisticated. (Overshot flakes are common whenever facially working techniques were used, as they were in many times and places in the prehistory of the world.) The Solutrean bifaces come in a variety of forms: long, narrow "willow leaves," classic bipointed, convex-sided "laurel leaves," rhomboidally shaped pieces, different classes of asymmetrical bifaces, pieces with a slight central tang, ones with a rounded base, others with a straight base, and bifaces (and some unifaces) with a concave base. *Bases are never fluted.* There also exist a variety of shouldered points, which are integral components of the Solutrean arsenal: these include both fully and partially invasively retouched (mostly unifacial) pieces in a variety of standardized forms, as well as pieces whose tang has been formed by abrupt retouch and which are otherwise (marginally) retouched. Finally there are true stemmed points in various forms and sizes that resemble (and may actually have been) "arrowheads".

One of the most distinctive aspects of this wide array of Solutrean projectiles is their regionally-specific character; while standard "laurel leaves" are fairly ubiquitous, many others have very limited geographic distributions. Notably, the true stemmed points are found in Mediterranean Spain (from Catalonia to Cádiz) and in southern Portugal. The basally concave points are mainly found in the eastern half of Asturias and in Cantabria, with a handful of outliers (exchange items, curiosities?) that have been found in the adjacent Basque Country and French Pyrenean foreland. (The concavities are slight–rarely deep, as in many Clovis points. According to Collins, "complete, pristine [Clovis] points generally exceed 100 mm in length," whereas the average length of whole Solutrean concave base points is 634 mm.) There are different shouldered point types peculiar respectively to Asturias-Cantabria, Dordogne-Charentes, Gascogne, Girona, and, more generally, the Mediterranean regions. This regional point style phenomenon is suggestive of an increase in territorialism associated with a compressed, circumscribed area of human occupation during the Last Glacial Maximum in southwestern Europe.

But Solutrean lithic technology is far more than just projectile elements. There are many different kinds of endscrapers, perforators, knives, and true burins (i.e., pieces from which one or more lateral spalls have been struck by the burination technique). This diversity of lithic tools and production strategies is accompanied by an organic technology that includes a couple of major Solutrean innovations: the eyed bone needle and the antler spearthrower—in addition to a wealth of beveled antler points and possible foreshafts (or even self-barbed point). Antler and bone artifacts, while not as common as in the subsequent Magdalenian, are not at all rare in the Solutrean. They are in Clovis.

Most significantly, Solutrean technology is thus very different from both the well-known Clovis and much less-understood pre-Clovis industries of North America, both in its specific artifact forms (e.g., true burins, backed bladelets) and in its diversity of projectile types, as well as other lithic and organic implements and fabrication techniques.

Insofar as it is formally described, Clovis technology can be characterized as follows: bifaces (some of which are concave base, *fluted* projectile points, others probably knives) and unifaces, both made either on flakes or blades depending on local raw material availability; a limited variety of other lithic tools including end- and sidescrapers, gravers, but very few true burins; rare ivory and bone points or foreshafts, *one* example of a bone shaft wrench. Microblades, tanged and shouldered points—all common in various Solutrean assemblages—are absent in the far more limited technological repertoire of Clovis. While there are superficial similarities (e.g., some concave base foliate projectile points, some organic points or foreshafts with anti-skid engraved lines on basal bevels), these are most parsimoniously explainable as independent developments—similar solutions to similar functional problems, given limited available lithic and osseous materials and manufacturing techniques. The fact that red ochre was used by people in both techno-complexes—as cited by Stanford—is meaningless, as such pigment use is virtually a cultural universal among *Homo sapiens* foragers worldwide.

Subsistence: Marine Resource Exploitation?

The transatlantic migration hypothesis would require that people in western Europe during the Last Glacial Maximum have a highly specialized maritime adaptation.

At La Riera Cave, a two-hour walk from the pleniglacial shore of the Cantabrian Sea during the Solutrean, we documented evidence of significant marine mollusc collection and minor fishing (of salmon and trout, which are anadromous to varying degrees and could have been taken at the shore or in nearby estuaries or freshwater streams). Similar evidence exists at other Solutrean sites in the region (e.g., Cova Rosa, Altamira), and presages a major boom in aquatic resource exploitation during the Magdalenian. However, there is no evidence in Cantabrian Spain (or elsewhere) for Solutrean predation on deep sea fish or marine mammals. (There is *one* rear first phalanx of a common seal in the Solutrean collection from Obermaier's 1924–25 excavations at Altamira that could well represent a scavenged animal. No additional seal remains were found in the recent Altamira excavations of González Echegaray and Freeman.) Humans were certainly acquainted with the seacoast, as attested by the penguin drawings and seal engravings of possible Solutrean age in Cosquer Cave, coastal southeast France, as well as fish and seal images in a number of other caves, such as Candamo in Asturias, La Pileta and Ardales in Andalusia, attributable for stylistic and archaeological reasons to the Solutrean. However, there are no representations of boats and no evidence whatsoever either of seafaring or of the ability to make a living mainly or solely from the ocean during the Solutrean. For Vasco-Cantabria and Aquitaine, at least, this is not surprising, as the Bay of Biscay, with its very steep thermal gradient, due to the clash of polar and latitudinally depressed Gulf Stream waters off the coast of Galicia, was a cold, windy and intensely stormy sea during the Last Glacial Maximum. In sum, there is simply no empirical support for assertions that Solutrean people could have survived on pack ice or navigated across the open Atlantic. The Solutrean was essentially a terrestrial adaptation, despite the peri-coastal distribution of many of its Iberian sites.

Depending on the region, hunter-gatherers during the Solutrean subsisted in largely treeless grasslands and heaths, mainly hunting medium to large terrestrial ungulate game: principally reindeer and horse in France, red deer and ibex in Iberia, with smaller numbers of bison, chamois and other mammals in all regions. There are trace quantities of mammoth remains in a few Solutrean sites of southwest France and Cantabrian Spain, but these are mainly pieces of worked ivory that could have been scavenged. The mammoth was already a rare creature on the landscape by this time in southwest Europe. There is no evidence for any degree of Solutrean mammoth hunting (specialized or not), in contrast to at least several classic Clovis sites.

Whereas Clovis pyrotechnology is said not to have included the use of stones to bank heat or to roast, such techniques are common in the Solutrean.

Art & Ornamentation

A major distinction between the Solutrean and Clovis lies in the area of artistic and decorative activity.

Although not as reknowned for works of portable or rock art and ornamentation as its successor the Magdalenian, the Solutrean is in fact better endowed with such images and artifacts than had been widely recognized until recently. Direct AMS dating of some of the charcoal drawings in Cosquer Cave prove that they were executed about 18,000–19,000 B.P., and new dates from La Pileta and Nerja in Andalusía yield ages of ca. 20,000 B.P. There are strong stratigraphic and/or indirect (but closely associated) radiocarbon arguments for attributing cave art in a number of other sites in France and Spain (e.g., Le Placard, Cougnac, Tête de Lion, Les Escabasses, Peña de Candamo, El Buxú) to the Solutrean. Even some of the spectacular limestone bas relief or deeply engraved friezes in Southwest France (e.g., Roc de Sers, Fourneau du Diable, Isturitz) are be [sic] attributable to this period.

Of the over 5,000 engraved and painted limestone or slabs from Parpalló Cave in Valencia, more than half are from Solutrean levels. By comparison with the Parpalló portable art objects, other rock art sites (notably the open-air figures of the Côa Valley in northeast Portugal, together with similar manifestations in nearby areas of Spain, as well as Portugal's only cave art site, Escoural) have been attributed to the Solutrean. Engraved stone slabs have been found in other Solutrean deposits, and engraved and "tick-marked" bones and ivory lamellae, perforated animal teeth and shells are common.

In short, one of the defining cultural characteristics of the Solutrean, along with the foliate and tanged points, is a wealth of both wall and portable art and ornamentation typical of neither Clovis nor "pre-Clovis." The facts that bones *are* well-preserved in many Clovis sites and that Solutrean rock art includes *open-air* examples (not just caves), are arguments against this distinction being merely one of differential preservation between the two cultural phenomena.

Discussion and Conclusions

The Solutrean represents the material evidence of the cultural adaptations of human groups surviving in the refugia of southwest Europe during the Last Glacial Maximum. This was a time of inventiveness and ingenuity under environmental and resource stress. The creativity of the Solutrean extended beyond the "arms race" that is attested by the plethora of lithic and antler point sizes and types (and even backed micro-blade elements) and by the invention of the spearthrower. It included new strategies for specialized, land-based, herd game hunting (including the swift, wary, cliff-dwelling ibex), supplemented by the use of littoral and riverine (but *not* oceanic) food resources. It also was characterized by a wealth of artistic and "marking" activities, no doubt related to social and ideological developments that helped humans to cope with hard times.

Significantly, Solutrean hunter-gatherers did not extend their range anywhere far enough north to put them in a geographic position to ever cross the North Atlantic to America (either on ice floes or in boats). Nor is there any evidence that they were skilled seafarers or marine mammal hunters.

Located 5,000 km from the U.S. eastern seaboard, the Solutrean techno-complex ended 5,000 radiocarbon years (over 200 human generations!) before the appearance of Clovis. Far more diverse in its lithic and organic technologies than Clovis, and characterized by an artistic tradition that is absent from Clovis, what the Solutrean would mainly seem to "share" with Clovis are concave base, bifacially-worked points. Yet such pieces in the Solutrean are found only at a handful of sites in a small area of northern Spain—not in France or in the rest of Iberia. Nor are the Solutrean points fluted, a feature which is absolutely diagnostic of Clovis points. Shouldered and stemmed points, as well as micro-blades, all so common in the Solutrean, are completely absent from the Clovis lithic repertory. And beveled antler points (or foreshafts), common in the Solutrean, are very rare in Clovis.

Thus, the most parsimonious explanation for the (superficial) similarities between the Solutrean and Clovis is the well-known (but under-acknowledged) phenomenon of technological convergence or parallelism. In short, there are only a limited number of ways in which to make a projectile point (or knife) out of stone. Invasive retouch (by pressure flaking or by hard or soft, direct or indirect percussion), including ribbon removals with overshooting for bifacial thinning, is among them. As has long been known, the prehistory of the world is replete with examples of bifacial foliate points. Just within Europe (not to mention Africa and Siberia), bifacial foliates reoccurred in the Middle and Upper Paleolithic (as well as in the Chalcolithic and Bronze Age) in different regions. It is a technological practice that has been invented and reinvented time and time again to fulfill a set of specific purposes, namely the killing and/or butchering of animals. Such convergence is recognized today in Europe, since bifaces span such vast distances of space and time that the search for "genetic" relationships is now seen to be a futile exercise. Similarly there are only limited numbers of effective hafting treatments possible for large lithic points; the basal concavity is one of them, independently invented not only in Clovis and in the Cantabro-Asturian Solutrean, but also in other prehistoric traditions (e.g., in Russia). One or two technical attributes are insufficient to establish a *cultural* link or long-distance interconnection.

While basal thinning has been used in various regions since Middle Paleolithic times, fluting is apparently a peculiar, specific and difficult-to-master technique for basal thinning that seems to have been a genuinely Native American invention. There is simply nothing like this form of basal thinning among the concave base Solutrean points made 9,000–5,000 years earlier. Credit should be given where credit is due: Native Americans, descended from diverse Asian populations, were the makers of Clovis and "pre-Clovis" lithics. The Solutrean of southwestern Europe was another story altogether. It seems to me particularly irresponsible–in the absence of any credible scientific evidence for prehistoric European settlement of the New World–for some professional archeologists to be suggesting that Native Americans are not the descendents of the first colonizers of this land.

Note

1. All dates given here are approximations based on generally large numbers of uncalibrated radiocarbon determinations. See the cited publications for exact dates.

EXPLORING THE ISSUE

Did Humans Migrate to the New World from Europe in Early Prehistoric Times?

Critical Thinking and Reflection

1. What evidence is there for the Solutrean migration hypothesis?
2. What evidence is there for the more orthodox view of the Asian migration hypothesis?
3. How should the techniques for making stone tools be evaluated for comparing the Solutrean and Clovis points?
4. Would the lack of evidence for the Solutrean migration hypothesis prove the Asian migration hypothesis? Would lack of evidence for the Asian migration hypothesis prove the Solutrean migration hypothesis?
5. Would it be possible for both hypotheses to be correct but incomplete? What kinds of evidence should we look for?

Is There Common Ground?

Other scholars are pursuing other lines of evidence. Biological anthropologists continue to study the bones of the oldest humans in the Americas, including Kennewick Man, whose bones have only recently been made available for study after a long legal battle between scientists and the Umatilla Indians, who wanted to rebury the bones. Some geneticists are studying the DNA of Native Americans to try to determine which Old World populations are their closest relations, whether they are descended from one or more founding populations, and how long they have been in the Americas. Some linguists are using the similarities and differences among the languages of indigenous Americans to work out whether the languages come from one or several sources and how long they have been evolving in the Americas. So far the results of these studies are inconclusive, as different scholars have reached different conclusions, but the genetic and linguistic studies generally suggest pre-Clovis entry of humans into the Americas.

Both positions on the Solutrean hypothesis suffer from limited evidence, which may or may not emerge in coming years. These two positions represent an orthodox view and a new hypothesis. The newer position always feels somewhat controversial, until more data becomes available and feels more routine. But there is no reason to believe that both positions could not conceivably be true in their broad outlines, with immigration from both the east and the west. It is even possible, but by no means demonstrated, that some humans had arrived in the New World much earlier and the sites at Monte Verde and few other early sites represent descendants of these earliest settlers. We do need more data to fully answer the question, "who settled the Americas?"

Additional Resources

For more on the Solutrean–Clovis controversy see:

Bradley, Bruce A. and Stanford, Dennis. 2006. "The Solutrean–Clovis Connection: Reply to Straus, Meltzer and Goebel," *World Archaeology* 38(4).

Straus, Lawrence, Melzer, David J., and Goebel, Ted. 2005. "Ice Age Atlantis?: Exploring the Solutrean–Clovis 'Connection,'" *World Archaeology* 37(4).

For discussions of some of the important pre-Clovis sites and their implications for our understanding of the arrival of humans in the Americas see:

Adovasio, James and Page, Jake. 2002. *The First Americans: In Pursuit of Archaeology's Greatest Mystery.* New York: Random House. (This volume discusses the Meadowroft Rockshelter.)

This volume discusses Monte Verde:

Dillehay, Tom D. 2000. *The Settlement of the Americas: A New Prehistory.* New York: Basic Books.

For more on the possibility that the first immigrants to the Americas came down the west coast in boats see:

Dixon, E. James. 1999. *Bones, Boats and Bison: Archeology and the First Colonization of Western North America.* Albuquerque: University of New Mexico Press.

For a discussion of Kennewick Man and his significance see:

Chatters, James C. 2001. *Ancient Encounters: Kennewick Man and the First Americans.* New York: Simon and Schuster.

Popular accounts of the controversies surrounding the initial migration into the Americas include:

Begley, Sharon and Murr, Andrew. 1999. "The First Americans," *Newsweek* April 26.

Hadringham, Evan. 2004. "America's First Immigrants," *Smithsonian* November 2004.

Lemonick, Michael D. and Dorfman, Andrea. 2006. "Who Were the First Americans?" *Time* March 13.

ISSUE 5

Did Climate Change Rather Than Overhunting Cause the Extinction of Mammoths and Other Megafauna in North America?

YES: Donald K. Grayson and David J. Meltzer, from "A Requiem for North American Overkill," *Journal of Archaeological Science* (May 2003)

NO: Stuart Fiedel and Gary Haynes, from "A Premature Burial: Comments on Grayson and Meltzer's 'Requiem for Overkill'," *Journal of Archaeological Science* (January 2004)

Learning Outcomes

After reading this issue, you should be able to:

- Understand that the end of the last ice age corresponds to major changes in the North American climate and environment as the earth was warming, ice sheets were melting, and humans were reaching the New World. At more or less the same time period large mammals like the wooly mammoths and mastodons were dying out.
- Discuss the possible role of humans in causing the extinction of megafauna at the end of the ice age.
- Discuss the possible role of climate change in causing the extinction of megafauna at the end of the ice age.
- Explain the use of evidence in the overkill hypothesis and the use of evidence in the climate change hypothesis for explaining the extinction of megafauna.
- Understand how evidence and logical deduction are combined in archaeological explanations and model building.

ISSUE SUMMARY

YES: Archaeologists Donald Grayson and David Meltzer argue that the evidence for human predation as the cause of the Pleistocene megafauna's extinction is circumstantial. They contend that this explanation is based on four premises that find little archaeological evidence to support them. Since there is limited evidence to support the overkill hypothesis, they suggest that climate change is a more likely explanation for these extinctions in North America as they seem to have been in Europe.

NO: Archaeologists Stuart Fiedel and Gary Haynes are strong supporters of the overkill hypothesis that argues that humans overhunted large mammals to extinction in North America. They contend that Grayson and Meltzer have misinterpreted older archaeological evidence and largely ignore more recent data. They maintain that there is little evidence for climate change as the cause of the extinctions, which happened within a relatively short period of about 400 years. They feel the empirical evidence supports the "overkill hypothesis."

Between 10,000 and 30,000 years ago the first wave of settlers swept into the New World. The exact date of this immigration is uncertain and archaeologists continue to suggest different dates for first settlement. During this period the global climate was changing. The cool, dry conditions of the last ice age (the Pleistocene) were gradually giving way to the warmer and wetter conditions of the Holocene (the geological period in which we currently live). It is still not clear how these first immigrants to the New World got here or from which direction they came—Asia or Europe. But it is fairly certain that whenever they arrived the most successful groups of mammal they encountered were the large megafauna (literally, "huge animals"), most notably the mastodon and wooly mammoth.

When humans were first arriving in the New World, glacial ice was retreating as the earth's climate warmed. About this time the mastodon and wooly mammoth, both of whom were characteristic of the cool Pleistocene, appear to have gone extinct. These Pleistocene megafauna were well-adapted to the cool, dry conditions of the last ice age. The large size of these animals allowed them to lose their warmth more slowly, which would have been an important adaptation during the last glacial maximum. But they had never had to deal with human predators until people started migrating to the New World from Asia. The question that several generations of archaeologists have confronted is what caused these extinctions? Were they simply the result of a warming climate? Or, were these species overhunted to extinction by humans?

After the ice age ended, megafauna had also gone extinct in Eurasia and Australia, but it was the archaeologist and geoscientist Paul S. Martin (1928–2010) who first attempted to address this question systematically for the North American context. In the 1930s, archaeologists had found a distinctive type of flint projectile point at Clovis, New Mexico, associated with bones from one of these large mammals. The assumption was that people who had made and used these tools were the first immigrants to the New World from Asia, and that they lived at least partly by hunting mastodons and mammoths. Some years later Martin reasoned that because these large mammals had not been exposed to human predation before, perhaps humans had been responsible for their decline and ultimate extinction. After all, in the nineteenth century Americans had seen the American bison hunted to the brink of extinction because of human predation. Could this not also have been the fate of the megafauna? Martin called this explanation the "overkill hypothesis."

Using computer modeling as well as the archaeological record, Martin argued that human predation could have caused the extinction of the Pleistocene megafauna. There were actually rather few sites in which artifacts from paleoindians had been found associated with mastodon or wooly mammoth bones. So Martin reasoned that this lack of data was because these early Indians had swept across North America so rapidly that they left rather little evidence in their wake. To explain this pattern of dispersal and overkill he developed a computer model that both settled the continent and overhunted the megafauna. But like any computer simulation, Martin's model is only as good as its assumptions and premises. These assumptions are what Grayson and Meltzer challenged.

Here Donald Grayson and David Meltzer challenge Martin's explanation for the extinction of these large animals. They argue that the archaeological evidence is extremely weak and most of what has been uncovered does not support the overkill hypothesis. In fact, they contend that the archaeological data actually *contradicts* the overkill hypothesis. They are especially skeptical that the lack of sites where humans killed megafauna is evidence in support of Martin's model. Martin had suggested that there were few such archaeological remains because the Pleistocene hunters had migrated into and spread out across North America so quickly. Grayson and Meltzer argue that Martin's interpretation of the "negative evidence" removes his proposal from the realm of theory since it cannot be tested. In place of the overkill hypothesis, Grayson and Meltzer suggest that the best explanation for the extinctions is drastic climate change, a period of rapid global warming.

Here Stuart Fiedel and Gary Haynes defend the overkill model. They remain unbothered by the lack of archaeological sites, since they argue that there would never have been large herds of megafauna in the first place, and bone preservation is so poor over much of their range. They contend that Grayson and Meltzer have ignored most of the evidence—both archaeological and climatological—that supports the overkill hypothesis. In particular, the rapid extinction of these large mammals over a period of about 400 years suggests to them that climate change could not have played as central a role as Grayson and Meltzer suggest. Fiedel and Haynes argue that the Pleistocene extinctions were contemporaneous with the arrival of the first humans but predated the Pleistocene—Holocene warming period by as much as 1000 years.

At the heart of the debate about the extinction of Pleistocene megafauna is the question of whether or not correlation is the same as causation. Both the overkill hypothesis and the climate change hypothesis are plausible models, and there is some evidence in support of each of the models. But the evidence is not unambiguous for either of these models. But in neither case do the researchers see direct evidence of what caused the extinctions. Instead, they see the arrival of humans at the same time that the large mammals died out in one case, or see a period of warming at the same time as the extinctions. These correlations in time may be the result of causation, but they are not proof of causation.

Grayson and Meltzer argue that the drastic climate change would have driven the megafauna—who were adapted to the cool, dry Pleistocene climate—to extinction. Their main evidence is that the beginning of the Holocene and its warmer climate coincided with the extinctions. They also argue that there is so little archaeological evidence that links humans and megafauna that it makes no sense to use this absence of data to support the overkill hypothesis. Fiedel and Haynes oppose this view citing Martin's original argument as a justification for the lack of archaeological data. These scholars then argue that the overkill hypothesis *expects* or *predicts* limited archaeological data. For them the relatively large number of preserved sites is strong evidence in favor of Martin's model. Fiedel and Haynes likewise contend that the end of the Pleistocene did not coincide with the extinction of the megafauna, but that the main warming phase happened much later.

The extinctions raise two concerns in the prehistoric world of ancient North America that parallel events in the twentieth and twenty-first centuries: human-caused extinctions and global climate change. Martin was clearly influenced by near extinction of the American bison since Theodore Roosevelt initiated conservation effort to protect the species. And since the mid-twentieth century, hundreds of smaller animal species have been threatened by human activities, mostly by degrading natural habitats. For the last 20 years, Americans have become increasingly aware of global climate change, which has brought a burst in the population of the mountain pine beetle that has killed vast pine forests in Montana and other western states.

This debate has raised a number of questions important to both prehistoric and contemporary societies. Can small-scale societies (e.g., hunter-gatherers) have impacts on their environment? How important is the impact of climate change on natural species? Can both the overkill and climatological hypotheses be synthesized? Are human beings wasteful? What implications does the overkill hypothesis have on the traditional image of Native Americans?

YES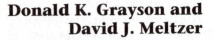

**Donald K. Grayson and
David J. Meltzer**

A Requiem for North American Overkill

Introduction

Toward the end of the Pleistocene, some 35 genera of primarily large mammals became extinct in North America, either in the sense that they no longer exist anywhere in the world (29 genera), or that they ceased to exist here while living on elsewhere (six genera). More than 40 years ago, Paul S. Martin began to develop what has become the most visible explanation for these losses: the extinctions, he argues, were due entirely to the impacts of human hunting.

Few speculations about the prehistoric past have achieved as much celebrity as this one. Hardly a textbook or popular scientific treatment of New World archaeology, ecology, and environmental history misses the opportunity to discuss it, with many understandably keen to use this apparent illustration of human destructiveness to teach a well-intentioned lesson in conservation. Yet despite this popularity, Martin's position gains virtually no support from the North American late Pleistocene archaeological and paleontological records. As a result, it gains almost no support from the scientists who specialize in these records. Here, we provide a brief historical background to Martin's argument, and then turn to the empirical record that shows it to be incorrect.

The Heart of the Argument

In developing what has become known as the 'overkill hypothesis', Martin was tackling a problem that has intrigued scholars ever since the former existence of such now-extinct mammals as mammoth and ground sloths became known, a process of recognition that began as the 18th century came to an end. Martin's particular approach to explaining the extinctions, however, became popular only after 1860, the year it was demonstrated in Europe that people had walked the earth with such beasts as the woolly rhinoceros, woolly mammoth, and 'Irish elk'. Soon after that acceptance occurred, it became so routine to attribute European extinctions to human hunting that, by 1872, this argument was being referred to as 'the favorite hypothesis.'

From *Journal of Archaeological Science*, vol. 30, 2003, pp. 585–593. Copyright © 2003 by Elsevier Science Ltd. Reprinted by permission via Rightslink.

While the intellectual roots of the overkill approach to explaining Pleistocene extinctions lie in 19th-century western Europe, our current understanding of the archaeology, vertebrate paleontology, and late Pleistocene climate history of that region is such as to leave the hypothesis no strong adherents there. Instead, it lives on elsewhere, most notably in Australia and North America. The situation in Australia is in considerable flux, and we therefore do not comment on it but instead focus on North America, the area we know best.

In North America, the contemporaneity of humans and extinct Pleistocene mammals was not demonstrated until the early 1930s, at Clovis, NM, where the evidence suggested that people had hunted the animals involved. A series of similar sites were discovered during the decades that followed. That several of those sites on the North American Plains and in the southwest contained the remains of mammoth clearly warranted the inference that Clovis groups at least occasionally hunted this animal. This reasonable observation was then transformed into the generalization that Clovis groups were specialized big-game hunters, even though there was (and is) no evidence for such specialization. Once that had occurred, a number of scholars found it reasonable to attribute North American Pleistocene extinctions at least in part to human hunting.

The contemporary North American version of the overkill hypothesis is due almost entirely to Martin, who has developed the hypothesis in sufficient detail to make it convincing to many, although its most vocal adherents are primarily those whose expertise lies outside the place and time period involved. Martin's hypothesis has changed somewhat over the years, but it has always included four major premises:

1. It has been well established through archaeological and paleontological research that the prehistoric human colonization of islands was followed by often massive vertebrate extinctions.
2. The archaeological phenomenon known as Clovis, marked by well made and distinctive fluted points and well dated to about 11,000 radiocarbon years ago, is extremely likely to have been created by the first peoples to have entered North America south of glacial ice, and represents the first peoples known to have hunted large-mammals in this huge area.
3. Clovis peoples preyed on a diverse variety of now-extinct mammals.
4. The late Pleistocene North American mammal extinctions occurred at or near 11,000 radiocarbon years ago.

From these key premises, Martin concludes that Clovis hunters caused these extinctions. Direct human predation, he argues, removed the herbivore contingent, while the loss of the herbivores led to the extinction of such carnivores as the saber-tooth and scimitar cats and the giant short-faced bear.

As we have noted, the overkill hypothesis was born in 19th-century Europe, only to be rejected as our understanding of western European archaeology, vertebrate paleontology, and climate history became sufficiently well refined to make it clear that the comings and goings of large mammals in this region were tightly linked to climate change. The North American situation is quite different. Here, the late Pleistocene climate record is strong, but our understanding of the archaeology and paleontology of this period is not. We do, however, know enough to examine Martin's critical premises in detail, and, in doing so, to find his argument significantly wanting.

Island Extinctions

To establish that prehistoric humans not only could have caused extinction, but did so on multiple occasions, Martin turns to island settings. There is good reason for this, since it is extremely well documented that on island after island in nearly all parts of the world, prehistoric human colonization was quickly followed by vertebrate extinction.

The most famous example of this phenomenon is certainly provided by New Zealand, where some 11 species of moas—large, flightless birds that ranged in estimated weight from 20 to over 200 kg—succumbed within a few hundred years of permanent human colonization some 900 years ago. All agree that these extinctions resulted from human activities. At least 25 other species of smaller vertebrates—lizards, frogs, birds, and at least one species of bat—were lost with the moas, and the list of species lost will surely grow as our knowledge of the recent biotic history of New Zealand grows.

While New Zealand may provide the most famous example of human-caused vertebrate extinction in a prehistoric island setting, nearly every island whose archaeology and paleontology is well known illustrates the same phenomenon. In the Mediterranean, only two species of mammals—both shrews—remain of the mammals that were present just prior to the human arrival. On Mangaia, in the Cook Islands, 13 of 17 species of landbirds known archaeologically did not survive to be described in writing. In the West Indies, multiple species of hutias, rodents that had long been present in the region, became extinct after people arrived. No matter where we look, as long as terrestrial vertebrates were present, the outcome is the same.

In no case is the precise cause or causes of these extinctions known. This is because in all known cases, human colonization was associated with multiple possible impacts on the species that were lost. In New Zealand, for instance, people not only hunted moas, but they also set fires that quickly destroyed massive expanses of forest and introduced competitors and predators in the form of rats and dogs. Some combination of hunting, introduced species (including pathogens), and anthropogenic vegetational change caused the losses that are so well documented there. We cannot, however, say what that combination was. The same is true for all known prehistoric, human-caused island extinctions. Because this is the case, none of these extinctions can be securely attributed to hunting alone, although this may certainly have occurred.

The magnitude of prehistoric human-caused vertebrate extinctions on islands came as a surprise when it first began to be described in detail by such scientists as Storrs Olson, Helen James, and David Steadman during the 1980s. Nonetheless, it has long been known that island faunas are in general prone to extinction, and the reasons for this are well understood. Island vertebrates are vulnerable because their populations are small, because they are confined to well-delineated areas of land that may undergo rapid environmental change, because they may have lost (and in some cases have clearly lost) the behavioral mechanisms needed to cope with introduced predators, pathogens, and competitors, and because there is no ready source of conspecific individuals to replenish dwindling populations. Island faunas are, as Paulay has noted, "among the most vulnerable in the world."

Martin's first premise is, then, depressingly true. The initial human colonization of island after island was followed by vertebrate extinction. That this premise is true, however, does not mean that it is relevant to continental extinctions. After all, the factors that make islands prone to vertebrate extinction—small population sizes of resident vertebrates, the lack of a ready source of conspecific colonizers, and so on—do not apply to the continental setting.

What might make some of the lessons learned from the biotic history of islands applicable to the North American setting is evidence that Clovis-aged peoples caused massive environmental disruption of the sort routinely seen in island settings. Of this, however, there is absolutely no evidence. In addition, Martin's hypothesis relies on hunting and hunting alone, and island extinctions resulted not from hunting but from 'the manifold impacts of human colonization,' as Holdaway has so aptly put it for New Zealand.

Clovis First

Clovis dates to within a few hundred radiocarbon years of either side of 11,000 years ago. Until recently, most archaeologists accepted Clovis as the archaeological manifestation of the first people to have occupied the Americas south of glacial ice. With the recent and fairly general acceptance of the validity of the 12,500-year-old human occupation at the southern Chilean site of Monte Verde, this view has largely crumbled. Given that there is no reason to doubt that people entered the Americas via the Bering Land Bridge, it follows that they must have been in North America long before they reached southern South America. Nonetheless, it remains true that Clovis is the earliest well-accepted archaeological phenomenon known from North America. Clovis also provides the earliest secure North American evidence that people did, in fact, encounter now-extinct large mammals.

Clovis Hunters

If Martin is correct in blaming Clovis hunters for late Pleistocene mammal extinctions in North America, it would seem to follow that these people must have hunted all of the animals whose extinction they are argued to have caused.

How many of those genera can be shown to have been human prey during Clovis times? The answer is two—mammoth and mastodon—and there are only 14 sites that securely document this relationship. As has long been known, this is not a sampling fluke. There are more late Pleistocene occurrences of horse than there are of mammoth or mastodon, and nearly as many for camel as for mastodon, yet there are no demonstrable kill sites for horse or camel or for any of the remaining genera. This is not for want of looking. Given the high archaeological visibility of the remains of extinct Pleistocene mammals, and their great interest to archaeologists and Quaternary paleontologists alike, if such sites were out there, they would surely be found. Indeed, there is a strong bias in the Clovis archaeological record toward just such sites.

The rarity of megafaunal kill sites is such an evident feature of the late Pleistocene archaeological and paleontological records of North America that Martin has had to address it. After all, other parts of the world—Late Pleistocene Europe, for example—are littered with sites that document human predation on large mammals.

Martin has attempted to account for the virtual absence of kill sites in an extraordinary way. He argues that it all happened so fast that we should not expect to find empirical evidence of that process. That is, he has been forced to argue that "much evidence of killing or processing of the extinct fauna is not predicted" by his position. It is a rare hypothesis that predicts a lack of supporting evidence, but we have one here, and we have it only because evidence for it is, in fact, lacking. Martin argues quite differently for New Zealand, where he calls on the abundance of archaeological sites containing moa remains to bolster his position that human hunting played a role in the extinction of these animals.

The Extinctions Occurred 11,000 Years Ago

Obviously, if Clovis-age hunters caused the extinctions, either directly (the herbivores) or indirectly (the carnivores) of some 35 genera of mammals, those extinctions must have occurred at or soon after Clovis times. However, of the 35 genera involved, only 15 can be shown to have lasted beyond 12,000 years ago. This leaves open the possibility that many of the remaining genera became extinct well before Clovis times. In western Europe, late Pleistocene extinctions were scattered in time and space, and there is little in the North American record to suggest that the same thing did not happen here.

This possibility causes difficulties for the overkill position. Martin and Steadman, for instance, have suggested that the Aztlan rabbit might have been 'large enough' to have been hunted to extinction by Clovis-age peoples. This genus, however, cannot be shown to have survived the last glacial maximum some 18,000 years ago. Clovis hunters are thus asserted to have driven the extinction of a very small animal that, as far as we can tell, predated Clovis by at least 7000 years.

But let us assume that as the years go by, more of the mammals will be shown to have become extinct during or soon after Clovis times. How unique would this make the North American extinctions?

The answer is 'not very'. The Northern Hemisphere, in general, saw substantial large mammal extinctions at the end of the Pleistocene. In Ireland, the latest radiocarbon date for the giant deer (sometimes called the 'Irish Elk') falls at 10,610 years ago; the latest date for reindeer falls at 10,250 years ago. In southwestern France, reindeer, mammoth, saiga, and the giant deer (among others) disappeared at about the same time that Clovis appeared in North America. In the southern Jura and northern French Alps, reindeer disappeared sometime between 12,000 and 11,000 years ago. In the Taimyr Peninsula of northern Siberia, mammoth disappeared from the mainland shortly after 10,000 years ago, although they persisted well into the Holocene on Wrangel Island. While all this was happening, Harrington's mountain goat and the Shasta ground sloth disappeared from the American Southwest, caribou (North American reindeer) retreat from their late Pleistocene ranges in the American midwest and southeast, and mammoth and mastodon (among others) are lost from the American landscape. Genetic data even suggest that cheetahs in Africa and cougars in North America may have undergone severe population declines as the Pleistocene ended.

Human hunting had nothing to do with the Eurasian losses. Martin cannot blame human hunters for the disappearance of reindeer and giant deer in Ireland since there were no people in Ireland at the time. In France, reindeer were an important part of the human diet for tens of thousands of years but were not lost until the Pleistocene ended. There were no Clovis hunters in Siberia, yet large mammal extinctions occurred here anyway. Large mammal extinctions occurred at the end of the Pleistocene with or without Clovis, with or without the presence of human predators.

The End of North American Overkill

Martin has recently noted that "archaeologists have always washed their hands of human complicity in large [mammal] extinction" in North America, and he is right. He might also have added that vertebrate paleontologists who specialize in late Pleistocene North America have also cleansed themselves of this notion. The reason is straightforward. There is no evidence for it and much against it. While Martin claims that a lack of evidence provides strong support for his position, others have different expectations of the empirical record.

Given that archaeologists and paleontologists have washed their hands of North American overkill, who accepts it and what explains its popularity? As we have mentioned, those who praise overkill are, by far and large, scientists who are not familiar with the details of the North American late Pleistocene. . . .

Our point is simple. The North American version of the overkill hypothesis lives on not because of archaeologists and paleontologists who are expert in the area, but because it keeps getting repeated by those who are not. As to why it remains popular in those circles, there are likely several reasons, but one seems especially compelling.

The first detailed development of the overkill hypothesis came in 1967, the same year that the Environmental Defense Fund was launched. Five years earlier, Rachel Carson's *Silent Spring* had appeared; a year later, in 1968, Paul Ehrlich produced *The Population Bomb*. By 1970, the US National Environmental Policy Act had been passed and Earth Day created. We are not suggesting that the overkill argument emerged as an integral part of the environmental movement; after all, Martin first raised the idea a decade earlier, and overkill models emerged in mid-19th century England in a very different historical context. Instead, we suggest that the overkill argument captured the popular imagination during a time of intense concern over our species' destructive behavior toward life on earth. It retains that grasp today.

It is easy to show that overkill's continued popularity is closely related to the political uses to which it can be put. Take, for instance, Peter Ward's recent discussion of the matter. Ward—a superb paleontologist whose scientific research focuses on fossils that are between about 300 million and 60 million years old—is convinced by Martin's arguments, concluding that "the ravages of hungry people surely were involved in the destruction of many species now extinct." In this conclusion, he finds "tragic validity for times approaching": "the Snake River salmon is virtually extinct . . . king crab fishing in Alaska has been essentially terminated because the stocks are gone; the great shellfish fisheries of Puget Sound have been halted because the oysters and mussels are too poisoned by industrial wastes to eat." For Ward, the overkill position is inextricably linked to modern times and to the homily of ecological ruin.

Ward is not alone in taking this approach. In *The Third Chimpanzee*, ecologist Jared Diamond enthuses over Martin's argument and ends the chapter with a brief discussion of "the blitzkriegs by which modern European hunters nearly exterminated bison, whales, seals, and many other large animals." The next chapter begins with a discussion of "the risk of a nuclear holocaust."

For these discussions, and others like them, overkill provides powerful political capital. That we may agree with the political goals of these authors is immaterial. Our concern here is that both science and environmental concerns are being done a disservice by relying on claims that have virtually no empirical support. We are not suggesting that those who use overkill in this way do so in disregard of the facts against it. We do believe, however, that they are insufficiently familiar with the archaeological and paleontological records bearing on overkill, and so cannot properly judge Martin's claims of its explanatory power.

In fact, Martin's recent writings suggest to us that he is no longer trying to approach this issue within a scientific framework. As we have noted, he explicitly maintains that the North American overkill position does not require supporting evidence. He is unconcerned that archaeologists 'wash their hands' of his ideas. He criticizes the search for pre-Clovis sites in the New World as "something less than serious science, akin to the ever popular search for 'Big Foot' or the 'Loch Ness Monster.'" As one of us has observed elsewhere, Martin's position has become a faith-based policy statement rather than a scientific statement about the past, an overkill credo rather than an overkill hypothesis.

By emphasizing the nature of the problem and by focusing research on the latest Pleistocene archaeology and paleontology of North America, Martin's arguments have led to a good deal of productive science. Now, however, it has become quite clear that things did not happen the way that Martin has envisaged. Martin's arguments drawn from islands are not relevant to continental settings, especially given that in every known instance, island extinctions were accompanied by massive habitat disruption. Northern Hemisphere mammal communities saw substantial extinctions at the end of the Pleistocene, with or without Clovis and even with or without a human presence. There are no kill sites for 26 of the 28 genera of North American herbivores and only 14 sites for the remaining two. It remains fully possible that the North American extinctions were not confined to the very end of this period, but were scattered across thousands of years, as occurred in Europe. Unless we can somehow accept that the very absence of evidence demonstrates that overkill occurred, it is time to focus on understanding what really did happen.

Unfortunately, what did happen is not at all clear. Although a number of climate-based hypotheses have been forwarded for North America, none have gained widespread acceptance, since none connect particular climate variables with particular organisms in powerful ways. Doing so is likely to be a daunting task, since it is very likely that an adequate explanation will have to be built by treating each organism on its own. Nonetheless, experience in other parts of the world shows that it can be done. It is clearly time to begin the task in a North American context.

Stuart Fiedel and
Gary Haynes

 **NO**

A Premature Burial: Comments on Grayson and Meltzer's "Requiem for Overkill"

In a recent JAS article ("A requiem for North American overkill"), Donald Grayson and David Meltzer attack Paul Martin's "overkill" hypothesis that humans caused America's Terminal Pleistocene megafaunal extinctions. This is one of three similar recent articles by these authors in which, by scrupulous evaluation of the archaeological record, they have reduced the list of unambiguous instances of human interactions with now-extinct mammals in North America to 14 proboscidean kill sites. We applaud their informed skepticism about the evidence, especially since one of us (Haynes) wrote a set of strict standards that Grayson and Meltzer used in their analyses. . . .

Although their critical assessment of the Late Pleistocene archaeological record is laudable, Grayson and Meltzer unfortunately make numerous mistakes, indulge in unwarranted ad hominem rhetoric, and thus grossly misrepresent the overkill debate. In this comment, we first briefly address those aspects of their papers that represent mere theatrical posturing, and then we turn our attention to their more serious errors of fact and interpretation.

First, the theater. A phrase repeated or paraphrased in each of the articles is that overkill is "a faith-based policy statement rather than a scientific statement about the past, an overkill credo rather than an overkill hypothesis." By thus denying the very scientific legitimacy of the overkill hypothesis, Grayson and Meltzer seek to preclude any further serious engagement with its advocates. Science is not advanced by such dogmatic dismissal of competing hypotheses. Also theatrical but unfounded are three points Grayson and Meltzer chose to emphasize in their article summary: (1) overkill has been rejected for western Europe (it has decidedly not been rejected by knowledgeable experts, such as A.J. Stuart and colleagues, (2) Paul Martin is the only reason overkill is still discussed for North America and Australia (also wrong—see, for example, the recent work of Alroy Flannery, and O'Connell, and (3) "there is virtually no evidence" to support overkill, which, as we show in this reply, is absolutely wrong. In fact, we think there is far more support for overkill than for climate change as the principal cause of the extinctions.

From *Journal of Archaeological Science*, vol. 31, 2004, pp. 121–122, 123–24, 125, 126–128.
Copyright © 2004 by Elsevier Science Ltd. Reprinted by permission via Rightslink.

Is There No Evidence of Overkill?

It seems as though it should be simple enough to test the overkill hypothesis. If, as hypothesized, Paleoindian hunters killed thousands of giant mammals, there ought to be lots of kill sites with unambiguous evidence of hunting and butchering (e.g., broken, cut, and burned bones, semi-disarticulated skeletons at hearth areas, associated stone tools). But in reality, such sites are very rare. Martin has responded to archaeologists' disappointment over the scarcity of megafaunal kill sites by stating that,

> Sufficiently rapid rates of killing could terminate a prey population before appreciable evidence could be buried. Poor paleontological visibility would be inevitable. In these terms the scarcity of known kill sites on a landmass which suffered severe megafaunal losses ceases to be paradoxical and becomes a predictable consequence of the special circumstances which distinguish *invasion* from cultural development within a continent. Perhaps what is remarkable in America is not that so few, but that *any* kill sites of extinct mammals have been found.

In short, the absence of kill sites is just as expectable as their presence. Thus, the overkill hypothesis seems immune from any simple and conclusive archaeological testing. For this reason, Grayson and Meltzer condemn Martin's theory as unscientific, driven by ideology not evidence. They also contend that the circumstantial evidence used by Martin to support a global overkill model is weak or nonexistent.

Grayson and Meltzer present their opinions ex cathedra; trust us, they advise the reader, because we are experts on Pleistocene North America, whereas overkill advocates such as Martin, John Alroy, and Tim Flannery are not. To the extent that they attempt to substantiate their opinions with actual evidence, they provide outmoded data and interpretations and ignore or deliberately omit the most recent chronological, archaeological and climatic data.

While Grayson and Meltzer mostly restrict their "requiem" to North America, which is the region of their self-proclaimed exclusive authority, they also deign to pronounce upon evidence from other parts of the world and in so doing reveal deficiencies in their knowledge. We are glad to provide a less biased overview of the recent literature, which tends to contradict their case. Regarding the European record, in which extinctions cluster at 40–20,000 and 14–10,000 rcbp, they write that "Human hunting had nothing to do with the Eurasian losses" of several megafaunal species, extinctions which were "scattered in time and space." Although they cite A.J. Stuart's recent informed assessment of the European record in support of their assertion that overkill is today rejected by European scientists, in fact, Stuart concludes that "the staggered pattern probably results from the interplay of climatic change and overkill by human hunters." . . .

Grayson and Meltzer strangely omit from their discussion the ca. 150 radiocarbon dates run on bones of megafauna by Tom Stafford, Russ Graham and Holmes Semken. Although there has been a delay in the formal publication of those dates, oral presentations have been given in several public venues. A brief summary of the new dates was published in *Quaternary Times,* the newsletter of AMQUA, in June 1999. Indeed, Grayson demonstrates an awareness of the new dates for proboscidean extinction. Although they do not cite the new dates, presumably Grayson and Meltzer allude to them when they assert that "to date, of the 35 genera involved, only 15 can be shown to have survived beyond 12,000 years ago. As a result, it is possible, though certainly not demonstrated, that a significant number of the losses predated the Clovis arrival." This is misleading sophistry, as it leaves the false impression that the extinctions of the 15 well-dated genera (17, actually) might have occurred sporadically over the millennium between 12,000 rcbp and Clovis expansion at 11,000 rcbp [or were even "scattered across thousands of years, as occurred in Europe"]. In fact, the 17 genera all disappear abruptly and simultaneously at 10,800–11,400 rcbp. Grayson and Meltzer do not acknowledge that these dates fatally undermine their arguments for gradual climate change as the cause of the extinctions. As they have recognized, demonstration that the extinctions were synchronous "requires that we attribute to the extinction 'event' . . . speed and taxonomic breadth. . . . Once that is done, explanations of the extinctions must be structured to account for these assumed properties, whether those explanations focus on people, climate . . . or disease." . . .

The abruptness and synchroneity of the extinction event are also clearly manifest in stratigraphic sequences on both site-specific and regional scales. As Vance Haynes has emphasized in the Southwest, megafauna (mammoth, horse, camel) fossils are found below the ubiquitous "black mats" (spring-laid organic layers), and never above them. These layers demarcate the Terminal Pleistocene extinction event as clearly as the K-T boundary marks the dinosaur extinction. The mats typically date to ca. 10,700 rcbp, early in the Younger Dryas chron. It should also be noted that, at locations frequented by megafauna throughout the late Pleistocene, their dung disappears at 11,000 rcbp or soon thereafter. . . .

Is There Evidence for Climate Change as the Cause of Extinctions?

Grayson and Meltzer advocate a vague theory of climate change in place of overkill, while candidly admitting that for now, "none (of the climate change hypotheses) connect particular climate variables with particular organisms in powerful ways."

Climate change has always been the main theoretical alternative to human predation. Grayson and Meltzer offer no new refinements to the climate model, and seem unaware of recent developments in the study of latest Pleistocene climates. It must be emphasized that a drastic revision of the climatic hypothesis has occurred recently, which they do not acknowledge. Formerly, the demise of megafauna was attributed to dramatic yet rather gradual changes in temperature and vegetation that occurred during the transition from the Pleistocene to the Holocene. But we now understand that the Holocene warming was delayed in the northern hemisphere by the 1100 or 1300-year Younger Dryas. This near-glacial cold interval ended abruptly, in only a few decades, with a sudden warming at 11,570 cal BP (10,000 rcbp) that occurred more than 1000 years after the crash of the megamammals; so, obviously, neither the concomitant temperature, climate, nor vegetation changes can have played an immediate causal role in the extinction. For this reason, Russell Graham, one of the foremost and best-informed proponents of climatic causation, now cites the Younger Dryas *onset* as the straw that broke the collective backs of the megafauna. . . .

In view of the new paleoclimate data, to make any case for climate as the killer, one would now have to show that the *Ice Age* (!) megafauna, having survived for 2 million years in climates often much colder than the present, were fatally stressed by rapid *cooling*, not warming. The Younger Dryas never got as cold, for a sustained period, as the many typical full glacial episodes that preceded it. True, the Younger Dryas caused the congregation of plants into anomalous communities with no precise modern analogues, and in some areas of North America, annual temperature extremes during the Younger Dryas were unprecedented in the previous 10,000 years (although conditions during numerous earlier stadial events were probably quite similar). However, except for an insignificant species of southeastern spruce—not demonstrably critical to the diet of any megamammal—no Terminal Pleistocene plant extinctions are recorded. Available dietary evidence (e.g., Columbian mammoth and ground sloth dung shows that megafauna were not overly picky eaters). They would not have been challenged by a shift in relative percentages of local plant species; and in response to geographic retraction, expansion, or translocation of plant communities on a decadal scale, these big animals were perfectly capable—as are modern proboscideans—of moving hundreds of miles ([There is] evidence of mastodon migration between Florida and Georgia). . . .

Apart from reduction in numbers and migration into hospitable refugia, another way that animal species may react to environmental stresses over time is reduction in body size, presumably the mechanism by which *Bison antiquus* was transformed into *B. bison* in the mid-Holocene (although an interesting alternative possibility is that an immigrant bison species from eastern Beringia replaced *B. antiquus* about 10,000 rcbp)—in which case we could add giant bison, often hunted by Clovis Paleoindians (e.g., at Murray Springs and Jake Bluff to the list of extinct megafauna). . . . If climate alone wiped out giant mammals, we might expect smaller collateral or descendant forms of those genera to have survived to the present: monkey-sized ground sloths, little ponies, or tapir-sized proboscideans. Sadly, this did not happen on the American mainland. . . .

For now, as Grayson and Meltzer admit, there is no testable climate change hypothesis. If climate change is to be taken seriously as the sole cause of extinction, its advocates must show that the challenges posed to American fauna by the Bølling–Allerød warming (14,700 cal BP) and Younger Dryas cooling (12,900 cal BP) were unique and more severe than in any past episodes. But the GRIP and GISP2 ice core records of past climates show that the Terminal Pleistocene changes were not unique in either their abruptness or severity. . . .

The Younger Dryas episode is unique in its faunal consequences only because its onset coincided with the arrival of human hunters.

Why Are There So Few Killsites if Overkill Is the Better Explanation for the Extinctions?

To summarize the argument to this point, it is clear that, at the very least, a purely circumstantial case can be made that humans played some role in Terminal Pleistocene extinctions in the Americas. One simply cannot ignore the fact that rapid human expansion is coeval with unprecedented faunal collapse. Plus, the "smoking spear" is there to see for anyone without conceptual blinders. In the very brief interval of Clovis hunting of megamammals, humans left behind at least 14 unambiguous kill and butchery sites in North America, by Grayson and Meltzer's own conservative estimate, and possibly many more than that according to other authorities. In view of the extremely narrow time interval, this is a phenomenally rich record.

With respect to the scarcity of non-proboscidean killsites, the taphonomic probability is extremely low that natural processes ever would preserve upland sites containing the butchered carcasses of horses, camels, ground sloths, and smaller megafaunal taxa. One of us (Haynes) can speak with authority on this matter, having devoted 25 years to neotaphonomic studies of large-mammal skeletons in Africa, Australia, and North America. Haynes has spent much of his professional career comparing fossil sites with the modern death sites of hundreds of African elephants and other large mammals that died as a result of non-cultural processes such as die-offs or carnivore predation, as well as government-sponsored killing operations. Even in protected situations such as permanent waterholes where burial may be rapid, very (very!) few modern mammal skeletons are preserved whole or meaningfully associated with evidence about the condition of their death, whether it was cultural or non-cultural. In general, modern death sites containing bones are very rarely preserved—in fact, depending on the local conditions, the proportion of large-mammal death sites (cultural or non-cultural) that will be preserved may be as low as 0.01% or less of total numbers being killed or dying naturally.

Grayson and Meltzer show that 25 of the extinct North American genera are represented by fewer than 50 FAUNMAP occurrences dated to the last millennia of the Pleistocene. Given likely human kill rates and preservation factors, there is an infinitesimal probability that even one of these few cases would be a provable kill site. It is thus remarkable that, for eight of these genera, there should be even ambiguous human involvement.

So there actually *is* empirical evidence, from analogous modern cases, that overkill would leave few fossil remains behind to indicate the very processes involved in the extinctions. Why then is the osseous evidence of human predation on non-proboscidean taxa so much more abundant in European archaeological sites? One reason is that almost none of these are actual kill sites; the bones occur in camps and settlements, often rockshelters that were occupied for long periods and repeatedly, where occupational debris is thick and abundant. North American Paleoindians, in contrast, rarely occupied rockshelters. Another reason is that hominid predation has a history of some 500,000 years in Europe, as against the few hundred years of Clovis megafauna hunting. The "scores" of bone-bearing archaeological sites in Europe must be only a small remnant of the tens of thousands of original occupational loci, the overwhelming majority of which were not preserved.

It is important to observe that, while there are at least two good Terminal Pleistocene kill sites east of the Plains (the Kimmswick mastodon in Missouri and, probably, the Wacissa River bison in Florida), we know of none involving any large mammal from the entire subsequent 12,500-year span of the Holocene. If archaeologists in eastern North America have not yet stumbled upon the remains of any butchered carcasses of elk, deer, bear, or woodland bison of Holocene age—*12,500 years with no discoveries*—what is the likelihood of finding a butchered Terminal Pleistocene ground sloth, stag-moose, horse, or musk-ox? Should we infer that Clovis hunters never preyed upon those animals? Faunal preservation in the east is generally poor; the common assumption that eastern Paleoindians focused almost exclusively upon caribou hunting is based upon a total of seven minute fragments of cervid bone from three early Paleoindian sites (Udora, Whipple and Bull Brook). This sparse evidence does not allow confident reconstruction of early Paleoindian hunting behaviors in the east.

Although we contend that human predation was instrumental in the collapse of American megafauna, we are not saying that Martin's original model was correct on all the particulars of the process. Available archaeological and ecological data suggest that, in several respects, the simulation models of overkill presented by Mosimann and Martin (blitzkrieg at the front of the wave of advance) and more recently by Alroy are rather unrealistic and require modifications of details:

1. Human populations of the Clovis era never approached 500,000–1 million or more; probably, there were no more than 50,000 people in North America at 12,900 cal BP.
2. Extinction of most species in North America probably was complete within about 400 years after human entry; thus, overkill had to be accomplished by many fewer people, and over a much shorter time, than Martin or Alroy postulates.
3. Humans probably did not advance in a wavefront across the continent; rather, exploratory stations (marshaling camps, staging areas) were established at favorable loci, such as game refugia, lakes and river confluences, and bands "leapfrogged" from one amenable spot to the next. Thus, the dragnet effect that Martin imagined, squeezing surviving megafauna into an ever-smaller safe haven ahead of the wavefront, is improbable. Some other circumscription factor—imperative access to potable water under drought conditions, perhaps—would have prevented the animals' escape from human hunting.
4. Clovis hunters may have either specialized in predation on mammoths, in which case collapse of this keystone species could have set in train a cascading collapse of Late-glacial ecosystems; or Clovis hunting may have been more generalized, in which case low levels of additional predation pressure may have had wider synchronous effects on many genera. A more diverse dietary base would also mean

that hunters did not have to curtail hunting in any one region as the numbers of available mammoths dwindled.

5. Various simulations show that a very small increase in predation loss due to humans (less than 5%) can wreak havoc upon animal populations. This is not the non-stop killing spree that overkill opponents often caricature.

6. We cannot ascertain the precise density of large mammal populations of the Late Pleistocene. We do not think there were vast herds or high-density populations. Some critics of overkill have wondered how Paleoindians armed only with spears ever could have wiped out large numbers of megafauna, when 18–19th century hunters with rifles took so long even to put a dent in American bison populations. The great herds of bison witnessed in the Contact period may have been a brief anomaly, reflecting both Little Ice Age climatic change and the decimation of Native American populations by European diseases after AD 1550. Was Terminal Pleistocene North America really comparable to the Serengeti? Or to a densely stocked cattle ranch? Or, were there pockets of animals in scattered clearings and river bottoms amid the taiga-like forests covering much of the continent? Patchy distribution of small prey populations makes overkill more imaginable, given very low-density, mobile human populations.

7. Before arrival of human hunters, the size of megaherbivore populations may have been limited more stringently by native carnivores rather than by food supply. Several authors have suggested that interactions between humans and indigenous animal predators (dire wolf, short-faced bear, sabertooth cats, lions, cheetahs) may have played some role in rapid megafauna extinction. These could have entailed either human eradication of direct competitors, as argued by Whitney-Smith, or disruption and dislocation of longstanding prey-predator relationships. Either way, modeling suggests that the consequent collapse of both herbivore and carnivore populations can be dramatic and very rapid.

8. It may never be possible to unambiguously extricate the relative causative roles of abrupt climate oscillations between 14,700 and 11,570 cal BP and of contemporaneous human hunting after 13,400 cal BP in instigating the megamammal collapse. Thus, North America cannot serve as the best laboratory-like example of a pure overkill process. Then again, climate is always changing, so there will probably always be some minor effect that can be temporally associated with any instance of extinction.

It seems that for Grayson and Meltzer, their intellectual problem with overkill may ultimately be an issue of scale. They have no qualms about accepting the central role played by humans in the demise of island faunas (e.g., the extinction of the moas within 150 years after humans arrived on New Zealand). We agree with them that, even in these cases, pure predation need not be the sole human impact. Species that accompany humans (e.g., dogs, rats, pigs) and pathogens played a role in island extinctions, as did anthropogenic transformation of the vegetation by felling and burning.

We are willing to entertain and investigate the possibility that the American case also may have entailed similar factors in addition to hunting per se (e.g., introduction of dogs accompanying the first Paleoindian migrants; possible spread of canine distemper or other zoonotic diseases, perhaps initially to carnivores; landscapes altered by burning in Central and South America and perhaps the Northeast, ca. 11,000 rcbp). However, for some intuitive reason, which they do not clarify by quantitative modeling, Grayson and Meltzer are incredulous that these processes could have operated at the scale of an entire continent. We wonder if they would classify Australia, at about 7 million km^2, as an island or a continent. As noted above, extinction of megamarsupials, giant reptiles and giant birds appears coincident with the rapid expansion of humans across the entire land mass around 48,000 BP. Sure, America is big, but within 500 years or less after their arrival, Paleoindians had explored the whole of America south of the ice sheets, depositing their distinctive and remarkably uniform tools in Washington State, Nova Scotia, Florida, Sonora, and from Panama to Tierra del Fuego by ca. 12,900 cal BP. Really, a continent is ultimately just a gigantic island. Animals could retreat from human predators for a while, but not indefinitely.

In the end, we do not understand why Meltzer and Grayson have elected to launch their concerted assault upon Martin's theory just at this moment. Within the last decade, paleoclimate studies, focused on ice cores and lake bed sediments, have achieved an unprecedented decadal precision in chronology, and ingenious use of proxy measurements now allows accurate estimates of temperature and precipitation at a micro-scale. Surely, anyone seriously propos- ing "climate" as the critical factor in megamammal extinctions should avail themselves of the new data. Yet, Grayson and Meltzer do not. Exciting new Paleoindian sites, some with relevant faunal data, are being reported every year from North and South America. Apart from their dogged defense of the ambigu- ous Monte Verde site, Grayson and Meltzer do not concern themselves with the rapidly accumulating South American evidence. Their failure to make any use of the new radiocarbon evidence of Stafford et al. has already been noted. . . .

The best explanation for American megafaunal extinctions right now is some form of human predation. As at least one leading archaeologist has rec- ognized, "The right question probably isn't whether people were involved, but how?". We have begun to outline realistic scenarios entailing human hunt- ing in a time of dramatic climate oscillations. At the same time, we are eager to employ the latest evidence from many Quaternary subdisciplines to test a plausible competing hypothesis of extinction triggered solely by climate change, but none has been put forward.

If Meltzer and Grayson have a compelling new climate change hypoth- esis to offer, it behooves them to set it out, in adequate detail, for scien- tific assessment. Instead, they have published an indefensibly abusive and unsubstantiated ad hominem attack on Paul Martin's research. If they or any- one else ever does present a climate change hypothesis that purports to fit the rapidly expanding body of evidence, then we can all proceed to do real sci- ence. Until then, in the words of Monty Python, "This isn't an argument—it's just contradiction."

EXPLORING THE ISSUE

Did Climate Change Rather Than Overhunting Cause the Extinction of Mammoths and Other Megafauna in North America?

Critical Thinking and Reflection

1. What sort of evidence is offered by proponents of the traditional view that mammoths and mastodons died out from overhunting by early human immigrants to the New World? To what extent is this hypothesis more of a thought-experiment based on deduction than a hypothesis driven by empirical evidence?
2. What are the limitations in the evidence offered for the overkill hypothesis? Could these limitations be confirmed with a few more excavations?
3. What sort of evidence is offered by proponents of the climate change hypothesis? To what extent is this hypothesis more of a thought-experiment based on deduction than a hypothesis driven by empirical evidence?
4. What limitations can be found in the climate change hypotheses? Could these limitations be overcome with more data? Where might we find this data?
5. How might archaeologists try to resolve this debate? Is there any specific new data set that might help resolve the question?

Is There Common Ground?

Currently, there is no definitive answer to whether mastodons and wooly mammoths died out because of overhunting or as a consequence of warming. Fiedel and Haynes contend that the most significant warming occurred well after the period of extinctions. The problem with this analysis is that we do not fully understand how warm the climate would have to be to have a significant impact on the Pleistocene environment, at least enough to make it difficult for the megafauna to thrive. On the other hand, we do not know precisely how large the populations of megafauna were and how many would need to be hunted to make the breeding populations unsustainable, particularly given the fact that the glacial ice was melting and retreating.

One possible resolution to the overkill debate combines the two explanations so that human activity combined with gradual warming led to unsustainable populations of megafauna. While this argument is not the only obvious explanation, it is one that might be considered as more data emerges.

Additional Resources

For further reading on Martin's original formulation of the overkill hypothesis see:

Martin, Paul S. 1967. "Prehistoric Overkill," in (edited with Henry Wright) *Pleistocene Extinctions: The Search for a Cause.* New Haven, CT: Yale University Press.

This idea was repeated in Martin's later works, most notably in a co-authored article:

Steadman, D. W. 1999. "Prehistoric Extinctions on Islands and Continents," in *Extinctions in Near Time.* New York: Plenum Press.

For a more updated overkill simulation see:

Alroy, John. 2001. "A Multispecies Overkill Simulation of the End-Pleistocene Megafaunal Mass Extinction," *Science* 292:1893–1896.

Grayson has written many papers dealing with late Pleistocene extinctions, climate change, and the overkill hypothesis, including:

Grayson, Donald K. 1991. "Late Pleistocene Extinctions in North America," *Journal of World Prehistory* 5:193–232.

Grayson, Donald K. 2001. "Reassessing Overkill: Early Americans and Pleistocene Mammals," *Bulletin of the Florida State Museum of Natural History* 29:1439–1449.

For less quantitative and more agency-based models, see David Webster and Gary Webster's use of optimal foraging theory:

Webster, David and Webster, Gary.1984. "Optimal Hunting and Pleistocene Extinction," *Human Ecology* 12:275–289.

A less technical overview of this debate and a good synthesis of the overkill and climatological theses can be found in:

Krech III, Shephard. 1999. *The Ecological Indian: Myth and History.* New York: W.W. Norton.

ISSUE 6

Can Archaeologists Determine the Cultural Background of the Earliest Americans from the Ancient Skeleton Known as Kennewick Man?

YES: James C. Chatters, from "The Recovery and First Analysis of an Early Holocene Human Skeleton from Kennewick, Washington," *American Antiquity* (vol. 65, no. 2, pp. 291–316, 2000)

NO: Michelle D. Hamilton, from "Colonizing America: Paleoamericans in the New World," in Heather Burke, Claire Smith, Dorothy Lippert, Joe Watkins, and Larry Zimmerman, eds., *Kennewick Man: Perspectives on the Ancient One* (Left Coast Press, 2008)

Learning Outcomes

After reading this issue, you should be able to:

- Understand the importance of finding an 8000–9000 year old skull along the Columbia River in Washington state.
- Discuss the significance James Chatters gave to this skull's dissimilarity from modern Native American skulls.
- Outline the significance that Native Americans from all over the United States gave to Chatters's original claim that the Kennewick skull was Caucasoid-like.
- Understand the significance that Native Americans place on referring to the Kennewick skull as Paleoamerican rather than Paleoindian.
- Discuss how difficult it is to explain the Kennewick skull's apparent difference from modern Native American skulls and why some Indian groups might be angered by some of these interpretations.

ISSUE SUMMARY

YES: In 1997, biological anthropologist and archaeologist James Chatters set off a firestorm when he described one of the earliest skeletons found in North America as "Caucasoid-like," based on a very preliminary analysis of what has come to be known as Kennewick Man. Here, he provides a more thorough analysis and a much more cautious analysis of this same skeleton, finding that these remains are not similar to any modern Native American skeletons. He concludes that the 8000+ year old Kennewick skeleton, together with several other early skeletons, indicates that settlement of North America was not by a single Asian population, but a much more complex pattern of in-migration from multiple populations than most archaeologists and biological anthropologists have assumed.

NO: Forensic anthropologist Michelle Hamilton challenges Chatters's original description of the Kennewick skull as "Caucasoid." She argues that Chatters and others have subsequently backed away from this description in favor of a new model they have called the "Paleoamerican Paradigm." She contends that this new paradigm implies that the ancestors of modern Native Americans are not the first human settlers on the continent, much as in Chatters's original assessment. After considering the analysis of the Kennewick skull and Native American reactions to the entire controversy, she concludes that the strident approach by Chatters and his colleagues has increased tensions between archaeologists and Indians like no other event in the past 20 years.

In 1996, biological anthropologist James Chatters was called in to consult on a skeleton found along the banks of the Columbia River in Kennewick, Washington. After determining that the bones were not recent and therefore not evidence of some modern crime, he concluded that the skeleton was quite old and perhaps from the early Holocene (the early part of the modern geological era that followed the end of the last great ice age, roughly beginning about 10,000–12,000 years ago). He published a brief report ("Encounter with an Ancestor") in the *Anthropology Newsletter* claiming that this early skull bore more resemblance to a Caucasoid skull than to contemporary Native American's skull.

These claims set off a firestorm of reactions from anthropologists and Indians alike. Although there have always been a few anthropologists insisting that at least some early Americans may have come from Europe as well as Asia, this assessment seemed to demonstrate that they were correct, and that Paleoindians may not have been the first settlers of North America. Most other anthropologists challenged whether there was enough evidence to identify the cultural background of this skull in the first place. There was after all only a single artifact associated with the skeleton, a projectile point—probably from a spear—that had killed the man. Whether this spear was wielded by friend or foe, by people biologically similar to him or not, remained an open and at this point in time an unanswerable question.

Native Americans were especially outraged by what seemed to them a hasty cultural attribution. For them white Americans had taken their lands and many of their cultural artifacts, forcing Indians to abandon their languages and traditional cultures. The one thing Indians had for certain was the fact that they were the first settlers to North America, and now Chatters wanted to take that away from Indians as well!

We should note that many Indians have wanted to rebury all human remains that were associated with Native American sites, but never before has there been such a powerful drive to take custody and rebury a skeleton as the Kennewick skeleton. Since the skeleton was found by U.S. Army Corps of Engineers, the Corps had some rights over the remains, and when local Umatilla Indians complained the Corps of Engineers halted any ongoing analysis of the bones. The Umatilla claimed the bones because they were the local Native American tribe that traditionally held rights to the site where the skeleton was found. If a skeleton was only 2000 years old, they would under normal circumstances be able to claim the remains under the Native American Graves Protection and Repatriation Act of 1990.

It is not fully clear why the Umatilla chose to seek these remains, and they clearly could not demonstrate any direct relationship to this long deceased individual. But they were the local Indians and would be the most likely group to press a claim. What was striking was the insistence they had for an early reburial, and they were happy to stop the analysis before it had gotten fully under way. Some archaeologists suspected that they wanted to rebury the remains quickly because they did not want any final report that would establish Caucasians not Indians as the earliest inhabitants of any part of their territory.

As suggested by Chatters in the YES article, when the Corps of Engineers halted research, a group of prominent biological anthropologists sued the Corps seeking an injunction against the Corps so that a full and complete analysis could be performed. In the end the scientists won the suit and the Department of the Interior arranged for the skeleton to be studied by appropriate scholars. Other anthropologists were called in to determine if there was any way to link this deceased individual with any local tribe on cultural and linguistic grounds. All of these studies have been published online on the U.S. Park Service Web site along with detailed documentation of the skeleton and its geomorphological setting.

In the first selection, Chatters documents what is known about the Kennewick skeleton, its original position, and its cultural affiliations. Published in the refereed archaeology journal *American Antiquity* three years after his first preliminary report in the *Anthropology Newsletter,* this account is fully cognizant of the firestorm his earlier publication had set in motion. It is far more cautious in the conclusions it reaches and some may be concerned that it does not ever come to a conclusion.

Chatters concludes that this skeleton is not similar to any known community either in the New World or in Europe or Asia. Indeed, one of his main findings is that this early skeleton, like the several others found in early sites older than 8000 years ago, do not resemble modern Native American skeletons. The key finding is that these early skeletons are as different from Native skeletons as they are from other modern populations. From this finding, he concludes that the peopling of North America probably came from more than one source community in the Old World, perhaps a number of waves of settlement from Asia and Europe.

In the second selection, forensic anthropologist Hamilton challenges the entire enterprise that Chatters and his various colleagues have been engaged in. She recognizes that Chatters's earliest report was too hasty and incomplete and sees this report and several others made by R. Bonnichsen, R. L. Jantz, D. W. Owsley, and a few other scholars as part of an agenda to establish a new model of North American settlement. She refers to this new model as the "Paleoamerican Paradigm." This new paradigm, just like Chatters's earlier claim that the Kennewick skull was "Caucasoid-like," was an attempt to claim that modern Native Americans were not the earliest human settlers on the continent, even though Native Americans were unambiguously in possession of this continent when European settlers first arrived in the fifteenth, sixteenth, and seventeenth centuries.

After considering the various analyses of the Kennewick skull and Native American reactions to the entire controversy, Hamilton concludes that the strident approach that Chatters and his colleagues have pursued has increased tensions between archaeologists and Indians like no other event in the past 20 years. Her essay also provides some follow up on the court case brought by the biological anthropologists.

When reading these two selections, students should consider the possible biases that each author has brought to this extremely delicate case study. But beyond the tensions between archaeologists and Native Americans, the Kennewick skeleton and the dozen or so early sets of remains found in scattered North American sites do present a surprising set of facts. They do not show close affinities with modern Indian biology from the last thousand years. This set of facts does require some explanation. How come these early skulls are not more obviously linked to modern Indians, even if they are not much closer to Asian and European populations? Do skeletons like Kennewick Man indicate a complex network of early settlement from many different sources? Or do they suggest more biological change over the past 8000–9000 years in North America than we have expected? Alternatively, was there more biological variation among the early settlers of this continent than we typically see in human populations today? In short, if Hamilton's challenge to the Paleoamerican Paradigm is to be taken seriously, we must consider all the possible explanations for the scanty facts currently available to us.

YES ↵ James C. Chatters

The Recovery and First Analysis of an Early Holocene Human Skeleton from Kennewick, Washington

The peopling of the Americas is the most prominent and contentious archaeological issue in the Western Hemisphere. A large and rapidly growing body of literature addresses where the immigrants came from, how they made the trip, when they arrived, what technologies they possessed, and who they were. Research into the "who" question has largely been focused on the genetic traits and languages of modern peoples in an attempt to reconstruct history from its end point. Actual physical remains have largely been ignored, partly because they are so rare and partly because of a prevailing view that early skeletal material was indistinguishable from later Amerindians. Within the past decade, however, study after study of Paleoamerican skeletal material is showing not only that early people are physically distinct from their modern counterparts, but also that the earliest remains are unexpectedly diverse.

Unfortunately, most of these studies remain limited by the tiny sample of ancient skeletal material. Whereas there are tens of thousands of North American skeletons dating to the past 2,000–3,000 years, no more than 37 individuals predate 8000 B.P. Accepting the earliest arrival at sometime before 14,000 years ago and calibrating 8000 B.P. to ca. 9000 years, this is an average of 8 individuals per thousand years. The number of complete skeletons and fully measurable crania thus far discovered is no more than 10. The opportunity to add one more—to increase the number by 10 percent—arose and nearly disappeared with a recent discovery in the eastern Washington town of Kennewick.

In July 1996, the nearly complete, well-preserved skeleton of what later proved to be an Early-Holocene Paleoamerican was discovered by spectators during a hydroplane race. The coroner of Benton County, Washington, in whose jurisdiction the bones were found, called on me to conduct a forensic investigation. The remains appeared to resemble modern western Eurasians more than recent Amerinds and were associated with debris from a late nineteenth-to early twentieth-century homestead. However, a stone projectile point was embedded in the pelvis, putting the individual's affiliation in doubt. A radiocarbon date was ordered on bone from the skeleton to solve the conundrum and established the Early-Holocene age. Soon thereafter, all studies were ordered to a halt by the U.S. Army Corps of Engineers (COE), from whose land the skeleton had eroded. Within two weeks the COE announced its intent

From *American Antiquity,* April 2000, excerpts from pp. 291–312. Copyright © 2000 by Society for American Archaeology. Reprinted by permission.

to repatriate the remains to five local tribes, but the action was halted when Robson Bonnichsen, C. Loring Brace, George Gill, C. Vance Haynes Jr., Richard Jantz, Douglas Owsley, Dennis Stanford, and D. Gentry Steele filed suit. At this writing, the case remains unresolved.

This paper describes the recovery, treatment, and initial analysis of the remains now popularly known as Kennewick Man.

The Site

Human bones were discovered at the base of a 2-m-high cutbank on the shore of a 6.4-km-long public area known as Columbia Park. The remains were disarticulated and scattered, clearly having eroded from a collapsed portion of the cut bank, and were distributed along more than 30 m of beach. Bones lay in the soft, secondary mud of the reservoir, often seeming to float at the water-mud contact. All larger fragments, including the skull, longbones, scapulae, os coxae, complete vertebrae, and larger rib and foot bones, occurred in the 12-m area between two prominent grass tussocks. Smaller bone fragments also were concentrated in this area, but scattered westward (upstream) for another

Figure 1

Topographic Map Showing the Locality Where the Kennewick Skeleton was Found.

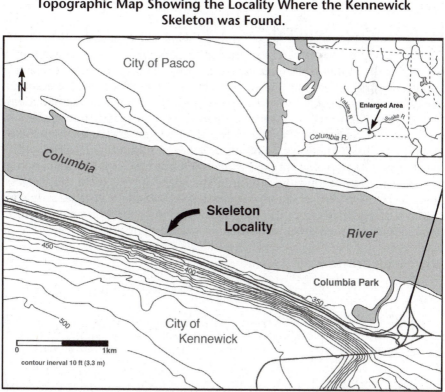

20 m. An inspection of the cut bank below which the skull had rested was unrevealing; no in situ bones or evidence of a grave pit could be found, nor was any found during the many later inspections.

The site is located on the . . . south bank of the Columbia River 531 km upstream from the Pacific Ocean. At an elevation of 104 m, it lies near the center of a broad lowland known as the Columbia Basin. The climate is maritime influenced, but the rain shadow effect of the Cascade Range, to the west, creates semiarid conditions that support a shrub-steppe ecosystem. Three great rivers meet within a short distance of the site. The Yakima enters the Columbia 5.5 km upstream and the Snake River joins it 10.3 km downstream. All three are important salmon streams.

The confluence of major rivers, with their water and fish, made the area an important aboriginal center, at least in later times, and archeological sites are plentiful. The Tri-Cities Archaeological District, which encompasses the area around the Yakima River mouth, contains 20 documented sites, including 6 villages and 5 cemeteries of the Late Period and an assortment of campsites of undetermined age. Excavations at one site, opposite the mouth of the Yakima River, revealed deposits dating to the later middle Holocene, but no earlier components have yet been identified. . . . Thus far, however, no habitation site coeval with the Kennewick skeleton has been identified in the vicinity.

Geoarchaeology

Local Geomorphology

During the late Wisconsinan Glaciation, the Columbia Basin was swept by a series of outburst floods from glacial lakes Missoula and Columbia, which terminated around 11,250 B.P. The Missoula events, which were the larger floods, ceased by 12,500–13,000 B.P., while smaller outbursts from Lake Columbia continued. With the ablation of the Okanogan lobe of the Cordilleran glaciation, the Columbia River, which had been the primary meltwater drain, found itself under-fit for its channel. By 10,000 B.P., it began filling this channel with a fine-textured flood-plain that can be identified from the U.S.-Canadian border downstream well beyond the mouth of the Snake River, . . . In most places, fluvial deposition on this landform ceased after 8000 B.P. . . . frequently contains a stratum of ash from the 6850 B.P. eruption of Mt. Mazama, capp[ing] the floodplain as the river underwent a downcutting phase. . . .

Site Stratigraphy

. . . Stratigraphy of the Kennewick Man Site is similar to that of other Early Holocene floodplain deposits. . . .

COE geologists obtained radiocarbon dates on bulk carbon from four fluvial strata below the modern beach level and from two samples of freshwater mussel shell from Unit I. . . . With increasing depth, these dates are 9010 ± 50, 12,460 ± 50, 15,330 ± 60, and 14,560 ± 50 B.P. The lowest three dates predate the Glacier Peak ashfall and are clearly too old, which also casts doubt on the uppermost date, despite its general consistency with a position between the

Mazama and Glacier Peak ashes. Shell dates from Unit I were 6230 ± 60 and 6090 ± 80 B.P. (Beta 113997), which is consistent with their stratigraphic position [above the others]. . . .

Interment or Natural Deposition

In the absence of a burial pit and associated grave goods, we do not know whether the skeleton was intentionally buried or incorporated in a fluvial deposit. However, the comparison of sediment from the bones with *in situ* strata provides some clues. If the depositional process was intentional burial in a stratified sedimentary setting, then we would expect the soil from the bone surfaces to represent a mix of strata; no clear match would be expected to a single stratum. If fluvial deposition was the process, then we *would* expect such a match. The result is again somewhat ambiguous, but the data do seem to lean toward the single-stratum, fluvial deposition hypothesis. Countering this interpretation, however, are two seemingly irreconcilable facts. First, the skeleton is unusually well preserved. Second, textural data indicate that the fluvial strata are typically less than 20 cm thick. It would seem that shallow deposits and good preservation are unlikely partners. However, we know neither how much time elapsed between deposition events nor, because of the secondary context, the topography of the surface onto which the skeleton might have been laid. Rapid deposition and/or deposition in a sediment trap of any kind, whether a depression, bush, or mass of debris, could have led to burial deep enough for good preservation. The issue remains unresolved.

Artifacts

The Projectile Point

The only cultural object found in direct association with the Kennewick skeleton is the fragmentary projectile point embedded in his pelvis. The surfaces of the point were visible through two bone windows, one in either surface of the ilium. The edges were largely, but not entirely, obscured by bone. Segments of edge could be seen along the upper rim of the posterior window and along a portion of the lower rim of the anterior window, at the base of the point. Because it was so extensively obscured, the point's shape, cross-section, and measurements could only be determined radiographically. Multiple X-ray "slices" were taken with a Picker® CT scan parallel and perpendicular to the plane of the blade at 1-mm intervals for a plan view and cross-section. Because object edges are somewhat blurred in the CT scans, measurements based on the radiographs must be understood to be approximate to within 1 mm.

The projectile point is leaf-shaped and made from a siliceous gray stone that appears to be of igneous origin, probably andesite or dacite. It has a narrow, slightly convex, apparently edge-ground basal margin, ca 10 mm wide, and expands to a maximum width of 18 mm near the broken blade edge. The cross-section is plano-convex in some areas to biconvex in others, with a maximum thickness of 6 mm. The entire visible edge of the blade is serrated, beginning within a few millimeters of the basal margin. Additional serrations are visible in some CT scan views, indicating the blade edge was completely serrated. The distal end of the blade is impact fractured into an irregular, chisel-like edge. That is, it is sheared-off obliquely to the (cross-section) but perpendicular to the long axis of the blade.

In summary, this is a fragment of a long, broad, thin, leaf-shaped point with a distally expanding blade, sharp, serrated edges and a slightly convex base. When complete, it would have been at least 70 mm long. This point fits the definition of a Cascade Point, a willow-leaf type often with serrated edges and a plano-convex cross-section. It is the hallmark of the local Cascade Phase, which dates between 5000 and 8000 BP., although some similar forms persist into the Historic period in some parts of the Northwest. Serrated variants of the type dominate components of the Cascade Phase that predate the Mazama ashfall. If we go by the reservoir-corrected age of the skeleton, the radiocarbon date and projectile point style together place the Kennewick skeleton at the very beginning of the Cascade Phase.

The impact fracture and depth of penetration of the point indicate that it was attached to a high velocity weapon. In arrow wounds there is a tendency for the tip of the point to be shattered on impact with bone and apparently remain in soft tissue. The blade, driven by the weight of the shaft, then penetrates bone. Since the bow and arrow were not introduced to the Columbia Plateau until 2400 B.P. at the earliest this point was almost certainly the tip of an atlatl-propelled dart.

Chronology

Age of the skeleton can be established relatively by stratigraphy and artifact chronology, and absolutely by the radiocarbon date on the bone itself. All evidence is consistent with an early Holocene age.

Relative Age

Geologic and cultural dates overlap. The remains came from the uppermost meter of the Early-Holocene alluvium, deposition of which ceased well before deposition of the eolian sediment of Unit I. As noted above, this alluvium ordinarily dates between 10,000 and 8,000 B.P. Locally, deposition certainly commenced after 11,200 B.P. and ceased well before the 6850 B.P. age of the Mazama tephra. The projectile point is of the Cascade style, which begins at ca 8000 B.P.; its serrations indicate a pre-6850 B.P. date. Thus, the skeleton comes from the period of overlap between these chronologies, or close to 8000 B.P.

Radiocarbon Age

A single radiocarbon date on bone collagen has been obtained for the Kennewick skeleton. As part of the Coroner's initial investigation, the fifth metacarpal of the left hand was submitted to the University of California, Riverside for ^{14}C dating. This bone was chosen because it had come from inside the neurocranium, where it presumably had been moved by rodents, and lacked the mineral deposits found on all other bone fragments. Free of precipitates, it apparently had been shielded from percolating water, and was, therefore, the most likely element to retain intact collagen and lack contaminants. Graphite prepared from total amino acids was submitted to Lawrence Livermore National Laboratory and produced an isotopically-corrected date of 8410 ± 60 B.P. . . . If we assume, that the carbon isotope signature results from the intake of marine protein and not C4 plants (an assumption we would need nitrogen isotope information to confirm), a value of −14.9 per mil indicates approximately 70 percent of the man's protein came from marine fish, in this case probably salmon or steelhead (*Oncorhynchus* spp.). If we further assume that the marine reservoir effect has remained constant during the Holocene, then the correction corresponding to this dietary fraction is 530 ± 150 years. The actual radiocarbon age would thus be 7880 ± 160 years B.P., which calibrates to 8340 to 9200 cal. years ago. Until evidence is obtained confirming either of the assumptions, however, it would be prudent to continue to cite the uncorrected age, with caveats.

The Skeleton

Recovery and Treatment

Remains were collected by me and various helpers on ten occasions between July 28 and August 29, operating under an Archaeological Resources Protection Act permit issued by the COE. . . .

Bones were taken to the Applied Paleoscience laboratory, where saturated fragments were first laid out to drain. . . .

General Description

The skeleton was recovered in approximately 350 fragments, representing at least 143 elements. Included originally were the nearly-complete cranium and mandible, all but two teeth (third molars) all complete cervical vertebrae,

Figure 2

The Skeleton of "Kennewick Man" in Approximate Anatomical Position. Small Fragments of Ribs, or Coxae, and Other Larger Trabecular Bones Are Not Shown.

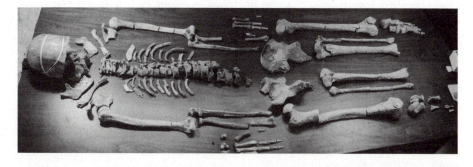

Figure 3

The Kennewick Skull Viewed in Right Profile.

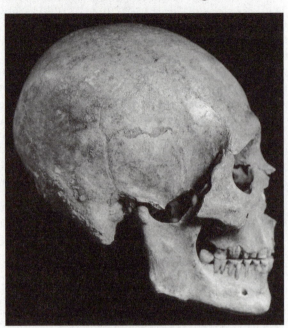

all thoracic and lumbar vertebrae (complete or fragmentary), parts of the sacrum, fragments of the manubrium, numerous fragments of 22 ribs, portions of both scapulae, complete humeri, complete right and nearly-complete left radii and ulnae, the majority of both os coxae, complete femora, tibiae, and fibulae, and parts of all hands and feet. All major bones were present in multiple fragments. . . .

The face is long, especially when the mandible is included, and relatively narrow. Prominent supercilliary arches and unusually thin supraorbital margins border high, rounded, horizontally-oriented orbits. . . . Canine roots are long and posteriorly curving, resulting in prominent ridges and deep canine fossae. The most striking feature of the face is the broad, projecting nose, which dominates the mid-face. . . .

The postcranial skeleton is that of a tall (for an early hunter-gatherer), moderately muscled individual. The legs are long, with relatively unbowed femora exhibiting low torsion and a high platymeric index (85 right, 80 left). A strong asymmetry is evident in the humeri, which have robusticity indices of 20.6 for the right and 18.5 for the left. Small head diameters indicate that both humeri are rather gracile for the man's size and sex. Distal limb segments are long in proportion to the proximal in both upper and lower extremities, with a radiohumeral index of 76 and a crural (tibia/fibula) index of 86. . . .

Sex

This individual was male, as indicated by the morphology of the os coxae and skull, metrics of the femur and humerus, and general robusticity of the skeleton. In the os coxae, the greater sciatic notch is narrow. The bodies of the pubic bones are well preserved, exhibiting no ventral arc, but the ischiopubic rami are not sufficiently intact for the subpubic outline or the ischiopubic ridge to be observed. Observable features are characteristically male. The skull is characterized by moderate nuchal development, a large, though narrow, mastoid process, a prominent supra-orbital ridge, and square (if narrow) chin. The supraorbital margin is unusually sharp for a male, however and there is a shallow, narrow preauricular sulcus in the ischium. Both of these traits are more common in females, but overall morphology is strongly male.

. . . Although we lack a representative sample of the population from which this skeleton came, the overall size and observed degree of robusticity would be interpreted as male in all modern populations.

Age

The complete union of all epiphyses, including the basilar suture, and the eruption and occlusion of all teeth clearly establish this male as a mature adult. Beyond that, the evidence is somewhat ambiguous, but death probably occurred between 35 and 45 years of age. Data were obtainable from the pubic symphysis, auricular surface, sternal end of the fourth (or fifth) rib, and the degree of ectocranial suture closure. Dental wear, x-ray evidence for incipient osteoporosis, osteoarthritis, and ligament ossification were used as secondary indicators.

Biological Affiliation

The Kennewick skeleton differs markedly from modern American Indians, particularly those of the North-western U.S. Anthroposcopy, craniofacial morphometrics, and discrete dental traits were used to determine to which modern geographic group he was most similar. A fourth method, extraction of ancient mitochondrial DNA was begun by Frederika Kaestle but has not been completed.

When this out-of-context, disarticulated skeleton was discovered, I worked from the assumption one must always use in a forensic situation: that the remains were of recent origin and could therefore be identified to one of the common modern populations in eastern Washington. I proceeded to do this. . . . Even though human populations show a wide range of variability in size and shape, and overlap in their ranges of variability both metrically and in the expression of discrete traits, they do exhibit central tendencies that are useful for forensic identification. These facts in mind, I found that the Kennewick remains differed from late prehistoric American Indians of the Pacific Northwest in the direction of the recent European immigrants. Northwest native peoples tend from my observations to be brachycranic to mesocranic, with very broad, flaring, anteriorly-placed zygomatics, and slight prognath-ism. Orbits of the males are markedly rectangular and laterally drooping. Their palates are short, broad, and elliptical, with third molars set medialy relative to the seconds. Mandibles are robust, with near-90° gonial angles and broad, short rami. Chins are broad but blunt and lack bilaterality. Culturally deter-mined characteristics are marked occipital or lambdoidal flattening from cra-dle board use and rapid dental attrition. With his dolicocrany, projecting face, round, horizontally oriented orbits, distinct, diverging plate, bilateral chin, and gracile mandible with its reclining, narrow ramus, the Kennewick skeleton differed in almost every respect from this pattern. He also lacked cradle board-ing and had unusually light dental wear for his age. While any one Amerind skull might exhibit one or more of these characteristics, I have yet to see one that exhibits all or even most of them.

Other characteristics that can be used to distinguish among modern regional populations have been femoral shape and body dimensions. Femoral shafts of late prehistoric Native peoples tend to be distinctly curved in the anterioposterior axis, with high torsion and platymeria. The people also are short statured. For example, mean stature of males from Prince Rupert Harbor was only 162.8 ± 3.8 cm and a group of 22 Late Archaic males from the Dalles region of the Columbia was estimated at only 163.3 ± 1.8 cm. The Kennewick skeleton is significantly taller, with platymeria, and low femoral curvature and torsion. While these features distinguish him from local Amerind populations, the extent to which they are under genetic influence is poorly known. Cer-tainly, we know that body size is strongly influenced by health and nutrition and that femoral shape responds to mechanical stresses, both of which are to some degree under cultural control.

Cranial characteristics, femoral morphology and stature together led me, in the forensic venue, to suggest an affiliation with modern Euroameri-cans. Once the skeleton's age was known, however, I referred to the remains as "Caucasoid-like." I did not state, nor did I intend to imply, once the skeleton's age became known, that he was a member of some European group.

Forensic trait lists are intended to facilitate identification and have been developed only to distinguish among the most numerous or fre-quently encountered *modern* groups: east Asians, Amerinds, west Africans (African Americans), and western Eurasians. The overlap that develops when we move between these most populous demes or into the past makes affiliation of individuals by discrete traits problematic at best; at some point in the past we are approaching a common ancestral morphology. Ideally, if we are hoping to identify places and populations of post-diaspora origin, we should compare ancient people with their contemporaries and predecessors in various parts of the world, not with their successors. How-ever, given the dearth of skeletons predating the Kennewick specimen in eastern Asia, (the probable most recent place of geographic origin for his ancestors) this is not currently possible except in the most limited way. It is possible, however, to compare the specimen with modern groups in search of the population with the closest statistical similarity and thus a possible common ancestry.

This can be done using the craniofacial morphometry. . . . Applying this approach, Chatters et al. used principal components analysis to compare craniometrics of the Kennewick skull cast with the Ainu and the 18 modern populations that Howells believes comprise most of the metric variability of modern *Homo sapiens*. A graphic comparison of the first two components, which included size, placed him nearest the Pacific Islanders and Ainu— Jomon-Pacific cluster. When size was factored out, he was an extreme outlier, with no close relationship to any modern population. Powell and Rose reached the same conclusion using a wider array of techniques and a variety of human databases. These results are consistent with previous analyses, which find that the closest craniofacial morphometric affinity of northern Paleoamericans is generally to the Pacific Islanders and South Asians, and that when size is factored out, they are often far removed from modern peoples. In general appearance, the Kennewick skull does somewhat resemble Polynesians, particularly Easter Islanders, and Jomon/Ainu.

Dental discrete traits echo this Jomon-Pacific affinity. Turner has identified two Asian dental patterns, the Sinodont, which characterizes modern north Asians and Amerinds, and the Sundadont, which he believes to be an earlier pattern retained in south Asian and Pacific Island groups. Differences are seen in root numbers and crown characteristics of molariform teeth, and winging and shoveling of incisors. The Sinodont pattern includes high frequencies of shoveled and double-shoveled incisors; winged upper central incisors; three-rooted lower first molars; single-rooted upper first premolars and lower second molars; reduced, pegged, or congenitally absent third molars; single lingual cusps on lower first premolars; and five-cusped lower first and second molars. Sundadonts tend to exhibit weak shoveling, two-rooted upper first premolars and lower first and second molars, two lingual cusps on the lower first premolar, and six cusps on the lower first molar and four on the lower second, and lack incisor winging. Cusp patterns and shoveling cannot be observed on the Kennewick teeth, but the remaining characteristics are those common to the Sundadont pattern. Thus, craniofacial and dental evidence converge to suggest an affinity—a common origin—with some modern coastal and maritime peoples of east Asia and the Pacific.

Stature and Body Mass

Stature is estimated from the length of the femur, as recommended by Waldron and body mass from the diameter of the femoral head. Stature estimation is dependent at the outset on the population from which an individual is derived, leaving a dilemma in this case. This skeleton is old enough to predate the modern populations on which stature formulae are based, and his physical characteristics distinguish him from Mongoloids in general and Amerinds specifically. Thus I had the dilemma of deciding which formula or formulae to use. . . . The Kennewick skeleton's crural index of 85.1 places him closest to African Americans, Arizona Amerinds, Melanesians, Egyptians, and Pygmies. Stature equations are available for African Americans and Mesoamericans, who are geographically close to Arizona Amerinds. Because of proximity and the great genetic distances between Africans and all other world populations the appropriate equations are Mesoamerican. Averaging estimates . . . gives a stature of 173.1 ± 3.4 cm.

I calculated body mass from the diameter of the femoral head . . . which gave an estimate of about 70–75 kg. The ratio of stature to mass indicates a man of moderate robusticity.

General Health and Nutrition

Strong, intact teeth, thick cortical bone in the limbs, and large size indicate an individual who was generally well fed, perhaps in part due to the anadro-mous fish diet suggested by the carbon isotope ratio of −14.9 per mil. . . .

Comparison With Other Paleoamericans

The Kennewick skeleton differs significantly from modern Amerinds, but he shares many features with other Paleoamerican males, when they are treated as a single population. Six males with radiocarbon dates older than 8000 B.P. are complete enough for comparison in one or more respects with the Kennewick skeleton. These are the specimens from Brown's Valley, Minnesota, Horn Shelter, Texas, Hourglass Cave, Colorado, Spirit Cave and Wizard Beach, Nevada, and Gore Creek, British Columbia. . . . Metric data, unless otherwise cited, have been collected by me from the original bones (Wizard Beach, Horn Shelter), a stereolithograph based on original radiometric data (Spirit Cave), or cited literature. Data are arranged longitudinally from east (Brown's Valley) to west (Gore Creek). Cranial, upper facial, nasal, orbital, crural, femoral and humeral robusticity, and platymeric and platycnemic indices are standard ratios. . . . Because several skulls lacked the cranial base, I could not compute standard height indices for all skulls. . . . Left elements are used for postcranial indices. Stature is computed in the manner described for the Kennewick skeleton because the crural indices are comparable. Ages are as published.

As a group the Paleoamericans tend to have high, dolicocranic skulls, medium to broad faces, and narrow to medium noses. Their faces are placed well forward on the cranium. . . . In the low, forward faces and high crural indices, they appear to retain vestiges of a tropical origin, even long past the original *Homo sapiens* emergence from Africa. Had they come from a fully arctic-adapted parent population, we would expect them to exhibit the longer, straighter face and shorter distal limbs that are common to high latitude populations.

The Kennewick skeleton compares favorably with this group, being significantly different from the other males in only two respects: stature and facial forwardness. He is taller and has an even more anteriorly placed face. His orbital, upper face, and cranial height indices, and his femoral robusticity are outside the group range, but not significantly so. Even in his age at death he is normal. Most Paleoamerican males died between the ages of 32 and 45; only three may have been younger at their deaths.

One interesting characteristic of the Kennewick skeleton is the difference between his humeral and femoral robusticities, when compared with the other males. Although he is the most robust in the femur, he is the second least robust in the left humerus. This may be due to his elbow injury, but even in the right arm he is no more robust than the Horn Shelter male, who has much lower femoral robusticity. Apparently, he had big legs but a rather slight upper body in comparison with his contemporaries.

Kennewick also is comparable to other Paleoamericans in his dissimilarity to modern Amerinds. There is a tendency for early North Americans to resemble South Asians and Pacific Islanders more closely than other modern peoples, but as with Kennewick Man, most individuals are dissimilar to any modern population. Exceptions are the Buhl woman, which has been shown through morphometric analysis to have cranial morphometry typical of an Ainu, and the Wizards Beach male, who is similar to modern Amerinds but also to Europeans and Polynesians. [These] suggest that there may have been multiple, physically distinct populations in Early-Holocene North America—groups too disparate to be derived from a single, recently-arrived parent population. Neves and his co-workers have found further that the earliest South Americans differ from the North Americans and most closely resemble ancient and modern peoples of Africa and Australo-Melanesia.

These observations are hinting that the early human history of the Western Hemisphere south of Alaska may be more complex than the single Amerind migration model can accommodate. Recent work in linguistics, molecular genetics, and archaeology are also revealing too much differentiation for a single terminal Pleistocene arrival. The technologies of Clovis and Monte Verde, for example, are much too disparate for either to be derived from the other or to have recently shared a common parent. Realization that the radiocarbon record has temporally compressed the evidence alleviates some of the pressure, but not all. If the early differentiation is to be reconciled with a terminal Pleistocene arrival, little earlier than 14,000 years ago, then it is mandatory that we acknowledge the possibility of multiple migrations by culturally and physically distinct peoples, some of whom have not persisted to the present day in recognizable form. The fact that early peoples do not resemble modern North Asians, but that many modern North American Indians do, further raises the possibility that post-Pleistocene gene flow and/or migration contributed significantly to the human biology of the Americas.

Summary

The Kennewick skeleton was the remains of a moderately-robust middle aged man who stood approximately 173.1 ± 3.6 cm tall and weighed approximately 70–75 kg. Geochronology, a projectile point of early Cascade style in his hip, and a radiocarbon date of 8410 ± 60 B.P. place his time firmly in the latter part of the Early Holocene. Although apparently well nourished and healthy in his youth, he suffered repeatedly from serious injuries, including a debilitating fracture of the left elbow, a massive thoracic trauma that caused a chronic flail chest, a spear wound in the right ilium that developed a chronic infection, and an acute infection in the left side of his head. The manner of his death cannot be pinpointed, but acute and chronic bone infections point to septicemia, and a possible, final, shoulder dislocating injury is a strong candidate. The man's dental and craniofacial characteristics show an affinity with Ainu and Pacific Island peoples, but make him stand out from modern American Indians, especially those who occupied Northwestern North America in later prehistory. He does, however, compare favorably with other Paleoamerican males, although he is significantly taller and has a more projecting face. The Kennewick man has offered a unique window into America's past, and with thorough, thoughtful, respectful, replicated study, will add significantly to our understanding of the origins, lives and deaths of America's earliest inhabitants.

Colonizing America: Paleoamericans in the New World

The protracted legal saga and subsequent 2004 court decision to permit analysis of the Kennewick skeleton has ongoing implications that highlight the continuing conflict between tribal peoples and anthropologists. For the scientific community, Kennewick Man represented the opportunity to analyze one of the oldest skeletons found on the North American continent. For American Indians, the battle symbolized a test of their legal right to control their own cultural and biological patrimony, including their ancestral dead. This disparity in perspective reveals why future access to ancient American skeletons will likely continue to be determined by federal courts, and not by cooperative agreements between tribal peoples and anthropologists.

The Paleoamerican Paradigm

Some specialists are now considering the possibility that different colonizing groups from Asia and possibly Europe are required to account for the biological, cultural, and linguistic diversity found [in the New World]. Many specialists believe that the future of First Americans research must focus on exploring the validity of this new paradigm.

Kennewick Man and other ancient remains are of importance to the scientific community because they lend insight toward understanding the earliest peopling of the Americas. Based on the physical appearance of Kennewick Man and other ancient American skeletal remains, some biological anthropologists have proposed a new scenario for the migration of humans into North America that removes American Indians as the New World's first inhabitants and replaces them with an older, unspecified population. They argue that the earliest humans on the North American continent share no biological continuity with modern American Indians and demonstrate phenotypic traits more similar to non-specific European, Indo-European, or Eurasian groups. Based on cranial measurements of approximately thirteen ancient American human remains dated older than 7,000 years (including Kennewick, Spirit Cave, Browns Valley, Pelican Rapids, Lime Creek, and Wizards Beach), proponents of this new theory argue that the earliest humans to inhabit the continent were not ancestral to American Indians and that there is no direct ancestor-descendant relationship. Because this theory is imprecisely defined in both the academic and public arenas, in this chapter it will hereafter be referred to it as the "Paleoamerican Paradigm."

The initial designation of Kennewick Man as "Caucasian" and the speculation regarding his possible European origin has had unfortunate consequences. The anthropologist who first examined the remains initially believed the skeleton was of an historic individual, based on the "presence of Caucasoid traits, [and] lack of definitive Native-American characteristics." This pronouncement, combined with a subsequent facial reconstruction that looked uncannily like *Star Trek*'s Patrick Stewart, immediately caught the imagination of the public, where the message ultimately received was that "Whites" were the first people to settle the Americas. Although anthropologists did not specifically claim that Kennewick Man was Caucasian, his ancestry is posited as something other than American Indian, usually in the direction of a putative European population. A sampling of speculation on the origins of the first Americans shows the avoidance of the term "Caucasian," but still arguing for a non–American Indian origin:

> It is absurd to argue about whether . . . Kennewick Man is Caucasian. The answer to that question is not informative. But if we can ascertain that Kennewick is more similar to contemporary European populations than to any others, that tells us something. (Richard Jantz)
>
> Initial studies have shown that the craniometric pattern departs from contemporary American Indians, often in the direction of European[s]. (Jantz and Owsley)
>
> The scientists have never said, "Kennewick Man is not Native American." He could be. Or he might not be. (Douglas Owsley)
>
> [I]n terms of its closest classification, [Spirit Cave] does have a "European" or "Archaic Caucasoid" look. (Preston)

Other anthropologists offered contrasting viewpoints on the practice or implication of characterizing Kennewick Man as European or Caucasian:

> I really do object to saying there is such a thing as a Caucasoid trait. . . . You can find changes in cranial size just within certain groups that lived in the same area. [In using the term Caucasoid to describe Kennewick Man] the hands of the anthropological clock had just been put back 100 years. Kennewick Man has become a textbook example of why race science is bad science. (Alan R. Goodman)
>
> The use of the term Caucasoid really is a red flag, suggesting that whites were here earlier and Indians were here later, and there's absolutely no reason to think that. (Donald K. Grayson)
>
> I don't think this will change our view of Native American ancestry. The fact that Kennewick Man doesn't look to some like a Native American . . . doesn't mean anything" (David J. Meltzer).

This transformation in thinking about the origins of founding American populations is apparent in recent academic literature, where the term "Paleoindian" is rapidly being replaced by "Paleoamerican." Although the term "Paleoamerican" is not new, having been used interchangeably with Paleoindian since the 1960s, what *is* new is the assertion that Paleoamerican now excludes American Indians. As Owsley and Jantz state: "[Early skulls] especially fall outside the range of American Indian populations and are so different that it may be more correct to refer to them as Paleoamerican rather than Paleoindian as many do."

Taken in a broader historical context, this new "geographical" naming shift has legal, cultural, and social consequences, as highlighted by Watkins:

> The change in terminology may have no impact on the study of early populations in North and South America, but the change certainly carries with it political implications since, by replacing "Indian" with "American," it illustrates the political aspects of naming. . . . If the naming of a geographic feature carries with it such power, imagine the power of being able to name the culture that used that geography.

The Craniometric Evidence

How did researchers arrive at the conclusion that Kennewick Man and other ancient American remains are not representative of ancestral American Indian populations? A series of cranial measurements were taken on the skulls and then statistical analyses performed to compare those measurements against those of eight historic American Indian groups (as well as twenty-six non–American Indian groups worldwide). Similarities in shape were found with the modern European samples but not with the modern American Indian samples, while three of the ancient skulls "provide evidence for the presence of an early population that bears no similarity to the morphometric pattern of recent American Indians." Researchers are in essence arguing that comparing the measurements of the ancient and modern skulls shows that the ancient skulls more closely resemble modern Europeans, inferring that the first people to arrive in the Americas were not related to American Indians but to a different unspecified population.

However, critics argue that what is reflected in the ancient American skeletal record is not indicative of colonization of the Americas by early European ancestors, but by the ancestors of American Indian populations who no longer resemble their descendant populations due to influences of chronology, evolution, environment, and adaptation. Some of the criticisms of the Paleoamerican Paradigm include the following five points.

1. Craniometric analyses are descriptive studies—there are no underlying models or theories to explain what is being observed. So, although such analyses are able to describe the ancient skulls as different from those of modern American Indians, they cannot provide

an explanatory mechanism to articulate why this is so. Without an underlying causal framework, the Paleoamerican Paradigm is not open to hypothesis testing or falsification. Because the model has no explanatory power, it is difficult to refute the following observation: "Even if the early people don't look like modern Indians, it's possible they are ancestral to today's Native Americans" (Joseph Powell).

2. A related critique is the utilization of craniometric methodology to make inferences about ancient and modern American populations. By the 18th century in America, craniometrics were used almost exclusively to promote a view of European superiority, especially as compared to American Indians. This soon paved the way for political legislation, such as enforced removal, and social agendas, such as Manifest Destiny, to play a large part in the destruction of formerly intact American Indian cultures. This is not to deny that craniometric and morphometric techniques are not capable of providing descriptive information, but their use as a typological seriating device to categorize human populations may carry underlying racial overtones. In 1935, Aleš Hrdlička warned anthropologists against an overreliance on cranial shapes to make inferences about the past:

> One of the greatest faults and impediments of anthropology has always been and is largely to this day, in spite of ever-growing evidence to the contrary, the notion of the permanence of skull types, and their changeability only through racial mixtures and replacements. It is time that this attitude be replaced by more modern and rational views on the subject, based on the steadily increasing knowledge of biological laws and processes. . . . (Hrdlička)

3. A significant but unknown component not satisfactorily addressed by the Paleoamerican Paradigm is the point at which American Indian cranial morphology over the last 10,000 or so years assumed its modern form, and what evolutionary processes and environmental constraints (at both the macro and micro levels) work to shape the human cranium over time. Researchers promoting the Paleoamerican Paradigm state that "when comparing early skulls with available modern populations, we note that most of them fall outside the normal range of recent population variation." This point is important because it is at the crux of the debate—comparing the shape of ancient human skulls to modern humans may be akin to comparing apples to oranges. Anthropologist David Hurst Thomas summarizes it this way:

> In North American Indian populations (and, indeed, human populations worldwide), there has been a distinct tendency for skulls to become more globular ("rounder") and less robust over the last 10,000 years. This being so, no experienced physical anthropologist should be surprised that the Kennewick skull has a longer, more robust face than recent Native Americans.

4. Another consideration not explained by the Paleoamerican Paradigm is the influence that pressures such as genetic drift, demographic growth, and sexual selection had on the cranial and skeletal morphology of the earliest Americans and to what degree these evolutionary forces changed the physical appearance of ancient Americans. Anthropologist Joseph Powell argues:

> There is a huge amount of variation among the first Americans. . . . Much of that is genetic, and it comes from the fact, I think, that these first Americans had very small colonizing populations, and they have a great degree of genetic variation due to genetic drift.

If left unaddressed, one of the underlying tenets of the Paleoamerican Paradigm must become that American Indians are an evolutionarily static group whose biology is fixed throughout time, and not subject to the same evolutionary processes as all other human groups.

5. Craniometric analysis by other researchers indicates that ancient New World remains have an overall skeletal morphology and pattern most similar to modern Southeast Asians and not Europeans. Even definitive Paleoindians (those known to be ancestral to certain American Indian groups) are unlike modern American Indian and European samples and show little or no evidence of a European component in craniofacial variation.

Kennewick Man in the Public Arena

The confusion over the racial attribution of the earliest Americans persists. The simplified message promulgated to the mainstream press—that Europeans were the first people on this continent—prompted public headlines in publications such as the *Washington Post* to proclaim: "Skeletons Suggest Caucasoid Early Americans," and the popular science magazine *Discover* to announce on its cover: "Europeans Invade America: 20,000 B.C." This theory has also found a very accepting audience among a segment of the population more than ready to embrace the underlying racial implications. Numerous white supremacist and nationalist groups point to research on Kennewick Man, Buhl Woman, Spirit Cave Man, Wizard's Beach, and others as proof of the inherent superiority and primacy of the white race. Many of their positions on the ancestry of Kennewick Man are similar to those promulgated in the mainstream press:

> The reasons for the American Indian sensitivity over the issue are obvious—proof that Whites—even if only in small numbers—walked the continent of North America before the Amerinds themselves would undermine the latter's claim to be the original "Native Americans." For the sake of political correctness, much valuable scientific data is being suppressed.

[Kennewick Man's] skull isn't an Indian skull at all, but is the kind of skull that white people have. . . . Suddenly, the Indians who have been claiming a moral high ground because "they were here first," have a rival. (H. Millard)

The question of the peopling of the Americas is acknowledged as a complex issue, but anthropologists must ensure that the meaning they convey is not simplistically reduced to "Europeans arrived in the Americas first," because in the eyes of the lay public and mainstream press this is the message received and currently accepted as fact. With this brief sketch of some of the complexities inherent in the conflict over the study of ancient American skeletal remains, I now turn to the perspectives of a tribal community to elucidate their positions on Kennewick Man, their ancestral dead, and their continuing conflict with anthropologists.

American Indian Perspectives

In partial response to the Paleoamerican Paradigm, and in an effort to avoid triggering another battle over ancient skeletons that may be discovered in the future, some tribal authorities have turned to legal remedies to avoid a repeat of the Kennewick Man outcome. Since 1990, federal cultural resource laws have changed the academic and scientific landscape of American bioarchaeology, and American Indian tribes are finding that a number of these laws are of great utility in their efforts to protect tribal resources, especially human remains. Two of the most powerful tools in their arsenal are the Native American Graves Protection and Repatriation Act (NAGPRA) and Section 106 of the National Historic Preservation Act. The ratification of NAGPRA was a defining (and restricting) event for the discipline of bioarchaeology, and the increasingly successful utilization of Section 106 by federally recognized sovereign tribes is resulting in further legal limitations on the collection of data from both American Indian skeletal remains and mortuary site settings.

I will examine the implications of the Kennewick Man court case for the relationship between anthropologists and American Indians by focusing on an example from the Eastern Band of Cherokee Indians, a federally recognized sovereign tribe based in North Carolina with an active Tribal Historic Preservation Office. As the former Section 106 Officer for the Eastern Band of Cherokee Indians, I have been able to learn first-hand about the tribe's perspectives in dealing with anthropologists, repatriation issues, and the Kennewick Man court judgment.

Like most North American Indian tribes, the Eastern Band of Cherokee Indians have a strong cultural ethos regarding mortuary behavior, with traditionally defined and clearly elucidated restrictions about the treatment of the dead. Cherokees oppose anthropological studies on American Indian skeletons; this opposition stems from a complicated avoidance proscription based on cultural theories of pollution and corruption as well as a deep conviction that it is degenerate activity to disturb the dead. These principles make up the

Cherokee philosophy regarding mortuary treatment and, in turn, influence their attitudes toward anthropological research. The Cherokee perception of corpses and their potential to influence the living are not necessarily representative of other tribal people's views, but a generalized American Indian sentiment can be distilled from the core of their belief—that the ancestral dead are not to be disturbed.

The Eastern Band's Response to the Kennewick Judgment

NAGPRA was intended as legislation that would provide American Indians with a legal mechanism to claim and repatriate affiliated tribal remains. As an article of cultural legislation that deals with Native American dead, NAGPRA has been employed for the benefit of tribal interests all across North America. But, as in the Kennewick Man case, tribes are finding that NAGPRA is not a perfect law, and in Cherokee experience, not without serious flaws.

Russell Townsend, the tribal historic preservation officer for the Eastern Band of Cherokee Indians, identifies the main failing of NAGPRA from a tribal viewpoint. This involves the contested process of ascertaining cultural affiliation, which proved to be the linchpin in the Kennewick Man court case that ultimately permitted scientists to study the remains and denied the tribes the right to rebury them:

> If a tribe cannot prove cultural affiliation, then the repatriation request cannot be successfully made. . . . In the list of NAGPRA guidelines there are no directions on how to discern cultural affiliation beyond broad categories such as direct lineal descent or geographic region. In this sense, establishing direct lineal descent beyond a time when birth certificates become commonplace is difficult. . . . Scientists define cultural affiliation based on ceramic traditions, settlement patterns, mortuary patterns, craniometrics, material culture, and landscapes. Each of these areas becomes more tenuous as one moves back in time. Tribes utilize language, landscape, parentage, behavioral culture, and specialized material culture to establish cultural affiliation. Again, these criteria are best suited to examination of only the recent past.

The Kennewick Man court proceedings were closely monitored by the Eastern Band of Cherokee Indians. The results further spurred the tribe to protect its dead by avoiding triggering NAGPRA entirely during the course of federal undertakings, via prearranged Memoranda of Agreement and Memoranda of Understanding initiated under Section 106 consultations that addressed the treatment of human remains prior to their possible discovery. The Tribal Historic Preservation Office of the Eastern Band of Cherokee Indians has used this technique to great effect, forming cooperative agreements with multiple federal, state, and local agencies, as well as with other tribes to ensure that, in the case of inadvertent human remains discoveries, NAGPRA is *never* activated, circumventing scientific study and research entirely. Avoidance or reburial occurs without ever determining cultural affiliation beyond "American Indian." This model is increasingly being utilized by other sovereign tribes as well, working in cooperation with each other to present federal agencies with a unified front when dealing with issues of avoidance, repatriation, and reburial.

The Future of Paleoamerican Studies

The recent debate over the remains of Kennewick Man . . . has done little to foster a reconciliatory relationship, rather it has probably done more to polarize the issues. (Society for American Archaeology)

In the wake of the Kennewick Man court ruling, scientists have now completed their studies on the skeletal remains, hopeful that the data gathered will illuminate what is known about the earliest human migrations to the North American continent. Tribal people have begun to reassess the utility of NAGPRA and are now turning to alternative legal measures to restrict scientific access to skeletal remains. These new shifts in tribal practices are a challenge to the discipline of anthropology, increasing by orders of magnitude as more federally recognized tribes and tribal historic preservation offices exercise growing control over their cultural, historical, and biological landscapes.

In 2007, tribal groups, enraged by the Kennewick Man outcome and continued appropriation and retention of their dead, were instrumental in introducing an amendment to NAGPRA that alters the current definition of Native American from "of or relating to, a tribe, people, or culture that is indigenous to the United States" to an all-encompassing "of or relating to, a tribe, people, or culture that is or was indigenous to the United States." If this bill passes, it will effectively render all human remains dated before 1492 as Native American, leading to further decreases in opportunities to study any ancient American remains. It is ironic that in winning the Kennewick Man decision, anthropologists may ultimately end up with a pyrrhic victory. Now on notice, tribes will avoid activating NAGPRA by ensuring a priori nondisturbance of human remains under Section 106 and mounting legal challenges and amendments to NAGPRA. It is likely that anthropologists may not be cognizant of the subtle shaping of their own discipline by these new tribal imperatives, all in direct response to the outcome of the Kennewick Man case.

EXPLORING THE ISSUE

Can Archaeologists Determine the Cultural Background of the Earliest Americans from the Ancient Skeleton Known as Kennewick Man?

Critical Thinking and Reflection

1. Would the Native American community be as outraged if Chatters's original reports had not referred to the skull as Caucasoid-like? What if he had merely suggested that it did not fit the patterns we see in modern Umatilla skeletal material?
2. Is there something useful that comes from referring to the early North American skeletons older than 8000 years as Paleoamerican skeletons rather than Paleoindian skeletons? Would Chatters and his colleagues lose anything in the analysis they are trying to make if they referred to these early remains as Paleoindian skeletons?
3. Are there possible explanations for why the Kennewick skull might not resemble modern Umatilla skulls?
4. Can we draw any conclusions about the history of settlement in North America from a dozen early skulls?
5. What possible explanations are there for the apparent differences between the Kennewick skull and modern Indian skull forms?

Is There Common Ground?

Whatever the origins of the Kennewick skeleton and its closest affiliations both within North America and in the Old World, referring to the skull as Caucasoid-like was clearly inflammatory, even if Chatters had not meant to be so. But beyond the firestorm it launched, this skull and the several skulls of similar age found in North America suggest that the continent's earliest pattern of settlement may have been somewhat more complex than archaeologists and Indians alike have long assumed.

Neither of these authors provide comparable data for Europe, Asia, and Africa to show how much human skeletons have changed in these regions over the same period. We might even expect that the glacial ice that covered so much of northern Eurasia and North America might have influenced which groups of early settlers survived and which did not. How much variation was present among the known North American skulls older than 8000 years and how does this compare with the similar variation in other regions?

It is not clear that referring to these early skeletal remains as Paleo-americans rather than Paleoindians adds anything substantive to the debate, although it most clearly has added to the tension between Indians and archaeologists. But one thing this nomenclature has enhanced if not created is to raise more suspicions among Native American communities about the intentions and goals of white anthropologists. One suspects that greater sensitivity to Indian perspectives might have helped the situation a great deal.

Additional Resources

Original report of Chatters can be found in:
> Chatters, James C. 1997. "Encounter With an Ancestor," *Anthropology Newsletter* (January):9,11.

A more complete statement of the current essay and Chatters's reaction to the controversy can be found in:
> Chatters, James C. 2001. *Ancient Encounters: Kennewick Man and the First Americans.* New York: Simon & Schuster.

The volume from which the second selection came is a collection of papers that generally take a perspective sympathetic to Native American concerns:
> Burke, Heather, et al., eds. 2008. *Kennewick Man: Perspectives on the Ancient One.* Walnut Creek: Left Coast Press.

The best summary of the debate over what to do with Native American skulls and why it is important to biological anthropologists and Indians alike can be found in:
> Thomas, David Hurst. 2000. *The Skull Wars: Kennewick Man, Archeology, and the Battle for Native American Identity.* New York: Basic Books.

Some of the analyses upon which Chatters and his colleagues rely include the following:
> Jantz, R.L. and Owsley, D.W. 2001. "Variation Among Early North American Crania," *American Journal of Physical Anthropology* 114(2):146–155.

Owsley, D.W. and Jantz, R.L. 2001. "Archaeological Politics and Public Interest in Paleoamerican Studies: Lessons from Gordon Creek Woman and Kennewick Man," *American Antiquity* 66(4):565–575.
> Watkins, Joe. 2004. "Becoming American or Becoming Indian: NAGPRA, Kennewick, and Cultural Affiliation." *Journal of Social Archaeology* 4(1):60–80.

The most recent set of documents about Kennewick Man can be found on the National Park Service Web site. This collection of official reports is the most comprehensive available: www.nps.gov/archeology/kennewick/Index.htm

ISSUE 7

Was There a Goddess Cult in Prehistoric Europe?

YES: Marija Gimbutas, from "Old Europe in the Fifth Millennium B.C.," in Edgar C. Polomé, ed., *The Indo-Europeans in the Fourth and Third Millennia* (Karoma Publishers, 1982)

NO: Lynn Meskell, from "Goddesses, Gimbutas, and 'New Age' Archaeology," *Antiquity* (March 1995)

Learning Outcomes

After reading this issue, you should be able to:

- Understand why some archaeologists have interpreted the presence of a large number of female figurines in early excavations as evidence for a cult that centered on a single female Goddess.
- Appreciate some of the similarities and differences between this interpretation and nineteenth-century interpretations of these societies as matriarchal.
- Outline the evidence Gimbutas has used to support her claims about a Goddess Cult.
- Offer examples of her evidence that other archaeologists challenge or find questionable.
- Explain why Meskell and others challenge Gimbutas's interpretation of evidence for a Goddess Cult.

ISSUE SUMMARY

YES: Archaeologist Marija Gimbutas argues that the civilization of pre-Bronze Age "Old Europe" was matriarchal—ruled by women—and that the religion centered on the worship of a single great Goddess. Furthermore, this civilization was destroyed by patriarchal Kurgan pastoralists (the Indo-Europeans), who migrated into southeastern Europe from the Eurasian steppes in the fifth to third millennia B.C.

NO: Archaeologist Lynn Meskell considers the belief in a supreme Goddess and a matriarchal society in prehistoric Europe to be an unwarranted projection of some women's utopian longings onto the past. She regards Gimbutas's interpretation of the archaeological evidence as biased and speculative.

The idea that prehistoric societies were matriarchal and worshipped a supreme Goddess has deep roots in European thought. The Greeks, like the Babylonians, regarded the earth as feminine and associated it with goddesses, a notion preserved in our expressions "Mother Earth" and "Mother Nature." In the nineteenth century, some cultural evolutionists, such as J.J. Bachofen (*Das Mutterrecht*, Benno Schwabe, 1861) and John Ferguson MacLellan (*Primitive Marriage: An Inquiry Into the Origin of the Form of Capture in Marriage Ceremonies*, 1865), postulated that the earliest human societies were woman-centered, but they became patriarchal ("male governed") before the beginning of written records. Coincidentally, some classicists began to see a single great Goddess lying behind the goddesses of classical Greece and they linked this Goddess to the female figurines ("Venus figures") being turned up in archaeological sites in the Balkans and southeastern Europe. In 1903, the prominent classicist Jane Ellen Harrison drew the threads together, postulating that in prehistoric southeastern Europe there existed a peaceful, woman-centered civilization where people lived in harmony with nature and worshiped a single female deity. This civilization was later destroyed by patriarchal invaders from the north, who brought war and male deities. By the 1950s, most archaeologists specializing in Europe accepted the view that a Goddess religion and matriarchal social system had spread throughout Europe before being replaced by the male-centered societies of the Bronze Age. But in the 1960s, a young archaeologist, Peter Ucko, challenged this view on the basis of extensive analyses of figurines from throughout eastern Europe and the eastern Mediterranean. He saw that there was great variation among figurines in time and space, and far from the general belief, all were female. This led the archaeological establishment to retreat to a more agnostic view, once again reserving judgment over the nature of the earliest European religions.

One archaeologist who retained and even elaborated on the theory of the ancient matriarchal society and the Goddess, however, was the late Marija Gimbutas. In the YES selection, Gimbutas presents her version of the theory and some of the evidence for it. She bases her interpretation on a large body of archaeological materials, especially the remains of buildings, clay models of buildings, and figurines. She contends that this matrifocal ("woman-focused") culture was destroyed by the invasions of patriarchal, nomadic pastoralists from the steppes of southern Russia, but traces of the earlier culture linger among the non-Indo-European peoples of Europe, like the Basques, and were mixed into the later patriarchal culture.

In the NO selection, Lynn Meskell, however, criticizes Gimbutas and her followers for adopting a highly speculative gynocentric ("female-centered") interpretation of the evidence, one that she believes consistently ignores contrary evidence and other possible interpretations. Meskell argues that Gimbutas has allowed her desire to affirm the existence of an ancient feminist utopia to color and distort her interpretation of the archaeological record, leading her, for example, to overlook the large numbers of figurines that are male or ambiguous in gender. She suggests that the current popularity of Gimbutas's view is due to "New Age" feminists hoping to ground their utopian visions in a past that they see as having been unfairly destroyed by men.

Over the past 20 years a popular women's movement, the "Goddess Movement," has grown up, especially in the United States, around the idea that the earliest organized religion was based on worship of a supreme Goddess. This is largely a reaction against the perceived androcentrism and antifemale bias of Christianity, Judaism, Islam, and other world religions and of the civilizations they underpin. Proponents believe that by reviving this religion, they can undo the cultural and psychological harm inflicted on women (and men) by our long history of patriarchal religions and cultures.

Many feminist archaeologists are ambivalent toward the Goddess Movement and Gimbutas's contribution to it. They believe, on the one hand, that Gimbutas's work helps to correct the imbalance in conventional presentations of human prehistory, in which women are usually portrayed as minor bit players. But they are concerned about the quality of her methodology and theories. Feminist archaeologists also worry that Gimbutas's "old-fashioned" ideas, such as the notion of universal stages of cultural evolution and her static view of gender relations, do not contribute to an archaeology in which feminist views are an integral part.

The YES and NO selections raise a number of questions that are important not only for our understanding of the prehistory of Europe, but also for archaeological interpretation in general. Are any other interpretations of this evidence possible? If so, how can we choose among the different possible readings? Can archaeologists insulate themselves from social and political currents of their day and provide "objective" interpretations of their findings? What is the proper role of imagination in creating a comprehensive picture of a vanished way of life from the small set of clues that have survived the vicissitudes of time?

YES ↵

Marija Gimbutas

Old Europe in the Fifth Millennium B.C.

With the growing realization of the necessity to distinguish the Neolithic and Copper Age pre-Indo-European civilization from the "Indo-Europeanized" Europe of the Bronze Age, I coined, ten years ago, the new term "Old Europe." This term covers, in a broad sense, all Europe west of the Pontic Steppe before the series of incursions of the steppe (or "Kurgan") pastoralists in the second half of the fifth, of the fourth, and the beginning of the third millennium B.C., for in my view Europe is not the homeland of the Indo-European speakers. In a narrower sense, the term Old Europe applies to Europe's first civilization, i.e., the highest Neolithic and Copper Age culture focused in the southeast and the Danubian basin, gradually destroyed by repeated Kurgan infiltrations. . . .

The two cultural systems are very different: the first is sedentary, matrifocal, peaceful, art-loving, earth- and sea-bound; the second is patrifocal, mobile, warlike, ideologically sky-oriented, and indifferent to art. The two systems can best be understood if studied before the period of their clash and mélange, i.e., before ca. 4500–4000 B.C. . . .

Social Organization

Theocratic monarchies? Old European societies were unstratified: there were no contrasting classes of rulers and laborers, but there was a rich middle class which rose as a consequence of metallurgy and expansion of trade. Neither royal tombs, distinct in burial rites from those of the rest of the population, nor royal quarters, distinguished by extravagance, have been discovered. I see no evidence of the existence of a patriarchal chieftain system with pronounced ranking of the Indo-European type. Instead, there are in Old Europe a multitude of temples with accumulations of wealth—gold, copper, marble, shells, and exquisite ceramics. The goods of highest quality, produced by the best craftsmen, belonged not to the chief, as is customary in chiefdoms, but to the Goddess and to her representative, the queen-priestess. The social organization represented by the rise of temples was a primary centrifugal social force.

From *The Indo-Europeans in the Fourth and Third Millennia* by Edgar C. Polome (Karoma Publishers, 1982), pp. 1, 7–14, 18–19 (notes omitted). Copyright © 1982 by Zivile Gimutas. Reprinted by permission of the estate of Marija Gimbutas.

The question of government organization is as yet difficult to answer. Central areas and secondary provinces can be observed in each culture group. Some of the foci were clearly more influential than others, but whether centralized government existed we do not know. I favor the theory of small theocratic kingdoms or city-states, analogous to Etruscan *lucomonies* and Minoan palaces, with a queen-priestess as ruler, and her brother or husband as supervisor of agriculture and trade. The basis of such a structure was more social and religious in character than civil, political, or military.

The matrilinear society.   There is absolutely no indication that Old European society was patrilinear or patriarchal. Evidence from the cemeteries does not indicate a subordinate position of women. There was no ranking along a patriarchal masculine-feminine value scale as there was in Europe after the infiltration of steppe pastoralists who introduced the patriarchal and the patrilinear systems. The study of grave equipment in each culture group suggests an egalitarian society. A division of labor between the sexes is demonstrated by grave goods, but not a superiority of either. The richest graves belong to both men and women. Age was a determining factor; children had the lowest number of objects.

A strong support for the existence of matrilinearity in Old Europe is the historic continuity of matrilinear succession in the non-Indo-European societies of Europe and Asia Minor, such as the Etruscan, Pelasgian, Lydian, Carian, and Basque. Even in Rome during the monarchy, royal office passed regularly through the female line—clearly a non-Indo-European tradition most probably inherited from Old Europe, Polybius, in the second century B.C., speaking of the Greek colony, Lokroi, on the toe of Italy, says, "all their ancestral honors are traced through women." Furthermore, we hear from Greek historians that the Etruscans and prehistoric Athenians had "wives in common" and "their children did not know their own fathers." The woman in such a system is free to marry the man of her choice, and as many as she pleases (there is no question of adultery—that was a male invention), and she retains control of her children with regard to their paternity. This evidence led George Thomson to the assumption that group marriage was combined with common ownership in prehistoric Aegean societies. Matrilinear succession on some Aegean islands (e.g., Lesbos, Skyros) is reported by written records in the eighteenth century and continues in partial form to this very day. Matrilinear succession to real property and prenuptial promiscuity were practiced in isolated mountainous regions of southwestern Yugoslavia up to the twentieth century. Such customs are certainly unthinkable in present patriarchal society; only a very deeply rooted tradition could have survived for millennia the counter-influence of the patrilinearity of surrounding tribes.

A matrifocal society is reflected by the types of Old European goddesses and their worship. It is obvious that goddesses, not gods, dominated the Old European pantheon. Goddesses ruled absolutely over human, animal, and plant life. Goddesses, not male gods, spontaneously generated the life-force and created the universe. As demonstrated by the thousands of figurines and temples from the Neolithic through the Copper Ages, the male god was an adjunct of the female goddess, as consort or son. In the models of house-shrines and temples, and in actual temple remains, females are shown as supervising the preparation and performance of rituals dedicated to the various aspects and functions of the Goddess. Enormous energy was expended in the production of cult equipment and votive gifts. Some temple models show the grinding of grain and the baking of sacred bread. The routine acts of daily existence were religious rituals by virtue of replicating the sacred models. In the temple workshops, which usually constitute half the building or occupy the floor below the temple proper, females made and decorated quantities of the various pots appropriate to different rites. Next to the altar of the temple stood a vertical loom on which were probably woven the sacred garments and temple appurtenances. The most sophisticated creations of Old Europe—the most exquisite vases, sculptures, etc., now extant—were women's work (the equipment for decoration of vases so far is known only from female graves). Since the requirements of the temple were of primary importance, production for the temple must have doubled or tripled the general level of productivity, both stimulating and maintaining the level of feminine craftsmanship.

Religion

Templesy.   The tradition of temple buildings begins in the seventh millennium B.C. A remarkable series of temple models and actual rectangular temples from the sixth and fifth millennia B.C. bear witness to a great architectural tradition.

At present about 50 models from various culture groups and phases are known. They are more informative than the actual temple remains, since they present details of architecture, decoration, and furnishings otherwise unavailable to prehistoric archaeology. Actual remains of sanctuaries suggest that miniature models in clay were replicas of the real temples. They almost always were found at the altars, probably as gifts to the goddess.

The seventh and sixth millennia temple models seemed to have conceived of the temple as literally the body or the house of the deity. Shrine models from Porodin near Bitola in Macedonia, for instance, have a cylindrical "chimney" in the middle of the roof upon which is modeled the masked features of a largeeyed Bird Goddess, a necklace encircling her neck ("chimney"). Other models have round openings fit for the goddess to enter in the shape of a bird or are made in the form of a bird's nest. . . .

The figurines portrayed (in clay models) and found in actual shrines are shown to perform various cult activities—ritual grinding, baking of sacred bread, attending sacrifices—or are seated on the altar, apparently used for the reenactment of a particular religious ceremony. In the mid-fifth millennium Cucuteni (Early Tripolye) shrine at Sabatinivka in the valley of Southern Bug in the Ukraine, 16 figurines were sitting on chairs on the altar, all with snake-shaped heads and massive thighs. One held a baby snake. The other group of 15 were in action—baking, grinding, or standing at the dish containing remains of a bull sacrifice. In the corner next to the altar stood a life-size clay throne with horned back support, perhaps for a priestess to supervise the ceremony. At Ovčarovo near Trgovište, northeastern Bulgaria, 26 miniature cult objects were found within the remains of a burned shrine. They included four figurines with upraised arms, three altar screens (or temple facades) decorated with symbols, nine chairs, three tables, three lidded vessels, three drums, and several dishes larger than figurines. Such objects vividly suggest ceremonies with music and dances, lustrations, and offerings.

The production of an enormous variety of cult paraphernalia—exquisite anthropomorphic, zoomorphic, and ornithomorphic vases, sacrificial containers, lamps, ladles, etc.—is one of the very characteristic features of this culture and may be viewed as a response to the demands of a theocentric culture where most production centered around the temple. The consideration of these creations is unfortunately beyond the scope of this article. Regarding the technological and aesthetic skills, nothing similar was created in the millennia that followed the demise of Old Europe.

Ceremonial costume and mask.   A wealth of costume details is preserved on the clay figurines. Deep incisions encrusted with white paste or red ochre affirm the presence of hip-belts, fringe, aprons, narrow skirts, blouses, stoles, a variety of hair styles, and the use of caps, necklaces, bracelets, and medallions. Whether these fashions were commonly worn, or were traditional garb for priestesses or other participants in ritual celebrations, can only be conjectured. The latter was probably the case; most of the figurines seem to have been characters in tableaux of ritual. But, ritual or not, the costumes reflect stylistic conventions of dress and taste characteristic of the period.

In the female costume several dress combinations recur persistently: partly dressed figures wear only a hip-belt, or a hip-belt from which hangs an apron or panels of an entire skirt of fringe, resembling a hula skirt; others wear a tight skirt with shoulder straps or a blouse.

A number of figurines show incised or painted stoles over the shoulders and in front and back. The skirt, which generally begins below the waist and hugs the hips, has a decorative texture of white encrusted incisions, showing net-pattern, zigzags, checkerboard, or dots. The skirt narrows below the knees, and on some figurines wrappings around the legs are indicated. It may be that the skirt was slit in front below the knees and fastened between the legs with woven bands. This type of skirt gives the impression of constraining movement and quite likely had a ritualistic purpose.

The figurines tell little about male attire; males are usually portrayed nude, except for a large V-shaped collar and a belt. In the last phase of the Cucuteni culture male figures wear a hip-belt and a strap passing diagonally across the chest and back over one of the shoulders. . . .

Special attention to coiffure and headgear is evidenced. The Bird and Snake Goddess in particular, or devotees associated with their images, had beautiful coiffures, a crown, or decorative headbands. VinCa and Butmir figurines have hair neatly combed and divided symmetrically in the center, the two panels perhaps separated by a central ribbon. Late Cucutenian figurines, primarily nude, but some wearing hip-belt and necklace, have a long, thick coil of hair hanging down the back and ending in a large, circular bun or with an attached disc, reminiscent of the style favored by Egyptian ritual dancers of the third millennium B.C. A typical item of dress is a conical cap on which radial or horizontal parallel incisions perhaps represent its construction of narrow ribbon-like bands.

Figurines were portrayed wearing masks representing certain goddesses, gods, or their sacred animals, or else they were simply shown as bird-headed (with beaked faces on a cylindrical neck), snake-headed (with a long mouth, round eyes, and no nose), or ram- or other animal-headed. Frequently-occurring perforations of the mask were obviously intended to carry some sort of organic attachment. Plumes, flowers, fruits, and other materials could have been employed in this way. . . .

Deities worshippedy.   In the literature on prehistoric religion the female figures of clay, bone, and stone are usually considered to be the "Mother Goddess." Is she indeed nothing more than an image of motherhood? The term is not entirely a misnomer if we understand her as a creatress or as a cosmogenic woman. It must be emphasized that from the Upper Paleolithic onward the persona of the Goddess splintered the response to the developing economy, and the images of deities portray not only the single maternal metaphor of the deity. Study of the several stereotypical shapes and postures of the figurines and of the associated symbolism of the signs incised upon them clearly shows that the figurines intend to project a multiplicity of divine aspects and a variety of divine functions.

There are, in my opinion, two primary aspects of the Goddess (not necessarily two Goddesses) presented by the effigies. The first is, "She who is the Giver of All"—Giver of Life, Giver of Moisture, of Food, of Happiness; she is also "Taker of All," i.e., Death. The second aspect of the Goddess is connected with the periodic awakening of nature: she is springtime, the new moon, rebirth, regeneration, and metamorphosis. Both go back to the Upper Paleolithic. The significance of each aspect is visually supported on the figurines by appropriate symbols and signs. The first aspect of the Goddess as Giver and Taker of All, that is, as both beginning and end of life, is accompanied by aquatic symbols—water birds, snakes, fish, frogs, all animals associated with water—and representations of water itself in the form of zigzag bands, groups of parallel lines, meanders, nets, checkerboards, and running spirals. The second aspect of the Goddess as Rebirth, Renewal, and Transcendance is accompanied by the symbols of "becoming": eggs, uteri, phalluses, whirls, crescents, and horns which resemble cornucopias. The Goddess often appears in the form of a bee, a butterfly, or a caterpillar. This second group involves male animals such as bulls and dogs.

The Giver of All, the Fish, Water Bird, and Snake Goddess

Hybrids of the human female with bird or snake dominated mythical imagery throughout the Upper Paleolithic, Neolithic, Chalcolithic, and Copper Ages from ca. 26,000 to the end of Old Europe at ca. 3000 B.C., but lingered in the Aegean and Mediterranean regions through the Bronze Age and later—at least 40 percent of the total number of figurines belong to this type. The Fish, Bird, and Snake Goddesses were interrelated in meaning and function. Each is Creatress and Giver. They are, therefore, inseparable from cosmogonic and cosmogenic myths such as water birds carrying cosmic eggs. She as the Mother or *Source* is the giver of rain, water, milk, and meat (sheep, their skin and wool). Her portrayals usually show exaggerated breasts marked with parallel lines, or a wide-open beak or round hole for a mouth. Her large eyes are a magical source, and are surrounded by aquatic symbolism (usually groups of parallel lines). Beginning in the Neolithic, the ram (the earliest domesticated animal, a vital source of food and clothing) became her sacred animal. The symbols of this goddess on spindle whorls and loom weights suggest that she was the originator or guardian of the crafts of spinning and weaving. Metaphorically, as "the spinner and weaver of human life," she became the Goddess of Fate.

Along with the life-giving aspect of the Goddess, her life-taking or death-giving aspect must have developed in preagricultural times. The images of vultures and owls are known from the Upper Paleolithic and from the earliest Neolithic (in the frescoes of Çatal Hüyük, in central Anatolia, vultures appear above headless human beings). The figurine type of the nude goddess with large pubic triangle, folded arms, and face of an owl, well known from Old European graves, may be representative of the Goddess in the aspect of night and death.

In early agricultural times, the Giver of All developed another function, a function vital to tillers of the soil—namely, that of "Giver of Bread." Her images were deposited in grain silos or in egg-shaped vases, where they were indispensable insurance for the resurgence of plant life. She also appears as a pregnant woman, her ripe body a metaphor of the fertile field. She was worshipped with her sacred animal, the pig. The fattening of the pig encouraged the growth and ripening of crops or fertility in general.

Richly represented throughout the Neolithic, Chalcolithic, and Copper Ages, still another aspect of the Goddess is, by natural association, that of "Birth-giving Goddess." She is portrayed with outstretched legs and upraised arms in a naturalistic birth-giving posture. This stereotypic image appears in relief on large vases and on temple walls; carved in black and green stone or alabaster, it was worn as an amulet.

The "Periodic Regeneration" aspect of the Goddess may be as ancient as the Giver of All aspect, since symbols of "becoming" are present in the Upper Paleolithic: crescents and horns appear in association with Paleolithic nudes. To regenerate the life-force was her main function; therefore, the Goddess was flanked by male animals noted for physical strength—bulls, he-goats, dogs. In her incarnation as a crescent, caterpillar, bee, or butterfly, she was a symbol of new life; she emerged from the body or horns of the bull as a bee or butterfly.

The female principle was conceived as creative and eternal, the male as spontaneous and ephemeral. The male principle was represented symbolically by male animals and by phalluses and ithyphallic animal-masked men—

goatmen or bull-men. They appear as adjuncts of the Goddess. The figurines of ecstatic dancers, goat- or bull-masked, may represent worshippers of the Goddess in rituals enacting the dance of life. . . .

Conclusion: The Kurgan Penetration

Old Europe was rapidly developing into an urban culture, but its growth was interrupted and eventually stopped by destructive forces from the east—the steadily increasing infiltration of the semi-nomadic, horse-riding pastoralists from the Pontic steppes. Periodic waves of infiltration into civilized Europe effected the disintegration of the first European civilization. Only on the islands, like Crete, Thera, and Malta, did the traditions of Old Europe survive for almost two millennia. The Bronze Age culture that followed north of the Aegean was an amalgam of the substrate and totally different elements of an eastern culture.

Thanks to a growing number of radiocarbon dates, archaeologists can ascertain the periods of Kurgan penetration into Europe. There was no single massive invasion, but a series of repeated incursions concentrated into three major thrusts:

- Wave No. 1, ca. 4400–4200 B.C.
- Wave No. 2, ca. 3400–3200 B.C.
- Wave No. 3, ca. 3000–2800 B.C.

The steppe (or "Kurgan") people were, above all, pastoralists. As such, their social system was composed of small patrilinear units that were socially stratified according to the strategic services performed by its male members. The grazing of large herds over vast expanses of land necessitated a living pattern of seasonal settlements or small villages affording sufficient pasturage for animals. The chief tasks of a pastoral economy were executed by men, not by women as was characteristic of the indigenous agricultural system.

It was inevitable that an economy based on farming and another which relied on stock breeding would produce unrelated ideologies. The upheaval of the Old European civilization is registered in the abrupt cessation of painted pottery and figurines, the disappearance of shrines, the termination of symbols and signs.

Old European ceramics are readily identified with the rich symbolic signs and decorative motifs that reflect an ideology concerned with cosmogony, generation, birth, and regeneration. Symbols were compartmentalized or interwoven in a myriad combination—meanders and spirals, chevrons and zigzags, circles, eggs, horns, etc. There were a multitude of pictorial and sculptural representations of goddesses and gods, of worshippers, and sacred animals. Kurgan pottery is devoid of symbolic language and of aesthetic treatment in general because it obviously did not serve the same ceremonial purposes as that of Old Europe. The stabbing and impressing technique is quite primitive and seems to focus on only one symbol, the sun. Occasionally, a schematized fir tree occurs which may symbolize a "tree-of-life."

Mythical images that were in existence on the Eurasiatic steppe dispersed now over a large part of Europe, and continued to the beginning of Christianity and beyond. The new ideology was an apotheosis of the horseman and warrior. The principal gods carry weapons and ride horses or chariots; they are figures of inexhaustible energy, physical power, and fecundity. In contrast to the pre-Indo-European cultures whose myths centered around the moon, water, and the female, the religion of pastoral, semi-sedentary Indo-European peoples was oriented toward the rotating sky, the sun, stars, planets, and other sky phenomena such as thunder and lightning. Their sky and sun gods were shining, "bright as the sky"; they wore starry cloaks adorned with glittering gold, copper, or amber pendants, torques, chest plates, belts. They carried shining daggers, swords, and shields. The Indo-Europeans glorified the magical swiftness of arrow and javelin and the sharpness of the blade. Throughout the millennia, the Indo-Europeans exulted in the making of weapons, not pottery or sculpture. The touch of the ax blade awakened the powers of nature and transmitted the fecundity of the Thunder God; by the touch of his spear tip, the god of war and the underworld marked the hero for glorious death.

Goddesses, Gimbutas, and "New Age" Archaeology

For a century a notion of a prehistoric Mother Goddess has infused some perceptions of ancient Europe, whatever the realities of developing archaeological knowledge. With the reverent respect now being given to Marija Gimbutas, and her special vision of a perfect matriarchy in Old Europe, a daughter-goddess is now being made, bearer of a holy spirit in our own time to be set alongside the wise mother of old.

Introduction

The field of archaeology, like many others, is prone to fads and fictions within the academic community and general public alike. A recurrent interest since the 19th century has been the notion of an omnipotent Mother Goddess, whose worship symbolizes a cultural continuity from the Palaeolithic era to modern times. The principle advocate for this theory over the past two decades, Marija Gimbutas, is seen to offer archaeological validity to these claims as a result of her recognized academic standing and long history of fieldwork in southeast European sites. From the material particulars of archaeology in her earlier work she moved toward an ideal vision of prehistory (compare Gimbutas 1965; 1970; 1971a; 1973 with interpretations in 1974; 1981; Gimbutas *et al.* 1989; 1989a; 1989b; 1991; 1992). Her widely published theories appeal to those committed to ecofeminism and the 'New Age' range of esoteric concerns, which include ancient religion and mythology. Whilst this vision of the past appears to embrace aspects of cognitive, gender and even feminist archaeologies, the interpretations it presents are simply hopeful and idealistic creations reflecting the contemporary search for a social utopia.

The concept of the Goddess is entangled within a larger, more complex, political phenomenon that involves regional and nationalist struggles (Chapman 1994; Anthony in press), linguistic aetiology (Renfrew 1987; Mallory 1989: 81), contemporary gender struggles and the feminist cause (Hallett 1993; Passman 1993). However, the revisionist histories on offer (Eisler 1987; Gimbutas 1974; 1989a; 1989b; 1991; 1992; Orenstein 1990; Spretnak

From *Antiquity*, vol. 69, no. 262, March 1995, pp. 74–86. Copyright © 1995 by Antiquity Publications Ltd. Reprinted by permission of Lynn Meskell.

1992; etc.) do not aim for a more complete understanding of ancient socie-ties *in toto*. Rather, they provide altogether alternative historical projections of what certain groups see as desirable. Re-writing the past from an engendered perspective is certainly long overdue, yet reweaving a fictional past with claims of scientific proofs (e.g. Gimbutas 1992) is simply irresponsible. Such 'new and improved' histories are more telling of contemporary socio-sexual concerns rather than their ancient antecedents.

Why the Goddess and Why Now?

Why has there been a proliferation of studies devoted to the concept of a Mother Goddess in recent years? Why has this appeal been so persistent, particularly to the general public? Whereas the academic study of figurines is usually integrated within regional culture studies, the notion of the God-dess has assumed larger proportions to the wider community. As a result, the literature of the Goddess lies at the interface where academic scholar-ship meets New Age gynocentric, mythologized interpretations of the past (Eisler 1987; Gimbutas 1974; 1989a; 1992; Spretnak 1992). This is a radically burgeoning field in women's studies and New Age literature, and its books must far outsell their scholarly counterparts. Since achieving icon status, The Goddess has been linked with movements and disciplines as diverse as christianity, feminism and ecofeminism, environmentalism, witchcraft and archaeology. In each of these the Goddess phenomenon is taken as a given rather than one speculative interpretation to be considered with alternative hypotheses. The past is being used in the present as an historical authority for contemporary efforts to secure gender equality (or superiority?) in spiri-tual and social domains.

. . . The current interest in the Goddess is not purely academic, but stems from a desire to remedy the results of millennia of misogyny and mar-ginalization (Frymer-Kensky 1992: vii) in both religious and secular spheres. My contention is that the connection has materialized in response to female disempowerment in our own recent history, particularly within religious power bases. The Goddess serves as a vehicle for women's groups and activists to reinforce legitimization of their position by means of an ancient anteced-ent. Contrary to the bloodied, materialist history and overt androcentrism of the Church, she is earth-centered, offering refuge and a counterbalance to the remote, punitive male god of western religions (Frymer-Kensky 1992; Spretnak 1992).

. . . Many of these initial gynocentric theories of prehistory share a fun-damental commonality to prior androcentric premises since they both employ 'sexist' paradigms in re-constru(ct)ing the past. Thus they do not promote credibility: rather they damage and delimit the positive attributes of gender-based research, due to their poor scholarship, ahistorical interpretations, fic-tional elements and reverse sexism. I see no detriment to current quests if we acknowledge that inequality was operative in the past, as it was in the historic cultures of the Near East and Mediterranean.

The Figurines as Archaeological Data

Figurines collectively termed Mother Goddesses or Venuses emanate from various regions and span an immense time-depth from the Palaeolithic to the Bronze Age and into historical periods, with considerable variability in form, style, decoration and context. This class of artefact—if that is an appropriate term—appears throughout much of Europe and southwest Asia, primarily southeast Europe and the Mediterranean islands from the Cyclades to Crete, Malta and Majorca (Ehrenberg 1989: 65; Malone *et al.* 1992: 76). The figures are generally accorded the status of 'art', although ethnographic evidence suggests that they do not form a distinct category. In a further tendency to project 20th-century biases of what constitutes 'good art', it has been suggested that carefully made sculptures were produced for important occasions by priestesses or mother figures (Gimbutas *et al.* 1989: 220). Conversely, the simple, schematic examples could have been made by any member of the community (male?). Figurines have been objectified, taken as devoid of spatial and cultural specificity; yet objects do not have inherent meaning divorced from their historically specific context of production and use (Hodder 1991; Dobres 1992a; 1992b).

For many figurines, provenience and context are lost due to poor excavation or non-archaeological recovery (for Cycladic figures see Gill & Chippindale 1993). Runnels (1990) and McPherron (1991) have noted the limits of excavation and recording by Gimbutas for her own site at Achilleion (Gimbutas *et al.* 1989), on which much of the larger picture is reliant. Dating, methodology, testing, typological and statistical analyses have all come under fire, not to mention artistic licence and over-interpretation. Weaknesses in scholarship have prevented Gimbutas' attempts, and the question of gender studies, to be taken seriously in archaeological circles (Tringham 1991: 97; 1993).

As part of a gynocentric agenda, female figurines have been considered largely to the exclusion of male and sexless examples (Gimbutas 1971b; 1974; 1986; 1989a; 1989b; 1992; Gimbutas *et al.* 1989), this selection shaping the vision of a single, omnipresent female deity. Her position is clear: male divinities were not prominent before the Indo-European invasion (see van Leuven 1993: 84). Many are undeniably female. Many are also male, androgynous, zoomorphic or indeterminate (see Marinescu-Bîlcu 1981; Hodder 1990; Milojkovic 1990; Pavlovic 1990; Talalay 1993); these are dismissed.

To her credit, Gimbutas assembled a large corpus of southeast European figurines in English publications, with copious photographs and illustrations. She aimed to investigate figurine attributes such as raw materials, production and form to some degree. However, studies of production have been undertaken more systematically by other scholars (Murray 1970), coupled with analyses of decorative motifs and positioning (Ucko 1968; Marinescu Bîlcu 1981; Pogozheva 1983) and patterns of breakage. It is unfortunate that Gimbutas did not incorporate findings from these studies into her later publications.

Mediterranean Matriculture and the Indo-European Debate

One key debate in 19th-century anthropology, currently experiencing a revival, hinges on the traditional matriarchal view of cultural evolution. Eminent scholars such as Morgan, Engels and Bachofen led the early debate, influenced by their own socio-intellectual biases, though failing to make the distinction between matriarchy, matrilinearity and matrilocality. Bachofen's evolutionist interpretations, long since discredited within academia, have now resurfaced in the Goddess literature. . . .

It has become popular in the past decade to view Neolithic cultures as matriarchal or matrifocal (Hayden 1986: 17), and to depict them as peaceful, harmonious and artistic in contrast to the more aggressive, destructive patriarchal societies that followed (Chapman 1991; Tringham 1991; Conkey & Tringham in press): the overthrowing of matriarchy by patriarchial society was the real Fall which has beleaguered Europe ever since. Childe raised a powerful analogue, arguing that using female figurines to substantiate matriarchal or matrilineal society was as accurate an indicator as the image of the Virgin Mary in the modern patriarchy (Childe 1951: 65). We should not ignore the possibility of matriarchy; rather we are not clear what form such evidence would take.

This line of reasoning ties directly into the polemic debate surrounding Indo-European archaeology and linguistics, in which Gimbutas was a major player (see Renfrew 1987: xiii; Mallory 1989: 182). Briefly, her view of Old Europe in the Neolithic period was characterized by its unfortified settlements (*contra* Marinescu Bîlcu 1981; Anthony in press) where a peaceful existence prevailed without threat of violence or fear of death itself. Within the matriarchy there were no husbands, yet men fulfilled important roles in construction, crafts and trade. Women's lives were liberal, socially and sexually, and inextricably bound to the rich religious system which ensured their prominence (Gimbutas 1992). Old Europe is portrayed as culturally homogeneous (*contra* Pavlovic 1988: 33; Mallory 1989: 22), socially egalitarian (*contra* Tringham 1990: 605; Anthony in press), devoid of human or animal sacrifice (*contra* Marinescu Bîlcu 1981; Anthony in press). Accordingly, this utopian existence was abruptly destroyed by Indo-European invasions: more specifically by the equocentric Kurgan culture from the Russian steppe. . . .

There is a striking congruence between Gimbutas' own life and her perception of Old Europe. Born in Lithuania, she witnessed two foreign occupations by 'barbarian invaders'; however, those from the East stayed. This prompted her immigration to the United States during which time the Soviet occupation of the Baltic states continued almost up until her death in 1994. In her own words, 'history is showing us between eight and ten million women had to die for her [the Goddess] . . . the wise people of the time . . . so it reminds me of the same [*sic*] what happened in Stalin's Europe when the cream of the society had to be removed and only fools were left to live. What happened in the twentieth century is the greatest shame of human history' (Gimbutas 1992). This strongly mirrors her view of Old Europe, a creative, matriarchal and *good* society which was invaded by men with weapons from the East.

Other writers (see Eisler 1987; Passman 1993) have run with Gimbutas' theories by stressing the superiority of assumed matristic cultures in Old Europe, Anatolia, Egypt and Minoan Crete on the basis of their peaceful, egalitarian, non-fortified communities and even their predisposition to vegetarianism (?) (Passman 1993: 187). Such a scenario is not borne out archaeologically. Walls and ditches at Nea Nikomedia, Dimini and Sesklo may have defensive functions. Both Neolithic and Chalcolithic sites like Tîrpesti, Ovcharovo, Polyanitsa and Tripolye clearly demonstrate fortification (Marinescu-Bîlcu 1981; Anthony in press: 20). Sites such as Dimini and Agia Sophia (Demoule & Perlès 1993) suggests status differentiation within communities, as does Selevac (Tringham & Krstic 1990: 206), with more evidence of social hierarchy from the cemeteries at Varna, Durankulak and other East Balkan sites (Anthony in press: 20). In addition, there is evidence of human sacrifice at Traian-Dealui, Fîntînilor (Marinescu-Bîlcu 1981: 135) and later from Knossos (Wall *et al.* 1986); animal sacrifices are attested at Poiana în Pisc and Anza. Artefactual evidence from Egypt indicates that weapons, in addition to items displaying battle scenes, were amongst the most common in the predynastic repertoire (see Davis 1992).

Even without the overwhelming archaeological data, historical evidence from Greece (Humphreys 1983; Hallett 1993), Egypt (Robins 1993) and Mesopotamia (Frymer-Kensky 1992) plus numerous ethnographic accounts suggest that cultures with strong female deities—if indeed they are deities—may still regard women in the profane world as a low-status group. The romanticized view of antiquity many feminists and pseudo-feminists present has more to do with creating an idealized past to contrast with our own secular, impersonal and industrialized present than with archaeological facts (Hays 1993: 84). Their visionary work links notions of 'ancient' and 'future', so enabling a richly figured heritage, once lived and lost, to be experienced again (Passman 1993: 182). This political reconstruction of a matristic past furnishes the seed for a return to Edenic conditions, ecological balance, healing the planet and matriculture itself, in opposition to the forecasts of Armageddon and the second coming (Starhawk 1982; Orenstein 1990; Passman 1993).

Cultic Figurines from a Sexist Perspective

Although proponents of post-processualism (e.g. Hodder 1987; 1990; 1991; Shanks & Tilley 1987) aim to understand symbolic systems, they still regard the archaeological record as a polysemous text that can be read (Hays 1993). Some have taken their position as reader to the extreme. Herein lies Gimbutas' attraction for a New Age audience, since she adopts the role of translator (channeller?) for a symbolic language stretching back millennia into the Neolithic mindset. In answer to Onians' claim that figurines represent ancient erotica, Gimbutas argues that 'love-making is clearly far from the thoughts of the ancient artist' (1981: 32). Knowing 'our European prehistoric forefathers were more philosophical than we seem to think' (1981: 39), she understands how they would be stunned to hear these new hypotheses. She further claims that the Achilleion figurines 'represent deities and their sacred animals, witness to continuous ritual performances in temples and at ovens in courtyards' (Gimbutas *et al.* 1989: 335). Her typological analysis was narrowed to fit these criteria, without mention of other functional interpretations. Similarly, she dismissed alternative explanations of Cycladic figures from mortuary contexts in favour of the Great Goddess (or stiff White Goddess) from a deeply rooted European tradition (1974: 158; 1992).

From the 1970s onwards Gimbutas presented arguments, with increasing fervour, to challenge a balanced and complementary view of the sexes in sacred and profane spheres (Hayden 1986; Chapman 1991). Her publications, including site reports (where one expects some attempt to discuss the data without a charged interpretation), were devoted to the Goddess and her manifestations; the gods are overlooked. At Anza 'only one [figurine] can possibly be male' (1976: 200), at Sitagroi 'only 1% can be considered as possibly portraying men' (1986: 226), at Achilleion the divine creatrix does not require male fecundity since 'her divine bisexuality stresses her absolute power' (Gimbutas *et al.* 1989: 196). In these reports every figure that is not phallic—and some that clearly are—are taken as symbols of the Goddess. This includes parallel lines, lozenges, zigzags, spirals, double axes, butterflies, pigs and pillars. Why this miscellany are self-evidently emblems of a female, much less a deity, is never explained. And indeed even the *male* may be symbolically *female:* 'although the male element is attached, these figurines remain essentially female' (1989a: 232). Gimbutas denied that phallicism was symbolic of procreation since Neolithic peoples did not understand the nature of biological conception (1974: 237).

Gimbutas was emphatic that Neolithic mythology was not polarized into male and female, due to the supremacy of the Mother. From this assumption she extrapolated, concomitantly, the role of women was not subordinate to men (Gimbutas 1974: 237; see Chapman 1991; Tringham 1991). Yet male, sexless and zoomorphic figures do exist, which makes the notion of an omnipotent Mother Goddess difficult to support. Ucko's examination of the later Knossos figurines demonstrated that androgynous examples were equal in number to the identifiable female statuettes (1968: 316; see Conkey & Tringham in press). Ucko (1968: 417) further concluded that most scholars treat male figures as exceptions, dismiss the sexless examples and regard female figurines as a singular deity without convincing explanation for their obvious variation.

The Goddess Contextualized

In addressing the archaeological context of finds at Anza, Sitagroi and Achilleion, Gimbutas interpreted partially excavated dwellings as 'house-shrines' and 'cult-places', and benches as 'altars' (1981; 1986; Gimbutas *et al.* 1989). She concluded human activities like grinding grain, baking bread, weaving and spinning were inseparable from divine participation (Gimbutas *et al.* 1989: 213–15). To Gimbutas it was 'obvious that the Goddess ruled over human, animal and plant life' (Gimbutas *et al.* 1989: 220). Perhaps these areas represented dwellings or workshops in view of associated finds like spindle whorls, a needle, awl and pottery discs? Indeed, few artefacts and features from these sites are assigned a mundane status (1981: 198–200; Gimbutas *et al.* 1989: 36–46, 213–15).

. . . Evidence from Anza, Selevac, Tîrpesti and Achilleion (see Gimbutas 1981; Gimbutas *et al.* 1989; Marinescu-Bîlcu 1981; Hodder 1990; Tringham 1990) indicates that figurines are found in every kind of context—refuse pits included. This would signify, as Gimbutas prefers, that the sacred is everywhere. Conversely, it could demonstrate that these figures are not sacred at all; or they may have multiple meanings which change as a figure is made, used and discarded.

Alternative Hypotheses

Recent work in Kephala (northern Greece) uncovered figurines near graves, which would indicate a possible function as territorial markers to reinforce ancestral ties in the Neolithic period (Talalay 1991: 49). Ethnographic reports from Africa over the past 200 years also suggest this kind of placement may be associated to ancestor cults. Further functions proposed include dolls, toys, tokens of identification, primitive contracts, communication or as part of birthing rituals (Talalay 1993: 40–43). Other plausible interpretations include teaching devices, tools of sorcery, magic, healing or initiation (Ehrenberg 1989: 75). Talalay proposes that clay legs from the northern Peloponnese served to symbolize social and economic bonds among communities like those of marriage contracts or identification of trading partners (1987: 161–2). These alternatives, as opposed to a universal deity, may explain the practice of discard. To assume *a priori* that there is a Goddess behind every figurine is tantamount to interpreting plastic figures of Virgin Mary and of 'Barbie' as having identical ideological significance. . . .

Conclusion: The Goddess, Pseudo-Feminism and Future Research

Whilst the concept of gender as a structuring principle is relatively new to archaeology, many progressive and scholarly studies have emerged in the last few years (e.g. Gero & Conkey 1991; Wylie 1991; Dobres 1992a; 1992b; Bacus *et al.* 1993; Brown 1993; Conkey & Tringham in press). However, many feminists feel that the establishment of an originary myth of the basis of scientific historical reality will facilitate the restoration of women's power. It then follows that the patriarchy will be dismantled and the lost pre-patriarchal culture can be regained (Passman 1993: 187). Matriculture is seen to give feminism the legitimacy the system demands.

Contrary to this position I argue, as feminist and archaeologist, that the approaches of Gimbutas and her advocates contrast markedly to many feminists (Brown 1993: 254), especially those involved in archaeological discourse. This is not to say that Gimbutas claimed to do feminist archaeology; rather that she has been adopted as an icon within the movement, more ardently outside archaeological circles. However, some feminists do not accept her methodology, since she was so steeped within the 'establishment' epistemological framework of polar opposites, rigid gender roles, barbarian invaders and cultural stages (Fagan 1992; Brown 1993) which are now regarded as outmoded. It is unfortunate that many archaeologists interested in gender are drawn to historical fiction and emotional narratives, which either replace or accompany serious archaeological dialogues. At this juncture sound feminist scholarship needs to be divorced from methodological shortcomings, reverse sexism, conflated data and pure fantasy, since this will only impede the feminist cause and draw attention away from the positive contribution offered by gender and feminist archaeologies. Gero & Conkey (1991: 5) assert that we are now in a position to draw from and contribute to emergent theoretical developments within archaeology, particularly post-processual directions that see social and symbolic theories as central. Gender, however, cannot be separated from other archaeological considerations and become the type of speciality area Gimbutas created.

In future studies we should not expect to delineate a rigid and unitary code which holds for all contexts (Hodder 1987), but rather to identify the dimensions of meaning pertaining to particular societies and to comprehend their social locus. It may prove more informative to ask 'how did the social production of this object contribute to its meanings and uses?', 'how did these meaningful objects enhance people's understanding of their lives?' and 'what other associated activities were operative that can inform us about social context?' (Dobres 1992a: 17–18). Naturally the multiplicity of manifestations relative to their archaeological contexts must be considered, coupled with the socioeconomic concerns of their manufacturers.

To conclude, academic and popular audiences alike need to review critically the evidence for a solitary universal Mother Goddess, along with other plausible interpretations. Although the post-processualists have stressed notions of pluralism, most now advocate that not *all* pasts are equal. The gynocentric narratives discussed above reveal more about our relationship(s) with the past and certain contemporary ideologies (Conkey 1992) than how these figurines were deployed in antiquity.

The Mother Goddess metanarrative presents a possible challenge to feminist archaeologies in that solidarity can often prevent us from contesting theories presented by women which seem to espouse pro-female notions: even if the evidence would suggest otherwise. Loyalty to a misrepresented picture of the past and our human heritage by dismissing or misconstruing the archaeological record cannot be supported under the guise of any political standpoint. Needless to say, many men feel that they are not in a position to engage in these issues and that only other women can do so. This exclusivity is not conducive to scholarly development; neither is failing to counter claims of a gendered superiority supported by 'scientific' archaeology that ultimately has filtered into mainstream society. An engendered re-balancing of the scales is long overdue and critically important to the trajectory of the discipline. However, emphasis on one sex to the exclusion of the other is not only detrimental to serious gender/feminist studies, but threatens the interpretative integrity of archaeology.

References

Anthony, D. W. In press. Nazi and ecofeminist prehistories: ideology and empiricism in Indo-European archaeology, in P. Kohl & C. Fawcett (ed.), *Nationalism, politics and the practice of archaeology*:1–32. Cambridge: Cambridge University Press.

Bacus, E.A. *et al.* 1993. *A gendered past: a critical review of gender in archaeology.* Ann Arbor (MI): University of Michigan Press.

Brown, S. 1993. Feminist research in archaeology. What does it mean? Why is it taking so long?, in Rabinowitz & Richlin (ed.):238–71.

Chapman, J. 1991. The creation of social arenas in the Neolithic and copper age of SE Europe: the case of Varna, in P. Garwood *et al* (ed.). *Sacred and profane*:152–71. Oxford: Oxford University Committee for Archaeology, Monograph 32.

—— 1994. Destruction of a common heritage: the archaeology of war in Croatia. Bosnia and Hercegovina, *Antiquity* 68:120–26.

Childe, V. G. 1951. *Social evolution.* London: Watts.

Conkey, M. W. 1992. Mobilising ideologies: the archaeologics of Paleolithic 'art'. Paper delivered to the American Anthropological Association, San Francisco.

Conkey, M. W. & R. E. Tringham. In press. Archaeology and the Goddess: exploring the contours of feminist archaeology, in A. Stewart & D. Stanton (ed.), *Feminism in the academy: rethinking the disciplines.* Ann Arbor (MI): University of Michigan Press.

Davis, W. 1992. *Masking the blow: the scene of representation in late prehistoric Egyptian art.* Berkeley (CA): University of California Press.

Demoule, J.-P. & C. Perles. 1993. The Greek Neolithic: a new review, *Journal of World Prehistory* 7(4):355–416.

Dobres, M.-A. 1992a. Re-presentations of Palaeolithic visual imagery: simulacra and their alternatives, *Kroeber Anthroplogical Society Papers* 73–4:1–25.

Ehrenberg, M. 1989. *Women in prehistory.* London: British Museum Publications.

Eisler, R. 1987. *The chalice and the blade: our history, our future.* San Francisco (CA): Harper Row.

Fagan, B. M. 1992. A sexist view of prehistory, *Archaeology* 45(2):14–16, 18, 66.

Frymer-Kensky, T. 1992. *In the wake of the goddess: women, culture and the biblical transformation of pagan myth.* New York (NY): Ballantine.

Gero, J. M. & M. W. Conkey. 1991. Tensions, pluralities and engendering archaeology: an introduction to women and prehistory, in Gero & Conkey (ed.): 2–29.

Gero, J. M. & M. W. Conkey (ed.). 1991. *Engendering archaeology: women and prehistory.* Oxford: Basil Blackwell.

Gill, D. W. J. & C. Chippindale. 1993. Material and intellectual consequences of esteem for Cycladic figures, *American Journal of Archaeology* 97:601–59.

Gimbutas, M. 1965. *The Bronze Age cultures in central and eastern Europe.* The Hague: Mouton.

—— 1970. Proto-Indo-European culture: the Kurgan culture during the 5th, 4th and 3rd millennium BC in G. Cardona *et al.* (ed.), *Indo-European and Indo-Europeans*: 155–97. Philadelphia (PA): University of Pennsylvania Press.

—— 1971a. *The Slavs*. London: Thames & Hudson.

—— 1971b (ed). *Neolithic Macedonia: as reflected by excavations at Anza, southeast Yugoslavia*. Los Angeles (CA): UCLA Institute of Archaeology. Monumenta Archaeologica 1.

—— 1973. The beginning of the Bronze Age in Europe and the Indo-Europeans—3500–2500 BC, *Journal of Indo-European Studies* 1(2):163–214.

—— 1974. *Gods and goddesses of old Europe*. London: Thames & Hudson.

—— 1981. Vulvas, breasts and buttocks of the Goddess Creatress: commentary on the origins of art, in G. Buccellati & C. Speroni (ed.), *The shape of the past. Studies in honour of Franklin D. Murphy*: 19–40. Los Angeles (CA): UCLA Institute of Archaeology.

—— 1986. Mythical imagery of Sitagroi society, in Renfrew *et al.* (ed.):225–301.

—— 1989a. *The language of the Goddess: unearthing hidden symbols of western civilisation*. London: Thames and Hudson.

—— 1989b. Women and culture in Goddess-oriented Old Europe, in J. Plaskow & C. C. Christ (ed.), *Weaving the visions*: 63–71. San Francisco (CA): Harpers.

—— 1991. *The civilization of the Goddess: the world of Old Europe*. San Francisco (CA): Harpers.

—— 1992. *The age of the Goddess: ancient roots of the emerging feminine consciousness*. Boulder (CO): Sounds True Recordings. Audio tape #A192.

Gimbutas, M., S. Winn & D. Shimabuku. 1989. *Achilleion: a Neolithic settlement in Thessaly, Greece 6400–5600* BC. Los Angeles (CA): UCLA Institute of Archaeology.

Hallett, J. P. 1993. Feminist theory, historical periods, literary canons, and the study of Greco-Roman antiquity, in Rabinowitz & Richlin (ed.):44–72.

Hayden, B. 1986. Old Europe: sacred matriarchy or complimentary opposition in A. Bonanno (ed.), *Archaeology and fertility cult in the Mediterranean*: 17–41. Amsterdam: B. R. Grunner.

Hays, K. A. 1993. When is a symbol archaeologically meaningful?: meaning, function and prehistoric visual arts, in N. Yoffee and S. Sherratt (ed.), *Archaeological theory: who sets the agenda?*:81–92. Cambridge: Cambridge University Press.

Hodder, I. R. 1987. Contextual archaeology: an interpretation of Çatal Hüyük and a discussion of the origins of agriculture. *University of London Institute of Archaeology Bulletin* 24:43–56.

—— 1990. *The domestication of Europe: structure and contingency in Neolithic societies*. Oxford: Basil Blackwell.

Humphreys, S. C. 1983. *The family, women and death: comparative studies*. London: Routledge & Kegan Paul.

Mcpherron, A. 1991. Review of Gimbutas *et al.* (1989), *American Antiquity 56*(3): 567–8.

Mallory, J. P. 1989. *In search of the Indo-Europeans*. London: Thames & Hudson.

Malone, C., A. Bonanno, T. Goulder, S. Stoddart & D. Trump. 1993. The death cults of prehistoric Malta. *Scientific American* (December):76–83.

Marinescu-Bilcu. 1981. *Tirpesti: from prehistory to history in eastern Romania*. Oxford: British Archaeological Reports. International series 107.

Milojkovic, J. 1990. The anthropomorphic and zoomorphic figurines, in Tringham & Krstic (ed.):397–436.

Murray, J. 1970. *The first European agriculture, a study of the osteological and botanical evidence until 2000* BC. Edinburgh: Edinburgh University Press.

Orenstein, G. F. 1990. *The reflowering of the Goddess*. New York (NY): Pergamon Press.

Pavlovic, M. 1990. The aesthetics of Neolithic figurines, in *Vinca and its world: international symposium. The Danubian region from 6000 to 3000* BC. *Belgrade, Smederevska Palanka, October 1988*:33–4. Belgrade: Academy of Arts and Sciences.

Passman, T. 1993. Out of the closet and into the field: matriculture, lesbian perspective and feminist classics, in Rabinowitz & Richlin (ed.):181–208.

Pogozheva, A. P. 1983. *Antropomorfnaya plastika Tripol'ya*. Novosibirsk: Akademiia Nauk, Sibirskoe Otdelenie.

Renfrew, C. 1987. *Archaeology and language: the puzzle of Indo-European origins*. London: Jonathan Cape.

Robins, G. 1993. *Women in ancient Egypt*. London: British Museum Press.

Runnels, C. 1990. Review of Gimbutas *et al.* (1989), *Journal of Field Archaeology* 17:341–5.

Shanks, M. & C. Tilley. 1987. *Re-constructing archaeology: theory and practice*. Cambridge: Cambridge University Press.

Spretnak, C. 1992. *Lost goddesses of early Greece*. Boston (MA): Beacon Press.

Starhawk. 1982. *Dreaming the dark: magic, sex and politics*. Boston (MA): Beacon Press.

Talalay, L. E. 1991. Body imagery of the ancient Aegean. *Archaeology* 44(4):46–9.

—— 1993. *Dolls, deities and devices. Neolithic figurines from Franthchi cave, Greece*. Bloomington (IN): Indiana University Press. Excavations at Franchthi Cave, Greece 9.

Tringham, R. E. 1991. Households with faces: the challenge of gender in prehistoric architectural remains, in Gero & Conkey (ed.):93–131.

—— 1993. Review of Gimbutas (1991). *American Anthropologist* 95:196–7.

Tringham, R. E. & D. Krstic (ed.). 1990. *Selevac: a Neolithic village in Yugoslavia*. Los Angeles (CA): UCLA Institute of Archaeology Monumenta Archaeologica 15.

Ucko, P. J. 1968. *Anthropomorphic figures of predynastic Egypt and Neolithic Crete with comparative material from the prehistoric Near East and Mainland Greece*. London: Andrew Szmidla.

Van Leuven, J. 1993. Review of Gimbutas (1991). *Journal of Prehistoric Religion* 7:83–4.

Wall, S. M., J. H. Musgrave & P. M. Warren. 1986. Human bones from a late Minoan 1b house at Knossos. *Annual of the British School at Athens* 81:333–88.

Wylie, M. A. 1991. Gender theory and the archaeological record: why is there no archaeology of gender?, in Gero & Conkey (ed.):31–47.

EXPLORING THE ISSUE

Was There a Goddess Cult in Prehistoric Europe?

Critical Thinking and Reflection

1. What evidence does Gimbutas offer for the existence of a Goddess cult in prehistoric Europe? Are there other ways to interpret this evidence?
2. What methodological concerns does Meskell raise about Gimbutas's analysis? Are other methodologies possible that might better support Gimbutas's interpretation?
3. What is the supposed association between Indo-Europeans and patriarchy? Why would Indo-Europeans have a patriarchal tradition while the previous inhabitants had a matriarchal tradition?
4. What is the association between female figurines excavated in many parts of Eastern Europe and the Middle East and the Goddess Cult? Are there other ways to explain the existence of these figurines without such a cult?
5. Why would feminists be attracted toward the Goddess Cult interpretation?

Is There Common Ground?

Certain aspects of this debate over the Goddess Cult concern evidence that both sides in the debate accept as facts. First, archaeological excavations have unearthed a number of plump female figurines in the region of the eastern Mediterranean and eastern Europe before the third millennium B.C.E. Second, there seems to be a major change in lifeways around the third millennium B.C.E. in this region. Scholars have traditionally associated this transition with the arrival of people from the Russian steppes, who it is presumed spoke early forms of Indo-European languages. Similarly, scholars have assumed that the earlier lifeways were associated with pre-Indo-European languages. Archaeologists have no evidence from their excavations about what language these early people spoke since writing had not appeared in any of these sites, but there are some non-Indo-European language like Hungarian, Finnish, Celtic, and Basque that seem to have predated the expansion of Indo-European languages. All of these are facts that need to be explained or accounted for, and suggest different ways to interpret the evidence and understand this region in the fourth millennium.

The argument against Gimbutas's interpretation is that she makes too much of the figurines. Seeing these figurines as ritual objects at the center of a major cult or religion is probably overinterpreting the evidence. It is probably best to consider what other interpretations might make sense of these figurines. Crucifixes and statues of the Virgin Mary are found in many Catholic households around the world. Both of these figures suggest the central relationship linking humans and God in Catholicism. But cultural anthropologists have observed that these figures and statues are often associated with much more dispersed personal cults than the rituals in a Catholic mass. Could these figures be personal ritual objects intended to assist women with fertility, pregnancy, safe delivery, healthy babies, and a swift return for the mother to productive activities? We cannot assert this interpretation as fact, but it is an alternative hypothesis that would have to be ruled out before we can accept Gimbutas's interpretations.

Similarly, before we can impute some characteristics to the societies before and after the transformation traditionally associated with the arrival of Indo-Europeans, we need to consider how we could know what the Indo-Europeans were like before they arrived in Europe. Again, these interpretations would seem to require considering alternative interpretations that can be evaluated in light of the evidence. Why, for example, would the Indo-Europeans have developed a patriarchal social organization, while other societies had a matriarchy? In sum, this issue hinges on evaluating different kinds of evidence in light of different possible interpretations.

Additional Resources

The early anthropological sources on the supposed prehistoric matriarchial societies are by Bachofen and MacLellan:

Bachofen, J. J. 1861. *Das Mutterrecht.* Benno Schwabe.

MacLellan, John Ferguson. 1865. *Primitive Marriage: An Inquiry into the Origin of the Form of Capture in Marriage Ceremonies.* A. & C. Black.

For background on the Goddess Movement's roots in European thought see:

Harrison, Jane Ellen. 1903. *Prolegomena to the Study of Greek Religion.* London: Cambridge University Press.

Hutton, Ronald 1997. "The Neolithic Great Goddess: A Study in Modern Tradition," *Antiquity* 71:7.

Beside the essay by Gimbutas above, her work is included in other publications:

Gimbutas, Marija. 1989. *The Language of the Goddess.* San Francisco: Harper & Row.

Gimbutas, Marija. 1991. *The Civilization of the Goddess.* San Francisco: Harper & Row.

Gimbutas, Marija. 1999. *The Living Goddess.* Berkeley: University of California Press.

The critiques of Gimbutas's theories include the following:

Baring, Anne and Cashford, Jules. 1991. *The Myth of the Goddess.* London: Viking Press.

Conkey, Margaret and Tringham, Ruth. 1995. "Archaeology and the Goddess: Exploring the Contours of Feminist Archaeology," in D.C. Stanton and A.J.

Stewart, eds., *Feminisms in the Academy*. Ann Arbor: University of Michigan Press. This essay provides an excellent overview of the controversy and discussion of its significance for feminist archaeology.

Ucko, Peter. 1968. *Anthropomorphic Figurines of Predynastic Egypt and Neolithic Crete with Comparative Material from the Prehistoric Near East and Mainland Greece*. London: Royal Anthropological Institute.

Ucko, Peter. 1992. "The Interpretation of Prehistoric Anthropomorphic Figurines," *Journal of the Royal Anthropological Institute*. 62.

Internet References . . .

An Interesting Site About Ebonics

This site provides a definition and a brief history of Ebonics.

www.lsadc.org/info/ling-faqs-ebonics.cfm

Ethnologue

This site produced by the Summer Institute of Linguistics gives information about 6,900 known languages in the world. Many of these are endangered and only about half of these have been well studied.

www.ethnologue.com/web.asp

Nonverbal Communication

This is a link that explores the nonverbal side of language. It is particularly relevant because the types of communication concerning the ape world are largely non-verbal ones.

http://nonverbal.ucsc.edu/

The Chimpanzee and Human Communication Institute Home Page

The Chimpanzee and Human Communication Institute provides information on this site about current research on teaching American Sign Language to chimpanzees. The site includes information about experiments with chimps as well as links to other sites dealing with the question of whether apes can learn a language.

www.cwu.edu/~cwuchci/

Useful Web Sites About the Sapir-Whorf Hypothesis

www.aber.ac.uk/media/Documents/short/whorf.html

www.nickyee.com/ponder/whorf.html

Linguistic Anthropology

*L*inguistic anthropologists study languages, particularly non-Western and unwritten languages. They also investigate the complex relationship between language and other aspects of culture. Language provides the categories within which culture is expressed and is the medium by which much of culture is transmitted from one generation to the next. Here we consider two classic questions that have confronted linguistic anthropologists for several decades. The first concerns whether chimpanzees and other apes have the innate ability to use symbols in ways that resemble human language. This question is important because if apes are capable of complex symbolic activity, then language and culture are probably not the exclusive capabilities of humans but have their origins in our primate past. The second question concerns what, if anything, scholars should do about the fact that many minority languages around the world are dying out as their last surviving speakers pass away. The problem is less about whether anything should be done about the elderly speakers themselves than about what could or should be done to encourage young people to learn the languages of their parents or grandparents.

- Can Apes Learn Language?

- Does Language Shape How We Think?

- Is Black American English a Separate Language from Standard American English, with Its Own Distinctive Grammar and Vocabulary?

ISSUE 8

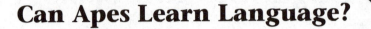

Can Apes Learn Language?

YES: E. S. Savage-Rumbaugh, from "Language Training of Apes," in Steve Jones, Robert Martin, and David Pilbeam, eds., *The Cambridge Encyclopedia of Human Evolution* (Cambridge University Press, 1999)

NO: Joel Wallman, from *Aping Language* (Cambridge University Press, 1992)

Learning Outcomes

After reading this issue, you should be able to:

- Understand several attempts to teach chimpanzees and other apes American Sign Language and some of the difficulties these researchers encountered.
- Discuss how ape-language projects in the laboratory are quite different from any study of ape communication in natural settings.
- Explain some of the criticisms other researchers have offered against these efforts to teach chimpanzees to use sign language as a symbolic system.
- Discuss why chimpanzees learning a small number of signs from American Sign Language might not suggest any inherent ability to use human language.
- Evaluate the arguments offered by those researchers who have trained apes to use signs and their relationship to the use of human language.

ISSUE SUMMARY

YES: Psychologist and primate specialist E. S. Savage-Rumbaugh argues that, since the 1960s, there have been attempts to teach chimpanzees and other apes symbol systems similar to human language. These studies have shown that although apes are not capable of learning human language, they demonstrate a genuine ability to create new symbolic patterns that are similar to very rudimentary symbolic activity.

NO: Linguist Joel Wallman counters that attempts to teach chimps and other apes sign language or other symbolic systems have demonstrated that apes are very intelligent animals. But up to now these attempts have not shown that apes have any innate capacity for language.

For more than a century, anthropologists have generally assumed that humankind's ability to make tools and use language were two characteristics that distinguished humans from all other animals. British anthropologist Kenneth P. Oakley, for example, first published his little volume entitled *Man the Tool-Maker* (London: Trustees of the British Museum) in 1949, which was republished in new or revised editions in the 1950s and 1960s by the University of Chicago Press for use as a supplementary college textbook. In the 1960s and 1970s, Jane Goodall and other primatologists convincingly demonstrated that chimpanzees, our nearest biological relatives, made simple tools, narrowing the gap between apes and humans.

Beginning in the 1940s a series of other scientists have worked with gorillas, chimps, and most recently the bonobo (or pygmy chimp) attempting to teach these apes simple forms of human-like language.

In the 1950s, the psychologist B.F. Skinner had argued that human children learned natural language through conditioning, such that positive responses to utterances from proud parents and other adults essentially trained children to recognize both grammatical patterns and vocabulary. But in the 1960s, linguist Naom Chomsky disproved Skinner's theory showing that human language is so highly complex that it must require some innate biological capability that he called a "language acquisition device." In several respects, all of the ape-language experiments since then have sought to understand when this biological capacity for language learning evolved in primates. If apes could use simple language then this biological capacity was present very early in our prehuman lineage.

The early years of the ape-language projects encountered one major difficulty. Try as they might, trainers could not get apes to vocalize human words reliably. This difficulty was a consequence of the fact that a chimp's vocal apparatus simply does not allow the possibility of human utterances. So efforts to teach apes how to use language had to overcome the problem of vocalization with some other means of communication.

Since Chomsky's studies of human language, linguists have generally accepted that the manipulation of symbols in systematic grammatical ways, rather than the ability to make utterances, is the most important and complex aspect of human language. Deaf people who have difficulty making recognizable linguistic utterances have no difficulty learning the grammar (phonology, morphology, and syntax) of normal language. Thus, if apes could manipulate symbols in linguistic ways, researchers hoped they could demonstrate that the ability to acquire language was a biological capacity shared by at least certain species of the apes and humans.

In the 1960s, researchers began using other media that would allow apes to use and manipulate symbols without vocalization. These approaches included plastic shapes on a board, symbols on a computer console, and American Sign Language, long used by deaf people. For more than 30 years, trainers have claimed that their chimp or gorilla students have learned symbols for hundreds of words or concepts and many of these researchers have claimed that such ability to manipulate symbols is analogous to symbol use among young human children.

If true, the ability to learn and use language, the last barrier that separates human beings from our non-human primate relatives has fallen away. This view has its supporters and detractors, many of whom—largely on political or religious grounds—would either like to see humans as just another of the great apes or would prefer to view human beings as unique in the animal kingdom. But at issue is whether the long series of ape-language projects has demonstrated that apes can learn to manipulate signs and symbols.

Psychologist and primate specialist Sue Savage-Rumbaugh and her husband Duane Rumbaugh have been among the most innovative researchers in this field at the intersection of anthropology, linguistics, and cognitive psychology. They have argued that a certain species of pygmy chimps, the bonobo, are biologically closest to *Homo sapiens* of all the great apes. Their recent work with a bonobo named Kanzi has been among the most successful of these ape-language projects. Here, after tracing the history of these projects, Savage-Rumbaugh concludes that Kanzi's ability to use symbols closely resembles similar abilities observed among small human children. Thus, she concludes that the ability to use symbols is a trait shared by apes and humans, even though this trait is most well developed among humans.

Linguist Joel Wallman interprets the evidence very differently from Savage-Rumbaugh. He acknowledges that the various gorillas, chimps, and bonobos are clever animals that have learned to respond to their trainers in important ways. But he argues that these animals have not learned anything resembling human language. Chimps and bonobos may be clever but they do not have full linguistic abilities, their abilities to use mental abstractions suggests only that very modest versions of these mental processes arose before our branch of the hominin lineage split off from the lineages of the great apes.

These selections raise a number of questions about the similarities and differences between apes and humans. What kind of linguistic ability do these ape learners exhibit? Do these symbolic strings genuinely parallel early childhood language acquisition? Most importantly, do these ape-language studies show that apes and human beings genuinely share a common ability for language? What are the minimal features that make up any natural language?

YES ↵

E. S. Savage-Rumbaugh

Language Training of Apes

Can apes learn to communicate with human beings? Scientists have been attempting to answer this question since the late 1960s when it was first reported that a young chimpanzee named Washoe in Reno, Nevada had been taught to produce hand signs similar to those used by deaf humans.

Washoe was reared much like a human child. People made signs to her throughout the day and she was given freedom to move about the caravan where she lived. She could even go outdoors to play. She was taught how to make different signs by teachers who moved her hands through the motions of each sign while showing her the object she was learning to 'name'. If she began to make a portion of the hand movement on her own she was quickly rewarded, either with food or with something appropriate to the sign. For example, if she was being taught the sign for 'tickle' her reward was a tickling game.

This training method was termed 'moulding' because it involved the physical placement of Washoe's hands. Little by little, Washoe became able to produce more and more signs on her own. As she grew older, she occasionally even learned to make new signs without moulding. Once Washoe had learned several signs she quickly began to link them together to produce strings of signs such as 'you me out'. Such sequences appeared to her teachers to be simple sentences.

Many biologists were sceptical of the claims made for Washoe. While they agreed that Washoe was able to produce different gestures, they doubted that such signs really served as names. Perhaps, to Washoe, the gestures were just tricks to be used to get the experimenter to give her things she wanted; even though Washoe knew how and when to make signs, she really did not know what words meant in the sense that people do.

The disagreement was more than a scholarly debate among scientists. Decades of previous work had demonstrated that many animals could learn to do complex things to obtain food, without understanding what they were doing. For example, pigeons had been taught to bat a ball back and forth in what looked like a game of ping pong. They were also taught to peck keys with such words as 'Please', 'Thank you', 'Red' and 'Green' printed on them. They did this in a way that made it appear that they were communicating, but they were not; they had simply learned to peck each key when a special signal was given.

From *The Cambridge Encyclopedia of Human Evolution,* Steve Jones, Robert Martin, and David Pilbeam, eds. (Cambridge University Press, 1992, 1999), pp. 138–141. Copyright © 1999 by Cambridge University Press. Reprinted by permission.

This type of learning is called *conditioned discrimination* learning, a term that simply means that an animal can learn to make one set of responses in one group of circumstances and another in different circumstances. Although some aspects of human language can be explained in this way, such as 'Hello', 'Goodbye', 'Please' and 'Thank you', most cannot. Human beings learn more than what to say when: they learn what words stand for.

If Washoe had simply signed 'drink' when someone held up a bottle of soda, there would be little reason to conclude that she was doing anything different from other animals. If, however, Washoe used the sign 'drink' to represent any liquid beverage, then she was doing something very different— something that everyone had previously thought only humans could do.

It was difficult to determine which of these possibilities charcterised her behaviour, as the question of how to distinguish between the 'conditioned response' and a 'word' had not arisen. Before Washoe, the only organisms that used words were human beings, and to determine if a person knew what a word stood for was easy: one simply asked. This was impossible with Washoe, because her use of symbols was not advanced enough to allow her to comprehend complex questions. One- and two-year-old children are also unable to answer questions such as these. However, because children are able to answer such questions later on, the issue of determining how and when a child knows that words have meanings had not until then been seen as critical.

Teaching Syntax

Several scientists attempted to solve this problem by focusing on sentences instead of words. Linguists argue that the essence of human language lies not in learning to use individual words, but rather in an ability to form a large number of word combinations that follow the same set of specific rules. These rules are seen as a genetic endowment unique to humans. If it could be shown that apes learn syntactical rules, then it must be true that they were using symbols to represent things, not just perform tricks.

Three psychologists in the 1970s each used a different method in an attempt to teach apes syntax. One group followed the method used with Washoe and began teaching another chimpanzee, Nim, sign language. Another opted for the use of plastic symbols with the chimpanzee Sarah. Still another used geometric symbols, linked to a computer keyboard, with a chimpanzee named Lana. Both Lana and Sarah were taught a simple syntax, which required them to fill in one blank at a time in a string of words. The number of blanks was slowly increased until the chimpanzee was forming a complete 'sentence'. Nim was asked to produce syntactically correct strings by making signs along with his teacher.

Without help from his teachers, Nim was unable to form sentences that displayed the kind of syntactical rules used by humans. Nim's sign usage could best be interpreted as a series of 'conditioned discriminations' similar to, albeit more complex than, behaviours seen in many less-intelligent animals. This work suggested that Nim, like circus animals but unlike human children, was using words only to obtain rewards.

However, the other attempts to teach sentences to apes arrived at a different conclusion, perhaps because a different training method was used. Both Sarah and Lana learned to fill in the blanks in sentences in ways that suggested they had learned the rules that govern simple sentence construction. Moreover, 6 per cent of Lana's sentences were 'novel' in that they differed from the ones that she had been taught. Many of these sentences, such as 'Please you move coke in cup into room', followed syntactical rules and were appropriate and meaningful communications. Other sentences followed the syntactical rules that Lana had learned, but did not make sense; for example, 'Question you give beancake shut-open'. Thus, apes appeared to be able to learn rules for sentence construction, but they did not generalise these rules in a way that suggested full comprehension of the words.

By 1980, Washoe had matured and given birth. At this time there was great interest in whether or not she would teach her offspring to sign. Unfortunately, her infant died. However, another infant was obtained and given to Washoe. This infant, Loulis, began to imitate many of the hand gestures that Washoe used, though the imitations were often quite imprecise. Washoe made few explicit attempts to mould Loulis's hands. Although Loulis began to make signs, it was not easy to determine why he was making them or what, if anything, he meant. Loulis has not yet received any tests like those that were given to Washoe to determine if he can make the correct sign when shown an object. It is clear that he learned to imitate Washoe, but it is not clear that he learned what the signs meant.

The question of whether or not apes understand words caused many developmental psychologists to study earlier and earlier aspects of language acquisition in children. Their work gave, for the first time, a detailed insight into how children use words during the 'one-word' stage of language learning and showed that children usually learn to understand words before they begin to use them. At the same time, there was a new approach to the investigation of ape language. Instead of teaching names by pairing an object with its sign or symbol and rewarding correct responses, there was a new emphasis on the communicative aspect of symbols. For example, to teach a symbol such as 'key', a desirable item was locked in a box that was given to the chimpanzee. When the chimpanzee failed to open it, he was shown how to ask for and how to use a key. On other occasions, the chimpanzee was asked to retrieve a key for the teacher, so that she might open the box.

This new approach was first used with two chimpanzees named Sherman and Austin. It resulted in a clearer symbolic use of words than that found in animals trained by other methods. In addition, because these chimpanzees were taught comprehension skills, they were able to communicate with one another and not just with the experimenters. Sherman and Austin could use their symbols to tell each other things that could not be conveyed by simple glances or by pointing. For example, they could describe foods they had seen in another room, or the types of tools they needed to solve a problem. Although other apes had been reported to sign in each other's presence, there was no evidence that they were intentionally signing to each other or that they responded to each other's signs.

Most important, Sherman and Austin began to show an aspect of symbol usage that they had not been taught; they used symbols to say what they were going to do *before* they did it. Symbol use by other apes had not included descriptions of intended actions; rather, communications had been begun by a teacher, or limited to simple requests.

Sherman and Austin also began to use symbols to share information about objects that were not present and they passed a particularly demanding test, which required them to look at symbols and answer questions that could be answered only if they knew what each symbol represented. For example, they could look at printed lexigram symbols such as 'key', 'lever', 'stick', 'wrench', 'apple', 'banana', 'pineapple' and 'juice', and state whether each lexigram belonged to the class of 'food' words or 'tool' words. They could do this without ever being told whether these lexigram symbols should be classified as foods or tools. These findings were important, because they revealed that by using symbols an ape can describe what it is about to do.

How Similar Is Ape Language to Human Language?

Even though it was generally agreed that apes could do something far more complex than most other animals, there still remained much disagreement as to whether ape's symbols were identical to human symbols. This uncertainty arose for two reasons: apes did not acquire words in the same manner as children—that is, by observing others use them; and apes did not appear to use true syntactical rules to construct multiple-word utterances.

The first of these differences between ape and child has recently been challenged by a young pygmy chimpanzee or bonobo named Kanzi. Most previous studies had focused on common chimpanzees because pygmy chimpanzees are very rare (they are in great danger of having their habitat destroyed in the coming decade and have no protected parks).

In contrast to other apes, Kanzi learned symbols simply by observing human beings point to them while speaking to him. He did not need to have his arms placed in position, or to be rewarded for using a correct symbol. More important, he did not need to be taught to comprehend symbols or taught that symbols could be used for absent objects as well as those present. Kanzi spontaneously used symbols to announce his actions or intentions and, if his meaning was ambiguous, he often invented gestures to clarify it, as young children do.

Kanzi learned words by listening to speech. He first comprehended certain spoken words, then learned to read the lexigram symbols. This was possible because his caretakers pointed to these symbols as they spoke. For example, Kanzi learned 'strawberries' as he heard people mention the word when they ran across wild strawberries growing in the woods. He soon became able to lead people to strawberries whenever they asked him to do so. He similarly learned the spoken names of many other foods that grew outdoors, such as wild grapes, honeysuckle, privet berries, blackberries and mushrooms, and could take people to any of these foods upon spoken request.

Unlike previous apes reared as human children, Kanzi was reared in a semi-natural woodland. Although he could not produce speech, he understood much of what was said to him. He could appropriately carry out novel spoken requests such as 'Will you take some hamburger to Austin?', 'Can you show your new toy to Kelly?' and 'Would you give Panzee some of your melon?'. There appeared to be no limit to the number of sentences that Kanzi could understand as long as the words in the sentences were in his vocabulary.

During the first 3 or 4 years of his life, Kanzi's comprehension of spoken sentences was limited to things that he heard often. However, when he was 5 years old, he began to respond to novel sentences upon first hearing them. For example, the first time he heard someone talk about throwing a ball in the river, he suddenly turned and threw his ball right in the water, even though he had never done this before. Similarly, when someone suggested, for fun, that he might then try to throw a potato at a turtle that was nearby, he found a potato and tossed it at the turtle. To be certain that Kanzi was not being somehow 'cued' inadvertently by people, he was tested with headphones. In this test he had to listen to a word and point to a picture of the word that he heard. Kanzi did this easily, the first time he took the test.

About this time, Kanzi also began to combine symbols. Unlike other apes, he did not combine symbols ungrammatically to get the experimenter to give something that was purposefully being held back. Kanzi's combinations had a primitive English word order and conveyed novel information. For example, he formed utterances such as 'Ball go group room' to say that he wanted to play with a specific ball—the one he had seen in the group room on the previous day. Because the experimenter was not attempting to get Kanzi to say this, and was indeed far from the group room, such a sentence conveyed something that only Kanzi—not the experimenter—knew before Kanzi spoke.

Thus Kanzi's combinations differed from those of other apes in that they often referred to things or events that were absent and were known only to Kanzi, they contained a primitive grammar and were not imitations of the experimenter. Nor did the experimenter ask rhetorical questions such as 'What is this?' to elicit them, Kanzi's combinations include sentences such as 'Tickle bite', 'Keep-way balloon' and 'Coke chase'. As almost nothing is yet known of how pygmy chimpanzees communicate, they could use a form of simple language in the wild. Kanzi understands spoken English words, so the ability that is reflected in language comprehension is probably an older evolutionary adaptation than is the ability to talk.

Studying ape language presents a serious challenge to the long-held view that only humans can talk and think. Certainly, there is now no doubt that apes communicate in much more complex and abstract ways than dogs, cats and other familiar animals. Similarly, apes that have learned some language skills are also able to do some remarkable non-linguistic tasks. For example, they can recognise themselves on television and even determine whether an image is taped or live. They can also play video games, using a joystick to catch and trap a video villain.

Scientists have only just begun to discover ways of tapping the hidden talents for language and communication of our closest relatives. Sharing 98 per cent of their DNA with human beings, it has long been wondered why African apes seem so much like us at a biological level, but so different when it comes to behaviour. Ape-language studies continue to reveal that apes are more like us than we ever imagined.

Aping Language

Experiments carried out over the past two decades . . . attempted to impart a language, either natural or invented, to an ape. The debate engendered by these projects has been of interest—consuming for some, passing for others—to all of those whose concerns include the enduring questions of human nature, among them anthropologists, psychologists, linguists, biologists, and philosophers.

An adequate treatment of the linguistic capabilities of apes entails consideration of a number of related issues, each of which is an interesting problem in its own right. Continuities in primate mentality, the relationship between language and thought in the individual and in the species, and the origin of language . . . are themes that . . . recur throughout this [debate].

. . . [N]one of the ape-language projects succeeded, despite employing years of tutelage far more intense than that experienced by most children, in implanting in an ape a capacity for language equal to that of a young child, let alone an adult. . . .

Why the Ape-Language Controversy Is a Controversy

All scientific arguments have in common at least these elements: (1) a minimum of two positions regarding the subject in dispute, positions generally held to be irreconcilable, and (2) an intensification of the normal emotional investment of the scientist in his or her position, due in some measure to the contending itself but perhaps also related to the ideological significance of the subject within the larger society. If, in addition, the argument includes suggestions of fraudulent or quasi-fraudulent procedures, the disagreement becomes a controversy. To the extent that this is an accurate characterization of scientific controversies, the ape-language debate is an exemplary one.

The radical opposition of opinion about the achievement of the various ape-language projects is well conveyed by the following quotations:

> [Washoe] learned a natural human language and her early utterances were highly similar to, perhaps indistinguishable from the early utterances of human children. (Gardner and Gardner 1978, p. 73)

The evidence we have makes it clear that even the brightest ape can acquire not even so much as the weak grammatical system exhibited by very young children. (Premack and Premack 1983, p. 115)

On measures of sign performance (form), sign order (structure), semantic relations (meaning), sign acts (function) and sign acquisition (development), apes appear to be very similar to 2 to 3 year old human children learning sign . . . Apes also appear to be very similar to 2 to 3 year old human children learning to speak. (Miles 1978, p. 114)

[The experimental chimpanzees] show, after years of training and exposure to signing, not the slightest trace of homological development parallel to that of human children. (Leiber 1984, p. 84)

After years of gentle teaching Koko has learned to use American Sign Language—the very same sign language used by the deaf. With her new-found vocabulary, Koko is now providing us with an astounding wealth of knowledge about the way animals view the world. (Patterson 1985a, p. 1) . . .

There are several sources of the stridency of the debate.

. . . [L]anguage, at least in the European intellectual tradition, is the quintessential human attribute, at once evidence and source of most that is transcendent in us, distinguishing ours from the merely mechanical nature of the beast. Language is regarded as the *sine qua non* of culture, and its presence in our species is the most salient behavioral difference between us and the other hominoids—with the relinquishing of tool use and, more recently, tool making (Goodall 1971; Beck 1980) as uniquely human capabilities, the significance of language as a separator has grown. And resistance to losing our quintessential attributes is, arguably, itself one of those uniquely human traits. Hence, some ape partisans (Linden 1974; Gysens-Gosselin 1979) have argued, the prevalent reluctance to accord the talking apes their due. An occasional variant of this interpretation is the accusation that those who refuse to recognize ape language are insufficiently committed to the Darwinian perspective or, worse, are anti-Darwinian. Thus Linden (1987) depicts those who question the likelihood of ape–human linguistic continuities as latter-day Wilberforces, averse to investigating "creatures who threaten to paralyze us by shedding light on the true nature and origins of our abilities" (p. 8).

A countervailing vector of our ideology, perhaps peculiar to our culture but possibly pancultural, consists of careless anthropomorphic projection and an irrepressively attractive vision of communication between our own and other species. In fact, it seems correct to observe that, at least until recently in the debate and probably up to the present, the majority opinion, both lay and scientific, regarding the linguistic capabilities of the apes has been positive. People seem not only accepting but positively desirous of the possibility of ape language.

Even if language did not have the sacrosanct status it does in our conception of human nature, the question of its presence in other species would still promote argument, for we are lacking any universally accepted, unassailable diagnostic criteria for language. There is no shortage of candidates for the indispensable attribute of language. For Katz (1976) and Limber (1977), the projective capability is crucial, the provision of language for the articulation of any conceivable new proposition through a novel combination of words. Savage-Rumbaugh (1981) holds the referential nature of individual symbols to be the essence of language, while Premack (1984) and Marshall (1971) see the capacity for representation of real-world situations to be paramount, and so on. The property most commonly invoked as definitive of language is its predication on a system of abstract rules for the production and interpretation of utterances—in other words, grammar. Hockett's (1959, 1960, 1963; Hockett and Altmann 1968) famous list of so-called design features of language—including rapid fading, duality of patterning, and displacement—has provided a useful orientation for those trying to capture the differences between human and nonhuman natural systems of communication. What is wanting, nonetheless, is consensus on what the necessary and sufficient, as distinguished from inessential, property or properties of language are and hence on how we might unequivocally identify language in another species.

This problem of defining features is more severe where the language of the young child is concerned, and it is the child's language that is taken by most parties to the debate to be the proper material for comparison with the apes. If the young child is not, in fact, capable of linguistically encoding anything she can think of, if her production and understanding of utterances do not suggest abstract grammatical constituents and processes, then can it be said that the child has language? Limber (1977) and Lightfoot (1982), at least, would say no.

This is a defensible position, its major problem found in the fact that the young child's language, which may not yet be language, will eventually become language. How is this discontinuity in development to be bridged? The difficulty is not the existence of a discontinuity per se—there are a number of others in human development. The physiological transition from prepubescence to pubescence, for example, poses a similar problem—the two developmental phases are identifiably distinct, yet there are no two adjacent points in time about which it could be said that the child was prepubescent in the first but pubescent in the second.

What makes the transition from "nonlanguage" (. . . early language) to language more problematic is that, unlike the case of puberty, in which the first phase is defined largely by the absence of characteristics of the later one, early language has its own, very salient features. Moreover, there are some striking functional and possibly structural similarities between these features and those of adult language. . . . And, contrary to those who would deny language to the young child, there is extensive evidence for grammatical structure in the earliest word combinations (Bloom 1970; Brown 1973), and, some have suggested (De Laguna 1927; McNeill 1970), in single-word utterances as well. (The proper characterization of this structure, however, is the subject of ongoing debate in developmental psycholinguistics—in fact, this may be the dominant concern of the field. . . .

Language, in summary, is central to our self-definition as a species, even though we have yet to derive an adequate definition of language itself, one that includes the essential but excludes the merely contingent.

Behaviorist Roots of the Ape-Language Experiments

There is an additional source of the contention surrounding the ape-language question. The issues in the debate tend to resonate along the long-standing cleavage within the behavioral sciences between those who advocate study of cognition and/or innately determined behavior, on the one hand, and those, on the other, who are behaviorist in method and theory.

Behaviorism, or stimulus–response psychology, came into being in the early decades of this century as an avowed antidote to the introspectionist trend in turn-of-the-century psychological investigation. Knowledge, thought, intention, affect, and all other unobservable mental phenomena were banished in favor of overt behavior as the only proper subject of a scientific psychology. To explain the behavior of animals, behaviorism, like the eighteenth-century empiricism from which it descends, posits a bare minimum of cognitive apparatus: (1) perception, (2) a capacity to represent in durable format the results of perception, and (3) the ability to form associations among those representations. In the behaviorist paradigm, the acquisition and strengthening of such associations constitute learning.

An association may be formed between a perceptual stimulus and an inborn response if that stimulus consistently accompanies another one that is innately connected to the response, as in the celebrated conjunction of the ticking of a metronome, food, and salivation in Pavlov's dogs. Or an animal may form an association between one of its own actions and a subsequent stimulus, as when a pigeon comes reliably to peck a button because its activation results in the dispensing of food. In this process, an association is created between an action and a following stimulus that "reinforces" that action. To qualify as a reinforcing stimulus, a consequence need not be one that we would regard a priori as satisfying or pleasant—in fact, any stimulus that increases the probability of the organism emitting the behavior that preceded it is, by definition, reinforcing.

In the behaviorist conception, all behavior is determined either by current stimuli or by past consequences. Language is verbal behavior; words function both as responses to stimuli and as stimuli themselves, eliciting further responses. Thus a sentence can be interpreted as a chain of stimulus–response events, each word a response to the preceding one and also a stimulus evoking the next, with the first word elicited by an environmental stimulus or an internal one, a "private event." Or, in some formulations, the entire sentence is regarded as one complex response to a stimulus.

The orthodox behaviorist account of learning has little use for traditional distinctions among types of behavior. Nor are species differences in behavioral mechanisms acknowledged. Although sometimes touted as such, the latter attitude is not an appreciation of evolutionary continuity, with the selectively and historically wrought similarities and divergences in behavior that such a theoretical affirmation entails. Rather, it reflects a commitment to cross-species *homogeneity*, a rejection of the notion that there are important differences across species in the processes that underlie the development and causation of behavior. . . .

Like other contemporary adherents of behaviorism, the ape-language experimenters embraced the various concessions to reality that the most primitive versions of behaviorism were forced to make over the years. The Gardners, for example, acknowledge that some parts of the innate behavioral repertoire of a species are more plastic and hence more readily conditioned than others, and also that species differ in their intrinsic propensities for various behaviors. Thus the chimpanzee's inborn motivation to communicate obviates conditioning as laborious as another behavior might require. That language acquisition in the chimpanzee and in the child are similarly dependent on extensive molding, shaping, and imitation, however, is an assumption that is fundamental to their research, and fundamentally erroneous. Indeed, their suggestion that the linguistic performance of the preschool child requires "intensive training" (1971, p. 188) is the *opposite* of one of the few claims to which virtually all language-acquisition researchers would assent. . . .

Lastly, it may be worth observing that the potential personal rewards of the ape projects have been substantial and emotional commitment commensurately high—the first person or team to give language to another species would certainly attain scientific immortality.

⋘◉⋙

. . . In describing their aspirations for Washoe, the first of the modern ape language pupils, the Gardners expressed pessimism about a direct assault on the question "Can an ape talk?" and . . . adopted instead an unabashedly behavioristic goal: "We wanted to develop behavior that could be called conversation" (1969, p. 665). And critics . . . have maintained that Washoe and her peers, though they may have simulated conversation, acquired neither a human language nor something crucially like one, but rather a system of habits that are crude facsimiles of the features of language.

Refuting the claim that apes have the ability to learn a language logically entails proving that they do *not* have it. This [selection] has not succeeded in doing something that cannot be achieved: proving that something does not exist. The relevant refutable claim, rather, is that one or more of the animals featured in these pages learned a language. Refuting this unequivocally, however, presupposes a set of definitive criteria for language and a demonstration that at least one of them was not met by each of the animals in question. . . . [S]uch criteria do not yet exist, either for adult forms or for children's forms of language. So it is not possible in principle to show that no ape *could* learn a language, and it is not possible in practice to show that none *has* learned a language. . . .

The ape-language experiments confirmed what students dating back at least as far as the gestalt psychologist Wolfgang Kohler have repeatedly demonstrated, which is that apes are highly intelligent creatures, probably second only to us, on measures of human intelligence. We may wonder how the evolutionary process engendered such a powerful mentality in the midst of the African rain forests, asking, like Humphrey (1976), of what use "conditional oddity discrimination" is to an ape in the jungle. But the cognitive prowess of the apes is a fact regardless of our inability to account for it.

That the apes, too, are reflexive and capable of impressively abstract mentation suggests that at least modest versions of these faculties arose before the ancestral hominoid lineage diversified into the African apes on the one hand and us on the other. Consider a modest assertion: a capacity for culture requires at least ape-level powers of abstraction. And a case could be made for self-awareness, too, as prerequisite to culture. To the extent that Freud's understanding of humanity's cultural creations as "immortality projects" is sound, an ego is presupposed. If the capacity for language, too, had arisen prior to that last hominoid divergence, then linguistics might have been a branch of comparative psychology, the ape-language experiments would never have been conceived, and this [selection] would have been about something else, say patterns of interspecies marriage. But, for that matter, had language arisen prior to the split that produced them and us—had we all spoken the same language—there might not have been a them and an us.

EXPLORING THE ISSUE

Can Apes Learn Language?

Critical Thinking and Reflection

1. What evidence does Savage-Rumbaugh offer that suggests that apes who use some signs from American Sign Language have any ability to use symbols or have any aptitude toward learning language?
2. Is there any evidence that these chimpanzees and other apes have actually learned to use symbols rather than just learning to respond to their trainers' behavioral cues?
3. Behavioral psychologists like B.F. Skinner argued that children learned language by being encouraged by their parents and other adults around them. How might these ape experiments with Sign Language be a test of Skinner's arguments?
4. If Wallman and the other critics of ape-language training are correct, have we learned anything from Savage-Rumbaugh's research and the efforts to train apes to use symbols? What would we expect of chimpanzees who separated from the human ancestral line about 8 million years ago?
5. If Wallman and the other critics of ape-language experiments are wrong, what would these studies demonstrate about human language capabilities?

Is There Common Ground?

The two sides on the issue of ape-language ability remain widely separated. Each side in the debate continues to have both its supporters and detractors. At the heart of the issue are several questions about (1) the biological nature of human beings and their nearest primate relatives, (2) the character of language and cognition, particularly among children who are just beginning to acquire language, and (3) the best and most unbiased methods for investigation of ape-language abilities.

Besides Savage-Rumbaugh's bonobo Kanzi, two other notable ape-language projects have received a considerable amount of attention. T. Beatrix and R. Allen Gardner began training their chimpanzee Washoe to use American Sign Language in the late 1960s with some success. Another researcher, Herbert S. Terrace trained his chimpanzee Nim Chimpsky to use 125 signs. Several other projects have used plastic tokens or computer symbols.

Another animal study is worth mentioning here because it did not have to overcome the inability to vocalize: animal psychologist Irene Pepperberg's 30-year study of her African gray parrot named Alex. Using plastic tokens of various shapes and colors, she demonstrated that Alex could identify different numbers, colors, and shapes using the parrot's natural ability to vocalize utterances that form simple strings that resemble sentences. None of these animal language studies have attempted to show that any of these species have natural language, but all of them are trying to show that the roots of linguistic competence may not have arisen with the rise of our genus *Homo*.

One of the strongest critics of the ape-language experiments is the cognitive psychologist Steven Pinker, who outlines his arguments in his book *The Language Instinct* (Harper Collins, 1994). Pinker argues that ape trainers have inadvertently used very subtle conditioning to train their primates. The sequences of symbols that even the most talented of the apes has produced are far simpler than normal children's linguistic abilities. His view is that Savage-Rumbaugh and other trainers have over interpreted the primate symbolic sequences so that ape abilities are merely conditioned responses. Chimps and bonobos may be clever animals, but their cleverness is conditioned along the lines that Skinner had proposed; it is not linguistic behavior as understood by Chomsky and most linguists. If true, Pinker's criticism suggests that all of the ape-language projects have been failures and at best trainers have tricked themselves into believing that apes can use symbols in linguistic ways.

Do the ape-language experiments introduce bias by interpreting symbolic strings too broadly and ambiguously? Are detractors of these experiments themselves biased, refusing to believe that apes are capable of any human-like linguistic or cognitive processes? And even if these experiments do not demonstrate an ability to use symbols in ways that precisely parallel child language use, can they not tell us a great deal about general patterns of cognition relevant to both humans and primates?

If Pinker is correct that humans use a different part of the brain for language than do apes when making natural vocalizations, then the efforts to demonstrate language ability in even the brightest of the great apes may ultimately be unsuccessful. Nevertheless, as Wallman and Savage-Rumbaugh suggest, however primitive apes' use of symbols may be, researchers may still learn a great deal about certain kinds of cognitive processes. If they do convincingly to show that apes have some kind of language capability, there is still much to be learned about ape cognition in several of the areas that Savage-Rumbaugh has suggested.

Such advances are possible only if the ape-language experiments can develop research methods that are completely free from bias and inadvertent human conditioning of their ape subjects. While Savage-Rumbaugh and the other researchers have tried to minimize the possibility of conditioning on their subject animals, as Pinker suggests, the context of the training makes it difficult to exclude the possibility of conditioning.

Up to now none of the ape-language projects have been able to tell us much if anything about ape communication in natural settings because all the projects were conducted in laboratory settings. Even though no language-like communication has been identified among wild chimps or bonobos, there is still much to be learned about how these species communicate. Such studies, particularly if they can be linked to the ape-language experiments, may have a great deal to offer about primate cognition and they may ultimately offer insights about process of language acquisition in human children.

Additional Resources

For a discussion of Washo and the other early ape-language projects, see the Web page on Washoe research at Central Washington University: www.cwu.edu/~cwuchci/publications.html.

Terrace, Herbert S. 1979. *Nim*. New York: Knopf.

Students may also have seen the recent film: *Project Nim* (directed by James Marsh), which documents the problems encountered when bringing a chimp into a human family.

Premack, David and Premack, Ann. 1983. *The Mind of an Ape*. New York: W.W. Norton.

Savage-Rumbaugh, Sue and Lewin, Roger. 1994. *Kanzi: The Ape at the Brink of the Human Mind*. New York: Wiley.

On child language acquisition see:

Pinker, Steven. 1984. *Language Learnability and Language Development*. Cambridge, MA: Harvard University Press.

For Skinner's original behaviorist model of language learning see:

Skinner, B. F. 1957. *Verbal Behavior*. New York: Appleton-Century-Crofts.

Chomsky's critique of Skinner appears in:

Chomsky, Naom. 1957. *Syntactic Structures*. 's-Gravenhage: Mouton.

Students may also enjoy Pinker analysis of what makes up language:

Pinker, Steven. 2011. *Words and Rules: The Ingredients of Language*. New York: Harper Perennial Editions.

For reviews of the state of ape-language experiments see:

Savage-Rumbaugh, Sue, Shaker, Stuart G., and Taylor, Talbot J. 1998. *Apes, Language, and the Human Mind*. New York: Oxford University Press.

Sergerdahl, Pär, Fields, William, Savage-Rumbaugh, Sue. 2005. *Kanzi's Primal Language: The Cultural Initiation of Primates into Language*. New York: Palgrave-Macmillan.

King, Barbara J., ed. 1999. *The Origins of Language: What Nonhuman Primates Can Tell Us*. Santa Fe: SAR Press.

King, Barbara J., ed. 1994. *The Information Continuum: Evolution of Social Information Transfer in Monkeys, Apes, and Hominids*. Santa Fe: SAR Press.

ISSUE 9

Does Language Shape How We Think?

YES: John J. Gumperz and Stephen C. Levinson, from "Introduction: Linguistic Relativity Re-Examined," and "Introduction to Part 1," in John J. Gumperz and Stephen C. Levinson, eds., *Rethinking Linguistic Relativity* (Cambridge University Press, 1996)

NO: Steven Pinker, from "Mentalese," in *The Language Instinct: How the Mind Creates Language* (Perennial Classics, 2000)

Learning Outcomes

After reading this issue, you should be able to:

- Understand the arguments about how language might shape the way people understand the world.
- Discuss the relationship between language and cognition.
- Explain the role that the structure of our language might have on interpretations that people make from the words or sentences they hear.
- Understand some of the implications of linguistic relativism on understanding the role of language in culture.
- Evaluate the pros and cons of the Sapir–Whorf hypothesis in a general way.

ISSUE SUMMARY

YES: Sociolinguists John Gumperz and Stephen C. Levinson contend that recent studies of language and culture suggest that language structures human thought in a variety of ways that most linguists and anthropologists had not believed possible. They argue that culture through language affects the ways that we think and the ways that we experience the world.

NO: Cognitive neuropsychologist Steven Pinker draws on recent studies in cognitive science and neuropsychology to suggest that Edward Sapir and Benjamin Whorf were wrong when they suggested that the structure of any particular language had any effect on the ways human beings thought about the world in which they lived. He argues that previous studies have examined language but have said little, if anything, about thought.

For more than a century, anthropologists and linguists have observed that the world's languages differ in a number of significant ways. While some languages, such as French or Spanish, require speakers to mark the gender of most nouns, English does not. While European languages require some sort of tense marking in the verb, Indonesian and a number of Native American languages do not need to indicate whether the action was currently happening, would happen in the future, or had happened in the past. Some languages in Africa, New Guinea, and Latin America have only two, three, or four basic color terms, while English has eleven. Some languages are rich in cover terms such as tree, bird, or animal, while others have many terms for the different species but may lack any single term that would include all kinds of trees, birds, or animals. For years, anthropologists have claimed that Eskimo languages have many terms for "snow," while English has only one. Do such differences among the world's languages have any effect on how different people think about the world in which they live? Does the lack of distinctive or general terms in our language influence what people can think about? Or do the grammatical necessities of a language, such as tense, number, or gender, lead us to notice some aspects of our world and ignore others?

The idea that human thought changes with different languages has come to be known as the question of linguistic relativity. It is most widely associated with the linguistic anthropologist Edward Sapir and his sometime student Benjamin Lee Whorf. Early in the century, Sapir had drawn on his studies of Native American languages to suggest that different lexical (vocabulary) items and different grammatical features did lead various Indian groups to view the world differently from English-speaking Americans. Several years later, Whorf published several papers expanding on Sapir's ideas. By the 1950s, the idea that the language people spoke shaped the way they were inclined to think about the world had become known as the Sapir–Whorf hypothesis.

Although the Sapir–Whorf hypothesis had been generally accepted by most American anthropologists, few accepted the hypothesis in its strongest and most deterministic form. Derived from Whorf's writings, the strong version implied that humans were prisoners of their native language and could only think in terms of that language's grammatical and lexical categories. Since most anthropologists learned these exotic languages and with training were themselves able to understand both the words and the exotic world views, most anthropologists inevitably recognized that language could not be so deterministic. On the other hand, most anthropologists recognized that their informants approached the world quite differently from themselves. Clearly such differences were cultural, but it remained unclear just how much of such differences were the result of linguistic differences.

The first formal test of linguistic relativity came in 1969 when cognitive anthropologists Brent Berlin and Paul Kay published *Basic Color Terms* (Berkeley, University of California Press). Examining the color terminologies of more than 100 languages from around the world, they concluded that the number of key or basic color terms a language might have was highly variable, from as few as two to as many as twelve. They interpreted the linguistic relativity argument, suggesting that human languages might adopt any set of linguistic categories; for them, relativity suggested no pattern whatever. What Berlin and Kay found for color categories was that the basic color terms were anything but random. If a language had only two colors, they would be black and white (or perhaps dark and light), whereas if it had three basic terms, the language would invariably have only black, white, and red. If there were four terms, that would include black, white, and red and either blue/green or yellow. Languages with five terms had black, white, red, blue/green, and yellow, and so on.

Berlin and Kay did not claim that people with three basic color terms could not distinguish the same range of colors as Americans could, but that the categories they used were fewer and these were used for a much larger range of shades than American categories. Red, for example, in languages with few color terms, generally includes many shades of brown and purple that Americans would never accept as red. But the red in American English covers many hues besides "pure" red also. The basic colors brown, purple, pink, and gray are relatively rare and only occur in languages with seven or more basic colors. Berlin and Kay suggested that although all people perceived colors the same, how they assigned particular color chips to different color terms was anything but arbitrary.

In the 1970s, these and other studies of how different people classified their natural, biological, and social worlds suggested to most anthropologists that language's role in culture was primarily limited to prescribing how people classified the world they inhabited rather than on people's thought processes. Thus, for about two decades, the Sapir–Whorf hypothesis was relegated to the dustbin of bad anthropological theories. But in the 1990s, a growing number of linguists and linguistic anthropologists began to reevaluate the hypothesis and a growing number have come to see the relationship between language and thought in a variety of new ways. Many have suggested that studies of color terms and other classificatory systems do not really examine the hypothesis at all. What is needed, they argue, are more detailed studies of lexical and grammatical systems.

Here the first selection by linguists John Gumperz and Stephen C. Levinson examines some of these new studies, suggesting that new findings on the issue of linguistic relativity are emerging from many quarters in linguistics and anthropology. Accepting a nondeterministic reading of Sapir and Whorf, they explore some of the directions this new research is taking.

As anthropologists and linguists began to reexamine the Sapir–Whorf hypothesis, new criticisms have arisen from the new field of cognitive neuroscience. Here, cognitive neuroscientist Steven Pinker evaluates the linguistic relativity question, drawing on recent studies by cognitive neuroscience.

He tends to view the relativity problem in more deterministic terms than do Gumperz, Levinson, and most of the anthropologists who are currently working on this problem.

These two selections raise questions about what possible role language can play in thought. Does the language we speak control how we think or does language merely shape our thoughts by suggesting some interpretations of the world as more plausible than others? Alternatively, does the vocabulary or grammar we employ have little influence either on what we perceive or on the interpretations most readily available to us?

YES ⮐

John J. Gumperz and
Stephen C. Levinson

Rethinking Linguistic Relativity

Introduction: Linguistic Relativity Re-Examined

Language, Thinking, and Reality

Every student of language or society should be familiar with the essential idea of linguistic relativity, the idea that culture, *through* language, affects the way we think, especially perhaps our classification of the experienced world. Much of our experience seems to support some such idea, for example the phenomenology of struggling with a second language, where we find that the summit of competence is forever over the next horizon, the obvious absence of definitive or even accurate translation (let alone the ludicrous failure of phrasebooks), even the wreck of diplomatic efforts on linguistic and rhetorical rocks.

On the other hand, there is a strand of robust common sense that insists that a stone is a stone whatever you call it, that the world is a recalcitrant reality that imposes its structure on our thinking and our speaking and that the veil of linguistic difference can be ripped aside with relative ease. Plenty of subjective experiences and objective facts can be marshalled to support this view: the delight of foreign friendships, our ability to "read" the military or economic strategies of alien rivals, the very existence of comparative sciences of language, psychology, and society.

These two opposing strands of "common sense" have surfaced in academic controversies and intellectual positions over many centuries of Western thought. If St. Augustine (354–430) took the view that language is a mere nomenclature for antecedently existing concepts, Roger Bacon (1220–92) insisted, despite strong views on the universal basis of grammar, that the mismatch between semantic fields in different languages made accurate translation impossible. The Port Royal grammarians of the seventeenth century found universal logic thinly disguised behind linguistic difference, while the German romantics in a tradition leading through to Humboldt in the nineteenth century found a unique *Weltanschauung*, "world view," in each language. The first half of our own century was characterized by the presumption of radical linguistic and cultural difference reflecting profound cognitive differences, a presumption to be found in anthropology, linguistics and behaviourist psychologies, not to mention philosophical emphasis on meaning as use. The second half of the century has been dominated by the rise of the cognitive sciences, with their treatment of mind as inbuilt capacities for information processing, and their associated universalist and rationalist presuppositions. St. Augustine would probably recognize the faint echoes of his views in much modern theorizing about how children acquire language through prior knowledge of the structure of the world.

There is surely some spiral ascent in the swing of this pendulum. Nevertheless it is important to appreciate how little real scientific progress there has been in the study of lexical or morphosyntactic meaning—most progress in linguistics has been in the study of syntax and sound systems, together with rather general ideas about how the meaning of phrases might be composed out of the meaning of their constituents. Thus there is still much more opinion (often ill-informed) than solid fact in modern attitudes to "linguistic relativity."

There are three terms in the relation: language, thought, and culture. Each of these are global cover terms, not notions of any precision. When one tries to make anything definite out of the idea of linguistic relativity, one inevitably has to focus on particular aspects of each of these terms in the relation. This [selection] will show how each can be differently construed and, as a consequence, the relation reconsidered. In addition the connecting links can be variously conceived. Thus by the end of the [selection] the reader will find that the aspects of language and thinking that are focused on are selective, but also that the very relation between culture and community has become complex. Readers will find the original idea of linguistic relativity still live, but functioning in a way that differs from how it was originally conceived.

Linguistic Relativity Re-Examined

The original idea, variously attributable to [Wilhelm von] Humboldt, [Franz] Boas, [Edward] Sapir, [and Benjamin Lee] Whorf, was that the semantic structures of different languages might be fundamentally incommensurable, with consequences for the way in which speakers of specific languages might think and act. On this view, language, thought, and culture are deeply interlocked, so that each language might be claimed to have associated with it a distinctive worldview.

These ideas captured the imagination of a generation of anthropologists, psychologists, and linguists, as well as members of the general public. They had deep implications for the way anthropologists should conduct their business, suggesting that translational difficulties might lie at the heart of their discipline. However, the ideas seemed entirely and abruptly discredited by the rise of the cognitive sciences in the 1960s, which favoured a strong emphasis on the commonality of human cognition and its basis in human genetic endowment. This emphasis was strengthened by developments within linguistic anthropology, with the discovery of significant semantic universals in color terms, the structure of ethnobotanical nomenclature, and (arguably) kinship terms.

However, there has been a recent change of intellectual climate in psychology, linguistics, and other disciplines surrounding anthropology, as well as within linguistic anthropology, towards an intermediate position, in which more attention is paid to linguistic and cultural difference, such diversity being viewed within the context of what we have learned about universals (features shared by all languages and cultures). New work in developmental psychology, while acknowledging underlying universal bases, emphasizes the importance of the socio-cultural context of human development. Within sociolinguistics and linguistic anthropology there has also been increasing attention to meaning and discourse, and concomitantly a growing appreciation of how interpretive differences can be rooted as much in the systematic uses of language as in its structure.

. . .[T]he ideas we associate today so especially with Whorf and Sapir have a long and distinguished lineage on the one hand, while perhaps being no more than one of two opposing perennial strands of thought, universalism vs. relativism, on the other. Nevertheless, they crystallized in a particular fashion in American intellectual life of the 1940s. The idea of a close link between linguistic and conceptual categories took on a new meaning in the context of three further background assumptions characteristic of the first half of the century. One was the presumption of a (sometimes tempered) empiricist epistemology, that is, the view that all knowledge is acquired primarily through experience. The other was the structuralist assumption that language forms a system of oppositions, such that formal distinctions directly reflect meaning distinctions. The third was the idea of an unconscious mental life, and thus the possibility of linguistic effects beyond conscious awareness. It was the conjunction of these background ideas together with the specific formulation of the" linguistic relativity" hypothesis that gave the hypothesis its particular character in the history of ideas.

Sapir may have originated the phrase, but the *locus classicus* (though by no means the most careful statement) of the concept of linguistic relativity is the popular articles by Whorf, where the following oft-quoted passages may be found which illustrate all the central themes.

Epistemology

We dissect nature along lines laid down by our native languages. The categories and types that we isolate from the world of phenomena we do not find there because they stare every observer in the face; on the contrary, the world is presented in a kaleidoscopic flux of impressions which has to be organized by our minds—and this means largely by the linguistic systems of our minds.

— (1956:213) . . .

Unconscious Thought

[T]he phenomena of language are to its own speakers largely of a background character and so are outside the critical consciousness and control of the speaker.

— (1956:211)

Linguistic Relativity

> The phenomena of language are background phenomena, of which the talkers are unaware or, at most, dimly aware . . . These automatic, involuntary patterns of language are not the same for all men but are specific for each language and constitute the formalized side of the language, or its "grammar" . . .
>
> From this fact proceeds what I have called the "linguistic relativity principle," which means, in informal terms, that users of markedly different grammars are pointed by their grammars toward different types of observations and different evaluations of externally similar acts of observation, and hence are not equivalent as observers, but must arrive at somewhat different views of the world.
>
> — (1956:221) . . .

The boldness of Whorf's formulation prompted a succession of empirical studies in America in the 1950s and early 1960s aimed at elucidating and testing what now became known as the Sapir–Whorf hypothesis. Anthropological and linguistic studies by Trager, Hoijer, Lee, Casagrande, and others have been well reviewed elsewhere. These studies hardly touched on cognition, but in the same period a few psychologists (notably Lenneberg, Brown, Stefflre) did try to investigate the relation between lexical coding and memory, especially in the domain of color, and found some significant correlations. This line of work culminated, however, in the celebrated demonstration by Berlin & Kay of the language-independent saliency of "basic colors," which was taken as a decisive anti-relativist finding, and effectively terminated this tradition of investigations into the Sapir-Whorf hypothesis. There followed a period in which Whorf's own views in particular became the butt of extensive criticism.

It is clear from this background that the "Sapir-Whorf" hypothesis in its classical form arose from deep historical roots but in a particular intellectual climate. Even though (it has been closely argued by Lucy) the original hypothesis has never been thoroughly tested, the intellectual milieu had by the 1960s entirely changed. Instead of empiricism, we now have rationalistic assumptions. Instead of the basic tenets of structuralism, in which each linguistic or social system must be understood first in internal terms before comparison is possible, modern comparative work (especially in linguistics) tends to presume that one can isolate particular aspects or traits of a system (e.g. aspect or subjecthood) for comparison. The justification, such as it is, is that we now have the outlines of a universal structure for language and perhaps cognition, which provides the terms for comparison. It is true that the assumption of unconscious processes continues, but now the emphasis is on the unconscious nature of nearly all systematic information processing, so that the distinctive character of Whorf's habitual thought has been submerged.

In this changed intellectual climate, and in the light of the much greater knowledge that we now have about both language and mental processing, it would be pointless to attempt to revive ideas about linguistic relativity in their original form. Nevertheless, there have been a whole range of recent intellectual shifts that make the ground more fertile for some of the original seeds to grow into new saplings. It is the purpose of this [selection] to explore the implications of some of these shifts in a number of different disciplines for our overall view of the relations between language, thinking, and society.

The Idea Behind the Present [Selection]

This [selection] explores one chain of reasoning that is prompted by these recent changes in ideas. The line of argument runs in the following way.

Linguistic relativity is a theory primarily about the nature of meaning, the classic view focusing on the lexical and grammatical coding of language-specific distinctions. In this theory, two languages may "code" the same state of affairs utilizing semantic concepts or distinctions peculiar to each language; as a result the two linguistic descriptions reflect different construals of the same bit of reality. These semantic distinctions are held to reflect cultural distinctions and at the same time to influence cognitive categorizations, an issue re-examined . . . below.

Assuming that there is such a link between linguistic structure and conceptual categories, the possibility of conceptual relativity would seem at first sight to depend on whether linguistic codings are significantly different across languages. Very little, however, is actually known about substantive semantic or conceptual universals. It is true that there are demonstrations of universal semantic principles in a few domains like color terminology, ethnobiological taxonomies, perhaps also in systems of kinship terminology. However, these demonstrations carry no necessary general implications, and the same holds for studies of grammatical meaning. . . .

Yet, on further reflection, distinctive linguistic (grammatical or lexical) codings are not the only ways in which "meanings" or interpretations can vary systematically across cultures. This is brought out by recent developments in the theory of meaning. These developments show that "meaning" is not fully encapsulated in lexicon and grammar, which provide only schematic constraints on what the speaker will be taken to have meant in a particular utterance. . . .

A large part of the burden of interpretation is thus shifted from theories of context-free lexical and grammatical meaning to theories of use in context. Some important principles of the use of language may plausibly be argued to be universal. . . . Yet others seem much more clearly culture-specific. For example, the ethnography of speaking has shown how diverse can be the principles governing the production and interpretation of utterances in specific speech events—court proceedings, formal greetings, religious rituals, councils, and the like. . . .

This [selection] therefore spans a large terrain, from the classic Whorfian issues of the relation of grammar to thought on the one hand to consideration of language use in sociolinguistic perspective on the other. One key idea that supports this span is the notion of indexicality, conceived not just in terms of the contextual dependence of deictic items, but also in the broader Peircean sense, as a broad relationship between interpreters, signals, and the context of interpretation. Indexicality necessarily anchors meaning and interpretation to the context of language use and thus to wider social organization. Issues of linguistic relativity are in this way directly related to the variable cultural structuring of contexts. . . .

Introduction to Part I . . .

The Very Idea: Causal Links Between Language and Thinking

Might the language we speak affect the way we think? Generations of thinkers have been intrigued by this idea. Aarsleff summarized Humboldt's influential views thus: "Humboldt's entire view of the nature of language is founded on the conviction that thinking and speaking, thought and language form so close a union that we must think of them as being identical, in spite of the fact that we can separate them artificially. Owing to this identity, access to one of the two will open nearly equal access to the other."

Whorf, as we saw [earlier], brought to the idea a new and heady mix of an empiricist epistemology, an insistence on the underlying systematicity of language as a structured semantical system, and an emphasis on the unconscious influence of language on habitual thought. . . .

The phrase "linguistic determinism" has come to stand for these views that there is a causal influence from linguistic patterning to cognition. Despite phrases like "linguistic conditioning," "linguistic legislation," "inexorable control," etc., Whorf's own considered position seems to have been that language influences unconscious habitual thought, rather than limiting thought potential. Thus the phrase "linguistic determinism" should be understood to imply that there is *at least some* causal influence from language categories to nonverbal cognition; it was not intended to denote an exclusive causal vector in one direction—probably no proponent has held the view that what cannot be said cannot be thought.

The idea that language could determine (however weakly) the nature of our thinking nowadays carries more than a faint whiff of anachronism; rather it seems to belong to an altogether different age, prior to the serious study of mind as an information processing device. That device, in the predominant metaphor of our time, is instantiated in "wetware," whose properties are in turn dictated by the genetic code of the species. Although those properties are only dimly understood, still it is generally presumed, as Fodor has influentially put it, that the mind is "modular," composed of subsystems specialized to the automatic unconscious processing of particular kinds of information, visual, auditory, haptic, and so on. Since we can, for example, talk about what we see, the output of these specialized systems must, it seems, be available to some central information processing system, where "thinking," in the sense of ratiocination and deliberation, occurs. This picture (a close analogy of course to the computers of the day) of a single generalized central processor with specialized input/output devices is beginning to give way to a more complex version: each specialized input/output device is itself a system of modules, while "central processes" may themselves be differentiated into different "languages of thought" (propositional, imagistic, and so on). . . . Nevertheless the essentials of the Fodorean view are very generally held.

Thus, on this widespread view, we can expect thinking in all essentials to have universal properties, to be couched in an inner language structurally the same for all members of the species, and to be quite unrelated to the facts of linguistic diversity. The tenor of the anti-Whorfian assumptions can be gauged from the following quotations: "For the vocabulary of the language, in and of its self, to be a moulder of thought, lexical dissections and categorizations of nature would have to be almost accidentally formed, rather as though some Johnny Appleseed had scattered named categories capriciously over the earth"; "Whorf's hypothesis [of linguistic determinism] has engendered much confusion, and many circular arguments. Its converse often seems more plausible" and "there is no evidence for the strong version of the hypothesis—that language imposes upon its speakers a particular way of thinking about the world"; "The discussions that assume that language determines thought carry on only by a collective suspension of disbelief."

In short, many authors find the thesis of linguistic determinism wildly adventurous or even ridiculous. On the other hand, others have recently claimed to find it sober and plausible. It is therefore useful to attempt to clarify the issues by dissecting the relativity hypothesis into its component parts, and in particular by isolating the "determinism" hypothesis from other linked ideas. Clearly, the hypothesis of linguistic relativity relies on the presumption of linguistic difference. Thus the discovery of universals may have a bearing on that hypothesis. But the hypothesis that linguistic categories might determine aspects of non-linguistic thinking is quite independent of facts about linguistic difference. Let us therefore spell out the nexus of interlinked hypotheses (where the numbers [1] and [2] refer to the premises and the number [3] to an implied conclusion).

[1] Linguistic Difference

Languages differ substantially in their semantic structure: both the intensions (the senses) and extensions (the denotations) of lexical and morpho-syntactic categories may differ across languages (and may do so independently).

[2] Linguistic Determinism

Linguistic categorizations, implicit or explicit, may determine or codetermine or influence aspects of non-linguistic categorization, memory, perception or thinking in general.

This is often said to have a "strong" and a "weak" form: under the strong claim, linguistically uncoded concepts would be unattainable; under the weak form, concepts which happen to be linguistically coded would be facilitated or favored (e.g. would be more accessible, easier to remember, or the default coding for non-linguistic cognition).

❧❦❧

The mechanisms whereby semantic distinctions may have an influence on cognition can be left open; a prior task is to show that there is indeed some correlation. Whorf himself of course held the view that the unconscious "compulsive patterning" of grammatical oppositions would play a special role in habitual unreflective patterns of thought.

Linguistic Relativity
Given that:

(1) differences exist in linguistic categories across languages;
(2) linguistic categories determine aspects of individuals' thinking; then:
(3) aspects of individuals' thinking differ across linguistic communities according to the language they speak.

Note that the conclusion here will hold even under the weakest versions of (1) and (2). Thus if there is *at least some* aspect of semantic structure that is not universal, *and at least some* cognitive effect of such distinctive semantic properties, then there must be *at least some* systematic cognitive variation in line with linguistic difference. That would seem . . . to be as trivially true as the strongest version of linguistic relativity (that one's semantic inventory of concepts provides one's total vocabulary of thoughts) is trivially false. Thus the central problem is to illuminate the degrees of language difference, and the ways in which semantics and cognitive categories and processes interact.

Now notice that modern views complicate this picture by apparently subscribing to various aspects of these propositions while robustly denying the conclusion in the syllogism above. For example, a common modern stance is:

(1') languages differ in semantic structure, but only at a molecular level— at an atomic level, the conceptual "atoms" (e.g. "male," "adult," etc.) are identical, and are merely assembled into some culture-specific notion like "uncle";
(2') "determinism" between semantic categories and conceptual categories is in a sense trivially complete, since they are one and the same—the meanings of words are expressed in a "language" that is identical to the "language of thought." . . .

Thus although the identity of linguistic and conceptual categories in (2') alone might be thought to entail linguistic relativity, it is in fact usually associated with some claim (often implicit) like that in (1'), allowing subscribers to presume that the "language of thought" (alias: system of semantic representations) is universal. Then the conclusion in (3) no longer follows. In schematic form we may now oppose the two views thus:

The Whorfian Syllogism

(1) Different languages utilize different semantic representation systems which are informationally non-equivalent (at least in the sense that they employ different lexical concepts);
(2) semantic representations determine aspects of conceptual representations;
> *therefore*
(3) users of different languages utilize different conceptual representations.

The Anti-Whorfian Syllogism

(1′) Different languages utilize the same semantic representation system (if not at the molecular then at least at the atomic level of semantic primes);

(2′) universal conceptual representations determine semantic systems, indeed THE semantic representation system just is identical to THE propositional conceptual system (the innate "language of thought");
    therefore

(3′) users of different languages utilize the identical conceptual representation system.

Despite the fact that the doctrines appear diametrically opposed, they are nevertheless, on suitable interpretations, *entirely compatible*, as long as one subscribes to the distinction between atomic and molecular levels of semantic representation. Then, on an atomic level, semantic representations, and their corresponding conceptual representations, are drawn from a universal language of thought, while on the molecular level there are language-specific combinations of universal atomic primitives, which make up lexical meanings (and meanings associated with morpho-syntactic distinctions) and which may have specific conceptual effects.

Most semantic analysts in practice work with an assumption of such "semantic decomposition" of linguistic expressions. But it is worth pointing out that there are in fact fundamental problems with that assumption which have long been recognized, and some of those who subscribe enthusiastically to (2′) might lose some of their enthusiasm if they realized that without (1′), (2′) implies the strongest version of linguistic relativity.

Let us take stock. Proposition (1) is evidently true, in the sense that languages clearly employ distinct lexical meanings. (1′) may or may not be tenable, but is in fact compatible with (1). Likewise (2) and (2′) are compatible if we make a distinction between atomic and molecular concepts: the inventory of concepts in the language of thought could determine the range of possible lexical concepts, but such lexical concepts once selected could in turn determine the concepts we employ when solving non-linguistic problems. (3) would be the conclusion from (1) and (2). All thus hinges on (2). Is it even remotely plausible?

Although the thesis of linguistic determinism seems at first sight to have an anachronistic flavor, it can easily be brought to bear on modern theorizing in a way that makes it look anything but silly. First, note that there is considerable psychological evidence that our working memory is restricted to about half a dozen chunks of information, but is indifferent to the underlying complexity of those chunks. Thus mental operations are facilitated by grouping elementary concepts into larger chunks. And this is just what lexical items do for us. Thus there is every reason to think that such chunks might play an important role in our thinking. . . .

Within such a framework, it is quite easy to show that in certain respects and for certain phenomena linguistic determinism *beyond* thinking-for-speaking is not only plausible, but must be correct. The reasoning can be exemplified as follows. Consider a language that has no words for *'in front,'* *'behind,'* *'left,'* *'right,'* and so on, preferring instead to designate all such relations, however microscopic in scale, in terms of notions like 'North,' 'South,' 'East,' 'West,' etc. Now a speaker of such a language cannot remember arrays of objects in the same way as you or I, in terms of their relative location from a particular viewing angle. If I think of the visual array currently in front of me, I think of it as, say, "boy in front of tree, dog to left of tree." Later I can so describe it. But that will not do for the speaker of the language with 'North'/ 'South'/'East'/'West' notions: remembering the array in terms of notions like 'front' and 'left' will not allow him to reconstruct the cardinal directions. So if he remembers it that way, he will not be able to describe it later; while if he remembers the array in a way congruent with the linguistic coding (in terms of 'North' and 'East,' etc.), then he will be able to code it linguistically. So it seems *prima facie* quite clear that the speaker of such a language and I simply MUST code our experiences differently for memory in order to speak our different languages. In short, thinking in a special way for speaking will not be enough: we must mentally encode experiences in such a way that we can describe them later, in the terms required by our language.

There are in fact just such languages that require the use of cardinal directions. Furthermore, this *prima facie* argument about the cognitive consequences of speaking such different languages can be backed up by empirical investigation: it turns out that in non-linguistic tasks speakers of languages that use 'North'/'South'/'East'/'West' systems instead of 'front'/'back'/'left'/'right' systems do indeed remember spatial arrays differently, in ways that can be demonstrated experimentally and observationally.

Is this a peculiar case? One needs to think afresh to assess the possibilities. From the perspective of speech production, there are three different kinds of ways in which a particular language might determine how we think. First, the grammatical or lexical categories may force a specific way of thinking at the time of speaking (the "regimentation" of thoughts described above). Second, such thinking-for-speaking may itself require the coding of situations in specific forms at the time that they are experienced. This is clearly so in the North/South/East/West case above. It is also clearly so in many other cases: for example, obligatory coding of number in languages with plural marking will require noticing for all possible referents whether or not they are singletons—some languages without plural marking will let one say in effect "I saw bird on the lawn," but in English I must say either a *bird* or *birds* and must therefore have remembered how many relevant birds there were; or in systems of honorifics based on relative age, I must have ascertained before speaking whether the referent is senior or junior to me; or in systems of aspect requiring distinctions between perfective and imperfective, I must attend to the exact nature of event-overlap. These are language-specific distinctions that seem to require noticing special properties of the world so that one is ready to encode them linguistically should the need arise. Such examples suggest that those theorists who reluctantly subscribe to a relativity in thinking-for-speaking, will have also to subscribe to a consequent relativity in thinking at the time at which events are experienced. Thirdly, one may also go on to consider the consequences, or after-effects, of thinking-for-speaking in a particular way. There may for example be memory effects: it may be easier to remember aspects of events that have been coded for speaking during prior verbalization (hence we may indulge in speaking-for-thinking). Since some languages will enforce particular codings (e.g. in systems of aspect, honorifics, number-marking, etc.), they may ensure that their speakers recall certain features of situations better than others.

Steven Pinker ➡ **NO**

Mentalese

Is thought dependent on words? Do people literally think in English, Cherokee, [or] Kivunjo . . . ? Or are our thoughts couched in some silent medium of the brain—a language of thought, or "mentalese"—and merely clothed in words whenever we need to communicate them to a listener? No question could be more central to understanding the language instinct.

In much of our social and political discourse, people simply assume that words determine thoughts. Inspired by [George] Orwell's essay "Politics and the English Language," pundits accuse governments of manipulating our minds with euphemisms like *pacification* (bombing), *revenue enhancement* (taxes), and *nonretention* (firing). Philosophers argue that since animals lack language, they must also lack consciousness—[Ludwig] Wittgenstein wrote, "A dog could not have the thought 'perhaps it will rain tomorrow'"—and therefore they do not possess the rights of conscious beings. Some feminists blame sexist thinking on sexist language, like the use of *he* to refer to a generic person. Inevitably, reform movements have sprung up. Many replacements for *he* have been suggested over the years, including *E, hesh, po, tey, co, jhe, ve, xe, he'er, thon*, and *na*. The most extreme of these movements is General Semantics, begun in 1933 by the engineer Count Alfred Korzybski and popularized in long-time best-sellers by his disciples Stuart Chase and S. I. Hayakawa. (This is the same Hayakawa who later achieved notoriety as the protest-defying college president and snoozing U.S. senator.) General Semantics lays the blame for human folly on insidious "semantic damage" to thought perpetrated by the structure of language. Keeping a forty-year-old in prison for a theft he committed as a teenager assumes that the forty-year-old John and the eighteen-year-old John are "the same person," a cruel logical error that would be avoided if we referred to them not as *John* but as $John_{1972}$ and $John_{1994}$, respectively. The verb *to be* is a particular source of illogic, because it identifies individuals with abstractions, as in *Mary is a woman*, and licenses evasions of responsibility, like Ronald Reagan's famous nonconfession *Mistakes were made*. One faction seeks to eradicate the verb altogether.

And supposedly there is a scientific basis for these assumptions: the famous Sapir-Whorf hypothesis of linguistic determinism, stating that people's thoughts are determined by the categories made available by their language, and its weaker version, linguistic relativity, stating that differences among languages cause differences in the thoughts of their speakers. People who

From *The Language Instinct: How the Mind Creates Language* (Perennial Classics, 2000), pp. 45–57, 69–73. Copyright © 1994 by Steven Pinker. Reprinted by permission of HarperCollins Publishers.

remember little else from their college education can rattle off the factoids: the languages that carve the spectrum into color words at different places, the fundamentally different Hopi concept of time, the dozens of Eskimo words for snow. The implication is heavy: the foundational categories of reality are not "in" the world but are imposed by one's culture (and hence can be challenged, perhaps accounting for the perennial appeal of the hypothesis to undergraduate sensibilities).

But it is wrong, all wrong. The idea that thought is the same thing as language is an example of what can be called a conventional absurdity: a statement that goes against all common sense but that everyone believes because they dimly recall having heard it somewhere and because it is so pregnant with implications. (The "fact" that we use only five percent of our brains, that lemmings commit mass suicide, that the *Boy Scout Manual* annually outsells all other books, and that we can be coerced into buying by subliminal messages are other examples.) Think about it. We have all had the experience of uttering or writing a sentence, then stopping and realizing that it wasn't exactly what we meant to say. To have that feeling, there has to be a "what we meant to say" that is different from what we said. Sometimes it is not easy to find *any* words that properly convey a thought. When we hear or read, we usually remember the gist, not the exact words, so there has to be such a thing as a gist that is not the same as a bunch of words. And if thoughts depended on words, how could a new word ever be coined? How could a child learn a word to begin with? How could translation from one language to another be possible?

The discussions that assume that language determines thought carry on only by a collective suspension of disbelief. . . .

As we shall see in this [selection], there is no scientific evidence that languages dramatically shape their speakers' ways of thinking. But I want to do more than review the unintentionally comical history of attempts to prove that they do. The idea that language shapes thinking seemed plausible when scientists were in the dark about how thinking works or even how to study it. Now that cognitive scientists know how to think about thinking, there is less of a temptation to equate it with language just because words are more palpable than thoughts. By understanding *why* linguistic determinism is wrong, we will be in a better position to understand how language itself works. . . .

❧✿❧

The linguistic determinism hypothesis is closely linked to the names Edward Sapir and Benjamin Lee Whorf. Sapir, a brilliant linguist, was a student of the anthropologist Franz Boas. Boas and his students (who also include Ruth Benedict and Margaret Mead) were important intellectual figures in this century, because they argued that nonindustrial peoples were not primitive savages but had systems of language, knowledge, and culture as complex and valid in their world view as our own. In his study of Native American languages Sapir noted that speakers of different languages have to pay attention to different aspects of reality simply to put words together into grammatical sentences. For example, when English speakers decide whether or not to put

-ed onto the end of a verb, they must pay attention to tense, the relative time of occurrence of the event they are referring to and the moment of speaking. Wintu speakers need not bother with tense, but when they decide which suffix to put on their verbs, they must pay attention to whether the knowledge they are conveying was learned through direct observation or by hearsay.

Sapir's interesting observation was soon taken much farther. Whorf was an inspector for the Hartford Fire Insurance Company and an amateur scholar of Native American languages, which led him to take courses from Sapir at Yale. In a much-quoted passage, he wrote:

> We dissect nature along lines laid down by our native languages. The categories and types that we isolate from the world of phenomena we do not find there because they stare every observer in the face; on the contrary, the world is presented in a kaleidoscopic flux of impressions which has to be organized by our minds—and this means largely by the linguistic systems in our minds. We cut nature up, organize it into concepts, and ascribe significances as we do, largely because we are parties to an agreement to organize it in this way—an agreement that holds throughout our speech community and is codified in the patterns of our language. The agreement is, of course, an implicit and unstated one, *but its terms are absolutely obligatory*; we cannot talk at all except by subscribing to the organization and classification of data which the agreement decrees.

What led Whorf to this radical position? He wrote that the idea first occurred to him in his work as a fire prevention engineer when he was struck by how language led workers to misconstrue dangerous situations. For example, one worker caused a serious explosion by tossing a cigarette into an "empty" drum that in fact was full of gasoline vapor. Another lit a blowtorch near a "pool of water" that was really a basin of decomposing tannery waste, which, far from being "watery," was releasing inflammable gases. Whorf's studies of American languages strengthened his conviction. For example, in Apache, *It is a dripping spring* must be expressed "As water, or springs, whiteness moves downward." "How utterly unlike our way of thinking!" he wrote.

But the more you examine Whorf's arguments, the less sense they make. Take the story about the worker and the "empty" drum. The seeds of disaster supposedly lay in the semantics of *empty*, which, Whorf claimed, means both "without its usual contents" and "null and void, empty, inert." The hapless worker, his conception of reality molded by his linguistic categories, did not distinguish between the "drained" and "inert" senses, hence, flick . . . boom! But wait. Gasoline vapor is invisible. A drum with nothing but vapor in it looks just like a drum with nothing in it at all. Surely this walking catastrophe was fooled by his eyes, not by the English language.

The example of whiteness moving downward is supposed to show that the Apache mind does not cut up events into distinct objects and actions. Whorf presented many such examples from Native American languages. The Apache equivalent of *The boat is grounded on the beach* is "It is on the beach pointwise as an event of canoe motion." *He invites people to a feast* becomes

"He, or somebody, goes for eaters of cooked food." *He cleans a gun with a ram-rod* is translated as "He directs a hollow moving dry spot by movement of tool." All this, to be sure, is utterly unlike our way of talking. But do we know that it is utterly unlike our way of thinking?

As soon as Whorf's articles appeared, the psycholinguists Eric Lenneberg and Roger Brown pointed out two non sequiturs in his argument. First, Whorf did not actually study any Apaches; it is not clear that he ever met one. His assertions about Apache psychology are based entirely on Apache grammar—making his argument circular. Apaches speak differently, so they must think differently. How do we know that they think differently? Just listen to the way they speak.

Second, Whorf rendered the sentences as clumsy, word-for-word transla-tions, designed to make the literal meanings seem as odd as possible. But look-ing at the actual glosses that Whorf provided, I could, with equal grammatical justification, render the first sentence as the mundane "Clear stuff—water—is falling." Turning the tables, I could take the English sentence "He walks" and render it "As solitary masculinity, leggedness proceeds." Brown illustrates how strange the German mind must be, according to Whorf's logic, by reproducing Mark Twain's own translation of a speech he delivered in flawless German to the Vienna Press Club:

> I am indeed the truest friend of the German language—and not only now, but from long since—yes, before twenty years already. . . . I would only some changes effect. I would only the language method—the lux-urious, elaborate construction compress, the eternal parenthesis sup-press, do away with, annihilate; the introduction of more than thirteen subjects in one sentence forbid; the verb so far to the front pull that one it without a telescope discover can. With one word, my gentlemen, I would your beloved language simplify so that, my gentlemen, when you her for prayer need, One her yonder-up understands.
>
> . . . I might gladly the separable verb also a little bit reform. I might none do let what Schiller did: he has the whole history of the Thirty Years' War between the two members of a separate verb inpushed. That has even Germany itself aroused, and one has Schiller the permission refused the History of the Hundred Years' War to compose—God be it thanked! After all these reforms established be will, will the German language the noblest and the prettiest on the world be.

Among Whorf's "kaleidoscopic flux of impressions," color is surely the most eye-catching. He noted that we see objects in different hues, depending on the wavelengths of the light they reflect, but that physicists tell us that wavelength is a continuous dimension with nothing delineating red, yellow, green, blue, and so on. Languages differ in their inventory of color words: Latin lacks generic "gray" and "brown"; Navajo collapses blue and green into one word; Russian has distinct words for dark blue and sky blue; Shona speak-ers use one word for the yellower greens and the greener yellows, and a dif-ferent one for the bluer greens and the nonpurplish blues. You can fill in the rest of the argument. It is language that puts the frets in the spectrum; Julius Caesar would not know shale from Shinola.

But although physicists see no basis for color boundaries, physiologists do. Eyes do not register wavelength the way a thermometer registers temperature. They contain three kinds of cones, each with a different pigment, and the cones are wired to neurons in a way that makes the neurons respond best to red patches against a green background or vice versa, blue against yellow, black against white. No matter how influential language might be, it would seem preposterous to a physiologist that it could reach down into the retina and rewire the ganglion cells.

Indeed, humans the world over (and babies and monkeys, for that matter) color their perceptual worlds using the same palette, and this constrains the vocabularies they develop. Although languages may disagree about the wrappers in the sixty-four crayon box—the burnt umbers, the turquoises, the fuchsias—they agree much more on the wrappers in the eight-crayon box—the fire-engine reds, grass greens, lemon yellows. Speakers of different languages unanimously pick these shades as the best examples of their color words, as long as the language has a color word in that general part of the spectrum. And where languages do differ in their color words, they differ predictably, not according to the idiosyncratic taste of some word-coiner. Languages are organized a bit like the Crayola product line, the fancier ones adding colors to the more basic ones. If a language has only two color words, they are for black and white (usually encompassing dark and light, respectively). If it has three, they are for black, white, and red; if four, black, white, red, and either yellow or green. Five adds in both yellow and green; six, blue; seven, brown; more than seven, purple, pink, orange, or gray. But the clinching experiment was carried out in the New Guinea highlands with the Grand Valley Dani, a people speaking one of the black-and-white languages. The psychologist Eleanor Rosch found that the Dani were quicker at learning a new color category that was based on fire-engine red than a category based on an off-red. The way we see colors determines how we learn words for them, not vice versa.

The fundamentally different Hopi concept of time is one of the more startling claims about how minds can vary. Whorf wrote that the Hopi language contains "no words, grammatical forms, constructions, or expressions that refer directly to what we call 'time,' or to past, or future, or to enduring or lasting." He suggested, too, that the Hopi had "no general notion or intuition of TIME as a smooth flowing continuum in which everything in the universe proceeds at an equal rate, out of a future, through a present, into a past." According to Whorf, they did not conceptualize events as being like points, or lengths of time like days as countable things. Rather, they seemed to focus on change and process itself, and on psychological distinctions between presently known, mythical, and conjecturally distant. The Hopi also had little interest in "exact sequences, dating, calendars, chronology."

What, then, are we to make of the following sentence translated from Hopi?

> Then indeed, the following day, quite early in the morning at the hour when people pray to the sun, around that time then he woke up the girl again.

Perhaps the Hopi are not as oblivious to time as Whorf made them out to be. In his extensive study of the Hopi, the anthropologist Ekkehart Malotki, who reported this sentence, also showed that Hopi speech contains tense, metaphors for time, units of time (including days, numbers of days, parts of the day, yesterday and tomorrow, days of the week, weeks, months, lunar phases, seasons, and the year), ways to quantify units of time, and words like "ancient," "quick," "long time," and "finished." Their culture keeps records with sophisticated methods of dating, including a horizon-based sun calendar, exact ceremonial day sequences, knotted calendar strings, notched calendar sticks, and several devices for timekeeping using the principle of the sundial. No one is really sure how Whorf came up with his outlandish claims, but his limited, badly analyzed sample of Hopi speech and his longtime leanings toward mysticism must have contributed.

Speaking of anthropological canards, no discussion of language and thought would be complete without the Great Eskimo Vocabulary Hoax. Contrary to popular belief, the Eskimos do not have more words for snow than do speakers of English. They do not have four hundred words for snow, as it has been claimed in print, or two hundred, or one hundred, or forty-eight, or even nine. One dictionary puts the figure at two. Counting generously, experts can come up with about a dozen, but by such standards English would not be far behind, with *snow, sleet, slush, blizzard, avalanche, hail, hardpack, powder, flurry, dusting,* and a coinage of Boston's WBZ-TV meteorologist Bruce Schwoegler, *snizzling.*

Where did the myth come from? Not from anyone who has actually studied the Yupik and Inuit-Inupiaq families of polysynthetic languages spoken from Siberia to Greenland. The anthropologist Laura Martin has documented how the story grew like an urban legend, exaggerated with each retelling. In 1911 Boas casually mentioned that Eskimos used four unrelated word roots for snow. Whorf embellished the count to seven and implied that there were more. His article was widely reprinted, then cited in textbooks and popular books on language, which led to successively inflated estimates in other textbooks, articles, and newspaper columns of Amazing Facts.

The linguist Geoffrey Pullum, who popularized Martin's article in his essay "The Great Eskimo Vocabulary Hoax," speculates about why the story got so out of control: "The alleged lexical extravagance of the Eskimos comports so well with the many other facets of their polysynthetic perversity: rubbing noses; lending their wives to strangers; eating raw seal blubber; throwing Grandma out to be eaten by polar bears." It is an ironic twist. Linguistic relativity came out of the Boas school, as part of a campaign to show that nonliterate cultures were as complex and sophisticated as European ones. But the supposedly mind-broadening anecdotes owe their appeal to a patronizing willingness to treat other cultures' psychologies as weird and exotic compared to our own. As Pullum notes,

> Among the many depressing things about this credulous transmission and elaboration of a false claim is that even if there *were* a large number of roots for different snow types in some Arctic language, this would *not*, objectively, be intellectually interesting; it would be a most mundane

and unremarkable fact. Horsebreeders have various names for breeds, sizes, and ages of horses; botanists have names for leaf shapes; interior decorators have names for shades of mauve; printers have many different names for fonts (Carlson, Garamond, Helvetica, Times Roman, and so on), naturally enough. . . . Would anyone think of writing about printers the same kind of slop we find written about Eskimos in bad linguistics textbooks? Take [the following] random textbook . . . , with its earnest assertion "It is quite obvious that in the culture of the Eskimos . . . snow is of great enough importance to split up the conceptual sphere that corresponds to one word and one thought in English into several distinct classes . . ." Imagine reading: "It is quite obvious that in the culture of printers . . . fonts are of great enough importance to split up the conceptual sphere that corresponds to one word and one thought among non-printers into several distinct classes . . ." Utterly boring, even if true. Only the link to those legendary, promiscuous, blubbergnawing hunters of the ice-packs could permit something this trite to be presented to us for contemplation.

If the anthropological anecdotes are bunk, what about controlled studies? The thirty-five years of research from the psychology laboratory is distinguished by how little it has shown. Most of the experiments have tested banal "weak" versions of the Whorfian hypothesis, namely that words can have some effect on memory or categorization. Some of these experiments have actually worked, but that is hardly surprising. In a typical experiment, subjects have to commit paint chips to memory and are tested with a multiple-choice procedure. In some of these studies, the subjects show slightly better memory for colors that have readily available names in their language. But even colors without names are remembered fairly well, so the experiment does not show that the colors are remembered by verbal labels alone. All it shows is that subjects remembered the chips in two forms, a nonverbal visual image and a verbal label, presumably because two kinds of memory, each one fallible, are better than one. In another type of experiment subjects have to say which two out of three color chips go together; they often put the ones together that have the same name in their language. Again, no surprise. I can imagine the subjects thinking to themselves, "Now how on earth does this guy expect me to pick two chips to put together? He didn't give me any hints, and they're all pretty similar. Well, I'd probably call those two 'green' and that one 'blue,' and that seems as good a reason to put them together as any." In these experiments, language is, technically speaking, influencing a form of thought in some way, but so what? It is hardly an example of incommensurable world views, or of concepts that are nameless and therefore unimaginable, or of dissecting nature along lines laid down by our native languages according to terms that are absolutely obligatory . . .

⋗⟨◉⟩⋗

People can be forgiven for overrating language. Words make noise, or sit on a page, for all to hear and see. Thoughts are trapped inside the head of the thinker. To know what someone else is thinking, or to talk to each other about the nature of thinking, we have to use—what else, words! It is no wonder that many commentators have trouble even conceiving of thought without words—or is it that they just don't have the language to talk about it?

As a cognitive scientist I can afford to be smug about common sense being true (thought is different from language) and linguistic determinism being a conventional absurdity. For two sets of tools now make it easier to think clearly about the whole problem. One is a body of experimental studies that break the word barrier and assess many kinds of nonverbal thought. The other is a theory of how thinking might work that formulates the questions in a satisfyingly precise way. . . .

⋯⊙⋯

Now we are in a position to pose the Whorfian question in a precise way. Remember that a representation does not have to look like English or any other language; it just has to use symbols to represent concepts, and arrangements of symbols to represent the logical relations among them, according to some consistent scheme. But though internal representations in an English speaker's mind don't *have* to look like English, they *could*, in principle, look like English—or like whatever language the person happens to speak. So here is the question: Do they in fact? For example, if we know that Socrates is a man, is it because we have neural patterns that correspond one-to-one to the English words *Socrates, is, a*, and *man*, and groups of neurons in the brain that correspond to the subject of an English sentence, the verb, and the object, laid out in that order? Or do we use some other code for representing concepts and their relations in our heads, a language of thought or mentalese that is not the same as any of the world's languages? We can answer this question by seeing whether English sentences embody the information that a processor would need to perform valid sequences of reasoning—without requiring any fully intelligent homunculus inside doing the "understanding."

The answer is a clear no. English (or any other language people speak) is hopelessly unsuited to serve as our internal medium of computation. Consider some of the problems.

The first is ambiguity. These headlines actually appeared in newspapers:

- Child's Stool Great for Use in Garden
- Stud Tires Out
- Stiff Opposition Expected to Casketless Funeral Plan
- Drunk Gets Nine Months in Violin Case
- Iraqi Head Seeks Arms . . .

Each headline contains a word that is ambiguous. But surely the thought underlying the word is *not* ambiguous; the writers of the headlines surely knew which of the two senses of the words *stool, stud*, and *stiff* they themselves had in mind. And if there can be two thoughts corresponding to one word, thoughts can't be words.

The second problem with English is its lack of logical explicitness. Consider the following example, devised by the computer scientist Drew McDermott:

Ralph is an elephant.
Elephants live in Africa.
Elephants have tusks.

Our inference-making device, with some minor modifications to handle the English grammar of the sentences, would deduce "Ralph lives in Africa" and "Ralph has tusks." This sounds fine but isn't. Intelligent you, the reader, knows that the Africa that Ralph lives in is the same Africa that all the other elephants live in, but that Ralph's tusks are his own. . . .

A third problem is called "co-reference." Say you start talking about an individual by referring to him as *the tall blond man with one black shoe*. The second time you refer to him in the conversation you are likely to call him *the man*; the third time, just *him*. But the three expressions do not refer to three people or even to three ways of thinking about a single person; the second and third are just ways of saving breath. Something in the brain must treat them as the same thing, English isn't doing it.

A fourth, related problem comes from those aspects of language that can only be interpreted in the context of a conversation or text—what linguists call "deixis." Consider articles like *a* and *the*. What is the difference between *killed a policeman* and *killed the policeman*? Only that in the second sentence, it is assumed that some specific policeman was mentioned earlier or is salient in the context. Thus in isolation the two phrases are synonymous, but in the following contexts (the first from an actual newspaper article) their meanings are completely different:

- A policeman's 14-year-old son, apparently enraged after being disciplined for a bad grade, opened fire from his house, *killing a policeman* and wounding three people before he was shot dead.
- A policeman's 14-year-old son, apparently enraged after being disciplined for a bad grade, opened fire from his house, *killing the policeman* and wounding three people before he was shot dead.

Outside of a particular conversation or text, then, the words *a* and *the* are quite meaningless. They have no place in one's permanent mental database. Other conversation-specific words like *here, there, this, that, now, then, I, me, my, here, we,* and *you* pose the same problems, as the following old joke illustrates:

First guy   I didn't sleep with my wife before we were married, did you?
Second guy   I don't know. What was her maiden name? . . .

These examples (and there are many more) illustrate a single important point. The representations underlying thinking, on the one hand, and the sentences in a language, on the other, are in many ways at cross-purposes. Any particular thought in our head embraces a vast amount of information.

But when it comes to communicating a thought to someone else, attention spans are short and mouths are slow. To get information into a listener's head in a reasonable amount of time, a speaker can encode only a fraction of the message into words and must count on the listener to fill in the rest. But *inside a single head*, the demands are different. Air time is not a limited resource: different parts of the brain are connected to one another directly with thick cables that can transfer huge amounts of information quickly. Nothing can be left to the imagination, though, because the internal representations *are* the imagination.

We end up with the following picture. People do not think in English or Chinese or Apache; they think in a language of thought. This language of thought probably looks a bit like all these languages; presumably it has symbols for concepts, and arrangements of symbols that correspond to who did what to whom. . . . But compared with any given language, mentalese must be richer in some ways and simpler in others. It must be richer, for example, in that several concept symbols must correspond to a given English word like *stool* or *stud*. There must be extra paraphernalia that differentiate logically distinct kinds of concepts, like Ralph's tusks versus tusks in general, and that link different symbols that refer to the same thing, like the *tall blond man with one black shoe* and *the man*. On the other hand, mentalese must be simpler than spoken languages; conversation-specific words and constructions (like *a* and *the*) are absent, and information about pronouncing words, or even ordering them, is unnecessary. Now, it could be that English speakers think in some kind of simplified and annotated quasi-English, with the design I have just described, and that Apache speakers think in a simplified and annotated quasi-Apache. But to get these languages of thought to subserve reasoning properly, they would have to look much more like each other than either one does to its spoken counterpart, and it is likely that they are the same: a universal mentalese.

Knowing a language, then, is knowing how to translate mentalese into strings of words and vice versa. People without a language would still have mentalese, and babies and many nonhuman animals presumably have simpler dialects. Indeed, if babies did not have a mentalese to translate to and from English, it is not clear how learning English could take place, or even what learning English would mean.

EXPLORING THE ISSUE

Does Language Shape How We Think?

Critical Thinking and Reflection

1. Gumperz and Levinson suggest a rather mild version of the Sapir–Whorf hypothesis that language shapes our possible interpretations and expectations rather than dictating what is possible for us to perceive. Does this softer version of the hypothesis make it more plausible an argument than the more deterministic view?

2. If our language shapes how we think about the world, how is it possible that humans can learn two or more languages? Would this mean that second or third languages would have no effect on broadening what might seem to us as possibilities? Is this not comparable to what happens when undergraduates travel on either vacation or with a foreign study program at their university?

3. In what ways might the Sapir–Whorf hypothesis be understood as expanding the more or less traditional anthropological view that our cultural background shapes how we interpret new events in the world?

4. What data does Steven Pinker use to support his critique of the Sapir–Whorf hypothesis?

5. What kind of evidence is required for a more systematic assessment of the Sapir–Whorf hypothesis?

Is There Common Ground?

In many respects these two positions on linguistic relativity differ largely on whether they accept the so-called: "strong" version of the Sapir–Whorf hypothesis or the more widely held "weaker" version in which language provides people with the concepts with which they can view the world. Edward Sapir almost certainly accepted a weak reading of the hypothesis in some of his early work from the 1920s. It is not clear that he or anyone before Whorf accepted the strong deterministic position that our language limits what we can think of or imagine. It is not even clear that Benjamin Whorf ever accepted the most deterministic position that has often been attributed to him. Steven Pinker and other critics from neuropsychology typically frame the question in its strongest and most deterministic reading, but this sometimes produces a straw man, which is one of the critiques that has been raised against Pinker's analysis.

Current thinking among linguistic anthropologists suggests that color terms, kinship terms, and other classification systems or taxonomic schemes demonstrate that human languages are not free to classify colors or kin terms in any idiosyncratic way. We know that the basic color terms are patterned just as the number of cousin terms. There are limits to human creativity in classifying, which may emerge from the nature of our optic nerves in the case of color terms and the logical possibilities of biological relatives. None of this, of course, changes how different groups understand the meaning of red or black, for example, which still fits the cultural relativism that most anthropologists accept.

Additional Resources

A summary of the Sapir–Whorf hypothesis:
> Kay, Paul and Kempton, Willett. 1984. "What Is the Sapir–Whorf Hypothesis," *American Anthropologist* 86:65–79.

A related view by a cognitive psychologist:
> Fodor, Jerry A. 1975. *The Language of Thought*. Cambridge: Harvard University Press.

In mainstream anthropology, the relativity question has often been framed in terms of language's effect on a people's world view, which is another version of the weak hypothesis. This essay is an example of this position:
> Hill, Jane and Mannheim, Bruce. 1992. "Language and World View," *Reviews in Anthropology* 21:381–406.

Two books by linguists suggest ways in which the weak version of linguistic relativity can help us understand the relationship between language and culture even in our own language:
> Lakoff, George. 1987. *Women, Fire and Dangerous Things*. Chicago: University of Chicago Press.

> Lakoff, George and Johnson, Mark. 1980. *The Metaphors We Live By*. Chicago: University of Chicago Press.

The most important early statements by Benjamin Lee Whorf can be found in a volume of his papers from the 1930s collected in 1956 in:
> Whorf, Benjamin Lee. 1997. *Language, Thought, and Reality: Selected Writings*, John B. Carroll (ed.). Cambridge: Technology Press.

For a more recent and detailed survey of anthropological approaches to the Sapir–Whorf hypothesis see:
> Lucy, John A. 1997. "Linguistic Relativity," *Reviews in Anthropology* 26: 291–312.

ISSUE 10

Is Black American English a Separate Language from Standard American English, with Its Own Distinctive Grammar and Vocabulary?

YES: Ernie Smith, from "What Is Black English? What Is Ebonics?" in Theresa Perry and Lisa Delpit, eds., *The Real Ebonics Debate: Power, Language, and the Education of African-American Children* (Beacon Press, 1998)

NO: John H. McWhorter, from "Wasting Energy on an Illusion," *The Black Scholar* (vol. 27, no. 1, 2001)

Learning Outcomes

After reading this issue, you should be able to:

- Understand what is meant by Ebonics and some of the ways in which Black English differs from standard English.
- Discuss the role that linguists and linguistic anthropologists might play in determining whether the language spoken in poor African American communities is a dialect of standard English or a separate and distinct language.
- Outline some of the ways that language can prevent people from disadvantaged communities from entering the middle class.
- Interpret some of the nonlinguistic issues that are embedded in the Oakland School District's decision to label African American English as a separate and distinct language.
- Understand how linguistic anthropology can help unravel the role of language and language use in social, economic, and political concerns of contemporary life.

ISSUE SUMMARY

YES: Linguist Ernie Smith argues that the speech of many African Americans is a separate language from English because its grammar is derived from the Niger-Congo languages of Africa. Although most

215

of the vocabulary is borrowed from English, the pronunciations and sentence structures are changed to conform to Niger-Congo forms. Therefore, he says, schools should treat Ebonics-speaking students like other non–English-speaking minority students.

NO: Linguist John McWhorter counters that Black English is just one of many English dialects spoken in America that are mutually intelligible. He argues that the peculiar features of Black English are derived from the dialects of early settlers from Britain, not from African language. Because African American children are already familiar with standard English, he concludes, they do not need special language training.

Most Americans now know that some African Americans, predominantly inner-city poor, speak differently and use different body language than middle class white Americans. As African Americans have gained greater exposure through television, films, sports, and music—especially rap and hip-hop— the general population has become familiar with the distinctive vocabulary, rhythm, and style of speaking that has been termed Ebonics or Black English. While this manner of speaking has become popular with some young white Americans and members of minorities in other parts of the world, such as the Maori of New Zealand, it has been criticized as substandard English by others, especially educators. Comedian Bill Cosby created a stir by advising young African Americans to "speak English!" How should we think about this distinctive manner of speaking? Is it ordinary English but full of mistakes and slang? Is it a dialect of English, a variant associated with a particular region or social group, like "Brooklynese"? Or is it an entirely separate language with its own grammar and vocabulary, a vocabulary largely borrowed from standard English but transformed by special rules of pronunciation?

The question of whether Ebonics is a dialect or a language (or something else) would normally be of little interest to anyone but linguists, and maybe not even to them. But the question gained significant social importance because of its implications for education. In December 1996, the school board of Oakland, California's Unified School District passed a resolution stating that Ebonics is not merely a dialect of English, but a separate language, and it is the primary language of the majority of African American students in the district. Therefore, they argued, African American students should be given special classroom instruction in standard English (English as a Second Language), just like students from other ethnic groups whose home languages were not English. They hoped that this would help improve the low test scores African American children in the district received on standardized English tests.

The resolution caused a media sensation and elicited criticism and even ridicule from people throughout the country, including politicians who feared that the Oakland school district would try to claim federal funds for the teaching of English as a foreign language to Ebonics speakers. In January 1997, the board issued several amendments meant to clarify some of the ambiguous points in the resolution, such as whether students were supposed to be actually taught in Ebonics, but they reaffirmed their belief that Ebonics is a separate language from English. Thus, the question of whether Ebonics is an English dialect or a separate language has major practical consequences for students across the country. Is that a question for school boards or other legislative bodies to answer, or should it be left to experts on language?

Linguists generally do not draw a sharp distinction between languages and dialects. The general idea is that most languages encompass multiple dialects, which can be distinguished by grammar, vocabulary, or pronunciation. These dialects are usually associated with particular regions or with social groups (ethnic groups, social classes, occupational groups, etc.) within the population speaking the language. Which dialect is considered the "standard" version of the language depends on several social and political factors, such as which dialect is spoken by a politically dominant ethnic group, rather than purely linguistic characteristics. For example, Cockney English is just as adequate for communication as BBC English, but the latter is considered the standard in Britain because it is spoken by the upper class.

Among the criteria used to decide whether two modes of speech are dialects or languages are mutual intelligibility (whether people can understand each other), percentages of same or similar words, and similarity of grammars. But distinctions on these bases are not always clear-cut or consistent with each other.

Mutual intelligibility is often difficult to measure or determine because humans learn whatever languages they are exposed to. For example, if two people have grown up in a neighborhood where two closely related languages are spoken, both may speak different languages in their homes, but they may each understand the other's language because they have grown up hearing it in the neighborhood.

When words in two related languages (such as English and German) have systematic similarities in words for the same things, we call these cognate words: hound and Hund, mother and mutter. Linguists assume that the two languages were once the same language but have gradually changed in different directions over the centuries. Counting or measuring the number of cognate words in two languages can be difficult because a large number of loan words can confuse the situation. We know, for example, that all languages borrow words from neighboring languages, especially from dominant languages. Linguists call these borrowings "loan words" and it is often difficult to determine whether the similar words are similar because of their shared history or from loan words. Similarities in grammar are also complicated when two languages are spoken in the same or neighboring areas. Nowhere is linguistic change more rapid and more complicated than in modern cities, adding to the complexity of the relationship between standard English and Black English.

In the YES selection, Ernie Smith makes the case that Ebonics is a separate language from English because, he argues, its grammar is based on the Niger-Congo languages of West Africa. He acknowledges that most of the vocabulary of Ebonics is borrowed from English, but points out that the pronunciation of the words has been altered to fit Niger-Congo forms. In the NO selection, John McWhorter, on the other hand, argues that Black English is just one of many dialects of English spoken in America. He points out that Black English and standard English are mutually intelligible, and he argues that the grammatical peculiarities of Black English can be traced to regional dialects in Britain more convincingly than to African languages.

As you read the following selections, ask yourself whether there is any objective basis for deciding whether two modes of speech are separate languages or just dialects of the same language. What should the criteria be? What kind of evidence would apply? Do you think Black English is more different from standard American English than, say, the speech of white, middle-class teenagers or the speech of poor white people in the rural south?

What Is Black English?
What Is Ebonics?

The features of the language of African Americans—U.S. slave descendants of West and Niger-Congo African origin—have been recognized, described, and discussed for decades. While in recent years the appellations *Vernacular Black English, Black Vernacular English, Black English Vernacular, and African American Vernacular English* have gained some popularity, the phrase most prevalently used is Black English.

In the 1970s and 1980s, several books appeared on the language of slave descendants of African origin with *Black English* as their title. . . .

Conspicuously, in none of these works is "Black English" defined. By using the word *English*, these works inherently posit that the language of African Americans is "English." And they also tacitly postulate that, being a variant of English, there is a genetic kinship between the language of African Americans with the Germanic language family to which English belongs. Yet, from a historical linguistic perspective, in terms of the "base" from which the grammatical features of "Black English" derive, nothing could be further from the truth. As a number of scholars have argued since the 1930s, African-American speech is an African Language System—the linguistic continuation of Africa in Black America.

What Is "Black English"?

In an attempt to find empirical data supporting the view that the language of African Americans is a dialect of English, I searched the literature on "Black English." Although I found ample debate on whether "Black English" emerged as a result of a pidgin/creole hybridization process or as a result of African slaves being taught Old English "baby talk," I found no empirical evidence that English is even the "base" from which "Black English" derives. This brings us to the issue of what criteria are used for defining and classifying any language, including English, in terms of its "genetic" or familial kinship.

In the *American Heritage Dictionary*, the word English is defined, in part, as "the West Germanic language of the English (people) divided historically into Old English, Middle English, and Modern English and now spoken in the British Isles, the United States and numerous other countries." While the definition tells us that English is a West Germanic language, the question remains: By what criteria was it discerned and decided that English is related to or akin to German and belongs to the West Germanic family of the Indo-European languages? Was it based on grammar rules, vocabulary, historical origins, or what?

According to Leonard R.Palmer in his text *Descriptive and Comparative Linguistics: A Critical Introduction,* to establish a kinship or "relationship" between languages, one must go beyond vocabulary and look at grammar:

> For . . . words are often borrowed by one language from another as a result of cultural contact. . . . What constitutes the most certain evidence of relationship is resemblance of grammatical structure, for languages retain their native structure even after their vocabularies have been swamped by foreign borrowing, such as has been the case for English. . . .

This prompts the question: What precisely is meant by the words *grammar* or *grammatical structure*? . . .

In linguistics—and for purposes here—the word *grammar* means the phonetic, phonological, morphological, syntactic and semantic systems of a language. Therefore, if English is defined and classified as a Germanic language based on a criterion of continuity in the rules of grammar, then it stands to reason that "Black English" is defined and classified as a dialect of English because there is continuity in the grammar of "Black English" and the English of non-Blacks.

There is, however, an incongruence in the empirical evidence. Those who believe that Black America's language is a dialect of "English" have not documented the existence of a single Black dialect in the African diaspora that has been formed on an English grammar base.

For the sake of argument, let us accept the view of some that "Black English" is a hybrid dialect invented by English-speaking European people during the colonial era as a "contact vernacular" or trade "lingua franca." If one accepts this view, the dialect would have to be based on the grammar of the "English" language. English-speaking people would not have known the grammar of the Niger-Congo African languages and thus could not have invented a hybrid dialect on an African grammar base.

The problem with this view is that there is not a single example of a hybrid dialect that uses African words superimposed on an English grammar. If this view were valid, surely there would be at least one such dialect documented in the diaspora of Niger-Congo African slaves taken by the English.

The fact is, when one analyzes the grammars of the so-called "Black English" dialect and the English spoken by the Europeans and Euro-Americans, the grammars are not the same. While there has been extensive borrowing or adoption of English and other European words, the grammar of the language of the descendants of Niger-Congo African slaves follows the grammar rules of the Niger-Congo African languages. In other words, based on a criterion of continuity in the rules of grammar, there is no empirical evidence that "Black English" ever existed.

An alternative thesis could be that it is not continuity in the rules of "grammar" but the etymology and continuity of the "lexicon" that is the criterion for defining and classifying languages as being related. Logically, if the etymology of the lexicon is the criterion for establishing familial kinship, and the bulk of the vocabulary of "Black English" has been borrowed or adopted from the English language stock, then "Black English" is a dialect of English.

But if one uses such a criterion one must ask: Why is there a double standard? It is universally accepted that English has borrowed the bulk of its lexicon from the Romance or Latin language family. Yet English is not classified as being a Latin or Romance language but as a Germanic language.

Actually, the use of *vocabulary* to classify the language of African Americans is just as incongruent. That is, since Latin and French are the origin of the bulk of the English lexicon, how is it that African-American speech is even classified as an English dialect at all? If the dominant lexicon of the English language is Latin and French, then ipso facto the etymology of the dominant lexicon of so-called "Black English" is Latin and French. By this criterion, it logically follows, that the dialect being called "Black English" would more properly be called "Black Latin" or "Black French."

There is however, another possible definition or meaning of the phrase "Black English"—one that does not hinge on the criteria for classifying a language but rather one that has to do with how the word *Black* is perceived and defined. Those who posit this view contend that "any definition of Black English is closely bound to the problem of defining 'Blackness.'" They posit that there is a wide range of characteristics and experiences among Black people, from those in the street culture to those in the middle class.

Concomitantly, there are many Blacks who are exposed to the English of the upper class and of educated native English speakers, while other Blacks have only been exposed to the dialects of English of the poorer whites. And there are Black people who, though they have not lived in close proximity to Euro-Americans, have had the benefit of an excellent English language instruction.

The argument is made that "Black English" is not merely the Black idiom of the particular English dialect to which a Black has been exposed. "Black English" refers to the English spoken by a Black person who has "mastered" and is ideally competent in his or her use of the grammar and vocabulary of Standard American English.

It must be stressed, however, that this "Black English" is not the "Black English" that is often described as having characteristics distinctively different from the Standard American English idiom. In fact, in terms of its grammatical structure, the "Black English" spoken and written by Blacks who are fluent or ideally competent in Standard American English is identical to that of the Euro-American's Standard American English.

Thus, a critical examination of the literature reveals there are at least three distinct connotations that the appellation "Black English" can have. The first is that "Black English" is a dialect of African Americans that is "based" on mutant ("baby talk") Old English and Middle English archaic forms. The second connotation is that "Black English" is a hybrid dialect of African Americans that has as its genesis the transactional or pidgin/creole language of the West and Niger-Congo African slaves. The third connotation is that "Black English" is the English spoken by mulattoes, house Negroes, and Black bilinguals who have "mastered" the grammar and vocabulary of Standard English.

Let us now turn to the perspective of the Africologist or Africanist scholars that the native language or mother tongue of the descendants of West and Niger-Congo African slaves is not a dialect of English.

The Meaning and Misuse of the Appellation Ebonics

The term *Ebonics* was coined in January 1973 by Dr. Robert L. Williams, a Professor of Psychology at Washington University in St. Louis, Missouri. Dr. Williams coined the term *Ebonics* during a small group discussion with several African American psychologists, linguists, and speech communications professionals attending a conference convened by Dr. Williams entitled "Cognitive and Language Development of the Black Child."

Etymologically, "Ebonics" is a compound of two words: "Ebony," which means "Black," and "phonics," which means "sounds." Thus Ebonics means, literally, "Black Sounds." As an all encompassing, nonpejorative label, the term *Ebonics* refers to the language of West African, Caribbean, and U.S. slave descendants of Niger-Congo African origin.

In the sense that Ebonics includes both the verbal and paralinguistic communications of African-American people, this means that Ebonics represents an underlying psychological thought process. Hence, the nonverbal sounds, cues, gestures, and so on that are systematically used in the process of communication by African-American people are encompassed by the term as well. This is the original and only intended meaning of the term *Ebonics*.

The consensus among the African-American scholars at the conference was that, owing to their history as slave descendants of West and Niger-Congo African origin, and to the extent that African Americans have been born into, reared in, and continue to live in linguistic environments that are different from the Euro-American English-speaking population, African-American children are not from home environments in which the English language is dominant. The consensus was that, as evidenced by phonetic, phonological, morphological, and syntactical patterns, African-American speech does not follow the grammar rules of English. Rather, it is a West and Niger-Congo African deep structure that has been retained. It is this African deep structure that causes African-American children to score poorly on standardized scales of English proficiency.

In essence, the "genesis" or "origin" of the African-American child's language is the West and Niger-Congo languages of Africa. While being segregated, denied, deprived, and socioeconomically disadvantaged certainly has limited the African American's exposure to and acquisition of Standard English, segregation and poverty is not the "origin" or root cause of the African-American child's limited English proficiency.

When the term *Ebonics* was coined it was not as a mere synonym for the more commonly used appellation *Black English*. Rather, the term *Ebonics* was a repudiation of the lie that Niger-Congo Africans had no fully developed languages originally and that the genesis of human speech for English-speaking African slaves is an Old English "baby talk" or European-invented pidgin/creole vernacular.

An African Grammar with English Words

Since the 1930s, a number of scholars have posited that African-American speech is an African Language System. . . . These scholars have consistently maintained that in the hybridization process, it was the grammar of the Niger-Congo African languages that was dominant and that the extensive word borrowing from the English stock does not make Ebonics a dialect of English. In fact, they argue, because it is an African Language System, it is improper to apply terminology that has been devised to describe the grammar of English to describe African-American linguistic structures.

For example, the scholars who view African-American speech as a dialect of English describe the absent final consonant clusters as being "lost," "reduced," "weakened," "simplified," "deleted," or "omitted" consonant phoneme.

But viewed as an African Language System that has adopted European words, African-American speech is described by Africologists as having retained the canonical form, or shape, of the syllable structure of the Niger-Congo African languages. Thus, in Ebonics homogeneous consonant clusters tend not to occur. This is not because the final phoneme has been "lost," "reduced," "weakened," "simplified," "deleted" or "omitted," but because *they never existed in the first place*. Hence it is by relexification (that is, "the replacement of a vocabulary item in a language with a word from another, without a change in the grammar," that in Ebonics English words such as *west, best, test, last* and *fast* become *wes, bes, tes, las* and *fas*; the words *land, band, sand* and *hand* become *lan, ban, san* and *han*; the words *left, lift, drift* and *swift* become *lef, lif, drif* and *swif*—and so forth.

Similarly, the canonical form, or shape, of syllable structure of Ebonics is that of the Niger-Congo languages of Africa, that is, a strongly consonant vowel, consonant vowel (CV, CV) vocalic pattern. Again, by relexification, in Ebonics entire sentences will have a CV, CV vocalic pattern. In Ebonics a sentence such as, "Did you eat yet?" will exhibit the CV vocalic pattern /ǰ i ǰ E t/ or /ǰ u w i ǰ E t /. The reply "No" or "Naw did you?" will exhibit the CV vocalic pattern /n ó ǰ u /. The sentence "Did you eat your jello?" will by relexification exhibit the CV pattern / ǰ u w i č o ǰ E l o /.

Because they view African-American speech as an English dialect, Eurocentric scholars contend that in sentences such as "You the teacher" and "That teacher she mean" a copula verbal or the verb *to be* has been "deleted," "dropped," or "omitted." In contrast, because Africologists view the language of African descendants as an African Language System, they contend that there has been no "deleted," "dropped," or "omitted" copula or verb *to be* in the sentences "You the teacher" and "That teacher she mean." As an African Language System that has an equational or equative clause phrase structure, the verb *to be never existed in the first place*.

Absolutely convinced that it is a vernacular dialect of English, Eurocentric scholars have also posited the existence of "double subjects" in so-called Black English. Viewing Ebonics as an English dialect, Eurocentric scholars mistakenly divide sentences such as "That teacher she mean" and "My sister she smart" into noun phrase (NP) and verb phrase (VP) constituents—as English would be properly divided. In contrast, equally convinced that Black American Language is in fact an African linguistic system, the Africologists do not divide sentences such as "That teacher she mean" and "My sister she smart" into NP and VP constituents. As an African system, the division of an equative clause sentence structure is into "topic" and "comment" constituents. Hence, the pronoun *she* that follows the common nouns *teacher* and *sister* in each sentence is not a constituent of the "topic" segment of the sentence. It is a recapitulative pronoun that belongs to the "comment" segment.

In sum, Ebonics is not a dialect of English. The term *Ebonics* and other Afrocentric appellations such as *Pan African Language* and *African Language Systems* all refer to the linguistic continuity of Africa in Black America. Eurocentric scholars use the term *Ebonics* as a synonym for "Black English." In doing so, they reveal an ignorance of the origin and meaning of the term *Ebonics* that is so profound that their confusion is pathetic. . . .

Eurocentric scholars lack any logical explanation for why, in the entire African diaspora, there is not a single hybrid English and Niger-Congo African dialect that has an English grammar as its base with African words superimposed. They also lack any logical reasons for using vocabulary as their basis for classifying Black American speech, while using grammar as their basis for classifying English. In the process, they are exposed for the academic charlatans they are.

The imperative, however, is to recognize that all pupils are equal and hence, all pupils should to be treated equally. Limited-English-Proficient (LEP) Asian-American, Hispanic-American, Native-American, and other pupils who come from backgrounds where a language other than English is dominant are provided bilingual education and English as a second language (ESL) programs to address their LEP needs. African-American LEP pupils should not, because of their race, be subtly dehumanized, stigmatized, discriminated against or denied. LEP African-American pupils are equally entitled to be provided bilingual education and ESL programs to address their LEP needs.

John H. McWhorter
→ **NO**

Wasting Energy on an Illusion

It is a fact that Black English is not different enough from standard English to pose any significant obstacle to speaking, reading, or writing it. Black English is simply a dialect of English, just as standard English is. Any language is actually a bundle of dialects—varieties which all share a core of vocabulary and structure which make them variations on a single theme, even though they differ from one another in particulars. Southern English, Appalachian English, Brooklyn English, and standard English itself are all dialects of English.

Of course, the boundary between dialect and language is not a stark one. Sometimes a variety can diverge so far from the common core of a language X that it becomes impossible to say whether it is a dialect of X or a new language Y. One useful indication of this is when the variety is no longer mutually intelligible with other dialects of X, although this can also happen when varieties remain closely related. There are also cases where geopolitics obscures linguistic reality: Swedish, Norwegian and Danish are really dialects of a single language "Scandinavian," but are considered separate languages because they are spoken in separate countries. Meanwhile, the "dialects" of Chinese, like Mandarin and Cantonese, are actually separate, mutually unintelligible languages, but since they share a writing system and a culture are treated as "dialects."

However, none of this means that there is any "debate" among linguists as to the status of Black English, which is a case in which there is no ambiguity. It is mutually intelligible with standard English both on the page and spoken, and its speakers do not occupy a separate nation. Supporters of the Oakland resolution have often attempted to wave this away by claiming that whether Black English is a dialect or a separate language is merely an arcane issue which we should leave linguists to idly bicker over while the Board "gets on with teaching standard English." However, again, there is no "debate": no credentialed linguist would disagree that Black English is a dialect of English. More importantly, the issue is directly pertinent to the Oakland resolution, not arcane: if Black English were a separate language, the Oakland resolution would be valid. If Black English is simply a dialect, this casts the resolution in a different light.

From *The Black Scholar,* vol. 27, no.1, 2001, excerpts pp. 9–14. Copyright © 2001 by The Black Scholar. Reprinted by permission.

However, it must be clear that in arguing against the Oakland resolution on the grounds that Black English is simply a dialect of English, I am not saying that it is a sloppy deviation from the standard. All dialects of all languages are rich, coherent systems. The standard English dialect, like all standard dialects, was chosen out of many solely because of bygone political accidents, not because it is somehow more logical than Black English or any other dialect. Like standard English, Black English is a subtle and complex affair.

To take one of many examples, contrary to popular belief, Black English speakers do not simply insert the verb *be* where standard speakers use conjugated forms like *am, is,* and *are.* In Black English, *be* has the very specific meaning of *habituality.* A Black English speaker would only say *My sister be walkin' by my window* to mean that she walks by on a regular basis. They would never say this to indicate that their sister was walking by at that moment, and anyone who did would sound "funny"—the proper Black English in such an instance would be *My sister walkin' by my window*, with no verb *be* at all. Thus the use of *be* is quite subtle in Black English, and would easily confuse anyone attempting to "learn" the dialect non-natively.

We also must not make the mistake of equating Black English with mere "street slang." Black English speakers indeed often use a colorful slang (lately, *phat* for "good", *fine* for "beautiful," *mackin'* for "cruising for a date," etc.) just as standard English speakers use slang (think of the Valley Girl-speak made popular by the movie *Clueless*, or the parents in the early 1960s' musical *Bye Bye Birdie* despairing of understanding a word their teenage children said). All dialects of all languages have always had slang. Slang, however, changes constantly, and is mere decoration upon an eternal underlying structure. African Americans have been using *be* in the same way for centuries, for example. Black English differs from standard English not only in terms of superficial, evanescent slang, but in fundamental structure.

❦

All of this said, however, Black English simply does not differ *enough* from standard English to impede its child speakers from acquiring the standard. One needs no advanced training to decide on the language/dialect issue here. The very fact that African Americans are often unaware of the very existence of a "Black English" beyond slang words is a clear demonstration that Oakland's resolution is misrepresenting what is in fact an inch-wide gap between two closely related dialects. . . .

❦

The folly of pretending otherwise is revealed by a thought experiment. Imagine that rural, low-income white children were falling similarly behind in Mississippi. The first things we would address would be sociological conditions and quality of schools. African Americans are often aware of the similarity between black speech and that of poor Southern whites. Indeed, such speech is essentially as different from standard English as Black English is. Nevertheless, what would we think of the person who suggested that the reason these children were falling behind was because of the difference between the local dialect and standard English? At best, this would make it into the footnotes of the final resolution addressing the problem.

Thus even without training in linguistics or education, one can perceive the mistake in attributing the poor showing of black students to minor dialect differences. Yet many educators and academics see the Black English situation as somehow an exception. . . .

◈

Another factor which misleads many into conceiving of Black English as a case apart is the highly vaunted "African influences" upon it. While never explicitly stated, the implication is that these influences have left traits so exotic that the jump between Black English and the standard is somehow more difficult to negotiate than that between other dialects and the standard. It is time, however, that the whistle be blown on this claim, which is a vast exaggeration of the facts, based on superannuated and marginal literature. African influence on Black English is light and indirect. Most non-standard features in Black English are directly traceable not to Mende, Yoruba or Kikongo but to regional dialects spoken by the British settlers whose English was what African slaves in America were exposed to. The habitual *be* described above, the use of *done* as in *He done seen her already*, double negation such as *There ain't nothin' stoppin' you*, the simplification of consonant clusters as in *wif* for *with*, the use of *-s* with verbs other than in the third person singular, as in *I walks with Sally*—all of these things can be heard today in Great Britain, and one can sometimes even be surprised by the oddly "African American" sound of some up-country white Britishers.

There are indeed "African Englishes." However, they are spoken not in Detroit, Oakland or Philadelphia, but in the Caribbean and Africa. Examining these reveals the shocking misrepresentation in the claim that Black English is any sense an "African Language System," as the Oakland resolution puts it. A creole language, Srnan, spoken in Surinam, was developed by African slaves, and superimposes English words upon a structure which is fundamentally that of West African languages such as Twi, Ewe, Yoruba and Igbo. Here is a sentence in Sranan: *A hondiman-dati ben bai wan oso gi en mati.* Every word in this sentence is from English: it means *That hunter bought a house for his friend*— literally "the hunter-that been buy one house give him mate." However, West African words tend to consist of sequences of consonant-plus-vowel, and the Surinamese slaves re-fashioned English words to fit this pattern, so that *that* became *dati, mate* became *mati.* The African languages many of the slaves in Surinam spoke place demonstratives like *that* after the noun instead of before it, and thus so does Sranan. Similarly, such languages string verbs together where English uses prepositions, and thus "buy one house give him friend" instead of "buy a house for his friend."

All claims that Black English is somehow an African language with English words must be measured against languages like Sranan. *House* in Sranan is *oso*. In Black English it is, well, *house*. In Sranan, *bought* is *ben bai*. In Black English—*bought*. And so on.

Of course, some have attempted to get around this by claiming that the "Africanness" of Black English is somehow "hidden," such that only trained scholars could identify it: "It looks like English, but it's not," as I have heard it put. Again, however, this could only be said by someone unfamiliar with, or willfully ignoring, creoles like Jamaican patois. Jamaican patois is not as deeply influenced by African languages as Sranan, but one could indeed say that it "looks like English but isn't." *You ran away from him* in Jamaican patois is *Yu ron go lef im*. All four words are English, but without the translation one would have to blink a few times to figure out the meaning, if one even could (this is another result of the tendency to string verbs in some West African languages). In Black English *You ran away from him* is *You ran away from 'im*. An African language?

⁕⟡⁕

. . . At best, African influence on Black English is largely restricted to intonation, some vocabulary items (most of them obsolete in urban culture) and patterns of social usage such as the famous call-and-response pattern. Terms such as "Nigritian Ebonics," and the subsuming of Black English into a "Pan-African Communication System," stem not from professional research by trained linguists on Black English, nonstandard British dialects, and several African languages, but from superficial, sociopolitically biased generalizations.

Thus, Black English is not "a case apart" among English dialects. Indeed, students have been castigated for speaking it, but programs have long been in place to address this. . . . Meanwhile, Black English is not in any sense of the term an "African language": it is simply a dialect of English.

At this point, however, some would argue that bridging Black English and standard English can only help, and that in such a desperate situation we must try anything that works. Indeed, a few scholars have found that black children's reading scores rise somewhat when the "bridging" approach is adopted. Presumably, however, this would be true with children speaking *any* non-standard dialect. The point is that other children do just fine without such help—bridging the gap between the home dialect and the standard is part of the challenge of education, and generally one so minor as to escape notice. Many teachers have told me that dialect was a nonissue when it came to black children's poor performance in schools like Oakland's.

This becomes clear with another thought experiment. Here is a passage in Brooklynese English: *Ain't it great, you an' me sittin' heah tuhgeddah?* Imagine Ed Norton, the sewer worker in *The Honeymooners*, saying it: The face is white, but the dialect is, in fact, as different from standard English as Black English is. Yet none of us are under the impression that the utterer of this sentence is at a disadvantage because school is taught in standard English; we simply imagine that they will unconsciously make the jump. Again, "African influence" does not transform Black English into a case apart: Ed Norton's together is *tuhgeddah*; a Black English speaking child's would be *tuhgethah*—which person is more "disadvantaged" in terms of access to standard English? Linguistically, neither is disadvantaged at all.

⋯⋘◉⋙⋯

It is natural that linguists might suppose that Black English bars children from the standard, minor dialectal differences having come to loom large in their minds as the result of the long-term study of such things which forms part of everyday linguistic inquiry. However, a wider view shows that this is a mere artifact of the frame of reference which linguistics inevitably creates, as such dialect differences have no effect upon school performance in contexts where sociopolitics and economics are healthy. Around the world, children often bring home dialects to school which are more different from the standard than we could possibly imagine in America. For example, Swiss children speak Swiss German and go to school in High German. The dialects are so divergent that even most Germans cannot understand Swiss German: *Not* is *nicht* in High German, *nüd* in Swiss; *been* is *gewesen* in High German, gsy in Swiss; language is *Sprache* in High German, *Muul* in Swiss. Yet Swiss children learn High German via immersion, and this is not considered oppressive, a slight, or an insult. There are countless similar contexts around the world. An example slightly closer to home is Scottish English: in the current film *Train-spotting*, the near-incomprehensibility of one Scottish-speaking man has attracted much comment. We must recall, however, that this man was schooled in standard English, and surely did not consider it an inconvenience. We are all aware of the alarming rapidity with which children pick up new languages. Imagine, then, how effortlessly they pick up mere dialects of their own language!

"But Swiss children live in a wealthy, well-ordered society," some will object. And this is exactly the point: the conditions under which many African American children in Oakland live are the problem, not Black English. . . .

⋯⋘◉⋙⋯

. . . [M]ost of these children already control standard English to a considerable degree. Television is a constant presence in most Americans' lives, and African Americans are no exception. More to the point, few African Americans speak nothing but standard English all day long. Black English and the standard are generally spoken together, often mixed within the same sentence: "I went to get my check today, but the place was closed—(shaking his head) every time I go down there they be closed, man." In other words, black children pick up standard English from parents and siblings right along with Black English. The children and teenagers interviewed by the networks and affiliates in covering the events in Oakland were vivid testimony to this, effortlessly switching between the two dialects and giving the lie to the Board's designation of such children as "Limited English Proficient." African American children resist speaking standard English in the classroom as an expression of the above-mentioned alienation from the mainstream culture. Language is indexed to identity, and thus naturally, children who associate standard English with selling out will refrain from speaking it. However, it is a misinterpretation to suppose that their home dialect has somehow barred them from acquiring a dialect they are bathed in daily from birth. Surely these children can watch "Full House" and "Seinfeld" without subtitles.

∘◉∘

. . . [G]iving African American children help they do not need would be to imply that they are among the stupidest children on earth. If Brooklynese children do not need translation exercises and readers in their home dialect, neither do African American children. If Swiss children are jumping from *Muul* to *Sprache* without a thought, surely African American kids can handle *She my sister* vs. *She's my sister*. African American children, knowing as we all do that their home language is a kind of English, would come to wonder why non-black children, many using non-standard features just as they do, were not given such "translation" lessons. Slavery and discrimination have done enough to create an inferiority complex in the African American race; we need not perpetuate it ourselves. Even worse, the "translation" approach would suppress a basic element of education, challenge—and in this case, a tiny one. Suckled on such overzealous accommodation to their ethnicity, these students would only feel cast adrift later. What felt like natural challenges to non-black students would seem more forbidding to many black students, having been introduced to school via a brand of unnecessary hand-holding which, for better or for worse, they will rarely encounter in the world as we know it.

∘◉∘

Finally, if the reader detects a larger philosophical problem lurking behind my statements, they are correct. The language of the Oakland resolution. . . betray[s] a Black Nationalist sentiment—of the paranoid, anti-intellectual sort—in many leading advocates. Most, I suppose, would dodge the explicit label. However, a depiction of Black English as a hitherto unknown African language spoken on the inner city streets of America is indubitably of a kind with the likes of Martin Bernal's pseudo-scientific *Black Athena*, conspiracy theories claiming that AIDS was set upon blacks by white scientists, and calls by some academics to pardon Al Sharpton's fabrication of the Tawana Brawley story as reflecting a "narrative" reasoning style indigenous to the "African" mind. Such separatist poison is already being taught seriously to African American college students in the guise of "education," turning legions of bright young black minds away from a constructive engagement with the world. More than a few African American academics, while not supporting such perspectives, wink and let them pass in the name of racial solidarity. In my opinion, however, this is settling for mediocrity. For this brand of pernicious nonsense to be extended to seven-year-olds should be chilling to all thinking people. . . .

. . . [T]he least appropriate thing to waste time, money and energy on, is "teaching" African American children how to translate from their "Nigritian Ebonics" tongue into a separate language known as English. Black children indeed bring a home dialect to the classroom, but so do most children across the country and around the world. We can be certain that if the real causes of educational failure among African American children were addressed, then to future historians, the attention presently paid to "Ebonics" would seem a peculiar little wrinkle in the American timeline.

EXPLORING THE ISSUE

Is Black American English a Separate Language from Standard American English, with Its Own Distinctive Grammar and Vocabulary?

Critical Thinking and Reflection

1. Although it is obvious that children from families where Spanish, Somali, or Khmer, rather than English are spoken start off with a social disadvantage in primary schools, do African American children, who speak nonstandard English begin with the same disadvantage? How are these disadvantages similar and different for the two types of children?

2. This issue illustrates how documenting the linguistic history of a group of languages is fraught with difficulty, largely because we have few early examples of how slaves actually spoke in the eighteenth century. Loan words from standard English have undoubtedly entered Black English for the past two centuries. Discuss how historical linguists and linguistic anthropologists might approach the question of whether Ebonics is simply a nonstandard dialect or a distinct language from standard English.

3. Although the Ebonics question is framed as a question about linguistic facts, it is really about social and political issues that have little to do with linguistics. Linguistic anthropologists today often study these factors outside of the details of the language to look at how language is used to distinguish and even discriminate against non-powerful groups. Outline these factors in the case of the Oakland School District, and how linguistic facts are being used in nonlinguistic ways.

4. Is it important to determine whether African American children in Oakland speak a nonstandard dialect of English or another language from English? What does this discussion contribute to our understanding of language's role in society?

5. The Ebonics issue raises a number of questions that illustrate that linguistic and cultural issues are usually deeply embedded in social, economic, and political questions. Why would activists in Oakland use the definition of Black American English as a way of focusing attention on the needs of African American children in the classroom. Is this really a linguistic question about the language these children speak or is the public debate about something else?

Is There Common Ground

This issue raises the questions of how languages come into existence and change over time. One well-documented process is language evolution and divergence. The general idea is that languages slowly change even during stable times, and when a population speaking a certain language splits apart, for whatever reason, their languages gradually become different because the changes taking place are independent. Most of the languages of Europe are thought to have evolved and diverged from a series of common ancestors (Proto-Indo-European, Latin, Proto-Germanic, etc.), which is why linguists can group them into language families (e.g., Germanic), subfamilies (e.g., German and English), and so on. But languages can also influence each other or even merge under some circumstances. For example, English absorbed a large number of French words after the Norman Conquest in A.D. 1066, which is why English now has a Germanic structure but a partially Romance vocabulary. Because these processes are gradual and continuous, sharp divisions between related languages usually do not exist.

Under some circumstances people deliberately create new languages, and these may eventually become the mother tongue of a group of people. This is the case with "pidgin" languages, such as Melanesian Pidgin English. Pidgins usually begin as trade languages between groups without a language in common. They have a simplified grammar and a vocabulary drawing on two or more existing languages. Occasionally, a pidgin language becomes the primary language of a group, in which case it is referred to as a "creole." It develops a more complex grammar and vocabulary to enable it to serve as a general purpose language, although its vocabulary may still betray its origin in other languages. McWhorter gives a vivid example of the creole language of the dominant population of Surinam in South America, who mostly descend from freed or escaped African slaves.

Linguists are uncertain whether Black English came from early English dialects in America and then diverged slightly from standard English because of the social isolation of the Africans and their descendants, as McWhorter implies, or from a creole derived from an African grammar combined with English vocabulary, the view Smith favors. Information on the speech of early African American slaves is scarce and hard to interpret. However, one African American language, Gullah, is quite certainly a creole that combines features of English and several African languages. It is spoken by small numbers of African Americans living on the Sea Islands and adjacent coastal areas of South Carolina, Georgia, and northern Florida.

At its heart, this issue is less about the characteristics of the language of Oakland's African American community than it is about the difficulty these families and their children have had in entering mainstream society. Language has clearly played some role in keeping these families in poverty, but it is hardly the only factor. Truancy, drug and alcohol use, high rates of crime, and families that have minimal education are also important factors. Nevertheless, speaking a nonstandard dialect of English or speaking a wholly different language (Ebonics) has not helped this community enter the mainstream. The two selections here, when taken together, suggest that these children may need more help getting an education than mainstream and middle-class children, and language has been at least one of many factors holding them back.

Additional Resources

A huge literature on Black English/Ebonics and education has sprung up over the last few decades, due most recently to the controversy arising from the Oakland school board resolution.

This offers a very useful bibliography of nearly 700 references. They code the references under a number of headings, some more relevant to educational issues and others to linguistics issues:

Rickford, John R., Sweetland, Julie, and Rickford, Angela E. 2004. "African American English and Other Vernaculars in Education," *Journal of English Linguistics* 32(3):pp. 230–320.

This edited volume from which Ernie Smith's selection is taken is an important general work on Black English and education:

Smitherman, Geneva. 2000. *Talking That Talk: Language, Culture and Education in African America.* New York: Routledge.

This volume contains a number of valuable articles and documents relating to the Oakland school board resolution:

Perry, Theresa and Delpit, Lisa. 1998. *The Real Ebonics Debate: Power, Language, and the Education of African-American Children.* Boston: Beacon Press in collaboration with Rethinking Schools.

This essay provides an excellent summary of the events in Oakland and the legal issues involved:

Jackson, Jacquelyne Johnson. 2000. "On Oakland's Ebonics: Some Say Gibberish, Some Say Slang, Some Say Dis Den Dat, Me Say Dem Dumb, It Be Mother Tongue," *The Black Scholar* 27(1).

Two recent edited volumes bring together a number of important articles on the history of Black English, based on many decades of research:

Poplack, Shana. 2000. *The English History of African American English.* Malden, MA: Blackwell.

Wolfram, Walt and Thomas, Erik R. 2002. *The Development of African American English.* Malden, MA: Blackwell.

Internet References . . .

Another Site About Ethnic Conflict

www.foreignaffairs.com/articles/64457/james-habyarimana-macartan-humphreys-daniel-posner-jeremy-weinst/is-ethnic-conflict-inevitable

Collisions of Religions and Violence: Redux

Collisions of Religions and Violence: Redux is a Web site that contains a special issue of the journal *Cross Currents* and deals specifically with the question of whether or not conflict and violence emerge from immutable religious and ethnic differences.

www.crosscurrents.org/violencespecial.htm

Margaret Mead's Anthropological Work

This site, created by the American Museum of Natural History, explores Margaret Mead's life and provides a history of her anthropological work. It also includes links to articles that discuss Mead's influence on anthropology.

www.amnh.org/exhibitions/expeditions/
treasure_fossil/Treasures/Margaret_Mead/mead.html

The following site has Margaret Mead's biography with lots of details.

www.interculturalstudies.org/IIS/Mead/ index.html

This site considers Margaret Mead's centennial and its significance.

www.interculturalstudies.org/IIS/Mead/2001centennial.html

Some Useful Sites About the Science/Humanities Debate

www.insidehighered.com/news/2010/11/30/anthroscience
http://chronicle.com/article/Anthropologists-Debate-Whether/125571

The Importance of Worldviews

http://anthro.palomar.edu/social/soc_2.htm

Cultural Anthropology

*C*ultural anthropologists study the culture and society of living communities. *Like other anthropologists, cultural anthropologists are concerned with developing and testing models about the human condition and the range of human possibilities, such as whether gender inequality or violence are inevitable in human societies. Some anthropologists have asked whether the lives of small hunting-gathering bands resemble the lifeways of early human groups with similar technologies. Other anthropologists have asked about the strength of other people's religious beliefs. But at the heart of anthropological debate today is whether anthropology should model itself on the natural sciences or whether anthropologists should see their role more as interpreters of human cultures.*

- Should Cultural Anthropology Stop Trying to Model Itself as a Science?

- Was Margaret Mead's Fieldwork on Samoan Adolescents Fundamentally Flawed?

- Do Men Dominate Women in All Societies?

- Does the Distinction Between the Natural and the Supernatural Exist in All Cultures?

- Is Conflict Between Different Ethnic Groups Inevitable?

- Do Native Peoples Today Invent Their Traditions?

ISSUE 11

Should Cultural Anthropology Stop Trying to Model Itself as a Science?

YES: **Clifford Geertz**, from "Thick Description: Toward an Interpretive Theory of Culture," in *The Interpretation of Cultures: Selected Essays* (Basic Books, 1973)

NO: **Robert L. Carneiro**, from "Godzilla Meets New Age Anthropology: Facing the Postmodernist Challenge to a Science of Culture," *EUROPÉA* (1995)

Learning Outcomes

After reading this issue, you should be able to:

- Understand how anthropology can be seen as scientific.
- Understand the role symbolic and interpretive approaches have played in sociocultural anthropology.
- Discuss the differences between an interpretive analysis and an analysis that explains human behavior in terms of its causes.
- Outline the current debate in the discipline between those who see anthropology as a science and those who see it as an interpretive field more closely belonging to the humanities.
- Gain an understanding of how anthropology can be seen both as a social science and as a humanity.

ISSUE SUMMARY

YES: Cultural anthropologist Clifford Geertz views anthropology as a science of interpretation, and he argues that anthropology should never model itself on the natural sciences. He believes that anthropology's goal should be to generate deeper interpretations of cultural phenomena, using what he calls "thick description," rather than attempting to prove or disprove scientific laws.

NO: Cultural anthropologist Robert Carneiro argues that anthropology has always been and should continue to be a science that

238

attempts to explain sociocultural phenomena in terms of causes and effects rather than merely interpret them. He criticizes Geertz's cultural interpretations as arbitrary and immune to disconfirmation.

For more than a century, anthropologists have viewed their discipline as a "science of humankind" or as a "science of culture." We study all aspects of the human condition, recording data on the economic, agricultural, and physical conditions in which our research subjects live, but from at least the early twentieth century, we have recognized that local cultures influence the ways that people choose to interact with their environment. For more than a century, anthropologists have recognized the importance of social relationships like kinship, marriage, friendship, and political allegiance in how peoples organize their use of the local environment. Until the 1960s, nearly all anthropologists understood anthropology as a social science that attempted to find regular patterns and relationships among the various aspects of any local cultural setting.

Biological anthropologists and archaeologists have tended to search for predictable and regular patterns using data from bones, DNA, the environment, and the material culture left behind by ancient peoples. Sociocultural anthropologists have typically relied much more heavily on data about human societies that is less easily quantifiable. Many sociocultural anthropologists collect data from participant observation that is rarely if ever replicable, yet often quite helpful in gaining insight into why people behave the way they do. In this sense, from the 1960s onward, many anthropologists have challenged whether anthropology is truly a science or whether it should be more properly interpreted with the humanities, like the disciplines of history and philosophy.

Not all anthropologists agree about what being a science should mean. At issue has been the question: If anthropology is a science, just what kind of science is anthropology?

Nineteenth- and early-twentieth-century anthropologists generally viewed anthropology as one of the natural sciences, and most early theorists—such as Edward Tylor, James Fraser, and Lewis Henry Morgan—saw anthropology as an extension of biology. Like biology, anthropology is a comparative discipline, and ethnographic descriptions of particular societies resemble the systematic descriptions that biologists provide of different species. Most early anthropologists were also attracted to the theories of the naturalist Charles Darwin, whose theory of natural selection attempted to explain how plant and animal species evolved. For anthropologists, evolution meant explaining how one social form or type of society developed into another.

In the 1920s, most sociocultural anthropologists abandoned evolutionary models as speculative and racist (white Europeans were always pictured as occupying the most "advanced" stage of cultural evolution), but new kinds of evolutionary models emerged after the Second World War. Leslie White proposed a unilineal model, arguing that cultural evolution could be explained in terms of how much energy a people could capture with their technology. Julian Steward proposed a rather different multilinear model to explain why societies in different environments evolved along different paths. Steward's idea that cultures could be explained as adaptations to particular environments became the theory of cultural ecology, which continues to be popular among many anthropologists, especially prehistoric archaeologists. In the 1960s, Marvin Harris combined cultural ecology and neo-Marxian ideas into a new paradigm, which he calls "cultural materialism." Harris and like-minded scholars, including Robert Carneiro, believe that anthropology's goal should be to explain the existence and characteristics of cultures and cultural features by means of verifiable laws, like those used in other scientific fields.

However, beginning in the 1920s, some anthropologists became more interested in what people thought than in what they did. Their definitions of culture emphasized shared beliefs and feelings more than shared behaviors. This trend developed in conjunction with the modern method of ethnographic fieldwork, which requires researchers to immerse themselves for a year or more in another society, to learn the local language, and engage in "participant observation." One objective of fieldwork is, in the words of Bronislaw Malinowski, to grasp the "native's point of view." Psychological anthropology (also called "culture and personality" studies) became very popular in American anthropology from the 1920s into the 1950s. Psychological anthropologists borrowed testing methods from psychology to "get inside the heads" of the people they studied. In the 1960s, studies of cultural classifications and religious beliefs, rituals, and symbolism, inspired in part by the French anthropologist Claude Levi-Strauss, helped maintain a focus on the mental aspects of culture. Clifford Geertz's "interpretive anthropology" grew out of this interest in cultural differences in thought worlds.

From the 1960s to the 1990s, few anthropologists have been as important in reframing the goals of anthropology as the cultural anthropologist Clifford Geertz. He had conducted field research on the Indonesian island of Java in the 1950s and 1960s and in the North African Arab country of Morocco in the 1960s. Many of Geertz's early publications focused on the symbolic lives of people in the communities he studied, focusing on religion and the world view of peasants. Geertz accepted that people in these communities had to deal with the material world in which they lived. But he argued that local approaches to the material world were shaped by the symbolic worlds in which people lived. Geertz often described these symbolic worlds as cultural systems that presented themselves as powerfully real as tangible as the characteristics of the soil, the patterns of rainfall, storms, and natural disasters. For the peasants of Java, for example, the economic concerns of farmers and petty traders could only be understood in terms of their expectations of the world and never about the agricultural or economic potential of the local region.

In the YES selection from his wildly popular essay "Thick Description" published in his book *The Interpretaion of Cultures,* Clifford Geertz believes that anthropologists should give up any attempt at positivist science because for him it is futile to seek scientific laws to explain human behavior. Instead, Geertz argues that anthropologists should produce interpretations of cultures in the form of "thick descriptions," which reveal the cultural meanings of what they have observed, heard, and experienced in the field. Thus, for Geertz, anthropology should be a science of interpretation, and by definition such a science cannot be based on verifiable laws, instead it depends on the personal interpretive abilities of each individual anthropologist.

In a similar way, Robert Carneiro has been at the forefront of the effort to defend anthropological research as a science since the 1970s. In the NO selection, he responds to scholars like Geertz that anthropology should try to *explain* sociocultural phenomena, not merely interpret what people think about them, just as natural scientists seek to explain the phenomena they study. He argues that human thought and behavior are part of the external world and that they are subject to laws of cause and effect like other natural phenomena. He rejects Geertz's form of cultural interpretation as art—the creation of meanings—rather than science. He saves his strongest criticism for the "postmodern" anthropologists, who take Geertz's interpretive anthropology to the next step, even of denying that a single objective reality exists. Postmodern anthropologists see science as just another cultural discourse, one that is used by powerful groups in the West to promote capitalism and imperialistic domination of non-Western peoples.

These selections pose several questions that lie at the heart of all sociocultural anthropologists. Should anthropologists try to explain the existence and characteristics of sociocultural phenomena, or should they merely seek to translate and make sense of other people's cultural beliefs and practices? Must we choose between these alternatives, or is anthropology broad enough to hold both of these perspectives and others as well? More specifically, to what extent is social action like a text? How can we know what interpretation of a practice is the correct one? Do humans have free will, and, if so, does that make the notion of laws of human behavior meaningless?

YES ↵

Clifford Geertz

Thick Description: Toward an Interpretive Theory of Culture

I

[Here I argue] for a narrowed, specialized, and, so I imagine, theoretically more powerful concept of culture to replace E. B. Tylor's famous "most complex whole," which, its originative power not denied, seems to me to have reached the point where it obscures a good deal more than it reveals.

The conceptual morass into which the Tylorean kind of *pot-au-feu* theorizing about culture can lead, is evident in what is still one of the better general introductions to anthropology, Clyde Kluckhohn's *Mirror for Man*. In some twenty-seven pages of his chapter on the concept, Kluckhohn managed to define culture in turn as: (1) "the total way of life of a people"; (2) "the social legacy the individual acquires from his group"; (3) "a way of thinking, feeling, and believing"; (4) "an abstraction from behavior"; (5) a theory on the part of the anthropologist about the way in which a group of people in fact behave; (6) a "storehouse of pooled learning"; (7) "a set of standardized orientations to recurrent problems"; (8) "learned behavior"; (9) a mechanism for the normative regulation of behavior; (10) "a set of techniques for adjusting both to the external environment and to other men"; (11) "a precipitate of history"; and turning, perhaps in desperation, to similes, as a map, as a sieve, and as a matrix. In the face of this sort of theoretical diffusion, even a somewhat constricted and not entirely standard concept of culture, which is at least internally coherent and, more important, which has a definable argument to make is (as, to be fair, Kluckhohn himself keenly realized) an improvement. Eclecticism is self-defeating not because there is only one direction in which it is useful to move, but because there are so many: it is necessary to choose.

The concept of culture I espouse . . . is essentially a semiotic one. Believing, with [German sociologist and political economist] Max Weber, that man is an animal suspended in webs of significance he himself has spun, I take culture to be those webs, and the analysis of it to be therefore not an experimental science in search of law but an interpretive one in search of meaning. It is explication I am after, construing social expressions on their surface enigmatical. But this pronouncement, a doctrine in a clause, demands itself some explication.

II

. . . [I]f you want to understand what a science is, you should look in the first instance not at its theories or its findings, and certainly not at what its apologists say about it; you should look at what the practitioners of it do.

In anthropology, or anyway social anthropology, what the practitioners do is ethnography [the study of human cultures]. And it is in understanding what ethnography is, or more exactly *what doing ethnography is,* that a start can be made toward grasping what anthropological analysis amounts to as a form of knowledge. This, it must immediately be said, is not a matter of methods. From one point of view, that of the textbook, doing ethnography is establishing rapport, selecting informants, transcribing texts, taking genealogies, mapping fields, keeping a diary, and so on. But it is not these things, techniques and received procedures, that define the enterprise. What defines it is the kind of intellectual effort it is: an elaborate venture in, to borrow a notion from [British philosopher] Gilbert Ryle, "thick description."

Ryle's discussion of "thick description" appears in two recent essays of his (now reprinted in the second volume of his *Collected Papers*) addressed to the general question of what, as he puts it, *"Le Penseur"* is doing: "Thinking and Reflecting" and "The Thinking of Thoughts." Consider, he says, two boys rapidly contracting the eyelids of their right eyes. In one, this is an involuntary twitch; in the other, a conspiratorial signal to a friend. The two movements are, as movements, identical; from an I-am-a-camera, "phenomentalistic" observation of them alone, one could not tell which was twitch and which was wink, or indeed whether both or either was twitch or wink. Yet the difference, however unphotographable, between a twitch or wink is vast; as anyone unfortunate enough to have had the first taken for the second knows. The winker is communicating, and indeed communicating in a quite precise and special way: (1) deliberately, (2) to someone in particular, (3) to impart a particular message, (4) according to a socially established code, and (5) without cognizance of the rest of the company. As Ryle points out, the winker has now done two things, contracted his eyelids and winked, while the twitcher has done only one, contracted his eyelids. Contracting your eyelids on purpose when there exists a public code in which so doing counts as a conspiratorial signal *is* winking. That's all there is to it: a speck of behavior, a fleck of culture, and—*voilà!*—a gesture.

That, however, is just the beginning. Suppose, he continues, there is a third boy, who, "to give malicious amusement to his cronies," parodies the first boy's wink, as amateurish, clumsy, obvious, and so on. He, of course, does this in the same way the second boy winked and the first twitched: by contracting his right eyelids. Only this boy is neither winking nor twitching, he is parodying someone else's, as he takes it, laughable, attempt at winking. Here, too, a socially established code exists (he will "wink" laboriously, overobviously, perhaps adding a grimace—the usual artifices of the clown); and so also does a message. Only now it is not conspiracy but ridicule that is in the air. If the others think he is actually winking, his whole project misfires as completely, though with somewhat different results, as if they think he is twitching. One can go further: uncertain of his mimicking abilities, the would-be satirist may practice at home before the mirror, in which case he is not twitching, winking, or parodying, but rehearsing; though so far as what a camera, a radical behaviorist, or a believer in protocol sentences would record he is just rapidly contracting his right eyelids like all the others. Complexities are possible, if not practically without end, at least logically so. The original winker might, for example, actually have been fake-winking, say, to mislead outsiders into imagining there was a conspiracy afoot when there in fact was not, in which case our descriptions of what the parodist is parodying and the rehearser rehearsing of course shift accordingly. But the point is that between what Ryle calls the "thin description" of what the rehearser (parodist, winker, twitcher . . .) is doing ("rapidly contracting his right eyelids") and the "thick description" of what he is doing ("practicing a burlesque of a friend faking a wink to deceive an innocent into thinking a conspiracy is in motion") lies the object of ethnography: a stratified hierarchy of meaningful structures in terms of which twitches, winks, fake-winks, parodies, rehearsals of parodies are produced, perceived, and interpreted, and without which they would not (not even the zero-form twitches, which, *as a cultural category,* are as much nonwinks as winks are nontwitches) in fact exist, no matter what anyone did or didn't do with his eyelids.

Like so many of the little stories Oxford philosophers like to make up for themselves, all this winking, fake-winking, burlesque-fake-winking, rehearsed-burlesque-fake-winking, may seem a bit artificial.

. . . In finished anthropological writings, . . . this fact—that what we call our data are really our own constructions of other people's constructions of what they and their compatriots are up to—is obscured because most of what we need to comprehend a particular event, ritual, custom, idea, or whatever is insinuated as background information before the thing itself is directly examined. . . . There is nothing particularly wrong with this, and it is in any case inevitable. But it does lead to a view of anthropological research as rather more of an observational and rather less of an interpretive activity than it really is. Right down at the factual base, the hard rock, insofar as there is any, of the whole enterprise, we are already explicating: and worse, explicating explications. Winks upon winks upon winks.

. . . The point for now is only that ethnography is thick description. What the ethnographer is in fact faced with—except when (as, of course, he must do) he is pursuing the more automatized routines of data collection—is a multiplicity of complex conceptual structures, many of them superimposed upon or knotted into one another, which are at once strange, irregular, and inexplicit, and which he must contrive somehow first to grasp and then to render. And this is true at the most down-to-earth, jungle field work levels of his activity: interviewing informants, observing rituals, eliciting kin terms, tracing property lines, censusing households . . . writing his journal. Doing ethnography is like trying to read (in the sense of "construct a reading of") a manuscript—foreign, faded, full of ellipses, incoherencies, suspicious emendations, and tendentious commentaries, but written not in conventionalized graphs of sound but in transient examples of shaped behavior.

III

Culture, this acted document, thus is public, like a burlesqued wink or a mock sheep raid. Though ideational, it does not exist in someone's head; though unphysical, it is not an occult entity. The interminable, because unterminable, debate within anthropology as to whether culture is "subjective" or "objective," together with the mutual exchange of intellectual insults ("idealist!"— "materialist!"; "mentalist!"—"behaviorist!"; "impressionist!"—"positivist!") which accompanies it, is wholly misconceived. Once human behavior is seen as (most of the time; there *are* true twitches) symbolic action—action which, like phonation in speech, pigment in painting, line in writing, or sonance in music, signifies—the question as to whether culture is patterned conduct or a frame of mind, or even the two somehow mixed together, loses sense. The thing to ask about a burlesqued wink or a mock sheep raid is not what their ontological status is. It is the same as that of rocks on the one hand and dreams on the other—they are things of this world. The thing to ask is what their import is: what it is, ridicule or challenge, irony or anger, snobbery or pride, that, in their occurrence and through their agency, is getting said.

This may seem like an obvious truth, but there are a number of ways to obscure it. One is to imagine that culture is a self-contained "super-organic" reality with forces and purposes of its own; that is, to reify it. Another is to claim that it consists in the brute pattern of behavioral events we observe in fact to occur in some identifiable community or other; that is, to reduce it. But though both these confusions still exist, and doubtless will be always with us, the main source of theoretical muddlement in contemporary anthropology is a view which developed in reaction to them and is right now very widely held—namely, that, to quote [anthropologist] Ward Goodenough, perhaps its leading proponent, "culture [is located] in the minds and hearts of men."

Variously called ethnoscience, componential analysis, or cognitive anthropology (a terminological wavering which reflects a deeper uncertainty), this school of thought holds that culture is composed of psychological structures by means of which individuals or groups of individuals guide their behavior. "A society's culture," to quote Goodenough again, this time in a passage which has become the *locus classicus* of the whole movement, "consists of whatever it is one has to know or believe in order to operate in a manner acceptable to its members." And from this view of what culture is follows a view, equally assured, of what describing it is—the writing out of systematic rules, an ethnographic algorithm, which, if followed, would make it possible so to operate, to pass (physical appearance aside) for a native. In such a way, extreme subjectivism is married to extreme formalism, with the expected result: an explosion of debate as to whether particular analyses (which come in the form of taxonomies, paradigms, tables, trees, and other ingenuities) reflect what the natives "really" think or are merely clever simulations, logically equivalent but substantively different, of what they think.

As, on first glance, this approach may look close enough to the one being developed here to be mistaken for it, it is useful to be explicit as to what divides them. If, leaving our winks and sheep behind for the moment, we take, say, a Beethoven quartet as an, admittedly rather special but, for these purposes, nicely illustrative, sample of culture, no one would, I think, identify it with its score, with the skills and knowledge needed to play it, with the understanding of it possessed by its performers or auditors, nor, to take care, *en passant,* of the reductionists and reifiers, with a particular performance of it or with some mysterious entity transcending material existence. The "no one" is perhaps too strong here, for there are always incorrigibles. But that a Beethoven quartet is a temporarily developed tonal structure, a coherent sequence of modeled sound—in a word, music—and not anybody's knowledge of or belief about anything, including how to play it, is a proposition to which most people are, upon reflection, likely to assent.

To play the violin it is necessary to possess certain habits, skills, knowledge, and talents, to be in the mood to play, and (as the old joke goes) to have a violin. But violin playing is neither the habits, skills, knowledge, and so on, nor the mood, nor (the notion believers in "material culture" apparently embrace) the violin. To make a trade pact in Morocco, you have to do certain things in certain ways (among others, cut, while chanting Quranic Arabic, the throat of a lamb before the assembled, undeformed, adult male members of your tribe) and to be possessed of certain psychological characteristics (among others, a desire for distant things). But a trade pact is neither the throat cutting nor the desire. . . .

Culture is public because meaning is. You can't wink (or burlesque one) without knowing what counts as winking or how, physically, to contract your eyelids, and you can't conduct a sheep raid (or mimic one) without knowing what it is to steal a sheep and how practically to go about it. But to draw from such truths the conclusion that knowing how to wink is winking and knowing how to steal a sheep is sheep raiding is to betray as deep a confusion as, taking thin descriptions for thick, to identify winking with eyelid contractions or sheep raiding with chasing woolly animals out of pastures. The cognitivist fallacy—that culture consists (to quote another spokesman for the movement, [anthropologist] Stephen Tyler) of "mental phenomena which can [he means "should"]—be analyzed by formal methods similar to those of mathematics and logic"—is as destructive of an effective use of the concept as are the behaviorist and idealist fallacies to which it is a misdrawn correction. Perhaps, as its errors are more sophisticated and its distortions subtler, it is even more so.

The generalized attack on privacy theories of meaning is, since early [Edmund] Husserl and late [Ludwig] Wittgenstein, so much a part of modern thought that it need not be developed once more here. What is necessary is to see to it that the news of it reaches anthropology; and in particular that it is made clear that to say that culture consists of socially established structures of meaning in terms of which people do such things as signal conspiracies and join them or perceive insults and answer them, is no more to say that it is a psychological phenomenon, a characteristic of someone's mind, personality, cognitive structure, or whatever, than to say that Tantrism, genetics, the progressive form of the verb, the classification of wines, the Common Law, or the notion of "a conditional curse" . . . is. What, in a place like Morocco, most prevents those of us who grew up winking other winks or attending other sheep from grasping what people are up to is not ignorance as to how cognition works . . . as a lack of familiarity with the imaginative universe within which their acts are signs. . . .

IV

. . . [T]he aim of anthropology is the enlargement of the universe of human discourse. That is not, of course, its only aim—instruction, amusement, practical counsel, moral advance, and the discovery of natural order in human behavior are others; nor is anthropology the only discipline which pursues it. But it is an aim to which a semiotic concept of culture is peculiarly well adapted. As interworked systems of construable signs (what, ignoring provincial usages, I would call symbols), culture is not a power, something to which social events, behaviors, institutions, or processes can be causally attributed; it is a context, something within which they can be intelligibly—that is, thickly—described. . . .

In short, anthropological writings are themselves interpretations, and second and third order ones to boot. (By definition, only a "native" makes first order ones: it's *his* culture.) They are, thus, fictions; fictions, in the sense that they are "something made," "something fashioned"—the original meaning of *fictiō*—not that they are false, unfactual, or merely "as if" thought experiments. . . .

V

Now, this proposition, that it is not in our interest to bleach human behavior of the very properties that interest us before we begin to examine it, has sometimes been escalated into a larger claim: namely, that as it is only those properties that interest us, we need not attend, save cursorily, to behavior at all. Culture is most effectively treated, the argument goes, purely as a symbolic system (the catch phrase is, "in its own terms"), by isolating its elements, specifying the internal relationships among those elements, and then characterizing the whole system in some general way—according to the core symbols around which it is organized, the underlying structures of which it is a surface expression, or the ideological principles upon which it is based. Though a distinct improvement over "learned behavior" and "mental phenomena" notions of what culture is, and the source of some of the most powerful theoretical ideas in contemporary anthropology, this hermetical approach to things seems to me to run the danger (and increasingly to have been overtaken by it) of locking cultural analysis away from its proper object, the informed logic of actual life. There is little profit in extricating a concept from the defects of psychologism only to plunge it immediately into those of schematicism.

Behavior must be attended to, and with some exactness, because it is through the flow of behavior—or, more precisely, social action—that cultural forms find articulation. They find it as well, of course, in various sorts of artifacts, and various states of consciousness; but these draw their meaning from the role they play (Wittgenstein would say their "use") in an ongoing pattern of life, not from any intrinsic relationships they bear to one another. . . .

A further implication of this is that coherence cannot be the major test of validity for a cultural description. Cultural systems must have a minimal degree of coherence, else we would not call them systems; and, by observation, they normally have a great deal more. But there is nothing so coherent as a paranoid's delusion or a swindler's story. The force of our interpretations cannot rest, as they are now so often made to do, on the tightness with which they hold together, or the assurance with which they are argued. Nothing has done more, I think, to discredit cultural analysis than the construction of impeccable depictions of formal order in whose actual existence nobody can quite believe.

If anthropological interpretation is constructing a reading of what happens, then to divorce it from what happens—from what, in this time or that place, specific people say, what they do, what is done to them, from the whole vast business of the world—is to divorce it from its applications and render it vacant. A good interpretation of anything—a poem, a person, a history, a ritual, an institution, a society—takes us into the heart of that of which it is the interpretation. When it does not do that, but leads us instead somewhere else—into an admiration of its own elegance, of its author's cleverness, or of the beauties of Euclidean order—it may have its intrinsic charms; but it is something else than what the task at hand—figuring out what all that rigamarole with the sheep is about—calls for. . . .

The ethnographer "inscribes" social discourse; *he writes it down.* In so doing, he turns it from a passing event, which exists only in its own moment of occurrence, into an account, which exists in its inscriptions and can be reconsulted. . . .

The situation is even more delicate, because, as already noted, what we inscribe (or try to) is not raw social discourse, to which, because, save very marginally or very specially, we are not actors, we do not have direct access, but only that small part of it which our informants can lead us into understanding. . . .

VI

So, there are three characteristics of ethnographic description: it is interpretive; what it is interpretive of is the flow of social discourse; and the interpreting involved consists in trying to rescue the "said" of such discourse from its perishing occasions and fix it in perusable terms. The *kula* is gone or altered; but, for better or worse, *The Argonauts of the Western Pacific* remains. But there is, in addition, a fourth characteristic of such description, at least as I practice it: it is microscopic.

This is not to say that there are no large-scale anthropological interpretations of whole societies, civilizations, world events, and so on. Indeed, it is such extension of our analyses to wider contexts that, along with their theoretical implications, recommends them to general attention and justifies our constructing them. . . .

It is merely to say that the anthropologist characteristically approaches such broader interpretations and more abstract analyses from the direction of exceedingly extended acquaintances with extremely small matters. He confronts the same grand realities that others—historians, economists, political scientists, sociologists—confront in more fateful settings: Power, Change, Faith, Oppression, Work, Passion, Authority, Beauty, Violence, Love, Prestige; but he confronts them in contexts obscure enough . . . to take the capital letters off them. These all-too-human constancies, "those big words that make us all afraid," take a homely form in such homely contexts. But that is exactly the advantage. There are enough profundities in the world already.

Yet, the problem of how to get from a collection of ethnographic miniatures— . . . an assortment of remarks and anecdotes—to wall-sized culturescapes of the nation, the epoch, the continent, or the civilization is not so easily passed over with vague allusions to the virtues of concreteness and the down-to-earth mind. For a science born in Indian tribes, Pacific islands, and African lineages and subsequently seized with grander ambitions, this has come to be a major methodological problem, and for the most part a badly handled one. The models that anthropologists have themselves worked out to justify their moving from local truths to general visions have been, in fact, as responsible for undermining the effort as anything their critics—sociologists obsessed with sample sizes, psychologists with measures, or economists with aggregates—have been able to devise against them.

Of these, the two main ones have been: the Jonesville-is-the-USA "microcosmic" model; and the Easter-Island-is-a-testing-case "natural experiment" model. Either heaven in a grain of sand, or the farther shores of possibility.

The Jonesville-is-America writ small (or America-is-Jonesville writ large) fallacy is so obviously one that the only thing that needs explanation is how people have managed to believe it and expected others to believe it. The notion that one can find the essence of national societies, civilizations, great religions, or whatever summed up and simplified in so-called "typical" small towns and villages is palpable nonsense. What one finds in small towns and villages is (alas) small-town or village life. If localized, microscopic studies were really dependent for their greater relevance upon such a premise—that they captured the great world in the little—they wouldn't have any relevance.

But, of course, they are not. The locus of study is not the object of study. Anthropologists don't study villages (tribes, towns, neighborhoods . . .); they study *in* villages. You can study different things in different places, and some things—for example, what colonial domination does to established frames of moral expectation—you can best study in confined localities. But that doesn't make the place what it is you are studying. . . .

The "natural laboratory" notion has been equally pernicious, not only because the analogy is false—what kind of a laboratory is it where *none* of the parameters are manipulable?—but because it leads to a notion that the data derived from ethnographic studies are purer, or more fundamental, or more solid, or less conditioned (the most favored word is "elementary") than those derived from other sorts of social inquiry. The great natural variation of cultural forms is, of course, not only anthropology's great (and wasting) resource, but the ground of its deepest theoretical dilemma: how is such variation to be squared with the biological unity of the human species? But it is not, even metaphorically, experimental variation, because the context in which it occurs varies along with it, and it is not possible (though there are those who try) to isolate the y's from x's to write a proper function. . . .

The methodological problem which the microscopic nature of ethnography presents is both real and critical. But it is not to be resolved by regarding a remote locality as the world in a teacup or as the sociological equivalent of a cloud chamber. It is to be resolved—or, anyway, decently kept at bay—by realizing that social actions are comments on more than themselves; that where an interpretation comes from does not determine where it can be impelled to go. Small facts speak to large issues, winks to epistemology, or sheep raids to revolution, because they are made to.

VII

There is an Indian story—at least I heard it as an Indian story—about an Englishman who, having been told that the world rested on a platform which rested on the back of an elephant which rested in turn on the back of a turtle, asked (perhaps he was an ethnographer; it is the way they behave), what did the turtle rest on? Another turtle. And that turtle? "Ah, Sahib, after that it is turtles all the way down."

. . . Cultural analysis is intrinsically incomplete. And, worse than that, the more deeply it goes the less complete it is. It is a strange science whose most telling assertions are its most tremulously based, in which to get somewhere with the matter at hand is to intensify the suspicion, both your own and that of others, that you are not quite getting it right. But that, along with plaguing subtle people with obtuse questions, is what being an ethnographer is like.

There are a number of ways to escape this—turning culture into folklore and collecting it, turning it into traits and counting it, turning it into institutions and classifying it, turning it into structures and toying with it. But they *are* escapes. The fact is that to commit oneself to a semiotic concept of culture and an interpretive approach to the study of it is to commit oneself to a view of ethnographic assertion as, to borrow W. B. Gallie's by now famous phrase, "essentially contestable." Anthropology, or at least interpretive anthropology, is a science whose progress is marked less by a perfection of consensus than by a refinement of debate. What gets better is the precision with which we vex each other. . . .

My own position in the midst of all this has been to try to resist subjectivism on the one hand and cabbalism on the other, to try to keep the analysis of symbolic forms as closely tied as I could to concrete social events and occasions, the public world of common life, and to organize it in such a way that the connections between theoretical formulations and descriptive interpretations were unobscured by appeals to dark sciences. I have never been impressed by the argument that, as complete objectivity is impossible in these matters (as, of course, it is), one might as well let one's sentiments run loose. As [economist] Robert Solow has remarked, that is like saying that as a perfectly aseptic environment is impossible, one might as well conduct surgery in a sewer. Nor, on the other hand, have I been impressed with claims that structural linguistics, computer engineering, or some other advanced form of thought is going to enable us to understand men without knowing them. Nothing will discredit a semiotic approach to culture more quickly than allowing it to drift into a combination of intuitionism and alchemy, no matter how elegantly the intuitions are expressed or how modern the alchemy is made to look.

The danger that cultural analysis, in search of all-too-deep-lying turtles, will lose touch with the hard surfaces of life—with the political, economic, stratificatory realities within which men are everywhere contained—and with the biological and physical necessities on which those surfaces rest, is an ever-present one. The only defense against it, and against, thus, turning cultural analysis into a kind of sociological aestheticism, is to train such analysis on such realities and such necessities in the first place. It is thus that I have written about nationalism, about violence, about identity, about human nature, about legitimacy, about revolution, about ethnicity, about urbanization, about status, about death, about time, and most of all about particular attempts by particular peoples to place these things in some sort of comprehensible, meaningful frame.

To look at the symbolic dimensions of social action—art, religion, ideology, science, law, morality, common sense—is not to turn away from the existential dilemmas of life for some empyrean realm of de-emotionalized forms; it is to plunge into the midst of them. The essential vocation of interpretive anthropology is not to answer our deepest questions, but to make available to us answers that others . . . have given, and thus to include them in the consultable record of what man has said.

Robert L. Carneiro

➡ **NO**

Godzilla Meets New Age Anthropology: Facing the Postmodernist Challenge to a Science of Culture

As we strive to understand nature, do we seek truth or solace?

Stephen Jay Gould

When I began working on the first incarnation of this paper, years ago, the greatest threat to a science of culture, it seemed to me, came from those anthropologists who considered themselves humanists. Today, though, the picture has changed radically. A much greater threat now comes from that large, amorphous host who march under the banner of postmodernism. Compared to the old-fashioned humanists, the threat they pose is as the Black Plague to the chicken pox. So it is against *them* that my major battle will be waged. By comparison, my engagement with traditional humanists will be but a preliminary skirmish.

Nonetheless, let me begin with the humanists, for, in their distaste for a science of culture, both humanists and postmodernists have much in common. If not genetically related, the two have at least sprouted from the same seedbed.

The antagonism between humanism and science is not only deep, but old. Almost two centuries ago the poet John Keats was provoked to cry "A Confusion on Newton!." Why? Because Newton had shown the rainbow to be caused by the refraction of light through raindrops, and *that*, for Keats, destroyed the wonder of it all. . . .

More recently, Joseph Wood Krutch has argued that "the experience of living is the thing which . . . has the greatest value, and . . . all the social sciences which tend to manipulate and regularize and unify human conduct result in a general lowering of the intensity of the experience . . . and . . . therefore, from my standpoint, they are bad."

Finally, E. E. Cummings expressed his contempt for science in this short verse:

While you and I have lips and voices which,
are for kissing and to sing with
who cares if some oneeyed son of a bitch
invents an instrument to measure spring with?

From *EUROPÉA*, 1995, I–1. Copyright © 1995 by Robert L. Carneiro. Reprinted by permission of the author.

That scientists and humanists should be antagonists is thus nothing new or unusual. What *is* anomalous is that within something calling itself a science, there should be a large nucleus of persons who reject the ways of science and profess to practice anthropology as a humanity.

Since science vs. humanism is such a major issue, let us look at its philosophical basis. Part of this basis is the distinction between science and art, a distinction which Leslie White has expressed very nicely:

> Science is one of two basic ways of dealing with experience. The other is art. . . . The purpose of science and art is one: to render experience intelligible. . . . But although working toward the same goal, science and art approach it from opposite directions. Science deals with particulars in terms of universals: Uncle Tom disappears in the mass of Negro slaves. Art deals with universals in terms of particulars: the whole gamut of Negro slavery confronts us in the person of Uncle Tom. Art and science thus grasp a common experience, or reality, (but) by opposite poles.

White's distinction strikes me as valid. At bottom, humanists do look at the world as artists. But there is more to it than that. Humanists are not content merely to *contemplate* their subject; they also *celebrate* it. If you doubt this, just look inside the front cover of the *Anthropology and Humanism Quarterly*, a new journal published by our Association. There you will read that humanistic anthropology "celebrates" the fact that "human reality" is something that "we creative primates construct."

Now, celebration is all well and good, but it is not part of science. No physicist "celebrates" acceleration, and no chemist "celebrates" carbon tetrachloride. This is simply not a function of science. Our job, as scientists, is not to celebrate, but to *explain*, to *account for.* That's what makes us scientists. Let a poet enrapture himself over a lily, admiring the symmetry of its petals, the delicacy of its stamens, and let him sigh over the subtle fragrance of its nectar, but let him not try to pass himself off as a botanist! . . .

Let us not think, though, that by asserting that humanists do not do science, we are puncturing their balloon. You cannot puncture what was never inflated to begin with, and the fact is that the humanists in our ranks do not *claim* to be doing science. On the contrary, they cheerfully admit that they are *not*. But they aren't content with this. They go on to assert that *we* cannot do science, social science, either. Indeed, many of them claim that social science *cannot* be done.

Clifford Geertz, the leading literary humanist in anthropology, finds those of us who consider ourselves social scientists "ignorant and pretentious usurpers of the mission of the humanities." So the gauntlet has been thrown down. Well, if Geertz says there can't be a social science, why not? Only two possibilities exist: either we cannot do it because it is intrinsically undoable, or, if it is theoretically possible, we cannot do it because, in practice, it is too difficult.

Let us look at each possibility in turn. To begin with, why should a science of culture be inherently impossible? The answer is, only if the things and events it studies are not subject to cause and effect. So then we must ask, is human behavior subject to strict causality? Not if there is free will.

No one has put the matter more concisely than the 19th century British historian James Anthony Froude:

> When natural causes are liable to be set aside and neutralized by what is called volition, the word Science is out of place. If it is free to a man to choose what he will do or not do, there is no adequate science of him. . . .

This is not the place to attempt a formal refutation of free will. Instead, I would like to try to convince the humanists among you that determinism is not such a bad thing after all. In fact, I would argue that when you look at it deeply enough, free will turns out to be rather uncongenial to the artist. Let me present my case.

First, though, some background. Several years ago, to help us with an exhibit at the museum in which I work, we hired an artist from San Francisco. During the course of his work, I became well acquainted with him, and in one of our conversations, the subject of free will came up. As you might expect, he and I were on opposite sides of the fence on this issue. We argued about it, but neither of us made much headway in convincing the other. His work completed, the artist returned to San Francisco, but we continued to correspond. And in one of my letters, I presented an argument which I hoped might persuade him to abandon free will and embrace determinism. Here is what I wrote:

> Dear ***,
>
> It is my contention that whenever an artist creates, he is never acting outside the stream of causation. What he engenders, no matter how novel, is never fortuitous. It is neither totally unforeseen nor unaccountable. It is, in fact, the product of lots of things swirling around in his psyche, conscious and unconscious. And—here's the kicker—I would argue that, from the artist's point of view, determinism, seen in this light, is better than free will! Genuine free will implies that, whatever you produce is entirely unconstrained by anything that went before. But if that were true, your creation would be completely out of your hands, entirely at the mercy of chance.
>
> And how could such a state of affairs possibly be satisfying to an artist? Isn't it much more congenial for you to think of your art as a summation and expression of everything that has gone into you, than for it to be unconnected and unrelated to you? Let's face it, free will—real free will—is completely depersonalizing and dehumanizing. It would work like a purely mechanical game of chance, in which you weren't even allowed to hold the dice. Surely the determinism I offer you, which puts you and your life experiences at the very heart of your artistic creation, should be much more congenial.
>
> Sincerely,

Now, if free will is merely an illusion, if human behavior is indeed strictly determined, there is no reason why, in principle, there cannot be a science of human behavior, a science of culture. Some humanists may grudgingly concede this, but then raise another objection: Whatever the case may be in *principle*, they say, in *practice*, human behavior is simply too complex for any genuine regularities, let alone any laws, to be teased out of it.

But is complexity of behavior solely a problem for the anthropologist? Not at all. The phenomena of physics are intricate and complex too. Of the thousands of leaves on a tree, no two fall to earth exactly the same way. Yet physics was able to see past the unique and erratic behavior of each fluttering leaf, and to formulate a general law of falling bodies. Could it be, then, that the anthropological humanist has given up finding any underlying laws in human behavior because he has not looked for them hard enough? When he triumphantly proclaims the impossibility of formulating any cultural laws, could he merely be making a virtue out of his own shortcomings? Could this, then, be nothing more than a case of the tailless fox preaching taillessness?

Having thus warded off the humanists, we come now to the main event: the challenge to the science of culture posed by postmodern anthropology. Humanism was a straightforward, innocent adversary. Postmodernism is anything *but*. Sometimes it appears quite amorphous, but at other times it has the head of a hydra and the arms of a squid. Nor is this only my opinion. C. Richard King, a not unsympathetic observer of the movement, has said that postmodernism "lacks a single, unitary definition . . . It appears to be, at once, everything and nothing." . . .

[W]hatever else postmodernism might aspire to be, it is, at bottom, one more manifestation of the old, familiar prejudice against science. Thus, in her book, *Postmodernism and the Social Sciences*, Pauline Rosenau tells us that the postmodernist "questions the validity of modern science and the notion of objective knowledge." Moreover, postmodernism's headlong retreat from science goes further than humanism's ever did. Not only does it disdain science, it declares science to be dead.

Although postmodernism has challenged anthropology on all fronts, its main attack has been leveled at ethnography. To give the devil his due, postmodernists have had a valid point to make here. Ethnographers have traditionally tended to round things off, to smooth things up. Their monographs often present a single "authoritative" statement of a particular custom or belief, as if that were all there was to it. Yet anyone who has ever done fieldwork knows that informants' versions of a custom or belief often vary all over the map. Thus, presenting only one version *masks* the actual complexity. This foreshortening of reality, though, is not done to deceive. It is done for practical reasons. Were a monograph to include 16 different versions of every custom and belief, it might be more "real," but would also become so cumbersome and wearying as to vitiate the effort. So ethnographers generally round off their accounts to the first decimal place, so to speak, and present a kind of "official" version.

But what does this "official" version of a culture really represent?, ask the critics of traditional ethnography. Is it the opinion of one's best-liked informant? Or the most reliable one? Is it the response of one informant or of several? And if several, and if their range of responses has been "averaged," then what is this "average" that gets printed in the monograph—the mean, the median, or the mode?

Postmodern critics contend that ethnography should stress the many "voices" that may be raised in a primitive society. It is certainly true that there may well be many such "voices," even in a small native village, and that most of them usually remain unheard. That, in itself, is an objective fact, and deserves to be duly noted. But to *dwell* on the myriad voices of informants—indeed, to make a *career* out of it—seems to me to attenuate and trivialize the craft of ethnography.

Yet this has become a dominant theme in postmodern anthropology. With full-throated voice, postmodernists proclaim that there is not *one* reality, but *multiple* ones. The trouble is, though, that as realities are multiplied, they are also divided; as they become more numerous, they become correspondingly smaller. And, there being more and more of them, facts now count for less and less, and so reality becomes progressively diluted and rarified. And it is but a small step from this to saying that there is *no* reality at all! And once *that* assertion has been made, the wheels come off the wagon.

⋅ᜦᑑᜦᴗ⋅

Let us look at this dissolution of reality a little more closely. Postmodern ethnography likes to call itself "dialogical." It puts a high premium on the *dialogue* that takes place between ethnographer and informant. James Clifford says that in the new ethnography "monophonic authority is questioned," and in its stead "dialogism and polyphony are recognized as modes of textual production." And Stephen Tyler, another leading voice in the movement, holds that postmodern ethnography "emphasizes the cooperative and collaborative nature of the ethnographic situation in contrast to the ideology of the transcendant observer." But Tyler goes a step further, claiming that the postmodern ethnographer "rejects the ideology of 'observer-observed,' there being nothing observed and no one who is observer." If this is literally true, one is left to wonder, with Richard King, whether "an anthropology which dismisses the distinctions between self and other . . . is possible or even imaginable?"

Setting that question aside, we come to the matter of "truth." Consider the following dilemma. If "truth" is a statement about reality, but reality has already been bargained away, where does that leave truth? "In cultural studies," says Clifford, "we can no longer know the whole truth, or even claim to approach it." But if the search for truth, the traditional objective of science, is left lying in the dust, what happens to science itself? The answer is inescapable. If, as Clifford says, "Cultures are not scientific 'objects,' the science of culture loses its subject matter, and with it, its identity and even its very existence. . . .

With ethnographic facts now having but a tenuous reality, they are being reassigned a place in the domain of literature, namely, fiction. Clifford puts his seal of approval on this change in the following words: "Ethnographic writings can properly be called fictions in the sense of 'something made or fashioned.' . . . But it is important to preserve the meaning not merely of making, but also of making up, of inventing things not actually real." So there we are, in the Land of Diggledy Dan.

⌖

Any serious study of literature naturally involves the use of *texts*. And texts have become a focus of postmodern ethnography. According to Geertz's oftquoted remark, culture itself is "an ensemble of texts, themselves ensembles, which the anthropologist strains to read over the shoulder of those to whom they properly belong." So the new ethnographer's field notes become his texts, and he proceeds to deal with them accordingly.

Yet, the more texts are scrutinized, the more they seem to proliferate, spawning *subtexts*. Now, teasing subtexts from a main text is surely slippery business, but it's also a lot of fun. It's a game *any*one can play, and *every*one can win, because there are no rules. There is no correct interpretation, no right answer. Any answer is as good as any other. . . .

Another offshoot of literary ethnography is narrative. Its practitioners focus on *stories* rather than customs. These "stories" started out as biographies, the life histories of one's informants. But it wasn't long before biography turned into *auto*biography, and the subject of one's research became, not one's informants, but oneself. As James Clifford put it, "With the 'fieldwork account' the rhetoric of experienced objectivity yields to that of the autobiography and the ironic selfportrait. The ethnographer, a character in a fiction, is at center stage." . . .

Practiced with fervor, this form of postmodern ethnography becomes supremely self-centered. The ethnographer focuses, not on what he is observing, but on what he *feels* about what he is observing! He is, in effect, watching the patient, but taking his own pulse! Thus, he has become more important than his subject matter. Or rather, he has turned himself *into* his own subject matter. So, by sleight-of-hand, ethnography has become autobiography. . . .

Needless to say, all of this is the very antithesis of science. The cornerstone of science has always been the premise that there is a real world out there, independent of our individual existences. And it is *this* world that, as scientists—as *anthropologists*—we should be studying. If anyone still doggedly prefers to contemplate his own navel, fine. But let him call his contemplation by a different name than anthropology. . . .

⌖

I find it quite ironic that persons so concerned with "meaning" as postmodern ethnographers claim to be, should show so little regard for the process of *conveying* meaning, namely, communication. Yet, "meaning" is certainly what they profess to be after. Listen to Clifford Geertz:

> Believing . . . that man is an animal suspended in webs of significance he himself has spun, I take culture to be those webs, and the analysis

of it to be therefore not an empirical science in search of law but an interpretive one in search of meaning.

Beware of those "webs of significance"! From them we have much to fear. The new ethnographer, like a spider, draws forth from his spinaret, threads of infinite subtlety, and with them, creates his own webs which, like those of the spider, are not only delicate, but sticky. And in them, he entraps his prey, holding it fast while he sucks out its meaning. Then, perhaps, he will discard the eviscerated carcass, leaving it to the old-fashioned ethnographer to find whatever vestige of structure and substance may be left in it.

Confronted with a choice between substance and meaning, it is perfectly clear that Geertz will take meaning any day. For him, nothing is what it *is*. It is what it *means*. The famous Balinese cockfight, for example, becomes, at his hands—and here I quote Geertz directly—"image," "fiction," "a model," "a metaphor." So far does he give flight to his fancies in this regard that even his fellow postmodernist, Vincent Crapanzano, feels it necessary to bring him to heel. Thus, Crapanzano says sharply, "Cockfights are surely cockfights for the Balinese—and not images, fictions, models, and metaphors." Indeed, Geertz's rendition of Balinese cockfights so disturbs Crapanzano that he characterizes it as "constructions of constructions of constructions," a simple, bloody fight between two roosters transmogrified into Cloud Cuckooland! . . .

⚜

In the frontal attack of postmodernism on anthropology, one major casualty has been . . . *ethnology.* So *fixated* are postmodernists at the level of ethnography, that they have failed to fulfill ethnography's traditional obligation to ethnology. From its earliest days, ethnography has always been the handmaiden of ethnology. It quarried and dressed the stones which ethnology then used to erect its larger stuctures. For it is here, in ethnology, that broad theories are built and generalizations crafted; where the major questions of anthropology are asked and answered. *Here* it is that we debate the origin of clans, the invention of agriculture, the function of crosscousin marriage, the role of age grades, the rise of chiefdoms, and the development of states. What have postmodernists contributed to the solution of these great problems? Nothing. Has anyone even *heard* of a postmodernist theory of the origin of the state? Alas, what will happen to such questions in an age of postmodern anthropology?

The new ethnographers are not, however, unaware that they're sidestepping these issues. George Marcus, for example, notes that "because of modern ethnography's commitment to social criticism, . . . it has rarely been directed to answering macrosociological questions about the causes of events or the constitution of major systems and processes." The new ethnographer, then, is like a mason so enamored of the peculiarities of each brick, that he turns them over in his hands, carefully studying them, but cannot bring himself to arrange them into some larger structure. He is a mason who has neglected to apply for his architect's license. And why not? Because he doubts that major edifices can ever be built anyway.

But it gets worse. Not only does the new ethnographer refuse to start building himself, he would deny the *ethnologist* a building permit too. He is not content to say what *he* can't do, he also tells us what *we* can't do. And why can't we? Because—among other things—the tools we choose to employ are defective. They are tools of our own devising—"hegemonic concepts"—rather than the simple adzes and digging sticks of our informants. And, Stephen Tyler tells us, "postmodern ethnography . . . seeks . . . to avoid grounding itself in the theoretical and commonsense categories of . . . Western tradition."

Were we to follow Tyler's injunction, though, we would be severely hamstrung. Consider this example. I regard the proportion of waking time that a society spends on subsistence to be of fundamental importance in determining the general level of its culture. Accordingly, I have tried to ascertain this figure for the Kuikuru of central Brazil during the course of my field work among them. However, not being a concept the Kuikuru themselves would be likely to think of, Tyler would rule such a calculation out of court as a "hegemonic Western category." Carried to this extreme, cultural relativism surely cuts us off at the knees. . . .

⚫

As we noted earlier, postmodernists are rather ambivalent about truth. At times, they assert there is no such thing; but at other times they tell us there are a thousand different truths. Where on earth does that leave us?

Needless to say, one can define truth any way one feels like. If one wants to define it as that which it is impossible to attain, fine. That takes care of the matter, once and for all. But what *good* does that do? It merely evades an important issue. Here's what I suggest instead. Truth need not be regarded as some mystical, vaporous essence; a holy grail to be sought for but never found. Truth can simply be defined as an *agreement* or *correspondence* between a proposition and something in the external world. As such, it becomes quite possible to attain it. In fact, it is, and has always been, the stated goal of science.

Another notion I rebel against is that truth, if allowed to exist at all, is at best tenuous and protean, and that anyone's "truth" is just as valid as anyone else's. The implications of this view for an ethnographer working in the field are jolting, to say the least. It implies that he should be satisfied with whatever answer he gets to a question, and not try to ferret out the "truest" truth he can. . . .

Is this really where we want to be? Suppose, for example, that Napoleon Chagnon had accepted at face value the genealogies first given to him by the Yanomamö as being as good as any other, and let it go at that. By eschewing verification he would, according to Tyler, have been following good, postmodernist procedure. But he would also have been sorely deceived, because, as he found out months later, the Yanomamö had purposely and systematically lied to him. Now, can any postmodernist seriously hold that the spurious genealogies Chagnon first obtained were just as good, just as true, just as valid, as the ones he got later? . . .

I have often been struck by the fact that there is no such thing as postmodern chemistry, or postmodern geology. Why not? To begin with, no serious science would be foolish enough to define itself out of existence. Nor could it afford to spend so much of its time dabbling in hairsplitting and pettifogging. No real science would devote itself so wholeheartedly to the inconsequential. To be sure, all the sciences have their many tiny facts, but these are gathered, not for their own sake, but to serve some larger purpose. And this purpose is to formulate a series of overarching propositions that seek to explain ever larger segments of nature. And are these aims not all we really need? . . .

So, what is to happen? What can we expect in the future? Despite my previous lamentations, I am not altogether worried; at least not in the long run. Why? Because I'm a firm believer in the principle of natural selection, and natural selection works on ideas just as it does on organisms. In the realm of ideas, as everywhere else, it's the payoff that counts. Ultimately, any intellectual movement will be judged by its results. If it produces nothing tangible, substantial, or enlightening, it will fall by the wayside, just as so many intellectual fads have before it. Thus I am ready to predict that postmodernism, like phrenology, prohibition, and free silver, will quietly fade away, and center stage will once more be occupied by less scintillating but more productive forms of inquiry. . . .

EXPLORING THE ISSUE

Should Cultural Anthropology Stop Trying to Model Itself as a Science?

Critical Thinking and Reflection

1. What difference does it make if anthropologists see their research as either a science or as one of the humanities? Does it change the questions one asks? Would it change the answers?
2. Why should we group cultural materialist and hypothesis testing research projects together as science? Is science only about hypothesis testing? Is there no room in science for observation-based research?
3. Why should interpretive projects like those that Geertz supports not be considered scientific? Do social science projects need to test hypotheses to be able to understand human societies and cultures more profoundly and in more depth?
4. Many anthropologists receive grants from both the National Science Foundation and the National Endowment for the Humanities or Wenner-Gren Foundation for Anthropological Research, both of which support interpretive research. Is it a contradiction to receive support from both sorts of funding agency?
5. Is there a middle ground for anthropology in this apparent battle between scientific and interpretive anthropology?

Is There Common Ground?

Cultural anthropology is often viewed as a big tent capable of embracing many diverse points of view, as the selections by Geertz and Carneiro suggest. Many anthropologists slip easily back and forth between humanistic and scientific approaches depending on the type of problem they are trying to solve. For example, one might use an interpretive approach to analyze a religious ritual and a scientific approach to work out the effects of globalization on a people's economy. But true partisans of the two paradigms, such as Geertz and Carneiro, would point out that the approaches are based on fundamentally incompatible epistemologies, totally different conceptions of what knowledge is and how we can get at it. This has not, however, been the dominant view in sociocultural anthropology.

While Geertz is an ardent champion of humanistic anthropology, he is not the harshest critic of anthropology as a law-based science. A number of so-called postmodern scholars—such as James Clifford, George Marcus, and Stephen Tylor—have been much more vocal in their attacks on positivism in anthropology. They have urged anthropology to become a self-reflective social science, practicing what has been termed "critical theory." For these scholars, anthropologists should seek out the implicit, underlying assumptions and motivations of the anthropologists who have produced what passes for anthropological knowledge. They have borrowed methods from literary criticism to "deconstruct" many classic ethnographic monographs, revealing the rhetorical techniques used by the authors to convince readers of the veracity of their accounts. Opponents have suggested that critical theorists are more concerned with studying the culture of anthropology than with understanding anthropology's traditional subject matter. Postmodernists have offered suggestions on how to improve the writing of ethnography, but do not offer any substitute for the kinds of explanations of sociocultural phenomena that natural science-minded anthropologists aim to produce.

Marvin Harris's cultural materialist approach, incorporating cultural evolution and environmental adaptation, is probably the most widely used scientific paradigm in anthropology. Carneiro uses this approach. Another scientific approach taken by some anthropologists (as well as biologists and psychologists) is "sociobiology." Sociobiologists argue that humans, like all animals, are genetically programmed to respond in certain ways, and cultural practices are just an external manifestation of inner biological drives.

Recently, in the 2010 meetings of the American Anthropological Association in New Orleans, the association modified its mission statement to delete the word science from the text, much to the dismay of many biological anthropologists and materialists. The widening rift among the membership was so striking that even the *New York Times* reported on it. Such tensions raise questions about what is at the root of this fissure in the discipline that has for so many decades seen itself as both *a science* and as *one of the humanities*.

Additional Resources

The selection we have used for this issue was written as the introduction to this collection of Geertz's writings. It is the most coherent statement outlining the breadth and scope of an interpretive anthropology. It contains what is probably his best-known interpretive essay, "Deep Play: Notes on the Balinese Cockfight."
Geertz, Clifford. 1973. *The Interpretation of Cultures.* New York: Basic Books.

Geertz's other important books about the interpretive approach include:
Geertz, Clifford. 1983. *Local Knowledge: Further Essays in Interpretive Anthropology.* New York: Basic Books.

Geertz, Clifford. 1988. *Works and Lives: The Anthropologist as Author.* Palo Alto: Stanford University Press.

This review essay offers a useful overview of the interpretive approach in cultural anthropology:
Fisher, Michael. 1977. "Interpretive Anthropology," *Reviews in Anthropology* 4(4).

A newspaper account that points out a growing rift in the discipline without really understanding what is behind the tension:
Wade, Nicholas. 2010. "Anthropology a Science? Statement Deepens a Rift," *New York Times* December 9, 2010. www.nytimes.com/2010/12/10/science/10anthropology.html

Important essays from a critical or postmodern perspective are contained in two edited volumes:

Clifford, James and Marcus, George E., eds. 1986. *Writing Culture: The Poetics and Politics of Anthropology*. Berkeley: University of California Press.

Marcus, George E. and Fisher, Michael M.J. 1986. *Anthropology as Cultural Critique: An Experimental Moment in the Human Sciences*. Chicago: University of Chicago Press.

Carneiro's other important works include:

Carneiro, Robert. 2000. *The Muse of History and the Science of Culture*. New York: Kluwer Academic/Plenum Publishers.

Carneiro, Robert. 2003. *Evolutionism in Cultural Anthropology: A Critical History* Boulder. CO: Westview Press.

Carneiro, Robert. 2010. *The Evolution of the Human Mind: From Supernaturalism to Naturalism, an Anthropological Perspective*. Clinton Corners, NY: Eliot Werner Publications.

This article provides a summary of his circumscription theory of state formation:

Carneiro, Robert. 1970. "A Theory of the Origin of the State," *Science* 169.

This volume offers an extended treatment of Harris's views on the science of culture:

Harris, Marvin. 1979. *Cultural Materialism: The Struggle for a Science of Culture*. New York: Random House.

ISSUE 12

Was Margaret Mead's Fieldwork on Samoan Adolescents Fundamentally Flawed?

YES: Derek Freeman, from *Margaret Mead and Samoa: The Making and Unmaking of an Anthropological Myth* (Harvard University Press, 1983)

NO: Lowell D. Holmes and Ellen Rhoads Holmes, from "Samoan Character and the Academic World," in *Samoan Village: Then and Now,* 2nd ed. (Harcourt Brace Jovanovich College Publishers, 1992)

Learning Outcomes

After reading this issue, you should be able to:

- Understand the criticisms that have been launched against Margaret Mead's groundbreaking research in Samoa.
- Discuss how theoretical concerns can shape the kinds of field data anthropologists collect during field research.
- Explain the basis of the Nature-Nurture question.
- Understand some of the limitations of anthropological field data and some of the possible ways of correcting these limitations.
- Discuss the role of the Mead–Freeman controversy for anthropologists.

ISSUE SUMMARY

YES: Social anthropologist Derek Freeman argues that Margaret Mead was wrong when she stated that Samoan adolescents had sexual freedom. He contends that Mead went to Samoa to prove anthropologist Franz Boas's cultural determinist agenda and states that Mead was so eager to believe in Samoan sexual freedom that she was consistently the victim of a hoax perpetrated by Samoan girls and young women who enjoyed tricking her. He contends that nearly all of her conclusions are spurious because of biases she brought with her and should be abandoned.

NO: Cultural anthropologists Lowell Holmes and Ellen Holmes contend that Margaret Mead had a very solid understanding of Samoan culture in general. During a restudy of Mead's research, they came to many of the same conclusions that Mead had reached about Samoan sexuality and adolescent experiences. They accept that Mead's description of Samoan culture exaggerates the amount of sexual freedom and the degree to which adolescence in Samoa is carefree but these differences, they argue, can be explained in terms of changes in Samoan culture since 1925 and in terms of Mead's relatively unsophisticated research methods compared with field methods used today.

In 1925, a student of anthropologist Franz Boas named Margaret Mead set off for a 9-month study of adolescent women in Samoa. At only 23 years of age, Mead was just barely beyond adolescence herself. For her research, she wanted to study a community outside the continental United States and looked to the South Pacific. Boas was concerned about Mead's safety in a remote and distant place, but arranged for her to stay with the Holt family, an American family at the small naval hospital in one of the outer islands of American Samoa. Here she could live in a European-style house, her physical safety would be ensured, and she could conduct research in one of the nearby villages. For the next several months, she could study the culture and lives of young Samoan women, and the patterns of their lives. By today's standards, Mead's field setting was not ideal, since she did not stay in the village where she could observe what was happening 24/7. But it is useful to remember that she was only the second American anthropologist to conduct an extended period of participant observation outside the mainland United States in the Pacific Islands.

On her return to New York in 1926, Mead completed revisions to her dissertation on *An Inquiry into the Question of Cultural Stability in Polynesia* (Columbia University Press, 1928), a library-based project that she had largely completed before her research in Samoa. Then she turned to writing up her experiences in Samoa, which she published as *Coming of Age in Samoa: A Psychological Study of Primitive Youth for Western Civilization* (William Morrow, 1928). Unlike her dissertation, written in a very technical style, this volume was written for the general public, and it addressed issues about adolescence that were framed in ways that attracted the public's interest. Mead concluded in *Coming of Age* that Samoan culture was much more relaxed about sexuality than Western culture, and Samoan girls routinely had sexual liaisons with young men. As a result of these relaxed attitudes, she argued that Samoan adolescents had a much more tranquil transition from childhood to adulthood than had been observed in America and other Western countries. For Mead, these findings demonstrated the dominance of nurture (cultural conditioning) over nature (understood as biological predispositions). Her book was focused rather narrowly on adolescent women, but she did publish other more scholarly works about Samoan kinship and social organization, which demonstrate her broad general understanding of Samoan society. *Coming of Age* was an immediate best-seller and it earned Mead renown for the rest of her life. She was the best-known scientist in the United States for several decades, and after Eleanor Roosevelt the second most respected woman until the 1960s.

Later, Mead studied several other societies in the South Pacific and Indonesia, returning repeatedly to questions of childrearing, sexuality and temperament, and culture change, publishing more than 50 books over her long career. She died in 1978 having served as a curator at the American Museum of Natural History in New York for some 50 years.

In 1983, some 5 years after Mead's death, the New Zealand-born anthropologist Derek Freeman published his book entitled *Margaret Mead and Samoa: The Making and Unmaking of an Anthropological Myth* (Harvard University Press), an excerpt of which is provided in the YES selection. Freeman argues that Mead was so eager to find support for her view of Samoa as a society with an ideal transition from childhood to adulthood that she blatantly biased the findings of her fieldwork, in effect falsifying her field data. These were strong charges against an important figure in American anthropology, and it prompted strong reactions from supporters and detractors alike.

Freeman had lived in Western Samoa from 1940 to 1943 as a school teacher. Here he learned the Samoan language and later decided to study anthropology in England. He conducted research for his dissertation in Sarawak in Malaysia and returned to western Samoa to conduct fieldwork from 1965 to 1967, with a followup visit. Because of his age, stature, and gender, most of Freeman's research was with the Samoan chiefs, and he spent relatively little time with young Samoan women. During this latter research, Freeman found evidence that he felt challenged some of Mead's published field data as well as a number of her conclusions regarding Samoan adolescence. He contends that Mead's young Samoan informants perpetuated a hoax on her by making up stories about their promiscuity. As older women, some of Mead's informants—now respected grandmothers and great-grandmothers—did not acknowledge the sexual freedom that Mead wrote about in the 1920s.

The NO selection that counter's Freeman's account is by anthropologists Lowell D. Holmes and his wife Ellen Rhoads Holmes, who in the 1950s conducted a restudy of the same community Mead had visited in 1925. Holmes and Holmes had expressly intended to test the reliability and validity of Mead's findings. They conclude that while Mead's characterizations of Samoans are in some ways exaggerated, the characterizations are by no means fundamentally wrong. They believe that adolescence for Samoan girls was more relaxed than it had been for girls and young women in America in the 1920s, even if it was not as carefree as Mead described it. In any event, they argue that Mead's description of the situation in this village was much closer than Freeman's depiction.

The response to Freeman's attack on Mead's findings was extraordinary and has included books, journal articles, editorials, and conference papers. Special sessions at the annual meetings of the American Anthropological Association were devoted exclusively to the Mead–Freeman debate. The first reaction was largely defensive as American anthropologists rushed to defend Mead from abroad. But as the initial shock of Freeman's assertions wore off, scholars began to address some of the specific points of criticism.

A number of scholars have pointed out that Samoan life has changed significantly since Mead's fieldwork. The Christian Church now exerts a much stronger pressure over the very same women that Mead had interviewed more than 50 years earlier. Another point is that these women were much more puritanical in the 1980s, when they were church elders and grandmothers, than they were as teenagers in the 1920s. These women now have reputations of social propriety to uphold that would not have concerned them in their youth. Can we say that they have the same views they had so many years earlier?

When Freeman visited Mead's village in 1981, he brought with him an Australian documentary film crew, specifically planning to interview some of Mead's now elderly informants. When asked what they had told Mead 60 years earlier, the women stated that they fibbed continuously to her, explaining that it is a cherished Samoan custom to trick people in these ways. Freeman and the film crew take such statements as incontrovertible evidence that Mead was hoaxed. But if it is Samoan custom to trick outsiders, how can Freeman and his film crew be certain that they are not victims of a similar hoax?

These selections allow us to ask a number of questions about Mead's research: Did Mead unintentionally exaggerate her findings about sexual freedom? Or did she intentionally falsify her field data, specifically so that she could support Boas's model of cultural determinism? Could Mead's excesses be explained as the consequence of her being a youthful and inexperienced field researcher? Or can difference between Mead's findings and those of the selection authors be explained in other ways?

These selections also raise a number of questions about the replicability of anthropological fieldwork. Is it possible to conduct a systematic restudy of another anthropologist's field subjects? Can an anthropologist working in another village or on another island reliably challenge the findings of another anthropologist?

This issue raises questions about the adequacy of Freeman's ethnographic data and his conclusions as much as it raises questions about Mead's. Did Freeman also have biases that fundamentally affect his conclusions? Should these selections encourage us to challenge his assertions? Do either Mead or Freeman provide data that could resolve the Nature-Nurture question that Mead had hoped to offer?

YES ↵

Derek Freeman

Margaret Mead and Samoa: The Making and Unmaking of an Anthropological Myth

Preface

By far the most widely known of Margaret Mead's numerous books is *Coming of Age in Samoa,* based on fieldwork on which she embarked in 1925 at the instigation of Franz Boas, her professor at Columbia University. Boas had sent the 23-year-old Mead to Samoa to study adolescence, and she returned with a startling conclusion. Adolescence was known in America and Europe as a time of emotional stresses and conflicts. If, Mead argued, these problems were caused by the biological processes of maturation, then they would necessarily be found in all human societies. But in Samoa, she reported, life was easy and casual, and adolescence was the easiest and most pleasant time of life. Thus in anthropological terms, according to Mead, Samoa was a "negative instance"— and the existence of this one counterexample demonstrated that the disturbances associated with adolescence in the United States and elsewhere had cultural and not biological causes. In the controversy between the adherents of biological determinism and those of cultural determinism, a controversy that was at its height in the 1920s, Mead's negative instance appeared to be a triumphant outcome for believers in the sovereignty of culture.

When *Coming of Age in Samoa* was published in 1928 it attracted immense attention, and its apparently conclusive finding swiftly entered anthropological lore as a jewel of a case. Since that time Mead's finding has been recounted in scores of textbooks, and through the vast popularity of *Coming of Age in Samoa,* the best-selling of all anthropological books, it has influenced the thinking of millions of people throughout the world. It is with the critical examination of this very widely accepted conclusion that I am concerned [here].

Scientific knowledge, as Karl Popper has shown, is principally advanced through the conscious adoption of "the critical method of error elimination." In other words, within science, propositions and theories are systematically tested by attempts to refute them, and they remain acceptable only as long as they withstand these attempts at refutation. In Popper's view, "in so far as a scientific statement speaks about reality it must be falsifiable," and rational criticism entails the testing of any particular statement in terms of its correspondence with the facts. Mead's classing of Samoa as a negative instance obviously depends on the adequacy of the account of Samoan culture on which it is based. It is thus very much a scientific proposition, for it is fully open to testing against the relevant empirical evidence.

While the systematic testing of the conclusions of a science is always desirable, this testing is plainly imperative when serious doubts have been expressed about some particular finding. Students of Samoan culture have long voiced such doubts about Mead's findings of 1928. . . . I adduce detailed empirical evidence to demonstrate that Mead's account of Samoan culture and character is fundamentally in error. I would emphasize that I am not intent on constructing an alternative ethnography of Samoa. Rather, the evidence I shall present has the specific purpose of scientifically refuting the proposition that Samoa is a negative instance by demonstrating that the depictions on which Mead based this assertion are, in varying degree, mistaken.

In undertaking this refutation I shall limit my scrutiny to those sections of Mead's writings which have stemmed from, or refer to, her researches on Samoa. My concern, moreover, is with the scientific import of these actual researches and *not* with Margaret Mead personally, or with any aspect of her ideas or activities that lies beyond the ambit of her writings on Samoa. I would emphasize also that I hold in high regard many of the personal achievements of Margaret Mead, Franz Boas, and the other individuals certain of whose assertions and ideas I necessarily must question in the pages that follow.

. . . When I reached Western Samoa in April 1940, I was very much a cultural determinist. *Coming of Age in Samoa* had been unreservedly commended to me by [Ernest] Beaglehole, and my credence in Mead's findings was complete.

After two years of study, during which I came to know all the islands of Western Samoa, I could speak Samoan well enough to converse in the company of chiefs with the punctilio that Samoan etiquette demands, and the time had come to select a local polity for intensive investigation. My choice was Sa'anapu, a settlement of 400 inhabitants on the south coast of Upolu. On my first visit to Sa'anapu I had become friendly with Lauvi Vainu'u, a senior talking chief. . . . I was to become his adopted son. From that time onward I lived as one of the Lauvi family whenever I was in Sa'anapu.

In my early work I had, in my unquestioning acceptance of Mead's writings, tended to dismiss all evidence that ran counter to her findings. By the end of 1942, however, it had become apparent to me that much of what she had written about the inhabitants of Manu'a in eastern Samoa did not apply to the people of western Samoa. After I had been assured by Samoans who had lived in Manu'a that life there was essentially the same as in the western islands, I realized that I would have to make one of the objectives of my research the systematic testing of Mead's depiction of Samoan culture.

Soon after I returned to Sa'anapu its chiefs forgathered one morning at Lauvi's house to confer on me one of the chiefly titles of their polity. I was thus able to attend all *fono*, or chiefly assemblies, as of right, and I soon came to be accepted by the community at large. From this time onward I was in an exceptionally favorable position to pursue my researches into the realities of Samoan life.

By the time I left Samoa in November 1943 I knew that I would one day face the responsibility of writing a refutation of Mead's Samoan findings. This would involve much research into the history of early Samoa. This task I began in 1945 in the manuscript holdings of the Mitchell Library in Sydney and later continued in England, where I thoroughly studied the Samoan archives of the London Missionary Society.

During 1946–1948, while studying anthropology at the University of London, I wrote a dissertation on Samoan social organization. . . . There then came, however, the opportunity to spend some years among the Iban of Borneo. With this diversion, . . . the continuation of my Samoan researches was long delayed.

I finally returned to Western Samoa, accompanied by my wife and daughters, at the end of 1965. Sa'anapu, now linked Apia by road, was once again my center of research. The chiefs of Sa'anapu immediately recognized the title they had conferred on me in 1943, and I became once again an active member of the Sa'anapu *fono*. My family and I remained in Samoa for just over two years, making frequent visits elsewhere in the district to which Sa'anapu belongs, as also to numerous other parts of the archipelago, from Saua in the east to Falealupo in the west.

Many educated Samoans, especially those who had attended college in New Zealand, had become familiar with Mead's writings about their culture. A number of them entreated me, as an anthropologist, to correct her mistaken depiction of the Samoan ethos. Accordingly, early in 1966 I set about the systematic examination of the entire range of Mead's writings on Samoa, seeking to test her assertions by detailed investigation of the particulars of the behavior or custom to which they referred. . . .

[I]n 1967 [I] organized a formal traveling party to [the island of] Ta'ū. We visitors were received as long-lost kinsmen, and in the company of chiefs from both Ta'ū and Sa'anapu I was able to review all those facets of Mead's depiction of Samoa which were then still at issue. In Ta'ū I also recorded the testimony of men and women who remembered the period to which Mead's writings refer. In many instances these recollections were vivid and specific; as one of my informants remarked, the happenings of the mid 1920s were still fresh in their memories.

As my inquiries progressed it became evident that my critical scrutiny of Mead's conclusions would have to extend to the anthropological paradigm of which *Coming of Age in Samoa* was a part. . . .

My researches were not completed until 1981, when I finally gained access to the archives of the High Court of American Samoa for the 1920s. Thus my refutation of Mead's depiction of Samoa appears some years after her death. In November 1964, however, when Dr. Mead visited the Australian National University, I informed her very fully, during a long private conversation, of the empirical basis of my disagreement with her depiction of Samoa. From that time onward we were in correspondence, and in August 1978, upon its first completion, I offered to send her an early draft of my refutation of the conclusions she had reached in *Coming of Age in Samoa*. I received no reply to this offer before Dr. Mead's death in November of that year.

In September 1981 I returned to Western Samoa with the specific purpose of submitting a draft of [my] book to the critical scrutiny of Samoan scholars. . . . In the course of the refutation of Mead's misleading account of their culture, which many Samoans encouraged me to undertake, I have had to deal realistically with the darker side of Samoan life. During my visit of 1981 I found among contemporary Samoans both a mature appreciation of the need to face these realities and a clear-headed pride in the virtues and strengths of the Samoan way of life. . . .

Mead's Misconstruing of Samoa

. . . [The] notion that cultural determinism was absolute was "so obvious" to Mead that . . . she also avowed it in *Coming of Age in Samoa,* in respect of adolescent behavior.

That this doctrine of the absoluteness of cultural determinism should have seemed "so obvious" to Mead is understandable. Anthropology, when she began its study in 1922, was dominated by Boas' "compelling idea," as Leslie Spier has called it, of "the complete moulding of every human expression—inner thought and external behavior—by social conditioning," and by the time she left for Samoa in 1925 she had become a fervent devotee of the notion that human behavior could be explained in purely cultural terms. Further, although by the time of Mead's recruitment to its ranks cultural anthropology had achieved its independence, it had done so at the cost of becoming an ideology that, in an actively unscientific way, sought totally to exclude biology from the explanation of human behavior. Thus as, [Alfred] Kroeber declared, "the important thing about anthropology is not the science but an attitude of mind"—an attitude of mind, that is, committed to the doctrine of culture as a superorganic entity which incessantly shapes human behavior, "conditioning all responses." It was of this attitude of mind that Mead became a leading proponent, with (as Marvin Harris has observed) her anthropological mission, set for her by Boas, being to defeat the notion of a "panhuman hereditary human nature." She pursued this objective by tirelessly stressing, in publication after publication, "the absence of maturational regularities."

In her own account of this mission, Mead describes it as a battle which she and other Boasians had had to fight with the whole battery at their command, using the most fantastic and startling examples they could muster. It is thus evident that her writings during this period, about Samoa as about other South Seas cultures, had the explicit aim of confuting biological explanations of human behavior and vindicating the doctrines of the Boasian school. By 1939 this battle, according to Mead, had been won. . . .

For Mead's readers in North America and elsewhere in the Western world, there could be no more plausible location for the idyllic society of which she wrote than in the South Seas, a region that since the days of Bougainville has figured in the fantasies of Europeans and Americans as a place of preternatural contentment and sensual delight. So, as Mead reports, her announcement in 1925 that she was going to Samoa caused the same breathless stir as if she had been "setting off for heaven." Indeed, there were many in the 1920s, according to Mead, who longed to go to the South Sea islands "to escape to a kind of divine nothingness in which life would be reduced to the simplest physical terms, to sunshine and the moving shadows of palm trees, to bronze-bodied girls and bronze-bodied boys, food for the asking, no work to do, no obligations to meet."

. . . How did the young Margaret Mead come so to miscronstrue ethos and ethnography of Samoa? The fervency of her belief in cultural determinism and her tendency to view the South Seas as an earthly paradise go some way in accounting for what happened, but manifestly more was involved.

The Ph.D. topic that Boas assigned to Mead was the comparative study of canoe-building, house-building, and tattooing in the Polynesian culture area. During 1924 she gathered information on these activities from the available literature on the Hawaiians, the Marquesans, the Maori, the Tahitians, and the Samoans. These doctoral studies did not have any direct relevance to the quite separate problem of adolescence in Samoa that Boas set her in 1925, and, indeed, the fact that her reading was mainly on Eastern rather than Western Polynesia concealed from her the marked extent to which the traditional culture and values of Samoa differ from those of Tahiti. Again, during the spring of 1925 she had little time for systematic preparation for her Samoan researches. Indeed, the counsel she received from Boas about these researches prior to her departure for Pago Pago lasted, she tells us, for only half an hour. During this brief meeting Boas' principal instruction was that she should concentrate on the problem he had set her and not waste time doing ethnography. Accordingly, when in the second week of November 1925 Mead reached Manu'a, she at once launched into the study of adolescence without first acquiring, either by observation or from inquiry with adult informants, a thorough understanding of the traditional values and customs of the Manu'ans. This, without doubt, was an ill-advised way to proceed, for it meant that Mead was in no position to check the statements of the girls she was studying against a well-informed knowledge of the fa'aSamoa [Samoan way of life].

It is also evident that Mead greatly underestimated the complexity of the culture, society, history, and psychology of the people among whom she was to study adolescence. Samoan society, so Mead would have it, is "very simple," and Samoan culture "uncomplex." . . .

As any one who cares to consult Augustin Krämer's *Die Samoa-Inseln*, Robert Louis Stevenson's *A Footnote to History*, or J. W. Davidson's *Samoa mo Samoa* will quickly discover, Samoan society and culture are by no means simple and uncomplex; they are marked by particularities, intricacies, and subtleties quite as daunting as those which face students of Europe and Asia. Indeed, the fa'aSamoa is so sinuously complex that, as Stevenson's step-daughter, Isobel Strong, once remarked, "one may live long in Samoa without understanding the whys and wherefores." Mead, however, spent not even a few months on the systematic study of Manu'a before launching upon the study of adolescence immediately upon her arrival in Ta'ū in accordance with Boas' instructions. Thus, she has noted that while on her later field trips she had "the more satisfactory task of learning the culture first and only afterwards working on a special problem" in Samoa this was "not necessary."

. . . Another problem was that of being able to communicate adequately with the people she was to study. Mead had arrived in Pago Pago without any knowledge of the Samoan language. . . . In this situation Mead was plainly at some hazard pursuing her inquiries in Manu'a, for Samoans, when diverted by the stumbling efforts of outsiders to speak their demanding language, are inclined not to take them seriously.

Mead, then, began her inquiries with her girl informants with a far from perfect command of the vernacular, and without systematic prior investigation of Manu'an society and values. Added to this, she elected to live not in a Samoan household but with the handful of expatriate Americans who were the local representatives of the naval government of American Samoa, from which in 1925 many Manu'ans were radically disaffected. . . . Of the immense advantage that an ethnographer gains by living among the people whose values and behavior he is intent on understanding there can be not the slightest doubt. Mead, however, within six weeks of her arrival in Pago Pago, and before she had spent any time actually staying in a traditional household, had come to feel that the food she would have to eat would be too starchy, and the conditions of living she would have to endure too nerve-racking to make residence with a Samoan family bearable. In Ta'ū, she told Boas, she would be able to live "in a white household" and yet be in the midst of one of the villages from which she would be drawing her adolescent subjects. This arrangement to live not in a Samoan household but with the Holt family in their European-style house, which was also the location of the government radio station and medical dispensary, decisively determined the form her researches were to take.

According to Mead her residence in these government quarters furnished her with an absolutely essential neutral base from which she could study all of the individuals in the surrounding village while at the same time remaining "aloof from native feuds and lines of demarcation." Against this exiguous advantage she was, however, depriving herself of the close contacts that speedily develop in Samoa between an ethnographer and the members of the extended family in which he or she lives. Such contacts are essential for the gaining of a thorough understanding of the Samoan language and, most important of all, for the independent verification, by the continuous observation of actual behavior, of the statements being derived from informants. Thus, by living with the Holts, Mead was trapping herself in a situation in which she was forced to rely not on observations of the behavior of Samoans as they lived their lives beyond the precincts of the government station on Ta'ū, but on such hearsay information as she was able to extract from her adolescent subjects. . . .

It is evident then that although, as Mead records, she could "wander freely about the village or go on fishing trips or stop at a house where a woman was weaving" when she was away from the dispensary, her account of adolescence in Samoa was, in the main, derived from the young informants who came to talk with her away from their homes in the villages of Lumā, Si'ufaga, and Faleasao. So, as Mead states, for these three villages, from which all her adolescent informants were drawn, she saw the life that went on "through the eyes" of the group of girls on the details of whose lives she was concentrating. This situation is of crucial significance for the assessment of Mead's researches in Manu'a, for we are clearly faced with the question of the extent to which the lens she fashioned from what she was being told by her adolescent inform-ants and through which she saw Samoan life was a true and accurate lens.

. . . [M]any of the assertions appearing in Mead's depiction of Samoa are fundamentally in error, and some of them preposterously false. How are we to account for the presence of errors of this magnitude? Some Samoans who have read *Coming of Age in Samoa* react, as Shore reports, with anger and the insistence "that Mead lied." This, however, is an interpretation that I have no hesitation in dismissing. The succession of prefaces to *Coming of Age* in Samoa published by Mead in 1949, 1953, 1961, and 1973 indicate clearly, in my judgment, that she did give genuine credence to the view of Samoan life with which she returned to New York in 1926. Moreover, in the 1969 edition of *Social Organization of Manu'a* she freely conceded that there was a serious problem in reconciling the "contradictions" between her own depiction of Samoa and that contained in "other records of historical and contemporary behavior." . . .

Mead's depiction of Samoan culture, as I have shown, is marked by major errors, and her account of the sexual behavior of Samoans by a mind-boggling contradiction, for she asserts that the Samoans have a culture in which female virginity is very highly valued, with a virginity-testing ceremony being "theo-retically observed at weddings of all ranks," while at the same time adoles-cence among females is regarded as a period "appropriate for love-making," with promiscuity before marriage being both permitted and "expected." And, indeed, she actually describes the Samoans as making the "demand" that a female should be "both receptive to the advances of many lovers and yet capa-ble of showing the tokens of virginity at marriage." Something, it becomes plain at this juncture, is emphatically amiss, for surely no human population could be so cognitively disoriented as to conduct their lives in such a schizo-phrenic way. Nor are the Samoans remotely like this, for . . . they are, in fact, a people who traditionally value virginity highly and so disapprove of premari-tal promiscuity as to exercise a strict surveillance over the comings and goings of adolescent girls. That these values and this regime were in force in Manu'a in the mid 1920s is, furthermore, clearly established by the testimony of the Manu'ans themselves who, when I discussed this period with those who well remembered it, confirmed that the fa'aSamoa in these matters was operative then as it was both before and after Mead's brief sojourn in Ta'ū. What then can have been the source of Mead's erroneous statement that in Samoa there is great premarital freedom, with promiscuity before marriage among adolescent girls, being both permitted and expected?

The explanation most consistently advanced by the Samoans themselves for the magnitude of the errors in her depiction of their culture and in par-ticular of their sexual morality is, as [Eleanor Ruth] Gerber has reported, "that Mead's informants must have been telling lies in order to tease her." Those

Samoans who offer this explanation, which I have heard in Manu'a as well as in other parts of Samoa, are referring to the behavior called *tau fa'ase'e*, to which Samoans are much prone. *Fa'ase'e* (literally "to cause to slip") means "to dupe," as in the example given by Milner, *"e fa'ase'e gofie le teine*, the girl is easily duped"; and the phrase *tau fa'ase'e* refers to the action of deliberately duping someone, a pastime that greatly appeals to the Samoans as a respite from the severities of their authoritarian society.

Because of their strict morality, Samoans show a decided reluctance to discuss sexual matters with outsiders or those in authority, a reticence that is especially marked among female adolescents. Thus, Holmes reports that when he and his wife lived in Manu'a and Tutuila in 1954 "it was never possible to obtain details of sexual experience from unmarried informants, though several of these people were constant companions and part of the household." Further, as Lauifi Ili, Holmes's principal assistant, observes, when it comes to imparting information about sexual activities, Samoan girls are "very close-mouthed and ashamed." Yet it was precisely information of this kind that Mead, a liberated young American newly arrived from New York and resident in the government station at Ta'ū, sought to extract from the adolescent girls she had been sent to study. And when she persisted in this unprecedented probing of a highly embarrassing topic, it is likely that these girls resorted, as Gerber's Samoan informants have averred, to *tau fa'ase'e*, regaling their inquisitor with counterfeit tales of casual love under the palm trees.

This, then, is the explanation that Samoans give for the highly inaccurate portrayal of their sexual morality in Mead's writings. It is an explanation that accounts for how it was that this erroneous portrayal came to be made, as well as for Mead's sincere credence in the account she has given in *Coming of Age in Samoa*, for she was indeed reporting what she had been told by her adolescent informants. The Manu'ans emphasize, however, that the girls who, they claim, plied Mead with these counterfeit tales were only amusing themselves, and had no inkling that their tales would ever find their way into a book.

While we cannot, in the absence of detailed corroborative evidence [but see addendum following], be sure about the truth of this Samoan claim that Mead was mischievously duped by her adolescent informants, we can be certain that she did return to New York in 1926 with tales running directly counter to all other ethnographic accounts of Samoa, from which she constructed her picture of Manu'a as a paradise of free love, and of Samoa as a negative instance, which, so she claimed, validated Boasian doctrine. It was this negative instance that she duly presented to Boas as the ideologically gratifying result of her inquiries in Manu'a. . . .

We are thus confronted in the case of Margaret Mead's Samoan researches with an instructive example of how, as evidence is sought to substantiate a cherished doctrine, the deeply held beliefs of those involved may lead them unwittingly into error. The danger of such an outcome is inherent, it would seem, in the very process of belief formation. . . .

In the case of Mead's Samoan researches, certainly, there is the clearest evidence that it was her deeply convinced belief in the doctrine of extreme cultural determinism, for which she was prepared to fight with the whole battery at her command, that led her to construct an account of Samoa that appeared to substantiate this very doctrine. There is, however, conclusive empirical evidence to demonstrate that Samoa, in numerous respects, is not at all as Mead depicted it to be.

A crucial issue that arises from this historic case for the discipline of anthropology, which has tended to accept the reports of ethnographers as entirely empirical statements, is the extent to which other ethnographic accounts may have been distorted by doctrinal convictions, as well as the methodological question of how such distortion can best be avoided. These are no small problems. I would merely comment that as we look back on Mead's Samoan researches we are able to appreciate anew the wisdom of Karl Popper's admonition that in both science and scholarship it is, above all else, indefatigable rational criticism of our suppositions that is of decisive importance, for such criticism by "bringing out our mistakes . . . makes us understand the difficulties of the problem we are trying to solve," and so saves us from the allure of the "obvious truth" of received doctrine.

Addendum: New Evidence of the Hoaxing of Margaret Mead

In my book *The Fateful Hoaxing of Margaret Mead* (1998) there is an account, based on the sworn testimony of Fa'apua'a, of how Margaret Mead in March of 1926 on the island of Ofu in American Samoa was hoaxed about the sexual mores of the Samoans by her two Samoan traveling companions, Fa'apua'a and Fofoa.

I [have recently discovered] direct evidence, from Mead's own papers, that Margaret Mead was indeed taken in by the "whispered confidences" (as she called them) of Fa'apua'a and Fofoa. This incontrovertible historical evidence finally brings to closure the long-running controversy over Margaret Mead's Samoan fieldwork. . . .

The crucially important direct evidence in question is contained in a little known book entitled *All True! The Record of Actual Adventures That Have Happened To Ten Women of Today* that was published in New York in 1931 by Brewer, Warren and Putnam. The "adventure" by Dr. Margaret Mead is entitled "Life as a Samoan Girl". It begins with a wistful reference to "the group of reverend scientists" who in 1925 sent her to study (Mead, 1925) "the problem of which phenomena of adolescence are culturally and which physiologically determined" among the adolescent girls of Samoa, with "no very clear idea" of how she was "to do this." It ends with an account of her journey to the islands of Ofu and Olosega in March of 1926 with the "two Samoan girls," as she calls them, Fa'apua'a and Fofoa. In fact, Fa'apua'a and Fofoa were both twenty-four years of age and slightly older than Dr. Mead herself. Dr. Mead continues her account of her visit to the islands of Ofu and Olosega with Fa'apua'a and Fofoa by stating: "In all things I had behaved as a Samoan, for only so, only by losing my identity, as far as possible, had I been able to become acquainted with the Samoan girls receive their whispered confidences and learn at the same time the answer to the scientists' questions."

 This account, by Mead herself, is fully confirmed by the sworn testimony of Fa'apua'a (cf. Freeman, 1998, Chapter 11). It can be found on p. 141 of the second and paperback edition (1999) of my book *The Fateful Hoaxing of Margaret Mead: A historical analysis of her Samoan research.* It is definitive historical evidence that establishes that Martin Orans is in outright error in asserting (1996:92) that it is "demonstrably false that Mead was taken in by Fa'apua'a and Fofoa." It is also evidence that establishes that *Coming of Age in Samoa,* far from being a "scientific classic" (as Mead herself supposed) is, in certain vitally significant respects (as in its dream-like second chapter), a work of anthropological fiction.

References

Freeman, Derek, 1999, *The Fateful Hoaxing of Margaret Mead,* Boulder: Westview, 2nd edition.

Mead, Margaret, 1925, Plan of Research Submitted to the National Research Council of the U.S.A. (Archives of the National Academy of Sciences).

Mead, Margaret, 1928, *Coming of Age in Samoa.* New York: Morrow.

Mead, Margaret, 1931, "Life as a Samoan Girl," in *All True! The Record of Actual Adventures That Happened to Ten Women of Today.* New York: Brewer, Warren and Putnam.

Orans, Martin, 1996, *Not Even Wrong: Margaret Mead, Derek Freeman and the Samoans,* Novato: Chandler and Sharp.

Lowell D. Holmes and
Ellen Rhoads Holmes

 **NO**

Samoan Character and the Academic World

On January 31, 1983, the *New York Times* carried a front-page article, the headline of which read, "New Samoa Book Challenges Margaret Mead's Conclusions." The book that precipitated this somewhat unexpected turn of events was *Margaret Mead and Samoa: The Making and Unmaking of an Anthropological Myth* by Derek Freeman, an emeritus professor of anthropology at Australian National University in Canberra. This work, which some claim set off the most heated controversy in sociocultural anthropology in one hundred years, is described by its author as a "refutation of Mead's misleading account" of Samoan culture and personality as presented in her 1928 ethnography, *Coming of Age in Samoa.*

The *New York Times* article was of special interest to me because, in 1954, I had conducted a year-long methodological restudy of the Mead data under attack. I had lived in Ta'ū village, where Mead had worked twenty-nine years earlier, and had used many of her informants in a systematic and detailed evaluation of every observation and interpretation she had made about the lifestyle of the people in that Samoan village. A methodological restudy, incidentally, involves a second anthropologist going into the field with the *express purpose* of testing the reliability and validity of the findings of a former investigator. This restudy is made in order to establish what kinds of errors of data collection or interpretation might have been made by certain kinds of people, in certain kinds of field research situations, researching certain kinds of problems. For example, Margaret Mead was a twenty-three-year-old woman investigating a male-dominated society that venerates age. She was a student of Franz Boas and, therefore, went equipped with a particular theoretical frame of reference. She was also on her first field trip—at a time when research methods were crude. My task in this methodological restudy was not only to analyze how my findings might be different from hers (if that would be the case), but I would also attempt to speculate on how differences in the status of the investigators (for example, sex, age, family situation, education) and other personal factors might affect the collection and interpretation of data.

My critique of Margaret Mead's study was presented in my doctoral dissertation, *The Restudy of Manu'an Culture. A Problem in Methodology,* which by 1983 had been collecting dust on a Northwestern University library shelf for some twenty-seven years. I was therefore eager to obtain a copy of Freeman's new evaluation of Mead's work from its publisher, Harvard University Press. In reading the book this is what I found.

In *Margaret Mead and Samoa: The Making and Unmaking of an Anthropological Myth* (1983), Derek Freeman argues that Mead perpetuated a hoax comparable in consequence to that of Piltdown Man when, in 1928, she described Samoa as a paradise where competition, sexual inhibition, and guilt were virtually absent. Refusing to believe that adolescents in all societies inevitably experience emotional crises—storm and stress—because of biological changes associated with puberty (as hypothesized in *Adolescence* in 1904 by psychologist G. Stanley Hall), Mead set out to discover a society where the passage to adulthood was smooth and without trauma. She described such a society in *Coming of Age in Samoa*. In delineating this "negative instance" (which challenged Hall's theory of universal adolescent rebellion and strife), Margaret Mead had in effect established that nurture (culture) is more critical than nature (biology) in accounting for adolescent maturation behavior in the human species. Derek Freeman, on the other hand, rejects the idea that human behavior is largely shaped by culture and believes that Mead and her mentor, Franz Boas (commonly called the "Father of American Anthropology"), were guilty of *totally* ignoring the influence of biological heredity. He believes that Mead's "negative instance" results entirely from faulty data collection and that Mead's Samoan findings have led anthropology, psychology, and education down the primrose path of pseudoscience. Freeman's book, therefore, is an attempt to set the record straight through his own, more accurate, observations of Samoa and Samoans—although his observations of Samoan behavior were in another village, on another island, in another country, and fourteen years later.

Freeman's main theoretical approach in this evaluation of Mead's work derives from the German philosopher of science, Karl Popper, who maintains that science should be deductive, not inductive, and that progress in scientific research should consist essentially of attempts to refute established theories. Thus, Derek Freeman is out to destroy the credibility of what he interprets as the "absolute cultural determinism" to be found in the work of Margaret Mead as well as in much of the work of Boas and his other students. This claim is, of course, spurious, as any student of American anthropological theory knows. For example, in Melville J. Herskovits' biography of Franz Boas, we find the statement that, because of his "rounded view of the problem Boas could perceive so clearly the fallacy of the eugenicist theory, which held the destiny of men to be determined by biological endowment, with little regard for the learned, cultural determinants of behavior." By the same token, he "refused to accept the counter-dogma that man is born with a completely blank slate, on which can be written whatever is willed. He saw both innate endowment and learning—or, as it was called popularly, heredity and environment—as significant factors in the making of the mature individual" (1953:28). Herskovits also points out that "numerous examples can be found, in reports on the various studies he conducted, of how skillfully Boas was able to weave cultural and biological factors into a single fabric" (*Ibid.*).

Marvin Harris concurs: "American anthropology has always been concerned with the relationships between nature (in the guise of habitat and genic programming) and culture (in the guise of traditions encoded in the brain, not in the genes). Neither Boas nor his students ever denied that *Homo sapiens* has a species-specific nature" (1983:26). In his book, *The Rise of Anthropological Theory,* Harris writes, "Boas systematically rejected almost every conceivable form of cultural determinism" (1968:283).

Evaluation of the Mead Data

My restudy experience in Ta'ū village in 1954 led me to conclude that Margaret Mead often overgeneralized; that, in many cases, we interpreted data differently; and that, because of her age and sex, some avenues of investigation apparently were closed to her—particularly those having to do with the more formal aspects of village political organization and ceremonial life. However, her overall characterization of the nature and dynamics of the culture were, in my judgment, quite valid and her contention that it was easier to come of age in Samoa than in America in 1925–1926 was undoubtedly correct. In spite of the greater possibilities for error in a pioneer study, Mead's age (only 23), her sex (in a male-dominated society), and her inexperience, I believe the reliability and validity of the Ta'ū village research is remarkably high.

I look upon an ethnographic account as a kind of map to be used in finding one's way about in a culture—in comprehending and anticipating behavior. Mead's account never left me lost or bewildered in my interactions with Samoan islanders, but I also felt that if one were to come to a decision about the comparative difficulties of coming of age in Samoa and the United States, it would be necessary to know something about what life was like for adolescents in America in 1925–1926. Joseph Folsom's book, *The Family,* published in 1934, but researched about the time Mead was writing *Coming of Age in Samoa,* provided that information. Folsom describes the social environment in which children came of age at that time as follows:

> Children are disciplined and trained with the ideal of absolute obedience to parents. Corporal punishment is used, ideally in cold blood. . . . All sexual behavior on the part of children is prevented by all means at the parents' disposal. . . . For the sake of prevention it has been usual to cultivate in the child, especially the girl, an attitude of horror or disgust toward all aspects of sex. . . . Premarital intercourse is immoral though not abhorrent. . . . Violations are supposedly prevented by the supervision of the girl's parents. . . . Illegitimate children are socially stigmatized. . . . The chief stigma falls upon the unmarried mother, because she has broken an important sex taboo (1934:10–25). . . .

While Freeman contends that Mead was absolutely wrong about nearly everything (partly, he maintains, because the teenage girls she used as informants consistently lied to her), I found discrepancies mainly in such areas as the degree of sexual freedom Samoan young people enjoy, the competitive nature of the society, the aggressiveness of Samoan behavior, and the degree of genuine affection and commitment between lovers and spouses.

I saw Samoan culture as considerably more competitive than Mead, although I never considered it as inflexible or aggressive as Freeman does. I observed a great preoccupation with status, power, and prestige among men of rank and, on more than one occasion, was present at fierce verbal duels between Talking Chiefs trying to enhance their own prestige and, incidentally, that of their village. . . .

I also found that Samoan culture was not as simple as Margaret Mead claimed, nor was Ta'ū village the paradise she would have us believe. She often romanticized, overgeneralized, and, on some occasions, took literary license in her descriptions of Samoan lifeways. For example, her very dramatic chapter, "A Day in Samoa," crowds typical activities (some of which occur only at particular times of the year) into a typical day and thereby presents a village scene that was much more vibrant, bustling, and picturesque than I ever encountered in any twenty-four hour period. Mead's chapter is good prose, but is it good anthropology? . . .

I also did not agree with Mead on the degree of sexual freedom supposedly enjoyed by her informants, but I believe her characterization comes closer to the truth than that of Freeman. Samoans have a very natural and healthy attitude toward sex. Judging by the number of illegitimate children in Ta'ū village when I was there and by the fact that divorce frequently involved claims of adultery, I would conclude that, while Samoans are far from promiscuous, they are not the puritanical prudes Freeman paints them to be. However, I must admit that it was difficult to investigate anything of a sexual nature, primarily because of pressure from the London Missionary Society church. Even today, older Samoans seem more distressed over Mead's claims that they are sexually active than Freeman's claims that they are aggressive with strong passions, even psychopathological tendencies. I would assume, however, that Mead was better able to identify with, and therefore establish rapport with, adolescents and young adults on issues of sexuality than either I (at age 29—married with a wife and child) or Freeman, ten years my senior.

Freeman maintains that Mead imposed her own liberated ideas of sexuality onto the Samoans and that her teenage informants consistently lied to her about these matters solely out of mischief. He has recently made contact with one of Mead's informants, Fa'apua'a Fa'amu, who lived in Fitiuta while Mead was working in Ta'ū village. Freeman believes this informant when she says that she consistently lied to Mead (while also identifying her as a good friend), but Freeman does not seem to consider the possibility that she may be lying to him. The possibility of Mead's informants being successful at such long-term deception is simply not credible considering the fact that Mead was an extremely intelligent, well-trained Ph.D. who constantly cross-checked her data with many informants. Anyone who has studied her field notes in the Library of Congress, as I have, must be impressed with her savvy and sophistication.

I must also disagree with Mead's statements that all love affairs are casual and fleeting, and no one plays for very heavy emotional stakes. Custom dictates that displays of affection between spouses and between lovers not take place in public. However, expressions of love and affection were often observed in the families of my informants. . . .

Although I differed with Margaret Mead on many interpretations, the most important fact that emerged from my methodological restudy of her Samoan research is that, without doubt, Samoan adolescents have a less difficult time negotiating the transition from childhood to adulthood than American adolescents. . . .

Critique of the Freeman Refutation

My objections to Derek Freeman's picture of Samoa are much more substantial than to the picture presented by Margaret Mead. Basically, I question Freeman's objectivity and believe he is guilty of an age-old temptation in science, which was recognized as early as 1787 by Thomas Jefferson—no slouch of a scientist himself. In a letter to his friend Charles Thomson, Jefferson wrote, "The moment a person forms a theory, his imagination sees, in every object, only the traits which favor that theory" (Martin 1952:33).

Not only does Freeman ignore counterevidence, he also ignores time and space and assumes that it is legitimate to assess data obtained by Mead in Manu'a in 1925–1926 in terms of the data he collected in Western Samoa in the 1940s, 1960s, and 1980s.

Time differences.   Freeman plays down the fact that Mead did her study of Ta'ū village in the Manu'a Island group of American Samoa fourteen years before he arrived as a teacher (not as an anthropologist) in Western Samoa and that he did not return to Samoa with the express purpose of refuting Mead's study until forty-three years after her visit. Minimizing this time gap, he arbitrarily states that "there is no . . . reason to suppose that Samoan society and behavior changed in any fundamental way during the fourteen years between 1926, the year of the completion of Mead's inquiries, and 1940, when I began my own observation of Samoan behavior" (1983:120).

However, Freeman did not visit Ta'ū village, the site of Mead's research, until 1968. Having established to his satisfaction that there had been few changes in Samoan culture during this long period of time, Freeman went on to state that he would "draw on evidence of my own research in the 1940s, the years 1965 to 1968, and 1981" (1983:120). I might add that he would draw upon historical sources, some of which go back as far as the early eighteenth century, to prove his points. My own analysis of Samoan cultural change, as published in *Ta'ū, Stability and Change in a Samoan Village* (1958), indicates, however, that while there was relative stability in the culture from 1850 to 1925 and from 1925 to 1954, change definitely did take place, particularly in the twentieth century. There is absolutely no basis for Freeman's dealing with Samoa as though it existed in a totally static condition despite its long history of contact with explorers, whalers, missionaries, colonial officials and bureaucrats, entrepreneurs, anthropologists, and, more recently, educators with Western-style curricula and television networks.

Place differences.   It also must be kept in mind that Sa'anapu (where Freeman observed Samoan culture) is not Ta'ū village (where Mead did her study). They are different villages, on different islands, in different countries, and there are great historical and political differences between the island of Upolu in Western Samoa and Ta'ū island in the isolated Manu'a Group of American Samoa. Western Samoa has experienced a long and often oppressive history of colonialism under Germany and New Zealand, while the Manu'a Group and American Samoa in general have been spared this. The U.S. Navy administration (1900–1951) exerted little influence outside the Pago Pago Bay area on the island of Tutuila, and the Department of the Interior, which took over from the Navy, has been an ethnocentric—but still benevolent—force in the political history of the territory. While Sa'anapu is on the opposite side of Upolu from Apia, it has daily bus communication with that port town, with all of its banks, supermarkets, department stores, theaters, bookstores, and nightclubs. Cash cropping has always been more important in Western Samoa than in American Samoa, and today, the economies of the two Samoas are vastly different. . . . On five separate research trips to Manu'a, I have never witnessed a single physical assault or serious argument that threatened to get out of hand. However, urban centers such as Apia in Western Samoa and Pago Pago in American Samoa have a very different character. As early as 1962, there were delinquency problems in the Pago Pago Bay area involving drunkenness, burglary, assaults, and rapes. Young people who migrate to urban areas such as Pago Pago and Apia are no longer under the close supervision and control of their *matai* [chief of the family] and often behave in very nontraditional ways. It is difficult, indeed, to make a blanket statement that all villages in Samoa are the same and that all behavior within the two Samoas is comparable. I have studied several villages during my thirty-seven-year contact with Samoa, and I find each unique in numerous, social, ceremonial, economic, and political respects.

Freeman's subjective use of literature.   A serious scientist considers all the literature relating to his or her research problem. One does not select data that [is] supportive and ignore that which is not. Freeman violates that principle repeatedly. . . . When [Ronald Rose's book, *South Seas Magic* (1959)] can be used to corroborate or advance Freeman's position, he is quoted; however, where Rose's statements concerning Samoan sexual behavior run contrary to Freeman's claims, and fall in line with Mead's observations, his work is ignored. For example, while Freeman insists that Samoans are puritanical and sexually inhibited, Rose writes that "sexual adventures begin at an early age. Although virginity is prized, it is insisted on only with the taupo. . . . If a girl hasn't had a succession of lovers by the time she is seventeen or eighteen, she feels she is 'on the shelf' and becomes the laughing stock among her companions" (1959:61).

With regard to the matter that Freeman believes was Mead's spurious example of a "negative instance"—a culture where coming of age is relatively less stressful—Rose writes (but understandably is not quoted by Freeman) as follows:

> Mental disturbances, stresses and conflicts occur at puberty but, as might be expected, these are not quite as common as in our society where taboos associated with sex abound (*Ibid.*: 164).

One can question the objectivity of a scientist who describes Samoans as "an unusually bellicose people" (1983:157) and attempts to substantiate the claim with citations from the eighteenth century, but fails to quote the favorable impressions of the very first European to come in contact with Samoan islanders from the village of Ta'ū, the very village Mead studied. In 1722, Commodore Jacob Roggeveen anchored his vessel off the village of Ta'ū and allowed a number of the islanders to come aboard. After a two-hour visit, the Commodore wrote in his log:

> They appeared to be a good people, lively in their manner of conversing, gentle in their deportment towards each other, and in their manners nothing was perceived of the savage. . . . It must be acknowledged that this was the nation the most civilized and honest of any that we had seen among the Islands of the South Sea. They were charmed with our arrival amongst them, and received us as divinities. And when they saw us preparing to depart, they testified much regret (Bumey 1816:576).

Rather than quote Roggeveen, Freeman chooses to discuss, as an example of Samoan bellicosity, the La Perouse expedition's visitation at Tutuila in 1787 that ended in tragedy. It is true that Samoans in the village of A'asu attacked a shore party, killing several crew members, but what Freeman fails to mention is that the attack occurred only after crew members punished a Samoan for pilfering by hanging him by his thumbs from the top of the longboat mast. . . .

It also should be noted that the eminent writer, Robert Louis Stevenson, who lived among Samoans the last four years of his life, recorded in his chronicle of Samoan events, *A Footnote to History*, that Samoans were "easy, merry, and pleasure loving; the gayest, though by no means the most capable or the most beautiful of Polynesians" (1892:148) and that their religious sentiment toward conflict was "peace at any price" (*Ibid.*: 147).

Observers contemporary with Mead in Samoa also record descriptions of Samoan chararacter that do not square with Freeman's allegations or his citations from early literature. For example, William Green, the principal of the government school in American Samoa in the 1920s writes:

> Personal combats and fist fights are rather rare today. I believe there has been no murder case in American Samoa since our flag was raised in 1900. Natives will suffer indignities for a long time before resorting to a fight but they remain good fighters. Boxing contests are held occasionally. . . . Respect for elders and magistrates has, I suppose, tended to discourage frequent combats. Life is easy, and one's habitual tendencies and desires are seldom blocked (1924:134).

Professional Reactions

. . . It is questionable whether any anthropology book to date has created such a media circus or produced such a media hero as *Margaret Mead and Samoa, The Making and Unmaking of an Anthropological Myth*. It is also doubtful whether any academic press ever mounted such a campaign of Madison Avenue hype to market a book as did Harvard University Press. The early reviews of the book and feature articles about the controversy were primarily penned by journalists and tended to be highly supportive of Freeman's critique, but once the anthropologists began evaluating the Freeman book, the tide took a definite turn. George Marcus of Rice University called the book a "work of great mischief," the mischief being that Freeman was attempting to reestablish "the importance of biological factors in explanations of human behavior" (1983:2). . . . Marvin Harris observed in his review that Freeman "seems obsessed with the notion that to discredit Mead's Samoan material is to discredit any social scientist who holds that 'nurture' is a more important determinant of the differences and similarities in human social life than nature" (1983:26).

It is only fair to point out that Derek Freeman had, and continues to have, a cadre of anthropological supporters, mostly in Europe and Australia, and the Samoans are mixed in their support of Mead or Freeman. . . .

Like most American anthropologists, and a few scholarly Samoans, we believe the Freeman book has done a disservice to Samoans and to the memory of Margaret Mead. *Margaret Mead and Samoa* is not an objective analysis of Mead's work in Manu'a, but an admitted refutation aimed at discrediting not only Margaret Mead, but Franz Boas and American cultural anthropology in general. Anthropology has often been referred to as a "soft science" throughout much of this rhubarb over Samoa and nature/nurture. It is little wonder, since Freeman's diatribe, published by a supposedly scholarly press, has been accepted by the media, by a select group of anthropologists, and by a number of distinguished ethologists and sociobiologists as legitimate anthropology. Margaret Mead would have loved to have debated the issues with Derek Freeman, but unfortunately, the book was not published while she was alive. It would have been great sport and good for the science of anthropology. As a friend wrote immediately after the publication of Freeman's book, "Whatever else she was, Margaret was a feisty old gal and would have put up a spirited defense which would quickly have turned into a snotty offense." We would have put our money on the plump little lady with the no-nonsense attitude and the compulsion to "get on with it."

References

Burney, James. 1816. *A chronological history of the voyages and discoveries in the South Seas or Pacific Ocean*. London: Luke Hansard and Sons.

Folsom, Joseph K. 1934. *The family: Its sociology and psychiatry*. New York: J. Wiley and Sons.

Freeman, Derek. 1983. *Margaret Mead and Samoa: The making and unmaking of an anthropological myth*. Cambridge, MA: Harvard University Press.

Green, William M. 1924. "Social traits of Samoans." *Journal of Applied Sociology* 9:129–135.

Hall, G. Stanley. 1904. *Adolescence: Its psychology and its relations to physiology, anthropology, sociology, sex, crime, religion and education*. New York: D. Appleton and Company.

Harris, Marvin. 1968. *The rise of anthropological theory.* New York: Thomas Y. Crowell Company.

———. 1983. "The sleep-crawling question." *Psychology Today* May:24–27.

Herskovits, Melville J. 1953. *Franz Boas.* New York: Charles Scribner's Sons.

Holmes, Lowell D. 1958. *Ta'ū̆.: Stability and change in a Samoan village.* Reprint No. 7, Wellington, New Zealand: Polynesian Society.

Marcus, George, 1983. "One man's Mead." *New York Times Book Review* March 27, 1983:2–3, 22–23.

Martin, Edwin T. 1952. *Thomas Jefferson: Scientist.* New York: Henry Schuman.

Rose, Ronald. 1959. *South Seas magic.* London: Hale.

Stevenson, Robert Louis. 1892. *Vailima papers and a footnote to history.* New York: Charles Scribner's Sons.

EXPLORING THE ISSUE

Was Margaret Mead's Fieldwork on Samoan Adolescents Fundamentally Flawed?

Critical Thinking and Reflection

1. Why was the attack on Margaret Mead so important for American anthropologists that it would lead to intense discussion and debate within the discipline? Why did newspapers in nearly every major American city cover the debate?
2. Outline the positions of Mead and Freeman on the Nature-Nurture question. What kinds of field data is required to test this hypothesis?
3. Why did Howell go to Mead's village in American Samoa specifically to restudy the community in which she worked? Why was a restudy necessary? Was Howell's research truly a study of the same community?
4. What are the limitations of anthropological research in a single community at a single moment in time? How might anthropologists overcome these limitations?
5. According to Freeman, what led him to attack Mead's field data and conclusions? Why did he wait until 5 years after her death to launch his attack?

Is There Common Ground?

Much of the commentary about the Mead–Freeman controversy has been by anthropological partisans defending either Margaret Mead or Derek Freeman. The emerging consensus by the mid-1990s was that Mead had exaggerated some of her findings and Freeman had overstated his criticisms of Mead. This consensus allowed anthropologists to consider how anthropological fieldwork was subject to exaggeration and misinterpretation by fieldworkers themselves.

The more important questions that both Mead and Freeman agreed were significant for anthropology, even though they disagreed on the answer. This was the Nature-Nurture question. Were human beings driven by their innate biology or were they more fundamentally shaped by the societies and cultures in which they grew up. Mead argued that her field data showed that Samoan adolescence was shaped by the relaxed attitude Samoans had toward sexuality. Freeman, who had adopted a sociobiological approach in the early 1980s, took the opposite position, namely that Samoans were as contentious as anyone else around the world. Adolescent men had high rates of minor criminal behavior and adolescence for Samoans was anything but placid as Mead had described it.

Anthropologist and Samoan specialist Martin Orans is the one scholar who has specifically examined the field notes and publications of both Mead and Freeman to ask whether data from either Mead or Freeman could prove their stance on the Nature-Nurture question. In his book *Not Even Wrong: Margaret Mead, Derek Freeman, and the Samoans* (Chandler & Sharp, 1996), Orans shows how neither Mead nor Freeman had framed the Nature-Nurture question in testable ways. His well researched volume is a must read for anyone who confronts this debate in more than superficial ways. His conclusion was not that either data set was wrong, instead he felt that neither data set systematically and testably addressed whether biology or culture were most important in shaping human behavior.

While there have been a steady trickle of journal articles about various aspects of the Mead–Freeman controversy since the mid-1990s, the only new development has been the recent book by anthropologist Paul Shankman, *The Trashing of Margaret Mead: Anatomy of an Anthropological Controversy* (University of Wisconsin Press, 2009). His position was outlined in several journal articles before his book was finished, but in essence his book changes the conversation, turning anthropological interpretation away from whether Mead's research was flawed to whether Freeman was engaged in character assassination. His argument is more complex than this simple summary, but he raises questions about how careful other anthropologists have been about taking sides on a scandal.

Additional Resources

Derek Freeman launched his initial attack on Mead in his book:
> Freeman, Derek. 1983. *Margaret Mead and Samoa: The Making and Unmaking of an Anthropological Myth*. Cambridge: Harvard University Press.

Freeman also assisted with a documentary film about Mead's research:
> Heimans, Frank. 1988. *Margaret Mead and Samoa*. A film produced for the Discovery Channel. Videorecording.

A few years later, he brought out a second edition of his original book with only minor revisions but a new title:
> Freeman, Derek. 1996. *Margaret Mead and the Heretic: The Making and Unmaking of an Anthropological Myth*. New York: Penguin.

He pursued his attack on Mead in yet another volume a few years later that picked up on themes developed in the documentary film:
> Freeman, Derek. 1999. *The Fateful Hoaxing of Margaret Mead: A Historical Analysis of Her Samoan Research*. Boulder: Westview Press.

Most of the response to Freeman's attack on Mead's research came in the form of a large number of journal articles. But one of the best assessments of Mead's field findings came from Howell 3 years after the original attack. This very fair assessment is not really from a supportive acolyte of Mead's, since Holmes did not always get along with Mead during her lifetime.
> Holmes, Lowell D. 1986. *Quest for the Real Samoa: Assessing the Mead–Freeman Controversy*. South Hadley, MA: Bergin & Garvey.

The best analysis of the Nature-Nurture question remains:

Orans, Martin. 1996. *Not Even Wrong: Margaret Mead, Derek Freeman, and the Samoans*. Novato, CA: Chandler & Sharp Publishers.

For the most recent version of the controversy see:

Shankman, Paul. 2009. *The Trashing of Margaret Mead: Anatomy of an Anthropological Controversy*. Madison: University of Wisconsin Press.

ISSUE 13

Do Men Dominate Women in All Societies?

YES: Steven Goldberg, from "Is Patriarchy Inevitable?" *National Review* (November 11, 1996)

NO: Kirk M. Endicott and Karen L. Endicott, from "Understanding Batek Egalitarianism," in *The Headman Was a Woman: The Gender Egalitarian Batek of Malaysia* (Waveland Press, 2008)

Learning Outcomes

After reading this issue, you should be able to:

- Understand how innate behavioral tendencies might influence human behavior, which in turn could shape social institutions.
- Understand how children's learning of particular cultural practices and values might influence how innate behavioral tendencies are expressed or even suppressed.
- Discuss the problems involved in defining such concepts as "male dominance" and "gender equality."
- Evaluate arguments for and against the existence of egalitarian societies, ones in which there are no significant differences in power, prestige, or possessions.
- Discuss the relationship between human nature and cultural variation.

ISSUE SUMMARY

YES: Sociologist Steven Goldberg contends that in all societies men occupy most high positions in hierarchical organizations and most high-status roles, and they also tend to dominate women in interpersonal relations. He states that this is because men's hormones cause them to compete more strongly than women for status and dominance.

NO: Cultural anthropologists Kirk and Karen Endicott argue that the Batek people of Peninsular Malaysia form a gender egalitarian society in the sense that neither men nor women as groups control the other sex, and neither sex is accorded greater value by society as a whole. Both men and women are free to participate in any activities, and both have equal rights in the family and camp group.

In most of the world's societies, men hold the majority of leadership positions in public organizations—from government bodies, to corporations, to religious institutions. In families, husbands usually serve as heads of households and as primary breadwinners, while wives take responsibility for children and domestic activities within the household. Is the predominance of men in these public areas of a family's life universal and inevitable, a product of our human nature, or is it a cultural fact that might vary or be absent under different circumstances and conditions? Is it even possible for any human society to be sexually egalitarian? Are there any societies in which men and women are equally valued and have equal access to possessions, power, and prestige?

Some nineteenth-century cultural evolutionists, including J. J. Bachofen and J. F. MacLellan, postulated that the patriarchal (male-dominated) societies known from history had been preceded by a matriarchal stage of evolution in which women held the dominant social roles in society. Today, nearly all anthropologists doubt that any matriarchal societies ever existed. It is well established, however, that some societies trace descent matrilineally, through women, and that in these societies women generally play a more prominent public role than in patrilineal societies, where descent is traced from father to children. For example, among the early contact period Iroquois, matrilineages owned the land, husbands came to live with their wives, women managed and controlled the longhouse economies, and, while they could not serve as sachems (leaders), the women nominated and deposed the male sachems.

European and American societies have never been either matrilineal or matriarchal; they are examples of societies that are firmly patriarchal. Most Europeans and Americans have long considered this state of affairs both natural and God-given. Both Christian and Jewish religions can offer scriptural justification and support for the predominance of men and the subordination of women.

The anthropology of women (later termed "feminist anthropology") arose in the 1970s and challenged claims that the subordination of women was either natural or inevitable. Feminists took up the rallying cry that "Biology is not destiny." They argued that women could do anything that society permits them to do, and patriarchal society, like any other social institution, could be changed.

Some feminist anthropologists considered male dominance to be universal, but attributed it to universal cultural, not biological, causes. The groundbreaking volume *Women, Culture, and Society,* edited by Michelle Rosaldo and Louise Lamphere, (Stanford University Press, 1974), presents some possible cultural reasons for universal male dominance. Rosaldo proposed that all societies distinguish between "domestic" and "public" domains and that women are always associated with the domestic domain, with the home and raising children, while men are active in the public domain, where they have opportunities to obtain wealth, power, and ties with other men. In the same volume, Sherry Ortner argued that all societies associate women with nature—because they bear and nurse children—and men with culture, which is universally regarded as superior to nature.

Other anthropologists claimed that sexually egalitarian societies once existed (e.g., Eleanor Leacock's "Women's Status in Egalitarian Society: Implications for Social Evolution," *Current Anthropology,* vol. 19, 1978). They attribute the scarcity of such societies today to historical circumstances, especially the spread of European patriarchal culture to the rest of the world through colonialism and Christian missionization.

During the last 30 years, anthropologists have conducted many studies focused on gender roles and indigenous ideas about gender in specific societies. The most provocative of these studies have been in non-Western and tribal societies, usually the kinds of societies we might describe as small scale or preindustrial societies. The general finding of these studies is that gender relations are much more complicated and variable than scholars thought in the early days of feminist anthropology. For example, a number of studies have shown that not all societies make a simple distinction between domestic and public domains, associate women exclusively with a domestic domain, or evaluate activities outside the home as superior to those inside it. And studies have shown that the association of women with nature and men with culture is not universal either. Scholars have also realized that analytical concepts like "male dominance" and the "status of women" are too crude to describe the range of variation found in all human societies. They have attempted to break up these categories into several different components that can be identified and measured in more systematic ways in ethnographic field studies.

The question of whether or not males are dominant in a particular society is not as clear-cut as it may once have seemed. The Endicotts argue that, among the Batek, the two genders seem to be about as equal as one could imagine men and women to be. But part of this egalitarianism can be explained by the fact that as nomadic hunter-gatherers, the Batek have few material possessions and no social hierarchy or stratification such as we find in most agricultural and industrial societies. In sedentary societies where individuals and families can amass larger quantities of material possessions the situation is more complex. For example, in her book *Fruit of the Motherland: Gender in an Egalitarian Society* (Columbia University Press, 1993), anthropologist Maria Lepowski has argued that the *Vanatinai* of Papua New Guinea are sexually egalitarian. Compared to many other New Guinea societies, status differences between the genders are indeed quite modest. But as a horticultural and fishing people, the *Vanatinai* do have minor forms of social ranking, and men tend to take on more of the elevated social positions than do women. In some societies, men's and women's spheres of activity and control are separate and independent and therefore not easy to compare. In many small scale societies, anthropologists have shown that women and men may have similar amounts of influence over daily life, but the cultural ideology (or at least men's ideology) portrays women as inferior to men, just as it portrays the things women do as less important than what men do. Some societies have competing ideologies, in which both men and women portray their gender as superior. The Hua of Papua New Guinea have multiple ideologies, which simultaneously present women as inferior, superior, and equal to men (see Anna Meigs's book *Food, Sex, and Pollution: A New Guinea Religion* [Rutgers University Press, 1984]). Despite these complications, it may still be useful to describe or refer to a culture as "gender egalitarian" when neither sex as groups has control over the other and neither sex is accorded greater value than the other by society as a whole.

In the YES article, Steven Goldberg claims that males are dominant in all societies, and he presents a biological explanation for male dominance, contending that males have more of the hormone that causes individuals to strive for dominance than women do. In his book *Why Men Rule: A Theory of Male Dominance* (Open Court Publishing, 1993), he specifies that the hormone in question is testosterone, which is produced by the testicles and which has a masculinizing effect on the brain both in utero and in puberty. This supposedly makes males more competitive than females in competitions for status and prestige. Thus, regardless of cultural variations, men will occupy most high-status and high-ranking positions in any society. He also says that men are biologically programmed to dominate women in interpersonal relations in all societies. In his book, he specifies that the dominance of men and deference of women are manifested both behaviorally and emotionally, the feeling that both men and women have that men are in charge and women can only get their way by working around the authority of the men. He does not deny that humans vary in the strength of their dominance tendency and that some women may be more dominant than some men, although this is very unusual.

In the NO article, Kirk and Karen Endicott present evidence that neither males nor females are dominant among the Batek of Malaysia. They consider the Batek to be an example of a gender egalitarian society. Males and females participate in most of the same daily activities, and both men and women are involved with children and domestic affairs. There are no high-status roles in this society, although informal leadership does exist. Significantly, the natural leader of the hunter-gatherer band with whom they lived was a woman, not a man. The Endicotts claim that the Batek case challenges the generalization that men are dominant in all societies.

The authors of the two selections also disagree on whether biological or cultural forces more powerfully determine relations between the sexes and how men and women interact interpersonally. For Goldberg, it is the presence of certain hormones in males that have conditioned them to be competitive, assertive, and dominating. For the Endicotts, gender equality emerges from a complex interplay of local cultural factors. Every woman can forage and hunt for her own food as well as for food to feed her children. Every Batek man, woman, and child shares what they have with all others in the community, creating an egalitarian ethos in nearly every aspect of social life. Another key feature of Batek society is their prohibition on violence, which protects both sexes from coercion, a prohibition that is rare in societies with complex economies and social hierarchies. For the Endicotts, if male hormones and biology played a role in Batek life, these have been overshadowed by their obligation to share, the social requirement to be noncompetitive, and their avoidance of violence.

YES ↰
Steven Goldberg

Is Patriarchy Inevitable?

In five hundred years the world, in all likelihood, will have become homogenized. The thousands of varied societies and their dramatically differing methods of socialization, cohesion, family, religion, economy, and politics will have given way to a universal culture. Fortunately, cultural anthropologists have preserved much of our present diversity, which may keep our descendants from too hastily allowing their natural human ego- and ethno-centricity to conclude that theirs is the only way to manage a society.

However, the anthropological sword is two-edged. While diversity is certainly apparent from anthropological investigations, it is also clear that there are realities which manifest themselves no matter what the varied forms of the aforementioned institutions. Because these universal realities cut across cultural lines, they are crucial to our understanding of what society *by its nature* is and, perhaps, of what human beings are. It is important, then, that we ask why, when societies differ as much as do those of the Ituri Pygmy, the Jivaro, the American, the Japanese, and a thousand others, some institutions are universal.

It is always the case that the universal institution serves some need rooted in the deepest nature of human beings. In some cases the explanation of universality is obvious (e.g., why every society has methods of food gathering). But there are other universalities which are apparent, though without any obvious explanation. Of the thousands of societies on which we have any evidence stronger than myth (a form of evidence that would have us believe in cyclops), there is no evidence that there has ever been a society failing to exhibit three institutions:

1. Primary hierarchies always filled primarily by men. A Queen Victoria or a Golda Meir is always an exception and is always surrounded by a government of men. Indeed, the constraints of royal lineage may produce more female societal leaders than does democracy—there were more female heads of state in the first two-thirds of the sixteenth century than there were in the first two-thirds of the twentieth.

2. The highest status roles are male. There are societies in which the women do most of the important economic work and rear the children, while the men seem mostly to hang loose. But, in such societies, hanging loose is given higher

From *National Review*, November 11, 1996, pp. 32, 34–36. Copyright © 1996 by National Review, Inc., 215 Lexington Avenue, New York, NY 10016. Reprinted by permission.

status than any non-maternal role primarily served by women. No doubt this is partly due to the fact that the males hold the positions of power. However, it is also likely that high-status roles are male not primarily because they are male (ditch-digging is male and low status), but because they are high status. The high status roles are male because they possess—for whatever socially determined reason in whichever specific society—high status. This high status exerts a more powerful influence on males than it does on females. As a result, males are more willing to sacrifice life's other rewards for status dominance than are females.

In their *Not in Our Genes,* Richard Lewontin, Leon Kamin, and Stephen Rose—who, along with Stephen Jay Gould are the best-known defenders of the view that emphasizes the role of environment and de-emphasizes that of heredity—attempt to find fault with my work by pointing out that most family doctors in the Soviet Union are women. However, they acknowledge that in the Soviet Union "family doctoring [had] lower status than in the United States."

Which is precisely the point. No one doubts that women can be doctors. The question is why doctors (or weavers, or load bearers, etc.) are primarily women only when being a doctor is given lower status than are certain roles played mostly by men—and furthermore, why, even when this is the case (as in Russia) the upper hierarchical positions relevant to that specific area are held by men.

3. Dominance in male–female relationships is always associated with males. "Male dominance" refers to the feeling, of both men and women, that the male is dominant and that the woman must "get around" the male to attain power. Social attitudes may be concordant or discordant with the reality of male dominance. In our own society there was a time when the man's "taking the lead" was positively valued by most women (as 30s' movies attest); today such a view is purportedly detested by many. But attitudes toward male-dominance behavior are causally unimportant to the reality they judge—and are not much more likely to eliminate the reality than would a social dislike of men's being taller be able to eliminate men's being taller.

⋅⦿⋅

Over the past twenty years, I have consulted every original ethnographic work invoked to demonstrate an exception to these societal universalities. Twenty years ago many textbooks spoke cavalierly of "matriarchies" and "Amazons" and pretended that Margaret Mead had claimed to find a society in which sex roles were reversed. Today no serious anthropologist is willing to claim that any specific society has ever been an exception.

It is often claimed that "modern technology renders the physiological differentiation irrelevant." However, there is not a scintilla of evidence that modernization alters the basic "motivational" factors sufficiently to cast doubt on the continued existence of the universals I discuss. The economic needs of modern society probably do set a lower limit on the status of women; no modern society could give women the low status they receive in some non-modern societies. But modernization probably also sets an upper limit; no modern society is likely to give women the status given to the maternal roles in some other matrilineal societies.

Scandinavian nations, which have long had government agencies devoted to equalizing women's position, are often cited by social scientists as demonstrating modernization's ability to override patriarchy. In fact, however, Norway has 454 municipal councils; 443 are chaired by men. On the Supreme Court, city courts, appellate courts, and in Parliament, there are between five and nine times as many men as there are women. In Sweden, according to government documents, men dominate "senior positions in employer and employee organizations as well as in political and other associations" and only 5 of 82 directors of government agencies, 9 of 83 chairpersons of agency boards, and 9 per cent of judges are women.

One may, of course, hope that all this changes, but one cannot invoke any evidence implying that it will.

Of course, there are those who simply try to assert away the evidence. Lewontin *et al.* write, "Cross cultural universals appear to lie more in the eye of the beholder than in the social reality that is being observed." In fact, with reference to the universalities mentioned above, they do not. If these universals were merely "in the eye of the beholder," the authors would merely have to specify a society in which there was a hierarchy in which males did not predominate and the case would be closed.

The answer to the question of why an institution is universal clearly must be parsimonious. It will not do to ascribe causation of a universal institution to capitalism or Christianity or modernization, because many hundreds of societies lacked these, but not the universal institutions. If the causal explanation is to be at all persuasive, it must invoke some factor present in every society from the most primitive to the most modern. (Invoking the male's physical strength advantage does meet the requirement of parsimony, but does not counter the evidence of the central importance of neuro-endocrinological psycho-physiological factors.)

When sociologists are forced to acknowledge the universals, they nearly always invoke "socialization" as explanation. But this explanation faces two serious problems. First, it does not explain anything, but merely forces us to ask another question: *Why* does socialization of men and women always work in the same direction? Second, the explanation implicitly assumes that the social environment of expectations and norms acts as an *independent* variable capable of acting as counterpoise to the physiological constituents that make us male and female.

In individual cases, of course, anything can happen.

Even when a causation is nearly entirely hereditary, there are many exceptions (as tall women demonstrate). Priests choose to be celibate, but this does not cast doubt on the physiological basis of the "sex drive." To be sure, there is also feedback from the environmental to the physiological, so that association of physical strength with males results in more males lifting weights. However, in principle, a society could find itself with women who were physically stronger than men if women lifted weights throughout their lives and men remained sedentary.

But, in real life, this can't happen because the social environment is a *dependent* variable whose limits are set by our physiological construction. In real life we all observe a male's dominance tendency that is rooted in physiological differences between males and females and, because values and attitudes are not of primary causal importance here, we develop expectations concordant with the male–female behavioral differences.

Most of the discussion of sex differences has emphasized the neuroendocrinological differentiation of males and females and the cognitive and behavioral differentiation this engenders. This is because there is an enormous amount of evidence demonstrating the role of hormones in fetally differentiating the male and female central nervous systems, CNS response to the potentiating properties of certain hormones, and the thoughts and actions of males and females.

There is not room here for detailed discussion of the neuroendocrinological mechanism underlying dominance behavior. But a useful analogy is iron and magnet. Iron does not have a "drive" or a "need" to find a magnet, but when there is a magnet in the area, iron, as a result of the very way it is built, tends to react in a certain way. Likewise, the physiological natures of males and females predispose them to have different hierarchies of response to various environmental cues. There is no response that only one sex has; the difference between men and women is the relative strengths of different responses. Males react more readily to hierarchical competitiveness than do females; females react more readily to the needs of an infant-in-distress. Norms and socialization do not cause this difference, but reflect it and make concrete a specific society's specific methods for manifesting the response. (Cleaning a rifle and preparing Spaghetti-Os are not instinctive abilities).

The iron–magnet analogy makes clear the role of social environment. Were there to be a society without hierarchy, status, values, or interdependence of the sexes, there would be no environmental cue to elicit the differentiated, physiologically rooted responses we discuss. But it is difficult to imagine such a society and, indeed, there has never been such a society.

Even if we had no neuro-endocrinological evidence at all, the anthropological evidence alone would be sufficient to force us to posit a mechanism of sexual psycho-physiological differentiation and to predict its discovery. We do, however, possess the neuro-endocrinological evidence and the anthropological evidence permits us to specify the institutional effects—the limits of societal variation that the neuro-endocrinological engenders.

For thousands of years, everyone, save perhaps some social scientists and others ideologically opposed to the idea, have known perfectly well that men and women differ in the physiological factors that underlie masculine and feminine thought and behavior. They may not have known the words to describe the linkage of physiology with thought and behavior, but they knew the linkage was there. (I recently read a comment of a woman in Pennsylvania: "They keep telling us that men and women are the way they are because of what they've been taught, but you can go a hundred miles in any direction and not find a single person who really believes that.") And even the most feminist parent, once she has children, can't help but notice that it is nearly impossible to get small boys to play with dolls not named "Killer Joe, the Marauding Exterminator," or at least with trucks—big trucks.

None of this is to deny tremendous variation on the level of roles. Even in our own society, in just a century the role of secretary changed from virtually solely male to virtually solely female. With the exception of roles associated with child nurturance, political leadership, warfare, security, and crime, virtually every specific role is male in some societies and female in others. No one doubts that the women who exhibit the dominance behavior usually exhibited by men encounter discrimination. But the question remains: why is dominance behavior usually exhibited by *men*?

The implication of all this depends on context. Clearly the correctness or incorrectness of the theory I present is important to an understanding of human behavior and society. But to the individual man or woman, on the other hand, the universals are largely irrelevant. The woman who wishes to become President has a sufficient number of real-life equivalents to know that there is not a constraint rendering impossible a female head of state. But there is no more reason for such a woman to deny that the motivation to rule is more often associated with male physiology than there is for the six-foot woman to pretend that women are as tall as men.

Kirk M. Endicott and
Karen L. Endicott

➡ **NO**

Understanding Batek Egalitarianism

The Batek were remarkably egalitarian in the social and cultural treatment of the sexes. This was so as recently as 2004, despite economic changes due to government-sponsored development projects. There was no area of Batek culture or social life in which men controlled women or subjected them to asymmetrical systems of evaluation. Batek concepts of males and females recognized the physical differences between the sexes without imposing evaluative or symbolic significance on them. In daily social life, men and women had equal control over themselves and an equal voice in the affairs of the camp-group. Men and women were equal partners in marriage: the choice of spouse was left to the individuals involved, husbands and wives cooperated economically but were not exclusively dependent upon each other, decision making was a shared responsibility, and divorce could be initiated by either spouse. The political system did not favor men over women except in the headmanship system imposed by outsiders. In the economic sphere, males and females had equal access to the sharing network, which included the foods brought in by both men and women. Neither sex was prohibited from participating in any activity, except for the prohibition among a few Aring River people in 1990 against women doing blowpipe hunting and men weaving pandanus. The contributions by each sex to the food supply differed between 1975–76 and 1990, but in both periods both sexes contributed to the material well-being of the group, and neither sex group thought it was being exploited by the other. Socialization to gender roles occurred without coercion or preferential treatment of either sex.

In this chapter we attempt to bring out the features of Batek culture and circumstances that fostered their gender egalitarianism. We think of these features as leveling mechanisms that prevented the rise of male dominance, for we accept the premise that in societies in which there is competition for control, males are at an advantage because of their greater physical strength and their freedom from childbearing and nursing. We do not mean to imply that the conditions enabling the Batek to be gender egalitarian are the only conditions that could do so. Gardner argues that a number of different combinations of cultural and natural circumstances can lead to individual autonomy—which we see as a key feature of gender equality—in hunting and gathering societies.

From *The Headman was a Woman: The Gender Egalitarian Batek of Malaysia* (Waveland Press, 2008), pp. 147–152. Copyright © 2008 by Waveland Press. Reprinted by permission of Waveland Press. All rights reserved.

The Bases of Batek Gender Egalitarianism

We define . . . a gender egalitarian society as one in which neither sex has overall control over the other or greater cultural value than the other. Control can be based in the economic system (e.g., the ability to withhold a resource necessary for survival), the system of authority (authority may be vested in such areas as political offices, kinship relationships, and religious ideologies), and in direct force. With these possible bases of control in mind, let us turn to a consideration of how the Batek prevented men from gaining control over women.

Economic Security

We believe that the key economic reason Batek men did not dominate Batek women is that no woman was dependent on a specific man—such as a father, husband, brother, or son—for survival. Women were economically secure, surviving through their own foraging efforts and through direct participation in the camp-wide food-sharing network. In 1975–76 most of the staple foods in the Batek diet, including rice and flour obtained in trade, could be procured by both men and women using skills, knowledge, and tools that were readily available to all. No rights of exclusive ownership over resources restricted women's access to any foods or other necessities, and the flexible division of labor permitted them to harvest any resources they came upon. Women also had full rights in the food-sharing network, and they retained these rights even when men obtained most of the food, as was the case in 1990. By contributing to and drawing from the food-sharing network, women could usually be certain of getting some food—including the foods ordinarily obtained by men, such as honey and arboreal game—even when they were ill or when their own food-getting efforts failed. Thus, the economic security of Batek women was based on their being able to depend upon the group as a whole in addition to their own efforts. Although Batek women—and men—could survive by their own efforts alone for limited periods of time, they were not economically *independent* like Hadza and Paliyan women, who gathered most of their own food and shared little even with their husbands.

Because Batek women were economically secure, women could withdraw from unsatisfactory marriages without suffering economic hardship. Both in 1975–76 and in 1990 we saw divorced women with children living happily for extended periods without remarrying, even when they had persistent suitors.

Some scholars have claimed that external trade and other economic processes that involve a delay between when the work is done and when the reward is received undermine the autonomy and equality of women in hunting and gathering societies. Leacock argues, following Engels, that when hunter-gatherers begin to produce commodities for trade, in addition to goods for consumption, families become isolated from each other, and women come to depend on their husbands and sons for survival, rather than on the group as a whole. Woodburn contends that "delayed-return" economic processes, which include collecting goods for trade, enmesh women in a system of binding commitments that place them under the authority of men.

Why, then, hasn't trade led to male dominance among the Batek? The answer is certainly not that trade is a recent innovation; there is good reason to suppose that the ancestors of the Batek have traded forest produce to horticulturalists for cultivated foods and other goods for the last 3000–4000 years, and commercial trade goes back at least to the 1930s. Rather, the reason seems to be that the Batek practiced trade in ways that were compatible with the general conditions ensuring women's economic security. Among the Batek, both men and women could and did collect and trade forest produce in 1975–76, although men generally spent more time at it than women. Trade in forest produce was just one of several sources of food for the Batek, and it was compatible with the other forms of food getting they practiced and with their general nomadic, egalitarian way of life. Most importantly, they shared all food obtained by trade just as they shared all food obtained directly from the forest. Thus, women benefited from external trade in the same way as men.

Dispersed Authority

Another characteristic of Batek society that seems to have inhibited the development of male dominance was the broad dispersal of authority. What little authority existed was spread among all adult men and women and consisted mainly of the authority to govern oneself and one's young children. Leadership was based on persuasion; there was no possibility of coercion. In these circumstances it was the qualities of the individual—including eloquence, intelligence, and tact—that determined what, if any, influence a person had over others. Group decisions were usually based on open discussion, and individuals had the right to ignore the consensus and follow their own desires. Batek ethics promoted extreme respect for personal freedom, constrained only by a general obligation to help others—as exemplified by the food-sharing requirement. Men, women, and children could all express their ideas and wishes and act on them as they saw fit.

Nonviolence

Another feature of Batek culture that seems to have inhibited male dominance was their suppression of all physical aggression. Like the horticultural Semai Orang Asli, who also appear to be gender egalitarian, the Batek abhorred violence and claimed that they would abandon anyone who was habitually aggressive. They regarded violent behavior as a sign of madness. They were usually successful at defusing potential violence through their methods of conflict resolution, and they took great pains to teach their children to avoid all aggressive behavior. Because no aggression was tolerated, Batek women were safe from coercion based on physical force or the threat of physical force.

Is Batek Culture a Result of Encapsulation?

The conditions we have identified as making gender egalitarianism possible among the Batek are largely cultural. Some scholars would go further to the question of why the Batek culture took the form it did in the first place. Why were Batek nomadic forager-traders and why were they organized in a fashion that permitted egalitarian relations between the sexes?

A number of scholars have argued that basic cultural features of some contemporary foraging peoples—including egalitarian gender relations where they exist—result from the societies being "encapsulated," surrounded and politically dominated by more numerous and powerful people. The Batek and other Semang could be categorized as encapsulated because they are surrounded by Malays. The encapsulation theory implies that egalitarian relations in foraging societies are an "abnormal" social condition and did not exist before the societies came under the influence of more powerful neighbors. Although the various proponents of the theory agree that the influence of the surrounding society shapes the culture of the foraging group, they do not agree on exactly how this takes place.

In an early formulation of this idea, Gardner describes the foraging Paliyan of India as being extremely individualistic, noncompetitive, nonviolent, noncooperative (to the point of not even sharing food with spouses), independent, and egalitarian even between the sexes. They show little emotion for others, and they hold idiosyncratic rather than shared views about the world. He postulates that these characteristics are due to the Paliyan having been subjected to centuries of abuse, threats, exploitation, and contempt from surrounding peoples. He argues that the relative helplessness of the Paliyan "made withdrawal or subservience more realistic than attempts at retaliation" and that their repression of aggressive impulses led to their particular cultural characteristics. He claims that a whole category of similarly surrounded and subordinate foragers ("refugee gathering peoples") share similar characteristics.

Testart defines a category of hunter-gatherers as *chasseurs-cueilleurs enclaves,* "enclaved hunter-gatherers," who are surrounded by more numerous and powerful farmers or herders with whom they trade. He says that the political domination of the outsiders promotes nomadism among the foragers: they keep moving to escape their tormentors. The foragers are egalitarian, he asserts, because continuous exploitation in trade equally impoverishes all of them. Woodburn also examines the relations between foragers and surrounding peoples. He asks: "Have their sharing and egalitarian leveling mechanisms developed in opposition to domination by outsiders? Have we here a sort of moral oppositional solidarity of low-status groups, akin to the egalitarian solidarity manifest in some working-class or millenarian movements?" Some writers have argued that the cultures of most if not all contemporary foraging peoples are predominantly shaped by their position in the larger surrounding society. The cultural characteristics of a people such as the Ju/'hoansi of southern Africa, they contend, are determined by their position as an impoverished rural proletariat in the class-stratified societies of Botswana and Namibia.

Could it be that the Batek were gender egalitarian because they were encapsulated by Malays? We think the answer is no. In fact, Malays could never have exercised real control over Semang as long as the latter were nomadic, economically self-sufficient, and had a vast empty forest to hide in. Even before Malay villages were removed from the Lebir watershed, local Malays were far from numerous enough or well-organized enough to have politically dominated the Batek. In recent years the Malaysian government, with all the resources of a modern nation-state, has been unable to exercise control over them. And the Batek never depended on trade with Malays for their survival, so trade with Malays was voluntary for both parties. If Batek had been coerced or abused by traders, they could have moved to remote areas or to areas near more congenial Malay villagers.

However, the Batek case does support Testart's claim that abuse or the potential for abuse by a more numerous and powerful people may reinforce the nomadism of some foraging groups. Frequent movement was probably the most effective defense the Semang had against the slave raiding that went on in some areas into this century. But the Batek economy also required nomadism, and there is no reason to suppose that they would have—or could have—settled down had there been no threat from Malays. Most Batek remained nomadic as recently as 1990, even though slave raiding ceased in the 1920s.

The Batek culture did not show the kinds of distortions and gaps that would suggest that they were merely a subdivision of the larger surrounding society, like some of the Indian foraging groups that appear to be occupational subcastes of forest produce collectors within Hindu society. The Batek had a strong sense of unity and a complete and distinctive culture, including a separate language, religion, and way of life. They considered Malays to be the archetypical "outsiders" with whom they often contrasted themselves. There is no reason to doubt that the Batek could have existed as an independent society with much the same form of culture before the Malays came on the scene.

In our opinion the most plausible reason that the Batek were nomadic forager-traders, with a culture supporting egalitarian relations between the sexes—and the reason that most closely resembles the Batek's own views of why they live the way they do—is that they were filling an ecological and social niche that provided them with a relatively secure and satisfying way of life, one that had some advantages over swidden horticulture, the main alternative possibility in their environment. For example, foraging was a more reliable way of getting food than farming in the deep forest, where birds, monkeys, wild pigs, elephants, and crop diseases could easily destroy the results of an entire season's labors. As Benjamin argues, the Semang are probably the descendants of the Hoabinhians who, after the advent of agriculture in the Malay Peninsula, opted to pursue a way of life based on nomadic foraging combined with trade with their farming neighbors. Until the arrival of the Malays in the interior in the last few hundred years, those neighbors were mainly Senoi Orang Asli, the descendants of other Hoabinhians who opted to concentrate on horticulture. Both groups became skilled specialists who shared the fruits of their respective modes of adaptation by means of trade. Pursuing complementary ways of life reduced the possibility of intergroup friction that could have arisen had they been competing for the same resources. No doubt there have been individual crossings back and forth across the Senoi–Semang boundary, especially when intermarriage has been involved, but the two ways of life have nevertheless remained distinct into the twenty-first century. As we have shown in this book, egalitarian relations between the sexes were an integral feature of the foraging-trading mode of adaptation the ancestors of the Batek chose.

EXPLORING THE ISSUE

Do Men Dominate Women in All Societies?

Critical Thinking and Reflection

1. Do you think the Batek case actually contradicts Goldberg's assertion that males are dominant over women in all societies? Is it really possible for a society to be egalitarian in every aspect of social life and thus to provide no venue for status competition?
2. If, as Goldberg contends, hormones cause the differences between male and female behavior in all societies, how can we understand the differences in gender roles that exist in different societies?
3. Would the existence of a single egalitarian society disprove Goldberg's thesis that differences between males and females in their striving for power and prestige result from differences in male and female hormones?
4. If you accept Goldberg's contention that males have an innate tendency toward domination, can you think of any cultural arrangements that might neutralize male superiority or at least keep it in check?
5. How would you explain the changing roles of women in American society over the last 50 years, such as their move into jobs outside the home, including occupations with high prestige and power (e.g., medical doctors and CEOs of corporations)?

Is There Common Ground?

Anthropologists have long debated how much weight to give to biologically based behavioral tendencies ("nature") versus learned behaviors, norms, and values ("nurture") in explaining individual behavior and cultural institutions in specific societies. In these two selections, Goldberg and the Endicotts disagree on the amount of influence each of these forces has in shaping the attitudes and actions of human males and females.

Goldberg contends that all societies are dominated by males because males have more of the hormones that drive them to compete for power, status, and prestige than women do. Furthermore, because most if not all men behave in this way, all societies contain status differences, and more men will inevitably find their way into the higher positions in the hierarchy than women.

The Endicotts, on the other hand, see the social system more as an independent variable to which the process of socialization adjusts the behaviors of individuals. This does not necessarily dismiss the influence of male hormones in the competition for status in hierarchical societies, but, unlike Goldberg, they consider some societies to be egalitarian—without significant hierarchies of power, wealth, or prestige—so there are no high-status positions for men and women to compete over. Most such societies are small-scale "tribal" societies, especially nomadic hunters-gatherers and slash-and-burn farmers. These societies, which are well represented in the hinterlands of Southeast Asia (see, e.g., T. Gibson and K. Silander, eds., *Anarchic Solidarity: Autonomy, Equality, and Fellowship in Southeast Asia* [Yale Southeast Asia Studies, 2011]; J. C. Scott, *The Art of Not Being Governed: An Anarchist History of Upland Southeast Asia* [Yale University Press, 2009]), deliberately undermine status and wealth differentials by means of what anthropologists call "leveling mechanisms" (e.g., an obligation to share food). In such cultures, a highly competitive person would be shunned as a deviant.

If we leave aside Goldberg's notion that the innate competitiveness of men inevitably lead all societies to be hierarchical, but accept his claim that men are inherently more competitive than women, then it is possible to say that in *societies in which hierarchy does exist,* male hormones may be responsible for men predominating in the most prestigious and powerful positions. However, other explanations are possible, such as the biological fact that only women can bear and nurse babies, thus limiting the amount of time they can compete for high positions.

Additional Resources

For a full explication of Goldberg's theory of innate male dominance see:
Goldberg, Steven. 1993. *Why Men Rule, A Theory of Male Dominance.* Chicago and La Salle, IL: Open Court.

For discussions of the literature on the influence of hormones on sex differences see:
McIntyre, Matthew H. and Edwards, Carolyn Pope. 2009. "The Early Development of Gender Differences," *Annual Review of Anthropology* 38, pp.: 83–97.

Worthman, Carol M. 1995. "Hormones, Sex, and Gender," *Annual Review of Anthropology* 24, pp.: 593–616.

For two views on the biological evolution of male–female differences in humans see:
Huber, Joan. 2007. *On the Origins of Gender Inequality.* Boulder, CO: Paradigm Publishers.

Smuts, Barbara. 1995. "The Evolutionary Origins of Patriarchy," *Human Nature* 6, pp.: 1–32.

For the full study of gender among the Batek see:
Endicott, Kirk M. and Endicott, Karen L. 2008. *The Headman Was a Woman: The Gender Egalitarian Batek of Malaysia.* Long Grove, IL: Waveland Press, Inc.

For a discussion of gender equality and inequality among hunter-gatherers in general see:
Endicott, Karen L. 1999. "Gender Relations in Hunter-Gather Societies," in Richard B. Lee and Richard Daly, eds., *The Cambridge Encyclopedia of Hunters and Gathers* Cambridge: Cambridge University Press.

For an up-to-date collection of articles on the anthropology of gender see:
Brettell, Caroline B. and Sargent, Carolyn F. 2009. *Gender in Cross-Cultural Perspective.* 5th ed. Upper Saddle River, NJ: Pearson Prentice Hall.

ISSUE 14

Does the Distinction Between the Natural and the Supernatural Exist in All Cultures?

YES: Roger Ivar Lohmann, from "The Supernatural Is Everywhere: Defining Qualities of Religion in Melanesia and Beyond," *Anthropological Forum* (November 2003)

NO: Frederick P. Lampe, from "Creating a Second-Storey Woman: Introduced Delineation Between Natural and Supernatural in Melanesia," *Anthropological Forum* (November 2003)

Learning Outcomes

After reading this issue, you should be able to:

- Understand what anthropologists mean by the term supernatural.
- Discuss the role of beliefs in the supernatural in everyday life.
- Outline some of the definitions of religion that anthropologists have used since the mid-nineteenth century.
- Interpret the role of the supernatural in modern American culture.
- Discuss the differences between the concepts of the supernatural and of religion according to an anthropologist.

ISSUE SUMMARY

YES: Cultural anthropologist Roger Ivar Lohmann argues that a supernaturalistic worldview or cosmology is at the heart of virtually all religions. For him, the supernatural is a concept that exists everywhere, although it is expressed differently in each society. For him, supernaturalism attributes volition to things that do not have it. He argues that the supernatural is also a part of Western people's daily experience in much the same way that it is the experience of the Papua New Guineas with whom he worked.

NO: Lutheran pastor and anthropological researcher Frederick (Fritz) P. Lampe argues that "supernatural" is a problematic and inappropriate term like the term "primitive." If we accept the term "supernatural," it is all too easy to become ethnocentric and assume that anything supernatural is unreal and therefore false. He considers a case at the University of Technology in Papua New Guinea to show how use of the term "supernatural" allows us to miss out on how Papua New Guineans actually understand the world in logical, rational, and naturalistic terms that Westerners would generally see as illogical, irrational, and supernaturalistic.

Making sense of other people's religions has been an interest of anthropology from the beginning of the discipline. In his book *Primitive Culture* (J. Murray, 1871), Sir Edward B. Tylor offered the first anthropological definition of religion: the belief in supernatural beings. Since the age of enlightenment in the eighteenth century, after Sir Isaac Newton and other scientists began to identify systematic patterns in the natural world, scientists had adopted the view that all phenomena could be explained in rational, naturalistic terms. Thus, for Tylor, the belief in ghosts, spirits, demons, demigods, and gods was evidence of irrational thought and lack of a correct understanding of the natural world. For him, primitive religion was based on a fundamental error. He reasoned that people in all societies had dreams, but primitive people interpreted these dreams as reality and the characters in them as spirits, souls, or demons. Tylor's interest in religious phenomena was part of his larger interest in explaining the evolution of culture from primitive cultures into modern, civilized ones. Belief in the supernatural in the form of spirits and ghosts was evidence for early evolutionary anthropologists that the society was "primitive." As societies developed and evolved into more civilized societies, religion took on more complex forms of the supernatural, in which a whole host of spirits and ghosts gave way to various gods and goddesses. Ultimately, polytheism with its many gods gave way to monotheism with its singular god.

Eventually, many of the early evolutionary anthropologists assumed that Christianity would give way to reason and rationality, abandoning the supernatural once and for all for reason and science. In a similar way, Bronislaw Malinowski had distinguished between science on the one hand and magic and religion on the other in his book *Magic, Science, and Religion* (Beacon, 1948). In 1966 the American anthropologists Anthony F. C. Wallace defined religion as "beliefs and rituals concerned with supernatural beings, forces, and powers."

But aside from the definitions provided by anthropologists like Tylor, Malinowski, and Wallace, there is no necessary reason why the notion that there is a distinction between the natural and the supernatural should be present in all societies. Whether people in all societies accept the distinction between the natural and the supernatural is an empirical question that we should be able to answer by observing whether all societies have ideas about the supernatural.

The issue is whether all societies around the world actually do believe in the supernatural as a category of reality distinct and separate from the natural world. Both essays provided for this issue were presented as part of a panel that was addressing an issue raised by anthropologist Morton Klass in his book *Ordered Universes: Approaches to the Anthropology of Religion* (Westview, 1995). Klass argued that the use of the term "supernatural" is problematic because the ways that most scholars use the term suggests a distinction between the natural world that is real and a supernatural world that is not really appreciated as authentic and real in the same way. In this sense, the concept of the supernatural has many of the same problems that the terms "primitive" and "race" have. At issue for Klass is a universe that feels as real and authentic to its participants as the natural world may feel to Western anthropologists. From this point of view, anthropologists will never understand the world of New Guineans, Africans, Hindus, or Catholics, if they begin by defining their subjects' religious beliefs in terms of a dichotomy between the realistic (the natural) and the fantastic (the supernatural). However we describe the nonnatural forces that many societies accept as present in the world; anthropologists must acknowledge that the peoples we study accept these forces as being as tangible and real as any rock or tree.

The two positions presented in this issue provide empirical examination of whether these nonnaturalistic forces, so typically called the supernatural, exist in all societies. They do so by examining the presence of the supernatural in particular societies. Both authors have conducted field research in Papua New Guinea, in the southwest Pacific north of Australia. This region has attracted the attention of anthropologists for more than a century because its people generally had simple forms of agriculture but a diverse array of different languages and cultures. In the decades following World War II, it had the largest number of societies that had not encountered Western culture. Its diverse peoples typically had religions that involved ghosts, spirits, and magic. In these selections, both Lohmann and Lampe accept that the supernatural consists of nonnaturalistic thinking. In other words, they accept that the supernatural should feel real to its participants. Its key trait, however, is that it does not use naturalistic notions of cause and effect.

Here, anthropologist Roger Ivar Lohmann argues that the core of the supernatural is attributing volition to things that do not have it. For him this is the central feature of religious thinking in all societies around the world. He distinguishes the supernatural as a concept that can be observed empirically in all societies, although its particular cultural expression will vary quite widely in the diverse cultures around the world. For him, attributing volition to things that cannot have volition or to things that do not exist is at the heart of the supernatural. Thus, the supernatural is not limited to spirits, gods, or ghosts but can also include "luck," "kharma," or "the mystical." He argues that even in North America most people "cross the border between naturalism and supernaturalism several times each day" when we see patterns of volition in otherwise random events.

Lutheran Pastor Frederick (Fritz) P. Lampe was chaplain at the University of Technology in Papua New Guinea for four years in the 1980s. He draws upon these experiences to challenge whether these Papua New Guineans are using supernatural thinking in responding to such issues as traditional notions of the polluting quality of female menstrual blood for men. For Europeans the idea that menstrual blood is dangerous is self-evidently wrong; therefore, it is classified as supernatural idea. But Lampe shows that these New Guinean ideas are based on a naturalistic worldview, not a supernaturalistic one.

In reading these selections, consider how each author understands what is meant by "the supernatural." Do the several cases mentioned by Lohmann demonstrate that the supernatural concept is present in every society? What about our own society? Does Lampe's case study actually demonstrate that the supernatural is not a salient part of the people's worldview he discusses? If it did, would this finding dismiss Lohmann's claim about universality? Even if in one or another case "the supernatural" is not a salient concept, would we necessarily want to abandon the concept as we have the term "primitive?"

YES ↩

Roger Ivar Lohmann

The Supernatural Is Everywhere: Defining Qualities of Religion in Melanesia and Beyond

Supernaturalism depicts conscious will or volition as the ultimate cause of phenomena. Supernaturalistic cosmologies are at the heart of virtually all religions. All humans seem to sense a supernatural realm, yet we are unable to detect it scientifically. It is an imagined dimension where volition can exist without brains, and control the physical world. I argue that the concept of 'supernatural' is necessary both to describe particular worldviews accurately, and to understand spirit belief and religion as ubiquitous in human experience.

In conceptualising the supernatural, it is very important at the outset to distinguish between the etic perspectives of scientific observers and the emic views of cultural participants. The supernatural can be viewed as a universal assumption among humans, or as the unique spiritual reality of a given culture. The supernatural is in this regard like sex, which, like all realms of common human experience, is modelled differently in different traditions to produce different gender systems. The distinction between sex and gender is necessary to understand the relationship between objective physicality and cultural models of the physically real. For the same reason that we need to distinguish etic and emic perspectives on reproductive capacity, we need to separate etic and emic definitions of 'supernatural'. As a technical term in anthropology, 'supernatural' serves best as an etic concept describing a universal human experience that is elaborated differently in different traditions.

I define the etic category of supernatural as a ubiquitous mental model that depicts one or more sentient, volitional agencies that are independent of a biological substrate and understood to be the ultimate cause of elements of physical reality. Individual cultural models of the supernatural, like the various forms of gender, are distinctive in different societies. Ethnographers should describe these differences carefully. Some anthropologists, however, argue that the spiritual worlds posited by different peoples are so distinctive that generalising about them with terms like 'supernatural' is inaccurate. I make the case to the contrary that, whereas there is indeed much variation in the spiritualities of different peoples, they are all similar enough to one another

From *Anthropological Forum,* vol. 13, no. 2, 2003, pp. 175–180, 182–184. Copyright © 2003 by Taylor & Francis Journals. Reprinted by permission via Rightslink.

that we can recognise virtually all of them as variants of a common human tendency to assume that a supernatural world exists. For example, many Melanesian peoples model the supernatural world as a hidden realm existing inside the material world. While Melanesians typically consider the supernatural to be immanent, some other peoples model the supernatural as being separate from its creation.

People everywhere learn that volition can find expression in physical phenomena, because they routinely experience and witness human creativity. For example, when a man desires a house, his volition brings about the construction of a house. One might call the mental model of this sort of agentive causation the 'volition schema.' Supernaturalism is the extension of the volition schema to phenomena that do not in fact result from will and choice, like the origin of the world. Belief in an afterlife, to give another example, results from extending the volition schema to the dead, who are no longer volitional, to explain our ongoing memories of them.

'Supernatural' is a venerable term in anthropology. However, some criticise it as ethnocentric or misleading, because many peoples do not think spiritual powers are separate from the 'natural' world. Moreover, they point out that, in its etic sense, the term implies that only the natural is real, while the supernatural is not, which does not represent the view of those who believe in a spirit world. These critiques do not demonstrate a problem with the category of 'supernatural'; rather, they point to the dangers of conflating various etic and emic *definitions* of the supernatural. When these are distinguished, the supernatural concept both clarifies a scientific position on a major source of religious behaviour and improves our ability to understand religious worldviews. The supernatural, as I define it, is a real phenomenon with physical causes and effects, which people model differently from one culture to the next. I suggest that all people can distinguish supernaturalistic ideas from naturalistic ones, though they may not find the distinction salient. The distinction is expressed using various idioms, including transcendent vs. tangible, real vs. illusory, sacred vs. profane, living vs. lifeless, ethereal vs. material, and, as I suggest is widespread in Melanesia, hidden vs. exposed, and inside vs. outside.

Critiques of 'Supernatural'

Critics of the supernatural concept have two basic arguments. First, they say that it implies condescension toward credulous believers in non-existent beings. Second, they argue that by using the term we erroneously assume that all religions share the West Asian assumption, found in Judaism, Christianity, and Islam, that the natural world is separate from a supernatural creator. These are valid critiques of certain ways of using the term 'supernatural', but they do not damn its usefulness when employed with respect, precision, and a distinction between etic and emic.

To see that this is so, consider an eloquent critique by Morton Klass. Klass points out the similarity between a farmer's offering to the deceased first owner of a field and his rent payment to an absentee landlord. Why, he asks, should we classify the former as supernatural and the latter as natural, when both the first owner and the landlord are invisible and ostensibly require compensation? To do so, he says, merely underlines our disbelief in the efficacy of the offering, and ethnocentrically smears our understanding of the farmer's worldview.

I do not think that seeking an etic explanation requires one to disregard or disrespect the emic one. Nor do we distort the emic perspective by asserting that the farmer can distinguish between dealings with spirits and people. Klass, however, does us a service by emphasising that this distinction may not be salient to the believer, and this should be described in the ethnography.

Having made an analogy with sex above, I consider one with language. In the same way as the pan-human cognitive capability for language is expressed locally as specific languages, and individually as speech, supernaturalism is expressed in local variants as religions, and individually as spirituality. The thousands of different languages all represent one kind of cognitive and behavioural capacity made possible by our neurological apparatus for language. Just as one can distinguish linguistic thought from purely image-based thought, one can likewise distinguish supernaturalism from naturalism. This is so even though both occur simultaneously, mix freely, and may be conflated in ethnopsychologies.

The disregard of Klass's farmer for a distinction that an anthropologist would notice is analogous to a native speaker's inattention to the difference between a voiced and an unvoiced consonant in a language in which this distinction does not carry meaning. Anyone can be made aware of the objective (phonetic) difference between the two sounds, and, for linguists, attention to phonetics is vital. Likewise, for practical purposes, the farmer may not think about the difference between an offering to a dead person and a payment to a living one, but he could make that distinction were it relevant to his task. For anthropologists, it is central to ours. Different peoples emphasise or de-emphasise the distinction between supernatural and natural causation, or mark it in different ways, and critics of the fuzzy use of the concept rightly bring this to our attention.

[Anthropologist Benson] Saler observes that anthropologists often use the term 'supernatural' without defining what they mean, possibly to appear respectful of local beliefs that they in fact consider erroneous. I concur with his view that, if by 'supernatural beings' we mean imaginary ones, we should go ahead and say so. One can openly disagree with others without disrespecting their views. During my fieldwork among the Asabano, a Papua New Guinea people who are enthusiastic Christians, I truthfully told them that I do not believe that Christianity or other religions are true, but that I am nevertheless interested in why they have found them convincing. We had a very amicable and productive exchange of views. Of course, we often disagree with the peoples among whom we work—we are culturally different. Mutual respect and friendship across cultural boundaries are possible, as any anthropologist knows. Cultural relativism serves well as a method to understand another's point of view, but, if used to limit our ability to make comparisons, generalisations, and scientific advances, it closes the mind it has only just opened.

Supernaturalism and the Imagination

Granted our right to draw etic conclusions from studies of emic experiences, the question remains as to whether the supernatural is really a product of the human mind. There appears to be little controversy that the imagination is heavily engaged in religious life, but are supernatural worlds made up? [James] Lett declares that, though many anthropologists are loath to admit it, we already know all religious beliefs to be false because they are not based on rationality or objectivity. I am in sympathy with his conclusion about the objective truth of religious beliefs; however, to write supernaturalism off as mere irrationality strikes me as unrealistic. Greenfield shows that, depending on people's knowledge, supernaturalism can offer a reasonable account for cures, and may actually help effect them. A community of believers can agree because they share experiences grounded in similarly biased perception, leading them to see what they expect to see.

Like naturalism, supernaturalism is normally based on rationally structured models of experiential evidence. Supernaturalism is distinctive in that it is based on extended, serious productions of what [Michele] Stephen calls the 'autonomous imagination', imagined realities that we do not recognise as our own inventions. The autonomous imagination, working with the volition schema, produces experiences of and belief in supernatural realms, as revealed in anthropological studies of dreaming. Supernaturalism builds wondrous mental models that could not result only from irrationality and subjectivity gone wild; religions have too much in common for that.

Some anthropologists have referred to spirits as non-empirical beings. Relationships with supernatural beings are central to religion, but these beings are not non-empirical; they are imaginary. The distinction is important, for while the imagination's creations need not accurately *portray* the reality that exists outside of the cogitating brain, they are *themselves* empirical phenomena in that human mental and motor behaviour can be studied scientifically.

Spirit beings are mental models of reality to which the imagination has granted volition. Spirits resemble the objectively real, but are clearly different. We cannot show our friends a spirit the way we can show them a rock. We cannot photograph spirits. Of course, showing a rock and saying it is *really* a spirit allows the listener to create a mental image partially based on the rock; but the imagination must also be invoked to give the rock life. Supernaturalistic models make scientific sense when we see them as arising from the imagination. This is why supernatural beings are often harder to see or touch, act at variance with our everyday knowledge of physics, and are so relevant to human fears and desires.

In so far as volition is a characteristic of humans, and spirits are imagined and related to as though they were people, anthropomorphism is a necessary component of supernatural models, but not all anthropomorphism is supernaturalistic. Non-supernaturalistic anthropomorphism recognises human-like qualities in the exterior or current form of an object that can be directly perceived with the senses, such as a bottle resembling a man in form or function. It includes playful, consciously metaphorical, and surface attributions of human-like qualities to the non-human. However, if one understands the anthropomorphised bottle to have sentience or to have been the result of an extra-biological volition, then one is engaging in supernaturalism. Supernatural anthropomorphism is long-lasting and serious (like the earnest belief among the Asabano that tree spirits are responsible for deaths), rather than brief misapprehensions (such as mistaking a sack for a person), or playful, purposeful fantasy anthropomorphism (like advertisements that endow products, such as Mr Clean cleanser, with human qualities).

Animism, however, defined as attributing spirits (foundational sentient agency) to materials, is by definition the stuff of supernaturalism. More depersonalised notions of mysterious power and meaning, known as *mana*, luck, or animatism—or reverence for persons, places, and things because of their history or symbolic significance . . . are not necessarily supernatural. There is a fine line between thinking that one is lucky because of personal circumstances, and attributing one's frequent success to a caring or powerful spirit. Likewise, a place can seem mystical because it evokes strong memories or feelings, with or without the additional notion that this indicates some kind of spiritual presence. Most of us probably cross the border between naturalism and supernaturalism several times each day.

The scientific theory that the supernatural is a natural product of the imagination is supported by the fact that spiritual experiences occur more easily in states of consciousness that allow the autonomous imagination greater play, such as trance and dreams. They also seem more plausible when socially supported: if everyone in the village says that witches are responsible for unfortunate events, witches come to seem very real indeed, as Evans-Pritchard discovered. The weight of tradition grants supernatural beings a veneer of objective reality. A community of believers can see the same spirit, not because it exists as an external being, but because all have similar imaginative hardware and tendencies, and shared instructions on what to picture.

The universality of spiritual experience indeed reveals that there is objective truth to the supernatural. That truth, however, is that the 'spirits' are found *inside* all our heads and not outside any of them. In the same way, all of us experience and can verify with one another that the earth appears to be flat, so it was not unreasonable when people made the jump to conclude that the earth is flat. This conclusion is wrong, of course, as an etic glance from above can show. The more distant perspective and the greater, but never perfect or absolute, objectivity it affords make it plainly visible that the universal experience of flatness, like that of supernaturalism, does reveal a more objective truth, and the truth is not what it first appeared. . . .

Recognising the Supernatural in Melanesia

Melanesians are sometimes characterised as lacking a supernatural concept (e.g., see Lampe). They are not alone in this. In this issue, White argues that supernaturalism can appear and disappear in the history of groups; Shorter notes that others do not divide the world into a supernatural/natural dichotomy; and Aragon points out that some peoples have imminent spiritualities and lack a transcendent supernaturalism in which events are understood to be miraculous. All these authors question the universality of the supernatural on an emic level, and therefore question its status as an etic category. It should be clear from my argument so far that I disagree with these positions in so far as they are using a definition of 'supernatural' similar to my own. I agree with Aragon that the notion of a miracle does not jibe with monistic worldviews but, as her paper makes very clear, even monists habitually apply the volition schema to nonliving things. The Tobaku do not perceive the spirits as miraculously breaking natural laws when they make the land fertile, but, in envisioning the land's fertility as coming from its spirit 'owners', they are attributing volition to something that does not, to the best current scientific knowledge, have it. Thus, by my definition of 'supernatural', Sulawesi highlanders are supernaturalists, but by Aragon's they are not. I prefer my own definition because it captures a universal human propensity that manifests itself within a range of variation.

I am clearly a lumper, while some of my colleagues are splitters, when it comes to categorising spiritual behaviours. To support my position that some lumping (as well as a clear definition) is called for in the case of supernaturalism, I wish to demonstrate that, even in a place that has been considered free of supernaturalism by excellent ethnographers, we can identify versions of the etic supernaturalism that I am at pains to argue exists. It is valuable to examine the bases on which claims of supernatural-free cultures are made. [Peter] Lawrence and [Mervin] Meggitt, for example, rightly note an interpenetration of spiritual and physical among Melanesian peoples. Elaborating, [Peter] Lawrence correctly states that 'gods, spirits, and totems were regarded as a real, if not always visible, part of the ordinary physical environment . . . described as more powerful than men but always as corporeal, taking human, animal, or insect form at will'. Based on these characteristics of Melanesian religions, he further describes them as lacking a concept of the supernatural. Yet what he is actually documenting is a conception of supernatural beings as not necessarily separate or ethereal, *not* a lack of supernaturalism per se. Then, somewhat contradictorily, he refers to these rather solid Melanesian spirits as 'non-empirical'.

Many Melanesian peoples believe that spirits can take physical form (*bodi devel* in Tok Pisin) rather than merely inhabiting an object. Kaluli, for example, consider birds to be dead people. Melanesians understand at least some spirits to be tangible and visible, so supernatural beings (volitional entities that are independent of brains and cause physical phenomena) *do* appear in their cosmologies. Stephen observes that Melanesian belief in physical spirits contradicts characterisations of Melanesian spirit beings as either non-empirical or unseen. Both believers and outsiders can verify birds' existence; it is the *significance* of physical phenomena that is disputed. To Kaluli, birds are really the dead, in spite of outer appearances. Interpreting birds as an expression of deceased human volition is supernaturalism. Ethnographers, unable to see the volition, but only its supposed physical manifestation, might conclude that the spirits themselves are non-empirical or unseen. However, even human volition originating in biochemical processes is not visible with the naked eye; only our skins and behaviours are.

Stephen reports that the Mekeo believe in a disembodied 'hidden self', perceived to leave the body in dreams. While avoiding the terms 'supernatural' and 'natural', Stephen identifies the main idiom in which Melanesians express the dichotomy: hidden vs. external realms. This accords closely with a large Melanesianist literature emphasising the religious role of secrecy and disclosure. To say something is hidden is not to say that it is invisible, ethereal, or non-empirical. A hidden thing, though usually obscured, can appear on occasion. The Asabano described certain beings and powers as hidden. Forest sprites, for example, called *wobuno* ('wild ones'), are alternatively called *balebaleno* ('those who hide'). Traditional Asabano religious knowledge was secret by definition. *Walemaw* means simultaneously secret and sacred. Asabano also believe the dead can become birds who may appear or hide. As reported widely in Melanesia, some Asabano felt at first contact that Whites were spirits: they had great technological and productive powers like the ancestors, and had been hidden until then.

Associated with the idea of hidden in Melanesia is the notion that interiors are more powerful and genuine than exteriors. Ngaing, for example, associate Whites with supernatural power because of their idea that interiors are light, while exteriors are dark. Ngaing discovered in dreams that the land of the Whites is really inside their own land. Inside themselves, they discover, they are white. I recorded an Asabano dream narrative in which the dreamer pulled down a zipper to reveal white skin underneath: an indication of what will happen in the afterlife. This interest in obscured interiors as the locus of the supernatural also resonates with widespread gender separation in Melanesia. Thus, men retain and fan their supernatural powers by isolating and hiding themselves, their rituals, and their sacra from women—a concern with 'purity' that makes sense when seen as an effort to maximise contact with hidden, supernatural interiors. The Telefol male's sacred net bag, for example, is covered with feathers to conceal the human bone sacra secreted inside from the profaning and withering female gaze.

While Melanesian worlds of inside and outside, of hidden and exposed, are deeply intertwined, they are nevertheless distinguished one from the other. Melanesians do not conceive of the distinction as non-empirical vs. empirical, or necessarily as ethereal vs. material or transcendental vs. immanent. Rather, they model the supernatural as a living inside truth, cause, and potential that, like the supernatural envisioned by transcendentalist Christians, is a volition that makes things happen, but is not always visible. Melanesians definitely recognise the supernatural as distinct from the natural, as I have defined the terms.

Conclusion

The natural/supernatural distinction is necessary for understanding religions, from both etic and emic points of view. From a scientific etic perspective, the distinction is between a physically perceived universe of ultimately non-volitional origins (the natural realm) and an imagined universe depicted as having ultimately volitional origins (the supernatural realm). The refined etic category 'supernatural' defines what ideal typical religions refer to, which all peoples, even those with an immanent spirituality, can recognise, but model differently.

All humans can use the volition schema to think about things. Scientists studying consciousness have to do the opposite and apply physical-chemical schemas to human minds in order to understand how physical matter can give rise to volition. You might find some of those same scientists believing in an afterlife. Klass's farmer, too, knows physical cause and effect: that rain must fall on his crops if they are to grow. He may also think that the ultimate reason the rain falls is because the guardian spirit of the field is pleased with his offering. The supernatural is real, but it is also imaginary, and, while prayer may move spiritual mountains, only work can move physical ones.

Supernaturalism attributes volition to things that do not have it; in this sense it is a kind of cognitive 'dirt'. [Mary] Douglas defines dirt as matter 'out of place', and explains the human fascination with purity as an effort to remove what cannot be placed into our categories. Similarly, the supernatural is *volition* out of place, and this in no small measure accounts for the human fascination with the anomalous idea of spirits. People strive to clean up dirt in order to make their environment 'conform to an idea'. In the realm of religion, however, they accomplish this same parity between ideal and physical worlds by projecting the supernatural—imagined volition out of place—onto the physical world.

Frederick P. Lampe

NO

Creating a Second-Storey Woman: Introduced Delineation Between Natural and Supernatural in Melanesia

Words matter. The use of the term 'supernatural' to describe social activities related to the ethereal maintains a dichotomy that may not be appropriate at this stage in the history of anthropology. I join Morton Klass in suggesting that the time has come to set aside the term 'supernatural', as we have other seemingly descriptive terms like 'race' and 'primitive'. Our continued distinction between natural and supernatural is problematic in that it is relatively easy to succumb to the temptation of labelling natural as real and supernatural as unreal.

In the 1980s, I spent 4 years as the Lutheran chaplain in and around the University of Technology in Lae, Papua New Guinea. The University of Technology, Unitech, was, at that point, one of two government-funded, degree-granting universities in Papua New Guinea. This paper considers the classificatory term 'supernatural' as it relates to men, women and housing at Unitech. The case in point involves the security arrangements for female students, the considered power of vaginal secretions, and the Enlightenment-driven, unilineal, evolutionary schema that contextualises economic and social development in Melanesia. Assuming there to be no natural reason to do otherwise, student living arrangements were organised by administrators without regard, or perhaps in spite of, social taboos prohibiting such things.

The question before us is the descriptive classification 'supernatural'. My argument suggests that on a macro-scale the propensity for anthropologists to impose imprecise distinctions, such as between natural and supernatural, for the sake of classificatory (etic) evaluation is akin to the colonial disregard for social practices and traditions. I contend that its continued use perpetuates an unhealthy power differential between researcher and subject. The use of supernatural retains elements of the colonial legacy that may not be particularly helpful or accurate.

The exploration, colonisation, and conversion of Melanesia by Europeans brought a highly segmented worldview into conflict with a largely cohesive collection of ideas about reality. The European propensity to distinguish between profane and sacred spheres effected a dichotomous differentiation between

From *Anthropological Forum*, vol. 13, no. 2, 2003, pp. 167–173. Copyright © 2003 by Taylor & Francis Journals. Reprinted by permission via Rightslink.

'natural' and 'supernatural' in Melanesia. Current higher education in Papua New Guinea reflects this distinction. Melanesian university students participate in a highly differentiated academic context representing a distinct and artificial social experience. An undifferentiated coalition of symbolic elements, with no distinction between supernatural and natural, is forced to contend with a highly differentiated system based upon a post-Enlightenment model of education.

I assume two things: the first is that the Enlightenment is the intellectual and cultural context for those who came to Papua New Guinea as colonisers; the second is that there is power associated with the sexual fluids of women within Melanesian society.

These two frame the subsequent structure for issues that surrounded student housing in the 1980s. The University's housing arrangements, like the intellectual climate of the Enlightenment, effected an artificial ordering of being. The culturally constructed explanation of women's power effects an unauthentic sense of what it means to be human in Melanesia. I join Shorter in this collection, suggesting that as interpreters of culture we must be cautious in our ethnographic reporting, so that we do not perpetuate power differentials through the use of distinctions that are no longer helpful or beneficial. The context of European contact and colonisation and the ontological nature of women vis-à-vis men force a false dichotomy between natural and supernatural. Klass (emphasis in original) observes the following regarding 'supernatural':

> that there is on the one hand a natural—real—universe, and on the other hand there are notions about aspects of the universe that are situated outside the natural and real and are therefore labeled supernatural by the person who *knows* what belongs in which category.

It must be noted that this analysis relies upon a very broad use of the term 'supernatural'. In *Miriam-Webster's collegiate dictionary,* Nature is defined, first, as 'the inherent character or basic constitution of a person or thing' and, second, 'as a creative controlling force in the universe', but neither of these really gets at what this debate is fundamentally about. The second definition of 'natural' states: 'a: being in accordance with or determined by nature b: having or constituting a classification based on features existing in nature'. 'Super' connotes something that is above or beyond. Thus, 'supernatural' refers to something above or beyond that which is a classification of features existing in nature. By using the term to distinguish one thing from another, we separate that which is united in the minds of those with whom we work. This separation is natural in the minds and socio-cultural experience of Europeans but not, perhaps, in the experience of others, specifically Melanesians.

As [Morton] Klass and [Maxine] Weisgrau, [Bengt] Sundkler and [Christopher] Steed and others have argued, the complex of symbols used by social groups was in constant flux. [Deborah] Gewertz and [Fred] Errington, [Donald] Tuzin, [Andrew] Lattas and others documented this creative reflexivity in their recent work in Melanesia. Thus, the introduction of a natural/supernatural dichotomy is one of many imported material and social elements that included technology, ideology and social practice. To suggest that colonial

incursion and influence represent a new phenomenon would discount precolonial experience in Melanesia. Change is not the point. Rather, it is the ways
in which Melanesians think about themselves, and organise and categorise
their universe. What is at issue here is the representation by social scientists
of the Melanesian experience. Klass and Weisgrau note: 'One of the most serious problems in the comparative study of religion is the ultimate tendency to
impose values and categories deriving from the anthropologist's culture upon
the one being studied.' This is at the core of my argument against applying a
macro-level classificatory term for the sake of etic clarity.

The Colonial Context

The Enlightenment played a significant role in the relationship that developed
between Melanesians and Europeans. Rationality was a dominant ideology underlying colonial attitudes up to and through 1975 Independence in Papua New
Guinea as the country negotiated nationhood and economic development. In its
pure form, Reason demanded dissociation from spirits, magic, and polluting
elements that were inextricably interwoven in the cultural complex of Melanesia.

Significant European contact on the eastern half of New Guinea began
in the mid-nineteenth century. The distinctions between sacred and profane,
supernatural and natural, religious and pagan, permeated life among the colonisers. The rationalised dissection of what had previously been undifferentiated meant that, in the minds of colonisers, a clear order of natural facts
existed. Understanding what happened in European colonies such as the Territories of Papua and New Guinea is as much about those who came expecting,
facilitating and forcing change as it is about the people who lived there. John
and Jean Comaroff have reflected on this as it relates to South Africa.

The symbolic systems of Melanesia were under significant pressure
to adapt to this incursion. The ways in which food was produced, illness
explained, healing facilitated, rites of passage practised, death explained, origins identified, and differences understood existed in a mass of cultural peculiarities. Spirits existed, power was recognised, and social organisation was
regulated. There was no distinction between the natural and the supernatural.
The ontological nature of men and women in society was defined within this
complex social structure. Each ethnic group had a distinct social construction
of gender, creating fluid yet distinct references about what it meant to be a
man or woman. These ontological constructions reflect distinct ideas about
human relationships, the world of spirits and power.

Women of Power in Melanesia

One cannot speak of a trans-Melanesian understanding of adult gendered relationships. Yet areas in which male cults were active include respect for the power
of the menstrual fluid of women, although the specificity of taboos surrounding female body fluid varies. [Polly] Wiessner and [Akii] Tumu suggest that 'the
idea that contact with menstruating females and menstrual blood is harmful to
men is widespread throughout the highlands'. General prohibitions are linked

to space and time. The preparation or handling of food, physical contact and specific sexual relations between men and girls once they have begun menses appear to be highly regulated. [Terence] Hays and [Patricia] Hays describe the Kwaasi initiation rite among the Ndumba as a time of realisation:

> It is only when a girl becomes a kwaasi that she discovers the extent of men's vulnerability and, because of it, the threat she represents to all. In the seclusion house and in subsequent life, a maturing woman learns that no man is immune to the forces she possesses. From the moment her menstrual blood begins to flow, the new responsibilities attendant upon being the custodian of a lethal weapon are placed squarely upon the initiate's shoulders.

When a woman is menstruating, she retires to the menstrual hut to protect the community. [Philip] Newman and [David] Boyd note that the initiation of Awa women includes warnings to:

> watch where they walk and sit and to be particularly careful in the handling and preparation of food. Menstrual blood is especially dangerous, they are told, and when the signs of a menstrual period appear, they must immediately go to the menstrual hut, [and] remain there until the flow stops.

The consequences of women ignoring these precautions include incapacitation and death for the men: the bones weaken, muscles atrophy and the body withers. Precautions include prohibition of food handling by women in menses, separate and distinct living arrangements, separated sleeping quarters or spaces, spatial orientation including physically higher male position (walking across slopes, within buildings, on ladders, elevations, and so on) and care of waste fluid.

[Mary] Douglas's hypothesis of inter-related symbolic systems of particular societies suggests that, in the case of women's sexual fluids, there appears to be a relationship between prohibitions and the structure of the wider society. More recently, [Thomas] Buckley and [Alma] Gottlieb suggest that menstrual prohibitions reflect the power of women over and against the danger they offer to society. Menstrual rules bring with them social arrangements that are desirable as well as problematic. [Marla] Powers proposes that, when individual rites (seclusion, for example) are taken in isolation 'rather than as a part of the dynamic whole', the result is 'misinterpretation'. Ritual seclusion thus must be viewed within the entire complex of the female life cycle—birth to menarche to death—all associated with creative birth power.

University Practicalities and Cosmological Constructions

The University's distinction between natural and supernatural, as embodied in housing arrangements, fostered an artificial systematic ordering of being and social order in Melanesia.

The University of Technology was founded in 1967, eight years before Independence. In the late 1980s, the faculty was largely expatriate, but the administration and support staff were Papua New Guinean. Unitech served the professional needs of a country that was then, and is now, emerging in global networks of economic trade and resource development. The training of engineers and professionals to work with national and transnational corporations with interests in gold, copper, silver, natural gas, timber, oil and fisheries was the central University mission.

In its early years, the student body was exclusively male. As a part of nation building, Papua New Guinea instituted countrywide educational opportunities for both boys and girls. The goal was to train Papua New Guinean professionals in the technical skills necessary to develop the country socially, politically and economically. These highly trained graduates were ultimately to replace imported expatriates. The student body was composed of men and women from much of Oceania. A Higher School Certificate from a National High School, awarded upon successful completion of Grade 12, was a prerequisite for entry.

Students who attended the University of Technology did so at the invitation of the PNG Department of Education. Papua New Guinea has, along with many former British colonies, adopted a national examination system in which a student's ability to continue beyond Grade 6 is determined through testing. In this land of over 700 languages, English is the language of education.

Female students at Unitech presented a security dilemma for the institution. With a student body that was predominantly male, there was an interest in protecting female students from attack or sexual assault. To this effect, female students were housed on the second floor of two cinderblock dormitories in 1986. Window bars and cyclone-fenced gates secured with heavy chains and padlocks secured these women each night. First-year male students were housed beneath their female counterparts.

The folklore of the campus indicated that this housing arrangement was intentional—upper-division students refused to be housed beneath women; first-year students did not have a choice. Informal interviews I conducted with first-year male students brought to light discomfort at living beneath women. In some cases, these students would sleep on the floor of upper-class male compatriots' dormitories for the duration of the year rather than stay in their own rooms. Upper-division students would regale others with stories about the lengths to which they and current students would go to avoid their housing assignments. Glee was evident in noting the consternation of newly arrived male students who discovered their dormitory arrangements. Upon the successful completion of their first year, male students then moved out to lodge-style dormitories on the outer perimeter of the campus.

The solution to women's security in the late 1980s included ignoring customary cautions regarding the power of highly charged female sexual fluids, and subjecting first-year male students to potential danger. Science, nature, and reason became the primary criteria for distinguishing between things considered to be true.

The Dilemma of Position

[Edward] Tylor speaks of the ritual practices and beliefs of the 'primitive' as parts of systems that are 'devised by human reason', in other words, of 'natural religions' as those that exist 'without supernatural aid or revelation'. He includes Christianity in this analysis. Belief systems are formed as part of a rational system of thought to make sense of the human place in the cosmos. This position appears to be at the heart of our dialogue here. To follow Tylor suggests that outsiders are able to explain what really occurs in religious systems (etic) vis-à-vis the explanations of participants (emic). In doing so, however, we risk denigrating that which is very real for the actors. At issue is power. In spite of an enlightened postmodern anthropological sensitivity to cultural contexts, distinctive phenomena, reflective positioning, and comparative inclinations, we have not moved far beyond Tylor. [Russell] McCutcheon notes that 'the Enlightenment provides the foundation of a strong outsider position in the study of religion', and goes on to suggest that the study of religion, rooted in the Enlightenment, 'consists in submitting the irrational aspects of human behavior to rational analysis'. Irrationality and rationality, however, exist only within the 'enlightened' etic perspective.

This differential analysis of an integrated system suggests that the human desire for synthesis is mistaken:

> [The Enlightenment's approach] has gone by such names as the scientific or the naturalistic study of religion. By 'naturalistic' one does not mean that this approach is more natural but simply that it presumes from the outset that religion is not *sui generis*, not a special case. Instead, it presumes that when religious people claim to have had supernatural experiences that defy rational explanation they are mistaken in some way.

In the attempt to synthesise the dichotomous relationship between natural and supernatural, European scholars seized upon ritual activity and accompanying mythological construction to define, organise and arrange their cosmos. The study of this language and activity is a recent project. As [Jonathan Z.] Smith (emphasis in original) notes: 'Simply put, the *academic study of religion is a child of the Enlightenment*'.

The issue of power is clearly present in this conversation as it relates to the category of supernatural. By continuing to use 'supernatural' as a classificatory term we perpetuate a false and imposed distinction. While the scientific minds thought they had solved the problem of providing security for arriving female students (their arrival being a significant step in itself), we anthropologists must avoid the temptation to shortcut cultural complexities by creating classifications that are imprecise and alien to the people with whom we work. The natural and supernatural are part of a cultural composite. In the case of housing and higher education in Papua New Guinea, the differentiation may only exist in our own minds.

The histories of both Melanesians and Europeans bring together ideas, practices, and constructions about what it means to be human. Such is the case with descriptive classificatory language that is introduced from without. As anthropologists, we may well be stuck with the awkward yet appropriate obligation of recognising and honouring the complex synthesis of human experience. By avoiding the use of a classificatory schema that perpetuates the positivist tendencies of the Enlightenment, we open the door for honest dialogue about the continual evolution of social experience. The indigenisation of the modern experience can, as a result, proceed with reflective analysis on the part of both insiders and outsiders, using common symbolic imagery that honours the whole.

EXPLORING THE ISSUE

Does the Distinction Between the Natural and the Supernatural Exist in All Cultures?

Critical Thinking and Reflection

1. What are the key features of the supernatural discussed in this issue? How is the supernatural related to religion?
2. What kinds of nonnaturalistic thinking do Americans participate in? Are these sufficient to demonstrate a belief in the supernatural in our society?
3. Is there a danger in using words like "primitive" or "supernatural" that undermines our understanding of people who think about the world differently from us?
4. Do Lampe and Lohmann really disagree that some irrational behaviors are based on assumptions about the world that are not empirical?

Is There Common Ground?

For nearly half a century, most anthropology textbooks have presented variations of Anthony F. C. Wallace's definition of religion as fact: beliefs and behaviors with regard to supernatural forces, power, and beings. Central to this definition is the concept of the supernatural. Both Lohmann and Lampe accept that the supernatural is an element typically identified by scholars as an element of religion.

But while this is a typical element in anthropological definitions of religion, two other definitions have been suggested that see religion from the perspective of a community's broader worldview, rather than some particular detail of that worldview like the supernatural. The first was suggested by anthropologist Clifford Geertz in his essay "Religion As a Cultural System." Geertz is less concerned with whether a community accepts that there are supernatural forces, but instead emphasizes that our cultural systems feel intensely real to us because they consist of symbolic elements that seem uniquely real. No matter how peculiar such symbolic elements—spirits, ghosts, gods, luck, good fortune, science, karma, or whatever—might seem to an outsider, they seem real and authentic to the members of the community.

About 20 years later, anthropologist Morton Klass picked up on essentially the same point in his book *Ordered Universes*. He stressed that the term "supernatural" seems to us fantastic, unreal, and unrealistic as in a fantasy or delusion. For Klass, as with Geertz, religion does not feel delusional to its practitioners, but feels authentic and realistic.

Klass's approach emerged from a theme that swept through anthropology beginning in the late 1960s. Many anthropologists challenged the use of many Western terms such as "primitive," "savages," and "barbarism" on the grounds that such terms were pejorative, and that they were based on an ethnocentric bias that prevented anthropologists from understanding other cultures. By the mid-1970s, some anthropologists suggested that even basic categories like kinship, politics, law, art, and religion need to be reexamined because they were based on the fundamental categories of Western societies that were not present in non-Western languages. The argument was that just because we find kinship, politics, or religion in America, there is no reason to believe that in radically different societies such as those in Africa, the Amazon, or New Guinea people understand or view their societies in these terms. Indeed, several of these abstract categories such as "art," "kinship," and "religion" have no indigenous terms in many societies. The debate presented here about the supernatural should be understood as emerging from these other debates.

These two essays cannot claim to have surveyed all societies, but merely give an example from some cases familiar to the authors. Nevertheless, these essays are useful in suggesting how scholars might approach the problem of the supernatural in human societies.

Additional Resources

The debate between Lohmann and Lampe appeared in a special issue of the journal *Anthropological Forum*, edited by Roger Ivar Lohmann (*Anthropological Forum*, vol. 13, no. 2, November 2003). This volume included eight other essays that take slightly different positions from the two in this issue.

Although Morton Klass's following book initiated one of the first debates discussing whether the supernatural is a universal human category, similar questions were raised about kinship by David M. Schneider in his following essay:

Klass, Morton. 1995. *Ordered Universes: Approaches to the Anthropology of Religion* Boulder, CO: Westview Press.

Schneider, David M. 1972. "What Is Kinship All About?" in *Kinship Studies in the Morgan Centennial Year*. Washington: Anthropological Society of Washington.

Several of the essays in this volume address similar concerns:

Klass, Morton and Weisgrau, Maxine K., eds. 1999. *Across the Boundaries of Belief* Boulder: Westview.

Earlier discussions of these topics would include:

Bird-David, Nurit. 1999. "'Animism' Revisited: Personhood, Environment, and Relational Epistemology," *Current Anthropology*, 40(Suppl), S67–S91.

Boyer, Pascal. 1994. *The Naturalness of Religious Ideas: A Cognitive Theory of Religion*. Berkeley: University of California Press.

Guthrie, Stewart. 1993. *Faces in the Clouds: A New Theory of Religion*. New York: Oxford University Press.

Kennedy, John S. 1992. *The New Anthropomorphism*. Cambridge: Cambridge University Press.

ISSUE 15

Is Conflict Between Different Ethnic Groups Inevitable?

YES: Sudhir Kakar, from "Some Unconscious Aspects of Ethnic Violence in India," in Veena Das, ed., *Mirrors of Violence: Communities, Riots, and Survivors in South Asia* (Oxford University Press, 1990)

NO: Anthony Oberschall, from "The Manipulation of Ethnicity: From Ethnic Cooperation to Violence and War in Yugoslavia," *Ethnic and Racial Studies* (November 2000)

Learning Outcomes

After reading this issue, you should be able to:

- Distinguish between the primordialist and circumstantialist perspectives on ethnicity and ethnic violence.
- Explain why some ethnic traits are more basic or primordial than others.
- Understand how circumstances can enhance or defeat cooperation across ethnic boundaries depending on the economic and political advantages of recognizing or denying ethnic and cultural differences.
- Discuss how the Indian case study presented by Sudhir Kakar draws on primordial ties.
- Explain how circumstances can change the importance of primordial ties like kinship, language, or religion.

ISSUE SUMMARY

YES: Indian social researcher Sudhir Kakar analyzes the origins of ethnic conflict from a psychological perspective to argue that ethnic differences are deeply held distinctions that from time to time will inevitably erupt as ethnic conflicts. Ethnic anxiety arises from preconscious fears about cultural differences. In his view, no amount of education or politically correct behavior will eradicate these fears and anxieties about people of differing ethnic backgrounds.

NO: American sociologist Anthony Oberschall considers the ethnic conflicts that have recently emerged in Bosnia to conclude that primordial ethnic attachments are insufficient to explain the sudden emergence of violence among Bosnian ethnic groups. He adopts a complex explanation for this violence, identifying circumstances in which fears and anxieties were manipulated by politicians for self-serving ends. It was only in the context of these manipulations that ethnic violence could have erupted.

Since the 1960s anthropologists and other social scientists have debated the causes, origins, and necessary conditions that led ethnic differences to erupt into ethnic violence. Such discussions have built on an older debate about the origins of ethnicity. In the earlier debate, two key positions emerged: the *primordialist* view in which ethnic attachments and sentiments emerge from the fact of being members of the same cultural community. Although cultural in origin, the primordialists saw kinship, language, and customary practices as the source of ethnic identity and social bonds between people of the same ethnicity. Ethnicity in this view was something one was born with, or at least born into, because it developed as one learned kinship, language, and culture. A second position, often called the *circumstantialist* perspective, was developed by the Norwegian anthropologist Fredrik Barth in his book *Ethnic Groups and Social Boundaries* (Little Brown, 1969). For Barth, a person's ethnicity was neither fixed nor a natural condition of his or her birth. One's ethnicity could be (and often was) manipulated under different circumstances. By dressing differently, by learning a different language, and by intermarriage, people in many ethnic groups could within a generation or two become members of another ethnic group and have a different ethnic identity. Later, if it became advantageous to be members of the first ethnic group, these same people could acknowledge their past and become members of the first group. Anthropologist Edmund Leach (*Political Systems of Highland Burma,* London School of Economics, 1954) described a similar case in highland Burma, where individuals shifted ethnic identity from Shan to Kachin and back again almost routinely as their circumstances and conditions changed.

Researchers in the United States have typically accepted the primordialist perspective, because ethnic differences in this country seem so difficult to alter or modify. For example, it is generally very difficult for an African American to "pass" as white. But in most parts of the world, ethnic differences are not readily marked by such obvious physical differences as in the United States, where ethnic differences are a historical byproduct of immigration from several distinct and distant places. In Malaysia, for example, non-Malays can become Malay simply by becoming Muslim, learning the Malay language, and adopting Malay dress and other daily practices.

These selections shift the ethnicity debate to the problem of whether ethnic conflict is inevitable. Sudhir Kakar uses a psychological approach to develop a primordialist argument to explain the frequent and almost continual problems of ethnic violence in India. For Kakar, ethnic sentiments and attachments emerge from deep psychological concerns at the unconscious or even pre-conscious level. He contends that psychologically there are primordial differences between Indians of different ethnic backgrounds and such differences lead to conflicts over access to resources, jobs, and the like.

Although Kakar's argument draws heavily on psychology, he clearly adopts a primordialist perspective that ethnic differences are inherently threatening. Such differences lead to tension and will ultimately emerge as conflict. Individuals may keep their fears and anxieties in check for the time being, but these preconscious fears and anxiety will eventually emerge. For him, no amount of education or politically correct training will eliminate these anxieties or permanently overcome them.

Anthony Oberschall considers possible explanations for the sudden appearance of ethnic conflict in the former Yugoslavia. He acknowledges that the primordialist variables of kinship, religion, and language may play some role in explaining why Serbs, Croats, and Bosnian Muslims behaved as they did once ethnic conflict broke out. These were traditional animosities that had existed for centuries in the Balkins, and they reemerged suddenly after 50 years of peace and cooperation. But such variables cannot explain why these groups started fighting with one another in the first place after nearly half a century of living together peacefully, regularly socializing, and even intermarrying with one another. Such ties as kinship, language, and religion do not explain why tensions flared up or why neighbors suddenly tried to eliminate people of other ethnic backgrounds from their towns and villages. Drawing on a complex pattern of circumstantial variables, Oberschall develops a circumstantialist model, arguing that politicians were manipulating local sentiments for their own ends. In the context of great uncertainty and crisis, people of all ethnic backgrounds bought into the anxieties suggested by their different leaders.

Oberschall's argument accepts the reality of primordialist variables such as kinship, language, and religion as more important than Fredrik Barth did in his original formulation of the circumstantialist perspective. But for Oberschall, such primordialist variables must be triggered by circumstantialist factors before they can be aroused. The Balkins case is a particularly apt one, as ethnicity in Bosnia is largely based on religious differences. All three "ethnic" communities have emerged from essentially the same pool of genetic material. The language spoken by all three groups is essentially the same language, often called Serbo-Croatian by linguists, though the Serbs use a Cyrillic alphabet and the Croats use a Roman one. The main "ethnic" differences emerge from their three different religions: Eastern Orthodox, Roman Catholic, and Islam. Religious differences in Bosnia correspond to traditional political alliances, but, as in the conflict in Northern Ireland they are not fundamentally based on significant biological or linguistic differences. In Bosnia, unlike Northern Ireland, people of all three ethnicities had lived and worked side by side for decades. In Sarajevo they socialized together, lived in the same apartment buildings, looked after one another's children, and had even intermarried. In Oberschall's view the primordialist variables are insufficient to trigger the ethnic violence and brutality that erupted in Bosnia. Ethnic violence, massacres, and ethnic cleansing could only have emerged if the sentiments and anxieties of people in the towns and villages were manipulated into fearing their neighbors.

As you read these selections, ask yourself what leads people to hate people of different ethnic backgrounds? Is it deeply held fears of cultural differences? Or, does conflict emerge because individuals fear losing what they have worked hard to obtain? How could people in Yugoslavia live together harmoniously for 50 years and then suddenly participate in the "ethnic cleansing" of their neighborhoods? Could the willingness to commit such acts of violence against neighbors have been suppressed for half a century by a strong central government? What is the source of this kind of group hatred, since differences in skin color and physical features are largely not present in either the Indian or Yugoslavian cases?

YES ⤶

Sudhir Kakar

Some Unconscious Aspects of Ethnic Violence in India

The need to integrate social and psychological theory in the analysis of cultural conflicts, i.e. conflicts between ethnic and religious groups, has long been felt while its absence has been equally long deplored. Though everyone agrees on the theoretical questions involved—how do these conflicts originate, develop, and get resolved; how do they result in violent aggression—a general agreement on the answers or even on how to get these answers moves further and further away.

A large part of the problem in the study of these questions lies with the nature of and the crisis within the social sciences. The declining fortunes of logical positivism, hastened in the last twenty years by the widespread circulation and absorption of the views of such thinkers as Gadamer, Habermas, Derrida, Ricouer and Foucault, has led to a plethora of new models in the sciences of man and society. The dominant model of yesteryears—social science as social physics—is now only one among several clamouring for allegiance and adherents. It incorporates only one view among many on the nature of social reality and of social science knowledge. Anthropology, sociology, political science, psychology and even economics are all becoming more pluralistic and scattering into frameworks. In such a situation, the calls for a general theory of ethnic violence or indeed (as Clifford Geertz has remarked) of anything *social,* sound increasingly hollow, and the claims to have one science seem megalomaniacal. Thus, without taking recourse to other disciplines and even ignoring the grand theories of human aggression in psychology itself—those of animal ethology, sociology, Freudian Thanatos and so on—I would like to present some limited 'local knowledge' observations on ethnic violence in India from a psychoanalytic perspective.

In the manner of a clinician, let me begin with the concrete data on which I base my observations on the first question, namely the origins of ethnic conflict. The data for these observations, and those which follow, come from diverse sources: spirit possession in north India, dreams of psychotherapy patients, eavesdropping on group discussions at the Golden Temple complex in July 1984, and finally, personal participation in large religious assemblies.

The Other in Ethnic Conflict

Some years ago, while studying the phenomenon of possession by spirits in rural north India, I was struck by a curious fact. In a very large number of cases, 15 out of 28, the *bhuta* or malignant spirit possessing Hindu men and women turned out to be a Muslim. When, during the healing ritual, the patient went into a trance and the spirit started expressing its wishes, these wishes invariably turned out to be those which would have been horrifying to the patient's conscious self. In one case, the Muslim spirit possessing an elderly Brahmin priest vigorously insisted on eating kababs. The five women surrounding the man who had engaged the *bhuta* in conversation were distinctly disheartened that he had turned out to be a *Sayyad* and one of them lamented: 'These Mussulmans! They have ruined our *dharma* but they are so strong they can withstand our gods.' In another case, the *bhuta* inhabiting a young married woman not only expressed derogatory sentiments towards her 'lord and master' but also openly stated its intentions of bringing the mother-in-law to a violent and preferably bloody end.

Possession by a Muslim *bhuta,* then, seemed to reflect the afflicted person's desperate efforts to convince himself and others that his hunger for forbidden foods and uncontrolled rage towards those who should be loved and respected, as well as all other imagined transgressions and sins of the heart, belonged to the Muslim destroyer of taboos and were furthest away from his 'good' Hindu self. In that Muslim *bhutas* were universally considered to be the strongest, vilest, the most malignant and the most stubborn of the evil spirits, the Muslim seemed to symbolize the alien and the demonic in the unconscious part of the Hindu mind.

The division of humans into mutually exclusive group identities of tribe, nation, caste, religion and class thus seems to serve two important psychological functions. The first is to increase the feeling of well being in the narcissistic realm by locating one's own group at the centre of the universe, superior to others. The shared grandiose self, maintained by legends, myths and rituals, seems to demand a concomitant conviction that other groups are inferior.

India has not been exempt from this universal rule. Whatever idealizing tendencies we might have in viewing our past history, it is difficult to deny that every social group in its tales, ritual and other literature, has sought to portray itself nearer to a purer, divine state while denigrating and banishing others to the periphery. It is also undeniable that sharing a common ego-ideal and giving one's own group a super-individual significance can inspire valued human attributes of loyalty and heroic self-sacrifice. All this is familiar to students of culture and need not detain us further here.

For the psychoanalyst it is the second function of division into ethnic groups, namely the need to have other groups as containers for one's disavowed aspects, which is of greater significance. These disavowed aspects, or the demonic spirits, take birth during that period of our childhood when the child, made conscious of good and bad, right and wrong, begins to divide himself into two parts, one that is the judge and the other that is being judged. The unacceptable, condemned parts of the self are projected outside, the projective processes being primitive attempts to relieve pain by externalizing it. The expelled parts of the self are then attached to various beings—animals and human—as well as to whole castes, ethnic and religious communities. This early split within our nature, which gives us a future license to view and treat others as if they were no better than the worst in ourselves, is normally completed by the time the child is six to seven years old. The earliest defenses for dealing with the unacceptable aspects of the self—namely their denial, the splitting from awareness and projection onto another group—require the active participation of the members of the child's group-parents and other adults who must support such a denial and projection. They are shared group defenses. The family and extended group of a Hindu upper-caste child, for instance, not only provides him with its myths and rituals which increase his sense of group cohesion and of narcissism in belonging to such an exalted entity, but also help him in elaborating and fleshing out his demonology of other ethnic and religious groups. The *purana* of the Muslim demon, for instance, as elaborated by many Hindu groups, has nothing to do with Sufi saints, the prophet's sayings or the more profound sentiments of Islam. Instead, its stories are of rape and pillage by the legions of Ghazni and Timur as well as other more local accounts of Muslim mayhem.

The Muslim demon is, so to say, the traditional container of Hindu conflicts over aggressive impulses. It is the transgressor of deeply-held taboos, especially over the expression of physical violence. Recent events in Punjab, I am afraid, are creating yet another demon in the Hindu psyche of north India. Over the last few years, tales of [Sikh militant leader] Bhindranwale's dark malevolence and the lore of murderous terrorists has led to a number of reported dreams from patients where Sikhs have appeared as symbols of the patient's own aggressive and sadistic superego. A group of Sikhs with raised swords chasing a patient who has broken into an old woman's shop, a Nihang stabbing a man repeatedly with a spear on the street while another patient as a frightened child looks down upon the scene from an upstairs window—these are two of many such dream images. Leaving aside the role played by these images in the patients' individual dramas, the projection of the feared aggressive parts of the self on the figure of the Sikh is an unhappy portent for the future relationship between the two communities. The fantasy of being overwhelmed by the frightening aggressive strength of the Sikhs can, in periods of upheaval and danger—when widespread regression in ego takes place and the touch with reality is weakened—lead to psychotic delusions about Sikh intentions.

Sikh Militancy

Until this point I have used some psychoanalytic, especially Kleinian, concepts of splitting and projective identification to understand data that bears on the question of ethnic conflict. More specifically, I have outlined the origins of certain pre-conscious attitudes of Hindus towards Muslims and Sikhs. These attitudes reflect the psychological needs of the child, and the adult, to split off his bad impulses, especially those relating to violence, and to attach them to other communities, a process supported and reinforced by other members of

the group. Let me now use another set of analytical concepts of group identity and narcissism, narcissistic hurt and rage, to understand the phenomenon
of Sikh militancy. To avoid any misunderstanding let me state at the outset
that I am primarily talking about the militant Sikh youth of Punjab, not of
all Sikh youths, and certainly not of the Sikh community as a whole. Also,
the word narcissism in psychoanalysis is not used in a pejorative sense but,
together with sexuality and aggression, as the third major and fundamental
motivational factor in human beings which is concerned with the mainte-
nance of self-esteem. The data for these observations comes from being an
observer of heated and anguished discussions among randomly formed groups
which were being spontaneously held all over the Golden Temple complex in
Amritsar, five weeks after Operation Blue Star.* Said elsewhere, the aftermath
of Blue Star, which heightened the awareness of their cultural identity among
many Sikhs, also brought out in relief one of its less conscious aspects. I have
called it the Khalsa warrior element of Sikh identity which, at least since the
tenth guru and at least among the Jats, has expressed itself in images of 'lifting
up the sword' against the 'oppression of a tyrannical ruler,' and whose associated legends only countenance two possible outcomes—complete victory
(*fateh*) or martyrdom (*shaheedi*) of those engaged in the battle. The surrounding society has of course reinforced this identity element over the years by
its constant talk of Sikh martial process and valour. The Sikh youth's acceptance of these projections of heroic militancy made by the Hindu can lead to
his overestimation of this aspect of his identity as he comes to feel that it is
his very essence. All other qualities which may compromise heroic militancy,
such as yearnings for passivity, softness and patience, will tend to be denied,
split off and projected onto other, despised groups. The damage done to the
Akal Takht—as much a symbol of corporate militancy as of religious piety—
reinforced the two M's—militance and martyrdom—the inner counterparts of
the well-known five K's which constitute the outer markers of the Khalsa warrior identity. The exaggerated value placed on martyrdom is hard to understand for Hindus since oppressors in their mythology—the Hindu equivalent
of Sikh legendary history—tended to be destroyed by divine intervention
rather than by the sacrifice of martyrs.

The army action was then a hurt to Sihk religious sentiments in a very
different way from the sense in which a Hindu understands the term. It was
an affront to group narcissism, to a shared grandiose self. The consequent feelings were of narcissistic hurt and rage. This was brought home to me again
and again as I listened to groups of anguished men and women in front of the
ruins of the Akal Takht. Most men stood in attitudes of sullen defeat, scorned
and derided by the women with such sentences as 'Where is the starch in your
moustache now?'

Given the collective need for the preservation of this core of the group identity, the Golden Temple action automatically completed a circle of associations.

---

* [Operation 'Blue Star' was the code name for the army action to clear the Golden Temple of
Sikh militants in June 1984, in which Bhindranwale died. The operation resulted in extensive
damage to the sacred site.—Ed.]

The army action to clear Akal Takht from desperadoes became an attack on the Sikh nation by a tyrannical 'Delhi durbar.' It was seen as an assault designed to wipe out all its traces, its *nishan*—since this is how it was in the past. The Sikhs killed in the attack were now defenders of the faith and martyrs—since this too is a pattern from the past. The encounter was viewed as a momentous battle, an oppressive empire's defeat of the forces of the Khalsa. The relatively heavy army losses are not a consequence of its restraint but a testimony to the fighting qualities of the Khalsa warrior. Paradoxically, the terrorist losses were exaggerated to simultaneously show the overwhelming strength of the army and the Khalsa readiness to die in martyrdom when victory is not possible.

Bhindranwale, in dramatically exemplifying the two M's of militancy and martyrdom, has touched deep chords. His status with much of the Sikh youth today is very near that of an eleventh guru. Initially, Bhindranwale may have been one of many *sants,* though more militant than most, who dot the countryside in Punjab. What began the process of his elevation was his successful defiance of the government—echoes, again of Sikh history, of defiant gurus contesting state authority. In setting the date and terms of his arrest ('*Santji* gave arrest,' and not 'He was arrested,' is how the people at the Temple complex put it), and predicting the day of his release, Bhindranwale began to be transformed from a mortal preacher to a 'realized' saint with miraculous powers. (And the reputation of being able to work miracles is, we know, essential for those aspiring to enter the portals of gurudom in all religious traditions.) His 'martyrdom' has now cemented the transformation and made his elevation into the Sikh militant pantheon irreversible. The tortures and murders in the Temple complex or outside are no longer his responsibility, being seen as the doings of deluded associates, acts of which Santji was, of course, unaware.

It is obvious that after the army action there was a threat to the cultural identity of at least a section of the Jat Sikh youth. This led to regressive transformations in the narcissistic realm, where reality is interpreted only as a balm to narcissistic hurt and as a coolant for narcissistic rage. It needs to be asked what precisely constituted this threat. I would tend to see the threat to the Jat Sikh group identity as part of a universal modernizing process to which many groups all over the world have been and continue to be exposed. This group though has preferred to change a social-psychological issue into a political one. The cultural decay and spiritual disintegration talked of in the Anandpur resolution are then viewed as an aspect of majority-minority relations rather than as an existential condition brought on by the workings of a historical fate. A feeling of inner threat is projected outside as oppression, a conflict around tradition and modernity as a conflict around power.

Narcissistic rage, then, is the core of the militancy of Sikh youth and Sikh terrorism. As Kohut says about this rage: 'The need for revenge, for righting a wrong, for undoing a hurt by whatever means, and a deeply anchored, unrelating compulsion in the pursuit of all these aims, gives no rest to those who have suffered a narcissistic injury.' For the analyst, this becomes paramount in the understanding of youthful militancy, the foreground, while political, social and other issues recede into the background.

Let me now make a few observations on the question of ethnic conflict resulting in violent aggression, i.e on mob violence. My data for these remarks is, paradoxically, personal participation in largely peaceful and loving groups engaged in religious and spiritual endeavours. Yet many of the psychological processes are common to the two kinds of groups. Both emotionally charged religious assemblies and mobs on the rampage bring out in relief the vulnerability of human individual ego functions confronted with the power of group processes. In the face of these, the 'integrity,' 'autonomy,' and 'independence' of the ego seem to be wishful illusions and hypothetical constructs. Mobs, more than religious congregations, provide striking examples of the massive inducement, by group processes, of individuals towards a new identity and behaviour of the sort that would ordinarily be repudiated by a great majority of the individuals so induced. They illustrate, more clearly than in any other comparable social situation, the evanescence of rational thought, the fragility of internalized behavioural controls, values, and moral and ethnical standards.

The most immediate experience in being part of a crowd is the sensual pounding received in the press of other bodies. At first there may be a sense of unease as the body, the container of our individuality and the demarcator of our boundaries in space, is sharply wrenched away from its habitual way of experiencing others. For, as we grow up, the touch of others, once so deliberately courted and responded to with delight, increasingly becomes a problem. Coming from a loved one, touch is deliciously welcomed; with strangers, on the other hand, there is an involuntary shrinking of the body, their touch taking on the menacing air of invasion by the other.

But once the fear of touch disappears in the fierce press of other bodies and the individual lets himself become a part of the crowd's density, the original apprehension is transformed into an expansiveness that stretches to include others. Distances and differences—of class, status, age, caste hierarchy—disappear in an exhilarating feeling that individual boundaries can indeed be transcended and were perhaps illusory in the first place. Of course, touch is only one of the sensual stimuli that hammers at the gate of individual identity. Other excitations, channelled through vision, hearing and smell, are also very much involved. In addition, there are exchanges of body heat, muscle tension and body rhythms which take place in a crowd. In short, the crowd's assault on the sense of individuality, its invitation to transcend one's individual boundaries and its offer of a freedom from personal doubts and anxieties is well nigh irresistible.

The need and search for 'self-transcending' experience, to lose one's self in the group, suspend judgement and reality-testing, is, I believe, the primary motivational factor in both religious assembly and violent mob, even though the stated purpose is spiritual uplift in one and mayhem and murder in the other. Self-transcendence, rooted in the blurring of our body image, not only opens us to the influx of the divine but also heightens our receptivity to the demonic. The surge of love also washes away the defences against the emergence of archaic hates. In psychoanalytic terms, regression in the body image is simultaneous with regression in the superego system. Whether the ego reacts to this regression in a disintegrated fashion with panic that manifests itself (in a mob) in senseless rage and destructive acts—or in a release of love encompassing the group and the world outside—depends on the structure provided to the group. Without the rituals which make tradition palpable and thus extend the group in time by giving assurances of continuity to the beleaguered ego, and without the permanent visibility of leaders whose presence is marked by conspicuous external insignia and who replace the benign and loving functions of the superego, religious crowds can easily turn into marauding mobs. Transcending individuality by merging into a group can generate heroic self-sacrifice but also unimaginable brutality. To get out of one's skin in a devotional assembly is also at the same time to have less regard for saving it in a mob.

Some Implications

The implications of my remark, I know, are not too comforting. The need for communities, our own to take care of our narcissistic needs and of others to serve as recipients for our hostility and destructiveness, are perhaps built into our very ground-plan as human beings. Well meaning educative efforts in classrooms or in national integration seminars are for the most part too late and too little in that they are misdirected. They are too late since most of the evidence indicates that the communal imagination is well entrenched by the time a child enters school. They are misdirected in that they never frankly address the collective—and mostly preconscious—fears and wishes of the various communities. Demons do not much care for 'correct' interpretations of religious texts by scholars, nor are they amenable to humanist pleas of reason to change into good and loving beings. All we can do is accept their existence but reduce their potential for causing actual physical violence and destruction. The routes to this goal, the strategies for struggle with our own inner devils, are many. One strategy strives for the dissolution of small group identities into even large entities. Sikhs and Hindus in Punjab can move towards a group identity around 'Punjabiyyat,' in which case the despised demon shifts outside to the *Purubia* or the *Madrasi*. One can go on to progressively larger identities of the nationalist Indian whose *bete-noire* can then be the Pakistani or the Chinese. One can envisage even larger groupings, for instance of the 'Third World,' where the sense of narcissistic well being provided by this particular community needs a demonic West as the threatening aggressor.

A second strategy is, in a certain sense, to go the opposite way. By this I mean less the encouragement of various ethnic identities than in ensuring that all manifestations of ethnic group action—assemblies, demonstrations, processions—are given as much religious structure as possible in order to prevent the breakout of archaic hate. Vedic chants and Koranic prayers, *mahants, pujaris* and *mullahs* in their full regalia and conspicuous by their presence, are fully encouraged to be in the forefront of religious processions and demonstrations. Traditional religious standards, flags and other symbols are liberally used to bind the religious assemblies.

Yet another strategy (and let me note that none of these are exclusive) is to concentrate all efforts at the containment of the communal demon on the dominant community. We know that the belief of the dominant party in a relationship often becomes a self-fulfilling prophecy, involuntarily changing the very consciousness of the weaker partner. In India the Hindu image of himself and of other communities is apt to be incorporated in the self image of non-Hindu minorities. Even when consciously accepted, the denigrating part of the image is likely to be a source of intensive unconscious rage in other communities. Their rage is stored up over a period of time, till it explodes in all its violent manifestations whenever historical circumstances sanction such eruptions.

Anthony Oberschall

The Manipulation of Ethnicity: From Ethnic Cooperation to Violence and War in Yugoslavia

Four views on ethnicity and ethnic violence are common. In the 'primordial' view, ethnic attachments and identities are a cultural given and a natural affinity, like kinship sentiments. They have an overpowering emotional and non-rational quality. Applied to the former Yugoslavia, the primordialist believes that despite seemingly cooperative relations between nationalities in Yugoslavia, mistrust, enmity, even hatred were just below the surface, as had long been true in the Balkans. Triggered by fierce competition for political power during the breakup of Yugoslavia and driven by the uncertainties over state boundaries and minority status, these enmities and hatreds, fuelled by fear and retribution, turned neighbour against neighbour, and district against district, in an expanding spiral of aggression and reprisals. Although the primordial account sounds plausible, and it is true that politicians activated and manipulated latent nationalism and ethnic fears, some evidence contradicts it. Ethnic cleansing was more commonly militias and military against civilians than neighbour against neighbour. In seventeen assaults against villages during the ethnic cleansing of Prijedor district in Bosnia in May/June 1992, we found that the aggressors wore military and paramilitary uniforms and insignia. In fourteen assaults, the survivors did not recognize any of the aggressors, who did not bother to wear masks or disguises. These 'weekend warriors' from central Serbia openly bivouacked at the Prijedor police station. The primordial theory omits the fact that ethnic hatreds can subside as a consequence of statecraft and living together. [President Charles] de Gaulle and [Chancellor Konrad] Adenauer managed to reconcile the French and German people. Why no lasting conciliation in Yugoslavia after forty years of ethnic peace?

In the second, 'instrumentalist' view, ethnic sentiments and loyalties are manipulated by political leaders and intellectuals for political ends, such as state creation. For Yugoslavia, the instrumentalist explanation highlights Serb nationalists' goal of a Greater Serbia, and a similar Croat nationalism. Ethnic cleansing resulted from a historical longing by Serbs in Croatia at first backed moderate nationalists, for a Greater Serbia, with deep cultural roots. [Slobodan] Milosevic and Serb nationalists tried to implement it when the opportunity

From *Ethnic and Racial Studies* by Anthony Oberschall, November 1, 2000, pp. 982–999.

arose in the late 1980s and early 1990s. Greater Serbia required ethnic cleansing of non-Serbs from areas inhabited by a majority of Serbs and the corridors linking Serb population clusters. Although there is evidence that ethnic cleansing was a state policy, orchestrated by the highest authorities in Serbia and the Bosnian Serb leadership, this explanation ignores that many Bosnian Serbs did not want secession, that many Serbs in Croatia at first backed moderate nationalists, and that many Serbs evaded the draft. The instrumentalist view assumes an ethnic consensus that initially does not exist. But if many were reluctant to wage war and to participate in ethnic cleansing, how did ethnic extremists prevail over these moderates?

The third 'constructionist' view of ethnicity and ethnic conflict was originally formulated by [Leo] Kuper. It supplements the insights of the primordial and of the instrumentalist views. Religion or ethnicity are very real social facts, but in ordinary times they are only one of several roles and identities that matter. There is a great deal of variance in a population on ethnic attachments and identities. In the words of [Juan J.] Linz and [Alfred] Stepan 'political identities are less primordial and fixed than contingent and changing. They are amenable to being constructed or eroded by political institutions and political choices.' The constructionist view offers insights but is incomplete. How are nationality and ethnicity constructed and eroded by political mobilization and mass media propaganda?

A fourth model of ethnic violence centres on state breakdown, anarchy, and the security dilemma that such conditions pose to ethnic groups who engage in defensive arming to protect their lives and property against ethnic rivals, which then stimulates arming by other ethnic groups like an arms race between states. The driving motivations are not ethnic hatreds but fear and insecurity. In the Yugoslav crisis Michael Ignatieff puts it thus:

> Once the Yugoslav communist state began to split into its constituent national particles the key question soon became: will the local Croat policeman protect me if I am a Serb? Will I keep my job in the soap factory if my new boss is a Serb or a Muslim? The answer to this question was no, because no state remained to enforce the old ethnic bargain.

There is a security dilemma in ethnic conflict, but why so much ethnic violence without state breakdown? Can insecurity and fear be spread by propaganda even when daily experience contradicts the allegations of ethnic hostility and threat? Can the powerful fear the weak?

Building on the four views and mindful of [Rogers] Brubaker and [David] Laitin's criteria for a satisfactory theory of ethnic violence, I use the idea of latent nationalism at the grass roots, and show how it was activated; I highlight ethnic manipulation by political leaders, and explain why manipulation was successful; I take into account the variance in ethnic identities and analyse why extremists prevailed over moderates; I focus on the security dilemma and ethnic fears and insecurity, and show how fears and insecurity grew from lies and propaganda. To this arsenal of concepts and models for generating the dynamics of ethnicization and collective violence, I add 'cognitive frames.' Combining all, I seek to explain how forty years of cooperative ethnic relations ended with collective violence and war.

Prijedor: A Case-Study

To get a sense of what is to be explained about ethnic conflict and violence at the grass roots, consider the Prijedor district in Northwest Bosnia where major ethnic violence took place in the spring of 1992. In the 1991 Census, Prijedor district was 42.5 percent Serb and 44 percent Muslim. It was surrounded by districts that had either a slight Serb majority or were close to even, as Prijedor was. Prijedor Serbs were not an isolated Serb minority island surrounded by a sea of Muslims and Croats.

There had been no Serb complaints of mistreatment, discrimination, or intimidation in Prijedor by non-Serbs, or vice versa. On the contrary, as a bewildered Muslim refugee from Prijedor stated:

> In Prijedor there were no conflicts between nationalities. We didn't make the distinctions. My colleague at work was an Orthodox Serb, we worked together. When we were children we went to the Orthodox church or the mosque together . . . I don't understand. Before there were never any problems between us. We lived together. My sister is married to a Serb, and a brother of my wife is married to a Croat.

According to the [United Nations] Bassiouni Report, Serbs held the leading positions in Prijedor in 1991, as they had done for decades. . . . In the 1991 elections, the predominantly Muslim SDA [Party of Democratic Union in Bosnia] won thirty seats; the Serb SDS [Serbian Democratic Party] twenty-eight, and thirty-two went to other parties. The Muslims refrained from taking over a number of leading posts to which their electoral victory entitled them because they believed in power-sharing. Even so, the SDS blocked the work of the Prijodor Assembly and organized a parallel governance for Serbs, in alliance with the SDS leaders in nearby Banja Luka. In Bosnia as a whole, the Serbs shared political power and controlled the most important military forces.

As in other towns and cities in Bosnia, the SDS in Prijedor organized a successful Serb plebiscite for Greater Serbia. A parallel Serb governance, called the 'Crisis Committee,' secretly created an armed force of Serbs with weapons obtained from Serbia. Serb crisis committees were also formed among Serbs in some of Prijedor district's towns and villages. On the night of 29 April 1992, without any provocation or a shot being fired, 1,775 well-armed Serbs seized the city of Prijedor in a *coup d'état*. By this time the Prijedor local government had completely lost power to various Serb groups. Paramilitaries had seized the radio and television transmitters and cut off all but Serb transmissions. The Serb *coup d'état* in Prijedor is similar to what happened elsewhere in Northern Bosnia.

Non-Serb leaders were arrested and shortly afterwards disappeared, presumed executed. The Muslim police and other officials were fired from their posts. Schools closed; the newspaper ceased publication, and a Serb paper was started. Non-Serbs were harassed, intimidated, fired from their jobs. Amid incessant house searches, weapons, mostly hunting guns, belonging to non-Serbs, were rounded up. After the attempt on 30 May by the Patriotic League of Croats and Muslims—an armed formation of 150 fighters—to retake the old city, many non-Serb inhabitants were arrested and sent to the infamous Omarskca camp. At Omarska, prisoners were tortured, brutalized, starved and killed. The guards were rural Serbs from nearby villages; the interrogators were Prijedor police inspectors. . . . People were rounded up and some were executed: those shot were Muslim leaders whose names appeared on a list. Atrocities took place elsewhere in the district.

Several observations should be made about the events in Prijedor. Muslims and Serbs had lived in peace before the conflict erupted. The Serbs were neither a numerical minority, nor discriminated against. They not only had a share of power, but they had the biggest share, and they were well armed. Why, then, did Serbs fear their fellow citizens in Prijedor? A cartoon from this period expresses the puzzle well. It shows a bearded Serb paramilitary, armed to the teeth, with guns, hand-granades, ammunition belts, knives, waving a machine gun, looking worried, and yelling at the top of his voice, 'I am being threatened!' There was no anarchy, no state breakdown in Prijedor. The Serbs used the police and military of a functioning government to subdue the non-Serbs. Serbs may have been apprehensive about their future in an independent Bosnia, but even in Bosnia they had a big presence—numerical, military, political, economic. There was no spontaneous violence initiated by Serb civilians against non-Serbs, nor vice-versa. Instead, there was a highly organized, secretly prepared *coup d'état*, like the 1917 Bolshevik seizure of power in Russia. . . . As in the Russian revolution with the Soviets, the Serb parallel government was not only an instrument for seizing power from non-Serbs but of stripping the moderate Serbs of any influence and authority.

What was the reaction of ordinary Serbs to these events? Though there is no information on Prijedor itself, one can learn from what observers recorded in nearby Banja Luka. Peter Maas reports that a Serb lawyer there estimated that 30 percent of Serbs oppose such things [ethnic cleansing], 60 percent agree or are confused and go along with the 10 percent who 'have the guns and control the television tower.' . . . An armed, organized 10 percent who control mass communications can have its way when the majority supports it overtly or tacitly or is confused, and when the opposition is unorganized, divided, and scared. One has to explain how it was that 60 percent were supportive of or confused on ethnic cleansing, since their support and quiescence were necessary for the success of the extremist 10 percent.

Was Violent Conflict Inevitable?

In a multinational state such as Yugoslavia, nationality will be a salient dimension of political contention, and there will be leaders and intellectuals with a nationalist ideology and agenda. The Yugoslav constitution and its political institutions were delicately balanced and crafted to deal with nationality. A nationalist challenge would inevitably zero in on stateness, minority rights and power-sharing: if accepted boundaries of political units are renegotiated or remade, who decides which peoples and territories belong to new and old political entities? Will all peoples in the new units be equal citizens for governance, or will majority ethnonational affiliation become the admission ticket for full citizenship?

Once unleashed, nationalism in Yugoslavia set on a collision course the two largest nationalities, the Serbs and the Croats. With a quarter of Serbs living outside Serbia; a centralized Yugoslav state was a guarantor of Serb security. For Croats and their history of opposition to Hapsburg rule, a decentralized state and weak federation meant control of their own destinies, unencumbered by inefficient state agencies and enterprises staffed and controlled by Serbs. Nevertheless, nationality issues could have been sorted out with democratic institutions in a confederation, with collective rights for minorities, and with systems of political representation in elections and collective decision rules in assemblies that would protect minority voice and favour coalitions rather than majority domination. With these reforms, nationalist leaders would have found it difficult to rally the citizenry to their cause.

In a country with great differences in economic development and standards of living between the Republics, there will be disagreements over economic policies, taxation, transfer, subsidies across regions, and abandoning socialism for a market economy. All Republics had experienced dramatic economic gains since World War II. Yugoslavia was not beyond economic repair.

As in other communist states in the late 1980s, the Yugoslav communist leaders wanted to remain in power. Some reprogrammed as reform communists, and hoped to move into European-style social democracy. Others chose ethnonationalism as the issue that would carry them to power and create a new principle of legitimacy for the post-communist regime. Moderate nationalists stood for conciliation among nationalities; extremists were willing to pursue their goals with force and violence. The defeat of the moderates was not inevitable. Why did xenophobic nationalism resonate with the citizenry? How is it that when the media unleashed the war of words and symbols before the war of bullets, so many believed the exaggerations, distortions and fabrications that belied their personal experiences?

Ethnic Relations Before the Crisis

Survey research on ethnic relations in mid-1990 found that in a national sample of 4,232 Yugoslavs, only 17 percent believed that the country would break up into separate states, and 62 percent reported that the 'Yugoslav' affiliation was very or quite important for them. On ethnonational relations, in workplaces, 36 percent characterized them as 'good,' 28 percent as 'satisfactory,' and only 6 percent said 'bad' and 'very bad.' For ethnonational relations in neighborhoods, 57 percent answered 'good,' 28 percent 'satisfactory,' and only 12 percent chose 'bad' and 'very bad.' For the majority of Yuogoslavs, on the eve of the Yugoslav wars, nationalist contention in the public arena did not translate into hostile interpersonal ethnic relations. . . .

Ignatieff is puzzled, 'What is difficult to understand about the Balkan tragedy is how . . . nationalist lies ever managed to take root in the soil of shared village existence. . . . In order for war to occur, nationalists had to convince neighbors and friends that in reality they had been massacring each other since time immemorial.'

The Manipulation of Ethnicity

For explaining ethnic manipulation one needs the concept of a cognitive frame. A cognitive frame is a mental structure which situates and connects events, people and groups into a meaningful narrative in which the social world that one inhabits makes sense and can be communicated and shared with others. Yugoslavs experienced ethnic relations through two frames: a normal frame and a crisis frame. People possessed both frames in their minds: in peaceful times the crisis frame was dormant, and in crisis and war the normal frame was suppressed. Both frames were anchored in private and family experiences, in culture and in public life. In the normal frame, which prevailed in [Josip Broz] Tito's Yugoslavia, ethnic relations were cooperative and neighbourly. Colleagues and workers, schoolmates and teammates transacted routinely across nationality. Some did not even know or bother to know another's nationality. Intermarriage was accepted. Holidays were spent in each others' Republics. Except in Kosovo, the normal frame prevailed for most Yugoslavs throughout the 1980s.

The crisis frame was grounded in the experiences and memories of the Balkan wars, the first and second world wars—and other wars before that. In these crises, civilians were not distinguished from combatants. Old people, children, women, priests were not spared. Atrocities, massacres, torture, ethnic cleansing, a scorched-earth policy were the rule. Everyone was held collectively responsible for their nationality and religion, and became a target of revenge and reprisals. . . .

Tito had wanted to eradicate the crisis frame, but it simmered in the memories of older people, the families of victims, intellectuals and religious leaders. Milosevic, Tudjman and other nationalists did not invent the crisis frame; they activated and amplified it. . . .

If the normal frame prevailed in the 1980s as shown by . . . survey findings, how did nationalists activate and amplify the crisis frame after decades of dormancy? The emotion that poisons ethnic relations is fear: fear of extinction as a group, fear of assimilation, fear of domination by another group, fear for one's life and property, fear of being a victim once more. After fear comes hate. The threatening others are demonized and dehumanized. The means of awakening and spreading such fears in Yugoslavia were through the newsmedia, politics, education, popular culture, literature, history and the arts.

The crisis frame in Yugoslavia was first resurrected by Serb intellectuals over the plight of the Kosovo Serbs. . . .

Fear of extinction was spread with highly inflated figures on the ethnic killings in World War II. . . .

In my interview with a Serb refugee one can trace how the atrocities discourse switched on the crisis frame: 'We were afraid because nationalists revived the memory of World War II atrocities . . . nationalist graffiti on walls awakened fears of past memories; it was a sign that minorities [Serbs in Croatia] would not be respected and safe.'

Fears of domination, oppression and demographic shrinkage were roused by the incessant rape and genocide discourse. . . .

Ordinary people echo the intellectuals' and the media crisis discourse. . . . Peter Maas asks a Serb refugee couple why they had fled their village. Their answer: Muslims planned to take over, a list of names had been drawn up, Serb women were to be assigned to Muslim harems after the men had been killed. They had heard about it on the radio; the Serb military had uncovered the plan. The journalist probes: 'Did any Muslims in the village ever harm you?' They reply, 'Oh no, our relations with the Muslims in the village were always good, they were decent people.' In the minds of the Serb couple, the crisis frame had eclipsed the normal frame. What under peaceful circumstances were totally implausible events—young women become sexual slaves in harems for breeding janissaries; a fifteenth- and sixteenth-century style Turkish/Islamic invasion of Europe—become credible narratives of ethnic annihilation and domination within the crisis frame.

Fear and the crisis frame provided opportunities for nationalists to mobilize a huge ethnic constituency, get themselves elected to office, and organize aggressive actions against moderates and other ethnics. . . .

Populist nationalism worked. The Vojvodina and Montenegro party leaderships resigned and were replaced by Milosevic loyalists. Abolishing the autonomous provinces of Kosovo and Vojvodina precipitated a constitutional crisis. . . . The nationality balance in Yugoslav politics was thus disturbed. Serbia gained control of over half the votes in all federal bodies and institutions. Slovenes and Croats reacted with their own nationalism.

There was grass-roots resistance to nationalism and to activation of the crisis frame. A content analysis of news stories in *Oslobodjenje* for 1990 indicates that municipalities, youth and veterans' organizations, and trade unions repeatedly protested against ethnic polarization and hatreds. . . . Important as this opposition was, it was countered by the spread of populist nationalism. *Oslobodjenje* in 1990 is full of affirmations of national symbols and identities: the renaming of localities; the reburial of bones of atrocity victims from World War II; nationalist graffiti on churches, mosques, monuments and in cemeteries; fights over flags, ethnic insults, nationalist songs, ethnic vandalism. To many, these were signs that normal times were sliding into crisis, and the authorities had lost control.

Mass communications and propaganda research help to explain why ethnic manipulation worked and why the crisis frame eclipsed the normal frame. First, . . . fear arousing appeals, originating in a threat, were powerful and effective in changing opinion and belief. Furthermore, the most important reaction to fear is removing the source of threat, precisely what nationalists were promising to do in Yugoslavia. Second, studies of propaganda routinely find that repetition is the single most effective technique of persuasion. It does not matter how big the lie is, so long as it keeps being repeated.

Third, much of what we know is vicarious knowledge and not based on personal experience. We accept the truths of authorities and experts whom we respect and who have socially recognized positions and titles. Who could really tell or check how many Serbs had been massacred by Ustasha? Fourth, outright falsehoods were common and intentional. According to a media analyst, 'In Serbia and Croatia, TV fabricated and shamelessly circulated war crime stories . . . the same victims would be identified on Zagreb screens as Croat, on Belgrade screens as Serb.' . . .

Fifth, mass communications studies of the two-step flow of communication show that in ordinary circumstances crude propaganda from 'patriotic journalism' is discounted because people are exposed to a variety of broadcast messages and because they check media messages against the beliefs and opinions in their social milieus in interpersonal relationships and conversations. Ethnic crisis politics breaks down the two-step flow. . . .

Nationalists Win the 1990 Elections

Second only to the mass media wars for the revival of the crisis frame were the 1990 elections. Every town and city experienced the founding of political parties, often at a huge rally in a public building or a sports stadium, during which speaker after speaker gave vent to exaggerated nationalist rhetoric and hostile pronouncements and attacks against other nationalities. . . .

Nationalists persuaded voters not to 'split the ethnic vote' but to vote as a bloc for the nationalists because the other nationalities would bloc-vote and gain power. Bloc-voting became a self-fulfilling prophecy. . . . The politicians elected were more nationalist than their voters. . . .

Repression of Minorities and Moderates

The demise of the moderates was due to a combination of electoral defeats, loss of credibility about being effective in a crisis, and intimidation and threats from extremists. . . .

The nationalist winners purged their ethnic opponents and moderates of their own nationality from party and state positions. The targets were sent anonymous threat letters, were fired from their jobs, forced into military service, charged with treason, subversion and plotting armed rebellion, and subject to office and house searches for weapons, radio transmitters and 'subversive' literature. . . . In a Bosnian example reported by [Tadeusz] Mazowiecki, 'According to a witness [from Bosanska Dubica], the elected authorities who were moderates and who tried to prevent acts of violence were dismissed or replaced by Serbian extremists.'

Other methods were cruder. . . . Ordinary people could not escape ethnic polarization. In an interview a Serb taxi driver explained: 'No one wanted the coming war, but if I don't fight, someone from my side [Serb] will kill me, and if my Muslim friends don't fight, other Muslims will kill them.'

The overthrow of moderates by extremists or radicals is well known in the great revolutions: Girondins were overthrown by the Jacobins in the French revolution and all groups were overthrown by the Bolsheviks in the Russian revolution. The means of seizing power are similar. The radicals create parallel governance to the state and come to exercise *de facto* authority in many institutions, and militias and mutineers execute a *coup d'état*. Then the remaining moderates are purged. It happens in ethnic violence as well. It did so in the mixed ethnic districts of Croatia and Bosnia, and it happened in Prijedor.

Militias Take Over

Militias and paramilitaries roamed far and wide and perpetrated ethnic cleansing, massacres, atrocities and other war crimes, as in the Prijedor district. . . .

Militiamen were not necessarily fanatics filled with hatred to start with. [Tim] Judah described how a Serb militiaman got recruited by his peers from the local SDS who pressured him for weeks: 'We've all got to take up arms, or we'll disappear from here.' He had Muslim and Croat friends. Would they protect him against extremists of all nationalities? Not likely, if it got violent. So he 'took out a gun.' Peer pressure, fear, not only of Muslims but of extremist Serbs who might finger him as a 'traitor,' were the major reasons for joining a militia. Some of these men were unemployed and expected a job in the coming Serb government as militia or police.

Once the young man 'took out a gun' he became encapsulated in a quasimilitary unit subject to peer solidarity and ethnic loyalty. He was trained in weapons and indoctrinated with the beliefs and norms of the crisis frame about other ethnics:

a. *Collective guilt:* 'They' act in unison; children grow into adults; women give birth to future warriors; even old people stab you from behind; 'they' will never change.
b. *Revenge and retaliation:* 'They' massacred 'us' in the past, and are about to do it again, in fact they have already started. A setting of scores is justified; an eye for an eye.
c. *Deterrence/first strike:* Disable them before they strike, which is what they are about to do, despite appearances, because they are secretive and treacherous.
d. *Danger/survival:* These are extraordinary times, one's entire nationality is threatened, and extreme measures are justified.
e. *Legitimacy:* Ordinary people and militias are justified in taking extreme measures because the constituted authorities have not come to the defence of our people.

These are the rationalization and the justifying norms for unrestrained, collective, ethnic violence. Other motives for collective violence were economic gain, peer pressure and lack of accountability. From being an ordinary man in normal times the militiaman changed into being a killer at crisis times.

The Bassiouni report (UN Security Council 1994) counted eighty-three paramilitaries in Bosnia alone operating between June 1991 and late 1993, fifty-three for Serbs, with an estimated 20,000–40,000 members, thirteen for Croats, with 12,000–20,000, and fourteen for Bosniac, with 4,000–6,000 men. In view of 700,000 Bosnian Serb men aged fifteen to thirty-five, militiamen were 10–20 percent of the Serb men of military age in Bosnia. Ten to 20 percent of adult males in militias, added to the military and police, are more than enough for death and destruction against civilians on a massive scale.

Conclusion

My account is not a narrative of events but an analytic explanation for the breakup of Yugoslavia amid collective violence. . . . On the eve of the wars, Yugoslavs reported cooperative interpersonal ethnic relations and opposed a breakup of the state. Nationalist leaders succeeded in manipulating ethnicity by spreading fear, insecurity and hatred, which advanced their political agenda of separate national states.

To explain their success I draw on elements from the primordialist, instrumentalist and constructionist views on ethnicity and on the theory of ethnic violence originating in fear and insecurity. To these I add the concept of a cognitive frame which clarifies élite-grass-roots linkage and ethnic manipulation. Nationalism, ethnic identity and attachment alone, however intense, do not explain grass-roots ethnic actions. Yugoslavs possessed two frames on ethnic relations: a cooperative frame for normal, peaceful times, as in the decades of the fifties to the eighties. They also possessed a dormant crisis frame anchored in family history and collective memory of wars, ethnic atrocities and brutality. Threats and lies that were implausible and dismissed in the normal frame could resonate when the crisis frame was switched on: they became persuasive, were believed, and inspired fear.

In the waning days of Communism, nationalists activated the crisis frame on ethnicity by playing on fears of ethnic annihilation and oppression in the mass media, in popular culture, in social movements, and in election campaigns. Élite crisis discourse resonated at the grass roots, made for ethnic polarization, and got nationalists elected. Once in office, nationalists suppressed and purged both moderates in their own ethnic group and other ethnics. They organized militias who perpetrated acts of extreme violence against innocent civilians. They conducted war according to the crisis script. Without the tacit, overt or confused support of the majority, the nationalist leaders could not have escalated ethnic rivalry and conflict into massive collective violence.

EXPLORING THE ISSUE

Is Conflict Between Different Ethnic Groups Inevitable?

Critical Thinking and Reflection

1. In the Indian case study, why does Kakar draw upon kinship, language, and religion as the key variables for explaining ethnic violence? Why not consider economics and control of resources?
2. In the Bosnian case study, why does Oberschall dismiss the underlying religious and linguistic differences as the explanation to ethnic violence?
3. When Fredrik Barth proposed the circumstantialist explanation for ethnic identity he pointed to cases in which people of one ethnic group could pass as members of another. Is this kind of ethnic shifting (or passing) generally possible in the United States? Is it sometimes possible?
4. One common theme for explaining the sudden rise of violence in Serbia is the death of President Tito, who is often said to have ruled Yugoslavia with an iron fist. Does this explanation fit the circumstantialist model or the primordialist model better?
5. Can you develop a general explanation for ethnic violence that is not exclusively circumstantialist nor exclusively primordialist that will explain both the Indian and the Balkans cases?

Is There Common Ground?

Anthropologists and sociologists have long recognized that racial and ethnic tensions in the United States and other countries are linked to issues about access to jobs, land, resources, and opportunities. They have also recognized that the primordial ties of kinship, language, and religion have a powerful effect on people's sentiments and views about people from other backgrounds.

Thirty years ago many anthropologists championed one or the other of these two positions, but by the 1980s positions softened and anthropologists generally lost interest in the debate altogether. Neither the circumstantialists nor the primordialists won the debate, but both sides knew that there really was not clear evidence that one or the other was singularly correct. The problem here had to do with the fact that primordial traits like language, biology, and religion often seem more basic to people around the world, but they rarely prevent intermarriage, trade, or social interaction unless passions are inflamed and there are economic or political issues at stake. Thus, in most cases of ethnic tension and violence both the primordialist and circumstantialist positions are both implicated.

Additional Resources

For further reading on genocide and ethnic cleansing see:

Hinton, Alexander L., ed. 2002. *Annihilating Difference: The Anthropology of Genocide*. Berkeley: University of California Press.

For another view on ethnic conflict in India, see:

Varshney, Ashutosh. 2002. *Ethnic Conflict and Civic Life: Hindus and Muslims in India*. New Haven: Yale University Press.

For a recent perspective about ethnicity see:

Burguière, André and Grew, Raymond, ed. 2001. *The Construction of Minorities: Cases for Comparison Across Time and Around the World*. Ann Arbor: University of Michigan Press.

For more circumstantialist discussions of ethnic conflict see:

In Crawford, Beverly and Lipschutz, Ronnie D., ed. *The Myth of "Ethnic Conflict": Politics, Economics, and "Cultural" Violence*. California: Berkeley: International Area Studies, University of California.

Eller, Jack. 1999. *From Culture to Ethnicity to Conflict*. Ann Arbor: University of Michigan Press

ISSUE 16

Do Native Peoples Today Invent Their Traditions?

YES: Roger M. Keesing, from "Creating the Past: Custom and Identity in the Contemporary Pacific," *The Contemporary Pacific* (Spring/Fall 1989)

NO: Haunani-Kay Trask, from "Natives and Anthropologists: The Colonial Struggle," *The Contemporary Pacific* (Spring 1991)

Learning Outcomes

After reading this issue, you should be able to:

- Understand why some anthropologists have argued that native "traditions" have been "invented" recently to support the position of elites in native communities.
- Appreciate why native scholars and educated elites find these pronouncements by white anthropologists' racist attacks on their knowledge and authority.
- Discuss the kind of evidence that Keesing and Trask have used to support their positions on whether native peoples invent their traditions.
- Understand why Trask may be taking Keesing's arguments a bit more personally than he intended.
- Suggest ways in which both Keesing's and Trask's arguments about the "invention of tradition" may be correct in some respects.

ISSUE SUMMARY

YES: Cultural anthropologist Roger M. Keesing argues that what native peoples in the Pacific now accept as "traditional culture" is largely an invented and idealized vision of their past. He contends that such fictional images emerge because native peoples are largely unfamiliar with what life was really like in pre-Western times and because such imagery distinguishes native communities from dominant Western culture.

NO: Hawaiian activist and scholar Haunani-Kay Trask asserts that Keesing's critique is fundamentally flawed because he only uses Western documents. She contends that native peoples have oral traditions, genealogies, and other historical sources that are not reflected in Western historical documents. Anthropologists like Keesing, she maintains, are trying to hold onto their privileged position as experts in the face of growing numbers of educated native scholars.

In 1983, Eric Hobsbawm and Terence Ranger published a collection of essays entitled *The Invention of Tradition* (Cambridge University Press). For many anthropologists trained in a structural-functionalist style of research, this volume was striking because it suggested two points that seemed to fly in the face of many cherished anthropological ideas. First, they argued that traditions in all societies change as a response to the political, economic, and social needs of the community. Second, they contended that the "historical" traditions societies celebrated were often invented in the recent past as a way of distinguishing one indigenous group from a dominant one. By 1983 most anthropologists accepted the axiom that all societies change over time. Culture and social traditions may work to inhibit changes and keep society functioning as it had in the previous generation, but innovations inevitably occurred. What made Hobsbawm and Ranger's book so important was that it used several Western examples to demonstrate that even in Western countries with rich historical documentation, institutions such as Scottish tartans could become routinized and accepted as a traditional and essential marker of Scottish ethnicity, even though the custom had existed for barely a century. They argued that the idea that tartans had ancient origins was particularly appealing to the Scots because it distinguished them from the dominant English culture that had long oppressed them. Ironically, it was the English owners of textile factories who had first introduced colorful wool tartans as a way of getting work for their factories and the weavers they employed. These English industrialists designed tartans for each of the traditional highland Scottish clans. Scottish highlanders liked the idea of having their clans recognized in public displays, even though the English government had stripped these clans of their most productive land and of the relevance of these clans in organizing political and economic life. But the distinctive plaid cloth recognized the traditional clan affiliations of Scottish citizens, allowing Scotts to express traditional social distinctions in a totally new way: cloth. The cloth was new, as were the relationships among clans and between the clans and the English government that ruled them. But the colorful tartans were built on one traditional element, highland clans, that had a deep cultural meaning for Scottish people, even if they no longer functioned as they traditionally had.

In the YES selection, social anthropologist Roger M. Keesing builds on Hobsbawm and Ranger's argument by turning his attention to the "invention of tradition" in Pacific Island countries. Keesing argues that throughout the

Pacific, people now accept a variety of traditions and customs as historical practices, even though he argues that these practices could only have emerged following the invasion of these islands by Western peoples. He contends that because colonial intrusion has been so comprehensive, most aspects of traditional customs have either disappeared or have been radically transformed. As a result islanders have very little understanding what their societies were like before contact with outsiders.

Keesing's point is that because their societies have been transformed Pacific Islanders have accepted idealized images of how their traditional societies were structured and the kinds of rituals and cultural practices their ancestors practiced. Certain of the themes and motifs they accept are appealing today because they celebrate the distinctiveness of traditional island cultures with respect to the dominant Western culture with its control over resources, economies, and political processes. These idealized and largely fictional images have great political power for oppressed people, and they have often become a rallying point for various social movements. But for Keesing, as appealing as these images of traditional island life may be for islanders, they find little support in historical documents and should largely be understood as modern mythmaking for the political ends of modern Pacific elites. In essence, the importance of these new "traditions" is their ability to construct histories that support indigenous leaders today.

Hawaiian activist Haunani-Kay Trask wrote the NO selection in response to the first. She rejects the view that modern Pacific Islanders have invented their traditions. Instead, she turns Keesing's argument on its head by claiming that assertions about the "invention" of Hawaiian traditions are themselves an example of Western colonialism, racism, and white presumptions of superiority over Pacific Islanders. She contends that Keesing only accepts Western sources as historical, completely ignoring oral traditions, local mythologies, genealogies, and rituals. In Trask's view, Western historical sources are biased by Western culture and often represent an inaccurate and limited understanding of native culture and its social institutions. She questions whether or not white anthropologists have a privileged view of native customs, suggesting that most of Keesing's claims are racist attempts to further belittle native understanding and appreciation of the past.

As a professor at the University of Hawaii, Trask seems especially bothered by the absence of native authors in Keesing's references. She points to Keesing's lack of nuance when he discusses native views of the past as an idealized golden age. For her, it is clear that Hawaiians understand their own past as a complex one with different statuses as interests for commoners and chiefs, women and men, and for those who worked the land and those who interacted with the spirit world. She challenges and rejects Keesing's claims that there never was a "Golden Age" or a spiritual attachment to the land. She argues that he knows nothing about Hawaii and Hawaiians but seems to accept the naïve ideas he may have heard from the tourist industry.

Building on Hobsbawm and Ranger's notion of the "invention of tradition," Keesing makes the case that in most—if not all—Pacific societies, the history and cultural traditions that are regarded as authentic are substantially different from the events and practices that actually occurred. In his mind, there can also be little doubt that controlling what is accepted as tradition has become politically important. How does Trask's concern over professional bias impact Keesing's other arguments? What criteria would Trask suggest as a substitute as a way of judging which practices are authentic traditions and which are modern innovations?

The YES and NO selections raise several questions for anthropologists to consider. Do native peoples or Western anthropologists have a better understanding of the native past? Have native traditions changed since Western peoples first encountered Pacific Islanders? Have these traditions changed as much as Keesing suggests? Have these changes been the direct result of Western colonialism or have native peoples been active agents in such changes or have they been passive victims in the face of Western domination? Are Western historical sources biased and inaccurate when describing native practices? Are native oral traditions today accurate and authentic visions of traditional ways of life? Is there an authentic cultural tradition in any society, or, as both Keesing and Trask seem to suggest, are there different traditions for chiefs and for commoners, for men and for women? And, finally, are these "traditions" powerful as tools to fight oppression?

YES ↵

Creating the Past: Custom and Identity in the Contemporary Pacific

Across the Pacific, from Hawai'i to New Zealand, in New Caledonia, Aboriginal Australia, Vanuatu, the Solomon Islands, and Papua New Guinea, Pacific peoples are creating pasts, myths of ancestral ways of life that serve as powerful political symbols. In the rhetoric of postcolonial nationalism (and sometimes separatism) and the struggles of indigenous Fourth World peoples, now minorities in their own homelands, visions of the past are being created and evoked.

Scholars of Pacific cultures and history who are sympathetic to these political struggles and quests for identity are in a curious and contradiction-ridden position in relation to these emerging ideologies of the past. The ancestral ways of life being evoked rhetorically may bear little relation to those documented historically, recorded ethnographically, and reconstructed archaeologically— yet their symbolic power and political force are undeniable.

Perhaps it does not matter whether the pasts being recreated and invoked are mythical or "real," in the sense of representing closely what actual people did in actual times and places. Political symbols radically condense and simplify "reality," and are to some extent devoid of content: that is how and why they work. Perhaps it matters only whether such political ideologies are used for just causes, whether they are instruments of liberation or of oppression. In the contemporary Pacific they are being used both to recapture just rights and to deny them. The question is less simple than that.

The process of recapturing the past, of reconstructing, of questioning Western scholarship—historical and anthropological—is important and essential. My intention is neither to defend established versions of the past from a standpoint of vested scholarly interest, nor to debunk emerging political myths by comparing them to actual pasts to which I claim privileged access. Rather, in showing contradictions in this process of political mythmaking and in showing how in many ways the contemporary discourses of cultural identity derive from Western discourses, I seek to promote a more genuinely radical stance in relation to both the more distant and the more recent past—and to Western domination, of minds as well as societies.

From Roger M. Keesing, "Creating the Past: Custom and Identity in the Contemporary Pacific," *The Contemporary Pacific,* vol. 1, nos. 1 & 2 (Spring/Fall 1989). Copyright © 1989 by University of Hawaii Press. Reprinted by permission. Notes and references omitted.

The discourse of identity, legitimacy, and historical origins—the political mythmaking of our time—is not as different from the political mythmaking of the pre-European Pacific as it might seem.

The "invention of tradition" has been extensively explored in recent years . . . , in relation to theoretical issues of ideology and representation, questions of political economy (such as the invention and evocation of a symbolically constructed Scottish Highlands culture, replete with woollen kilts from British mills as well as bagpipes) . . . , and the dynamics of national-identity construction in postcolonial nation states. These phenomena have not been extensively explored for the Pacific. Nonetheless, they have occurred in other times and places and are going on at present in other settings. Contemporary Malaysia, where a mythic "Malay culture," a conflation of indigenous (but heavily Indianized) court traditions and Islam, is being used to persecute and disenfranchise Chinese and Indian minorities and indigenous ethnic groups, is a case in point.

Modern Mythmaking in the Pacific

Before I turn to some of the important theoretical issues raised by contemporary movements and ideologies of cultural identity, let me sketch briefly the range of phenomena I am concerned with.

Beginning with ideologies of *kastom* in contemporary Melanesia, I will illustrate four variants, or levels, mainly with reference to the Solomon Islands. These phenomena have counterparts in Vanuatu and Papua New Guinea.

First, at a national and regional level, are rhetorical appeals to "The Melanesian Way," and idealizations of custom (most often emanating from a Westernized elite). In Vanuatu in particular, the ideologies and charters of the postcolonial state enshrine customary law and institutions.

Second, are ritualized celebrations of custom in the form of the arts—music, dance, "traditional" dress—as dramatically enacted in art festivals, tourist events, and rituals of state.

Third, the rhetoric of custom is invoked with reference to a particular region or island or province within a postcolonial state. This may take the form of competition for state resources and political power, regional separatism, or even secessionist demands. . . . In the emergence of Papua New Guinea, secessionist claims by North Solomons and East New Britain were cast partly in terms of customary unity. . . .

Fourth, if the field of view is narrowed to particular language groups, particularly on islands like Malaita (or Tanna) where the commitment to "traditional" culture remains strong, we find ideologies of *kastom* used to resolve the contradictions between ancestral ways and Christianity. As Burt has documented, the Kwara'ae of central Malaita have produced origin myths that trace their ancestors back to wandering tribes of Israelites and codify ancestral rules in the style of Biblical commandments. The creation of mythical customs has been encouraged and even demanded by institutions of the postcolonial state that empower and legitimize "paramount chiefs" or other "traditional" leaders: contemporary Melanesia is now filled with "paramount chiefs" in areas that in precolonial times had no systems of chiefly authority or hereditary rank. . . .

In Australia, idealized representations of the pre-European past are used to proclaim Aboriginal identity and the attachment of indigenous peoples to the land, and are being deployed in environmentalist as well as Aboriginal political struggles. In New Zealand, increasingly powerful and successful Maori political movements incorporate idealized and mythicized versions of a precolonial Golden Age, the mystical wisdom of Aotearoa.

Hawai'i and New Caledonia exhibit further variants on the themes of Fourth World political struggle, with idealized representations of precolonial society deployed to assert common identity and to advance and legitimate political demands. In the Hawaiian case, a cultural tradition largely destroyed many decades ago must be reconstituted, reclaimed, revived, reinvented. A denial that so much has been destroyed and lost is achieved by political mythology and the sanctification of what survives, however, altered its forms. In New Caledonia, the issues are not simply the desperate struggle for political power and freedom from colonial oppression, but also the creation of both common bonds and common cultural identity among peoples whose ancestors were deeply divided, culturally and linguistically, into warring tribes speaking mutually unintelligible languages.

Some Theoretical Themes

These discourses of cultural identity in the contemporary Pacific, although they depict the precolonial past and claim to produce countercolonial images, are in many ways derived from Western ideologies.

. . . [C]ontemporary Third World (and Fourth World) representations of their own cultures have been shaped by colonial domination and the perception of Western culture through a less direct reactive process, a dialectic in which elements of indigenous culture are selected and valorized (at the levels of both ideology and practice) as *counters to* or *commentaries on* the intrusive and dominant colonial culture. That is, colonized peoples have distanced themselves from (as well as modeling their conceptual structures on) the culture of domination, selecting and shaping and celebrating the elements of their own traditions that most strikingly differentiate them from Europeans.

. . . Pacific Island elites, and Aboriginal Australians, Maori, and Hawaiians in a position to gain leadership roles and become ideologues, have been heavily exposed, through the educational process, to Western ideologies that idealize primitivity and the wisdom and ecological reverence of those who live close to Nature. Idealizations of the precolonial past in the contemporary Pacific have often been derivatives of Western critiques of modern technology and progress; ironically, those in the Pacific who in their rhetorical moments espouse these idealized views of the past are mainly (in their political actions and life-styles) hell-bent on technology, progress, materialism, and "development."

In the process of objectification, a culture is (at the level of ideology) imagined to consist of "traditional" music, dances, costumes, or artifacts. Periodically performing or exhibiting these fetishized representations of their cultures, the elites of the new Pacific ritually affirm (to themselves, the tourists, the village voters) that the ancestral cultural heritage lives on.

. . . [A]ssertions of identity based on idealizations of the ancestral past draw heavily on anthropological concepts—particularly ideas about "culture"—as they have entered Western popular thought. It is ironic that cultural nationalist rhetoric often depicts anthropologists as villains who appropriate and exploit, although that anti-anthropological rhetoric is itself squarely shaped by anthropology's concepts and categories. . . .

European scholars are implicated in a more direct way in some of the misrepresentations of ancestral cultures. Some of the classic accounts and generalizations about the cultures of Polynesia and Melanesia by expatriate scholars—to which Islanders have been exposed through books and other media—are misleading. Western scholars' own misrenderings and stereotypes have fed back into contemporary (mis)representations of the Pacific past.

In questioning the political myths of our time, I am not defending the authority of anthropological representations of the Pacific past, or the hegemonic position of scholarly discourse in relation to the aspirations of indigenous peoples to recapture their own pasts. The past . . . is contested ground. I am urging that in contesting it, Pacific Islanders be more relentlessly radical and skeptical—not that they relinquish it to the "experts." (We who claim expertise, too, can well reflect on the politics and epistemology of our privileged authority.)

Finally (and critically), if I seem to imply a gulf between the authenticity of actual precolonial societies and cultures and the inauthenticity of the mythic pasts now being invented in the Pacific, such a characterization in fact perpetuates some of anthropology's own myths. The present political contexts in which talk of custom and ancestral ways goes on are of course very different from precolonial contexts. Nonetheless, such mystification is inherent in political processes, in all times and places. Spurious pasts and false histories were being promulgated in the Pacific long before Europeans arrived, as warrior leaders draped veils of legitimacy over acts of conquest, as leaders sought to validate, reinforce, [and] institutionalize, . . . and as factions battled for dominance. Ironically, then, the "true" and "authentic" cultures of the Pacific past, overlain and distorted by today's political myths, represent, in part at least, cumulations of the political myths of the ancestors.

In Pacific communities on the eve of European invasion, there were multiple "realities"—for commoners and for chiefs, for men and for women, for young and for old, for free persons and for captives or slaves, for victors and for vanquished. Genealogies, cosmologies, rituals were themselves contested spheres. The "authentic" past was never a simple, unambiguous reality. The social worlds of the Pacific prior to European invasion were, like the worlds of the present, multifaceted and complex.

Moreover, however the past may be constructed as a symbol, and however critical it may be for historically dominated peoples to recapture this ground, a people's cultural heritage poses a challenge to radical questioning. We are all to some degree prisoners of "real" pasts as they survive into the present—in the form of patriarchal values and institutions, of patterns of thought, of structures of power. A deeply radical discourse (one that questions basic assumptions) would aspire to liberate us from pasts, both those of our ancestors and those of (colonial or other) domination, as well as to use them as political symbols.

Let me develop these arguments. . . .

The Fetishization of "Culture"

Not only in the Pacific are dramatizations and ritual enactments of cultural traditions being celebrated—in the form of dress, music, dance, handicrafts—while actual cultural traditions are vanishing. The two processes—the celebration of fossilized or fetishized cultures and the destruction of cultures as ways of life and thought—are going on in the Soviet Union, eastern Europe, and China and also in the Andean states, Brazil, Malaysia, and Indonesia. Perhaps it is an essential element in the process of nation building, where populations are ethnically diverse. Most often, a dominant national population imposes its language and cultural tradition on minority groups while appearing to value and preserve minority cultures: they are preserved like specimens in jars. . . . What greater alienation than watching those who dominate and rule you perform symbolically central elements of your cultural heritage: selling *your* culture?

What makes the Pacific distinctive here is the way, particularly in the Melanesian countries, the specimens in the jars are the cultures those with political power have themselves left behind. Members of the Westernized elites are likely to be separated by gulfs of life experience and education from village communities where they have never lived: their ancestral cultures are symbols rather than experienced realities. Bringing the specimens out of the jars on special occasions—cultural festivals, rituals of state—is a denial of alienation at a personal level, and a denial that cultural traditions are being eroded and destroyed in the village hinterlands. . . .

By the same logic, the "cultures" so commoditized and packaged can be sold to tourists. I have commented elsewhere on the way this commoditization shapes Pacific cultures to fit Western fantasies:

> Mass tourism and the media have created a new Pacific in which what is left or reconstructed from the ruins of cultural destruction of earlier decades is commoditized and packaged as exoticism for the tourists. The Pacific [is] Fantasy Land for Europe and the United States (and now for Japan) . . . to be symbolically constructed—and consumed by a consumerist society, to serve its pleasures and needs.
>
> The commoditization of their cultures has left tens of thousands of Pacific Islanders as aliens in their own lands, reduced to tawdry commercialized representations of their ancestors, histories and cultures. Beneath the veneer of fantasy, the Islanders are pauperized in village hinterlands or themselves commoditized as menial employees. Serving the comforts as well as the fantasies of rich tourists, they are constrained to smile and "be happy," because that is part of their symbolic image.

We need only think of tourism in Fiji. There, at least, the elements of culture enacted for tourists represent a version, if an edited and Christianized one (no strangling of widows in the hotel dining rooms), of a past that actually existed. The representations of "Hawaiian culture" for tourists, with hula dances, ukuleles, and pineapples, illustrate that where there is a gulf between historical realities and the expectations of tourists, the fantasies will be packaged and sold.

Invented Pasts and Anthropology

The objectification of a way of life, the reification of the customs of ancestors into a symbol to which a political stance is taken—whether of rejection or idealization—is not new in the Pacific, and is not confined to Islanders who have learned the Western concept of "culture." The so-called Vailala Madness of the Gulf Division of Papua in 1919, where villagers destroyed cult objects in a wave of iconoclasm, and proclaimed their rejection of the ways of ancestors who had withheld material riches from them, is but one example. Other classic "cargo cults" echoed the same theme.

The political stances being taken toward the ways of the ancestors in the contemporary Pacific reflect some of the same mechanisms. When massively confronted with an engulfing or technologically dominating force—whether early colonial invaders or more recently the world capitalist system and late-twentieth-century technology and wealth—one is led to take an objectified, externalized view of one's way of life that would hardly be possible if one were simply *living* it. Land, and spiritual connection to it, *could not* have, other than in a context of invasion and displacement and alienation, the ideological significance it acquires in such a context.

The ideologies of our time, unlike cargo cult ideologies, are phrased in terms of "culture" and other anthropological concepts, as they have passed into Western popular thought and intellectual discourse. This is hardly surprising, given the educational experiences of Pacific Island leaders, but it is problematic nonetheless, because the concepts that have been borrowed oversimplify in ways that have bedeviled anthropology for decades. First, "culture" represents a reification. A complex system of ideas and customs, attributed a false concreteness, is turned into a causal agent. Cultures are viewed as doing things, causing things to happen (or not happen).

In the framework of functionalist anthropology, societies and cultures have been attributed a spurious coherence and integration and portrayed in a timeless equilibrium. The timelessness and integration of the ideologically constructed Pacific pasts represent in part a projection of anthropology's own conceptual simplifications into contemporary political myths.

. . . Pacific Island peoples asserting their identity and their continuity with the past are led to seek, characterize, and proclaim an "essence" that has endured despite a century or more of change and Westernization.

In a different and older anthropological tradition—one that lives on in anthropology museums, hence is represented in the contemporary Pacific—a culture is metonymically represented by its material artifacts. This museological tradition, which has old roots in the nineteenth-century folklorism of Europe, has fed as well into the discourse on cultural identity, as I have noted. From it derives the view that in preserving the material forms and performance genres of a people, one preserves their culture.

In borrowing from anthropological discourse, ideologies of cultural identity in the contemporary Pacific have not only acquired conceptual oversimplifications but have incorporated some empirical distortions and misinterpretations for which anthropologists (and other European scholars) are ultimately responsible.

It is not that Aboriginal or Maori activists, or contemporary Samoans or Trobriand Islanders, are uncritical in their acceptance of what anthropologists have written about them. In Aboriginal struggles for land rights, for example, one of the battles has been waged against orthodox views, deriving ultimately from Radcliffe-Brown, of the patrilineality of local territorial groups—views incorporated into federal land rights legislation. The ironies and contradictions of Aboriginal peoples being denied rights they believe are culturally legitimate on grounds that they do not fit an anthropological model have chilling implications for those of us who would claim privileged authority for our "expertise" or *our* constructions of the past.

There is a further twist of irony when scholarly interpretations that may be faulty, or at least misleadingly oversimplified or overgeneralized, have been incorporated by Pacific Islanders into their conceptions of their own pasts. Let me illustrate with the concept of *mana* in Oceanic religion. . . . When I was at the University of South Pacific in 1984 and spoke on *mana*, I discovered that Polynesian students and faculty had been articulating an ideology of a common Polynesian cultural heritage and identity in which *mana* was central. Yet, as I pointed out, in many languages in Western Polynesia *mana* is used as a noun only to describe thunder, lightning, or other meteorological phenomena. Where *mana is* used as a noun to refer to spiritual power, in a number of Polynesian languages, it seems to be a secondary usage, less common than its usage as a stative verb ('be effective,' 'be potent,' 'be sacred').

Mana in the sense it has acquired in anthropology seems centrally important only in a few languages of eastern Polynesia, notably Maori and Hawaiian. . . .

The imputation of mystical wisdom to Polynesians (who in the process were distinguished from their dark-skinned, savage, cannibal neighbors to the west) has roots in European theories of race. The construction of the Polynesians in European thought, a process going back to the early explorers, has been brilliantly examined by Bernard Smith. Most striking has been the construction of Maori culture in European imagination. . . . The cosmic philosophy of the Maori, the mystical worldview, is as much a European as a Polynesian creation. Even though contemporary Maori ideologues attempt to discredit some aspects of the representation of Maori culture by Western scholars, the counterrepresentation advanced as authentic seems deeply infused by early Western romanticizations of the Maori. . . .

Political Mythology and Cultural "Authenticity": A Wider View

So far, I have implied that there is a wide gulf between the authentic past—the real ways of life that prevailed in the Pacific on the eve of European invasion—and the representations of the past in contemporary ideologies of cultural identity. This gulf requires a closer look.

. . . My point is . . . that the real past was itself highly political. Pacific societies, in pre-European times, were far from stable and static . . . : they were, as the archaeological record makes very clear, marked by political expansions and contractions, regional systems, warfare, trade—and change. Anthropological models have by and large failed to capture the dynamics of cultural production and change. Cultures are often imagined to be like coral reefs, the gradual accumulation of countless "polyps." . . . To the contrary, . . . cultural production is a highly political process. The symbolic material of cultures—rules imputed to ancestors, rituals, myths—serves ideological ends, reinforcing the power of some, the subordination of others.

From such a viewpoint, the authentic ancestral cultures of the past begin to appear in a different light. The rituals, the myths, the ideologies of hierarchy and the sanctity of chiefs, served political purposes. Conquering chiefs—or their priestly retinues—invented genealogies connecting them to the gods, and discrediting fallen rivals. Those individuals or classes acquiring sufficient political power to control symbolic production could bend cultural rules and roles to their own ends, reinforcing and legitimating their power. (The old Polynesian process whereby ascendant chiefly factions produce and impose versions of the past that legitimate their ascendancy in cosmic and genealogical terms has clearly continued into the latter twentieth century, notably in Tonga.) "Ancestral cultures" themselves represented legitimations of political power and aspirations; cultures were contested spheres. In this sense, the political myths of the contemporary Pacific that refashion the past to advance the interests of the present are not so different from the political myths of the past, dutifully recorded by the early ethnographers.

There are political contexts where it is important for an idealized vision of the past to be used as counter to the present: to the world capitalist system as it incorporates poor Third World countries on its margins as primary producers and consumers; to mindless materialism, disintegration of bonds of kinship and community, narcissistic individualism, destruction of environments for short-term profit. There is a place for pastoral visions, in the West and in the Pacific.

And there is certainly a place for discourses of resistance cast in terms of cultural identity. For Fourth World indigenous minorities in the Pacific—Maori, Aboriginal Australians, Kanaks, Hawaiians—a reverence for what survives of the cultural past (however altered its forms), and for a lost heritage, is a necessary counterpoint to deep anger over the generations of destruction.

But such ideologies become self-delusory if they are not interspersed with visions of "real" pasts that cast into relief not simply their idealized virtues, but their cracks of contradictions. . . . European scholars of the Pacific have been complicit in legitimating and producing male-oriented and elitist representations of societies that were themselves male- and (in many cases) elite-dominated. A critical skepticism with regard to pasts and power, and a critical deconstruction of conceptualizations of "a culture" that hide and neutralize subaltern voices and perspectives, should, I think, dialectically confront idealizations of the past. I am encouraged by the emergence, in the last several years, of critical writings in this vein by Pacific Islanders, including Epeli Hau'ofa and a number of feminist critics.

This is not the time to leave the past to the "experts," whether of the present generation or their predecessors. . . .

A more radical Pacific discourse would also be more deeply self-reflexive about the hegemonic force of Western education, of Christianity (an integral part of the colonial-imperialist project), of Western pastoral myths as appropriations of Otherness. . . .

A similar self-reflexivity is a continuing challenge for scholars working in the Pacific. Both the political implications and epistemology of our projects and representations are deeply problematic. The frame of certainty that surrounds scholarly expertise—like mythical history—is less solid than it seems: it dissolves in the right mixture of astute skepticism and self-reflexivity. But specialists on the Pacific do not best serve the interests of a less hegemonic scholarship or best support the political struggles of decolonizing and internally colonized Pacific peoples by suspending their critical judgment or maintaining silence—whether out of liberal guilt or political commitment—regarding mythic pasts evoked in cultural nationalist rhetoric. Our constructions of real pasts are not sacrosanct, but they are important elements in a continuing dialogue and dialectic.

Natives and Anthropologists: The Colonial Struggle

As a Hawaiian, a long-time outspoken defender of my people's claim to nationhood, a scholar, and a Native who knows her history and people, I found Roger Keesing's article . . . a gem of academic colonialism. Knowing oldfashioned racism too crude to defend but bitterly clinging to his sense of white superiority, Keesing plows the complaining path of the unappreciated missionary who, when confronted by ungrateful, decolonizing Natives, thinly veils his hurt and anger by the high road of lamentation: Alas, poor, bedeviled Natives "invent" their culture in reaction to colonialism, and all in the service of grimy politics!

Keesing's peevishness has a predictably familiar target: Native nationalists—from Australia and New Zealand through the Solomons and New Caledonia to Hawai'i. The problem? These disillusioned souls idealize their pasts for the purpose of political mythmaking in the present. Worse, they are so unoriginal (and, by implication, unfamiliar with what Keesing calls their "real" pasts) as to concoct their myths out of Western categories and values despite their virulent opposition to same. Thus the romanticization of pre-European Native pasts (the "Golden Age" allegedly claimed by the Maori); the assertion of a common Native identity (eg, Fijian "culture"); the "ideology" of land as spiritually significant (supposedly argued by Hawaiians, Solomon Islanders, Kanaks, and Aborigines). The gospel, according to Keesing, is that these claims are "invented." To be specific, there never was a "Golden Age," a common identity, or a spiritual attachment to the land.

Proof? Keesing supplies none, either on the charge that Native nationalists have made such claims or that their claims are false. He merely asserts fabrication then proceeds to belabor, through the mumbo jumbo of academic "discourse," the crying need for Natives (and academics) to face "our" pasts with "skepticism," while pursuing a "critical deconstruction of conceptualizations" to achieve "dialectical confrontation." The final intention should be to "liberate us" from our pasts.

Well, my answer to Keesing has been said by modern-day Natives to wouldbe White Fathers many times: What do you mean "us," white man?

Among Hawaiians, people like Keesing are described as *maha'oi haole,* that is, rude, intrusive white people who go where they do not belong. In

Keesing's case, his factual errors, cultural and political ignorance, and dismissive attitude qualify him perfectly as *maha'oi*. Unlike Keesing; I cannot speak for other Natives. But regarding Hawaiian nationalists, Keesing neither knows whereof he speaks, nor given his *maha'oi* attitude, does he care.

Example.   Keesing only cites works by *haole* academics on the current situation in Hawai'i. Obviously, he hasn't bothered to read our Native nationalists and scholars, including those, like myself, who have been very critical of these same *haole* academics. Indeed, most of his comments on Hawaiian nationalists come from one problematic and contested article (contested by Natives, that is) by anthropologist Jocelyn Linnekin, hardly a sound evidentiary base for sweeping claims that we invent our past.

Beyond his poverty of sources, there is Keesing's willful ignorance of solid evidence from Native forms of history—genealogy—which reveal that in pre-*haole* Hawai'i our people looked on land as a mother, enjoyed a familial relationship with her and other living things, and practiced an economically wise, spiritually based ethic of caring for the land, called *mlāma 'āina*.

Contrary to Linnekin's claims, and Keesing's uncritical acceptance of them, the value of *mālama 'āina* has been "documented historically," and "recorded ethnographically," (as Keesing might learn if he read Native sources), two of the criteria Keesing cites as central to any judgment of the accuracy of "ancestral ways of life being evoked rhetorically" by Native nationalists today.[1] If Natives must be held to Keesing's criteria, why should he be allowed to escape them?

The answer is that Keesing, with many Western academics, shares a common assumption: Natives don't know very much, even about their own lifeways, thus there is no need to read them. (The only "real" sources are *haole* sources, hegemony recognizing and reinforcing hegemony).

Keesing's racism is exposed here. Not only has he refused to read what we Native nationalists write and say, he has refused to look at our sources of knowledge. But then, Keesing believes, Natives are so colonized, why bother?

Example.   Keesing has also failed to distinguish between what Hawaiian nationalists say about our ways of life and what the mammoth tourist industry advertises "Hawaiian culture" to be, including "hula dances, ukuleles, and pineapples." Because he is totally ignorant of modern Hawaiian resistance, he is also totally ignorant of the Native criticism of the tourist industry, including the myth of happy Natives waiting to share their "culture" with tourists. In fact, after years of Native resistance to tourism, the churches in Hawai'i (with the push of Native nationalists and international ecumenical groups) sponsored a conference on the impact of tourism on Hawaiian people and culture in 1989. At that conference, Hawaiians from each of our major islands spoke eloquently of tourism's damage to Hawaiian sites, dance, language, economics, land, and way of life. The declaration issued from that conference listed ways to halt this damage, including a ban on all resorts in Hawaiian communities. Keesing should be reading this kind of primary evidence if he wants to learn what Hawaiian nationalists think about tourism and our culture.

Example.   Keesing claims that Native nationalists hark back to an "authentic," "simple, unambiguous reality," when, in fact, "there were multiple 'realities'— for commoners and chiefs, for men and for women . . ." in cultures where "genealogies, cosmologies, rituals were themselves contested spheres."

As usual, the critical reader finds not a single reference here to a single Native nationalist statement. More *haole* sources follow, especially Keesing on Keesing. But where are the Natives?

In the dark, naturally.

The truth is that Keesing has made a false charge. Those of us in the current Hawaiian nationalist movement know that genealogies are claimed and contested all the time. Some of the chiefly lineages have legal claims on lands taken by the United States government at the American annexation of Hawai'i in 1898, which means that genealogies have an impact beyond the Hawaiian community. Cosmologies are also contested, with nationalists citing and arguing over accuracy and preferability.[2]

Finally, at the Center for Hawaiian Studies—which generates nationalist positions, sponsors nationalist conferences, and teaches the historical background and political substance of nationalist arguments—students are required to take a course on genealogies.

Given Roger Keesing's shameless claims about us Hawaiian nationalists, I invite him to take this course, or any other offered at our center. We Natives might teach him something.

Example.   Keesing asserts that "cultural nationalist rhetoric often depicts anthropologists as villains who appropriate and exploit." In a note, he adds that anthropologists are "imagined to be appropriating and profiting from other people's cultures. . . ."

In Hawai'i, contract work is a major source of funding for archaeologists and anthropologists. These people are hired by investors and state or private institutions to survey areas and deem them ready for use. In highly controversial cases regarding removal of Hawaiian bones and destruction of Hawaiian temple and house sites, many archaeologists and anthropologists have argued *for* development and *against* preservation while receiving substantial sums of money. At its worst, these controversies have exposed the racist paternalism of anthropologists who pit (in their own words) *emotional* Hawaiians who try to stop disinterment and development against *scientific* anthropologists who try to increase the store of (Western) knowledge.

Of course, these *haole* anthropologists would be outraged were we Hawaiians to dig up *their* relatives for osteological analysis, search for evidence of tuberculosis and other diseases, and, not coincidentally, get paid handsomely for our troubles. To my knowledge, no anthropologist has ever dug up missionary bones, despite their plentiful presence. Nor has any haole "expert" ever argued that missionary skeletons should be subjected to osteological analysis, despite historical evidence that missionaries did bring certain diseases to Hawai'i. White colonialism in Hawai'i ensures that it is the colonizers who determine disinterment. Since we are the colonized, we have no power to disinter the bones of the colonizer. Thus,

Native remains are dug up and studied. Missionary and explorer remains are sacrosanct.

Apart from contract work, anthropologists make academic careers and employment off Native cultures. Keesing may not think this is "profiting," but anthropologists who secure tenure by studying, publishing, and lecturing about Native peoples are clearly "profiting" through a guaranteed lifetime income. Of course, Keesing is disingenuous, at best. He knows as well as Native nationalists that anthropologists without Natives are like entomologists without insects.

For Hawaiians, anthropologists in general (and Keesing in particular) are part of the colonizing horde because they seek to take away from us the power to define who and what we are, and how we should behave politically and culturally.[3] This theft testifies to the stranglehold of colonialism and explains why self-identity by Natives elicits such strenuous and sometimes vicious denials by members of the dominant culture.

These denials are made in order to undermine the legitimacy of Native nationalists by attacking their motives in asserting their values and institutions. But motivation is laid bare through the struggle for cultural expression. Nationalists offer explanations at every turn: in writing, in public forums, in acts of resistance. To Natives, the burst of creative outpouring that accompanies cultural nationalism is self-explanatory: a choice has been made for things Native over things non-Native. Politically, the choice is one of decolonization.

The direct links between mental and political decolonization are clearly observable to representatives of the dominant culture, like Keesing, who find their status as "experts" on Natives suddenly repudiated by Natives themselves. This is why thinking and acting like a native is a highly politicized reality, one filled with intimate oppositions and psychological tensions. But it is not Natives who create politicization. *That* was begun at the moment of colonization.

In the Hawaiian case, the "invention" criticism has been thrown into the public arena precisely at a time when Hawaiian cultural and political assertion has been both vigorous and strong willed. Since 1970, Hawaiians have been organizing for land rights, including claims to restitution for the American overthrow of our government in 1893 and for forced annexation in 1898. Two decades of struggle have resulted in the contemporary push for Hawaiian sovereignty, with arguments ranging from complete secession to legally incorporated land-based units managed by Hawaiians, to a "nation-within-a-nation" government akin to Native American Indian nations. The US government has issued two reports on the status of Hawaiian trust lands, which encompass nearly half the State of Hawai'i. And finally, a quasi-governmental agency—the Office of Hawaiian Affairs—was created in 1978, partly in response to Hawaiian demands.

This kind of political activity has been accompanied by a flourishing of Hawaiian dance, a move for Hawaiian language immersion schools, and a larger public sensitivity to the destructive Western relationship to the land compared to the indigenous Hawaiian way of caring for the land.

Non-Native response to this Hawaiian resistance has varied from humor, through mild denial that any wrong has been committed against the Hawaiian people and government, to organized counteraction, especially from threatened agencies and actors who hold power over Hawaiian resources. Indeed, representatives of the dominant culture—from historians and anthropologists to bureaucrats and politicians—are quick to feel and perceive danger because, in the colonial context, all Native cultural resistance is political: it challenges hegemony, including that of people like Keesing who claim to encourage a more "radical stance" toward our past by liberating us from it.

But Keesing obviously knows nothing about Hawaiians. He has failed to distinguish land claims from cultural resurgence, although both have nationalist origins. And he has little or no background regarding the theft of Hawaiian domain and dominion by the American government in the nineteenth century. Given this kind of ignorance of both our recent and distant past, Keesing would do better to take a "radical" look at the racism and arrogance of *his* culture which originated anthropology and its "search for the primitive."

As for nationalist Hawaiians, we know our future lies in the ways of our ancestors, not in the colonial world of *haole* experts. Our efforts at "liberation" are directed against the colonizers, whether they be political agencies, like the American government, or academics, like Keesing himself. We do not need, nor do we want to be "liberated" from our past because it is the source of our understanding of the cosmos and of our *mana*.

In our language, the past (*ka wā mamua*) is the time in front or before; the future (*ka wā mahope*) is the time that comes after. In the words of one of our best living Native historians, Lilikalā Kameʻeleihiwa (whom Keesing did not read), "The Hawaiian stands firmly in the present, with his back to the future, and his eyes fixed upon the past, seeking historical answers for present-day dilemmas. Such an orientation is to the Hawaiian an eminently practical one, for the future is always unknown whereas the past is rich in glory and knowledge."

Notes

1. In her article, Linnekin writes, "For Hawaiʻi, 'traditional' properly refers to the precontact era, before Cook's arrival in 1778." But later on the same page, she admits that "tradition is fluid . . ." Despite this confusion she criticizes Hawaiians for a "reconstruction of traditional Hawaiian society" in the present.

   But what constitutes "tradition" to a people is ever-changing. Culture is not static, nor is it frozen in objectified moments in time. Without doubt, Hawaiians were transformed drastically and irreparably after contact, but remnants of earlier lifeways, including values and symbols, have persisted. One of these values is the Hawaiian responsibility to care for the land, to make it flourish, called *mālama ʻāina* or *aloha ʻāina*. To Linnekin, this value has been invented by modern Hawaiians to protest degradation of the land by developers, the military, and others. What Linnekin has missed here—partly because she has an incomplete grasp of "traditional" values but also because she doesn't understand and thus misapprehends Hawaiian cultural nationalism—is simply this: the Hawaiian relationship to land has persisted into the present. What has changed is ownership and use of the land (from collective use by Hawaiians for subsistence to private use by whites and other non-Natives for profit). Asserting the Hawaiian relationship in this changed context results in politicization. Thus, Hawaiians assert a "traditional" relationship to the land *not* for political ends, as Linnekin (and Keesing) argue, but because they continue to believe in the cultural value of caring for the land. That land use is now contested makes such a belief political. This distinction is crucial because the Hawaiian cultural motivation reveals the persistence of traditional values, the very thing Linnekin (and Keesing) allege modern Hawaiians to have "invented."

2. In Hawai'i the Kawananakoa line contests the loss of governance, since they were heirs to the throne at the time of the American military-backed overthrow of Hawaiian Queen Lili'uokalani. The Salazar family lays claim to part of the Crown lands for similar reasons. Regarding land issues, the Ka'awa family occupied Makapu'u Point in 1988 in protest over its current use. Their argument revolved around their claim to ownership because of their genealogical connection to the Kamehameha line. Among nationalist organizations, 'Ohana o Hawai'i, led by Peggy Ha'o Ross, argues claims to leadership based on genealogy. These examples illustrate the continuity of genealogy as profoundly significant to Hawaiians in establishing mana and, thus, the power to command recognition and leadership. Keesing obviously knows nothing about any of these families or their claims.

3. The United States government defines Native Hawaiians as those with 50 percent or more Hawaiian blood quantum. Those with less than 50 percent Hawaiian blood are not considered to be "Native" and are thus not entitled to lands and monies set aside for 50 percent bloods. Hawaiians are the only human beings in the State of Hawai'i who are categorized by blood quantum, rather like Blacks in South Africa.

    While bureaucrats are happily dividing up who is and is not Native, the substance of *what* constitutes things Hawaiian is constantly asserted by anthropologists against Native nationalists. Of course, the claim to knowledge by anthropologists is their academic training applied to the field. Native nationalists' claim to knowledge is their life experience as Natives.

    The problem is more serious than epistemology, however. In a colonial world, the work of anthropologists and other Western-trained "experts" is used to disparage and exploit Natives. What Linnekin or Keesing or any other anthropologist writes about Hawaiians has more potential power than what Hawaiians write about themselves. Proof of this rests in the use of Linnekin's argument by the US Navy that Hawaiian nationalists have invented the sacred meaning of Kaho'olawe Island (which the US Navy has controlled and bombed since the Second World War) because nationalists need a "political and cultural symbol of protest" in the modern period. Here, the connection between anthropology and the colonial enterprise is explicit. When Natives accuse Western scholars of exploiting them, they have in mind the exact kind of situation I am describing. In fact, the Navy's study was done by an anthropologist who, of course, cited fellow anthropologists, including Linnekin, to argue that the Hawaiian assertion of love and sacredness regarding Kaho'olawe was "fakery." Far from overstating their case, Native nationalists acutely comprehend the structure of their oppression, including that perpetuated by anthropologists.

EXPLORING THE ISSUE

Do Native Peoples Today Invent Their Traditions?

Critical Thinking and Reflection

1. Give an example of the invention of tradition suggested by Keesing and evaluate the sources of the evidence he provides.
2. Give an example of how Keesing has gotten it wrong (according to Trask) and what evidence she draws upon to support her view.
3. If Keesing was overstating the argument for one of his examples, what would that mean for his other arguments? If Trask were perhaps overstating Keesing's position, would this invalidate her general argument?
4. How might a white anthropologist study changing traditions in Hawaii or other Pacific Island societies without offending or running afoul of Trask or some other native scholars?
5. How might native scholars defend their positions about the nature of native traditions without considering at least some white historical sources?

Is There Common Ground?

The YES and NO selections for this issue confront Hobsbawm and Ranger's notion of the "invention of tradition." It is clear that in mainstream American society, certain traditions have been invented and others have been transformed into new traditions. Shedding light on these innovations and changes in traditions often upsets people in mainstream society. For example, in the early 1800s national leaders introduced a series of what were essentially myths about the honesty of George Washington and cherry trees, and his ability to throw a silver dollar across the wide Potomac River, when he may actually have thrown it across a minor tributary near Mount Vernon. In the early twentieth century, Italian Americans introduced a national tradition in the celebration of Columbus Day, honoring the explorer—who never reached the North American mainland—as a national hero and founder of the nation. In a time when Catholics were often discriminated against, having a Catholic hero supported their national claims. More recently, as Native Americans have asserted their rightful role in American life, they have objected to celebrations of an explorer who killed or enslaved nearly all of the Native Americans he encountered in the Caribbean. In recent years, each December brings claims from some TV personalities that secular Americans have launched a "war on Christmas" when chain stores instruct their employees to greet customers with "Happy Holidays" rather than "Merry Christmas." These personalities claim

Christmas as an "American tradition." Despite their claims that Christmas was celebrated throughout colonial America, in colonial New England the Puritans had in fact outlawed any celebration of Christmas because the holiday had long been a holiday of drunkenness and debauchery among the poor and working class of England, until after Charles Dickens's published his story, "A Christmas Carol" in 1843. The point of all these examples is that many traditions change and some new "traditions" have been invented to serve certain political, social, or cultural ends.

Hobsbawm and Ranger, of course, had drawn on the invention of Western as well as non-Western "traditions." But here Keesing jumps from one Pacific Island group to another referring generally to traditions without unpacking any specific example in any detail. Trask takes issue with his approach, arguing that Keesing knows little or nothing about Hawaiian history and traditions. In fact, Keesing offers only casual references to "invented" Hawaiian traditions and there may be some merit in Trask's claims that Keesing is conflating Hawaiian tourist industry claims and more authentic (and more complex) sets of native understandings in Hawaii.

Hawaiian society clearly changed after the arrival of Western explorers, whalers, and missionaries. Some changes, such as the conquest of the entire archipelago by Kamehameha the Great, happened soon after Captain Cook arrived in the islands. Such conquest had to have transformed Hawaiian understandings of their society. Abandoning the "kapu system" of taboos in 1820 soon after Kamehameha the Great's death led to a comprehensive transformation of Hawaiian society. Thus, there can be little question that Hawaiian society and its traditions have changed. Trask is one of the leading figures in Native Hawaiian studies and is clearly aware of these changing traditions. So what is the basis of her concerns?

In some respects, Trask and Keesing seem to be talking past one another in these selections. Hawaiian leaders like Trask were deeply offended by an essay written by anthropologist Jocelyn Linnekin in 1983 and by her 1985 book Children of the Land (Rutgers University Press). In both of these works, Linnekin makes similar arguments to those of Keesing, and in many respects Keesing's selection here was inspired by Linnekin's work. Although Linnekin's work is carefully researched, she does rely more heavily on written Western sources than oral histories. But the main objection to Linnekin is that she does not support the views of native scholars like Haunani-Kay Trask and several others.

One of the most important concerns raised by Trask is whether white anthropologists feel intellectually superior to the native peoples and their intellectual elites.

Additional Resources

The key essays by Jocelyn Linnekin referred to above are:
Linnekin, Jocelyn. 1983. "Defining Tradition: Variations on the Hawaiian Identity," *American Ethnologist* 10:2–252.

Linnekin, Jocelyn. 1985. *Children of the Land*. New Brunswick, N.J. Rutgers University Press.

> Haunani-Kay Trask reviewed this book in the *Hawaiian Journal of History* (vol. 20, 1986).

Similar arguments have been made about other Pacific Island societies, including a more focused argument about the invention of tradition among the Maori of New Zealand:

> Hanson, Alan. 1989. "The Making of the Maori: Culture Invention and Its Logic." *American Anthropologist* 91(4).

Like Linnekin's and Keesing's works, Hanson's essay prompted a vigorous and at times hostile debate within New Zealand. At one point some Maori threatened to censure the American Anthropological Association because of this article, which some in New Zealand considered racist and anti-Maori. Stephen Webster discusses this topic in light of the so-called Maori renaissance, a revival of Maori cultural values within the modern bicultural state of New Zealand in his book:

> Webster, Stephen. 1998. *Patrons of Maori Culture: Power, Theory and Ideology in the Maori Renaissance*. Dunedin, N.Z. University of Otago Press.

Questions about the invention of traditions have become important in North America as well. Brian Haley and Larry Wilcoxon published an essay that argued that anthropologists and environmentalists had encouraged Chumash Indians to exaggerate claims that a site proposed for industrial development was traditionally sacred. The following year, archaeologist John McVey Erlandson published a reply to Haley and Wilcoxon. Like Keesing, Erlandson drew from historical (white American) sources to defend his position that the site was sacred.

Internet References . . .

American Anthropological Association Code of Ethics

Created by the American Anthropological Association, the largest organization of anthropologists in the world, this American Anthropological Association Code of Ethics Web site provides a code of ethics for its members and a handbook on ethical issues faced by anthropologists.

www.aaanet.org/committees/ethics/ethcode.html

Kennewick Man

This site contains an article on the controversy following the discovery of the bones of a 8400-year-old man, now called Kennewick Man. The article discusses whether the bones, which do not appear to be Native American, should be protected under the Native American Graves Protection and Repatriation Act (NAGPRA) and therefore be reburied. Links are provided to previous articles, which give further information from both sides of the debate on Kennewick Man.

www.archaeology.org/9701/etc/specialreport.html

Other Useful Web Sites on the Chagnon Fieldwork Debate

www.darwinwars.com/cuts/oddsnsods/chagnon_written.html

Smithsonian Institution Ethical Dilemmas

This site offers some examples of ethical dilemmas encountered by anthropologists during fieldwork.

http://anthropology.si.edu/outreach/Teaching_Activities/edethica.html

The National Park Service NAGPRA Web Site

www.nps.gov/nagpra/

The Yanomamö

Created by Brian Schwimmer, the first Yanomamö (also spelled *Yanomami*) Web site listed explores intergroup relations, alliances, and the role of warfare among the Yanomamö. The next two Web sites provide links to photos of the Yanomamö and pages that deal with aspects of change in these communities.

**www.umanitoba.ca/faculties/arts/anthropology/tutor/
case_studies/yanomamo/**

www.geocities.com/Athens/Academy/9118/yanomami.html

**www.trinity.wa.edu.au/plduffyrc/subjects/
sose/geography/respop/yano.htm**

Ethics in Anthropology

*T*he ethical treatment of other peoples has come to play an increasingly important role in contemporary anthropology. Ethical issues directly affect how cultural anthropologists should treat their living human subjects. But similar issues also affect archeologists and biological anthropologists because the artifacts of past communities often represent the ancestors of living communities. Here the interests of anthropologists and native peoples diverge, and we ask whether such bones should be reburied to respect the dead or if they should be studied for science. Similarly, we may ask what the ethical responsibilites of Western anthropologists should be when they find certain cultural practices abhorrent or unjust. Should anthropologists work to change these practices? All of these issues raise questions about how involved anthropologists should become with the peoples with whom they work. Should anthropologists take a passive, objective, and even scientific position or should they use what they know to support or change these native communities?

- Should the Remains of Prehistoric Native Americans Be Reburied Rather Than Studied?

- Did Napoleon Chagnon's Research Methods Harm the Yanomami Indians of Venezuela?

ISSUE 17

Should the Remains of Prehistoric Native Americans Be Reburied Rather Than Studied?

YES: James Riding In, from "Repatriation: A Pawnee's Perspective," *American Indian Quarterly* (Spring 1996)

NO: Clement W. Meighan, from "Some Scholars' Views on Reburial," *American Antiquity* (October 1992)

Learning Outcomes
After reading this issue, you should be able to: • Understand why Native Americans have fought so strongly for repatriation of human remains and other important cultural material currently housed in museums around the country.   • Discuss why archeologists have strived to keep control of museum collections of skeletal material and why they feel repatriation often represents the loss of scientific data.   • Explain the dispute between some Native American groups and some archaeologists and anthropologists over when to excavate Indian sites and what to do with the artifacts and remains found in these sites.   • Understand why Indians have made repatriation a political issue rather than just an issue of social justice, fairness, and religious freedom.   • Consider some ways for Indians and archaeologists to collaborate over excavations involving the prehistory of the United States.

ISSUE SUMMARY

YES: Assistant professor of justice studies and member of the Pawnee tribe James Riding In argues that holding Native American skeletons in museums and other repositories represents a sacrilege against Native American dead. Non-Native Americans would not allow their cemeteries to be dug up and their ancestors bones to be housed in museums. Thus, all Indian remains should be reburied.

NO: Professor of anthropology and archaeologist Clement W. Meighan believes that archaeologists have a moral and professional obligation to the archaeological data with which they work. Such field data are not just about Native Americans and their history but about the heritage of all humans. He concludes that such data are held in the public good and must be protected from destruction.

From the beginning, the relationship between Native Americans and anthropologists in the United States has been an uncertain one. For some anthropologists and some tribes the relationship has been mutually cooperative and supportive. For other anthropologists and other tribes the relationship has been an overtly hostile one, in which Native Americans deeply mistrust anthropologists and feel that Indian culture is being exploited for the professional and personal benefit of the researchers. For many Native American communities nonnative researchers represent just another group of outsiders who will take advantage of them. The ironic fact is that cultural anthropologists and archaeologists are often the one group of outsiders who actually understand and respect the cultural traditions of these Indians. Many archaeologists and cultural anthropologists have worked hard to establish strong rapport with the communities in which they work, collaborating on projects supported by tribal groups.

Despite these advances the one issue that disrupted the rapport between Indians and anthropologists concerns what to do with the skeletal remains excavated in Native American sites. Since archaeologists started excavating Native American sites in the mid-nineteenth century they have preserved human skeletal remains along with the other kinds of artifacts they have unearthed. Their goal was to protect these artifacts for future research, and natural history museums and state museums have been filled with projectile points, broken potsherds, stone tools, and the bones of ancient Native Americans.

The complete destruction of a nearly pristine gravesite spurred the U.S. Congress to pass a law that would protect Native American graves from desecration by amateur pot hunters just wanting to find artifacts they could sell to make money. The same legislation simultaneously dealt with another issue that had upset Indians for decades, storing skeletal remains and other sacred ritual paraphernalia in large public museums. Unlike the pot hunters who would destroy all of the information about the burials that could be learned from the context, setting, position, and dating of an early burial just to get to the complete pots, professional archaeologists studied the objects in their collections, contributing to the knowledge we have about particular regions. The same is true of the skeletons, many of which have been studied for what they can tell us about Indian peoples' precontact history. But for many Native American groups, such studies themselves are repugnant because for them the dead should not be disturbed in the first place.

The Native American Graves Protection and Repatriation Act of 1990 imposed severe penalties for disrupting any Native American archaeological site without permission from a state or federal agency. But it also required all public museums to return or repatriate to the tribes any skeletons or grave goods excavated with these skeletons if the tribes wanted to rebury these human remains. A complex method for notifying tribes about what was contained from their tribal group in each group was established and tribes were given the option of reburying these remains if they wished. A few groups have insisted on the return of all skeletal material, while a few others have wanted nothing to do with the remains fearing that more harm than good would come from reburial. But for archaeologists and biological anthropologists who work with skeletal remains reburial means that the data they have for their research is lost to science forever. This tension between Native American tribes who want to rebury their tribal remains and archaeologists who want to continue to study these remains persists.

James Riding In, himself a Pawnee, argues that anthropologists and archaeologists have consistently desecrated graves by excavating and studying the bones of Native Americans. He begins his discussion by outlining the history of man public museum collections of Native American skulls. Many of these he maintains were war dead from the Indian Wars of the 1870s, and they should have been buried on the spot after these battles. Riding In says that Native Americans believe that the bodies of the dead must be reunited with "Mother Earth."

Clement W. Meighan counters that the debate over what should be done with bones from archaeological excavations is a conflict between science and religion. In the case of very early prehistoric sites, there is usually no evidence that links living tribes inhabiting the surrounding areas with the early community; many of these groups would either be unrelated to living tribal members or might even be the remains of enemy groups.

For Meighan the requirement of science must be defended, and the unraveling of humankind's prehistory in the New World is of public interest to all Americans, whether Native or not. He contends that the public's right to know about the past is important, and any reburial of archaeological material represents the destruction of scientific data that can never be recovered. Arguing that political motives are at the heart of Native American claims to religious interests in archaeological remains, Meighan views reburial as an attempt to censor archaeological and anthropological findings that conflict with Native American legends and myths.

Riding In, on the other hand, feels that any excavation of a Native American grave site is a desecration in the first place, not science. He draws heavily on Pawnee understandings of what happens when people die, but frames his arguments around the worldwide oppression that all Native peoples have suffered at the hands of people from Europe who have seized and colonized their lands, taken their resources and pushed Native peoples to the margins of society. Studying the skeletons of Native peoples is simply another example of oppression. He acknowledges that the repatriation movement which has struggled to rebury all Native American remains was originally started by the American Indian Movement (AIM) in the early 1970s. The repatriation provisions in the NAGPRA legislation are a good beginning but he wants to see the scope of the legislation extended to all non-Indian organizations and entities, forcing them to repatriate whatever skeletal remains are in their possession.

Although NAGPRA has been the official law of the land for two decades now, several contentious concerns remain about just which bones should be repatriated and how should these bones be treated both legally and professionally. Riding In and Meighan raise a number of questions about the interests of the Native American community and the interests of the science of archaeology. We see here a tension between science and religion that is not entirely dissimilar to debates in fundamentalist Christian circles over the teaching of evolution in public schools, which they see as intrusion into their religious beliefs.

These selections raise questions of direct relevance to anthropologists generally. Are Native American religious beliefs more important than those of secular scientists? Can the concerns of science ever win out over the narrow religious interpretations of one social community such as fundamentalist Christians or the Pawnee? Do archaeologists desecrate Native American sacred sites whenever they excavate? Should the religious concerns of one ethnic or cultural community override either the professional concerns of another group or the intellectual rights of the general public? Who should control information about the past, Native Americans groups or scientists? Who should control depictions of any ethnic group's past? And who should control interpretation of the past anyway?

YES ⬅

James Riding In

Repatriation: A Pawnee's Perspective

My opposition to scientific grave looting developed partially through the birth of the American Indian repatriation movement during the late 1960s. Like other American Indians of the time (and now), I viewed archaeology as an oppressive and sacrilegious profession that claimed ownership over many of our deceased relatives, suppressed our religious freedom, and denied our ancestors a lasting burial. My first encounter with an archaeologist occurred at a party in New Mexico in the late 1970s. After hearing him rant incessantly about the knowledge he had obtained by studying Indian remains, burial offerings, and cemeteries, I suggested that if he wanted to serve Indians he should spend his time excavating latrines and leave the graves alone. Of course, he took umbrage at the tone of my suggestion, and broke off the conversation. While studying history at the University of California, Los Angeles [UCLA] in the mid-1980s, I became committed to pursuing the goals of the repatriation movement, which was gaining momentum. Like other reburial proponents, I advocated the reburial of all Indian remains warehoused across the nation in museums, universities, and federal agencies. I also promoted the extension or enactment of laws to protect Indian cemeteries from grave looters, including archaeologists.

While working to elevate the consciousness of the UCLA campus about the troubled relationship between archaeologists and Indians, a few of us, including students, staff, faculty, and community members, took advantage of opportunities to engage in dialogue with the anti-repatriation forces. During these exchanges, tempers on both sides often flared. Basically, the archaeologists were functioning on metaphysical and intellectual planes that differed from ours. We saw their professional activities as sacrilege and destructive, while they professed a legal and scientific right to study Indian remains and burial goods. We wanted the university to voluntarily return the human remains in its collections to the next-of-kin for proper reburial. They desired to protect excavation, research, and curatorial practices. Asserting profound respect for Indian concerns, beliefs, and values, members of the archaeology group offered a host of patronizing excuses for refusing to endorse our calls for repatriation. In this sense, the UCLA struggle mirrored the conflict over human remains ensuing throughout much of the country. In 1989, as the UCLA battle ensued, I accepted an offer to assist the Pawnee government in its efforts as a sovereign nation to reclaim the remains of its ancestors held at the

From *American Indian Quarterly* by James Riding In, Spring 1996, pp. 238–244, 246–249.

Smithsonian Institution. Being a citizen of this small and impoverished nation of Indians, I welcomed the opportunity to join other Pawnee activists in the repatriation quest. Earlier that year, Congress had enacted a repatriation bill that provided a legal mechanism for Indian governments to reclaim ancestral remains and burial offerings held at the Smithsonian.

Despite the law, obdurate Smithsonian personnel sought to frustrate Indian repatriation efforts with such tactics as stonewalling, deceit, and misinformation. Although Smithsonian personnel claimed that the true identities of six skulls classified as Pawnee could not be positively established, subsequent research on my part uncovered a preponderance of evidence confirming the authenticity of the accession records. This research also showed that, after U.S. soldiers and Kansas settlers had massacred a party of Pawnee men who had been recently discharged from the U.S. army, a Fort Harker surgeon had collected some of the victims' skulls in compliance with army policy and shipped them to the Army Medical Museum for craniometric study.

Since that report, I have written articles, given presentations, and, in conjunction with others, conducted research on behalf of Pawnee repatriation initiatives at Chicago's Field Museum of Natural History. I also have written a report from information found in the Native American Graves Protection and Repatriation Act (NAGPRA) summary letters showing the location of additional Pawnee remains, sacred objects, objects of cultural patrimony, and cultural artifacts.

This essay offers some of my views concerning the reburial aspect of the repatriation struggle. It seeks to show the intellectual and spiritual foundations behind the movement as a means for understanding the complexity of the controversy. It also attempts to demonstrate how repatriation advocates managed to effect discriminatory laws and practices. Finally, it conveys a message that, although old attitudes continue to function within the archaeology and museum communities, a concerted effort brought to bear by people who espouse cooperative relations is in place to bring Indian spiritual beliefs in conformity with non-Indian secular values.

At another level, I write with the intent of creating awareness about a pressing need to disestablish racial, institutional, and societal barriers that impede this country's movement toward a place that celebrates cultural diversity as a cherished and indispensable component of its social, political, and economic fabric. Despite the tone of skepticism, caution, and pessimism found within this study, I envision a society where people can interact freely, respecting one another without regard to race, color, ethnicity, or religious creed. Before this dream becomes a reality, however, America has to find ways to dissolve its racial, gender, cultural, and class barriers.

Pawnee Beliefs, Critical Scholarship, and Oppression

The acts committed against deceased Indians have had profound, even harmful, effects on the living. Therefore, as an activist and historian, I have had to develop a conceptual framework for giving meaning and order to the conflict. The foundation of my perspective concerning repatriation is derived from a combination of cultural, personal, and academic experiences. An understanding of Pawnee religious and philosophical beliefs about death, gained through oral tradition, dreams, and research, informs my view that repatriation is a social justice movement, supported by native spirituality and sovereignty, committed to the amelioration of the twin evils of oppression and scientific racism. Yet, I am neither a religious fundamentalist nor a left- or right-wing reactionary. Concerning repatriation, I simply advocate that American Indians receive what virtually every other group of Americans enjoys; that is, the right to religious freedom and a lasting burial.

My training as critical scholar provides another cornerstone of my beliefs about the nature of "imperial archaeology." My writings cast the legacy of scientific body snatching within the realm of oppression. Oppression occurs when a set or sets of individuals within the dominant population behave in ways that infringe on the beliefs, cultures, and political structures of other groups of people. Acts of stealing bodies, infringing on spirituality, and resisting repatriation efforts represent classic examples of oppression.

Although exposed to years of secular interpretations about the nature of the world and the significance of archaeology for understanding the past through formal Euroamerican education, I have continued to accept Pawnee beliefs about the afterlife. To adopt any other perspective regarding this matter would deny my cultural heritage. I cannot reconcile archaeology with tradition because of the secular orientation of the former as well as its intrusive practices. Unlike archaeologists who see Native remains as specimens for study, my people view the bodies of deceased loved ones as representing human life with sacred qualities. Death merely marks the passage of the human spirit to another state of being. In a 1988 statement, then Pawnee President Lawrence Goodfox Jr. expressed a common perspective stressing the negative consequences of grave desecration on our dead: "When our people die and go on to the spirit world, sacred rituals and ceremonies are performed. We believe that if the body is disturbed, the spirit becomes restless and cannot be at peace."

Wandering spirits often beset the living with psychological and health problems. Since time immemorial, Pawnees have ceremoniously buried our dead within Mother Earth. Disinterment can occur only for a compelling religious reason. Equally critical to our perspective are cultural norms that stressed that those who tampered with the dead did so with profane, evil, or demented intentions. From this vantage point, the study of stolen remains constitutes abominable acts of sacrilege, desecration, and depravity. But racist attitudes, complete with such axioms as "The only good Indian is a dead Indian," have long conditioned white society to view Indians (as other non-whites) as intellectually inferior subhumans who lacked a right to equal treatment under legal and moral codes. Complicating matters, value judgments about the alleged superiority of the white race became interlocked with scientific thought, leading to the development of oppressive practices and policies.

Consequently, orgies of grave looting occurred without remorse. After the Pawnees removed from Nebraska to Oklahoma during the 1870s, local settlers, followed by amateur and professional archaeologists, looted virtually every Pawnee cemetery they could find, taking remains and burial offerings. Much of the "booty" was placed in an array of institutions including the Nebraska State Historical Society (NSHS) and the Smithsonian Institution.

We have a right to be angry at those who dug our dead from the ground, those who established and maintained curatorial policies, and those who denied our repatriation requests. Last year, my elderly grandmother chastised white society in her typically reserved, but direct fashion for its treatment of our dead. After pointing to an Oklahoma bluff where many Pawnee relatives are buried, she declared, "It is not right, that they dug up all of those bodies in Nebraska." What she referred to can be labeled a spiritual holocaust. When anyone denies us our fundamental human rights, we cannot sit idly by and wait for America to reform itself. It will never happen. We have a duty not only to ourselves, but also to our relatives, our unborn generations, and our ancestors to act. Concerning repatriation, we had no choice but to work for retrieval of our ancestral remains for proper reburial and for legislation that provided penalties for those who disrupted the graves of our relatives.

Yet our initiatives sought redress in a peaceful manner. In 1988, Lawrence Goodfox expressed our goals, declaring "All we want is [the] reburial of the remains of our ancestors and to let them finally rest in peace and for all people in Nebraska to refrain from, forever, any excavation of any Native American graves or burial sites." In our view, reburying the disturbed spirits within Mother Earth equalizes the imbalance between the spiritual and physical worlds caused by the desecration.

National Challenges to Imperial Archaeology and Oppression

The Pawnee reburial struggle occurred within the context of a worldwide indigenous movement. What beset my people had affected Natives everywhere. In this country, few Indian nations escaped the piercing blades of the archaeologists' shovels or the slashes of the headhunters' knives. These operations infringed on Indian beliefs, burial rights, and sovereignty. The notion that this type of research had validity was so ingrained in the psyche of many non-Indians that rarely did anyone question the morality, ethics, or legality of these practices; that is, until the repatriation movement surfaced in the late 1960s. This movement stands on a paramount footing with the valiant struggles of African-Americans for civil rights and women for equality. Taking a leading role during the early stages of the repatriation movement, organizations such as the American Indian Movement (AIM), International Indian Treaty Council, and American Indians Against Desecration (AIAD) expressed in dramatic fashion Indian concerns about the excesses of archaeology and oppression. Committed to the causes of reburying all disinterred Indians and stopping grave disruptions, these groups often employed confrontational strategies. Near Welch, Minnesota, in 1972, for example, AIM members risked arrest by disturbing a dig site. In addition to burning field notes and tools, they confiscated unearthed artifacts and exposed photographic film. Throughout the 1970s and 1980s, AIAD challenged the human remains collections and curatorial policies of government agencies, museums, and universities. As time progressed, many college campuses saw a dramatic increase in tensions between Indians and archaeologists. These actions catapulted the repatriation movement into the consciousness of sympathetic politicians, newspaper editors, and members of the general public. Increased knowledge of the issues subsequently spawned unprecedented levels of non-Indian backing of repatriation.

As the 1980s progressed, more conciliatory Indians, often coming from the professions of law and politics, surfaced as leading figures in the movement. Unlike the universal reburial advocates, these moderates tended to see compromise as the most expedient means available to acquire the desired legislation. They often sought a balance between scientific study of Native remains and the need for Indians to gain religious, burial, and repatriation rights under the law. Organizations such as the National Congress of American Indians and the Native American Rights Fund espoused the moderate cause. Realizing that public sentiments increasingly favored the Indians' views, some archaeologists and museum administrators endorsed compromise as a means of cutting their losses and saving face. With common ground beneath their feet, individuals and organizations waged a series of intense political battles at the state and federal levels.

With moderates in control, reform transpired relatively swiftly. By 1992, more than thirty states had placed laws on the books extending protection to Indian cemeteries, including several with repatriation provisions. Congress passed two pieces of legislation, the National Museum of the American Indian Act in 1989 and NAGPRA the following year. Collectively, these national laws provided Indian nations a means to obtain human remains linked to them by a "preponderance of evidence" and associated funerary offerings held by institutions that received federal funding. NAGPRA also provides penalties for individuals convicted of trafficking in human remains.

Ongoing Reburial Initiatives

With legal avenues now open for Indian governments to reclaim stolen ancestral remains and associated burial objects, some of the old repressive policies fell by the wayside. The change enabled relatives to begin the task of reclaiming stolen bodies and grave offerings for reburial. Collectively, Indian nations thus far have interred thousands of stolen remains. To date (summer 1995), the Pawnees alone have placed nearly a thousand bodies back in Mother Earth. The total number of recovered bodies will surely reach the tens of thousands within a few years.

Reinterment ceremonies, along with funeral feasts, evoke a gamut of emotional expressions ranging from sorrow to joy. When conducting reburials, people rejoice at the fact that the repatriated remains are finally being returned to Mother Earth, but, like modern funerals, an air of sadness pervades the ceremonies. In particular, reinterring the remains of young children causes grieving and weeping. Mourning is part of the healing process in that reburials seek to restore harmony between the living and dead by putting restless spirits to rest. At another level, reburials bring closure to bitterly contested struggles.

Future Concerns

Legislation emanating from the repatriation movement has changed the customary ways that archaeologists and museums operate. Most notably, Indian governments now have established a sovereign right to reclaim the bodies of their ancestors from offending museums, universities, and federal agencies. In this capacity, they have the power to grant and deny access to their dead. Additionally, the new laws make face-to-face interaction routine between museums and Indian nations in certain repatriation matters. Several observers have proclaimed that the common ground signals the dawning of a new era of cooperative relations between Indians and museums. Despite changing attitudes and practices, it is too soon to assess the long-term ramifications of the reburial controversy. Six problematic areas cause me concern about the future of repatriation:

First, the laws do not provide for the reinterment of ancient, unclaimed, or unidentified remains. In other words, the fate of tens of thousands of bodies, along with associated funerary offerings, is uncertain. Will those with authority take steps to provide for a proper reburial for these bodies or will they allow the continuance of old practices and policies?

Second, the absence of legislation and aggressive enforcement of burial protection laws in some states may send a message that grave looting can resume without fear of arrest, prosecution, or punishment.

Third, NAGPRA's graves protection stipulations apply only to federal lands and entities that receive federal funding. In states without both progressive reburial legislation and a substantial Indian populace, large-scale acts of grave desecration may continue. . . .

Fourth, and perhaps most significant a pervasive attitude among elements of the archaeology and museum communities keeps repressive and archaic ideas alive. In fact, members of these groups have consistently disavowed any wrongdoing by themselves and their predecessors. Rather, some present their work to the public as neutral, impartial, and objective interpretations of distant Native American cultures. To counter claims that the digging and study is disrespectful, others assert that taking remains for study shows respect for Indian people and culture. In a twisted logic, still others insist that they are the "true spiritual descendants of the original Indians and the contemporary Indians [are] foreigners who had no right to complain about their activities." Like most other repatriation advocates, I reject these pleas as condescending and duplicitous acts of misguided people and lost souls. . . .

Anti-repatriation advocates echoed a common refrain. They viewed their pursuits as being under attack by narrow-minded and anti-intellectual radicals who sought to destroy archaeology. Equating repatriation with book burning, some alarmists often charged falsely that Indians would not rest until they had stripped museums and universities of their Indian collections. These strategies contain elements of self-delusion, arrogance, and racism. A tacit message found in these paternalistic defenses of imperial archaeology was that Indians must, for their own good, learn to respect the work of archaeology. Equally disturbing is the notion that Indians need archaeology. However, the exact opposite is true. Beneath the self-serving rhetoric lay a deceptive ambiance of cultural imperialism that masked the stark reality of how archaeology and museums infringed on Indian religion and burial rights.

Fifth, imperial archaeologists have had substantial levels of support from real and pretend Indians. The phenomena of co-optation and self-interest reverberates loudly here. Usually found working in museums, universities, and government agencies, some of these individuals claim a heritage complete with a Cherokee princess, but they embrace the secular views and values of Western science. Others belonging to this camp clearly have significant amounts of Indian blood, but they rely heavily on the goodwill of their non-Indian colleagues to promote and maintain their careers. Non-institutional advocacy surfaced from some grassroots Indians. At meetings, conferences, and confrontations, archaeologists rarely failed to produce a reservation Indian or two who spoke passionately against reburial in an effort to convince the public and policy makers that Native communities lacked unanimity on the subject. Whatever their motive, degree of Indian blood, or cultural orientation, their willingness to endorse oppressive archaeological practices marks a radical departure from traditional Indian philosophy.

Collectively, "wannabes" and misguided Indians may be able to damage reburial efforts. As the movement pushed for national repatriation legislation in the late 1980s, we found them sitting on committees convened by anthropology and museum associations that issued reports condemning repatriation. In a worst-case scenario, NAGPRA and other committees stacked with them and imperial archaeologists could conceivably frustrate or undermine repatriation requests.

Finally, it seems that archaeologists have launched a campaign to convince the public, tribal leaders, and others that skeletal investigations are necessary for a variety of reasons. According to a recent *Chronicle of Higher Education* article, "More and more of those kinds of opportunities will occur, many scholars agree, when researchers learn to persuade American Indians and others that skeletal remains and artifacts represent something other than a publication toward a faculty member's promotion and tenure." In other words, we are seeing archaeologists adopt less abrasive tactics to get their hands on our dead. Succumbing to subtle pressure, aimed at convincing us to accept a secular view of the dead as research objects, will erode a cherished part of our belief systems and cultures. In any event, some Indian nations have allowed the creation of archaeology programs on their reservations.

Clearly, the repatriation movement has won some major victories, but the war is unfinished. United States history teaches the lesson that individuals who face the threat of losing a privileged status often will devise rationalizations and strategies to resist change. Southern slave owners, for example, argued against abolitionism by making the outlandish claim that involuntary servitude was a benevolent institution that saved millions of blacks from the savagery of Africa. Historians repeated this claim well into the twentieth century.

It is conceivable that at some point someone will challenge the constitutionality of NAGPRA. If this occurs, will the courts respect Indian beliefs and burial rights? America's long history concerning issues of Indian religious freedom and political rights makes the possibility of a legal suit a scary thought. The Supreme Court has occasionally protected Indian sovereignty, as well as hunting, fishing, and water rights, but it also has incorporated such imperialistic notions as the doctrine of discovery and the plenary power doctrine into U.S. law. Its decisions also have eroded the power of Indian self-government by allowing the imposition of federal jurisdiction over certain crimes committed on Indian lands.

In recent years, conservative justices appointed by President Ronald Reagan have endangered Indian religious freedom. In *Lyng v. Northwest Indian Cemetery Protective Association* (108 S. Ct. 1319 (1988)) Justice Sandra Day O'Connor wrote the majority decision stating that the U.S. government had the right to build a road through an area on federal lands sacred to Yurok, Karok, and Tolowa Indians even if such a construction project would destroy the ability of those people to worship. In *Employment Division Department of Human Resources of Oregon v. Smith* (110 S. Ct. 1595 (1990)) the court held that a state could abridge expressions of religious freedom if the state had a compelling reason to do so. In this case, the court paved the way for states to deprive Native American Church (NAC) members of the right to use peyote in connection with their worship. Fortunately, in 1994, Congress addressed the religious crisis caused by the court by enacting a law that sanctioned peyote use for NAC services.

History demonstrates that promises made by white America to help Indians have not always materialized. The administrative branch of the federal government has entered into 371 treaties with Indian nations and systematically violated each of them. The legislative record is another cause of concern. The Indian Reorganization Act of 1934 authorized Indian nations to restructure themselves politically but only in accordance with models and terms acceptable to Department of Interior officials. During the 1970s, Congress declared that Indian government could exercise more powers of self-government. Federal bureaucratic controls over Indian governments, however, actually became more stringent, if not suffocating, in this era. During that decade, Congress also enacted the American Indian Religious Freedom Act of 1978 in a half-hearted effort to encourage federal agencies to accommodate customary Indian worship practices at off-reservation sites. The act provided virtually no protection because federal agencies and the Supreme Court, as we have seen, have followed a tradition that sees nothing wrong with suppressing Indian religious freedom. Although Indians are pursing a legislative remedy to resolve these problems, Congress has yet to enact a true religious freedom law for them.

Conclusion

Facing overwhelming odds, the repatriation movement has achieved many noteworthy successes. United States society, including a growing number of sympathetic archaeologists and museum curators, has finally recognized that Indians are not disappearing, and that Indians are entitled to burial rights and religious freedom. Nevertheless, under the new repatriation laws, many non-Indian entities still "legally" hold thousands of Indian remains and burial offerings. With many archaeologists and museum curators committed to upholding oppressive operational principles, values, and beliefs, the fate of these bodies remains in question. Moreover, others, perhaps best described as wolves in sheeps' clothing, are seeking to gain our cooperation, a euphemism meaning the delivery of another blow to our revered philosophies about the dead.

Given the durability of imperialist archaeology and the new approaches being used to gain access to the remains of our beloved ancestors, we must remain vigilant and monitor their operations. Protecting our dead must remain a moral and spiritual obligation we cannot callously abandon for we cannot allow further erosions of our beliefs and traditions. Thus a need still exists for maintaining the cultural traditions that inspired the repatriation movement.

Clement W. Meighan

Some Scholars' Views on Reburial

[T]here is something inherently distasteful and unseemly in secreting either the fruits or seeds of scientific endeavors.

— Judge Bruce S. Jenkins

Destruction of archaelogical collections through the demands for reburial presents a serious conflict between religion and science. Archaeologists should not deal with these matters by "compromise" alone, but must sustain their rights and duties as scholars.

The above quotation is from a court case having nothing to do with archaeology, yet if we believe that archaeology is a scientific endeavor we must agree that this statement applies to archaeology as well as medicine, chemistry, or other fields of scholarship. The recent increased attention given to the ethics of scientists and scientific organizations, with news accounts almost weekly in such journals as *Science,* requires archaeologists to examine their basic assumptions about the nature of science and their obligations to scholarship. This is brought forward most forcefully in the debate over the past 20 years about the problems of reburial of archaeological and museum collections.

The discussion by Goldstein and Kintigh (1990) is a valiant effort to unravel some of the strands of conflict inherent in the controversy over the destruction of museum collections in the name of Indian religious beliefs. They seek some sort of middle ground in which scholarly and ethnic concerns can coexist in a constructive way. However, in view of the massive losses of scientific data now legislated by the federal government and some of the states, it needs to be made clear that many archaeologists do not agree with some aspects of the philosophical position taken by Goldstein and Kintigh. In particular, their statement that "We must change the way we do business" (Goldstein and Kintigh 1990:589) is not justified, particularly since their suggestions for change involve the abandonment of scholarly imperatives and the adoption of an "ethical" position that accepts the right of nonscholars to demand the destruction of archaeological evidence and the concealment of archaeological data. Of course, changes in the way archaeology is done will inevitably take

From *American Antiquity,* October 1992, pp. 704–710. Copyright © 1992 by Society for American Archaeology. Reprinted by permission.

place, for both internal (professional) and external (social/legal) reasons. This does not mean that the basic rules of scholarly obligations to one's data should change as well.

Goldstein and Kintigh fall into the anthropological trap of cultural relativism. In asserting that we must balance our concerns for knowledge with "our professional ethic of cultural relativism," they argue that our values are not the only values or ethics, but only one legitimate belief system. The implication is that all belief systems are of equal legitimacy, therefore one cannot make a clear commitment to any particular values as a guide to action. However, most individuals do make a commitment to the values that will guide their personal action. Recognizing that other people may have other values does not mean that one must accept those values or compromise his/her own ethical standards. Indeed, the dictionary has a word for believing one way and acting another—it is "hypocrisy."

Those who affiliate with organized groups, whether the Church of the Rising Light or the Society for American Archaeology (SAA), supposedly accept the beliefs and goals of the organization as stated in their by-laws or scriptures. The SAA, as an organization dedicated to scholarly research in archaeology, is bound by the general rules of scholarship that require *honest reporting and preservation of the evidence*. If the research data are subject to censorship, how can there be honest reporting? If the evidence (collections) is not preserved, who can challenge the statements of the researcher? Who can check for misinterpretations, inaccuracies, or bias? Once the collection is destroyed, we have only an affidavit from the researcher; we can believe it or not, but there is no way that additional investigation or new laboratory techniques can be applied to the collection to gain a better understanding of the evidence. The astounding new methods for medical and genetic research on ancient populations require a piece of the bone—pictures and notes won't do. Similarly, laboratory advances in dating and determining the source of artifact materials require that the relevant objects be available for study. Since we commonly proclaim that archaeological collections are unique and irreplaceable, how can we ever justify the conscious and acquiescent destruction of our data?

The suggestion of Goldstein and Kintigh that we balance our own values with the professional ethic of cultural relativism by "compromise and mutual respect" is not realistic. Many archaeologists are not going to compromise away their most fundamental scholarly beliefs. Similarly, many Indian activists are not going to compromise away their beliefs (however unsupported by evidence) that every Indian bone of the past 12,000 years belongs to one of their ancestors. There are some instances in which compromise and mutual respect have led to satisfactory results for both sides; there are many more instances in which these valued qualities have been insufficient to prevent or postpone destruction of important archaeological finds.

Those who want to do away with archaeology and archaeological collections are of course entitled to their beliefs, and they are also entitled to use whatever political and legal machinery they can to bring about their stated goals. Originally, the goals were modest, but they have escalated every year since this discussion began more than 20 years ago, as reviewed by me in an earlier article (Meighan 1984). The present-day goals have repeatedly been made clear. For example, Christopher Quayle, an attorney for the Three Affiliated Tribes, stated in *Harpers* (Preston 1989:68–69): "It's conceivable that some time in the not-so-distant future there won't be a single Indian skeleton in any museum in the country. We're going to put them out of business." The "them" refers in this statement to physical anthropologists, but it is also extended to archaeologists. For example, the recent agreement between state officials in West Virginia and a committee representing Indian viewpoints (a committee which, incidentally, includes non-Indians) states that everything in an ongoing study of a 2,000-year-old Adena mound must be given up for reburial within a year—"everything" includes not only the bones of the mythical "ancestors" of the claimants, but also all the artifacts, the chipping waste, the food refuse, the pollen samples, the soil samples, and whatever else may be removed for purposes of scientific study. While the tax-payers are expected to pay for a 1.8-million-dollar excavation on the grounds that it is in the public interest for archaeological data to be preserved, *nothing* of the tangible archaeological evidence is to be preserved. Meanwhile, Indian activists are paid to "monitor" the excavation, and they were given the right to censor the final report and prevent any objectionable photographs or data from appearing.

If there is any doubt about the goals of the anti-archaeology contingent, consider the case of Dr. David Van Horn, charged with a felony in California for conducting an environmental impact study required by law, and being honest enough to report what he found in the site, including some small bits of cremated bone, which required hours of study by physical anthropologists to identify as human. Is the reporting of a legally mandated salvage excavation a felony? It can be in California, and there are many who would like to make archaeology a crime throughout the United States. Archaeologists who accept these situations or treat them as merely local concerns (apparently the position of most scholarly organizations including the SAA), have not just compromised, they have abandoned scholarly ethics in favor of being "respectful and sensitive" to nonscholars and anti-intellectuals. When the current round of controversy is over, this loss of scientific integrity will be heavily condemned.

So there are some situations in which compromise is not necessarily the best approach, and this is one of them. Archaeologists may well be legislated out of business, and museums may well lose all their American Indian collections, and indeed the Indians have been far more successful than the archaeologists in the political arena. Many archaeologists believe, however, that this should not occur with the happy connivance of the scholarly profession of archaeology. Over 600 of them are members of the American Committee for Preservation of Archaeological Collections (ACPAC), which has argued for over 10 years that archaeology is a legitimate, moral, and even useful profession, and that collections that were legally made should remain in museums as an important part of the heritage of the nation. Bahn may have had this group in mind in his news report on the "first international congress on the reburial of human remains," in his reference to "the extremists, who unfortunately did not attend the congress to put the case for rejecting the whole notion of reburial." Who are these extremists? Neither ACPAC nor any individual known to me has stated that no reburial of any kind should take place; everyone agrees that bones of known relatives should be returned to demonstrable descendants. The disagreement is over remains to which no living person can demonstrate any relationship. Museum materials 5,000 years old are claimed by people who imagine themselves to be somehow related to the collections in question, but such a belief has no basis in evidence and is mysticism. Indeed, it is not unlikely that Indians who have acquired such collections for reburial are venerating the bones of alien groups and traditional enemies rather than distant relatives.

If the present attacks on archaeological data were happening in engineering, medicine, or chemistry, they would not be accepted by the general public since destruction or concealment of the facts in those areas of scientific knowledge can lead to disastrous results for many living people. The general lack of public concern about the attack on archaeology arises from the perception that archaeological conclusions really do not matter—if someone's reconstruction of the ancient past is ridiculous or unsupported by evidence, who cares? It will not affect the daily lives of anyone now alive, no matter what we believe about what happened thousands of years ago. However, the principles of scholarship and scientific evidence are the same in all scholarly research, including archaeology and anthropology, and credibility of conclusions is an essential consideration for any field of scholarship, whether or not there are immediate practical effects of the conclusions that are reached.

In one of the polemics put forward by Indian spokesmen in the student newspaper at the University of California (Los Angeles), those of us on the archaeological faculty were accused of participating in an activity that was comparable to the "killing fields of Cambodia." Even allowing for the juvenile rhetoric characteristic of student newspapers, I was dumbfounded at such a statement. How could I harm any person who had already been dead for thousands of years? How could anything that my studies did with the bones of these ancient people harm any living person? The condemnation seems extreme for a "crime" that is merely a failure to invite mythical descendants to control my research and destroy museum collections held in the public interest. When issues of respect and sensitivity are raised, it needs to be pointed out that these work both ways.

Some Legal Issues: Constitutional Requirements

The first amendment states that Congress shall make no laws respecting an establishment of religion. Most state constitutions have similar clauses; that of California says the state will *never* pass such laws. Yet California, other states, and the federal government have numerous laws on the books that are specifically written to favor aboriginal tribal religious beliefs and compel others to act in accordance with them. Religious infringement also occurs when archaeologists are excluded from evaluating claims regarding repatriation because they do not hold particular religious beliefs. Until these statutes are challenged and overturned, they remain an opening for other groups to seek similar legislation making their religious beliefs enforceable by law. Creationists, for example, have been trying for over 60 years to outlaw the teaching of evolution because it is in conflict with their religious tenets.

That there is a science vs. religion aspect is clear in the religious justification for the claiming of bones and "sacred" artifacts, as well as the proclamation of many activists that archaeologists and museums are committing sacrilege in obtaining, storing, and studying archaeological remains. I discuss bone worship elsewhere (Meighan 1990). Tonetti (1990) provides a case study of the situation in Ohio, documenting the religious roots of the anti-archaeology movement. He also reports a survey of Ohio legislators that reveals a frightening ignorance of science in general and archaeology in particular: "As Zimmerman so dramatically stated in his op ed piece in the Columbus Dispatch, he does not want the General Assembly making law dealing with science issues when over 75% do not know what his 5 year old son has known for years—that dinosaurs and humans did not coexist" (Zimmerman [1989], as quoted in Tonetti [1990:22]; recent news reports state that some Indians are now claiming dinosaur bones recovered by paleontologists).

Some Legal Issues: Cultural-Resource Laws

There is a serious conflict between the laws mandating return and destruction of archaeological material (not just bones but also artifacts and anything deemed "ceremonial" by the claimants), and those laws mandating cultural-resource management and the study and conservation of archaeological sites and remains. The Van Horn case previously mentioned put Van Horn in the position of doing an environmental-impact report required by law, only to find himself spending thousands of dollars defending himself against a felony charge for violating laws based on Indian religious beliefs about cremated bones. The judge agreed with defense witnesses that there was no basis for a trial, but the state made its point that archaeologists will be heavily punished if "Indians" request it, regardless of the validity of their complaint.

The legal dichotomy between science and religion as it pertains to archaeology may be related, as Goldstein and Kintigh (1990:589) point out, to the fact that public perception does not include Indian history as part of the history of the United States, even though they recognize that public policy and law include the non-European past as an integral part of the history of the nation. That part of American history that is Indian history is largely the contribution of archaeology; *all* of it prior to 1492 is the contribution of archaeology. This has been recognized and supported by the government since the Antiquities Act of 1906, and it is the basis for all the environmental-impact laws dealing with archaeological remains.

Many opponents of archaeological-resource laws believe that since archaeology has no effect on public health or safety, it ought to be excluded from environmental impact laws. They are given considerable ammunition by laws that state that it is in the public interest to spend a lot of money to get archaeological materials, and then state that such materials are not worth preservation but are to be reburied as soon as possible after they are dug up, in some cases within a few days or weeks of the fieldwork. Further, the belief that archaeology belongs to Indians removes it from the heritage of all of the citizens and makes it less likely that the public will be interested in supporting activities not seen to be in the broad public interest. In these times of stringent budgets, it is hard enough to convince the taxpayers that they should finance archaeological excavations without having to convince them that they should also finance the reburial of the items recovered.

There are major negative results for archaeology in the present situation where not only the federal government, but states, counties, cities, and a plethora of political agencies believe that they should pass regulations controlling archaeological research. These laws and regulations conflict with one another and vary from jurisdiction to jurisdiction. In some states the conduct of archaeological research is a risky business. The smart archaeologist in California does not find certain things. If they are found, they are either thrown away or not mentioned in his/her reports. Field classes are also careful not to expose students or teachers to criminal charges, meaning that students in those classes will never expose a burial or deal with any "controversial" finds. Chipping waste is still a safe area for study.

This chilling effect on research is creating an underground archaeology of ill-trained students, dishonest researchers, and intimidated teachers who are afraid to show a picture of a burial to their classes, let alone an actual human bone. Students, who are often more perceptive than their professors, rapidly catch on and change their major or move their archaeological interests to parts of the world where they will be allowed to practice their scholarly profession. There is an increasing loss to American archaeology, and of course to the Indians whose history is dependent on it.

Some Museum Issues

A negative effect of the ongoing shift to tribalism and the right of anyone to claim anything in museums is already happening. In the past, most of the support for museums came from private donors, who contributed not only money but collections. Donors of collections had the tacit (and sometimes written) agreement that their materials would be preserved in the public interest. Who would contribute anything to a museum if they thought the museum was going to give their material away for reburial or destruction? When even Stanford University and other respected repositories of scientific collections decide that their first obligation is to whatever Indian claimant comes along, the donor who wants his/her material *preserved* will seek a repository in a state or country that is dedicated to that aim. It is a paradox that the National Park Service is busily developing new standards of curation for government collections at the same time the new National Museum of the American Indian is declaring that it will not keep anything that Indian claimants declare that they want.

Reviewers of this article believe that only a very small part of archaeological collections will be taken away from museums and archaeologists. This is a pious hope in view of the escalation of claims previously noted, reaching the apex in the West Virginia case in which *everything* recovered by archaeologists is to be given up for reburial. There are numerous cases in which archaeologists or museum employees have given up entire collections rather than negotiate with Indian claimants; for example, one prominent California case (the Encino excavation) included reburial of a number of dog skeletons, not required by any statute. It is true that the Smithsonian and some other museums now have committees to evaluate claims against their collections; perhaps these will protect scholarly and public interests, but it remains to be seen whether they can withstand the political pressures brought to bear. While I am sure that not all collections will entirely disappear, under current legislation all physical remains, all mortuary associations, and all items claimed to have religious or ceremonial significance are at risk—these are the major sources of information in many archaeological studies. When claimants can get museum specimens merely by using the word "sacred," it should be apparent that anything can be claimed by someone. It does happen, it has happened, and scholars can only hope that it will not happen in the future.

Conclusions

When scholarly classes in United States archaeology and ethnology are no longer taught in academic departments (they are diminishing rapidly), when the existing collections have been selectively destroyed or concealed, and when all new field archaeology in the United States is a political exercise rather than a scientific investigation, will the world be a better place? Certainly the leadership in archaeological research, which has been characteristic of the last 50 years of American archaeology, will be lost, and it will be left to other nations to make future advances in archaeological methods, techniques, and scholarly investigations into the ancient past.

One reviewer of this paper commented that I am engaged in a "futile attempt to resurrect a bankrupt status quo." In this view, not only can nothing be done to improve the present situation, but nothing *should* be done, and we should all meekly accept the regulations, limitations, and restrictions of academic freedom that are brought forward by politicians and pressure groups. For the last 20 years, those who have attempted to change these restrictions in favor of scholarly ethics and the preservation of collections have been dismissed as a small group of outmoded discontents who cannot adapt to a changing world. This is a mistake; I may represent a minority view, but it is not confined to a small number and is growing rapidly as archaeologists see more and more of their basic data destroyed through reburial. ACPAC's 600 members (in 44 states) include a sizeable fraction of the leading archaeologists in the United States as well as physical anthropologists, museum workers, and yes, Indians.

I am, however, triggered by the accusation that my comments lead to nothing but intransigence to offer a few suggestions for action other than "compromise," which so far has mostly meant giving in to political demands. My suggestions:

1. Archaeologists negotiating with Indians or other groups should make an effort to be sure that all factions of the affected group are heard, not merely the group of activists who are first in the door. Many archaeologists have been doing this for years, and nearly all of us can report that we had little difficulty in finding Indians who would work with us in a mutually agreeable and often rewarding relationship

that respected Indian interests but at the same time preserved the archaeological collections. Unfortunately, numerous instances can be cited of savage personal attacks on those Indians who agreed to share the archaeologists' task, with attempts to force the archaeologist to use other consultants and claims that the one chosen was not a real Indian (see an example in Tonetti [1990:21]). When money is involved, this is probably inevitable. However, there is no reason for archaeologists to be controlled by enemies of their discipline when they can work with friends. The existence of Indian physical anthropologists, archaeologists, and museum workers, as well as the increasing number of Indian-owned museums with scientific objectives and high standards of curation, should offer opportunities for real collaboration that do not require the destruction of evidence nor the censorship of scientific reporting.

2. Professional organizations should work to amend the legislation dealing with archaeology to get a time cut-off inserted: Remains older than a certain age should not be subject to reburial. The present laws, which ignore time and assume that everything, regardless of age, is directly related to living people, are not scientifically valid, and the scientific organizations are in a position to make this clear, if necessary in court. The recent reburial of an Idaho skeleton dated at 10,600 years ago should never have happened, but as reported by the State Historic Preservation Office of that state, Idaho law requires *no* demonstration of any relationship between Indians and archaeological remains.

3. Professional organizations should point out the disagreements between "preservation" laws and "religion" laws and should try to strengthen the former and eliminate the conflicts. If they are unable to resolve the issue by negotiation, they should support court cases that address the matter.

4. If scholarly organizations are unwilling or unable to make a clear statement of their position with respect to the giving up of archaeological collections and data, it is left to the individual archaeologist to decide his or her own professional ethics in this matter. A clear review of the moral issues is given by Del Bene (1990). This should be considered, particularly by young archaeologists entering the profession, so that they are consciously aware of the decisions they are making and the consequences for their professional future.

References

Del Bene, T.A. 1990. Take the Moral Ground: An Essay on the "Reburial" Issue. *West Virginia Archeologist 42*(2):11–19.

Goldstein, L., and K. Kintigh. 1990. Ethics and the Reburial Controversy. *American Antiquity* 55:585–591.

Meighan, C.W. 1984. Archaeology: Science or Sacrilege? In *Ethics and Values in Archaeology*, edited by E.L. Green, pp. 203–233. Free Press, New York.

1990. Bone Worship. *West Virginia Archeologist 42*(2):40–43.

Preston, D.J. 1989. Skeletons in Our Museums' Closets. *Harpers*. February: 66–75.

Tonetti, A.C. 1990. Ghost Dancing in the Nineties: Research, Reburial and Resurrection Among the Dead in Ohio. *West Virginia Archeologist 42*(2):20–22.

EXPLORING THE ISSUE

Should the Remains of Prehistoric Native Americans Be Reburied Rather Than Studied?

Critical Thinking and Reflection

1. Riding In uses his own Pawnee customs to explain his views on repatriation and reburial of human remains from all Native American sites. To what extent is this a reasonable position for remains from all Indian tribes? Is there a single religion for all Native Americans? Would it matter if one or another tribe had become Evangelical Christians, Catholics, or Lutherans?

2. When writing some 15 years ago, Meighan takes a more strident position than most archaeologists would voice today. What factors would tend to soften the archaeological position on repatriation today that were not present when these two essays were first published?

3. For Riding In the core of his argument is the moral and religious perspective, which places Native rights as equal to the rights of mainstream Americans. Meighan takes the position that science stands apart from issues of morality and religion, but is equally—if not more important. But both authors view the repatriation issue from at least one other perspective. What is this perspective? Why do they both acknowledge it and back off from it?

4. Is it likely that museums will be able to keep any of the Native American skeletal collections?

5. Interpretations of NAGPRA legislation suggest that any tribe can present a serious and credible claim that an object in a public museum has deep cultural significance for their tribe. This has been generally successful in reclaiming important objects, even though not an expressed intention of the original legislation. Will NAGPRA ultimately lead to the loss of all the great museum collections of cultural material in the United States?

Is There Common Ground?

In the early 1980s before passage of NAGPRA, some archaeologists had adopted very strident attitudes toward Native American groups demanding reburial of all skeletal remains. When these essays were written a number of issues were still unresolved. Since then a number of Indian groups have successfully requested the return of human remains from many museums. Other groups have expressed little interest in repatriation of skeletal remains because

397

they do not share the same religious beliefs as those expressed by Riding In. A number of museum curators and archaeologists have taken a much more tempered and conciliatory approach to dealing with these issues than the position expressed by Meighan. Some have even worked closely with Indians and have established a new rapport not widely seen before NAGPRA.

Such possibilities suggest that there are a variety of alternative approaches to the issue of reburial besides the diametrically opposed positions expressed in these two selections. Many groups, both from museums and universities, have urged compromise. More Native American students are obtaining professional training as anthropologists and archaeologists. And some archaeologists collaborate with local tribal groups whenever skeletal material is uncovered.

Despite these advances some contentious issues remain. What should be done with very early skeletons whose affiliation with modern tribes is suspect? Should the religious beliefs of one group of Native Americans stand for those of all Indians? Should modern Native American communities have rights to rebury any human remains found on their lands? What should happen to the remains of the very earliest settlers in North America who are unlikely to be biologically related to modern tribes?

Additional Resources

One of the most recent and current surveys of the issue can be found in:
Murray, Tim. 2011. "Archaeologists and Indigenous People: A Maturing Relationship," *Annual Review of Anthropology* 40:363–378.

Another view of collaboration between archaeologists and Native Americans can be found in:
Goodby, Robert G. 2006. "Working With the Abenaki in New Hampshire," in J. Kerber, ed. *Cross-Cultural Collaboration: Native Peoples and Archaeology in the Northeastern United States.* Lincoln: University of Nebraska Press.

For an excellent summary of anthropological interest in Native American remains supportive of Riding In's general position see:
Bieder, Robert. 1990. *A Brief Historical Survey of the Expropriation of American Indian Remains.* Native American Rights Fund.

Watkins, Joe. 2005. "Through Wary Eyes: Indigenous Perspectives on Archaeology," *Annual Review of Anthropology* 34:429–449.

A useful article from the archaeological community is:
Rose, J.C., Green, T.J., and Green, V.D. 1996. "NAGPRA Is Forever: Osteology and the Repatriation of Skeletons," *Annual Review of Anthropology* 25:81–103.

On the ethical issues involved in the reburial question see:
Goldstein, Lynn and Kintigh, Keith. "Ethics and the Reburial Controversy," *American Antiquity* 55(3):585–591.

Preston, Douglas. 1997. "The Lost Man: Umatilla Indians' Plan to Rebury 9,300 Year Old Kennewick Man with Caucasoid Features," *The New Yorker* June 16.

Thomas, David Hurst. 2000. *Skull Wars: Kennewick Man, Archeology, and the Battle for Native American Identity.* New York: Basic Books.

Vitelli, Karen D., ed. 1996. *Archaeological Ethics.* Walnut Creek: Altimira Press.

The most recent set of documents about Kennewick Man can be found on the National Park Service. This collection of official reports is the most comprehensive available: www.nps.gov/archeology/kennewick/Index.htm

ISSUE 18

Did Napoleon Chagnon's Research Methods Harm the Yanomami Indians of Venezuela?

YES: **Terence Turner,** from *The Yanomami and the Ethics of Anthropological Practice* (Cornell University Latin American Studies Program, 2001)

NO: **Edward H. Hagen, Michael E. Price, and John Tooby,** from *Preliminary Report* (Department of Anthropology, University of California, Santa Barbara, 2001)

Learning Outcomes

After reading this issue, you should be able to:

- Understand the debate over the ethics of Napoleon Chagnon's research among the Yanomami Indians of southern Venezuela.
- Discuss the possible effects a foreign anthropologist can have on a remote and isolated tribe.
- Explain some of the unintended consequences of anthropological fieldwork in remote areas.
- Understand some of the difficulties in conducting research with remote peoples with simple technologies.
- Discuss the ethical obligations that anthropologists have toward their study communities.

ISSUE SUMMARY

YES: Anthropologist Terence Turner contends that journalist Patrick Tierney's book *Darkness in El Dorado* accurately depicts how anthropologist Napoleon Chagnon's research among the Yanomami Indians caused conflict between groups and how Chagnon's portrayal of the Yanomami as extremely violent aided gold miners trying to take over Yanomami land.

NO: Anthropologists Edward Hagen, Michael Price, and John Tooby counter that Tierney systematically distorts Chagnon's views on Yanomami violence and exaggerates the amount of disruption caused by Chagnon's activities compared to those of such others as missionaries and gold miners.

In September 2000, a startling message flew around the e-mail lists of the world's anthropologists. It was a letter from Cornell University anthropologist Terry Turner and University of Hawaii anthropologist Leslie Sponsel to the president and president-elect of the American Anthropological Association, with copies to a few other officers, warning them of the imminent publication of a book that they said would "affect the American anthropological profession as a whole in the eyes of the public, and arouse intense indignation and calls for action among members of the Association." The book in question, which they had read in galley proofs, was Patrick Tierney's *Darkness in El Dorado: How Scientists and Journalists Devastated the Amazon* (W.W. Norton and Company, 2000). The letter summarized some of Tierney's charges that medical researcher James Neel, anthropologist Napoleon Chagnon, and others seriously harmed the Yanomami Indians of Venezuela, even causing a measles epidemic that killed hundreds.

The leaking of the letter and the subsequent publication of an article by Tierney in *The New Yorker* caused great excitement at the annual meeting of the American Anthropological Association in San Francisco in mid-November 2000. Discussion climaxed at a panel discussion that filled a double ballroom at the Hilton Hotel with several thousand anthropologists and media representatives from around the world present. The panel included Tierney, anthropologist William Irons (representing Chagnon, who declined to attend), and experts on the history of science, epidemiology, and South American Indians. (Neel could not defend himself, as he had died earlier that year.) Numerous members of the audience also spoke. During and after the meeting a consensus developed that Tierney was wrong in his claim that the measles epidemic in 1968 was caused by Neel's and Chagnon's inoculations, since measles vaccines are incapable of causing the actual disease. However, Tierney's accusations that Chagnon had treated the Yanomami in an unethical manner during his research and had distorted his findings were not so easily dismissed. Later, the Executive Board of the A.A.A. established a task force to examine the allegations in Tierney's book. The 300-page Task Force Final Report was completed on May 18, 2002 and posted on the A.A.A. Web site.

Why would a book about researchers' treatment of a small Amazonian tribe have caused such an uproar? The reason is that, due to the enormous sales of Chagnon's book *The Yanomamö* (now in its fifth edition) and the prize-winning films he made with Timothy Asch, the Yanomami (as most scholars spell their name) are probably the world's best-known tribal people and Chagnon is one of the most famous ethnographers since Margaret Mead. The image of Yanomami men as relentlessly aggressive, engaged in a never-ending struggle over women has been burned into the consciousness of generations of undergraduates. Chagnon's use of his Yanomami data to support his sociobiological explanation of human behavior has also had influence outside anthropology, for example, in evolutionary psychology. The idea that the most aggressive men win the most wives and have the most children, thus passing their aggressive genes on to future generations more abundantly than the peaceful genes of their nonaggressive brethren, is a cornerstone of the popular view that humans are innately violent.

Tierney's attack on Chagnon's credibility sent shock waves through the scholarly community. Part of the defensiveness on the part of anthropology professors was that so many of us had so often used Chagnon's films and monograph in our classes. The freshness of his films, in particular, made us feel that we understood the Yanomami Indians almost as well as the peoples we ourselves had studied. The charges that Chagnon had misrepresented the Indians with whom he lived meant that anthropology professors had similarly misrepresented the Yanomami to their students for several decades. The charges challenged everything we thought we knew about this previously obscure group deep in the rainforests of Venezuela.

This controversy raises a number of fundamental ethical questions for anthropological researchers. Are scholars responsible for how others use their findings? Should researchers always place the welfare of their subjects ahead of the success of their research? Do researchers have a moral obligation to compensate the people for their help and information? Are researchers responsible for the sometimes-harmful effects of those payments? Are there ways of doing research that are mutually beneficial?

In this issue, Turner argues that Tierney is correct in claiming that Chagnon failed to object when gold miners used his portrayal of the Yanomami as violent to hinder the establishment of a Yanomami reserve in Brazil, that Chagnon manipulated his demographic data to support his hypothesis that more violent Yanomami men have more wives and children than less violent ones, and that his fieldwork practices caused conflict between Yanomami groups. Turner agrees with journalist Patrick Tierney that Chagnon callously refused to disavow the image he created of the Yanomami as violent when gold miners and their supporters used that image against them. He also blames Chagnon for manipulating his data to contend that Yanomami are genetically programmed to be violent, due to violent males having more children than nonviolent ones, and for actually causing violence by his gift giving and violations of taboos. In addition, when Chagnon and his team gave villagers machetes and other Western goods to his closest friends, this gave them an unfair advantage over neighbors, inspiring both his friends and their enemy neighbors to greater violence.

Hagen, Price, and Tooby counter that Tierney deliberately misrepresents evidence in claiming that Chagnon violated Yanomami taboos in his fieldwork and that he manipulated his data to support his claim that killers have more offspring than nonkillers. They attribute Tierney's opposition to Chagnon to the latter's use of sociobiology, a theory that is unpopular with many anthropologists. Hagen and his colleagues contend that Tierney systematically selects and distorts his evidence to portray Chagnon in the worst possible light, and they argue that the amount of harm Chagnon did to the Yanomami pales compared to that caused by missionaries, gold miners, and other intruders into their territory. The period of contact in which Chagnon was living with the Yanomami was one of great social disruption because it was not just Chagnon, but miners, missionaries, and other outsiders who inspired the increased violence.

When reading these selections, consider what the ethical obligation of a field researcher is to the people one is studying. Should anthropologists try to prevent change from coming to their study communities? Or should they assist their informants with medicines and useful foreign goods?

YES ⬅

Terence Turner

The Yanomami and the Ethics of Anthropological Practice

Controversy over the mistreatment of the Yanomami, an indigenous people of Venezuela and northern Brazil, by scientific researchers and anthropologists had smoldered for over a decade before it burst into flame [in 2001] with the publication of Patrick Tierney's *Darkness in El Dorado*. The controversy over the issues raised in the book, and more broadly over what has been done to the Yanomami by anthropologists and other researchers, confronts the discipline of anthropology, as represented by its professional society, the American Anthropological Association, and several universities and learned societies with which some of the principals in the case were connected, with ethically fraught issues. How these issues are dealt may well set significant precedents for the ethical and scientific standards of the institutions and professions involved, particularly in regard to the responsibilities of professional associations for the conduct of their members, and of researchers in the field for their human subjects. . . .

My work as head of the AAA Special Commission to Investigate the Situation of the Brazilian Yanomami in 1990–91 was the original reason for my involvement in Yanomami affairs. Together with subsequent work with NGOs and anthropologists engaged in the struggle to support and defend the Yanomami, it remains the basis of my appraisal of much of Tierney's account of Chagnon's activities among the Yanomami, including his attacks on Yanomami-support NGOs and Yanomami leaders. I was appointed to head the Special AAA Commission on the Brazilian Yanomami by the then President of the AAA, Annette Weiner, on the basis of my work as an activist with Brazilian indigenous groups and indigenous support NGOs and my personal acquaintance, based on long-standing cooperation, with many actors and groups involved in the Yanomami struggle. My mission was to report back to the President and Executive Board of the Association on what if any action the Association should take on behalf of the Yanomami of Brazil. The context of this unusual appointment was the desperate, and at the time apparently losing battle to save the huge Yanomami Reserve. After a ten year struggle led by the Brazilian NGO, the CCPY (Committee to Create a Yanomami Park), the area had been studied, surveyed and tentatively demarcated by an official Brazilian governmental team, only to be invaded by 40,000 illegal gold miners in 1988. . . .

My investigation of the situation created by the multiple Yanomami crises of 1988 to 1991 for the AAA involved me in new or renewed contacts with Brazilian NGO workers, indigenous rights activists, medical doctors and health workers from governmental and private agencies, personnel of FUNAI, missionaries, progressive journalists, lawyers, politicians, and anthropologists (including officers of the Brazilian Anthropological Association, ABA). These encounters and consultations, together with further contacts and collaborations on subsequent visits to Brazil, comprise the basis of my published responses to Chagnon's unfounded calumnies against NGOs, Missions and the Yanomami leader Davi Kopenawa at the time of the gold miners' invasions and the campaign to dissolve the Yanomami Reserve from 1988 to 1991, his untruthful statements on the responsibility of the Salesians and the Yanomami themselves for the massacre at Haximu in December 1993, and his renewed diatribes against Davi Kopenawa at the 1994 AAA Meetings and on more recent occasions. They are also the basis of my evaluation of Tierney's account of the same events in his book, which I find substantially correct. . . .

The great majority of contemporary researchers who have worked with the Yanomami, or who have studied the effects of Chagnon's representations of the Yanomami in both Brazil and Venezuela, have critically challenged many of Chagnon's ethnographic and theoretical claims, his methods and actions in the field, and a number of his statements in popular media. . . .

The interdependence of ethical and empirical issues is unavoidable in dealing with Chagnon's work, in which factual claims of Yanomami aggressiveness and the link between killing and reproductive success are adduced, explicitly or implicitly, as "scientific" evidence for the sorts of statements he has made in the media that have been decried on ethical grounds. The issue becomes even more complex when one confronts the criticisms of Chagnon's data and analysis summarized and extended by Tierney. These criticisms, notably in Tierney's Chapter 10 that deals with Chagnon's 1988 article in *Science,* seriously imply the manipulation and withholding of data to support unsound but theoretically and ideologically desired conclusions. . . .

I will organize my discussion under five general headings [excerpt: from two are included here], designating general types of ethically problematic behavior, comprising representative instances from Tierney's text that seem to me to be sufficiently well documented and analyzed, and/or attested from other sources, to be considered "well founded." . . .

I. Statements and Silences by Chagnon Damaging to the Yanomami

I.A. Statements About "Fierceness" or Violent Aggressiveness as a Dominant Feature of Yanomami Society, and Silences (Failure to Speak Out Against Misuses of These Statements Damaging to the Yanomami)

Chagnon stood by virtually without demur during the drive to dismantle the Brazilian Yanomami reserve in 1988–92, while politicians, military leaders and journalists allied with mining interests employed his portrayal of the

Yanomami as ferocious savages involved in chronic warfare over women, to justify the dismemberment of Yanomami territory. Their argument ran that Yanomami communities needed for their own safety to be isolated from one another by "corridors" of open land, which would incidentally be accessible to gold miners. Chagnon's refusal to disown this use of his work in Brazilian media, where it might have had some effect, became understood by both sides in the struggle over the Yanomami reserve from 1988 to 1992 as a statement by omission in support of the miners and their political allies. This had a serious enough impact that the Brazilian Anthropological Association formally appealed to the American Anthropological Association in 1989 demanding that the U.S. Association investigate the ethics of its member's tacit support of those who were exploiting his statements. The American Association failed to take action, and this failure has come back to haunt it. . . .

The issue, as the Brazilian Association's new statement forcefully put it, is not simply that third parties exploited Chagnon's statements and silences for their own purposes. Anthropological researchers, its statement acknowledges, have an obligation to speak the truth about their research findings, and cannot control the uses to which others may put their findings. They do, however, have an ethical responsibility to speak out against the misuse of their findings by third parties, especially when such misuse directly damages the people referred to and most especially when these people were the subjects of the anthropologist's research. . . .

I.B. Repeated and Untruthful Attacks on NGOs, Anthropological Activists and Yanomami Leaders

I.B.1. Attacks on NGOs, Anthropological Activists

. . . Tierney . . . accurately reports Chagnon's shocking charge "that the very people who posed as defenders of the Indians were actually destroying them". This was Chagnon's allegation, which he repeated in the *Times Literary Supplement* and the *New York Times,* that the medical clinics and outreach programs instituted by missionaries and NGOs were not actually helping but rather "killing" the Indians ("killing by kindness"), in his words. Although primarily directed against the Salesians in Venezuela, this allegation was phrased so as implicitly to include missions and secular NGOs in Brazil. He further asserted that the Salesian missionaries, as well as unnamed Protestant missionaries at Mucajaí, were promoting warfare among Yanomami villages by giving or selling shotguns to the Indians on their mission stations. Yanomami leaders like Davi Kopenawa, he claimed, were not authentic leaders but "pawns" or "parrots", mindlessly repeating what their NGO and missionary manipulators told them to say. . . .

I.B.3. Chagnon's Attacks on Yanomami Leaders: (1) Davi Kopenawa

Chagnon has publicly charged on several occasions, beginning in the late 1980's and early 1990's, that the Brazilian Yanomami leader Davi Kopenawa was a mere "parrot" of NGOs, mouthing lines he was fed by the do-gooder organizations that supposedly kept him as a useful symbol for self-serving fund-raising campaigns (again, he never cited specific statements or texts). Davi Kopenawa was a major asset in these struggles, as virtually the only Yanomami leader capable of speaking out for Yanomami interests in the Brazilian and international political arenas, who at the same time commanded genuine support among the Yanomami of his own and other communities. Kopenawa was and remains the most important spokesman for the Brazilian Yanomami: he is a dynamic, effective, and independent person and leader. Chagnon's gratuitous and untruthful attacks damaged (or were clearly intended to damage) him. Chagnon is still at it: A CNN TV crew that interviewed Chagnon in November 2000 was startled to hear him call Kopenawa "a cigar store Indian". . . .

I.C. Ethnographic Misrepresentation as an Ethical Issue

Tierney analyzes a number of Chagnon's texts and statements that appear to involve possible manipulations of statistical data to support theoretical conclusions that would otherwise not follow, and the use of the same kinds of manipulations to implicate political enemies in causing the deaths of (or, in Chagnon's blunter term, "killing") Yanomami. Cases of the first kind may be considered to constitute a grey area between incorrect statistical analysis and deliberate manipulation. There seems little doubt, however, about the ethics of the much graver charges in the second category. . . .

Chagnon's article, "Life Histories, Blood revenge, and warfare in a tribal population", published in *Science* in 1988, has been taken by his critics and sociobiological supporters alike as the quintessential formulation of his theoretical claim that violent competition (fierceness) among males is driven by competition for sexual access to females, and that success in this competition, as measured by killing other men, therefore leads to increased reproductive success. Sociobiologists seized upon the Yanomami, as represented by Chagnon, as living examples of the evolutionary past of the race: the most direct links between the human present and the supposed primate heritage of Alpha male-centered harems and dominance hierarchies. . . . Tierney correctly points out that this notoriety, and the central misconception on which it was based, was overtly cultivated by Chagnon in public statements such as his presidential address to the Human Behavior and Evolutionary Society:

> I demonstrated that Yanomamo men in my 25 year study who had participated in the killing of other men had approximately three times as many children and more than two times as many wives as men their own ages who had not.

As Tierney also correctly says, this statement is thoroughly false. . . .

Tierney, relying partly on Lizot, somewhat more on Albert and most heavily on Ferguson, and contributing some findings of his own, provides a reasonably accurate summary of the criticisms of Chagnon's analysis. He reviews three fundamental criticisms of Chagnon's statistical manipulation of his data. Firstly, Chagnon's statistical comparison of the number of wives and children of "killers" (defined as "unokai", on the basis of their having undergone the ritual of purification for those who have participated in the killing of a person, *unokaimou*) to those of non-killers has been criticized as skewed by his inclusion of a large number of young men between 20–25 and 25–30 as members of the statistically relevant population. Very few Yanomami men of this age had killed anyone and almost none had wives or children. The result was to inflate the relative advantage of the killers, almost all of whom were older men, some over 30 and most over 40. When killers were compared with men of their own age-bracket, "the reproductive success of killers was not nearly as impressive—ranging between 40 to 67 percent, a fraction of the 208 percent advantage that Chagnon had broadcast to the press". In other words, age was a factor that accounted for much of the variation, and Chagnon had not taken it properly into account.

Another variable Chagnon left out of account, according to critics like Ferguson and Albert, was headman status (and the additional, partly overlapping status of shaman). In his 1988 paper, he simply classed all headmen as killers, *"unokai"*, but as Tierney says, that is a confusion of categories. Most Yanomami headmen have several wives, because of their status as headmen rather than their status as "killers" (*"unokai"*, in Chagnon's translation). Headman status, like age, is thus another variable that must be recognized as accounting for a significant part of the contrast in number of wives and children between men in the killers category and non-killers. Yet another important variable, explicitly excluded by Chagnon in his text, was the death of fathers. For reasons he did not explain, Chagnon excluded the children of dead fathers from his initial analysis. This turns out to have been a strategic point for his whole argument about reproductive success. According to Chagnon and other Yanomami ethnographers, successful killers become themselves the main targets of vengeance raids, and are highly likely to be killed in the midst of their reproductive years. As Brian Ferguson had been the first to point out, if this likelihood of killers to have their reproductive careers cut short were taken into account, the supposed reproductive advantage of killers might actually disappear to become negative. . . .

Tierney also raises a series of questions about manipulations of statistically strategic bits of data. Two young men in their twenties were listed in Chagnon's 1997 *Yanomamo Interactive* CD on The Ax Fight as having four and five children respectively. This was far more than the other men in their age category, and these two men had been identified as violent participants in the ax fight shown in the CD. Tierney checked Chagnon's original census and found that Mohesiwa was listed as born in 1938 and Ruwamowa in 1939, thus making them 33 and 32, respectively, rather than 24 and 27, as Chagnon now claimed, at the time of filming. Tierney "found no other mistakes in the census transfer. And if these were mistakes, they were statistically perfect ones"— as they seemed to show the greater reproductive success of violent men in contrast to their supposed age-mates in the under-30 categories.

There was also the case of the five young men Chagnon listed as killers in the under 25 age group, all of whom had wives. When challenged by Albert, however, Chagnon removed them to the 30-plus category, remarking that since the Yanomami do not count past three, the estimation of age is necessarily approximate. Their removal substantially altered the statistical predominance of killers as husbands and fathers in their age category. In sum, as Tierney remarks, "Minute manipulations in each age category could easily skew all the results"—and apparently had done so in the cases in question. . . .

Tierney also pointed out that although Chagnon had given the impression in his *Science* article that the three raids he described involved communities that were still living in a relatively traditional way, unaffected by the presence of missionaries and government agents that had led to the decline or suppression of warfare in other areas of Yanomami country, this was not the case. Chagnon had identified the villages in his article only by number, which Lizot had complained made them impossible to match up with any known (named) Yanomami communities. Tierney succeeded in identifying 9 of the 12 villages involved, showing that they were the same ones where he had done most of his fieldwork. . . .

Once identified and connected by Tierney to their known historical contexts, the three raids described in abstract terms in the *Science* article assumed different meanings. Pinning down the actual identities and locations of the villages showed that they were actually situated in an area of heavy contact with Venezuelan society and missionary influence. No longer abstract instances of violent competition for reproductive success, in an indigenous world whose essential patterns of warfare had not yet been affected by alien presences such as missionaries or anthropologists, they now appeared as significantly affected by Chagnon's own presence and activities. Chagnon himself, it transpired, had "filmed, transported, and coordinated" two of the three raiding parties over part of the distance to their targets. . . .

I.C. False Accusations Against Missions and NGO's of "Killing" Yanomami or Otherwise Being Responsible for Raising Their Death Rate

In an OpEd column in the New York Times of October 1993, Chagnon claimed that Yanomami were dying at missionary posts with medical facilities at four times the rate obtaining in "remote" villages. This was supposedly based on statistics Chagnon had collected and was the key data he cited in support of his shocking allegation that the Salesian missionaries were "killing the Yanomami with kindness". Tierney notes that this has become "one of the most frequently quoted statements in the Yanomami controversy," but shows that it is actually a misleading effect obtained by switching statistical data between categories of the study. He explains,

> Chagnon divided the villages in three categories of mission contact: "remote", "intermediate", and "maximum". The villages with maximum [mission] contact had a thirty percent *lower* mortality rate than remote groups, while the "intermediate" villages suffered four times as many deaths as the missions. Chagnon's data thus confirmed what all other researchers have found, but in the NYT Chagnon converted the "intermediate"

villages into "missions", which they are not. . . There is no doubt that the debate about mission mortality has been based on misinformation.

Tierney accurately chronicles Chagnon's attempt to spin the tragic episode of the massacre of twelve Yanomami from the village of Haximu by Brazilian gold miners in July 1993 into a series of spurious charges against the Yanomami from the village of Paapiu for being partly responsible for the massacre and the Salesian missionaries for trying to cover it up. The "cover up", in Chagnon's version, chiefly consisted in a campaign by the missionaries to block his "investigation" of the massacre, in order to prevent him from discovering and disclosing their role in "killing the Yanomami by kindness" at their mission stations (see preceding section). This was tantamount to accusing the Salesians of being accessories after the fact to mass murder.

Chagnon claimed he had the right to investigate the murders as a member of a Venezuelan Presidential Commission on Yanomami affairs. With his ally Brewer-Carias, Chagnon had in fact been appointed to a commission to supervise the projected Yanomami Biosphere Reserve by the transitional President who succeeded Carlos Andres-Perez after the latter's impeachment. This commission, however, lacked any specific investigative powers relevant to the massacre. An unprecedented national outcry, with massive street demonstrations and protests against Brewer's and Chagnon's appointments, specifically including their declared intention to conduct an investigation of the massacre, followed the announcement of these appointments. This historically unprecedented wave of opposition led the President to appoint a different commission specifically to investigate the massacre. The intent was clearly to remove Chagnon and Brewer from any connection with the Haximu investigation, and it was so understood by the Venezuelan media and public, although the President did not get around to formally dissolving the Brewer-Chagnon commission until later. . . . Chagnon, accompanied by Brewer, nevertheless attempted to go to Haximu to "investigate", regardless of the fact that the new Presidential investigating commission was already en route to the spot, and they lacked the necessary authorization to go to the area, let alone to conduct an investigation. When they landed at the village airstrip, two miles from the massacre site, they were summarily ordered to leave by the judge who headed the legitimate investigative commission. She gave Brewer and Chagnon a choice: get out of Haximu immediately or face arrest. The air force pilot who had flown them to the spot sided with the judge. He flew Chagnon straight to Caracas, confiscated his notes and told him to get out of Venezuela within twenty-four hours. Chagnon did so. . . .

Another of Chagnon's attempts to implicate missionaries in fomenting Yanomami killings by distributing shotguns was his attack, in the fourth edition of his book, on the Protestant Missionaries of the Evangelical Mission of Amazonia, supposedly stationed at Mucajaí. Tierney shows that this account is a fictional pastiche, combining aspects of the geography, personnel and history of the distant, and long-abandoned, mission station of Surucucu with those of Mucajaí, and adding elements of fantasy and distorted and displaced versions of actual actions. Indians lugging a washing machine over the mountain by the mission station at Surucucu becomes a single Missionary carrying a refrigerator on his back over a non-existent mountain at Mucajaí. The refusal of missionaries at Surucucu to sell shotguns to the Indians, and their abandonment of the mission post there rather than be obliged to do so, becomes the provision of shotguns by the Mucajaí missionaries to the Yanomami, their guilt supposedly redoubled by their subsequent refusal to inquire if the guns they had provided had been those used in an attack on a "remote" village (Chagnon suggests that if they found out that the guns they had provided had been the ones used, they would have to confiscate them, which would have made the Yanomami forsake the mission. As Tierney reports, everyone with any knowledge of these events, including the missionaries in question and others familiar with the different posts and mission families Chagnon had conflated, denounces Chagnon's account as fictional. . . .

II. Field Methods Disruptive of Yanomami Society

Drawing heavily on the writings of Brian Ferguson and his own data, Tierney documents charges that Chagnon's methods of obtaining the names of dead relatives, by exploiting enmities between factions and hostile communities, and above all by giving massive amounts of steel goods as presents, destabilized Yanomami communities and inter-communal relations, giving rise to conflicts, raids and wars. He also documents that Chagnon took a limited part in raids by transporting raiding parties in his motor launch. The issues here centrally involve the scale of operations and the time-pressure under which Chagnon was obliged to collect his pedigree data. Whether working for James Neel or on his own, his commitment to surveying the maximum possible numbers of villages in relatively minimal periods of time precluded normal anthropological methods of building rapport and finding culturally appropriate ways of obtaining culturally taboo information that have been used successfully by other anthropologists who have worked among the Yanomami. This forced him to resort to bullying and intimidation, including shooting off firearms and performing shamanic rituals of magical child-killing. It also led him to resort to bribery on a massive scale, using huge amounts of steel tools, pots, etc. These hoards of otherwise rare and highly valued items became foci of conflict between rival factions and villages, which on a number of documented occasions led to raids and wars in which people were killed.

As his work continued over the years, Chagnon, rather than modifying his modus operandi to diminish its destabilizing effects, continued to raise the ante, becoming a player in the regional system of conflicts and the struggle for dominance that were set off in part by quarrels over the wealth he brought with him. There began to be wars between "Chagnon's" village, containing Yanomami dependent on him for steel goods, and villages associated with other sources of goods, such as the anthropologist Lizot, and the independent Yanomami cooperative SUYAO. All of this, Tierney, Ferguson, Albert, and others have argued, represented a massive disruption of Yanomami social peace consequent upon Chagnon's field methods. If so, it may be considered to constitute a violation of clause III.A.2 of the AAA

Code of Ethics: "Anthropological researchers must do everything in their power to ensure that their research does not harm the safety, dignity, or privacy of the people with whom they work. . .".

The sheer scale of Chagnon's operations thus came to constitute a sui generis factor with ethical effects and implications not anticipated by the existing AAA Code of Ethics. Over a period of thirty years, according to anthropologist Brian Ferguson and others familiar with the political and historical aspects of his research, Chagnon has used methods to extract culturally sensitive data and biological specimens from Yanomami that have involved the violation of Yanomami cultural norms and caused dissension, and occasionally conflict, between communities and between factions of the same community. These conflicts, according to Ferguson, seconded by Tierney, have sometimes led to the breakup of communities and to inter-village raiding. Chagnon's tactics reportedly included giving large amounts of steel tools, the most esteemed presents, to certain villages or factions, thus inevitably destabilizing relations with non-recipients groups. The[se] also included, by his own account, deliberately lying to a village or faction that he had obtained the taboo names of their dead relatives from another village or faction, thus arousing anger and resentment that he could exploit to get the village or faction in question to give up the names of the deceased ancestors of the other group. After Chagnon got his data and departed, the villagers were left with bitter resentments that could aggravate existing tensions and provoke open conflicts. Chagnon seems also to have employed bullying and intimidation, brandishing weapons and shooting off firearms to make the Yanomami (who are usually the opposite of "fierce" in relations with non-Yanomami such as Venezuelans and Euro-North Americans) willing to give him information, if only to get rid of him.

The effectiveness of these tactics owed much to Chagnon's dramatic exploitation of the great discrepancy between his resources of wealth and power and those of the Yanomami as leverage to extract information, without regard to the ways this disrupted the social relations, stability and political peace of the communities of the people among whom he worked. The main authority for these allegations are the writings and public statements of Chagnon himself. One does not need to be a "left wing academic" or an "anti-science culturologist" to agree that these tactics raise questions of research ethics. . . .

IV.B. What Is to Be Done?

I believe that we as anthropologists owe it to the Yanomami, and to ourselves, to speak the truth publicly about what has been done to the Yanomami. In this sense, the role of the Association and its Task Force may be compared to that of truth commissions in places like South Africa or Guatemala: not to punish individuals, but to make principled public statements about what has been done, by whom, and in what ways the actions and statements in question may have violated the collective ethical standards of the profession. . . .

Anthropology as a discipline and as a profession can learn valuable lessons from analyzing what went wrong in Neel's and Chagnon's work, and why. I have suggested that a common thread connecting the ethical problems of both researchers is that concern with large-scale data collection under high time pressure, exacerbated in some cases by the institutional pressures of big scientific research projects, led both to make inadequate allowance for ethical and cultural standards, and in some cases, the social and physical well-being of the individual persons and communities comprising their subject populations. For anthropology, the lesson is that the pursuit of large amounts of quantitative data in abstraction from the cultural and social forms of life of the local people may become an end in itself that leads researchers to lose sight of or ignore the social standards and needs of the people they study. Such data, no matter how scientifically valuable, must never be pursued to the point of disruption of local social relations and cultural standards, or allowed to take priority over the well being of persons and communities. . . .

Edward H. Hagen, Michael E. Price, and John Tooby

→ **NO**

Preliminary Report

Introduction

As we will begin to show in this report, *Darkness in El Dorado* is essentially a work of fiction. Its author, Patrick Tierney, has very selectively quoted hundreds of sources in order to, first, caricature anthropologist Napoleon Chagnon's work on the Yanomamö, and second, to discredit what he claims is "Chagnon's ethnographic image of the ferocious Yanomami" by instead portraying them as meek, peaceful, helpless, and, ultimately, victims of Chagnon himself. Tierney's creative use of primary sources in this venture begins almost immediately. After a brief introductory chapter, Tierney wastes little time attempting to undermine Chagnon's portrayal of Yanomamö males as relatively healthy and frequently engaged in war:

> Before going into the jungle, I had read and admired The Fierce People. So it was surprising to see that the Yanomami—so terrifying and "burly" in Chagnon's text—were, in fact, among the tiniest, scrawniest people in the world. Adults averaged four feet seven inches in height, and children had among the lowest weight-height ratios on the planet.

References are supposed to support, not refute, the claims one is making. Tierney's reference above cites a relatively short paper by Rebecca Holmes on Yanomamö health. Although the paper does confirm the widely known fact that Yanomamö are short, it does not support one of Tierney's major themes: that Chagnon has exaggerated the frequency of Yanomamö warfare. What Tierney fails to mention here or anywhere else in his book is what Holmes says in her paper about Yanomamö war:

> Raids resulting in serious wounds and death occur *several times a year* in spite of missionary pressure to restrict warfare. About 20 warriors from Parima A, a two-day walk through the jungle from Parima B, raided one of the settlements in Parima B during our fieldwork. There were no injuries, although a study of the nurse's recent medical records indicates that these raids not uncommonly result in wounds from poison arrows. (Holmes 1985, p. 249; emphasis added).

Tierney cites Holmes' paper four times but he fails to mention her evidence on war and violence on any of these occasions, evidence which is

From *Preliminary Report on the Neel/Chagnon Allegations*, October 11, 2001. Published by Department of Anthropology, University of California, Santa Barbara. Reprinted by permission of the authors.

directly relevant to one of the major themes of his book. This failure is obviously deliberate. . . .

Preliminary Evaluation of Chapter 3

Naming the Dead

Tierney, in Chapter 3 (The Napoleonic Wars) and elsewhere in his book, fingers Chagnon's method of obtaining accurate genealogies as a source of conflict between individuals and villages, and, more generally, as an affront to Yanomamö dignity (Chagnon's recent statement on this issue can be found in Appendix XIV). What we will show below is that Tierney's account is substantially undermined by the very sources he cites.

First, however, it may be useful to note that most societies, including the US, have a 'name taboo.' In the US, for example, it is not wrong to mention one person's first name or nickname to another person who does not know it, but it is often considered rude to *use* the nickname or first name of someone if you do not know them well. For example, even if Judith Smith's friends call her 'Judy', she might be offended if a stranger used that name instead of 'Judith' or Ms. Smith. How many news articles on *Darkness* have referred to 'Pat' or even 'Patrick' instead of 'Patrick Tierney' or 'Mr. Tierney'? None. In professional contexts, it is also rude to use someone's first name instead of their title and last name (e.g., Dr. Smith). In court rooms, we do not even use the judge's name, but instead address him or her as 'your honor' even though it is perfectly OK to know the judge's name, or ask someone what his or her name is. So, Americans have a rather elaborate name taboo.

The Yanomamö 'name taboo' is quite similar to the American 'name taboo.' Names are *not* 'scared [*sic*] secrets' (almost everyone knows them, in fact), but their *use* in particular social contexts is considered rude and insulting, just as, for Americans, *knowing* someone's first name or nickname is not insulting or wrong, but the *use* of nicknames and first names is rude and insulting in certain social contexts. (For the Yanomamö, the improper use of names is much more insulting than for Americans, however.) Here is Chagnon explaining the name taboo:

> The taboo is maintained even for the living, for one mark of prestige is the courtesy others show you by not using your name publicly. This is particularly true for men, who are much more competitive for status than women in this culture, and it is fascinating to watch boys grow into young men, demanding to be called either by a kinship term in public, or by a teknonymous reference such as 'brother of Himotoma' (see Glossary). The more effective they are at getting others to avoid using their names, the more public acknowledgment there is that they are of high esteem and social standing. Helena Valero, a Brazilian woman who was captured as a child by a Yanomamö raiding party, was married for many years to a Yanomamö headman before she discovered what his name was. The sanctions behind the taboo are more complex than just this, for they involve a combination of fear, respect, admiration, political deference, and honor.

The Yanomamö were understandably concerned that if the stranger in their midst (Chagnon) learned their names, he might *use* them disrespectfully. Chagnon *never* did this. Chagnon *always* addressed individuals in the proper manner, and he never intentionally used names disrespectfully (nor does Tierney present any evidence that Chagnon used names disrespectfully). Chagnon always used the Yanomamö equivalent of 'Judith' when that was appropriate, 'Ms. Smith' when that was appropriate, and 'Your Honor' when that was appropriate. Because he was struggling with a foreign culture, Chagnon occasionally but *unintentionally* offended individuals. Unlike academics, the Yanomamö are forgiving; they knew his missteps were accidental, and took no lasting offence.

Chagnon also found that it was easier to obtain a person's name from non-kin or enemies. In the US, Judith Smith's friends might be reluctant to reveal Judith's nickname to a stranger—not because *knowing* the nickname is taboo, but because its improper *use* might offend their friend—but people who were not close friends of Judith's would feel no such reluctance, nor would they violate any taboo by revealing the nickname. The same applies to the Yanomamö—asking non-kin and enemies about names is *not* taboo (remember, these names are widely known, and there is no taboo against outsiders knowing these names).

Contrary to Tierney's claims, Chagnon did *not* play enemies or villages off one another to obtain names. Notice that in Tierney's account of Chagnon's method, these claims have no supporting citations:

> Chagnon found himself in a difficult predicament, having to collect genealogical trees going back several generations. This was frustrating for him because the Yanomami do not speak personal names out loud. And the names of the dead are the most taboo subject in their culture.
>
> "To name the dead, among the Yanomami, is a grave insult, a motive of division, fights, and wars," wrote the Salesian Juan Finkers, who has lived among the Yanomami villages on the Mavaca River for twenty-five years.
>
> Chagnon found out that the Yanomami "were unable to understand why a complete stranger should want to possess such knowledge [of personal names] unless it were for harmful magical purposes." So Chagnon had to parcel out "gifts" in exchange for these names. [Anthropologists have 'to parcel out gifts' for most interviews with most informants on most topics. Giving gifts in exchange for extensive genealogical information is common practice in anthropology] One Yanomami man threatened to kill Chagnon when he mentioned a relative who had recently died. Others lied to him and set him back five months with phony genealogies [both these events are discussed in detail by Chagnon]. But he kept doggedly pursuing his goal.
>
> Finally, he invented a system, as ingenious as it was divisive [no citation], to get around the name taboo [Chagnon was not trying to 'get around the name taboo,' a claim that makes no sense ('getting around the name taboo' would entail *using* names disrespectfully—something he never did, nor had any desire to do). Chagnon was trying, not only to get information necessary to his research, but also to integrate himself into Yanomamö society by learning what was common knowledge:

everyone's name, including those of ancestors]. Within groups, he sought out "informants who might be considered 'aberrant' or 'abnormal,' outcasts in their own society," people he could bribe and isolate more easily. These pariahs resented other members of society, so they more willingly betrayed sacred secrets [names are not 'sacred secrets'— they are public knowledge] at others' expense and for their own profit. [son-in-laws doing bride service—who are therefore not living with their kin—are a common example of what Tierney terms 'pariahs'] He resorted to "tactics such as 'bribing' children when their elders were not around, or capitalizing on animosities between individuals." [using children as informants is, again, common practice among anthropologists—usually because they have the patience for the all the tedious questions that anthropologists ask]

Chagnon was most successful at gathering data, however, when he started playing one village off against another. "I began traveling to other villages to check the genealogies, picking villages that were on strained terms with the people about whom I wanted information. I would then return to my base camp and check with local informants the accuracy of the new information. If the informants became angry when I mentioned the new names I acquired from the unfriendly group, I was almost certain that the information was accurate." [see below for the material that Tierney has omitted from this quote]

When one group became angry on hearing that Chagnon had gotten their names, he covered for his real informants but gave the name of another village nearby as the source of betrayal [no citation]. It showed the kind of dilemmas Chagnon's work posed. In spite of the ugly scenes he both witnessed and created, Chagnon concluded, "There is, in fact, no better way to get an accurate, reliable start on genealogy than to collect it from the enemies."

His divide-and-conquer information gathering exacerbated individual animosities [no citation], sparking mutual accusations of betrayal [no citation]. Nevertheless, Chagnon had become a prized political asset of the group with whom he was living, the Bisaasi-teri.

As usual, Tierney deliberately omits critical evidence that readers need to fairly evaluate his accusations and insinuations. With the exception of the quote from the Salesian missionary Juan Finkers, all of the cited information in the above quote comes from Chagnon's publications.

Tierney also conveniently fails to mention that Kaobawa, a Yanomamö headman, *demanded* that Chagnon learn the truth, even though he knew that would involve Chagnon learning the names of his dead kinsmen:

[Kaobawa's] knowledge of details was almost encyclopedic, his memory almost photographic. More than that, he was enthusiastic about making sure I learned the truth, and he encouraged me, indeed, *demanded* that I learn all details I might otherwise have ignored. . . . With the information provided by Kaobawa, and Rerebawa [another informant], I made enormous gains in understanding village interrelationships based on common ancestors and political histories and became lifelong friends with both. And both men knew that I had to learn about his recently deceased kin from the other one. It was one of those quiet understandings we all had but none of us could mention.

This information is in Chagnon's popular monograph, *Yanomamö* (which Tierney cites numerous times).

When Chagnon began his fieldwork with a Yanomamö village in the sixties, the Yanomamö did not know why Chagnon wanted to know their names, and were understandably quite reluctant to reveal this information to an outsider who might use it disrespectfully. Chagnon recounts the humorous and ingenious tactics the villagers used to deceive him about their real names during his initial stint in the field, and his own equally ingenious method of penetrating this deception by getting the information from other Yanomamö in enemy villages (see Appendix XIII for the monograph excerpt). Indeed, this is one of the major flaws in Tierney's account: he conveniently fails to mention that the methods that Chagnon discusses are those he used during the first six months or so of his fieldwork, before the Yanomamö had come to trust that Chagnon was not going to use the information disrespectfully. That Chagnon made strenuous attempts to avoid offending anyone while collecting names is clear from sentences that immediately follow those Tierney chooses to cite (material in bold not cited by Tierney):

> I began traveling to other villages to check the genealogies, picking villages that were on strained terms with the people about whom I wanted information. I would then return to my base camp and check with local informants the accuracy of the new information. If the informants became angry when I mentioned the new names I acquired from the unfriendly group, I was almost certain that the information was accurate. **For this kind of checking I had to use informants whose genealogies I knew rather well: they had to be distantly enough related to the dead person that they would not go into a rage when I mentioned the name, but not so remotely related that they would be uncertain of the accuracy of the information. Thus, I had to make a list of names that I dared not use in the presence of each and every informant. Despite the precautions, I occasionally hit a name that put the informant into a rage, such as that of a dead brother or sister that other informants had not reported. This always terminated the day's work with that informant, for he would be too touchy to continue any further, and I would be reluctant to take a chance on accidentally discovering another dead kinsman so soon after the first.**
>
> These were always unpleasant experiences, and occasionally **dangerous ones, depending on the temperament of the informant.**

Chagnon stresses his efforts to avoid mentioning the names of the dead to close kin in all five editions of his monograph, yet Tierney *deliberately* fails to mention this. . . .

However history may judge Chagnon's method of obtaining accurate genealogies (Native North Americans rely heavily on accurate genealogies in laying claim to valuable government benefits, etc.) it is important to properly represent what he did. Tierney instead deliberately omits key evidence that would allow the reader to evaluate his claims and improperly characterizes names as "sacred secrets" of the Yanomamö as a group; instead, their public *use* reflects the status and respect accorded to particular individuals. Using the same sources cited by Tierney, it is clear that Chagnon never used names disrespectfully, and soon came to be trusted on this matter by the Yanomamö. . . .

Detailed Evaluation of Chapter 10: To Murder and to Multiply

Brief Introduction

Chapter 10 of *Darkness in El Dorado* by Patrick Tierney is an extended attack on a well-known 1988 paper published by Chagnon in *Science* entitled "Life Histories, Blood Revenge, and Warfare in a Tribal Population." In this paper, Chagnon argues that warfare among the Yanomamö is characterized by blood revenge: an attack on one group by another prompts a retaliatory attack, which itself prompts retaliation, *ad infinitum*. In other words, Yanomamö war is quite similar to the patterns of conflict we see in the Balkans, the Middle East, Africa—anywhere ethnic groups come into armed conflict. In order to understand this pattern among the Yanomamö (and thus, perhaps, everywhere else), Chagnon presents data which suggest that successful Yanomamö warriors (unokai—men who have killed) are rewarded for their bravery and success. Among the Yanomamö, these rewards take the form of wives. Chagnon showed that unokai have more wives, and consequently more offspring, than non-unokai. Chagnon argued that if, over evolutionary time, cultural success lead [sic] to reproductive success, individuals would be selected to strive for cultural success. He further argued that cultural success is often achieved by engaging in successful military actions against enemies. Perhaps, then, the cycles of violence suffered by countless groups worldwide are driven, in part, by men who seek status and prestige by successfully attacking enemies.

This entire thesis has been assailed by Chagnon's critics, and Tierney hopes to bury it by demonstrating that Chagnon's research was shoddy, dishonest, and contradicted by other studies. In fact, whether or not Chagnon's theory is correct, *many* studies have demonstrated that, in small-scale societies, cultural success does lead to reproductive success, that cultural success is frequently associated with military success, and conflicts are often caused by conflicts over women. Tierney reviews almost none of these studies, and when he does, he omits key evidence that supports Chagnon's thesis.

Before we begin our analysis of Tierney's efforts in this chapter, we note that people often misconstrue Chagnon's work to mean that the Yanomamö are exceptionally violent, unlike other groups. Nothing could be further from the truth. In fact, we now know that most non-state societies have (or had) high rates of violence compared to state societies. Chagnon was one of the first to document in detail the profound impact of intergroup violence on a non-state society. . . .

Chagnon has also famously claimed that Yanomamö wars often start with conflicts over women. Tierney implies or states several times that this is either unimportant, "secondary," or a fabrication of Chagnon's. For example:

> Yet the popular image of the Yanomami waging war for women persisted. Chagnon deftly *created it* by repeatedly claiming that men went on raids, captured women, and raped them at will afterward.

If Chagnon had created this image, then there should be no independent reports of Yanomamö raiding for women, and there should especially be no such reports predating Chagnon's. There are, however, many accounts of Yanomamö raiding for women that predate Chagnon's, accounts that place more emphasis on wife-capture than Chagnon does (Chagnon has stated several times that it is often not the principle [sic] motivation for a raid). . . .

Selective Omission of Data Which Support Chagnon's Findings

Claim   Tierney argues against Chagnon's claim that warriorship and reproductive success are correlated in tribal societies, citing a study of the Waorani:

> Among the Waorani of the Ecuadorian Amazon, a tribe with the world's highest known rate of attrition of war, every known male has killed at least once. But warriors who killed more than twice were more than twice as likely to be killed themselves—and their wives were killed at three times the rate of other, more peaceful men. Most prolific killers lost their wives and had to remarry—which made it look as if they had more wives if they survived.

Misrepresentation   Here, Tierney omits important information which supports the validity of Chagnon's result. Tierney refers to a recent ethnography of the Waorani in which the authors actually went out and collected the data to test Chagnon's model. The problem was, since all Waorani males had participated in a killing, they could not separate killers from non-killers. Instead they categorized men based on how many killings they had participated in: 1–5, 6–10, and 11+. Then they compared the numbers of wives and offspring among men in each of these categories. They found that killers of 1–5 people averaged 1.35 wives and 4.37 offspring, killers of 6–10 people averaged 2.00 wives and 6.08 offspring, and killers of 11+ people averaged 2.25 wives and 8.25 offspring. Thus, these data are highly consistent with those of Chagnon. The Robarcheks have essentially replicated Chagnon's finding, although they have a different interpretation of this result. They go on to present data showing that more prolific killers are more likely to get killed themselves and to lose a wife to violence; the latter are the only data that Tierney chooses to report. Tierney thus omits what is both the crux of the Robarcheks' study, and also the most useful element for evaluating the reliability of Chagnon's result: the successful replication of that result. . . .

Insinuates That Chagnon Dishonestly Confounded
Unokais and Headmen

Claim   Tierney insinuates that Chagnon dishonestly includes headmen, in addition to unokais, in his sample and that the presence of headmen somehow skewed his results:

> "In his *Science* piece all headmen were also included as "killers," a confusion of categories; when the headmen were factored out, the study's statistical significance in one of its major age categories collapsed, Chagnon admitted. He would not say which category it was. . . . Again, Chagnon maintained a tenacious silence in the face of public challenge, this time by the anthropologist Brian Ferguson."

Misrepresentation   Chagnon does indeed include headmen in his sample of unokais, but only because these headmen are unokai, as Chagnon states clearly: "All headmen in this study are unokai." Tierney seems to suggest that Chagnon includes some headmen that he knows not to be unokai. Brian Ferguson, in *American Ethnologist,* did challenge Chagnon's inclusion of headmen in his study, saying that since headmen usually have more wives and children, and since all headmen in the study were unokai, the inclusion of headmen might increase the correlation between unokainess and reproductive success. Ferguson's point is actually misguided: the fact that all headmen were unokai is highly consistent with Chagnon's theory that in tribal societies "cultural success leads to biological success," i.e. good warriorship leads to high social status, which in turn leads to high reproductive success, and it is absurd to suggest that the presence of unokai headmen somehow contradicts a theory which it in fact strongly supports. Nevertheless, in a piece entitled "Response to Ferguson" which immediately followed Ferguson's challenge in the same issue of *American Ethnologist,* Chagnon agreed to reanalyze the data with headmen removed. Even with headmen removed, unokais (compared to non-unokais) had significantly more offspring in all four age categories, and more wives in three of four age categories ($ps < .05$). In one age category (ages 31–40), the difference between unokai and non-unokai wives was just barely not significant ($p = .07$). The statistical "collapse" to which Tierney refers is apparently the fact that $p = .07$ rather than $<.05$ for the 31–40 category, an extremely minor discrepancy misleadingly referred to as a "collapse." And there was no "tenacious silence" by Chagnon with regard to which age category was affected by the removal of headmen: Chagnon states clearly in his *American Ethnologist* piece that the category is "31–40." Tierney is clearly aware of this article (he cites it and it appears in his bibliography), so it is odd that he seems to overlook it here. . . .

Misrepresents Chagnon's Explanation for Unokai Reproductive Success

Claim   Tierney suggests that Chagnon claims that the link between killing and reproductive success is due solely to the fact that Yanomamö killers are more successful in abducting women in raids. Tierney notes that this link is "tenuous" because only a "low" number of women are actually abducted in raids:

Nor was there anything but the most tenuous connection between killing, raiding, and the capture of women. The number of women captured in the warfare of the Yanomami is low, despite their reputation. . . . Yet the popular image of the Yanomami waging war for women persisted. Chagnon deftly created it by repeatedly claiming that men went on raids, captured women, and raped them at will afterwards.

Misrepresentation   In fact, Chagnon has stated repeatedly that when he says the Yanomamö "fight over women," he does not mean that they usually initiate raids for the purpose of abducting women. He simply means that most conflicts begin as some kind of sexual dispute, and he makes this clear in the target article: "most fights begin over sexual issues: infidelity and suspicion of infidelity, attempts to seduce another man's wife, sexual jealousy, forcible appropriation of women from visiting groups, failure to give a promised girl in marriage, and (rarely) rape." On the same page he is clear that most wars are perpetuated by revenge, not the desire to abduct women: "The most common explanation given for raids (warfare) is revenge for a previous killing, and the most common explanation for the initial cause of the fighting is 'women'." In his famous ethnography—cited extensively by Tierney—Chagnon says "although few raids are initiated solely with the intention of capturing women, this is always a desired side benefit" and "Generally, however, the desire to abduct women does not lead to the initiation of hostilities between groups that have no history of mutual raiding in the past." Tierney completely ignores that Chagnon downplays the significance of abduction as a motivation to raid and then claims that Chagnon "deftly created" the image of the Yanomamö waging war in order to abduct women.

Further, by concentrating exclusively on abduction as the only explanation for the high reproductive success of unokais, Tierney ignores what Chagnon claims might be "the most promising avenue of investigation to account for the high reproductive success of unokais," the fact that "cultural success leads to biological success." Chagnon explains that unokais, because of their prowess and willingness to take risks in military matters, are regarded as more valuable allies than non-unokais: "in short, military achievements are valued and associated with high esteem." This high status of unokais makes them more attractive as mates. In a published response to criticism about the target article, Chagnon goes into even greater detail about how unokai status makes men more attractive as mates.

Why Has Tierney Been So Dishonest?

To conclude our preliminary report, we ask the obvious question, "Why has Tierney been so dishonest?" The short answer is, we don't know. We offer the following two speculations [one included here]—but we must stress that these are only speculations, speculations we ourselves find less than satisfying. . . .

The field of anthropology has been riven for at least the last two decades by a debate between 'scientifically oriented' anthropologists and 'humanistically oriented' anthropologists. The former tend to believe that there is an objective human reality and that scientific methods will help us discover it. The latter tend to believe that realities are relative, and socially or culturally constructed, and they are often extremely skeptical and critical of Western science. The debate between these two camps has frequently been so bitter that it has caused prominent anthropology departments, like Stanford's, to split in two. The debate is not confined to anthropology. It is widespread in the humanities and social sciences, and has come to be known as the Science Wars.

Tierney clearly hoped to successfully indict two of the most famous scientists to work with indigenous people in the Amazon, Chagnon and Neel, with serious crimes and breaches of ethics, and thus strike a blow against scientific, and particularly evolutionary, anthropology. For students and others, we provide our perspective on this issue, and how it may account, in part, for Tierney's dishonesty.

There are three fundamental aspects of Chagnon's career that place him at ground zero in the debate between 'scientific' anthropologists and 'humanistic' anthropologists. First, Chagnon has been a staunch and vocal proponent and practitioner of scientific anthropology, one whose books and films are widely assigned in anthropology courses around the world. Second, and even more galling to 'humanistically' oriented anthropologists (and disconcerting to many 'scientific' anthropologists as well) is Chagnon's use of sociobiological theory. Sociobiology is a set of theories and general principles about animal social behavior that derive from Darwin's theory of evolution by natural selection. Although biologists were excited by the sociobiological theories that appeared in the 1960's and 1970's, there was an immediate outcry by some biologists (e.g., Stephen J. Gould) and many social scientists when E. O. Wilson suggested that sociobiology might be useful for understanding *human* social behavior. It was 'obvious' to both sides in the sociobiology debate that the other side was motivated entirely by politics. In the ensuing war of words between supporters and critics of sociobiology, the field became stigmatized. Few social scientists are willing to use the theory, and even the many biologists employing sociobiology in their study of non-human animals avoid mentioning the word 'sociobiology.' Despite this, sociobiology is a standard part of the theoretical toolkit used by biologists in virtually every biology department in the world. It is, without doubt, the theory most widely used to study and understand the social behavior of all (non-human) living things. The world's most prestigious scientific journals, Science and Nature, routinely publish research articles using sociobiology, and hundreds of research articles using sociobiology are published every year in major biology journals. Applying sociobiology to humans, however, remains strictly taboo. Chagnon has openly violated this taboo by interpreting his data in light of sociobiological theories.

Finally, Chagnon has focused his career on one of the most contentious issues in anthropology: violence and aggression in small-scale, 'primitive' societies. Critiquing Western culture has been a popular topic in anthropology since the 1920's. (In fact, a widely used cultural anthropology text is titled *Anthropology as Cultural Critique.*) In order to critique Western culture, anthropologists often feel they must find non-Western cultures that do things better. Because violence and aggression in Western societies are well deserving of critique, anthropologists hoped to discover societies with little aggression or violence that could serve as examples of a better way of living. Chagnon, by contrast, argues that violence and aggression are common in most non-Western societies—even small-scale societies like the Yanomamö—and that violence and aggression are probably part of human nature. This has infuriated the many anthropologists who prefer practicing anthropology as cultural critique. The favorite alternative to Chagnon's interpretation of Yanomamö war is that of Brian Ferguson. Ferguson, unsurprisingly, blames Yanomamö war on the influence of Western culture.

By taking aim at Chagnon, Tierney has charged into the middle of this debate on the side of the humanists against the scientists, particularly against the tiny minority who apply Darwinian theory to people. The subtitle of his book is "How Scientists and Journalists Devastated the Amazon." The very first words in the book, in the frontpiece, are from Daniel Dennett: "It is important to recognize that Darwinism has always had an unfortunate power to attract the most unwelcome enthusiasts—demagogues and psychopaths and misanthropes and other abusers of Darwin's dangerous idea." (Although Tierney doesn't mention it, Dennett is actually a strong advocate of Darwinian approaches to social science, and has written in defense of Chagnon.) And much of the book is a muddled attempt to attack Chagnon's sociobiological approach to Yanomamö warfare. Tierney constantly inserts comments like "Chagnon picked up where Social Darwinists left off" (Ch. 2), and he is even willing to make unsupported accusations of murder: "the incredible faith the sociobiologists had in their theories was admirable. Like the old Marxist missionaries, these zealots of biological determinism sacrificed everything—including the lives of their subjects—to spread their gospel." (Ch. 2).

Maybe Tierney thought that if he could destroy Chagnon, arch-enemy of many humanistic anthropologists and culture critics, he would be a hero in the Science Wars. And maybe he really thought a victory in the Science Wars would help the Amazon and its peoples. But the Amazon is not being devastated by scientists. Or journalists. Or sociobiologists. It is being devastated by logging, mining, road building, and slash-and-burn farming by the region's burgeoning population. Character assassination will do precisely nothing to change this.

EXPLORING THE ISSUE

Did Napoleon Chagnon's Research Methods Harm the Yanomami Indians of Venezuela?

Critical Thinking and Reflection

1. What are the specific charges that Turner levels against Chagnon in this selection? Although we can assume that Turner has gotten some examples from Tierney's account, what is the logical basis for Turner's charges?
2. Why might some anthropologists have exaggerated the impact of Chagnon's research on the Yanomami?
3. Chagnon's use of his data to misrepresent the Yanomami is also implicated by Tierney and Turner. How are these charges of unethical behavior different from his distribution of machetes and other imported goods?
4. What general lessons are to be learned from this case if the charges against Chagnon are correct? What lessons are to be learned if the charges are overstated as Hagen and his colleagues assert?
5. To what extent is Chagnon responsible for how people interpret his findings and conclusions about the Yanomami?

Is There Common Ground?

This controversy exposed a deep rift in the anthropological community. The rift has been variously defined as between those who see anthropology as a science and those who consider it a humanistic discipline, between sociobiologists and cultural determinists, and, at the basest level, between scholars who personally like or dislike Neal and Chagnon. The battle lines are sharply drawn, and few anthropologists have remained neutral. The antagonists are pulling no punches in their charges and countercharges.

The El Dorado Task Force of the American Anthropological Association, which investigated Tierney's accusations, concluded, among other things, that Neel and his associates should be praised, not condemned, for vaccinating Yanomami against measles, an action that "unquestionably. . . saved many lives" (see the Final Report on the A.A.A. Web site at www.aaanet .org). However, it criticized Chagnon on ethical and professional grounds for working with a group of wealthy and corrupt Venezuelans to gain access to the Yanomami in 1990, despite having been denied a research permit by the Venezuelan government. It also criticized him for misrepresenting the

Yanomami as the "fierce people," a view used by others to justify violence against them, and for not correcting that image or supporting their human rights. Not surprisingly, the report has been criticized by Chagnon's supporters as too harsh and by his enemies as too lenient.

Additional Resources

Tierney's original article and book are what set this issue in motion. This controversy has generated a huge literature in a short time, the speed being due in large part to the widespread use of the Internet. The literature includes articles and book reviews in newspapers, popular magazines, and scholarly newsletters and journals; radio programs; and numerous documents and opinions posted on Web sites.

Tierney, Patrick. 2000. *Darkness in El Dorado: How Scientists and Journalists Devastated the Amazon.* New York: Norton.

Tierney, Patrick. 2000. "The Fierce Anthropologist," *The New Yorker* October 8.

The most comprehensive and balanced guide to sources is the Web site of Douglas Hume, a graduate student at the University of Connecticut. It includes a comprehensive bibliography of materials published from September 2000 to the present and links to relevant Web sites and documents:

http://members.aol.com/archeodog/darkness_in_el_dorado/index.htm

The Web site for public anthropology contains papers from a round table discussion among several scholars with varying points of view:

www.publicanthropology.org

The Department of Anthropology at the University of California at Santa Barbara Web site provides a number of documents and statements supporting Chagnon:

www.anth.ucsb.edu/chagnon.html

The paperback edition of Tierney's book contains an 11-page postscript responding to his critics. Other printed publications include the following, which presents comments by six scholars:

Current Anthropology Forum. 2001. "Reflections on Darkness in El Dorado," *Current Anthropology* 42(2):265–276.

A relevant earlier source is:

Sponsel, Leslie. 1998. "Yanomami: An Arena of Conflict and Aggression in the Amazon," *Aggressive Behavior* 24(2): 97–122.

Contributors to This Volume

EDITORS

ROBERT L. WELSCH is a professor of anthropology at Franklin Pierce University in Rindge, NH. For many years, he has been an adjunct curator of anthropology at The Field Museum in Chicago. More recently, he was appointed a research associate in the department of anthropology at the National Museum of Natural History at the Smithsonian Institution and a research associate in the department of anthropology at the American Museum of Natural History in New York. He received his BA in anthropology from Northwestern University in 1972, an MA in anthropology from the University of Washington in 1976, and a PhD from the same department in 1982. He has conducted field research among the Ningerum people of Papua New Guinea, the Mandar people of Sulawesi, Indonesia, the diverse peoples of the Sepik Coast of Papua New Guinea, and the varied peoples of the Papuan Gulf. He is the author of *An American Anthropologist in Melanesia* (University of Hawaii Press, 1998), *Coaxing the Spirits to Dance: Art and Society in the Papuan Gulf of New Guinea* (Hood Museum of Art, 2006), coeditor, with Michael O'Hanlon, of *Hunting the Gatherers: Ethnographic Collectors, Agents, and Agency in Melanesia* (Berghahn Publishers, 2000), coeditor, with Anita Herle, Karen Stevenson, and Nick Stanley, of *Pacific Art: Persistence, Change, and Meaning* (University of Hawaii Press, 2002), and coeditor, with Eric Venbrux and Pamela Sheffield Rosi, of *Exploring World Art* (Waveland, 2006).

KIRK M. ENDICOTT is an emeritus professor of anthropology at Dartmouth College. He received a BA in anthropology from Reed College in 1965, a PhD in anthropology from Harvard University in 1974, and a DPhil. in social anthropology from the University of Oxford in 1976. He has repeatedly conducted field research among the Batek people of Malaysia. He is the author of *An Analysis of Malay Magic* (Clarendon Press, 1970) and *Batek Negrito Religion: The World-view and Rituals of a Hunting and Gathering People of Peninsular Malaysia* (Clarendon Press, 1979), coauthor, with Robert K. Dentan, Alberto G. Gomez, and M. Barry Hooker, of *Malaysia and the "Original People": A Case Study of the Impact of Development on Indigenous Peoples* (Allyn and Bacon, 1997), and coauthor, with Karen L. Endicott, of *The Headman Was a Woman: The Gender Egalitarian Batek of Malaysia* (Waveland, 2008).

AUTHORS

C. LORING BRACE is a professor of anthropology at the University of Michigan. His research considers issues of morphological variability among human populations. He is the author of many articles and books, including *Evolution in an Anthropological View* (AltaMira Press, 2000) and *"Race" Is a Four-Letter Word: The Genesis of the Concept* (Oxford University Press, 2005).

BRUCE BRADLEY is a senior lecturer in the Department of Archaeology at the University of Exeter and a research associate in anthropology at Carnegie Museum of Natural History. He has published widely on Paleoindians, flaked stone technologies, and the American Southwest.

DAVID M. BUSS is a professor of psychology at the University of Texas. His research interests focus on various aspects of evolutionary psychology, such as human mating strategies, the emotion of jealousy, social conflict, and stalking. He is the author of many articles and books, including *The Dangerous Passion: Why Jealousy Is as Necessary as Love and Sex* (Free Press, 2000).

ROBERT L. CARNEIRO is a cultural anthropologist and an emeritus curator of anthropology at the American Museum of Natural History in New York. He has conducted field research in Brazil, Peru, and Venezuela, focusing on cultural evolution and political evolution. He is the author of many books and articles, including *Evolutionism in Cultural Anthropology: A Critical History* (Westview, 2003).

JAMES C. CHATTERS is owner of Applied Paleoscience, of Richland, WA, and a research professor of anthropology at Central Washington University, and deputy coroner of Benton County, WA. His principal research focus is the postglacial human and ecological history of the Columbia River Basin. He is the author of *Ancient Encounters: Kennewick Man and the First Americans* (Simon & Schuster, 2001).

KAREN L. ENDICOTT is director of communications at the Thayer School of Engineering at Dartmouth College. She was trained as a cultural anthropologist and conducted field research among the Batek of Malaysia, and is coauthor of *The Headman Was a Woman* (Waveland, 2008).

STUART FIEDEL is an archaeologist working with John Milner Associates in Alexandria, Virginia. He is the author of many books and papers, including *Prehistory of the Americas,* 2nd ed. (Cambridge University Press, 1992).

DEREK FREEMAN (1916–2001) was an emeritus professor of anthropology at the Research School of Pacific and Asian Studies at the Australian National University. He conducted field research among the Iban of Borneo and the Samoans of western Samoa. He is the author of many books and articles, including *The Fateful Hoaxing of Margaret Mead* (Penguin, 1999).

CLIFFORD GEERTZ (1923–2006) was a professor at the Institute for Advanced Study in Princeton, NJ. He conducted field research in Indonesia and Morocco. He was the author of *The Interpretation of Cultures* (Basic Books,

1973), *Works and Lives: The Anthropologist as Author* (Stanford University Press, 1988), and many other books.

GEORGE W. GILL is an emeritus professor of anthropology at the University of Wyoming. He is a biological and forensic anthropologist and has examined human skeletons from Mexico, Peru, Easter Island, and the Great Plains.

MARIJA GIMBUTAS is a late professor of European archaeology at the University of California at LosAngeles. She was the author of seventeen books and some two hundred articles on European prehistory, including *The Civilization of the Goddess* (HarperCollins, 1992).

STEVEN GOLDBERG is a professor of sociology at City University of New York. He has written many books and journal articles, including *Why Men Rule: A Theory of Male Dominance* (Open Court, 1993).

DONALD K. GRAYSON is a professor of anthropology at the University of Washington (Seattle). He is a specialist on prehistoric environments and has excavated many early sites in the Great Basin and in other western states. He is author of The Desert's Past: A Natural Prehistory of the Great Basin (Smithsonian Institution Press, 1993) and many other books.

JOHN J. GUMPERZ is an emeritus professor of anthropology at the University of California at Berkeley. His research interests have concentrated on sociolinguistics and issues about language and culture. He is the author of numerous books and articles, including *Discourse Strategies* (Cambridge University Press, 1982).

EDWARD H. HAGEN is an anthropologist in the Institute for Theoretical Biology at Humboldt University in Berlin. His research has focused on evolutionary approaches to depression. He has published several articles about biosocial science and sociobiology.

MICHELLE D. HAMILTON is a professor of forensic anthropology at Texas State University, San Marcos. She was formerly the Section 106 officer for the Tribal Historic Preservation Office of the Eastern Band of Cherokee Indians in Cherokee, North Carolina.

GARY HAYNES is a professor of anthropology at the University of Nevada at Reno. His research has focused on Paleoindians, the peopling of the New World, and North American large mammals. He is the author of *The Early Settlement of North America: The Clovis Era* (Cambridge University Press, 2002).

ELLEN RHOADS HOLMES has conducted field research in Samoa. She is coauthor, with her husband Lowell D. Holmes, of *Samoan Village: Then and Now* (Harcourt Brace, 1992) and *Other Cultures, Elder Years: An Introduction to Cultural Gerontology* (Sage, 1995).

LOWELL D. HOLMES is an emeritus professor of anthropology at Wichita State University. He has conducted field research in Samoa and in contemporary America. He is the author of many articles and books, including *Quest for the Real Samoa* (Bergin & Garvey, 1986).

SUDHIR KAKAR is widely known as the father of Indian psychoanalysis and has practiced for many years in New Delhi. He has been a visiting professor of psychology at the University of Chicago and is currently a senior fellow at the Center for the Study of World Religions at Harvard University. His books include *The Color of Violence: Cultural Identities, Religion and Conflict* (University of Chicago Press, 1996).

ROGER M. KEESING (1935–1993) was a professor of anthropology at McGill University. He is best known for his research among the Kwaio people of Malaita in the Solomon Islands and published four books and many articles about them, including *Custom and Confrontation: The Kwaio Struggle for Cultural Autonomy* (University of Chicago Press, 1992).

FREDERICK P. LAMPE was the Lutheran chaplain at Syracuse University, where he was also affiliated with the department of anthropology. He spent four years as a Lutheran missionary and chaplain at the University of Technology (Unitech) in Lae, Papua New Guinea.

STEPHEN C. LEVINSON is director of the Language and Cognition Group at the Max Plank Institute for Psycholinguistics at Nijmegen in the Netherlands. His research has focused on linguistic anthropology and cognitive anthropology. He is the author of numerous books and articles, including *Presumptive Meanings* (MIT Press, 2000).

ROGER IVAR LOHMANN is a professor of anthropology at Trent University, Oshawa, Ontario. He conducted research concerning the anthropology of religion among the Asabano of Papua New Guinea. He was the editor of *Dream Travelers: Sleep Experiences and Culture in the Western Pacific* (Palgrave Macmillan, 2003).

JOHN H. McWHORTER is a professor of linguistics at the University of California at Berkeley. His research has focused on creole and pidgin languages as well as dialect variations in North America. He is the author of many books, including *Doing Our Own Thing: The Degradation of Language and Music and Why We Should, Like, Care* (Gotham, 2003) and *Defining Creole* (Oxford University Press, 2005).

CLEMENT W. MEIGHAN (1925–1997) was a professor of anthropology at the University of California at Los Angeles (UCLA) and for many years director of UCLA's Archaeological Survey. He excavated numerous archaeological sites in California and Mesoamerica. He was coauthor of *Chronologies in New World Archaeology* (Academic Press, 1978).

DAVID J. MELTZER is a professor of prehistory at Southern Methodist University. He has excavated numerous sites in search of archaeological evidence of early Paleoindians. He is the author of *Folsom: New Archaeological Investigations of a Classic Paleoindian Bison Kill* (University of California Press, 2006).

LYNN MESKELL is an assistant professor of anthropology at Columbia University. Her archaeological research is focused on Egypt and the Mediteranean. She is the author of *Archaeologies of Social Life* (Blackwell, 1999).

ANTHONY OBERSCHALL is a professor of sociology at the University of North Carolina at Chapel Hill. He has written many books and articles dealing with social conflict, including *Social Movements: Ideologies, Interests, and Identities* (Transaction Books, 1993).

DALE PETERSON is a professor of English at Tufts University. He is the author, with Jane Goodall, of *Visions of Caliban: On Chimpanzees and People* (Houghton Mifflin, 1993) and, with Richard Wrangham, of *Demonic Males: Apes and the Origins of Violence* (Houghton Mifflin, 1996).

STEVEN PINKER is a professor of psychology at Harvard University. His research has focused on the relationship between language and cognitive function. He has written numerous books, including *Words and Rules: The Ingredients of Language* (Basic Books, 1999).

MICHAEL E. PRICE is an anthropologist and was a postdoctoral fellow at the University of Indiana, formerly a graduate student at the University of California at Santa Barbara. He has published several articles about biosocial science and sociobiology.

JAMES RIDING IN is a professor of justice studies and American Indian studies at Arizona State University. A historian by training, he is also a member of the Pawnee tribe.

E.S. SAVAGE-RUMBAUGH is a primatologist and for many years a professor of biology at Georgia State University. Recently, she moved to the Great Ape Trust in Des Moines, Iowa. Her research has focused on the ability of apes to learn human language. She is the author of many articles and books about apes and their capacity for language, including *Ape Language: From Conditioned Response to Symbol* (Columbia University Press, 1986).

ERNIE SMITH is a professor of linguistics at the California State University at Fullerton. He was an early supporter of Ebonics (Black English) and has been a consultant to the Oakland School District's program on Standard English Proficiency. He has written many essays and articles about Ebonics.

DENNIS STANFORD is a curator of archaeology at the Department of Anthropology at the National Museum of Natural History at the Smithsonian Institution. He has conducted excavations in the Arctic and High Plains.

LAWRENCE GUY STRAUS is professor of anthropology at the University of New Mexico. His research has focused on Old World adaptations during the Pleistocene. He is the author of *Iberia before the Iberians: The Stone Age Prehistory of Cantabrian Spain* (University of New Mexico Press, 1996).

ROBERT W. SUSSMAN is professor of physical anthropology at Washington University in St. Louis and was an editor of the *American Anthropologist*. He is the author of many articles and books, and editor of *The Biological Basis of Human Behavior: A Critical Review,* 2nd ed. (Prentice Hall, 1999).

CAROL TAVRIS is a social psychologist and writer. Her books include *The Mismeasure of Woman* (Touchstone, 1992) and *Mistakes Were Made (But Not By*

Me): Why We Justify, Foolish Beliefs, Bad Decisions, and Hurtful Acts (Harcourt, 2007).

JOHN TOOBY is a professor of anthropology at the University of California at Santa Barbara (UCSB**)** and codirector of UCSB's Center for Evolutionary Psychology. He is a specialist on the evolution of hominid behavior and cognition. He is the coeditor of *The Adapted Mind: Evolutionary Psychology and the Generation of Culture* (Oxford University Press, 1992).

HAUNANI-KAY TRASK is a professor of Hawaiian studies at the University of Hawai'i at Manoa. She is a well-known native Hawaiian activist with Ka Lahui Hawai'i, one of several organizations advocating native Hawaiian sovereignty. She is the author of *From a Native Daughter: Colonialism and Sovereignty in Hawai'i,* rev. ed. (University of Hawai'i Press, 1999).

TERENCE TURNER is an emeritus professor of anthropology at the University of Chicago. He is best known for his research among the Kayapo of the Amazon. His current research focuses on, among other topics, ethics and human rights. He has published many articles and book chapters about the Kayapo.

JOEL WALLMAN is a program officer at the Harry Frank Guggenheim Foundation in New York. In recent years, he has studied aggression and linguistic ability. He is the author of *Aping Language* (Cambridge University Press, 1992).

RICHARD WRANGHAM is a professor of anthropology at Harvard University. He studies primate behavior and ecology and evolutionary biology. He is the author, with Dale Peterson, of *Demonic Males: Apes and the Origins of Human Violence* (Houghton Mifflin, 1996).